W9-AFS-697

www.wadsworth.com

wadsworth.com is the World Wide Web site for Wadsworth/Thomson Learning and is your direct source for dozens of online resources.

At *wadsworth.com* you can find out about supplements, demonstration software, and student resources. You can also send e-mail to many of our authors and preview new publications and exciting new technologies.

wadsworth.com

Changing the way the world learns®

From the Wadsworth Series in Production

Albarran, Alan B., *Management of Electronic Media*, 2d Ed.

Alten, Stanley R., *Audio in Media*, 6th Ed.

Armer, Alan A., *Writing the Screenplay*, 2d Ed.

Craft, John, Frederic Leigh, and Donald Godfrey, *Electronic Media*

Eastman, Susan Tyler, and Douglas A. Ferguson, *Broadcast/Cable/Web Programming: Strategies and Practices*, 6th Ed.

Gross, Lynne S., and Larry W. Ward, *Electronic Moviemaking*, 4th Ed.

Hausman, Carl, Philip Benoit, and Lewis B. O'Donnell, *Modern Radio Production*, 5th Ed.

Hausman, Carl, Lewis B. O'Donnell, and Philip Benoit, *Announcing: Broadcast Communicating Today*, 4th Ed.

Hilliard, Robert L., *Writing for Television, Radio, and New Media*, 7th Ed.

Hilmes, Michele, *Connections: A Broadcast History Reader*

Hilmes, Michele, *Only Connect: A Cultural History of Broadcasting in the United States*

Mamer, Bruce, *Film Production Technique: Creating the Accomplished Image*, 3d Ed.

Meeske, Milan D., *Copywriting for the Electronic Media: A Practical Guide*, 4th Ed.

Stephens, Mitchell, *Broadcast News*, 3d Ed.

Stephens, Mitchell, *A History of News*, 2d Ed.

Viera, Dave, *Lighting for Film and Electronic Cinematography*

Zettl, Herbert, *Sight Sound Motion*, 3d Ed.

Zettl, Herbert, *Television Production Handbook*, 8th Ed.

Zettl, Herbert, *Television Production Workbook*, 8th Ed.

Zettl, Herbert, *Video Basics*, 3d Ed.

Zettl, Herbert, *Video Basics Workbook*, 3d Ed.

Zettl, Herbert, *Zettl's VideoLab 2.1*

Film Production Technique

Creating the Accomplished Image

THIRD EDITION

Bruce Mamer

Minneapolis College

THOMSON
™
WADSWORTH

Australia ■ Canada ■ Mexico ■ Singapore ■ Spain
United Kingdom ■ United States

Publisher: Holly J. Allen
Assistant Editor: Nicole George
Editorial Assistant: Mele Alusa
Technology Project Manager: Jeanette Wiseman
Marketing Manager: Kimberly Russell
Marketing Assistant: Neena Chandra
Advertising Project Manager: Shemika Britt
Project Manager, Editorial Production: Mary Noel
Print/Media Buyer: Judy Inouye
Permissions Editor: Robert Kauser
Production Service: Ideas to Images
Text Designer: Gary Palmatier, Ideas to Images
Art Editor: Gary Palmatier, Ideas to Images
Photo Researcher: Cheri Throop
Copy Editor: Elizabeth von Radics
Cover Designer: Gary Palmatier, Ideas to Images
Cover Image: © 2002 Cooper Andrew/Corbis Sygma
Compositor: Robaire Ream, Ideas to Images
Cover and Text Printer: Banta, Menasha

*To Ellen, Rebecka,
and David*

For more information about our products, contact us at:
Thomson Learning Academic Resource Center
1-800-423-0563

For permission to use material from this text, contact us by:
Phone: 1-800-730-2214
Fax: 1-800-730-2215
Web: http://www.thomsonrights.com

Wadsworth/Thomson Learning
10 Davis Drive
Belmont, CA 94002-3098
USA

Asia
Thomson Learning
5 Shenton Way #01-01
UIC Building
Singapore 068808

Australia
Nelson Thomson Learning
102 Dodds Street
South Melbourne, Victoria 3205
Australia

Canada
Nelson Thomson Learning
1120 Birchmount Road
Toronto, Ontario M1K 5G4
Canada

Europe/Middle East/Africa
Thomson Learning
Berkshire House
168-173 High Holborn
London WC1V 7AA
United Kingdom

Latin America
Thomson Learning
Seneca, 53
Colonia Polanco
11560 Mexico D.F.
Mexico

Spain
Paraninfo Thomson Learning
Calle/Magallanes, 25
28015 Madrid, Spain

ISBN 0-534-56477-1
Library of Congress Control Number: 2002101083

Contents

Chapter 3   **Constructing the Scene**   42

Chapter 4   **Crew Organization**   60

PART III   Shooting   183

Chapter 9   Composition   184

Preface

THIS book is about creating images. People embark on their first filmmaking projects for a variety of reasons. Some want to express a vision that is unique and challenging. Others have a story to tell or something they feel needs saying. Some want to entertain, whereas others are busy dreaming up ways to subvert mainstream commercial product. Regardless of what brings a person to the medium, the starting place in film is the moving image.

Whatever shape a beginning filmmaker's desire takes, his or her aims will be best served by a broad-based understanding of film technique. Anyone who has learned to play a musical instrument knows that before a musician is ready to play before an audience, a huge commitment of hours spent learning time signatures and practicing scales is required. An aspiring painter discovers the same requirement of apprenticeship: One cannot master any art form overnight.

Film is no different. But perhaps because Hollywood's images look so effortless, novice filmmakers are often shocked to discover how much attention each individual shot is actually given. Commercial film producers generally consider that a film crew has done a good day's work if it has produced a little more than a minute of what will wind up being finished film. The budgets for commercial films today are astronomical: $20 million is an average figure, which puts the cost of a 90-minute film at around $200,000 per minute. Although a film's budget would never be expressed this way, the figure reflects at least some of the extensive resources devoted to each image.

Clearly, beginning independent filmmakers need not, and in most cases could not, emulate this scale and approach. But even on the smallest scale, filmmaking is an extremely costly and complicated endeavor. For this reason a mastery of the technical elements of filmmaking—the ability to control the variables of focus, exposure, lighting, and composition, for example—is essential to creating images of worth, value, and weight, images that function within a film as parts of an integrated whole.

A common but unnecessary stumbling block for many beginning film students is "technophobia." Despite the computer revolution, the problem remains widespread among people regardless of age, gender, and background. This book takes a comprehensive approach to covering the technical aspects of filmmaking in a way that is practical and straightforward, yet there may nevertheless be portions that require study and rereading because of the complexity of the processes described. It is my hope that the text makes the process of mastering basic film technique an empowering rather than intimidating experience.

Another underlying assumption is the importance of understanding and mastering traditional technique. To that end this book focuses on conventional (Hollywood) film style: breaking down scenes for dramatic emphasis, lighting for atmosphere, editing for pace and efficiency, and so forth. Although more-adventurous and experimental techniques are encouraged, they could not be effectively addressed within the scope of this book without shortchanging and trivializing vital and complex issues. I encourage anyone interested in experimenting with film form and technique to follow that impulse, but I also advise that there are many reasons for understanding the workings of conventional narrative films. The most radical techniques often, though not always, evolve from conventional approaches and are effective precisely because the artist knows his or her way around the norm.

In film as in other fields, there is a tendency to divide people into "creative" and "technical" roles, in some cases subordinating the technical mastery of the craft as less important, perhaps less "artistic." Certainly, there are technical people who are not creative, but there are also creative people who are not productive because they do not understand the technical fundamentals. In filmmaking, which could reasonably be called the most "technical" of the arts, those who truly excel, whether as directors, cinematographers, editors, or other skill positions, are both technically expert and creatively engaged. It makes no sense and is indeed counterproductive to separate these qualities in any discussion of filmmaking. Another underlying assumption in this text, therefore, is that the creative ideas that work in film are grounded in technical understanding.

To that end this text approaches the process of making films from the perspective of projects that involve at least a small crew. It recognizes the contributions of individual crew members and the general common sense with which crews are organized. The desire to be an excellent gaffer (lead lighting electrician) or grip (the crew's jack-of-all-trades) is a worthy pursuit. Moreover, for those who aspire to direct, working from the bottom up and serving in a number of capacities provides both a fuller knowledge of the craft and a better understanding of the interpersonal dynamics on a set. Many aspiring filmmakers wish to create films on their own. If this is the case, this text still applies: You just have to be responsible for all the elements detailed herein (no easy task!).

This book distinguishes between working on productions with a big budget and working on smaller, low-budget projects. This represents an inescapable fact. As an independent or student, you are probably working without access to the resources and support equipment that filmmakers working on large productions take for granted. You are making films on the edge and have to scrape and struggle for everything you can get. This book's practical emphasis is on technologies to which most independent filmmakers can realistically gain access; it also encourages as much ambition as possible in obtaining advanced equipment. The tribulations of working outside the commercial mainstream notwithstanding, this book is being written on the crest of a new wave of vital independent films, and it is my fervent hope that the independent ethic will prosper and flourish.

Changes to the Third Edition

Expanded emphasis on digital technologies This third edition continues to explore and expand on digital technologies—particularly in the editing room. Digital nonlinear editing (NLE) systems that educational programs and independent filmmakers can afford are now finally the norm, with powerful editing software costing about the same as a good word processing program. Many film-trained editors were reluctant to abandon film editing for video editing, because of the instability, expense, and inflexible nature of most of the early systems. This reluctance has disappeared to the extent that, while image acquisition is still frequently on film, traditional film editing is being done by only a limited, though significant, number of people.

Shooting on film and posting in a digital environment has become standard, from the Hollywood feature with a gargantuan budget to cash-strapped students and independents. The conventional film edit receives coverage here because it is still being done, but this third edition continues the incorporation of extensive new information on film-to-video transfer and digital nonlinear editing.

Expanded coverage of the interplay of film and video   Another major change in this third edition is to start off with an overview of the current interplay between film and video in the realms of both production and exhibition. The past twenty years have been an exceptionally confusing time, with the integration of film and video posing many unsettling challenges. Although we may be nearing the end of this confusion, the night is always darkest just before the dawn. At no time have the options been so perplexing to the average individual who just wants to make a film.

The elements that give film such an exceptionally beautiful and resonant quality are also its great downfall: It is inflexible and difficult to manipulate. The things that give video its great advantages are also related to its shortcomings: The electronic nature of video allows it to be very flexible, and the image can be endlessly manipulated; but image quality has always been limited and is only now, debatably, remotely starting to approach the beauty of film.

So students and independents, not to mention many in the industry, are faced with some tough decisions. One of the great challenges of both teaching film and writing a textbook like this is that all initial filming decisions must be informed by a complex knowledge of how films are made in the present environment. As with any field, it takes a long and disciplined course of study to get where you want to go. Students must take baby steps—move sequentially—when they want to fly, a particularly grievous frustration when everyone and everything in their path seems to be flying.

Other specific changes include:

- An entirely new first chapter devoted to sorting out the many options for initiating and completing a media project; it explores the many decisions that have to be made before production begins

- Updated coverage of cameras in part II that includes general information on video cameras; it also provides lists of the different video formats and their positive and negative aspects

- Major additions to chapter 8, *Film Stocks, Processing, and Video Transfer and Capture,* that fully address transferring film to video and further consider matchback information and capturing video into NLE systems

- Additions to chapters 16 and 17 that further integrate NLE into the workflow of completing a film or video

The final consideration is not so much a change in the closed, interior world of a text, but a significant development in the media-making world. This is the introduction of the new Apple digital nonlinear editing program. Final Cut Pro is not a wonder product, but it has had an impact, particularly in the academic world. There is other NLE software that is probably as good, but the initial stability of Final Cut Pro and its pricing for students have made it very attractive. A major problem in film and video schools is that much of the media software has been very twitchy, with crashes, reinstallations, and lost media being all too common. So far Final Cut Pro has been both affordable and reasonably stable. This text is not proprietary to Final Cut Pro, but I use it as a general example in a number of contexts.

One of the major purposes of this book is to give the reader an appreciation of just what it takes to produce the images we see on-screen. It may take quite some time to achieve the recommended level of control. You may start out working with small lighting instruments or a cheap light meter. You may be working on your own or with insufficient help. But at all times, you want to be moving toward the basic goal presented: controlling the elements in and in front of the camera. My hope is that this book will help you develop the confidence that comes with an understanding of both the craft and the art of filmmaking.

Acknowledgments

This third edition owes its overall quality to many people, but the most significant contributions were from those who gave much-appreciated direction on the new sections on nonlinear editing. Jason Wallace has been an invaluable source, being one of the few people out there who really has his hands around the new digital world and the video/film interface. Daniel Geiger was also extremely helpful in talking about matchback and adding helpful information and insights. Rob Hahn of Ithaca College was an immense help on the second edition and his insights continue through this one.

There are also numerous people who have contributed to specific sections of the book. Craig McKay, A.C.E., the editor of *Something Wild,* was most gracious in giving pertinent details about the editing of the scene reproduced in chapter 5. Thanks to Margaret Berg for allowing me to use still frames from the shooting of her script *Broken* in the examples of NLE software. Jennifer Schou, Elizabeth Halliday, and Michael Romine were the actors who were most gracious in allowing their images to be used in those illustrations.

Del Olson of Delden Film Labs commented on general lab work and video transfer; Greg Meyers of Lighthouse, Inc., on lighting equipment; and John Fillwalk, Stephen Solum, and Homer Lambrecht of Minneapolis College on video and sound. Fred Ginsberg of Equipment Emporium; Gerard Bonnette, freelance sound mixer; and Andy Mayer, freelance sound technician, gave welcome input on location and studio recording issues. Brian McGraw of Cinequipt, Inc., and David Tufford of Lighthouse, Inc., were exceptionally helpful in providing details about camera equipment and logistical assistance in finding photographs. Colleagues Gary Reynolds and Abdel Hafidh Bouassida were generous with their time and comments on content and overall structure. Also of Minneapolis College, Chauncey Dunn has been immensely helpful as a source of video information and as an ear to listen in a challenging year. Matt Wilkinson of Kodak was also most useful in providing details about film stock, edge numbers, and a host of other issues.

Brian Jennings, Blake Rizk, and many others too numerous to mention have been invaluable in helping me keep my finger on the pulse of day-to-day production. Steve Pecchia-Bekkum and Josh Wright have also been most helpful in this regard. Chris Weaver, Benno Nelson, Anna Coates, and Brian Crewe have been instrumental in letting me know the lay of the land. Gregory M. Cummins, Gregory Winter, and Jay Horan have contributed to many of the insights and stories in the text. Dennis O'Rourke of Cinesound II in Minneapolis has been an ongoing source of information and is one of those rare and wonderful birds—a seasoned professional who loves to work with students and share his extensive knowledge of his field. Most significant thanks go to Miroslav Janek and Roger Schmitz, with whom I shared many hours lugging and using cameras, lights, and sound gear—necessary experience to obtain the unique perspective required to truly understand the filmmaking process.

From Wadsworth I would like to thank my publisher, Holly Allen, and my project editor, Mary Noel. I would particularly like to thank Gary Palmatier and Robaire Ream of Ideas to Images for their fine work in illustration and design, and copy editor Elizabeth von Radics, who was both thoughtful and diligent in helping manage and refine this at times overwhelming amount of information.

The reviewers for this third edition were immensely helpful: John G. Cooper, Eastern Michigan University; Karen Holmes, San Francisco State University; David K. Irving, New York University; Andrew Millington, Emerson College; Vaughn Obern, Los Angeles City College; and Fredric A. Weiss, San Antonio College.

For assistance in the earliest stages of this project, special credit must go first and foremost to my friend and developmental agent par excellence, Paul Nockleby. Paul was instrumental in making this text a reality. Readers of early versions of the first edition included Peter Bundy, Gwynneth Gibby, Mary Ahmann, Bill Caulfield, and Elizabeth von Radics. At various stages of the manuscript, Beth Berg, Tania Kamal-Eldin, and Martha Boehm were also invaluable in this regard. M. Walker Pearce and Charles Harpole were extremely helpful in both reading and supporting this project in its early stages. Martha Davis Beck, in particular, has been a friend and valued reader throughout the entire project.

Institutional support has been greatly appreciated as well. Minneapolis College was most gracious in giving me time to complete this project. Thanks for help on earlier editions go to Joe Anderson of Georgia State University and Chuck Berg and Ed Small of the Department of Theater and Film at the University of Kansas, who so generously gave their valued insights.

In the years since the publication of the first edition, the ongoing surge in the quantity and quality of work by my current and former students has been immensely gratifying. Tracking their many screenings, numerous awards, and credits on major films continually reminds me of what a great and important profession teaching is. Their frequently expressed appreciation has been very emotionally rewarding, and I would like to reiterate my many thanks to them. My parents, Donna and Stuart Mamer, have provided highly valued support in many ways, as has the rest of my extended family. And most of all, thanks go to my daughter, Rebecka, who has been compelling me to stay sharp by starting her own path in the film world; to my son, David, who is still deciding; and to my wife, Ellen, who with equal challenges in her own career and life still supports me in so many ways.

Bruce Mamer

Part I

Blocking for the Camera

1

Initiating the Process

The Future of Film

Ah, the great debate: Film and video—video and film—the chemical and the electronic. The third edition of this text warrants an overview of the present situation regarding film and the prospects for its continued use. The buzz in the late 1990s was that the future was digital. Film was indeed finally dead. The days of independent filmmakers' struggling against overwhelming odds to raise the huge amounts of capital needed to shoot a project on film were over. Inexpensive digital cameras and desktop digital editing would spark an outpouring of digital features that would revolutionize not only the content and delivery of the product, but the makeup of those who create the product as well. We would soon be inundated with smart, exciting digital features that were either beamed to digital theaters or available for download on the Internet. When the dot-com universe collapsed, this notion probably went with it. In fact, millions of feet of film continue to be shot every year, and film remains the standard mode of presentation in theaters as well. Although the revolution has failed to materialize, it nevertheless may still be lurking out there, waiting for a better moment.

Why does the revolution remain around the corner? If you think of the technology that appeared indispensable in 1980, why has film—almost alone—been able to hang on? The humble electric typewriter and the turntable make occasional appearances. Typeset printing, lithography, dial phones, and much more have all gone the way of the passenger pigeon. The economic downturn that started in July 2000 has probably been the biggest culprit. Theaters have been hit particularly hard, with at least one major exhibitor filing for bankruptcy. An industry that is under significant financial pressure is going to be hard-pressed to make the massive investment required to retool its primary vehicle of delivery.

Through it all, film remains. I am perhaps overly fond of telling my students that it was roughly twenty-five years ago that I first heard someone predict with great certainty that film would be dead in five years. It was right at the beginning of what could be called the second great video revolution: the widespread introduction of portable video gear and the ensuing transformation of the television newsgathering process from shooting on film to shooting on video. I was a film student chatting with television students and, with very little hard information to support my argument, fell back on an impassioned defense of the beauty, subtlety, and power of the film image as an expressive tool. To a certain extent, it was a question of art versus information. From the very start of this second transformation, video was clearly going to knock film out of the box in everything from news to social service promos to political agitprop. This is not to say that video was not making—and is not continuing to make—great strides as an art form. But video was clearly going to have a complete lock on the information aspect of visual media. The question has remained the same since then: Will the expressive quality of the film image allow it to coexist with video?

A quarter of a century later and in a new millennium, I find myself supplying the same answer. It seems that at roughly five-year intervals, I have been forced by some circumstance to reestablish my passion for the future of film. My favorite was in the mid-1980s, when a colleague with a dubious agenda made the assertion to students that you couldn't even track down 16mm film stock any longer. In November 2000 the waters were further muddied by an article in the *New York Times* about George Lucas and his newest S*tar Wars* epic. The article went overboard both in asserting the supremacy of new digital projection technology over film and in predicting the imminent demise of shooting and distributing on film. Indeed, Sony's new 24p system, a version of which Lucas uses, is getting results close to film but is also dauntingly expensive. The price will come down, but the question of how much and when remains. Several months later the *Times* printed a response from cinematographer John Bailey, saying that indeed digital cinema was going to make further inroads but that film would remain the medium of choice for projects that require the qualities of the film image. The choice between film and video would be project- and exhibition-specific. In reality, and as Bailey asserts, this has been clear from the outset. Either way, the argument refuses to die.

Another part of the problem is connecting with an audience. You can put a great movie on your Web site, but without expensive advertising only the most adventurous Web surfers are going to track it down. And then, how do you recoup your costs? Connecting is difficult enough, but the fundamental flaw in the whole argument is that inexperienced makers with small cameras, inadequate support equipment, limited budgets, untested actors, and dubious directing abilities cannot really be expected to consistently create product that ranks with the great or even the average works of American and international cinema. This is a bitter truth. What the digital world sparked was hundreds of marginally watchable digital features with barely audible sound, awkward execution, poor pacing, and myriad other technical and aesthetic problems. Certainly, there are wonderful exceptions, but they are vastly outnumbered by the countless videotapes that are lying on dusty shelves while their owners wax philosophical about how much was learned from the experience.

Simply stated, much of the new digital work was undisciplined and devoid of the elements that make commercial features successful entertainment experiences. We have this great democratizing technology, but technology does not make movies. People make movies, and the polished, engaging, consumer-friendly work still comes out of Hollywood. Many will complain about conditioning and monopolistic practices, but Hollywood films remain seamless, involving experiences that are replete with familiar actors whom general audiences enjoy watching. Whether some people like it or not, this experience is still highly valued by the majority of the moviegoing public. And the fact that Hollywood produces so few good films is not a function of lack of talent, lack of vision, or obeisance to perceived commercial requirements (although the latter two may in some limited sense have an impact). It is that making something good is incredibly difficult. A great film or even a good film represents the confluence of so many disparate factors that it is simply going to happen with relative infrequency. All the smart guys hanging around in bars berating the "hacks" need to get a life. Creating an aesthetically successful film starts to look more like chance than anything else. But remember the old saying: Chance favors the well-prepared mind.

Despite claims to the contrary, the bottom line on the future of film may hark back to my initial argument—that video has simply not achieved the qualities of the filmed image. Or if it has gotten close, it remains so expensive that one might as well shoot film anyway. When I embarked on the first edition of this book in 1992, a number of my peers in the field wondered aloud why I would put so much effort toward a medium that had such a limited future. Well, the future continues unabated. Oh, and by the way, many of the things predicted in the first few paragraphs will eventually come to pass. When the talented individuals who rushed to make digital features get some experience and start making more-polished and engaging work, we will see some of the much-anticipated democratization.

But Hollywood and film—not that the two can be equated—are not going away. A friend once likened Hollywood to the automobile industry in Detroit in the 1960s: on top of the heap, arrogant, and ripe to be plucked by smaller, more exciting carmakers. There may be some truth to this, but he said that fifteen years ago and it ain't happened yet. It would be nice to see work coming from other arenas, but that is not going to happen until people learn the hard lessons of commercial features; that is, one needs to create films that have good storytelling qualities, engaging performances, efficient pace, and logical scene structure. In other words films that have the elements that can involve and excite an audience.

I don't know if film will someday be a thing of the past, but its use will undoubtedly continue to decline and become more specialized. The question is how long this will take. I am betting on . . . well, let's say at least a while.

The Shape of Film Editing

Although film remains a potent force in production, the landscape for editing and finishing a visual project has changed dramatically over the past twenty years. Computer and video technologies have had a tremendous impact on the way projects are finished. As the use of the term *visual project* in the first sentence suggests, we are even having trouble knowing what to call things. Is a project shot with a digital camera and edited on a computer a film? Is a project shot on film but edited and finished on video a film? In both cases, no. The end product is the determining factor. A film is a film is a film. Is a project shot on film, edited digitally, then returned to a film format a film? Yes. A *film* is a work that can be projected photographically in a theater. Although video projection and its newer digital counterpart have been around for a while and have made great strides in the past few years, in essence the theatrical presentation of the video image is still in its infancy simply because each and every one of the 35,000 screens in the United States (not to mention internationally) still project film. Despite all the digital hullabaloo, if someone wants his work to receive extensive theatrical screenings, no matter what its potentially humble beginnings, it is going to have to be released on film.

Given this context, this book has a number of critical underlying assumptions. The first, and potentially most arguable, is that the reader does indeed want his or her final product to be a motion picture print that can be projected in a theater. This, of course, is by no means a foregone conclusion. You have to ask some very central and tough questions: Is a film print really going to be useful? Do you want festival screenings? Do you foresee theatrical release? Can your budget, or a distributor's budget, absorb the cost of the number of film prints required to give the film a general release? Would theatrical video projection be a possibility, or is your project's final destination going to be television showings or rentals in video stores? The latter two scenarios are both instances in which a video finish is all that's required, which is usually a decidedly less expensive option. If you do finish on video, can you absorb the cost of transferring to film if distributors are interested? All of these questions must be answered before you start shooting, which is unfortunately just the point when you have the most concerns about whether your film will be a success or a failure. If you want the traditional film presentation, the only option is a final motion picture print.

So there is the choice: film or video. One does not equal the other, and a knowledge of what you desire as a final product should inform your decisions from the very start. In addition, when video is considered, we need to first make the distinction between analog and digital. Further particulars of the differences between the two media will be considered in later chapters. *Analog video* is essentially the encoding of an electrical signal on a conventional magnetic tape. *Digital video* is the storage of a digital signal (0's and 1's), again on what is essentially a conventional magnetic medium. Digital video generally produces a higher-quality picture, without the generational loss that accompanies the copying of analog video. Digital video is also easier to manipulate in terms of color, exposure, and a host of other variables. In the editing world, digital *nonlinear editing (NLE)* has become the norm, as it is able to mimic film editing in all the nonlinear glory of computer technology. Analog video editing, in all honesty, was a complete mess for anything but the simplest of applications. It was great for newsfilming and informational videos, but in hindsight—and for many of us in foresight—its drawbacks made it a tough customer for complex projects. Analog video can be digitized, but images shot with digital cameras will generally provide a better and more stable source. Although we expend great effort making a distinction between film and video, for now we will lump analog and digital under one video umbrella.

In this environment it has become critical that before embarking on a project filmmakers understand all the questions surrounding the film versus video debate. This chapter lays out a framework for making those initial choices. Essentially, there are five possibilities for how you initiate, proceed with, and complete a visual project. The first question is whether to shoot film or video. Again this is project-specific, but feature films, specialty presentations such as IMAX and Omnivision, episodic television shows, commercials, and music videos are generally still shot on film. Although there are exceptions, pretty much everything else is shot on video. Of the five project types listed as shot on film, only features and specialty presentations are finished on film. Again, film editing in the student and independent world is a significant factor as well.

What are the options for initiating, proceeding with, and completing a visual project? They are:

1. Shoot on film, edit on film, and finish on film.

2. Shoot on video, edit on video, and finish on video.

3. Shoot on film, edit on video, and finish on video.

4. Shoot on film, edit on video, and finish on film.

5. Shoot on video, edit on video, finish on video, and transfer to film.

Because so much work is destined for a television screen, most projects employ methods number two or three. This is clearly where the bulk of the action is. From television shows to news to industrials to corporate promos, the majority of work in the industry revolves around video presentation. Even this long list leaves out some possibilities, specifically productions created in virtual environments and projects that are shot on film but not really finished for theatrical projection, such as NASA launches and the like. But these are the most common choices.

This text devotes energy to all five approaches, but several are given more attention relative to the others. For the most part, this text covers the last part of the equation: finish on film. The production chapters are pertinent to people proceeding with the third approach. Computer editing, which includes all the edit-on-video approaches, is a critical component of the text. Some space is devoted to digital shooting, but much of this is better left to video production and editing texts. The fifth option requires some explanation; it refers to finishing on video and converting the video to a film print. The technology for this has been around for many years,

1-1

A motion picture shot comprises individual frames
that when projected in succession provide the illusion
of movement

but the process of converting the video image to film has become a significant enough issue that it should be considered a distinct possibility. All this is covered in detail in later chapters, but, given the complexity of choices, a brief overview here will be a helpful starting point.

Shooting, Editing, and Finishing on Film

Although shooting on film is still commonplace, the conventional film edit—that is, cutting actual film pieces and their attendant sound tracks—is becoming relatively uncommon. Nonlinear editing, or computer editing, has largely supplanted it, but aspects of the conventional film edit nevertheless play a significant role in general production. In particular, the feature film world still integrates film editing with NLE in the postproduction phase, and students and independents often find it a viable approach. For this latter group, if a final film print that can be projected in a theater is the goal, there is a strong rationale for going ahead and cutting film. You may have to take this as an article of faith for now; the rationale is presented later. What is described in the following discussion is essentially the way films were finished, with some minor variations, from roughly the introduction of sound in 1926 to the relative consolidation of the digital revolution today.

Before proceeding, a few basic definitions are required. Motion picture film is made up of a series of still photographic images. **SEE 1-1** When projected in succession, these images provide the illusion of movement. Each individual photographic image is called a *frame*. A sequence of frames is called a *shot*, which is commonly defined as the footage created from the moment the camera is turned on until it is turned off. Despite several styles of film that have specialized approaches, the shot is generally considered the basic building block of a film. The industry standard for projection and shooting is 24 individual *frames per second (fps)*. Shooting at lower and higher frame rates yields fast and slow motion, respectively; all standard projection is at 24 fps.

In all stages of a conventional film edit, a project exists as a number of pieces. You do not really get to see the whole thing together until the film is finished. Editing is a process of moving toward an *answer print*. The answer print is checked to make sure everything is correct—color, exposure, and a host of other considerations. Once an acceptable answer print is achieved, it is used as the guide to make all subsequent prints, called *release prints*. The *original* film—the film that ran through the camera while shooting—is never handled or projected in the editing process. All work is done on frame-for-frame duplicate copies of the film called *workprints*. Original film, often though not always referred to as *negative,* is used only as a printing source. The version of the film that you are working on during the actual editing process is called the *edited workprint (EWP)*. All the truly creative editing work is done at this stage.

Sound complicates editing immensely. Although sound and picture are edited at the same time, all sound is handled on separate pieces similar to the film. Sound is generally recorded on location or in the studio on a conventional magnetic medium or digital audio recorder and then transferred to magnetic film stock, which is the same size, dimension, and construction as the film itself. This is referred to as *mag stock* or *fullcoat,* the latter being a name that actually implies a specific type of mag stock. For those who have done basic video editing, mag stock may appear awkward

1-2

Most film editing is done on flatbed editing machines
Moviola M-77AH flatbed editing table

1-3

The most common flatbeds have three film transports—one picture and two sound

and anachronistic until one understands the freedom it allows—a freedom now matched by digital editing technology.

Most film editing is done on *flatbed* editing machines. **SEE 1-2** Although there are bigger versions, the most common flatbeds have three film *transports,* one picture and two sound. **SEE 1-3** The *picture gate* is where each individual frame is projected. The sound transports have magnetic playback heads that correspond precisely with the picture gate in terms of frames. The film and sound can be run at 24 fps and in fast and slow motion, both forward and in reverse.

Once the sound is transferred to magnetic film stock, it is represented as a specific length of film. If we were to take an example, say, someone reading Lincoln's Gettysburg Address, we could build images against that transferred piece of sound. **SEE 1-4A** Indeed this figure is based on an oft-cited scene from Leo McCarey's *Ruggles*

1-4

Compiling mixtracks enables sound to be manipulated against picture and vice versa

Picture						
Laughton	Cowboys	Bartenders	Ruggles	Over the shoulder (Laughton)	Old men	Laughton

	Sound				
A	Fourscore and 7 years ago, our fathers... the last full measure of devotion... and for the people, shall not perish from the earth.				
B	Honkytonk piano...				
C				Clock chiming		
D		Horse galloping			Horse galloping	

of Red Gap (1935), where Charles Laughton reads the address to a saloon full of grizzled cowboys. If we wished to have specific images positioned against specific events in the speech, we would simply find the sound we wanted and cut the image we wanted on the picture roll across from it. If we wished to have some music in the background, it would be transferred to a separate piece of stock and positioned on another roll against the image and existing sound. **SEE 1-4B** The process of editing sound requires creating a number of separate rolls of mag stock, called *mixtracks,* to create the desired layering of sound. If the sound effect of a clock chiming in the background is desired, another track is required. **SEE 1-4C** This sound can also be very precisely positioned wherever it is wanted. If you want the sound of horses galloping by outside, that too is handled separately. **SEE 1-4D** Any sound that you want layered in requires another mixtrack.

The final product is one picture roll—the edited workprint—and a number of mixtracks—all the same length as the picture. The number of mixtracks depends on how complex and layered the sound is. A music video may have only one track—the music track. More-complex sound requires more-complex track building.

Once every element is where you want it, you start the final steps of finishing a film: *audio mixing,* or *final audio mixdown* (the creation of the final sound track), *negative cutting,* and the actual *printing* of the film. Although the filmmaker has substantial input, these three processes are handled either in a laboratory or by experienced professionals; all are expensive. When you start these processes, all the creative decisions of editing have been made. There is almost no turning back. These processes are a matter of locking all the elements into place and combining them on one piece of film—the answer print.

The final mix requires that the picture and the mixtracks be taken to a professional mixing facility, where all the tracks of sound are mixed down to a single sound track—the *master mix.* It is here that you finalize all the volume levels, any manipulations of sound quality, the sound fades planned by the editor, and so on. The master mix represents the final sound for the film. This used to happen with mag stock as the standard recording medium, but digitized sound has changed the procedure significantly.

Whether the master mix is on mag film or in a digital format, it is quickly turned into an *optical master*—a piece of film that is blank except for a narrow strip of diamond-shaped patterns opposite the side with the sprocket holes. **SEE 1-5** These patterns are the sound for the film, all sound in film being handled photographically. The optical master is used to print the sound track on the final film, where it is called an *optical track.*

You then return to the original footage for negative cutting; that is, you have it "conformed" to what you did in the edited workprint. The film is usually given to a professional, listed in credits as the *negative cutter* or *conformist,* who makes a master version of the film out of the original, using the edited workprint as a guide. The film has latent *edge numbers,* usually referred to as *key numbers,* which are exposed onto the original film by the manufacturer and then printed through to the workprint. They serve as a reference for the negative cutter. This is generally the only time the

1-5

The optical master is a piece of film that is blank except for a strip of patterns opposite the sprocket holes

Flowchart representing
the process of finishing
a film

original is handled and cut. This conformed original is still only a printing medium. Everything projected on a screen will be a print made from this edited original. These latent edge numbers are a critical component in any interface that we may contemplate between film and video.

In the negative matching process, the original film is actually cut into two separate rolls called *A & B rolls* (there can be more than these two). In the A & B rolls, the picture is set up with all the odd-numbered shots on one roll and all the even-numbered shots on the other. (This process is explored in chapter 18.) It is done mostly to achieve color and exposure control in the printing process and to facilitate dissolves, fades, and a few other effects. A & B rolling is standard procedure in 16mm but not 35mm film.

The process of finishing a film can be represented as a flowchart. **SEE 1-6** The sound and the image have two separate paths; they are cut at the same time but not represented on the same piece of film until the very end. An answer print is also descriptively called a *married print,* where the two entities are finally joined together.

To summarize, the mixtracks and the edited workprint are created in editing. The mixtracks are mixed down into a master mix, which is then converted into an optical master. The edited workprint is used as a guide to re-create the film out of the original, making the A & B rolls. The A & B rolls and the optical master are then used to create an answer print. Unless there are complications, the answer print is the guide for all subsequent release prints. Hollywood commercial films generally do not cut the precious original. The original starts to deteriorate after a small number of printings, so it is used as the head of a family tree of printing and projection versions of the film. Often what you see at the theater is many generations away from that original piece of film, particularly when films are released in numerous theaters simultaneously.

The final processes of completing a film, including conforming, mixing, and printing, are costly. The following estimates assume that you are finding vendors that will provide services at reasonable rates. If you want to mix the sound where George Lucas mixes his, multiply your costs by about five. The mix on a 5-minute 16mm film might cost $150 to $250, assuming reasonably uncomplicated sound. If your film has an average number of cuts and you can find a negative cutter who will negotiate, you might get conforming done for $200. A final print of a color film would be around \$200 to \$250, including the creation of the optical master. Black-and-white is cheaper. This does not include titles and a host of other hidden costs. Few students take their first films all the way to a final print. It is far more expensive than most tentative first efforts warrant.

Shooting, Editing, and Finishing on Video

Indeed, digital video has arrived. Gone are the days of Hi-8, Super 8 video, VHS-C, and all the other competing analog video formats hoping for a place at the table. The future remains uncertain but we have finally arrived at a point where we can invest in technologies that appear to have a clear application for some time to come. Although high-end gear remains expensive, technology has come down in price to the extent that many people can acquire hardware that will allow them to complete very low budget productions on their own. Digital video (DV) and Mini DV technology, with a camera or VCR interfacing with a desktop computer, have made a powerful production tool available to students and independents of modest means. **SEE 1-7** The \$60,000 digital editing systems have been undercut, or at least augmented, by software like Apple's Final Cut Pro, Adobe Premiere, and a host of other powerful low-cost programs that run on desktop computers. There will undoubtedly be semiannual upgrades and improvements, but the uncertainty that attended the introduction of so many new video formats and refinements may at last be abating. Although this technology may not support the image quality required for high-end productions, it has already absorbed an enormous amount of midrange work.

Again a few basic definitions are in order. Standard video, whether digital or analog, runs at a nominal 30 fps. This is called the *NTSC (National Television System Committee)* signal, which is the broadcast and recording standard in the United States, Canada, Japan, and a number of other countries. To many it is an awkward standard, due mainly to the fact that it does not translate well to film's 24 fps and it doesn't actually run at precisely 30 frames, but a fraction less. Unlike the film frame, the video frame is not a distinguishable entity; it is broken down into two separate fields of magnetic information stored diagonally on the videotape (see chapter 8 for a detailed explanation). The digital video signal is binary—a series of 0's and 1's—yet it emulates the frame configuration of analog video.

1-7

A typical basic NLE editing station
Macintosh G3 CPU and
Sony VX-1000 Mini DV camera

Time code—another critical aspect of video—is simply a perfect-time rolling clock that is recorded in conjunction with the image on a track of the videotape. It is recorded in hours, minutes, seconds, and frames and, like edge numbers in film, provides a "permanent address" for each individual frame of video. It is generated by the camera while shooting or it can be introduced in postproduction. In the editing suite, it is displayed, and all edit points are identified, input, and stored by their numbers. Time code is the driving force of all things video and is critical to any relationship between film and video.

Regardless of whether the source material is digital or analog, any NLE program must *capture* the footage to be edited. This is the process of transferring the footage onto the hard drive of a computer. If it is digital footage, it can be captured as is; but if it is analog, it must be digitized first. Video can be stored at a number of different *resolutions,* referring to the number of pixels dedicated to each individual image. Although software varies, at highest resolution 1 gigabyte of storage is required for roughly every four minutes of video footage. The benefit of digitizing at a lower resolution is that you reduce storage space, thus freeing up room for more footage. The downside is that it can be difficult to analyze the quality of low-res shots and you have to return to a higher-quality version to complete the project. With the expanding hard drives of most computers as well as external hard drives, storage is becoming less of a problem. Lengthier projects, however, can still become organizational headaches.

Although individual NLE software programs identify and exhibit many functions slightly differently, they all have reasonably similar applications. A good starting point is to first understand that digital editing emulates film editing: although one never handles any pieces, shots are trimmed and sound tracks are built using the same considerations. These are often referred to by different names, but most NLE editing programs will have four key *windows:* a bin, a viewer, a timeline, and a preview window.

Final Cut Pro (FCP) is typical, with the addition in the lower right of a toolbar, for common editing functions, and an Audio Meters indicator, to monitor sound levels. **SEE 1-8**

1-8

A representative window for NLE systems
Final Cut Pro

The bin is where all clips are stored
Final Cut Pro

In- and out-points can be determined in the viewer before a clip is brought into the timeline
Final Cut Pro

The *bin,* called the Browser in FCP, is where all the shots, referred to as *clips* in many systems, are stored. **SEE 1-9** Each clip is represented by a brief written description, a title, or an icon (often a frame of the shot). Sound, whether in conjunction with a shot or as a separate entity, is stored in the bin as well.

When a clip is selected, it will appear in the *viewer.* **SEE 1-10** This window will have the standard playback controls—*play, pause, reverse,* and so on. In the viewer one can analyze the shot to determine where it should begin and end. The software

Sound is typically represented as a waveform
Final Cut Pro

has the capability to *scrub* through the shot, that is, move over it frame by frame. Sound is played and scrubbed on just as the picture is. The various NLE systems handle this differently, but sound is often represented as some type of waveform. **SEE 1-11**

Each clip will have the rolling time code numbers, either created by the software or generated by the camera during shooting. Using these timings the editor determines the in- and out-points for the shot. The editor sets the edit points, then inserts the shot into the edited project.

The edited project, with the selected sections of clips, is represented on some form of *timeline.* **SEE 1-12** Shots and sound are dragged, or otherwise moved, onto the timeline and placed in the desired positions. The timeline usually has a zero point, representing the beginning of the show, and indicates how the show unfolds in hours, minutes, seconds, and frames. The editor can zoom in and out on the timeline to focus on anything from micro-representations of short segments

1-12

A representative timeline for NLE systems
Final Cut Pro

1-13

Many NLE systems use the "rubber band" method of setting audio levels

of the project to the complete show. The software's menus provide typical effects such as superimpositions, fades, dissolves, and many other transitions. The more sophisticated systems have what is called *nondestructive editing,* which means that, rather than going back into the bin to reset your in- and out-points, you can control the length of the clip on the timeline if you decide to make the shot longer.

Timelines generally have two to four audio tracks, with the option for more. The various programs handle volume control differently, but many use a method that one software producer calls "rubber bands." **SEE 1-13** With the vertical spread of the track representing a volume scale, you click at the bottom of the effects bar, "lasso" the sound, and drag it to the desired volume level. Most software also includes fairly crude to quite sophisticated controls for sound equalization and signal processing, giving the potential for cleanup and general manipulation of the sound. With the possibility of multiple audio tracks, equalization, and audio processing, an entire complex sound track can be built. Most NLE software allows the maker to mix the audio internally, thus bypassing an expensive commercial mixdown, although a strong rationale will be made later to do a professional mix.

As the picture and sound tracks are built on the timeline, the edited show can be viewed in the *preview window,* called the Canvas in FCP. **SEE 1-14** The finished program can be output to videotape and then broadcast or shown in whatever venue you desire. Again, taking the project to a commercial video postproduction facility may add a further dimension to the project.

NLE systems have a plethora of other capabilities. Novice makers, faced with so many options, will

1-14

The Canvas is where the editing decisions made in the timeline are played
Final Cut Pro

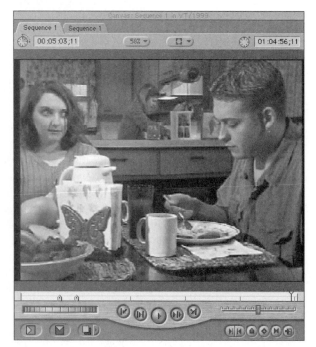

frequently make ill-informed decisions that have a negative impact on the project down the road. Talk to people who are using the programs and stay as well informed as you can about every step of the process. Perhaps the only downside of the digital revolution is that computers are by no means bulletproof, with crashes and computer "gremlins" causing no end of headaches. Learning curves on many of these systems can be quite lengthy, so be prepared to spend time mastering the extensive potential of some of these powerful programs.

Shooting on Film, Editing and Finishing on Video

This next approach is relatively straightforward. For reasons of image quality, stability of medium, and "if it ain't broke, don't fix it," a substantial percentage of work destined for television is still shot on film. The general path here is to shoot on film, transfer the film to video, then cut on an NLE system. The final product is output to video and broadcast. Next to originating on video to begin with, this is the most common approach. Because we do not have to go back to the original film for any reason, everything that was said about digital editing in the previous section applies here as well. There are a number of complications having to do with resolution, and in some instances projects will go back to film for a higher-quality transfer, but overall the process is relatively uncomplicated.

The only new wrinkle in all of this is the transfer of the film to video. Film-to-video transfers can range from using a cheap and crude setup where a video camera is essentially pointed into a film projector lens to high-end lab setups that cost hundreds of dollars per hour to use. Any professional or semi-professional project requires this latter approach, in which the conversion is done on a *telecine*—a high-end transfer machine at a film processing lab or video postproduction studio. The video is made straight from the original—using the negative as the source is the professional standard. The film can be transferred to either digital or analog videotape, which is then captured by the NLE system as described in the previous section.

In the telecine process, there is extensive opportunity to manipulate the image shot on location. The telecine is operated by a studio employee called the *colorist,* who can add a powerful dimension to the project, having control of the quantities of red, green, and blue; being able to manipulate exposure; and having a host of other options at his or her disposal. There are, as always, many considerations when the transfer is done, but the main goal is to get the film onto tape in as high and as consistent a quality as possible.

Video projection is also a consideration when finishing on video. Until recently, the quality of the image produced by commonly used video projectors has been severely lacking. The amount of definition in the image and the overall contrast have been based on the limitations of the NTSC signal. Recent technological advances, however, particularly digital projection, are quickly narrowing the gap between film and video projection. George Lucas is again at the forefront of this, with the stated intent of having the next *Star Wars* film projected digitally whenever possible. He will undoubtedly be making quite a few film prints for standard theatrical release both nationally and internationally, but the future of digital projection will further popularize this already widely used approach.

Shooting on Film, Editing on Video, and Finishing on Film

This is the domain of most feature films and it is where the world starts to get very complicated. Film and video are somewhat like squabbling siblings: They look like they want to talk to each other, and they can be made to talk to each other, but only if you lay the groundwork very carefully.

The process described here is referred to as *matchback,* wherein the project is cut on an NLE system, with the editing decisions made on video being replicated on the original film in order to make a final film print; that is, the video edit has to provide the information required for a negative cutter to conform the film that was originally shot. This translation between film and video is based on establishing and maintaining a relationship between the edge numbers of film and the time code of the videotape (other types of coding are used as well). Although it is premature to stress this particular aspect, the setup and data encoding for this relationship must be established absolutely scrupulously. Any flaws in the information will cause major problems later in the process.

The primary complications in the relationship between film and video are the aforementioned conversion from the 24 fps of film to the nominal 30 fps of video and the accommodations that must be made because video actually runs slightly less than 30 fps. In a perfect world, one film frame would translate to one video frame, but, alas, perfection and matchback are hard-fought end products. With film at 24 and video at 30, some conversion has to be made. The solution is to print more fields of some film frames than of others—a process called *three:two pull-down* (see chapter 8 for a complete discussion). This means that some video information does not have corresponding film frames, causing potential flaws in the matchback information. There can also be slight discrepancies in timing, given that the film and video frames actually represent different fractions of a second. The most high-end NLE systems have a way of eliminating this messy conversion, thus eliminating these concerns, but these systems remain very expensive with which to work.

In addition, because video actually runs at 29.97 fps, the film is slowed down ever so slightly in the transfer. This is of course imperceptible to the eye. The sound, on the other hand, which is recorded separately when shooting film, must also be slowed down when transferred to whatever editing or capture medium is being used. When we do matchback, the film goes back to running at exactly 24 fps and we must speed up the final sound track again. The pros have this down, but it is a lot to keep track of for novices and those who have done only video. Film schools and labs have countless horror stories of projects that had a breakdown somewhere in the chain, the result being an expensive film print in which the sound starts to slowly drift out of sync and winds up being several seconds off sync by the end of a lengthy project. This can be fixed but only at further expense.

Again, the starting point is to interrelate the edge numbers of the film with the time code of the video. This is generally established in the telecine process, and both the telecine operator and the editorial staff must monitor the process to ensure that all information is entered correctly. Not all NLE systems can handle matchback. And even the most sophisticated systems specifically designed to address this complex interrelationship often handle the exact details of frame and speed conversions differently. Whatever the specific strategy, the two critical goals are to provide a negative cutter with the information needed to go back to the original film and to create a sound track that will remain in sync. In the telecine process, a number of different things have to happen (this is addressed in detail later in the text). If there are any flaws in the way the initial information is created, there will be project-threatening problems down the line. Be sure that you understand all the issues and that all aspects of the system and software are compatible to handle all stages of production.

Shooting, Editing, and Finishing on Video and Transferring to Film

This final method is a bit more exotic, being that most students and independents would be hard-pressed to afford it, but because shooting and finishing on film has its own rather expensive aspects, this last approach is not beyond consideration. In essence the process follows the shoot/edit/finish-on-video model, but the wrinkle is that the final video product is converted to a film print by a lab.

This wrinkle is by no means new. Video broadcasting actually predates video recording, and the only way some of the earliest television shows still exist is because early engineers used a *kinescope,* a type of motion picture camera that literally filmed the picture off a television as it was being broadcast. Although different technologies have been developed and employed, the kinescope approach is still widely used.

The older kinescopes of TV shows are not particularly attractive, and kinescope and related technologies did not progress much until the mid- to late 1980s. Occasionally, in feature documentaries video was handy and inexpensive to shoot, and the small amount that was used in the final product was converted to film. A few specialty films, such as Emile De Antonio's *In the King of Prussia* (1983), used this approach, but the image quality was too limited to meet Hollywood standards—a hierarchically imposed standard but a standard nonetheless. One of the bitterest truths for independents is that Hollywood filmmaking will always be a benchmark for the majority of moviegoers. Steve James's *Hoop Dreams* (1994) was one of the first feature documentaries to successfully incorporate this model.

The approach picked up steam when features started incorporating digital animation techniques, often referred to as *CGI (computer-generated images).* James Cameron's *The Abyss* (1989) and *Terminator II* (1991) were some of the earliest examples of a very sophisticated technical approach. The base live-action image was shot on film on location. The shots that required special effects were digitized frame by frame and then individually manipulated. Each video frame was then scanned back onto a film frame, at great expense, and intercut with the footage that did not require special effects. Larry and Andy Wachowski's *The Matrix* (1999) and a host of other films have further developed this approach.

The appearance of films that originated entirely on video, like Thomas Vinterberg's *The Celebration* (1998) and Lars Von Trier's *Dancer in the Dark* (2000), both part of what has been called the Dogma 95 movement, were the beginning of a significant trend. The approach has become much more common with established makers like Spike Lee using quite a bit of video in his film *Bamboozled* (2000), Mike Figgis making the formally innovative *TimeCode* (2000), and "indies" like Miguel Arteta's *Chuck and Buck* (2000) gaining national attention. Although many such films have garnered well-deserved critical accolades, they have had only a marginal impact on the more typical commercial fare in American cinema. A recent film, *The Anniversary Party* (Jennifer Jason Leigh and Alan Cumming, 2001), may be an initial commercial test of this approach. One of the major tenets of the Dogma 95 movement and much of the entire video-to-film approach is a rejection of the slick, perfect Hollywood visual approach. Shot by one of Hollywood's most outstanding cinematographers, *The Anniversary Party* may be the first salvo in the high-end Hollywood "production values" approach to adopt the video-to-film approach. There will soon be many more, as Steven Soderbergh, Robert Rodriguez, and a host of others are embarking on projects.

Many labs are providing video-to-film transfer services, most employing some kind of kinescope. The results range from amazing to unacceptable. The kinescope approach can yield excellent results, but certain types of movement and lighting can still prove challenging to reproduce. Rates are quite expensive. Most labs transfer only to 35mm and charge from $250 to $1,000 per minute. Labs that transfer to 16mm charge from $200 to $250 per minute. Many of the previously mentioned films, such as *Dancer in the Dark,* have employed this approach. Using the higher-end transfers, a 2-hour feature would cost about $100,000. Given that audio tracks may require attention to be viable in a theatrical presentation, costs can only escalate.

Outside of kinescope transfers, the next step up is laser and related technology. Sony has been a leader in this field with its *EBR (electron beam recording)* system. Some form of this process has been around for a while, dating back to the excellent results in *The Abyss* and other films, and improvements to the technology have created results that, in many eyes, equal film. George Lucas's latest *Star Wars* saga—created, edited, and finished entirely in a digital environment—will undoubtedly be a major test of this approach. Lucas is planning as much digital projection as he can arrange, but many film prints will nevertheless be required for conventional distribution and exhibition. To create them Lucas will be using Industrial Light + Magic's proprietary and highly touted video-to-film transfer technology. Audience reactions to both the digital and conventional presentations will be of great interest.

Video-to-film is going to be a player for a while. The question, as suggested before, is if digital projection will become the clear winner and make film prints unnecessary. I think we can assume that it will happen, but again the question is *when.* In 1999 a lot of people were predicting that the conversion would be done in two years. Whatever the outcome, a great deal of research-and-development dollars will be expended toward this in the foreseeable future, given that theatrical distribution is still done with motion picture prints.

Potentially the biggest problem that makers have to face now is that there are simply too many options. Confronted with so many bewildering choices, making initial decisions can be problematic and lead to expensive regrets when complications appear down the road. Unfortunately, the only solution is to do your homework and learn as much as you can so that your decisions are as informed as possible. As suggested earlier, much of this hinges on the plan for your film's distribution—hard choices to make when you are just learning the lay of the land in the first place.

Although understanding the many technical options is critical, that is in a way only a small part of the story. If there has been a general shortcoming in the past ten years, it is the thinking that technology is an end in and of itself; but it is talented, creative people who make good movies, and experience in the craft is paramount. Directors from Steven Spielberg to Spike Lee are frequently noted for stating that it simply takes about ten years of working at it to get where you want to go. Too many people want to be there without the process of getting there; too many people think that they can become instant winners in the feature filmmaking sweepstakes. To quote the great final line from Jake Barnes in Ernest Hemingway's *The Sun Also Rises,* "Isn't it pretty to think so."

2

Creating the Shots

The Language of the Camera

Motion picture film is made up of a series of still photographic images. When projected in succession, these images provide the illusion of movement. Each individual photographic image is called a *frame*—a discrete entity that, just as in painting, has shapes and forms arranged in a *composition.* A sequence of frames is called a *shot,* which is commonly defined as the footage created from the moment the camera is turned on until it is turned off. Despite several styles of film that have specialized approaches, the shot is generally considered the basic building block of a film.

If the shot is the film's basic building block, the *setup* is the basic component of a film's production. Establishing a setup, also referred to as a *camera position, placement,* or, simply, *angle,* is just what the name suggests: arranging the camera to execute a shot. If you need a simple shot of a character saying "Yes," you have to set up the camera, do some basic set decoration, work out the lighting, record the sound, and so on. If you then want another character to respond "No," you have to go through the same process to execute that shot. A setup may involve something as simple as a single line of dialogue or it may cover extensive material that will be used throughout a scene.

Beyond these basic definitions, it is important to start thinking of the shots as accomplishing goals, dramatic or otherwise. A shot may show us a necessary piece of information or help create an atmosphere. It may serve as a simple delivery device for a line of dialogue, or produce associations that would not be elicited without its presence. A shot does not have to be discussed in a purely narrative (story) context. Like an abstract detail in a pointillist painting, it may be one piece in a grander abstract plan. It may add to the kinetic energy (movement) of a piece, such as in music videos. All shots have a purpose and must be thought out in terms of their relationship to the greater whole of the film. A shot has to do something because, whatever its content or purpose, its presence will have an impact.

When discussing shots, the idea of choice is key to the filming of any action— simple or complex, conventional or unconventional. Filmmakers repeatedly face a deceptively simple question: *Where do I put the camera to "cover" this action [this line of dialogue, this facial expression] in a way that is involving and dramatically effective?* Although covering the action implies a purely functional approach, there must be an internal logic to the way the camera is being used—a logic that fits the dramatic context and the formal approach of the material being shot. There must be a reason why a closer shot is used at a specific point. There must be a reason why you withdraw from the action with a wider shot at another point. A scene in which the presentation has not achieved some internal logic will appear shapeless and "undirected." The choices made will structure the viewer's perception of the scene and contribute to defining the shape and meaning of the film. The determining factors in choosing specific shots are the context of the material and the greater structure of shots in which each single shot participates.

Overshadowing this idea of choice should be an awareness that all the decisions made on a set (camera, lighting, sound, and so on) are driven by the demands of the editing room. Each shot must be approached with a sense of the whole film in mind—a process called *shooting for the edit*. A film crew comprises many skilled professionals, all of whom must at some level understand how the scene being filmed is going to cut together. The sound people must know what the editors need to cut the audio tracks. The cameraperson must think about what compositions will cut together and whether the scenes are being appropriately covered. The lighting crew needs to understand that the quality of light must be continuous from one shot to the next.

With the exception of a few specialized approaches, virtually every film—whether narrative, experimental, documentary, or animated—has to confront this question of the relationship of the camera to the subject and surroundings. Some common strategies for shooting scenes—and having a strategy is crucial—are developed throughout this text, but any plan must come from the filmmaker's understanding of the materials at hand and the dramatic needs of the subject matter. Whatever the approach to shooting, keep in mind that someone (possibly you) will have to fit all the pieces together. The beginning of the process must be informed by the end.

The Shots

Though this text devotes much attention to the *technical* elements of filmmaking, developing a thoughtful and intelligent approach to using the camera is the long-term goal. These first chapters propose the development of a menu of what many consider the resources—or the language—of cinema (see figure 3-1 for a summary). Such a list risks simplifying many complex issues, but the following should serve as an introduction to an array of commonly used shots employed to achieve specific dramatic goals within individual scenes. In determining a strategy for filming any action, whether straightforward or complex, the choices are limitless.

Proxemics

Proxemics, from *proximity,* refers to the distance between subject and camera. Essentially, there are three basic positions: long shot, medium shot, and close-up. There are many points in between and outside these three, such as medium close-ups and extreme long shots, but these alternative positions can be seen, and will be treated, as variations of the basic three. In studio television production, shot descriptions are very clearly defined and, especially when given as part of the instructions to a camera operator, have very specific meanings. In film production interpretation of specific positions is not always so rigid.

20   *Part I — Blocking for the Camera*

2-1

A long shot includes the full human body or more
Anthony Hopkins in Julie Taymor's *Titus* (1999)

2-2

A full-body shot, or full shot, includes just the person from head to toe
Charlie Chaplin's *One A.M.* (1916)

2-3

In an extreme long shot, subjects often look remote and isolated
Steve Buscemi in *Fargo*

LONG SHOT

A *long shot (LS)* is any shot that includes the full human body or more. **SEE 2-1** A shot that includes just the person from head to toe is alternately called a *full-body shot* or a *full shot*. A shot in which the subject is exceptionally far away from the camera is called an *extreme long shot (ELS)*.

The LS tends to be random in the information it presents. If there is a general shot of people in a space, it would be difficult for viewers to distinguish which character or characters are supposed to be the main subject of the shot. Momentarily discounting the notion that many elements, such as lighting, costume, and composition, can direct our attention to specific parts of the frame, we cannot logically value one character over another in a long shot. Closer shots are then used to convey much more specific information.

The full-body shot was much used by filmmakers in the early years of filmmaking but has fallen into modest disfavor in recent years. Director Charlie Chaplin shot almost exclusively in full-body shots. **SEE 2-2** He wanted the viewer to see both his body language and his facial expressions, without the involvement of closer shots or the clutter of complex editing.

The long shot, and even more so the extreme long shot, can also be used to diminish the subject. Presenting a lone figure in a vast landscape will make the figure appear overwhelmed by the surroundings. Westerns are well known for using both the LS and the ELS to achieve this effect, giving us rugged individuals within vast panoramas of untamed space. Other genres use this effect as well: In Ethan and Joel Coen's *Fargo* (1996), a character (Steve Buscemi) buries some money in a vast wasteland of snow and ice. **SEE 2-3** The emptiness and emotional aridity of the space give visual representation to the insanity of hiding a treasure with no visible landscapes for retrieval, serving as a metaphor for lives led with no visible relation to meaningful action—lives with no bearings.

MEDIUM SHOT

The shot of a person from the waist up gives more detail than the full-body shot but is generally neutral in its presentation of the subject. **SEE 2-4** The *medium shot (MS)* represents how we interact with people in life, at least in American culture. When two people speak, they generally address each other in something roughly approximating the medium shot, which literally puts the viewer on equal footing with the subject being filmed. We rarely get right up into other people's faces to speak. In current parlance that would be invading their space. On the other hand, we rarely address people in long shot except as part of a stiff, formal address or

2-4

A medium shot shows a person from the waist up
Bruno Ganz in Wim Wenders's
The American Friend (1977)

in the initial stages of being introduced to someone. In a medium shot, the subject is neither diminished nor unduly emphasized.

The key word in describing the MS is *neutral.* This is an arguable distinction because many see the full-body shot as equally neutral—if not more so—because it does not necessarily emphasize a particular element. There is merit to this argument, but the long shot's tendency toward randomness and diminishment often gives it additional dramatic baggage.

CLOSE-UP

The *close-up (CU)* is essentially a head shot, usually from the top shirt button up. **SEE 2-5** Anything closer than that is an *extreme close-up (ECU).* The *medium close-up (MCU),* which is from midchest up, is also frequently employed.

The CU is the shot that provides the greatest psychological identification with a character as well as amplifies details of actions. It is the point in which the viewer is forced to confront the subject and create some kind of internal psychological self. This identification in a CU can occasionally be so intense that the shot becomes claustrophobic. The close-up creates a tight and confined space. It has very strict boundaries both for an actor's performance and a viewer's sense of a character's freedom of movement. The viewer can get the sense of an oppressive and menacing closeness—an in-your-face effect.

Close-ups are also used to amplify details. The interrelationship of these shots can be particularly successful in creating suspense. A classic example of this is in

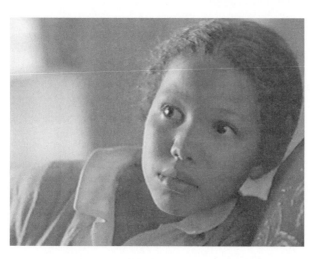

2-5

A close-up is essentially a head shot
Jurnee Smollett watches the adults from a
distance in Kasi Lemmons's *Eve's Bayou* (1997)

Alfred Hitchcock's *Sabotage* (1936), in which a woman (Sylvia Sidney) realizes that her husband (Oscar Homolka) was involved in the death of her younger brother. As she serves him dinner, she starts glancing at a large carving knife. The film cuts from close-ups of the carving knife to the woman looking at it. It then cuts to the man looking at the woman. She looks at the carving knife. He looks at the carving knife and then at her. This goes on for a brief period as the tension mounts. She finally takes the knife and stabs him. This type of editing is a very common and effective device for creating suspense.

It is clear that the sequence of LS-MS-CU represents a natural and logical progression of moving closer to a subject. The sequence also represents a general movement from information that is random and undifferentiated toward more-specific information. This simple progression is one of the mainstays of the conventional approach to scene construction. (Basic principles of scene structure are discussed in chapter 3.)

ANGLES

Although the term *angle* is often used on the set to designate simple camera position (setup), it also has a more limited meaning in terms of camera resources, that is, the height and orientation, or level, of the camera in relationship to the subject.

LOW-ANGLE SHOT

A *low-angle shot* is one in which the camera is below the subject, angled upward. **SEE 2-6** It has a tendency to make characters or environments look threatening, powerful, or intimidating. A classic example of the extended use of this shot is the presentation of Radio Raheem (Bill Nunn) in Spike Lee's *Do the Right Thing* (1989). **SEE 2-7** A scene involving a country kid's first day in the big city is another, albeit clichéd, example. The viewer is presented with low-angle shots of skyscrapers looming over the awed onlooker.

The low-angle shot can also give a distorted perspective, showing a world out of balance. This can produce a sense of both disorientation and foreboding. A good example comes from Alfred Hitchcock's *Vertigo* (1958). In an eerie cemetery scene, James Stewart is consistently filmed from below, making the framing of background

In a low-angle shot, the camera is below the subject, angled upward

The effect of this typical low-angle shot is to make the character seem powerful and intimidating
Bill Nunn in *Do the Right Thing*

2-8

This low-angle shot features distortion between the foreground and background, which can be intentionally disorienting

James Stewart in *Vertigo*

elements disorienting. The arrangement of the steeple and trees in the background gives the shot a very ominous tone. **SEE 2-8**

Foreground elements can also become distorted. Video artist Bill Viola used this notion to good effect in one of the movements of *Ancient of Days* (1978–81). The section has a lengthy shot of what is apparently a huge boulder in the foreground with a group of tourists milling around in the background. As the tourists move, we slowly start to realize that the perspective may be fooling us as to the size of the boulder. By the end of the shot, we realize that the rock is no more than a foot or so tall.

HIGH-ANGLE SHOT

The *high-angle shot* is obviously the opposite of low-angle, and its effects are the opposite as well. The camera is placed above the subject, pointing down. It tends to diminish a subject, making it look intimidated or threatened. This is the conventional way of making characters look insignificant.

Fritz Lang's masterpiece *M* (1931) has a classic exchange that incorporates both high- and low-angle shots. The film has a scene involving two men arguing, one of whom suspects the other of being the child murderer who is the focus of the film's story. One man is short (the accused) and the other tall (the accuser). The scene is then an interplay between high-angle and low-angle shots in which the viewer sees each man's perception of the other. **SEE 2-9**

2-9

A. Establishing shot
Fritz Lang's *M*

B. High-angle shot

C. Low-angle shot

EYE-LEVEL SHOT

Eye-level shots are those taken with the camera on or near the eye level of the character or subject being filmed. Eye-level shots tend to be neutral. Much like the medium shot, an eye-level shot puts the viewer on equal footing with the subject being filmed. It has none of the diminishing or exaggerating qualities of the high- and low-angle shots.

A significant majority of shots in theatrical films, as well as a high percentage of shots in episodic television, are shot at eye level. High- and low-angle shots can be misused, occasionally implying things about a character that are not justified dramatically. For all the stylistic bravura of the Radio Raheem shots in *Do the Right Thing*, some critics have wondered if the character should have appeared so threatening.

All of this said, most directors will tell you that they will not put the camera directly at eye level—they will position it just slightly above or below. True eye level is considered too confrontational, too direct to the audience.

BIRD'S-EYE VIEW

The *bird's-eye view*, also called an *overhead shot,* is actually a variation of the high-angle shot but is so extreme that it has an effect all its own. This shot is from directly above and tends to have a godlike, omniscient point of view; people look antlike and insignificant.

Many classic examples of the bird's-eye shot are, of course, found in Alfred Hitchcock's *The Birds* (1963). In one of the film's early bird attacks, the townspeople are gathered in a diner near a gas station. A gas station attendant is struck by a bird, and gas spills out around the pumps. It is ignited, and the birds start to attack as the firefighters and townspeople try to cope with the blaze. Suddenly, the film cuts to a perspective several hundred feet above the action. **SEE 2-10** As birds float serenely in the foreground, the futility and chaos of the human response to nature's revenge looks small and pitiful.

OBLIQUE SHOT (DUTCH ANGLE)

In an *oblique shot*, also called the *Dutch angle,* the camera is tilted laterally on a tripod so it is no longer parallel with the horizon. The oblique shot takes the straight lines of the world and presents them as diagonals. It is generally used to give an overwhelming sense of the world's being unbalanced or out of kilter. One of the classic employments of the oblique angle is in Carol Reed's *The Third Man* (1949), a mystery set in post–World War II Vienna. The tilted shot is largely responsible for the film's overall sense of a world where human values and actions are distorted. **SEE 2-11**

2-10

The bird's-eye view takes the high-angle shot to an extreme
Alfred Hitchcock's *The Birds*

2-11

The oblique shot (Dutch angle) is generally used to convey a world that is off balance or out of kilter
Carol Reed's *The Third Man*

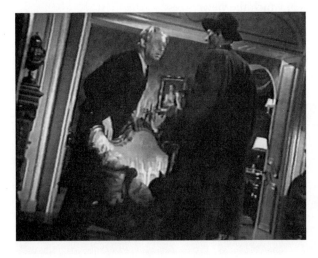

The 1960's "Batman" television show also used the oblique angle extensively. In this case the effect is campy, the action being highly stylized to exaggerate the effect. To a certain extent, the oblique angle is problematic for just this reason: It is so transparent in its effect that it virtually announces its own cliché. Many critics have found fault with *The Third Man,* claiming that the use of the oblique angle eventually becomes predictable and finally banal.

When a technique like the oblique angle is used, we must also recognize that employing a camera that is level with the world has certain aesthetic assumptions. With a level camera in such a high percentage of what we see in films, it begins to appear so natural that we rarely even question it. As with some of the other approaches, such as medium shots and eye-level shots, a level camera is used when subjective judgments are not desired. The level camera approximates our general perception of the world.

POINT-OF-VIEW SHOT

A *point-of-view shot* represents the perception or viewpoint of a specific character. It is not used as frequently as one might at first presume, primarily because camera vision and human vision are decidedly not the same. The eye has unselective focus—the constantly shifting gaze is somewhat random and chaotic in its focus of attention. If you watch a dance, your eye might randomly go from the dancer's feet to her hands, to her face, then back to her feet. The human gaze shifts with only minimal structure to the view it creates. A camera's vision is considerably more focused and selective.

Many films, however, use the point-of-view shot effectively. Horror films have come to use it quite extensively—for instance, replicating the point of view of the killer as he relentlessly stalks his prey. The selective focus actually seems to aid the effect, representing a maniacally focused perception. Robert Montgomery's *Lady in the Lake* (1946) is a classic exploration of the point-of-view shot. The entire film is played from a detective's perspective. The viewer sees what he sees. It is an interesting experiment, but eventually becomes so artificial that the approach is seldom duplicated except as snippets within a larger whole. Hitchcock's *Vertigo* has a much more common and successful approach to the point-of-view shot. The film constantly shifts from the looker (James Stewart) to what he is looking at. The film is very voyeuristic, as are many Hitchcock films, in its constant positioning of the viewer and the viewed.

Movement

Clearly, camera movement is a critical aspect of the way films work, in terms of both the kinetic energy it can provide and its employment as a storytelling device. The German filmmakers of the 1920s are credited with exploring and perfecting many of the effects that can be achieved with the moving camera. They are responsible for what is generally referred to as *fluid camera technique*—an approach to shooting that smooths out or eliminates entirely any bumpy camerawork, moving from composition to composition in an efficient and timely manner. This was the approach adopted by classic Hollywood cinema and, although challenged by more-informal camera techniques, remains an important philosophical approach to shooting. Later chapters address some of the character of the difficult-to-define kinetic aspects; focus here is on the employment of movement in a storytelling mode.

Pan and tilt controls enable you to swivel and tilt the camera

Pans and Tilts

A *pan* is a shot in which the camera is simply swiveled horizontally on a tripod. A *tilt* is similar to a pan except its movement is vertical. **SEE 2-12** Both pans and tilts can be used to reveal new elements within the frame—elements of which the viewer may have been unaware. A typical example might be a shot of a couple walking down a street hand in hand. The camera then pans over to show a crestfallen suitor, seeing them together for the first time.

   With that revelation we can create associations and in some cases a sense of causality. An example of the use of the pan to create an association comes from D. W. Griffith's *Birth of a Nation* (1914). There is one shot that starts with a wide view of a Civil War battle and then pans to a woman huddled with small children on a wagon. To emphasize the point further, Griffith includes a pan back to the battle. The conclusion is inescapable. The misery is a by-product of the battle. Some might argue that the same effect could be accomplished with a cut between the two subjects, but by panning the two subjects are spatially, and thus philosophically, connected.

   Although the pan can be employed as described, its extensive use may be problematic because it does not really duplicate the movement of the human eye. When following a lateral movement, your eyes move by themselves or in conjunction with head and body movement. The pan is somewhat like pivoting your head without moving your eyes. We occasionally view movement in this manner—such as at a tennis match—but it is often in specific circumstances and it feels and looks unnatural.

   Pans have to be carefully planned in terms of both their execution and their eventual use. The word *pan* will quickly become part of your everyday vocabulary, but the movement is generally used in conjunction with subject movement or as part of larger camera movements rather than as an expressive technique. You can prove this to yourself with a few simple shooting tests. Pan from one person sitting in a chair to another or go to a theater rehearsal and pan from subject to subject on the stage. Unless you are following movement, the pans will probably look mannered and stagy.

The general application of the tilt is similar to that of the pan—revealment and so on—except that it can also go from one angle to another, say, from eye level to low-angle. A common example would be a child running down a street and then straight into someone's knees. We then see the tilt from the knees to an intimidating low-angle shot of a disapproving adult.

WHEELED CAMERA SUPPORTS

The past several decades have seen a profusion of specialized devices to assist camera moves, with a trend toward electronically assisted movement. As technology evolves, distinctions between the following types of movements have blurred significantly. For example, many dollies have modest crane capabilities and cranes can be adapted to do other tasks. Although students rarely get their hands on the newest technologies, you should be familiar with what is available. This prepares you for professional experience and sets you to thinking about inexpensive ways of duplicating complex effects.

DOLLIES

A *dolly* is a wheeled vehicle with a camera-mounting device. **SEE 2-13** Dollies can be as simple as a go-cart–style platform with wheels on which to mount a tripod. The more sophisticated designs have seats for the camera operator and assistant,

Dollies can be as simple as a go-cart–style platform on wheels or as sophisticated as a computerized vehicle complete with seating
The Chapman Super PEEWEE II dolly

with movement manipulated by a variety of complex controls. The earliest dollies were large, heavy vehicles that were used almost entirely in the studio. The many new lightweight dollies make dolly work on location so easy that their use has almost become the norm. Dollies often require specially designed *tracks* to eliminate the bumpiness of moving over uneven surfaces. **SEE 2-14**

Dolly shots can be quite effective, because they can go from one proxemic position to another—from the random information of a long shot to the specifics of a close-up or vice versa. The camera moving in, called a *push-in,* can be used to clarify detail, identify objects of importance, or amplify emotion. Moving out, called a *pull-out,* can lose people in bigger spaces or, as with a pan, reveal elements heretofore unseen.

Milos Forman's *Amadeus* (1984) contains many examples of effective dolly shots. Although the elderly Salieri (F. Murray Abraham) narrates the film, his dialogue in the film's flashback story is quite limited. Much of the film is composed of reaction shots, often incorporating movement, of Salieri's responding to the impetuousness of the young Mozart. One sequence shows him seeing Mozart for the first time. **SEE 2-15** Salieri is hiding in the room as Mozart (Tom Hulce) flirts lewdly with his future wife (Elizabeth Berridge). Salieri is stunned by the sudden realization that this "dirty child," as he calls him, is the great composer. Here, Foreman uses the dolly to emphasize Salieri's reaction, the movement amplifying the shocked look on his face.

With the camera mounted on a dolly, it can also move alongside a stationary action in what is called a ***tracking shot.*** Although its distinction from a dolly shot may seem arbitrary, a tracking shot follows alongside, in front of, or behind a moving subject; the character's position in the frame remains roughly the same, and what

2-15

Dolly shots can be effective for going from the random information of an establishing shot to the specific information of a close-up

Milos Forman's *Amadeus*

A tracking shot follows alongside, in front of, or behind a moving subject

changes is the background. **SEE 2-16** Although this may not appear to be a significant difference, it can be played for some clever effects. Buster Keaton's *The General* (1925) has several good examples of this. **SEE 2-17** With the camera on a train running on parallel tracks, Keaton is on top of another train, furiously chopping wood and oblivious to his surroundings. Keaton's position within the frame remains relatively consistent, but in the background we see the entire Confederate Army pass behind him. Moments later the entire Union Army passes behind him as well, again entirely unnoticed. Thus, in one sequence, Keaton's character has unknowingly passed from behind friendly lines to behind enemy lines.

2-17

The background shifts in a typical tracking shot, whereas character position remains roughly the same
Buster Keaton's *The General*

2-18

A camera crane enables you to get above or below a subject, thus varying height in relationship to the subject

2-19

A camera crane has full freedom of movement both horizontally and vertically
The Chapman Mobile Titan crane

CRANES

A camera *crane* has a single elevating arm on a rolling vehicle. Cranes vary from the small ones incorporated into dollies to large vehicles that can get the camera high in the air. Cranes generally have seats for the camera operator and at least one assistant. The crane can accomplish many of the same things as the dolly; but whereas the dolly, in its strict definition, has only horizontal possibilities, the crane has full freedom of horizontal and vertical movement. The ability to get above or below a subject allows one to vary height in relationship to the subject. Frequently, the camera goes up to give the viewer an omniscient view. **SEE 2-18 AND 2-19**

A good example of a crane shot is an oft-cited one from Alfred Hitchcock's *Notorious* (1946). **SEE 2-20** The shot starts with a dollylike movement, showing a wide shot of a party scene. Filmed from a balcony, the

2-20

This classic crane shot goes from a general establishing shot to a very specific close-up
Alfred Hitchcock's *Notorious*

information is random and undifferentiated. It simply establishes the scene as a formal party. It appears to be a routine shot designed to create a simple transition between one scene and the next. Due to the conventional nature of this opening, what comes next catches the viewer off guard. The camera cranes all the way down to a tight shot of Ingrid Bergman's hand. We see that she is tightly grasping a key—a key stolen from her husband. The shot thus goes from a random view to a very specific piece of information that is crucial to the plot. The complexity of the technical execution of such a shot is breathtaking, given that the position of the key has to be coordinated to be in just the right place in the final composition. It is similar to shooting an arrow through the hole of a moving doughnut at fifty paces.

ARMS

There are many other types of movement devices, particularly modifications to the basic crane design. Lacking a seat for the operator, *arms* suspend the camera on the end of a crane-style device. **SEE 2-21** The camera operator uses a joysticklike remote control to execute pans and tilts while watching on a video monitor what the camera is recording.

Spike Lee's *Do the Right Thing* has a spectacular shot that was filmed with an arm or similar device. **SEE 2-22** The shot starts with Mother Sister (Ruby Dee) and the Mayor (Ossie Davis) sitting on a bed. They get up and start walking toward the camera. The camera pulls all the way back and out of a window. As they look out of the window, the camera cranes around to Mookie (Spike Lee) on the street. It is an exceptional shot, tying together many of the film's elements.

Arms suspend the camera on the end of a crane-style device
The Chapman Lenny Arm II

This spectacular shot was executed with a jib or an arm
Spike Lee's *Do the Right Thing*

HANDHELD CAMERA

With the *handheld camera*, shots lack the smoothness to which so many technical resources are devoted. The handheld camera can give a you-are-there feel to the shots, a sense of the viewer's being a participant in the action. This "camera as a participant" approach can lend a sense of urgency or chaos to the action. The handheld camera can also give scenes an informal and spontaneous tone, though its use to achieve this end has a number of pitfalls.

The handheld camera has been very popular in documentary and experimental films and has made inroads in feature films as well. The development of lightweight portable cameras and sound recorders in the late 1950s had a tremendous impact on documentary film, with filmmakers shooting handheld on location under almost any circumstances. A significant number of experimental films have used the handheld camera as an alternative to the often rigid formal approach of commercial cinema. In Jonas Mekas's *Reminiscences of a Journey to Lithuania* (1971), the filmmaker took a trip to his homeland, photographing short snippets of subjects that interested him. The resulting film, which Mekas narrates in a fragmented, poetic style, is a free-form collection of home movie–like shots, very few of which are more than a second or two long.

Although there are occasional early examples, the handheld camera has become more frequent in commercial feature films since the 1960s. Stanley Kubrick's *Dr. Strangelove* (1964) has some beautiful examples of thoughtful use of the handheld camera. It is used most effectively in the scenes of the attack on Jack D. Ripper's compound and in those of the crippled bomber as it wings for Russia. **SEE 2-23** The assault on Ripper's compound emulates the chaos of combat footage. It is particularly effective when intercut with the highly formal images of the war room, where the fate of the world is being decided.

The scenes in the bomber are even more effective. Just after the plane is hit, sparks and smoke are everywhere. The handheld camera charges in and gives the appearance of capturing the action as it happens. The images, when looked at individually, take on an almost abstract quality. Many of *Dr. Strangelove*'s scenes are played for comedy, and the handheld camera scenes play as a stark and effective contrast. Lars von Trier's *Breaking the Waves* (1997) is one of the most recent examples of a film that employs the handheld camera extensively for effect.

2-23

The free-form use of a handheld camera in this scene emulates the chaos of the action on-screen
Stanley Kubrick's *Dr. Strangelove*

SPECIALIZED RIGS

The many specialized rigs available today give smoothness and fluidity to shots that were previously impractical or impossible. New developments in technology undoubtedly allow filmmakers innumerable opportunities. Unfortunately, the use of these may not be feasible on smaller projects for some time to come.

Steadicam   The *Steadicam*™ was designed in recognition of the freedom of movement benefits offered by the handheld camera, while also recognizing the desire to eliminate its attendant shakiness. A device that mounts on the camera operator's chest, it incorporates balanced weight and reciprocating movement to give fluidity to what are essentially handheld shots. It is an expensive piece of equipment that requires a trained operator in top physical condition, and its use has become widespread, particularly in the shooting of commercials.

One of the first uses of the Steadicam in a theatrical feature was in John Schlesinger's *Marathon Man* (1976). In one scene Dustin Hoffman is chased on foot through New York's Central Park. He runs up and down stairs. He runs across cobblestone streets. The camera is with him everywhere he goes. These shots would have been almost inconceivable without the Steadicam, requiring either a handheld camera or extensive track. In the first case, the shot would have reflected each and every one of the camera operator's footsteps. In the second case, conventional track would often be in the shots and could not accommodate things like the shape of a staircase.

Car rigs   Scenes sometimes called for shots from moving vehicles. Often these are just standard close-ups or medium shots of the vehicle's occupants. They would be routine, except that engine vibration and road bumps are major complications. Specialized mounts are used to attach the camera securely to the vehicle and, with a design almost like a shock absorber, minimize pavement bumpiness.

Shooting out of the window of a moving vehicle can be employed to establish a sense of place or create an impression of great expanse. Terrence Malick's *Badlands* (1973) has many exceptional moving-vehicle shots of the arid northern plains as representations of the emptiness of the film's rootless and unconnected characters. Toward the end of the film, distant mountains serve as both an actual and a metaphorical destination that is continuously moved toward but never reached.

Aerial   Aerial shots (from planes and helicopters) have their own particular aesthetic and also need specialized mounts to reduce vibration. *Aerial shots* can be used as variations of crane shots, but the movement and the elevation set them apart. Ken Burns's television series "The Civil War" (1989) employed long aerial shots with the camera literally floating down some of the back-country rivers of the battle areas. These shots served as transitional devices, background for narrative, and a means of giving the viewer a strong sense of place. One lengthy shot traveling down a beautiful, hazy river at sunset is juxtaposed against a speech by Frederick Douglass about the openness and promise of America versus the reality of slave life.

Focus Effects

Occasionally, beginners expect that, as a rule, everything should be in focus. Although this is indeed the approach of many films, focus can be used to create many effects—from those so subtle that they are rarely noticed by the viewer to others so big that they demand to be interpreted on a thematic level. As should be expected, there are a number of approaches to using focus as an aesthetic expression.

DEEP FOCUS

The approach that keeps all elements in the frame sharp is called *deep focus*. It has been written about extensively and has many champions in the critical and theoretical world. Theorists interested in deep focus are usually champions of a realist approach to cinema. Orson Welles, Jean Renoir, and Alain Resnais, among others, have been generally recognized as creators of some of the great experiments in deep focus. Renoir's *The Rules of the Game* (1939) is often cited as an early example of the use of many different planes of focus to facilitate complex, multilevel action. Working with the technical elements that maximize focus is critical to achieving this goal.

SHALLOW FOCUS

Shallow focus is an approach in which several different planes of focus are incorporated within a single image. This can create a purposefully less realistic image—one that manipulates viewer attention and suggests different planes of action, both literally and figuratively. Shallow focus is less of a theoretical construct than deep focus is and it does not have as strong a critical following, probably because realist critics are so firmly committed to deep focus.

The play between soft and sharp focus can be used to achieve a number of different effects:

- Suggesting other planes of action without allowing them to dominate viewer attention

- Isolating a subject in a space

- Suggesting that a subject lacks clarity

- Shifting focus for a form of dramatic emphasis or to draw viewer attention to a specific part of the frame

- Acting as a transition from one scene to the next

Planes of focus can direct viewer attention to specific parts of the frame. Just as you can choose different shots—LS, MS, CU—you can choose different areas of the frame to be in focus. Gordon Willis's cinematography for Herbert Ross's *Pennies from Heaven* (1982) has a number of examples of this. When Arthur Parker (Steve Martin) meets a young blind woman in a tunnel, he is stunned by her purity and grace but has no context in which to articulate his feelings. As they emerge from the tunnel, Arthur is out of focus in the background, an effect that forces the viewer to focus on her. **SEE 2-24** This shot also amplifies the unfocused longings of Arthur, a character who is virtually made mute by the grimness of his surroundings.

Allowing the background to go out of focus to suggest peripheral action is a common effect. A scene in a diner from Jonathan Demme's *Something Wild* (1986) provides an excellent example of this. **SEE 2-25** When working in public places, it is generally desirable to use extras, or "atmosphere" as they are called, to

Focus isolates the background subject, forcing the viewer to concentrate on the subject in the close-up
Herbert Ross's Pennies from Heaven

2-25

Leaving the background action out of focus prevents
the viewer from being distracted by it
Ray Liotta in *Something Wild*

2-26

In a shallow-focus approach, several planes of focus are
incorporated within a single image
Bernardo Bertolucci's *The Last Emperor*

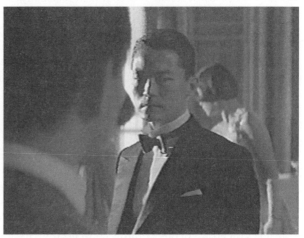

suggest the presence of other people. Placing them out of focus can achieve this
suggestion without attracting attention and diminishing viewer involvement with
foreground action.

Bernardo Bertolucci's *The Last Emperor* (1987) also has many examples of a
shallow-focus approach. The young emperor (John Lone) is frequently portrayed as
being alone and isolated. To emphasize this, both foreground and background
elements are often purposefully out of focus. **SEE 2-26**

SHIFTING FOCUS

The discussion of focus so far has left out an obvious complicating factor: movement.
Not only do subjects move, but camera movement is often incorporated into shots
as well. As either the subject or the camera moves, focus is necessarily going to have
to change. You therefore have to *rack focus,* which is physically shifting the focus
ring as the shot is being executed. Racks are usually done by the *first assistant
cameraperson (1st AC)*—the crew member who is responsible for the cleanliness
and proper operation of the camera. In British films there is actually a separate credit
for "focus puller," a recognition that suggests how frequently their talents are
employed. Planning and executing a rack focus usually requires setting up marks on
the floor and tape on the focus ring. Practical aspects of a rack focus are covered in
chapter 10.

The rack focus effect is employed frequently, although it is most often used to
keep a moving subject in focus. As such, it goes largely unnoticed. Occasionally, it is
used as a transitional device to get from one scene to the next: A shot will be slowly
racked out of focus, then the first shot of the new scene will start out of focus and be
racked into focus. Another technique is to start with some foreground element in
focus and then rack to a background element.

Focus can also be used effectively to delineate different elements of a shot—to
change the emphasis, and hence the viewer's attention, from one area of the frame
to another. Emphasis is created by shifting focus from one subject to another, not by
editing or by the camera's proximity to the subject.

A shot from Mike Nichols's *The Graduate* (1967) illustrates this effect well. **SEE 2-27** It occurs in a scene in which Elaine (Katherine Ross) learns that Benjamin (Dustin Hoffman) has been having an affair with her mother (Ann Bancroft). The revelation is handled visually: Benjamin looks at Mrs. Robinson, who is standing behind Elaine. Mrs. Robinson is out of focus. As Elaine turns, there is a rack focus to Mrs. Robinson that makes Elaine's sudden comprehension of the situation inescapable. As Elaine turns back to Ben, she remains out of focus for several seconds, serving to amplify her emotional confusion. Then she is racked back into focus. Focus racks are often timed to specific movements so they are less noticeable.

Racking focus between characters in conversation to achieve an effect similar to editing is occasionally tried. One character says her line, then focus racks to another character, who says his line, then it racks back again. This was a popular approach in a number of films in the 1960s and 1970s. It is occasionally employed today, though if overused the effect can appear mannered and artificial.

Lens Perspective and Characteristics

Lens perspective refers to the way lenses represent space. Different kinds of lenses have different effects on the way we perceive depth and dimensionality within an image. This aspect of lenses has a great impact on the process of choosing a lens. Directors and cinematographers generally do not choose lenses for how close they bring the viewer to the subject; that can be controlled by simple camera placement. Lenses are usually chosen for how they represent space.

WIDE-ANGLE

The defining characteristic of the *wide-angle lens,* also called a short lens, is that it elongates space; that is, objects appear more distant from each other than they actually are. A number of objectives can be accomplished with this. Like the long shot, which can diminish a character, the short lens can be a critical element in this effect. It can take a big space and make it even bigger. Using a short lens on a lone figure within a vast landscape can increase the effect of isolation and diminishment. Orson Welles's *Citizen Kane* was one of the first films to extensively explore the use of the short lens for effect. In *Kane*'s low-angle shots, the short lens adds to the sense of a cavernous and oppressive space. One impressive shot from Bernardo Bertolucci's *The Sheltering Sky* (1990) has a vista with characters looking off a cliff, the desert stretching out in

2-27

A rack focus can be used metaphorically, such as to symbolize a character's confusion and then sudden comprehension
Mike Nichols's *The Graduate*

2-28

The wide angle of this shot maximizes the sense of tiny figures against a vast landscape
Bernardo Bertolucci's *The Sheltering Sky*

2-29

This extreme wide-angle shot gives the interaction between the characters an unsettling subtext
Orson Welles's *Touch of Evil*

front of them. **SEE 2-28** It is clearly shot with a wide-angle lens to maximize the sense of tiny figures against a vast indifferent landscape.

Wide-angle lenses also bend lines in the composition outward. Orson Welles used an extreme wide-angle lens for several car shots in *Touch of Evil* (1958), giving the conversation between the two men an unsettling subtext. **SEE 2-29** Extreme wide-angle lenses bend corners and give almost funhouse-mirror distortion to the objects or people being filmed. They are rarely used for portraiture, because they balloon people's faces and make them look heavy or freakish. The closer the lens is to the subject, the more pronounced the effect. The most familiar distorting lens is called a *fish-eye*, which sees almost a full 180 degrees in front of the camera. Its effects are so extreme that it is not used frequently.

The most inappropriate use of a wide-angle lens that I can remember came from a film about a family farm being foreclosed. There was a shot of a character looking on sadly as all the household goods were being sold. The cinematographer shot the character with a wide-angle lens, which made her look grotesque and freakish. I have never been able to discern why the cinematographer made that choice. Possibly he thought it would make the woman look miserable and downtrodden. It was clearly a carefully considered decision on his part, because he had to get right up into her face to get the shot—something that made her, a nonprofessional, quite uncomfortable. Wide-angle lenses are used extensively, but care must be taken with some of their more extreme characteristics.

NORMAL

A *normal lens* basically gives a normal representation of perspective. Subjects look roughly the same size as they do from the camera, and the distances between subjects look unaltered. One must remember, however, that the film image is two-dimensional. Just because a normal lens is used does not mean that the image will accurately represent three-dimensional space. You have to think of many more issues, such as composition, focus, and lighting, if you want to create an image that appears to have some depth. As a developing pattern might suggest, the normal lens is probably the most commonly employed.

TELEPHOTO

The *telephoto lens* does the opposite of the wide-angle lens. Rather than elongate perspective, the telephoto lens squashes it, making things look closer together. This is a very common effect and many examples come to mind. In films set in big cities, directors and cinematographers like to use telephoto lenses to shoot crowd shots on streets. It makes people look crowded together and cramped and exaggerates the effect of people packed together like rats.

The long lens can also make movement toward the camera look distorted, giving a subject an almost dreamlike inability to reach its destination. Another shot from Mike Nichols's *The Graduate* provides an excellent example of this effect. Near the end, Benjamin (Dustin Hoffman) is running toward a church where Elaine is getting married. To amplify his desperation, one of the key shots is clearly executed with a long lens. Hoffman is running as fast as he can, but he does not appear to cover any appreciable space. **SEE 2-30**

As the shot starts, you can see how compressed the space appears. You can tell that the car and the telephone pole are at different distances from the camera, but you would be hard-pressed to tell how far apart they actually are. It is also very difficult to tell if Hoffman has passed the car or is still behind it. The second frame represents a point four seconds into the shot, four seconds being a much more substantial amount of screen time than it might seem. Again, it is impossible to judge how much distance he has covered. The third frame represented is eight seconds into the shot. The effect is not quite like he is running in place, but it does seem as though he is spending a great deal of time and exerting a tremendous amount of energy to cover what appears to be a very short distance. The entire action of this segment of the shot takes eighteen seconds. In the words of the Red Queen in *Alice in Wonderland*, "The faster I go, the behinder I get."

The effect can even jam things together to the extent that it almost makes the image appear abstract. Landscapes can take on an exaggerated and heightened form. Telephoto lenses also flatten surfaces in a way that can be considered the opposite of the ballooning effect of wide-angle lenses. The human face can appear narrow and compacted, with the nose flattened and the eyes closer together. This effect is not as unflattering as the wide-angle one.

ZOOM

The term *zoom* as it is meant here has existed long enough that most people understand what it means. The *zoom lens* includes all of the focal lengths discussed previously. Although it may strike some people as odd that the zoom lens was left out of the section on camera movement, it was left out because it is not truly a *movement*. The zoom effect is created by movable elements in the lens that either bring the subject closer to or push it farther away from a stationary camera. This

2-30

This telephoto shot gives a dreamlike aspect to the character's desperate yet seemingly futile pursuit
Mike Nichols's *The Graduate*

2-31

The perspective shifts in the zoom shots
Dustin Hoffman in *The Graduate*

allows shots, like some camera movements, to go from very random information to very specific information and vice versa.

The zoom has side effects, however, that are clearly specific to the zoom and that distinguish it from traditional camera movement. It includes a transition from the spatial characteristics of one focal length to the spatial characteristics of another. If we zoom in on a subject, we go from the elongation of the wide-angle lens to the squashed perspective of the telephoto. The dolly shot looks decidedly different because it is usually done with a fixed lens, so the perspective characteristics remain the same throughout the movement. The dolly gives the feeling of moving independently through a space, whereas the zoom gives the feeling of being mechanically moved through space. In effect, the dolly brings the viewer to the subject, and the zoom brings the subject to the viewer.

Despite this difference, many directors still tend to use the zoom like the dolly. It takes much less setup time and equipment, thus accomplishing roughly the same effect at a much cheaper price. In the faster working climate of television, it is particularly popular. As such it has gotten a reputation as the poor man's dolly or the hack director's dolly. It is rarely used thoughtfully as a means of representing different spatial approaches.

The previously mentioned shot from *The Graduate* of Dustin Hoffman running toward the church is one of the few good examples of how the spatial characteristics of both extremes of the zoom lens can be used to good effect. **SEE 2-31** Hoffman's run toward the camera is only one segment of a longer shot. When Hoffman reaches the camera, the camera pans and zooms out at the same time. **SEE 2-32** The result is the

2-32

The simultaneous pan and zoom changes the perspective from a squashed space to an elongated space

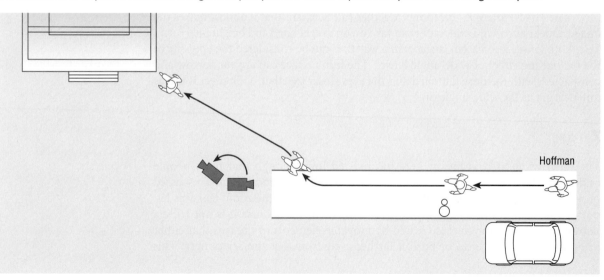

transition from a lens that squashes space to a lens that elongates space. Suddenly Hoffman is a tiny figure dwarfed by a huge church.

The zoom lens can also be used for what has become known as a "vertigo shot," popularized in the Alfred Hitchcock film of the same name. In a vertigo shot, the lens is zoomed in as the camera is dollied out or vice versa. If this is done carefully, the framing of the composition remains exactly the same while only the perspective characteristics change. The perspective of the shot is thus smashed or elongated like an accordion, which can give a very distorted or subjective sense of screen space. In *Vertigo* it is used to re-create the point of view of a man terrified of heights. In Martin Scorsese's *Goodfellas* (1990), the technique is employed to represent the subjective perspective of the Ray Liotta character in his most drug-addicted and paranoid state.

Choice of lens is a key part of all shooting decisions. The employment of a specific lens brings with it both the lens's representation of space and its inherent characteristics. Occasionally, someone comes up with the mistaken notion that telephoto lenses are used for close-ups and wide-angle lenses for long shots. You can use a telephoto lens for a full-body shot, but the field of view will be narrow and you will have to be some distance from the subject. Wide-angle lenses are often used for close-ups, though one must be aware of their distorting qualities. It is all dependent on what you are trying to achieve visually. If a director wants a scene to have a sense of open space, he or she will opt for a wide-angle lens. Scenes that seek a very constrained sense of space require the opposite. You must understand the properties of different lens types, because lens choice has a big impact on the image and thus occasions many preshooting discussions.

3

Constructing the Scene

Oᴎᴇ **of the necessary steps in planning** the filming of a scene is to develop a strategy for shooting. Although this involves developing a specific approach in the form of a storyboard or shot list, some basic principles of scene construction must be considered before trying to sketch anything out.

In theater production *blocking* refers to planning where the actors will be and how action occurs in relationship to the set and stage space. In film this is complicated by the presence of the camera. ***Blocking for the camera*** refers to staging action for the camera. As much or more than any other element, blocking for the camera must be done with a clear concept of how the scene is going to be edited. It might be useful to think of a film as a jigsaw puzzle, each piece of which must be created individually and have a specific place in the finished pattern. But unlike a puzzle, there is no single, correct way to put together a film. The design of each film bears the mark of the filmmaker's personal style, with the result being a unique piece of work.

The choices you make in terms of setups are entirely up to you, but seeing all choices as being equal is a mistake. Shooting a scene should be done with the knowledge not only of a wide set of rules intrinsic to film, but also of accepted, often-anecdotal folk wisdom that has evolved over the years and of many aesthetic principles developed by filmmakers and artists in other media. There may not be one right way to do a scene, but there are myriad wrong ways. There are approaches that many talented people have determined work; there are others that simply do not. If the goal is to create a scene that is clear and coherent to the viewer, understanding basic scene construction is crucial.

The Director

Directors are usually involved from near the beginning of a project all the way to, in some cases, the creation of the final print. A film is organized into three critical phases: preproduction, production, and postproduction. *Preproduction* constitutes the planning and preparation: the process of identifying and securing all the elements— aesthetic, human, and material—that will be needed for the film. This includes fine-tuning the script, casting, location scouting, set design, finding props, organizing the shooting into a series of manageable tasks, and whatever else it takes to get into a position to shoot. *Production* includes all the actual shooting. Producers often play a critical role here, but the director is usually the key decision-making force in both

3-1
The menu of the camera resources presented so far

Proxemics	Camera Movement	Lens Perspective and Characteristics
Long shot	Pan	Wide-angle
Medium shot	Tilt	Normal
Close-up	Dolly	Telephoto
Camera Angles	Tracking	Zoom
Low	Crane, arm, and so on	
High	Handheld	**Focus**
Eye level	Steadicam	Shifting focus
Bird's-eye view	Aerial	Deep focus
Oblique/level		Shallow focus
Point-of-view		

of these stages of a film. Some directors are also involved in *postproduction,* the editing and all the detailed finishing processes, which is covered in part V.

It is the director's choices that drive the rest of the crew's actions. On fictional films the director is responsible for determining the *look*—the visual character—of the film, rehearsing and organizing the actors' performances, selecting the setups and all attendant details, and marshaling all forces toward the completion of the material. Although other key crew members have varying levels of input, it is the director's responsibility to define the script in terms of both a theatrical, dramatic interpretation and the story's visual presentation.

The Menu

Before discussing scene construction itself, a summary of the visual resources presented so far is in order. **SEE 3-1** Lists such as this risk constant editorializing. On close scrutiny some of the categories begin to break down, and there are always exceptions to any suggested effect. Knowledge of these basics, however, can serve as a starting point for both those who want to learn conventional film techniques and those who want to go beyond them. That said, the implementation of certain techniques, such as close-ups, is often consistent from the most adventurous independent production to conventional television shows, even though the content of the shots may be radically different.

Certain patterns start to suggest themselves with these shots. If you want an essentially neutral portrayal, for example, you might choose specific approaches, such as a medium shot, at eye level, with a level camera. Most of the shots of Radio Raheem in Spike Lee's *Do the Right Thing* are from a low angle, but there are several that have even more extreme characteristics. One shot of the character is from a low angle, photographed with a wide-angle lens, with the camera at an oblique angle. **SEE 3-2** The wide angle exaggerates the character's features, and the oblique angle gives the sense of a world out of balance. Whether or not one agrees

3-2
An oblique, low-angle shot with a wide-angle lens exaggerates the character's features and conveys a world out of balance
Bill Nunn in *Do the Right Thing*

with the intimidating nature of the combination of these effects, one can appreciate how a shot like this figures into the grand plan of the film. One of the major elements of *Do the Right Thing* is the increasing tension caused by the hot and stifling day on which the action occurs. The shot of Radio Raheem, as well as many other elements of the film, creates an atmosphere where everything is distorted and on the edge.

Although lists like figure 3-1 can give valuable ideas, these effects should not be treated as a mix-and-match recipe. It is not a matter of getting diminishment by mixing two-thirds long shot with one-third high angle. That approach would most likely be stereotypical and clichéd. Rather, the camera should be approached as a meaning-producing instrument. A list like this should never be seen as an end. The myriad subtleties continue to be explored more than a century after the first frame of film saw a glimpse of light.

Basic Scene Structure

It is clear from the discussion of shots and other resources that where the camera is placed in relation to the scene plays a central role in guiding how the viewer interprets character and action. A long shot of a character responding to something, for example, does not draw us in as persuasively as the same response in a closer shot. The sequence of long shot/medium shot/close-up (LS-MS-CU) represents a process of moving closer to the action, of moving from a random view to much more specific information.

DRAMATIC EMPHASIS

The concept of dramatic emphasis lies at the heart of narrative filmmaking and can be a critical component of experimental and documentary film as well. Simply stated, *dramatic emphasis* refers to the director's using the camera to show us the action in the order and with the amplification that he or she wants. The director breaks down the scene into an interrelationship of dramatic perspectives (shots) that focus viewer attention on specific information, characters, dialogue, action, and so on.

Alfred Hitchcock's *Notorious* has many remarkable sequences, but one of its more subtle scenes provides a clear example of this concept. **SEE 3-3** The scene takes place about one-quarter of the way into the film and involves Alicia (Ingrid Bergman) trying to have a discussion with an unresponsive suitor, Dev (Cary Grant). Struggling with a shady past, Alicia is trying to start over—making the insult that Dev delivers in the middle of this scene all the more humiliating. The entire beginning of the scene is played in a *two-shot*, so named because it shows two people from roughly the waist up. The timing of the cut to the close-up is key to the scene's effect. The exact positioning of the cut is indicated by the horizontal line, right at the end of Dev's line of dialogue, and the camera subtly emphasizes the emotional deflation visible in Alicia's face.

The two-shot is played out for an unusually long period of time—almost forty-five seconds. Some argument could be made that the director could have broken down the scene into other shots to emphasize Grant's taciturn response or Bergman's attempt to draw him out; and yet the choice of playing this part of the scene in a two-shot has an unquestionable logic. There is nothing occurring that cries out for emphasis. It is just a simple exchange of dialogue, and a cut is not necessary until the intensity of the interchange increases. When the cut finally does come, its logic is inescapable. If anything, cutting the lengthy two-shot would dilute the impact of the cut when it finally does come.

Dramatic emphasis—when the camera shows the action in the order and with the emphasis that the director wants—lies at the heart of narrative filmmaking
Ingrid Bergman and Cary Grant in *Notorious*

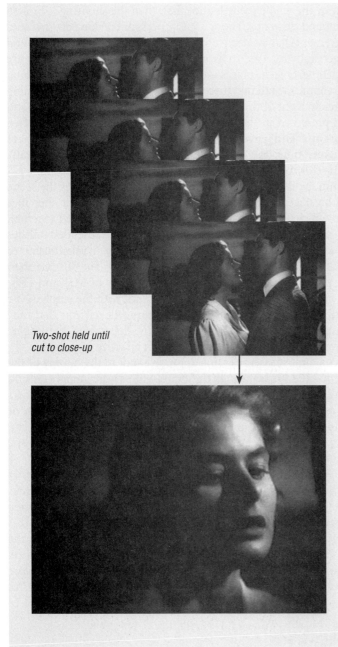

Two-shot held until cut to close-up

ALICIA

I wonder if it is too cold out here. Maybe we should eat inside.

She kisses him.

Hasn't something like this happened before? What's the matter? Don't look so tense. Troubles? Well, handsome, I think you'd better tell mama what's going on. All this secrecy is going to ruin my little dinner.

Pause.

Come on, Mr. D, what is darkening your brow?

DEV

After dinner.

ALICIA

No, now. Look, I'll make it easy for you. The time has come when you must tell me that you have a wife and two adorable children and this madness between us can't go on any longer.

DEV

I bet you've heard that line often enough.

ALICIA

Right below the belt every time. That isn't fair, Dev.

You need not look far to see examples of scenes that use shot selection for dramatic emphasis. The technique is pervasive. In the hands of a competent craftsperson, the approach is so natural to the logic of the scene that we barely notice it. Indeed, most commercial films are purposely designed so that the editing—how the scenes are constructed—is virtually invisible.

MASTER SCENE TECHNIQUE

As suggested, the sequence of LS-MS-CU represents a common movement from random, general information to very specific information. Scenes often begin with a relatively random long shot, then the focus becomes tighter and more specific. In most cases a wide view of the whole scene is shot first, then the shooting is broken down into medium shots and close-ups. Though this process of breaking down scenes into their constituent elements has a variety of permutations and goes under several different names, it is generally referred to as *master scene technique*. Elements are simply those things—people, objects, places—that are key aspects of the scene being shot. If a scene has two characters talking, there are two elements. If they are arguing over the restaurant check in front of them, the check might become a third element. The elements are then presented in the groupings and the order that the director desires to create dramatic and engaging scenes. Though there were others experimenting at the same time, the early filmmaker D. W. Griffith is generally credited with pioneering this concept.

Master scene technique is an approach in which the director stages the scene essentially as it would be staged in a theater. All or part of the scene is shot in a *master shot*—a shot in which all, or most, of the elements are presented together. This shot is also called, more descriptively, an *establishing shot,* because it establishes the space in which the scene is occurring, where the characters are in relationship to each other, any important objects that may be present, and so on. The director then stages the scene many more times, only shooting it in a variety of MSs and CUs. Medium shots convey more-specific information, though not with the emphasis or intensity that can be achieved with the close-up. Directors will tell you that they generally save close-ups for the most intense part of an individual scene—the climax. The material is then given to an editor, who cuts it into an effective sequence.

This method has an almost assembly-line approach and, in the heyday of the Hollywood studio system—the 1920s through the 1950s—films were literally ground out in a highly efficient factory. Indeed, one production unit at Warner Brothers even referred to itself as the "Sausage Factory." Directors who had some clout, or who worked on such low-budget films that no one paid much attention to them, were able to make films with some individual character, but the assembly-line approach influenced virtually all films of the day.

This method has been recognized under a variety of different names, such as *invisible editing, continuity style, classic Hollywood style,* and *master shot discipline,* among others. By whatever name, the approach was—and still is—standard operating procedure in American filmmaking. There is, after all, a certain logic to this progression of moving closer to a subject. As with so many other techniques in the Hollywood approach, this is a natural replication of human perceptual experience. When we are curious about something, we move closer to it. Different and more adventurous styles have been experimented with, particularly in the 1960s and 1970s, but the traditional approach still has profound influence.

SHOT/REVERSE SHOT

In its simplest and most common manifestation, called shot/reverse shot, master scene technique provides an easy way to handle a conversation between two or more characters. Once pointed out, the approach is familiar to everyone, particularly those who watch television interview programs such as "60 Minutes." It is the bread and butter of thousands of movies and countless television shows.

Quite simply, *shot/reverse shot* involves shooting all of person A's dialogue from setup #1, then picking up the camera and moving it to setup #2—called the *reverse*

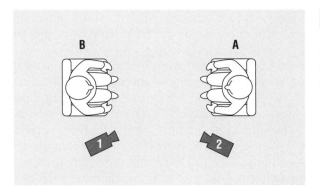

3-4

Shot/reverse shot involves shooting all of person A's dialogue from setup #1, then moving the camera to setup #2 and shooting all of person B's dialogue

shot—and shooting all of person B's dialogue. **SEE 3-4** The results are then intercut as a simple back-and-forth exchange. We have a shot of person A saying a line of dialogue, then a shot of person B responding. To keep things visually interesting, other types of shots are worked in, such as two-shots or *over-the-shoulder (OTS)* shots (done over a character's shoulder).

The usefulness of this basic approach in shooting interviews is obvious. Several hours of an interview with person A are shot. When the interview is over, the subject is excused and the camera is moved to the reverse shot (setup #2). Several minutes of the interviewer (person B) nodding in assent (or maybe staring blankly in disbelief) are then shot. The inevitable dull interludes in the actual conversation can simply be cut out in the editing, the resulting jump in the footage covered with a shot of the interviewer responding to what is being said. This method of shooting allows the footage to be manipulated into the desired order and length—which also extend to manipulating the context and content of what is said. Although many films, from Orson Welles's *Citizen Kane* to the work of Robert Altman, try to find more adventurous approaches, shot/reverse shot remains a common method of delivering dialogue.

Although they are relatively straightforward to describe, these techniques—master scene technique, shot selection for dramatic emphasis, and shot/reverse shot—require practical experience to truly understand and control. Moreover, it is important to recognize the function they serve. These techniques are essentially tools that enable you to communicate narrative information clearly and effectively. On occasion, a more adventurous shot selection may overcomplicate material that demands a straightforward presentation. These techniques also serve a purpose common to most narrative art forms: They start with a general view of the subject, then move to a closer, more specific perspective.

Continuity

Style in American film has largely been subservient to the goal of presenting seamless and involving stories that, at least in their parts, are portrayed as unfolding in real time. Scenes are put together in such a way that their construction—the shot selection, the editing—goes largely unnoticed by the viewer. In film criticism this has most aptly been referred to as *invisible editing*.

A substantial part of this approach is based on *continuity shooting*—the creation of shots that, when cut together, represent continuous action. The style employs both story structures and formal elements that do not deviate substantially from realistic portrayals of events. Although this style has indeed been pervasive, other traditions have evolved that either present alternatives or, in many cases, are conscious assaults on the ideological assumptions of this dominant approach. The remainder of this chapter explores some of the underlying principles of continuity shooting.

The general application of the concept of continuity in film is familiar to most viewers. It is most noticeable in scenes where it is lacking—sequences where the action does not match from shot to shot. For example, in one shot a character has on a tie; in the next shot, the tie is missing and the character's shirt is casually unbuttoned. In one shot a character reaches for a drink with her right hand; in the next she picks up the drink with her left hand. In a master shot, there is a full glass of beer on a table; in the medium shot, it is empty. The mistake reaches comical proportions when the master shows the glass full again. Some of the mistakes are so obvious that it seems unthinkable that someone could have missed the problem, but during the lengthy delays between setups and the press of never-ending competing demands, elements are easily shifted, lost track of, and mislaid.

Although these examples are common things that most observant viewers have noticed at some time or another, shooting in continuity has a broader definition that has wide-ranging implications for the way elements must be monitored while shooting a scene: When you are shooting in continuity, you are creating a real-time relationship among the shots. As should be clear by now, films are not shot in order, much less in real time. A scene that takes several minutes of screen time could easily have taken a day or more to shoot. Shooting in continuity means you are creating pieces of film that will later be cut together in such a way as to suggest that what the viewer is seeing is occurring in real time.

Continuity editing is dependent on the ***match cut,*** a very common type of cut in which the action matches from one camera angle to the next. If a person is going out of a door, he or she starts to open the door in the first shot, and the next shot picks up the action at the same point in time, from the opposite side of the door. In a cut from a long shot of someone sitting down in a chair to a closer shot, the action in the two pieces should match.

The opposite of a match cut is a jump cut, something that was virtually heretical in the golden age of the Hollywood studio system. The ***jump cut*** is a cut between shots in which there is a jump in time—an ellipsis—between the shots. In his landmark film *Breathless* (1959), French director Jean-Luc Godard incorporated the jump cut into a structure that both made narrative sense and subverted dominant stylistic approaches. In this formally radical approach, when Godard wanted to get a character from one side of town to another, he simply cut him from one place to the other. When he wanted to get from one part of a conversation to another, he simply cut out all the intervening material. The result is that characters jump from one place to another, creating a jumbled, chaotic sense of reality. These are cuts that draw attention to themselves and, by extension, to the process of making a film. Godard's film openly flouted the conventional approach, giving a highly subjective representation of space and action. American films in general still attempt to create a relatively seamless sense of real time and real space, but Godard's influence has had a profound impact on everything from the most typical Hollywood features to commercials to music videos.

CONTINUITY SHOOTING

Shooting out of sequence requires careful attention to detail to ensure that all the elements of a scene remain consistent from shot to shot. Something shot early in the morning may have to be matched with something you are going to shoot late in the afternoon. Even if you are doing shots relatively close together, you can run into problems. A student film from several years ago had an example of this. The film had a simple sequence of a woman entering a house. The student put the camera outside to shoot the first part of the movement. When that shot was completed, he moved the camera indoors to do the match shot of the completion of the entrance. The actor sat down to wait and, as it was a bright, sunny day, put on her sunglasses. When the next shot was done, she had forgotten to take off the sunglasses. One can appreciate the sinking feeling the student had on getting the film back and seeing the mistake which, as glaring as it was, would be noticed by most viewers.

In the old days, continuity was monitored by the "scriptgirl"—a hopelessly outdated credit. Now the continuity person is called a *script supervisor*. Continuity used to be monitored by making rough sketches and detailed notes describing the action, the elements within the frame, and the position of performers. Although sketches and notes are still essential, Polaroid cameras had a big impact on how continuity was accomplished. The script supervisor could produce an instant representation of how all the elements within a frame were arranged. The use of Polaroids quickly became commonplace. Their sole drawback is that they can represent only individual moments within larger movements, and their sound and frequently needed flash make them unusable during takes.

In recent years Polaroids have been partially replaced with a virtually foolproof method. The *video assist* is a tiny video pickup device mounted in the viewing system of the film camera; it gives a video representation of the shot, albeit not a particularly high-quality one. With it the script supervisor can go back to check where specific movements occurred in relationship to dialogue and action or to find the precise positioning within a frame. If the script supervisor and video assist person have to roll through a substantial amount of tape to find what they need, however, this can be quite time-consuming. If other people feel the need to get involved, the whole set can come to a standstill, and pretty soon everyone is standing around drinking coffee and watching the monitor. Nevertheless, the use of video assist on sets is becoming prevalent. Polaroids are still used extensively, particularly in the costume and makeup departments.

TYPES OF CONTINUITY

The script supervisor is actually involved in only a few types of continuity. Some elements, such as lighting, are so specialized that they are left to their respective departments. The following categories of continuity are general areas, rather than rigid classifications that have been defined and elaborated on over the years.

Action   The position of performers and other moving elements within the frame must be carefully monitored. This refers to matching action between closer and longer shots, as opposed to what characters are wearing or how props are arranged in a scene.

If an actor says his line in the master shot before sitting down but says it after he sits down in the MS, the two shots will be uncuttable. If he is scratching his chin in the MS but has his hands at his side in the master, the pieces again will be uncuttable. This is always a difficult issue because, although you have to communicate to the actors the need for continuity so their actions match between setups, you also do not want to inhibit them. Experienced professionals are generally very knowledgeable about the requirements of the medium. For nonprofessionals it can be quite disconcerting.

Props, costume, and makeup   Shooting a short scene can easily take a day or more. Invariably, elements are moved around as you light, and objects are moved to balance compositions. Costumes and makeup also require constant attention. Responsibility for the consistency of these elements is shared by the script supervisor and the crew members in the respective departments.

Apparently simple things such as candlelight can drive the script supervisor to distraction. Over the course of a shoot, candles will have to be carefully controlled so they remain consistent. If the candles are allowed to burn down, they may not match from the beginning of the scene to the end. A script supervisor would probably ask the prop person to bring a substantial number of extra candles. The prop person may burn some candles to certain lengths the night before, so as to substitute specific lengths. Assuming the standard delays between takes and setups, the candles might have to be blown out between shots. This is no problem, except it necessitates lighting them again. Because many smaller projects do not have a continuity person, or have one who has other responsibilities, something like this can easily be overlooked.

Historical Especially important in period pieces, historical continuity refers to checking that all elements are historically accurate for the context of the film. People reading printed books in a version of Chaucer's *The Canterbury Tales* would be inappropriate; similarly, television antennas in a film set in the Civil War period would be out of place. Many films play fast and loose with this. You will often hear of films including a song or some other element that was created after their action occurs. This is often a matter of research, the responsibility for which can fall on a number of different shoulders. For a song it may fall to the screenwriter or, if the song's inclusion is an editorial decision, the film's postproduction team. For elements in the frame, the research may be the purview of the **art department**, an umbrella term for everyone involved in the design elements of the image. Extensive researching abilities may be part of the job description for many crew positions, particularly for period pieces.

As with everything, purposefully breaking the conventions can create interesting results. Alex Cox's *Walker* (1988) is set in 1850 Nicaragua, with the title character installing himself as the imperialist president of the war-torn country. To emphasize parallels to modern events, the film includes such historical impossibilities as Walker and his men being saved by army helicopters, images that are eerily reminiscent of the fall of Saigon in 1975. There are many other improbable elements, including a computer-outfitted command center and Walker's pride in making the cover of *Time* magazine. The purpose is clearly to create parallels with modern events and break with realistic modes of historical interpretation. Baz Luhrmann's *Moulin Rouge* (2001) is another good example of a film that purposefully mixes historical periods for stylized effect.

As you watch films more carefully, you will notice unintentional historical continuity errors with some frequency. One of director Anthony Mann's great westerns, *The Far Country* (1955), has jet trails in the sky above scenes supposedly occurring in the 1880s. The more actual film production experience you get, the more you realize that things like this are usually not mistakes but rather the unavoidable compromises one must make when under time and budgetary constraints. Perhaps they were losing the light and were forced to shoot despite the conditions. The more you know, the more you may be amazed that films get made at all! The production of a film is such a complex tangle of marshaling elements to occur at just the right time that you are often forced to proceed, even when you do not have everything you want in place.

Lighting Matching will be a problem if shots that are to be cut together look different in terms of the color and quality of the light, an issue often referred to as *photographic consistency*. It will drive many of the technical considerations you need to be concerned with while shooting. The script supervisor is generally not involved in lighting continuity issues, other than occasionally taking notes for the lighting crew.

Continuity is one concern that delineates motion picture photography from still photography. Still photography is usually not sequential in its presentation.

Even if a still photographer is attempting to create some kind of photo montage, the images are nevertheless presented as discrete entities and anything but major differences in lighting is not going to be noticed. In film, however, if you want the illusion of shots occurring in real time, the quality and intensity of light must match from shot to shot.

Still photographers who visit film sets are often amazed at the complexity of the lighting approach. They invariably suggest that a simpler approach might work, until they are made aware of the kinds of matching that are being attempted. Even then some cannot grasp the difference. Still photographers usually have extensive control in the printing process, including dodging specific elements or areas of the image and manipulating exposure and processing times. When they are shooting, if they just get a decent negative they can create the kind of product they want. Although there is some room for image manipulation in film, these discriminations can generally be applied only to the whole shot and the entire frame. It is imperative that you work out all matching issues when you are shooting.

One story may give some sense of the kind of hoops one must jump through in this regard: I was once working on an exterior shoot in a midwestern state on one of those days that people who forecast the weather like to call "partly sunny"—an ambiguous term that leaves up to question whether there are going to be more clouds or more sun. This was definitely a "more clouds" day, weather that reminds one why filmmakers prefer the largely cloudless skies of southern California. It was a relatively simple scene that the *production manager (PM)*—the person responsible for all scheduling—had budgeted the morning for shooting, with the intent of shooting another scene in the afternoon. The problem in such a situation is that the quality and intensity of light between the sunny and the cloudy periods do not match. The scene would have proved uncuttable—that is, would have appeared awkward or poorly staged to the viewer—had we attempted to shoot under both conditions. The three- or four-hour shoot became a daylong ordeal in which a succession of hapless souls tried to estimate, with limited success, how much sunshine we were going to be blessed with at any given time. The production manager was tearing her hair out because the afternoon shoot, which was logistically complicated, had to be canceled and rescheduled while a large number of costly elements (actors, extras, props, and the like) waited idle.

If it had been a bigger shoot, we probably would have had the resources to overcome our difficulties. There are lights that, as their manufacturers love to boast, "outshine the sun at twenty paces." But our options were limited, and we spent substantial time just waiting. Natural light has a nasty habit of changing quite frequently. Artificial light requires a level of control that can be imposed only with experience and budget.

Sound   This refers to creating a sound track that is consistent, with no big shifts in either the volume or the quality of the recorded sounds. Although the location recordings must be as consistent and high quality as possible, sound continuity is largely an editorial issue. Many imperfections can be covered or fixed, either during the editing process or when mixing the final sound track in the studio.

Sound can also have implications for historical continuity. When doing period pieces, modern sounds can present problems. The sound mixer on a film set in the 1840s, for example, which was shot about forty yards from a major highway and a half mile from a private airport, had to jump through many hoops to get usable sound.

Performance   With action being shot from so many setups, performance must be standardized so that it matches between camera angles. This is generally not a problem on larger productions, where most actors, as well as the director, are experienced professionals. But on films where you may be working with nonprofessionals, it can be a big issue, both in terms of what a performer can produce and in how an inexperienced director evaluates that performance. Before shooting, details of a performance—the level and tone—should be completely worked out between the *talent* (actors) and the director. A director who asks for anything different between takes can cause enormous editing problems. Although this is not the script supervisor's domain, a good one will recognize glaring errors.

I had one job working with an inexperienced director who was directing a very emotional performance from an untrained actor, a bad mix if there ever was one. He was not getting from her what he wanted, but he started shooting anyway. We did several takes of the master shot of one of the actor's long speeches, then moved in for medium shots and close-ups. Between setups the director decided that her performance was too unrestrained in the master, so he asked the actor for less. The next time he got too little, so he asked for more. He got too much. He was trying to shape the performance as we were shooting, and the resulting footage proved uncuttable. The editor was eventually forced to play the whole thing in master, an option that suited neither the scene nor the shape of the film. If this kind of mistake were made on a larger project, the eventual outcome would probably be a reshoot (and people would be fired). On smaller budgets this option does not always exist.

Spatial continuity   This refers to creating an understandable sense of space and is the focus of the following section.

The Line

A director friend likes to call the line "the central organizing principle" of narrative cinema. The *line,* also called the *180-degree rule* or the *axis of action,* refers to a principle used to create an understandable sense of the space in which the action is occurring. The line is relatively easy to understand on a superficial level, but its application is something that takes on-set experience to truly comprehend. Simply stated, the rule says that *if shooting is begun on one side of an action, it must stay on that side.* If the camera jumps to the other side of the action—that is, crosses the line—the sense of an understandable and continuous space can be disrupted. Before doing storyboards or blocking the action for the camera, this line is drawn in the shooting space. The application of this rule has become less rigid in recent years, but if the goal is to create a logical and continuous sense of space, shooting with an understanding of the line is a must. As with anything painted with such a broad stroke, there are exceptions, but they are fewer than might be expected. Even if a distorted sense of space is desired, a knowledge of the line's effect is still necessary.

The location of the line is generally based on one of two factors: sightlines or direction of action.

SIGHTLINES

With *sightlines,* the line is created by drawing a straight line that represents a character's direction of vision. The line is based on the sightlines of the character who is on camera and it can change as his or her direction of view changes. Often the line is drawn between two people in conversation, though it applies to an individual character watching an action as well as to multiple-character situations.

If you start on one side of the sightlines between two characters, you must stay on that side. If you use a setup from the other side of the line, the characters will not appear to be looking at each other and may seem to have switched places.

If you start shooting from setup #1, the rest of the setups should be on that side of the sightlines. **SEE 3-5** If you cut to anything on the setup #2 side, you will

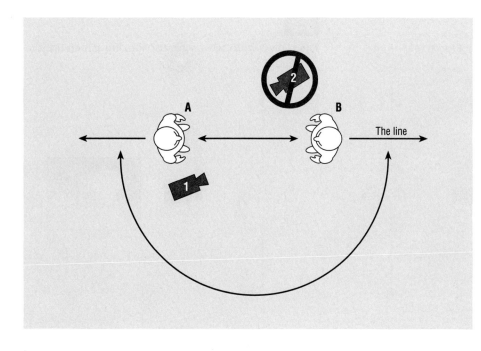

3-5
The "line" refers to a principle used to create an understandable space in which the action occurs

have problems with matching sightlines, and the characters will appear to be looking at some unseen third space. It does not make any difference on which side of the sightlines you start. That should be an aesthetic determination based on what you want to see in the background, which profile of the performers you want to film, and anticipated character movement. But once you have started on one side, you have to stay on that side.

This can be difficult to conceptualize, so taking the most extreme example should make it easier to understand. In this example setup #1 is at a right angle to person A, and setup #2 is at a right angle to person B on the opposite side of the line. **SEE 3-6**

The key to understanding this is to consider the direction that the character will be looking in the resulting film. If we can transpose the shot from setup #1 to see how it would look on the screen, the character would be looking screen-

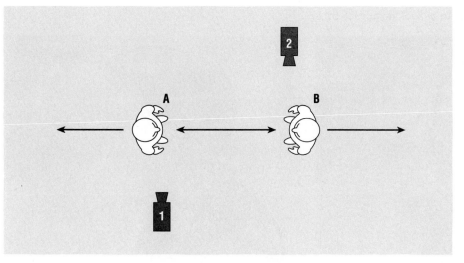

3-6
Mismatched camera positions help illustrate the concept of the line

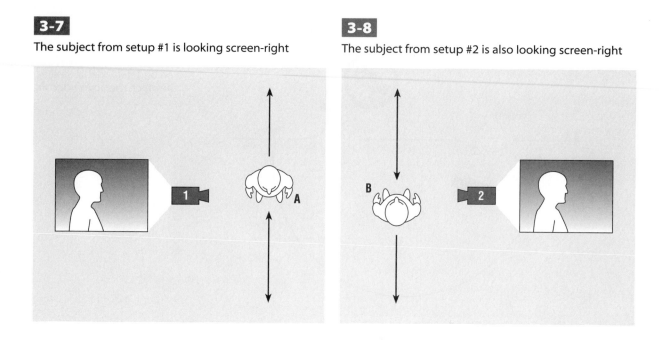

right. **SEE 3-7** If the same thing is done with setup #2, which way would the character be looking? This may be more difficult to visualize, but if we pull the camera around while moving the character with it, the direction can be determined. **SEE 3-8** Again, the character would be looking screen-right.

The problem comes when we attempt to cut the two pieces together. **SEE 3-9** It appears as though person A is talking to the back of person B's head. If the angles chosen are less extreme than in this example, the problem remains. This is more difficult to visualize, but characters will appear to be looking at some abstracted third space. Though audiences will not point to the screen and say, "Look, they crossed the line," on an unconscious level it will be difficult to discern a logical space, that is, understand where the characters are in relationship to each other and the space. This confusion, this sense that something is wrong with the scene, will disrupt viewer involvement with the drama.

3-9

The characters do not appear to be looking at each other

Clearly, there are many filmmakers who *want* to disrupt this seamless, unimpeded involvement, or they wish intentionally to create a confused sense of space and action. If you deliberately want to create a disrupted sense of space, you must understand the application of the line just as clearly as when you want a conventional representation. In many situations, a confused sense of space does not serve the narrative context, even if what you are doing is unconventional. The director who calls the line "the central organizing principle" of narrative cinema is no dull conventionalist—he has won international awards for some odd and unconventional stories—but he does not want confusion over spatial relationships to distract the viewer's attention from the action of his films. Planning out the entire scene in terms of setup, character position, and the line is a necessary component of scene construction.

Character movement complicates the line in regard to sightlines, although the line simply changes as a character's sightlines change. Sightlines also become more complicated when there are more than two characters. Usually, when filming a conversation involving multiple characters, one should try simply to stay to one side of the action or the other.

Action

In terms of action, the concept of the line is even more clear-cut. If you film a car driving down the street from its right side, it will be moving from left to right in the resulting shot. If you then cross the street and film the same car continuing in the same direction, it will be moving from right to left in the resulting shot. When you try to cut the two pieces together, the car will appear to have changed direction. **SEE 3-10**

D. W. Griffith certainly understood this idea by the time he made *Birth of a Nation.* The Civil War battle scenes would have been virtually incomprehensible without following this rule. In one sequence the Confederate troops charge the Union

3-10

Crossing the line in an action shot causes the car to appear to have changed direction

3-11

Setup showing action
moving left to right

3-12

Crossing the line reverses the action

lines. Because all setups are to the right of the charge, the Confederate troops are always moving from left to right. **SEE 3-11** What would happen if Griffith had tried to mix in some setups from the left side of the Confederate charge? The Confederate troops would have moved from right to left. **SEE 3-12** Clearly, they would look like they were retreating when intercut with shots from the other side. When shooting any action that depends on a continuous sense of direction, from battle scenes to football games, the line must be a chief consideration.

CONCEPTUAL ERRORS

Other than disregarding the line altogether, the biggest mistake beginning filmmakers make is thinking that the line is from the camera to a character, when it is actually between one character and another. As a character's sightlines change, the line changes. If person A shifts her gaze from person B to person C in setup #1, the line shifts across the camera with her

As a character's sightlines change, the line changes

Music video setup

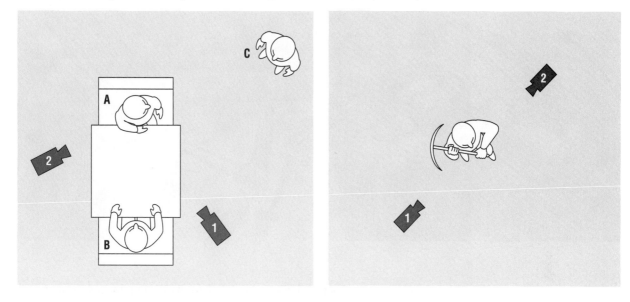

sightlines. **SEE 3-13** Whereas setup #2 would have been unacceptable previously, it is now perfectly within bounds. If person A returns her view to person B, you have effectively made a shift to the left side of the conversation.

Music videos have had a tremendous impact on many of these "rules" of film construction. Many music videos do not have a clearly thought-out strategy toward many issues such as the line, nor should they. Despite this there are still examples of the 180-degree rule being broken that clearly do not work. An editor friend recently showed me a video that eventually got some play on MTV which, were it not for video's inherent ability to manipulate the image, would have included a very disruptive *line jump*. **SEE 3-14**

The video had a sequence of shots of a gravedigger wielding a pickax. The director had made one of the most basic conceptual errors possible. He shot the full shot of the gravedigger from one side of the action (setup #1), then, inexplicably, he shot a close-up of the pickax gliding through the frame in slow motion from the other side of the action (setup #2). With an action of this nature, it is very easy to figure out what the line is. The direction of the motion matches the sightlines, and the line is the plane of the motion of the pickax. Imagine these two pieces cut together and you can get a sense of how incongruous some simple line jumps look. The arc motion of the pickax is from left to right in the first shot and from right to left in the second shot. **SEE 3-15** The scene was salvaged only because it is possible, with the appropriate high-end video gear, to flip the video image side to side, in much the same way as with many computer graphics software programs. Unaltered, though, these two pieces do not fit together except as a disjointed representation of a simple movement.

After several sessions of having the line concept drilled into him, one student was gloating about finding a line jump in Nicholas Ray's *Rebel Without a Cause* (1955). Occasional line jumps are found in classical-era Hollywood films. Sometimes they appear to be mistakes that could not be fixed; other times they simply represent the director's avoiding complicated steps to reposition the camera, assuming the audience will be able to follow the action. Indeed, when the space is straightforward or innately understood (a baseball field is a good example) certain leaps of faith can be taken with the camera. Some line jumps are simply not a big problem. It may be just as

3-15

Line jump results in the pickax's swinging from the other side of the action

well to brazen your way across, being more efficient than going through some fancy, schematic footwork to cross over. There are other line jumps, however, that cause noticeable breaks in continuity.

Sometimes line jumps can be part of a greater plan; other times they are just irreversible mistakes in conception with which one must live. There are films that owe their informal effect to a complete or partial disregard for the line. A line jump is essentially a jump cut, and, just as Godard employed jumps in time in *Breathless,* disruptions of conventional space can create specific effects, most notably confusion or chaos. At the other extreme is a film like Milos Forman's *Amadeus,* which is so dependent on emphasizing Salieri's responses to Mozart's actions—on Salieri watching Mozart—that the line is scrupulously observed. Whatever the approach, the line must be clearly understood to achieve desired spatial effects.

SCREEN DIRECTION

The concept of screen direction comes into play when a character leaves a shot and then has to reenter in another shot. This is essentially a function of the line, although the difference is that screen direction ties together separate spaces by direction of movement. Simply stated, the way to achieve consistent screen direction is by having characters enter the frame from the opposite side they exited. If they exit frame-left, they must enter the next shot frame-right. If this simple rule is not observed, it will look as though the characters have turned around and gone in the opposite direction. Of course, such screen direction can also be applied to deliberately create a discontinuous or confused sense of space.

When the spaces in which consecutive scenes are taking place are not closely related, failure to think out screen direction can create at most some modest disorientation. If a character's next scene is across town, the direction he exits and enters the frame may not make much difference. When spaces for scenes are closely related, however, failure to think out screen direction can be disastrous. A good example of the latter would be a sequence of shots of someone getting up and going from one room to another. **SEE 3-16** If you start the movement from setup #1, the character will exit the frame screen-right. If you make the mistake of shooting the next part of the movement from setup #2, the character will enter

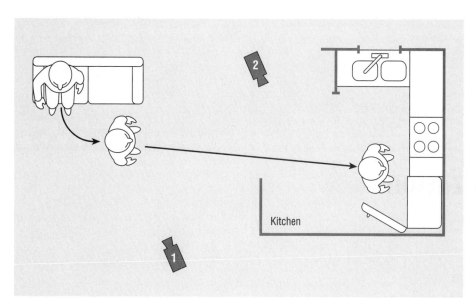

3-16
Screen direction comes into play when a character exits a shot and then reenters in a subsequent shot

from the right and move to the left. It will appear as though she changed directions rather than walked in a straight line. It may even appear that she walked around behind the camera.

Although this is only tangentially related, there are generally accepted expectations that certain types of movement go in specific directions. This is particularly true of points on the map. When characters travel east, we expect them to move from left to right; if they are traveling west, right to left. When Woody Allen flies to California in his 1977 film *Annie Hall,* viewers would probably not accept the plane moving from left to right. Westerns also incorporate substantial right-to-left movement, indicating a westward direction.

A number of film critics and theorists have suggested that the line is a byproduct of the theatrical heritage of film, that cutting to the far side of action would be tantamount to making the audience jump to the opposite side of the stage or suddenly view the play from backstage. Early filmmakers, realizing that the audience's closest frame of reference was watching stage productions, were loathe to disrupt conventional audience positioning relative to the action.

There is a certain amount of truth to this, but the 180-degree rule mainly serves to create matching sightlines and continuous direction of action. If the line is not observed, people will just not appear as though they are looking at each other, and action will appear discontinuous. Again, very few audience members will recognize this on a conscious level. As some of the rigid rules of narrative filmmaking break down, the line may become less important—or maybe filmmakers are just paying less attention to it. Nevertheless, it is crucial that its application be understood no matter what one is attempting to accomplish.

4

Crew Organization

Although creating a plan for shooting—thinking out the shots and the dramatic context of the scenes—is the primary goal during preproduction, the search for and hiring of a crew is also a necessity. A number of craft positions may not need to be filled until closer to the actual shooting, but many of the critical creative people should be hired in the film's earliest stages. Many crew members indeed will have invaluable creative input in planning out the conceptual approach to shooting. Although independents and students may not employ all of the positions described here, it is important to be familiar with all of the roles and their attendant responsibilities. As with so much else, even if there is no specific person on board for a certain job, it nevertheless has to be done. It's simply one more thing for which you, the filmmaker, must be responsible. The organization and sophistication with which a project is approached has a direct bearing on the final product.

The Sequence of Events

Although all three phases of a film's production have legitimate claims to being the most critical, a film that is not properly prepped is a disaster waiting to happen. Even films that appear very improvisational require input from key creative personnel.

Script The first step is coming up with an acceptable script. Scripts can come from many sources, ranging from original scripts, to adaptations of acquired short stories or novels, to simple story ideas that a producer wants a screenwriter to develop. However advanced the script is, the producer generally engages writers to rewrite, adapt, or develop the project.

Director and key people After the writers, the producer's next hire is usually the director, although *talent,* stars usually, may also be brought on board at earlier stages. The *director,* who is usually the key decision-making force in all stages of a film, then starts developing the script in terms of casting, locations, general visual style, and dramatic approach.

Once funding, script, and director are in place, the sequence of events is fairly straightforward. Putting a film together in preproduction has become something of a science. Very early in the process, the producer hires the *production manager (PM),* who is responsible for all the general organization of the crew as well as the practical planning and scheduling of the film. A good PM can break down a script and estimate costs to within a few percentage points.

The next step is usually to hire the other key personnel: the ***director of photography (DP)***, also called the *cinematographer,* a production designer, and anyone else whose input may be needed during the initial stages. Crew that is specific to actual shooting—sound engineers and people for props, costumes, makeup, and so on—can be hired closer to actual shooting, although almost everyone needs some prep time to anticipate the needs of a given production.

Once these central people are in position, the following tasks have to be undertaken, and personnel to assist in these stages must be hired as well.

Casting   Careful and thoughtful casting is critical to the aesthetic success of any narrative film. There are certainly films that do not rely heavily on the performers, like some action and horror movies, but most rely on the creation of credible characters in believable situations. Casting can be quite informal for independent and student projects, but it is a major undertaking for commercial films. Like so much else, casting has become specialized, with agencies playing a key role in auditioning. The casting crew can even separate into groups for casting main roles, peripheral roles, and even extras.

Union rules are a critical consideration in casting. Many actors are members of the Screen Actors Guild (SAG) or the American Federation of Television and Radio Artists (AFTRA), which have stringent rules about participation in films that don't pay the talent or that defer payments until later. You need to become familiar with these rules. Many independents choose to work with nonunion performers, although this obviously excludes many talented people.

Auditions are a must. For independents and students, this generally means putting a notice for an *audition call* in the want ads of a local newspaper. Major urban newspapers have a specific section for these, referred to as "cattle calls" by the insensitive, which actors frequently consult. It is also worthwhile to put up notices at local theater companies and at university drama departments. The notice can be general, although you may want to list the number of roles, the gender and age, and such issues as controversial subject matter. When scheduling auditions, be very up-front about what the actors' time investment will be, the subject matter, and the payment they can expect. If an actor finds anything objectionable, it is better to find out at this stage and not waste either your or the actor's time.

Actors are usually asked to do a *cold read* of a short section of the part for which they are being considered. A good approach is to explore the actor's ability by asking for different interpretations of the chosen selection. Find out how responsive the actor is and how sensitive to trying out different approaches to a character. In auditions for stage plays, actors are generally asked to perform a monologue from a play of their choice. Beginning directors may find these useful to evaluate how animated performers are and to get an example of their overall ability, although monologues are generally not required in film auditions. In this initial phase, ten to fifteen minutes should be allotted for each audition.

The director must bring thoughtful, interpretative skills to the casting session and be able to look at a script and perceive the character, motivation, and the nuances of every role. This is as true for a main character who is in every scene as it is for a bit role in one small scene. It takes an experienced eye to be able to evaluate individual talent for specific roles. The biggest mistake beginning directors make is evaluating performance in terms of an actor's interpretation of a part. This is usually because the director has not defined the character clearly in his or her mind before the casting session starts. It is imperative that the director do an interpretative session with the script, virtually writing a brief analysis of every character. Again, asking actors for different interpretations of the part is a clue to their general ability.

Sometimes an actor will show up at an audition and appear to be perfect for a specific part, perfect as you have visualized that particular character. Though this works occasionally, don't let superficial appearances determine character. Type is certainly important, but if the performer cannot be successful in the role, the approach is defeating.

The first auditions should produce a number of potential candidates for each role. *Callbacks* are generally needed to make final decisions, and spending more time and working with a larger section of the script should help identify the performers you want for the roles. As casting decisions are narrowed down, try to find some measure of the talents' commitment to the project. If you sense hesitation or a condescending attitude from an actor, those feelings may become magnified when shooting commences. Inexperienced performers often do not understand exactly what they are getting themselves into, and if their maturity level is low, this can cause such problems as tardiness, a lack of concentration, and so on. Although someone's attitude cannot be dictated, commitment is simply a requirement of performance. Once filming has started, disaffected talent are usually impossible to replace without starting over from scratch. Rather than struggle with a talented but balky actor, hiring a potentially less talented performer may make sense if that person is reliable and committed to the project.

Rehearsals Arranging as much time as possible for rehearsals is a good idea, but in reality they are rarely afforded as much time as the talent and director would desire. This is particularly true when actors work for free, as is often the case in independent situations. A stage play is often rehearsed for months before it is seen by the public. In film, however, actors must give a usable performance from the first day of shooting. Any rehearsal time is a bonus, but if none is possible, be ready to start producing at a high level right from the start. When preshooting rehearsals are not feasible, set aside time on the set to walk through the entire scene before commencing to shoot. This gives the actors a sense of the shape of the scene prior to breaking it down into the individual pieces.

Design In conjunction with the director and cinematographer, the *production designer (PD)* begins preliminary work to determine the overall design approach of the film. Many major decisions have to be made prior to shooting. One of the first has to do with the amount of studio versus location shooting. Certain scripts demand studio time, whereas others clearly require location work. Most films fall somewhere in the middle, where locations and studios have to be weighed in terms of costs and a variety of other factors. A common approach is to shoot the exteriors on location and all interiors on matching sets created on soundstages. Independents and students, unable to afford the costs of renting expensive studio space and creating sets, frequently do all work on location. Although locations do have cost advantages, they also frequently need some preparation, whether it be as complicated as a sophisticated interior design or as minimal as bringing in a few props and moving around some furniture.

Location shooting The responsibility of *location scouting* falls to the location scouts and includes searching for and assessing possibilities for specific scenes. Familiarity with the script is generally required, although some location scouts are armed with just a list of needed locations and their desirable features. Once suitable possibilities are found, the director, the DP, and, in some instances, the PD will visit the locations and evaluate their visual and technical appeal. With the input of the DP and the designer, not to mention the financial people, the producer and director make the final decision.

Permission to use locations must then be secured. Public spaces require contacting the appropriate authorities; use of private property must also be authorized. Most states have film boards, and many large cities have a liaison to facilitate film- and videomakers' needs in this regard. Cities where filming is common may require permits, location fees, insurance binders, and other guarantees. Security precautions may be stipulated as well. In smaller markets local people are generally more enthusiastic about movies, often letting students and independents use locations for free. This can be a great opportunity unless something happens, such as damage to property or an accident resulting in injury, which makes liability an issue. Industry practice is to have all bases covered when shooting on location. Many young filmmakers are tempted to grab locations without prior permission, thinking they can be in and out before anyone knows they are there. This is a bad idea. The entire shoot is spent looking over your shoulder to see if anyone is coming to throw you out. It invariably colors how the scene is executed.

Be honest with people about how long you expect shooting to take. Substantial sums are spent on commercial film projects to make the use of locations as simple and hassle-free as possible. They can simply clear everyone out and shoot in peace. For independents, shooting around the comings and goings of the rest of the world can be very trying. Independents frequently find themselves relying on the kindness of strangers to let them use locations, particularly when needing public spaces or businesses such as restaurants or bars. When a shoot that is sold as taking a couple of hours becomes an all-day ordeal, goodwill dissipate quickly.

Independents are often compelled to conform their needs to the conditions of a convenient location, whereas commercial features can manipulate existing spaces to conform to their needs. A colleague tells the story of how he had a location scout scouring a city for a professor's office, with nothing left in the budget for location fees. After days of searching, the scout turned up at my friend's office with the news that he had found the best possible spot. They were standing in it. It was the best possible spot because the price was right—free. My friend was stuck with a location forced upon him, rather than one that may have better suited his purposes.

Such are the decisions made in the independent world. For *The Long Goodbye* (1973), Robert Altman shot several scenes at his own beach house. Having a crew in your home is something akin to having scouts set up camp in your living room for a week. Heavy dollies and lighting instruments, rearranging furniture, and the constant parade of crew members can take its toll on any space. Building a set on a soundstage has many advantages; the biggest factor against it for independents is again the cost of space rental and the materials and labor involved in construction. Despite this, studio work should be carefully considered. Extended work in a single location can become stressful, with the disruption to neighbors and local businesses becoming an increasing source of irritation.

The Production Crew

Most film crews are put together from scratch, with skill positions being filled from a pool of experienced freelancers. In the studio days, all the crew members were in-house employees. The costume department may have been working on a half-dozen films at a time. The music department had an in-house orchestra that worked hand-in-glove with composers, songwriters, and the film editors. The grips were assigned to specific soundstages and worked on dozens of films a year.

Putting together a film crew today is somewhat akin to putting together an entire orchestra to perform an original composition one time. Many people have to be brought on board and their efforts coordinated toward achieving a common goal. Freelancers are known by their reputations and are sought out and hired for each new film. People who are fast, understand the needs of a set, and bring creative decision-making to their craft are always in demand. In general, being fast may be the most valued aspect.

Many newcomers to the process are seduced by stories of people who have started at the top, but most people start in entry-level positions: production assistants, cable pullers, or as the new guy or gal on the grip crew. Some stay there; others slowly work their way up to positions in which they are most able to demonstrate their skills. Most successful professionals tell of how humbly they started and what they had to go through to get where they are.

Established craftspeople frequently turn down work, whereas the newcomer struggles to get name recognition and nail down a few paying jobs. It is the old catch-22: You need proof of your ability to get work, but no one will give you the opportunity to prove yourself without a list of credits. Newcomers often have to work for free to get recognition, although one should be wary of abuses. Film companies love to get this free labor, but newcomers should put strict limits on how many freebies they are willing to do. The more you work for free, the more people tend to take advantage. After one or two projects, if you have not proven your worth so that someone is willing to pay you, you may want to look for another company.

Crew members generally have no more job security than the project of the moment and the network of employers who know and trust their work. Freelancers have to handle deductions for things like taxes, Social Security, health insurance, and retirement on their own. All the ramifications of being self-employed need consideration.

TEAM SPIRIT

Although sports metaphors can be irritating, team spirit is essential to making films. In the early 1960s, the *auteur theory* became popular in the United States. Derived from the writings of François Truffaut, Jean-Luc Godard, and other contributors to the influential French journal *Cahiers du Cinéma,* the major tenet was that the director is the "author" of the film, the key motivating force in the creative life of the work. Though the theory gave much deserved attention to such directors as Alfred Hitchcock, Howard Hawks, and John Ford, it has led to a significant misunderstanding about the role of the support crew members. It would seem unnecessary to repeat the cliché that filmmaking is a collaborative art, except that few people outside the industry truly understand what that means: Every crew member is faced with decisions large and small that contribute many elements to a film. If each person does not bring some measure of creativity to these decisions, the project as a whole will suffer.

Particularly in independent settings, the key to putting together a crew is to assemble a group that is basically compatible and, more important, committed to finishing the project. Nothing is more destructive than having people around who clearly want to be elsewhere, for whatever reason—be it immaturity, ignorance of their role, or other excuses for being unproductive. Film crews tend to be an amalgamation of iconoclasts and eccentrics, individualism and ego seemingly a necessary attribute to successfully staying in the field. Despite this, responsible crew members understand the need to move forward as a unified whole. They also do not make the mistake of over- or underestimating their contribution. Chronic complainers can poison the atmosphere on a set and make everyone wish they were somewhere else. If someone on the set does not want to be there, do yourself a favor and grant their wish.

A crew that is committed and harmonious is, of course, the ideal, although anyone remotely involved in the business has endless war stories about the stresses and personal frictions that occur. The creative process involves the clash of temperaments and visions that strong personalities bring to any venture. In addition, the amounts of money involved have become so astronomical that the whole enterprise can be suffused with the tensions produced by needing to get it right under intense pressure. I have been on sets where the bickering was constant. Despite this the goal of producing the necessary material was never lost. Those who are unproductive or who hinder productivity need to be shown the door.

The crew is there to maximize efficiency. An inefficient set results in inadequate footage, leaving the editor without enough to work with. In the final analysis, all the crew members exist to relieve the director of some of the decision-making pressure. Crews that force the director to focus on minutiae are not doing their jobs. The director must be able to focus on the important issues: performance and the camera. This is a major concern for independents, with the overwhelming technical and logistical considerations frequently detracting from what is occurring in front of the camera.

The Crew's Responsibilities

What follows are brief descriptions of some of the key positions on a film crew. Feature films have many more credits not covered here, including guarantee companies, bonding agents, and assistants to the stars. Although these people are important players in making a commercial feature film, many independent shoots consist of just camera and sound, some talent, and a location. The job descriptions outlined here represent the skill positions needed during actual shooting. Although the duties of a number of positions may fall to a single individual on a small crew, all these jobs must nevertheless be done. The effectiveness with which they are carried out has an impact on the overall quality of your work. For lack of an adequate crew, beginners may find themselves in the role of grip/boom operator/part-time script supervisor, or some similarly outrageous combination. This much multitasking is discouraged, certainly, but it represents the reality of working with limited resources.

Although credits for modern films have grown to exaggerated lengths, they still do not encompass all the people who work on a project. Crew sizes vary but are generally dependent on how logistically ambitious the scene being shot is. A scene between two people in an easily manageable location takes a relatively small number of people by feature film standards. Bigger scenes require hiring additional crew members, called *day players*. Carpenters, crowd control specialists, security guards, and a host of others may be needed for a few specific shots. Day players with specialized skills, such as Steadicam operators or animal handlers, get into the credits because they must market their specialty to other productions. Individual films have unique credits, for example a horse wrangler in a western or a prosthetics person in a horror film. One film listed a pigeon wrangler, which might appear absurd except that whenever an element that is difficult to control has to perform on cue, professional services are a must.

With crews as with performers, union rules often dictate the boundaries of a particular crew member's responsibilities, with other crafts being barred from doing specific jobs. These rules occasionally seem ridiculous, but the delineation of responsibilities clarifies who does what, and when division of responsibility is not clear, important things can slip through the cracks. Time spent haggling over who is responsible for what on a set is better devoted to productive pursuits.

Most independent shoots are nonunion, and the boundaries often blur into a "let's pitch in and get it done" approach. The sound crew's helping strike the lights is unheard of on a union shoot but not uncommon with a small crew. As suggested, the parameters of some positions can be fluid even within union rules. The moment someone says "a director does this," someone else interjects their own experience where there was an entirely different crew structure. General responsibilities of crew positions are outlined in the following discussion, and significant deviations are considered where appropriate.

Crews are broken down into departments—the art department, the grip department, and so on. Three key positions—the sound mixer, the boom operator, and the script supervisor—and their crafts and responsibilities are explained in appropriate chapters. Some of these roles, the director's for instance, have already been described, though a brief summary is in order. All editing personnel are discussed in part V.

The Producer's Team

The job of the *producer* is to shepherd a film from beginning to end, although that role can vary with the size and complexity of a project. *Supervisor* is probably the best description, although the job can range from being the pivotal figure in a film's entire life, to being a figurehead, to being the director's right-hand aide. On most commercial features, the producer ushers the film from initiation through to the editing, exhibition, and residual economic afterlife. Usually present from before it starts to long after it ends, the producer may be involved in hiring other decisive personnel, such as the director of photography, the production manager, the production designer, the assistant director, and so on. In many situations the producer hands this responsibility to the director, respecting the director's need to create a production team with whom he or she is comfortable.

In the traditional Hollywood path, the producer is the major organizing and capitalizing force in preproduction. On commercials, however, the producer may also be the ad agency executive who developed the ad concept, and he or she may be a very powerful presence on the set. The director in this situation may be a hireling whose sole job is to execute a highly developed storyboard. Although a film produced by George Lucas or Steven Spielberg may have as much of their imprint on the film as of the person who directed it, most producers are generally not involved in the day-to-day logistics of shooting except in a monitoring capacity.

PRODUCTION MANAGER

As stated, the *production manager (PM)* is responsible for initial budgeting and logistical planning and, once shooting starts, for managing the pragmatic aspects of a film's production. The PM works mostly out of the *production office*, the hub of communications for the entire shoot. Much of the work is done with the assistant director, both being responsible for scheduling the daily operations of the crew. Responsible to the producer, the PM also controls the production company's purse strings, approving most major cash expenditures.

Production management has been boiled down to a science of how most effectively to manage all the disparate elements it takes to create a film. Any film can be broken down into manageable tasks. The PM analyzes the script and subdivides the individual scenes into elements needed for their execution. This includes main players, locations, props, extras, vehicles, and anything else the script requires. The producer, director, and, in particular, the assistant director help the PM devise the most efficient schedule for shooting the film. From this they create a master plan in the form of a chart called the *production board* (see figure 5-8 for a description). On union shoots, the PM must consider overtime, night shooting, remote locations, and other factors to minimize costly crew holdovers. The PM's goal is to maximize production resources while maintaining cost efficiency.

When scheduling shoots, particularly with exteriors, the weather and acts of God can make the PM's job very demanding. Most PMs could probably write a dissertation on the accuracy of the weather-forecasting industry. When a shoot depends on such factors as weather, the production manager must consider what other scenes can be shot instead if the weather does not cooperate. The job is a constant juggling act, marshaling talent and resources to be at the right place at the right time.

A film I was involved with that was highly reliant on exteriors coincided with the rainiest month in the history of the film's location. This left intended locations flooded and made photographic matching of one day's shoot to the next difficult. Every rainy morning found the production manager scrambling to put together an interior shoot on obviously short notice. On overcast mornings she had to consult the DP to see whether the light matched previously filmed scenes and then formulate a plan. She eventually ran out of alternative interiors to shoot, and it was still raining. Rather than keep the full crew standing by, we wrapped and then returned with a smaller crew once the weather cleared.

CRAFT SERVICES

The notion that a film crew runs on its stomach is well worth remembering. Some directors can work a whole day without eating, running just on nervous energy. Crews' stomachs are not so forgiving. The student who gets all the pieces of the puzzle into position but forgets to feed the crew is courting dissension and possible mutiny. Small amenities like coffee can make the difference between a productive crew and a snarly one.

The time and expense involved in rounding up the required foodstuffs needs to be anticipated. Although this would never happen on a commercial shoot, time is not being spent wisely when the director has to stop somewhere before the shoot to get coffee and rolls for the rest of the crew. Someone who enjoys feeding other people may be interested in the job. Have this person poll the crew for any special dietary needs or preferences, such as vegetarianism. Get a sense of preferred beverages and provide as wide a range as possible. The crew is important, but the talents' needs should be particularly considered. A thirsty performer is one who is not focusing on the appropriate concerns.

The Director's Team

The people discussed here report to the director personally. Their major role is to take some of the pressure of the routine pragmatic decisions off the director's shoulders. Again, the director is one of the key forces in almost every phase of a film's production. The extent of his or her involvement in postproduction depends on contractual obligations. In the golden age of the studios, after shooting concluded many directors did not see the film again until it was on the screen. Contemporary directors generally have more power, though it is still a matter of the director's reputation. A director such as Woody Allen or Spike Lee is a strong presence in the editorial process; there are obviously others who cannot exert similar influence. Directors rarely do any actual cutting, because it is so time-consuming and painstaking, but will generally look at rough cuts of the film periodically and make suggestions.

First-time crew members are sometimes surprised at how unapproachable directors often are—some are brusque to the point of being rude. It was only when I started to direct that I understood this; there are so many details the director has to consider that it is not rudeness but simply the blinders of intense concentration. There is a story of a famous director who was re-creating a World War II conflict over a river bridge. Because it was the only bridge for miles, he was able to use it for only one morning. In the frantic preparations on the day of the shoot, a battery of assistants buffeted him with questions to which he answered a perfunctory "yes," assuming that most details were inconsequential in the grand scheme of things. But when he was asked if all the extras in the German uniforms were supposed to be on the near side of the bridge or the far side, he decided he had better stop and think for a moment.

ASSISTANT DIRECTOR

In commercial production, the assistant director is actually the producer's person; on independent and student shoots, where the lines of responsibility can get blurred, he or she tends to be the director's point person. The *assistant director (AD)* is the conduit and buffer between the overwhelming technical preoccupations of the crew and the director's need to focus on performance, action, and camera. The AD is the director's right hand and is responsible for communicating with all the departments, making sure the production is progressing. As suggested, the AD also works hand in hand with the production manager in scheduling all the needed elements for each scene. A good AD often has a reputation for toughness, being the one who comes down on crew members who are not producing at the level or speed expected of them. "What are we waiting on here?" is a question often heard on the set and it frequently comes from the AD.

The AD's major responsibility is making sure that all crew members are on the same wavelength, pursuing the same goals. The AD must let all crew members know what the next shot is and what is expected of them or things can deteriorate quickly. The AD must also make the crew aware of which shots are upcoming. Much of the ability to anticipate needs is left to the initiative of the individual crew members and departments, but they need to be told the essential blocking of the scene and the camera angles. The farther ahead each department plans, the more prepared they are for all eventualities.

The critical question that the AD is always asking is "What is standing between us and the camera rolling?" Is it a camera thing? Are there some costume issues? Lighting? Everything must be in position before the shot can be executed. A large part of filmmaking is problem solving, including the need to solve pragmatic, technical, and aesthetic questions. The AD is in the thick of the battle.

However important the AD's communication with the crew is, it depends on the director's ability to communicate with the AD. A disorganized director leaves the AD impotent in terms of arranging for what is going to be shot next. The goal is always forward movement. When people are donating their time, which is often the case on independent and student productions, it is crucial that their time be spent thoughtfully and productively.

TALENT

It is probably not appropriate to lump the performers in with rest of the crew. The role of the talent is not so much central to the creation of the image as it is to be the subject or focus of the image. They clearly exist for a much different reason than does everyone else. Despite this, how the actors interlock with the rest of the crew is critical.

Working with talent is one of the most challenging areas for the inexperienced director. The director's role is to guide the actors cooperatively in the evolution of an organic performance. In the best situation, this is a team effort in which the actor works out a suitable approach within the director's interpretation of the story. The most important thing a director can do is allow performers to find the characters on their own. If the director can create the conditions where trust is a given, talented actors will be able to find their characters. If young directors err, it is on the side of underdirection, leaving performers without firm footing in creating a consistent approach. Actors bring a tremendous amount to their roles, but it is the director's responsibility to help them shape a coherent performance.

The question is how to translate the words in the script into recognizable human behavior. What language does the director use to describe emotion? How is a response in the script qualified? If a character is told that the bank is going to foreclose on his home, what are the possible responses? Desperation? Passive acceptance? Rage? How many different ways are there to express rage? Is it quiet steaming, uncontrolled yelling, or throwing things? Clearly, the choices are many, and each defines the character in a distinct way. Think of Orson Welles's *Citizen Kane* and the way the title character destroys his wife's room.

In the final analysis, the actor must be responsive to the director's interpretation of the role, although actors occasionally balk at this. Both theater and film abound with stories of actors who have their characters clearly thought out before the director is even on board or have clashed with directors about interpretations. This usually represents the actions of a professionally secure actor and can in many instances yield productive results. Despite attendant tensions this does not diminish the need for directors to state their ideas forcefully.

The inability to pay actors often forces young, inexperienced directors into a marriage of convenience with young, inexperienced talent. Even though there are young actors who are as talented as established ones, they are still in the process of developing their craft, and as such their life experiences are often not broad enough or rich enough to offer a thoughtful and compelling performance. One can tell when a performer is emulating the common stereotypes he thinks typifies a specific group. Portrayal requires empathy, and empathy requires insight. When empathy is not present, acting takes on the character of impersonation. A performer must be capable of crawling inside the character's skin and creating visual signs of an inner life. Although the responsibility for an inorganic performance is usually laid at the actor's feet, it lies equally, if not more so, with the director.

Two key issues need to be addressed when working with either stage-trained or untrained performers. The first is the often remarked-upon difference between stage and film acting. On the stage the performer has to act for audience members in the back row. If this is done in film, the performance will be too intense and overblown for the intimacy of the camera. Almost invariably, performers from stage backgrounds are asked to give less; broad facial expressions and gestures must be made subtle so the performer does not "knock the camera over." Second, the pace of performances often looks much slower on the screen than when shooting; screen time is remarkable in how it makes normally timed events feel drawn out. To avoid slow sections on screen, performance must often be delivered a little faster than what at first appears normal.

If possible, it is better to use professional talent for even the most peripheral roles. Inexperienced production crews often try to get friends, family members, or significant others to do small roles. This is generally a mistake. People unfamiliar with the process often don't understand the timing necessary to create shots that are appropriately paced. Talent who can follow instructions and perform peripheral actions in the same way every time minimize delays and allow the director to focus on foreground action.

During shooting there should be a limit on how many people are communicating with the talent. Sound problems should be funneled through the AD. Discussions of continuity problems should probably follow the same route. To help talent focus on performance, stand-ins are useful for working out the pragmatic aspects of complex shots. For inexperienced directors, the technical elements of film often take over and become overriding forces to be dealt with; those technical factors can be so overwhelming that actors often get left to their own devices. Although it has been suggested that the crew is there to take pressure off the director, eventually you will realize that everything is there for the performers so they can do their job with as few distractions as possible. To a certain extent, the crew's major responsibility is to keep all the chaos of the film set under control so the actors can perform unhindered.

PRODUCTION ASSISTANTS

Production assistants (PAs) do all the general running around on the set and behind the scenes. They are responsible to the assistant director and do all the inevitable last-minute tasks that arise. They can be made available to other departments, but only at the direction of the AD.

Although PAs are not pivotal players, the assistance they provide is indispensable. The position warrants discussion because it has traditionally been where many beginners get their start on crews. These are excellent entry-level positions in which you can gain a vantage point, albeit an active one, on the inner workings of a film crew. Be aware that in recent years beginners have been forced to compete with a growing pool of professional PAs. The position has evolved to the extent that an experienced and knowledgeable PA can be a valuable asset on a set.

The Camera Crew

In most commercial productions, the director of photography does not actually look through the camera as the shot is being executed; all actual shooting is done by the *camera operator*. The DP calls the composition and relies on the operator to execute the correct framing. This distinction between job descriptions is the product of union rules. International cinematographers who have to conform to these working relationships often find them stifling. Nonetheless, the operator/DP relationship has become one that works relatively well.

The camera itself requires several highly skilled technicians. This crew is led by the *first assistant camera person (1st AC),* whose responsibility is the organization, handling, loading, transport, setup, maintenance, and cleaning of everything having to do with the film, camera, and lenses. This includes all tripods and other camera support equipment. Sometimes the grips will help, and additional personnel will be brought in for complex setups involving cranes, aerial mounts, and the like. On most projects there will be a *second assistant cameraperson (2nd AC),* also referred to as the *clapper/loader.* The 2nd AC is responsible for marking the scene and loading magazines, as well as for filling out camera reports, preparing the film for the processing lab, and assisting the 1st AC in any way possible. For a detailed explanation of the responsibilities of the AC and attendant assistants, see chapter 10.

On a set the ACs constantly attend to the needs of the camera, going to seemingly fastidious extremes to make sure it is clean and operating properly. If you are working by yourself, it's up to you to take care of all these concerns. Whether on your own or with a full crew, the camera is no small responsibility; if it does not perform as it should, you will not be successful. Ignoring the double negative, the commonly heard phrase is "if you ain't got the camera, you ain't got nothin.'"

THE DIRECTOR/DP RELATIONSHIP

Many directors have a very clear concept of the photographic aspect of a film, in which case the DP is there to implement that vision. Other directors may hand over the entire visual approach of the film to the DP. In the first case, the DP still brings rich talent and experience to the visuals. Alfred Hitchcock had an extremely clear visual sense, and yet you can see stylistic differences among his many cinematographers, particularly when looking at films shot by his longtime collaborator

Robert Burks. The directors who turn responsibility for composition and lighting over to the DP—and this is more often the case with contemporary than classic Hollywood directors—tend to see their role more as working with actors and story.

Very few directors shoot their own films, a fact that surprises many newcomers until they understand the complex demands of both positions, each discipline requiring competing sensibilities. Despite their far-ranging responsibilities, directors must focus on the performance when the camera is rolling. Rather than watch the performance, DPs tend to treat the entire field of camera vision as an abstract space, focusing on the movement of form and shape. The DP who focuses on the talent may miss other elements in the frame, such as background movement, lighting problems, mic boom shadows, and so on. Though not mutually exclusive, each approach requires treating the frame in different ways. Shooting and directing at the same time is more common in commercials, where more attention is paid to each image and less to issues of performance, continuity, and marshaling the many resources that it takes to make a feature.

GRIP/ELECTRIC

Outside of the ACs, the other major camera support crews fall into two distinct departments: grip and electric. These departments, which are often lumped together under the general heading of *grip/electric,* work closely together on lighting, although the grip crew is also responsible for all rigging involving the camera, from dolly and tracks, to camera mounts on cars, to setting flags for lens flares. The *gaffer* is the head of the electric crew, and the *key grip* is the head of the grip crew, although the grips' work with the instruments is generally at the direction of the gaffer.

The gaffer is responsible for locating all sources of electricity and directing the setup of the instruments. The name comes from the hooks, resembling those used by fishermen, that old-time electric company workers used to climb poles. The *best boy* is the gaffer's right hand. A number of *electricians* fill out the crew. The *grips* are the jacks-of-all-trades on the set. The name comes from the suitcases full of tools that the predecessors of today's generation of grips used to bring to the set every day. The skills needed by the grips range from basic carpentry, to metal working, to knot tying. The grips are the great practical problem solvers on the set.

A gaffer friend likes to joke that the electricians are the forces of light and the grips are the forces of darkness. The electricians erect the instruments and "fire them up." The grips then cover the light, shaping and manipulating it to create the details and shadows necessary for a complex image. Although the division is never quite so clear, the grips take care of everything in front of the instruments, and the gaffer and his crew take care of everything at and behind the instruments. If it is electric and produces light, the electricians do the work. If it needs rigging or is not electric and needs setting on a stand—silks, flags, and so on—it's the grips' job.

Although the two crews work together on lighting, they have very carefully delineated responsibilities. More than other positions, these distinctions tend to break down on small independent shoots. The grips do just about everything under the sun. Having a few people around who can troubleshoot and rig setups will expedite filming greatly.

THE ART DEPARTMENT

The art department is technically aligned with the camera. The previously mentioned production designer is responsible to the director but often works most closely with the DP. The production designer is the nominal head of the art department, which is an umbrella for a wide range of skilled people. The key personnel responsible to the production designer are those involved in the building and decoration of the set or location. The ***art director*** is an expert in materials and building and is responsible for executing the production designer's plans. Carpenters, painters, and other specialists assist in the actual creation of the set. The *set decorator* plans the small items on the set, the details that make the space look realistic. The *set dresser* executes the set decorator's conceptions. Loosely associated with this group are the *costume designer,* the *props master,* the *hair stylists,* the *makeup* people, and everyone involved in the nonphotographic content of the frame. On commercial features each skill position has a battery of assistants.

When away from the comforts of the soundstage, most locations need extensive prepping. The art department generally works several days ahead of the shoot, although assistants are present during the shooting to respond to the inevitable last-minute needs of the talent and set. They are all responsible for the myriad activities necessary to produce the kind of look that is desired.

Films vary dramatically in terms of how much the art department contributes to the process. A film with a contemporary setting shot largely in exteriors or locations may require modest prepping, ranging from painting to hiding, cheating, or changing the elements that are present. On films that are design heavy, particularly period pieces and futuristic or fantasy projects, the production designer is on board early in preproduction and can have a substantial impact, participating in discussions with the director and the DP to determine a general approach to the look of the film.

All the people in the previous two sections go under the broad sobriquet of "picture people." There are many people on a set devoted to the picture, and their efforts and skills facilitate much of the character and complexity of the image. They contribute to what is called the film's ***production values***—a general term referring to the overall quality of the image. Films in which the sets are cheap and poorly lighted are said to have poor production values; the opposite is the film in which the image is appointed appropriately to the dramatic context of the material.

5
Previsualization

ARMED with some basic principles, the next step is to formulate a strategy for shooting each individual scene. This strategy is largely the director's responsibility, although other craft positions will become involved. This strategy can take a variety of forms: shooting scripts, shot lists, storyboards, and so on. Whatever form the strategy takes, the key is to be prepared. Although this will be amplified throughout this chapter, nothing sows the seeds for failure more effectively than not being mentally and organizationally ready to shoot a scene.

Preparation

A prepared director has planned the visual and dramatic approach to the day's work, including thinking out the blocking of the scene, the setups, the personality and motivation of all the characters, and the importance of the action within the larger context of the script. There are a number of ways to prepare a scene. You can plan each shot meticulously, including the exact framing and incorporation of all movement, or determine the rough parameters of the shots, intending to work out the finer points on the set. You can also come in armed with only a clear mental picture of the scene, so long as that picture has been communicated to the key creative people. This last approach should not be attempted by beginners. Whatever the method of preparation, a director should walk "on the floor" knowing the movements of all the characters, where they should be when they deliver their lines, and how the camera is going to cover the script.

Maximum efficiency on the set is an important goal. In all but the most specialized circumstances, there is material from a script that must be accomplished—that is, a certain number of setups to be shot—and action to be covered. No matter how high the budget, you are always working with limited resources on a limited time schedule. On a practical level, a lack of organization causes lengthy delays, poorly communicated needs for props and technical setups, and frequent duplication of effort. This produces anxiety and tension on the set, inhibiting productivity in a way that usually shows in the final product. On a conceptual level, it can indicate fundamental flaws in the way a director is shaping the visual approach to the material. An unprepared director tends to create scenes that are shapeless and paceless, with the internal logic—the logic of dramatic emphasis—clearly missing.

A certain case can be made for a spontaneous approach to filming, although that case tends to be both overstated and overromanticized. In most instances it is a surefire way to create an uncuttable mess. Even films that appear informal are more planned than people realize. The simple fact is that a lack of preparation can be disastrous, particularly for inexperienced and independent directors. Independents often depend on the donation of time and materials from many people. Film schools abound with stories of talent or crew who left a project because they felt that their time was being wasted. There are few things more destructive to the morale on a set than crew members being forced to cool their collective heels while decisions that should have been made earlier are being pondered. These are particularly sticky issues for inexperienced directors, because they are still learning the organizational skills needed to avoid such problems in the first place.

Methods of Previsualization

Being able to visualize a film in advance, to dream it out, is a difficult skill to develop. Although it may be easy to come up with great ideas for individual shots, planning an entire scene is a formidable challenge. Previsualization requires experience and a knowledge of all the things that do and do not work in specific situations. There are a number of important tools to aid in previsualizing scenes, including overheads, storyboards, shot lists, and, to a lesser extent, shooting scripts. These tools also play an essential role in giving the appropriate crew members the information they need to do their jobs effectively.

These tools are invaluable in forming a strategy for covering the action. Presented with an action, what choices do you make to film it? If a character crosses a room, do you dolly or pan? Would planning a cut to a wider shot be a better strategy? If a character looks off-screen, an expectation is created of seeing what the character sees. Do you plan a cut to what is seen? Do you pan to it? An action can be uncomplicated—simply getting the character from one place to another—or it can be invested with all manner of figurative overtones, whether symbolic, metaphoric, or allegoric.

As the rationales for the following previsualization tools are being discussed, keep in mind that most scenes are shot with a single camera. This is done for a variety of reasons, most notably to avoid complications in lighting design and expenses of extra cameras and crew. With the cost of producing a film becoming so exorbitant, however, the preference for single-camera shooting has been changing. When it costs what it does to get a full crew onto a location and create the required look for a film, needing to go back for reshoots or missed shots may simply not be possible. Pressure to produce something cuttable increases, and a second or even third camera may ensure that enough material is generated. Despite this, these discussions will stay with the still-prevalent single-camera model.

OVERHEADS

Overheads, views of the scene from directly above, are the best starting place, being a good prelude to storyboarding. Draw an overhead of the location or set and start thinking out the movements of the characters as they go through actions or deliver dialogue, blocking the scene as though it were on a theatrical stage. In a best-of-all-possible-worlds situation, this blocking is developed with the actors in rehearsal. Once you have determined where the characters are going to be during the scene, you can devise a few potential setups. Then you can start deciding what material from the script you want to be covering from each individual setup. Drawing a vertical line on a copy of the script to denote the material covered is a good method for cross-referencing setups against the dialogue and action. For some directors this is

5-1

Overheads of scenes are helpful for blocking and determining camera setups and can be useful in identifying potential conceptual problems

all that is needed for an organized approach to a scene, although moving on to storyboarding is highly recommended.

Once some basic setups are worked out, other things start to fall into place. You can work in some complicated shots, some atmosphere shots, or a variety of other effective options. You might eventually wind up discarding the original setups altogether, but at least there is a starting point from which to develop engaging ideas.

Overheads will also help you with the line. When looking at a scene from above, the line can be drawn, based on sightlines or direction of action, and a determination can be made about where to start shooting. Having all this determined in advance can prevent getting worked into a corner. One beginning filmmaker was shooting a scene in which he made a central mistake that could easily have been avoided with some forethought. The scene involved a conversation between a person in a kitchen and another seated on a couch across the room. **SEE 5-1** Without carefully considering the ramifications, the filmmaker began shooting the person on the couch from an apparently logical place—setup #1. When he began to shoot the second character, he had a problem. Setup #2 would have been the logical place for shooting the second character, but this would create a sightline mismatch. To preserve the line, he wound up shooting this part from setup #3. This left the actor's back to the camera as he turned to talk to the character on the couch, a solution that neither pleased the actor nor made much sense in the final product. To incorporate setup #2 and preserve the continuity of sightlines, the appropriate place to shoot the first character would have been from roughly setup #4. The best solution may have been to rearrange the space.

When a specific setup is logical or desired for a scene, such as setup #2 in the previous example, it can be drawn on the overhead, then the other setups can be determined in relation to it. A basic, conventional approach to shooting a scene should be easy to work out.

STORYBOARDS

A *storyboard,* or simply *board,* has each shot drawn on one side of the page, with the script material it covers—dialogue, action, objects—on the other side. In a certain sense, it is the comic book version of the film. A standard storyboard form will have room for three storyboard frames vertically down one side of the page, with room for the dialogue and action on the other. Some commercial forms are quite elaborate, with space for camera directions, continuity notes, overheads, and whatever else is necessary. Computer software is available that can generate the forms, many programs having clip art based on common framings. Creating a simple storyboard form by hand or on a computer is not complicated; all that is needed are three rectangles arranged down the side of a page.

A good starting place is to determine a limited number of camera setups on the overhead and apportion the action and dialogue to those setups on the storyboard. Though this sounds similar to drawing vertical lines through the script, the storyboard gives the framing of the shots and all the movement of the camera and subjects. If six setups are envisioned, you can start assigning lines and action to those specific cameras. If a line of dialogue is to be done in a medium shot from a particular camera angle, the storyboard would include a drawing of the character in an MS, including rough positioning against the background, with the dialogue to the side. If the shot includes camera movement, the storyboard would have representations of key framings in the movement, with arrows indicating direction of movement. The storyboard draws out every shot, not just general positions or a few representative shots. The storyboard can represent action as simple as the delivery of a line of dialogue or as complicated as the opening 8-minute shot from Robert Altman's *The Player* (1992), a shot that, if indeed it were storyboarded, would have had many drawn frames representing all the specific points in the movement.

Storyboards can be formal, consisting of elaborate drawings indicating precise framing and movement. These are created according to the director's instructions and are usually the handiwork of *storyboard artists* hired specifically for the purpose. Storyboards can also be exceedingly simple, with stick figures and crude line drawings to show rough positioning. Whatever the form, the purpose of the storyboard is the same: to communicate the shooting strategy to the appropriate individuals.

Certain films demand scrupulous storyboarding, particularly those that employ extensive special effects. Robert Zemeckis's *Who Framed Roger Rabbit* (1988), with its carefully executed animation combined with live action, was storyboarded down to precise camera framing, character position, and even lens length. Some directors (Alfred Hitchcock was famous for this) have the entire film completely storyboarded before shooting a frame of film. Hitchcock used the storyboard like a blueprint for a building, seeing the actual shooting as a messy afterthought to the truly creative part of the process.

SHOOTING SCRIPTS AND SHOT LISTS

Initial scripts are relatively bare-bones affairs. Camera directions and the specifics of character movement are largely left to the discretion of the director. Once everything is determined in terms of camera and movement, the director puts together a detailed version of the script, called the ***shooting script,*** which is essentially an annotated version of the script, numbering the scenes for preparation and logging during shooting. This is not so much a previsualization tool as it is the *result* of previsualization, a formal version of the director's initial intentions.

The ***shot list*** is a less formal alternative to the storyboard. It lists brief written descriptions of the intended shots. Experienced directors frequently use the shot list because it is the minimum that will serve their purposes when, given their abilities to shape a scene, making a storyboard is unnecessary. For people who can visualize from it, the shot list can be as instructive as a storyboard.

A Typical Scene

Taking a simple script involving two characters as an example, these processes become clearer. **SEE 5-2** The numbers on the side of the heading denote the scene number from the shooting script.

    The first step is to draw an overhead of the chosen location with rough positioning of talent. **SEE 5-3** A typical approach is to plan a master shot for the first several lines—setup #1. Medium shots of both characters are also conventional options for the ensuing dialogue, shooting John from setup #2 and Andrea from setup #3.

    When the scene is storyboarded, the dialogue can be apportioned to the setups that have been devised. A potential storyboard, in this case, is a simple approach to shooting a few lines of dialogue. **SEE 5-4** The circled numbers in the upper right refer to the setup, although most storyboards do not cross-reference setups like this. The numbers on the left are scene numbers used to identify the location in the script. How they are generated is explained in chapter 10.

    Although this is a bare-bones example, with the shot being used as a vehicle for the dialogue, the same process that breaks this scene down in such a straight-

---

5-2

Sample script of a typical scene

Scene number

8.   INTERIOR. KITCHEN. EARLY EVENING.   8.

Andrea and John are cleaning up the kitchen after dinner. They have just finished washing the dishes in silence, reflecting on the tense discussion during dinner.

JOHN
I don't want to spend the evening at home. What do you want to do?

ANDREA
I should probably stay home. I've got a lot of work to do. What are you thinking about doing?

JOHN
(exasperated)
    Anything. I just want to get out of here. Do you want to go to the movies?

ANDREA
I don't know. What times are the shows?

5-3

Overhead of a typical scene

Storyboard of a typical scene

forward manner could be applied to more-elaborate ends as well. If the goal were in a more expressive realm, the shots would differ but the same basic reasoning applies.

This method, of course, represents the basic style of scene breakdown that D. W. Griffith pioneered: the interrelationship of shots for dramatic emphasis. Although this approach can be highly effective, it can leave out subtle shadings and the active participation of the camera. It is a functional approach that values covering a scene, though some would argue that it has the potential to be dull. Many of the shots outlined in this approach can be a useful jumping-off point, even when a director intends some adventurous shooting. Although this approach may sound easy, it is difficult to make even the simplest of scenes work. Even the most conventional television product requires facility and experience to pull off.

COVERAGE

Shooting the action and dialogue of a scene from more than one setup—called *coverage*—should always be built into your shooting plan. The initial storyboard examples may appear to suggest that lines in the script are shot from only one angle. This is not the case. Directors must direct the setups so that their vision shapes the material, but they generally shoot individual dialogue and action from at least a few different angles, as well as covering longer portions of the script from the setups. This provides options in the editing room if there are any conceptual errors in the way the scene was shot.

In the most excessive variation of this approach, the director (and only a very insecure director would do this) shoots the material from almost every conceivable angle. The footage is then handed over to the editor with a simple "good luck" as the only guide. Editors hate this. It forces them into the position of redirecting the film. The idea of coverage should not deny the logic of using specific camera setups. One first-time director, overcompensating for the coverage mistakes he had seen in his experience as an assistant editor, felt the necessity to shoot his scenes from just about every possible angle. Every time the principal shooting appeared to be over, he would think of one more angle that he absolutely had to have to edit the piece. The crew was looking for a noose and a sturdy tree. The director should shape the scene while still providing options.

You may have heard of the opposite extreme in which directors shoot specific parts of the script from one and only one angle, imposing ultimate control by not providing any options for the editors. Both Alfred Hitchcock and John Ford were famous for maintaining this kind of tight control. Before you fall into what many call "the Hitchcock syndrome," however, be aware that both Hitchcock and Ford achieved this control of the expressive powers of cinema only after directing many films. Ford made dozens of shorts and routine action films, many now lost, before making any of the films that contributed so much to his reputation. In Hitchcock's case, with a few notable exceptions, his first fifteen or so films are largely unremarkable.

Independents and students often attempt to conserve film to stay within miniscule budgets, forgoing some angles to stay within an arbitrary amount of footage allotted for a scene. This can sometimes lead to false savings. Missing key shots can diminish a scene's total effect. Although shooting must be economical, do not skimp on the necessary elements.

A Caveat

Preparing a script can be very methodical, and an increasing number of films appear overplanned and devoid of life, bland executions of meticulously thought-out storyboards. The shots in such films are machine engineered and factory assembled to the extent that they lose any semblance of being part of an organic whole. One episodic television program was so meticulously planned that it required only about one month's work from its star player. The star was in the studio for a week or two to shoot all the close-ups and mediums for the entire season. The rest of the cast was called in, and all the star's two-shots and masters were filmed. The star was then released, and the next several months were spent shooting the material for the rest of the cast. Thus, a shot of the star giving sage advice to a character may have had its reverse done weeks or even months later. Although the skills of the makers largely hid the approach, the result felt overly calculated.

Cautioning against overplanned films is important, but there is some danger of encouraging the opposite—completely spontaneous shooting. This approach rarely yields fruitful results. There is a tendency among some beginners to regard previsualization as overdetermined, somehow destroying the spontaneity of artistic creation. This perception can be a strong one. Marlene Dietrich was once reminiscing for a university audience about Orson Welles and his exceptional creative ability and vital imagination. Undoubtedly swept up in the moment, one questioner asked if Welles, being the instinctual genius that he was, ever stooped to working from storyboards and shooting scripts. After a stunned pause, Dietrich's response was a contemptuous "of course," which spoke volumes about the naïveté of the question. The notion that ideas just jump out of the brain straight onto the screen has occasioned more bad beginning films than any other single misconception. Clearly, some middle ground is required.

The storyboard is certainly a key previsualization tool, but it is not set in stone and should not intimidate thoughtful improvisation on the set. By the same token, any deviation from a well-thought-out game plan should be carefully considered in terms of how it will be integrated into everything else. After a long day, crews can get slaphappy and make decisions that at the time appear brilliant but later look ridiculous. Do not let yourself be put in a position in which wholesale changes occur, because the shape of a scene as a whole can get lost. All changes must be weighed and carefully incorporated into the shooting plan.

Production Design and Costume

Although they are not by definition storyboard issues, the planning for production design and costume is often done at the same time or is included in the storyboarding process itself. The *production designer (PD)*, the person responsible for designing all the film's settings, will often use the storyboards as a guide to create sketches of the settings. These elements often come under the general heading of *decor*, which also includes props, makeup, and any other element that is part of the physical content of the frame. German filmmakers of the 1920s are generally credited with the first significant explorations in the use of decor to create effect. In films such as F. W. Murnau's *Nosferatu* (1922) and Fritz Lang's *Metropolis* (1926), the directors investigated how external settings suggested or reflected internal states of mind. Both theater and painting have precedents for this kind of approach, and film's incorporation of many common devices from these traditions was inevitable.

Design for realistic films has a great deal to do with visual stereotypes—the way the viewer expects certain things to look. If a script calls for the establishment of an upscale home, certain elements can be used to create that effect. If the goal is to establish an isolated, dilapidated mountain cabin, other components can be incorporated to suggest that. The settings for a fantasy film may be more the creation of an imaginative designer, but even they are done within the context of what viewers expect, though some play against visual stereotype, such as the seedy, run-down futures of Ridley Scott's *Alien* (1979) and Terry Gilliam's *Brazil* (1985).

Production design can range from the relatively simple to the complex and costly. The war room scenes in Stanley Kubrick's *Dr. Strangelove* (Ken Adam, production designer) are dominated by strong design elements. **SEE 5-5** The peculiar credibility of the space makes the outrageous actions of the characters all the more absurd. The same designer's work on the early James Bond films both influenced—and was influenced by—modern design. Looking back at these films, one realizes that the novelty of their look was a substantial part of their appeal.

Visual environment helps define character. A messy, cluttered environment tends to establish similar traits in the character. The opposite is a very cold, empty environment as featured in films like Paul Schrader's *American Gigolo* (1980) and Woody Allen's *Interiors* (1978), both films about cold, emotionally empty people. **SEE 5-6** Clearly, many other elements contribute to the tone and atmosphere

5-5

Strong production design elements can add underlying meaning to a scene
Stanley Kubrick's *Dr. Strangelove*

5-6

Visual environment can define character and context
Mary Harron's *American Psycho*

The conservative costuming of the country women is juxtaposed with the stylish garb of the city women
Julie Dash's *Daughters of the Dust*

of a scene. Color plays an important role, with scenes being conceived in a variety of emotional tones, from warm tones, to cool tones, to earth tones, and so on.

Another factor used to define character is costume. Emil Jannings's doorman in F. W. Murnau's *The Last Laugh* (1924) is an oft-cited example. When the doorman has his uniform, he is a proud and overbearing character; when he loses the uniform, he becomes small and pitiful. A major contrast in Julie Dash's *Daughters of the Dust* (1991) is between the stiff and repressed country women and the independent city women. The country women are all costumed in reserved darks and lights, with straight and harsh lines. **SEE 5-7A** The city women are dressed in cream colors, with decorative frills and fashionable hats. **SEE 5-7B**

Makeup is somewhat different, because its use is often purely functional, although many films employ makeup as either a major design element or for purposes of character definition. In either case the employment of makeup is never simple. Beginners do not usually have experience with makeup, a fact that leads to a variety of pitfalls when they attempt basic effects. Many makeup people come to film with a theatrical background, and it is important to realize that the kind of makeup the performers need for an audience 20 to 100 feet away is vastly different from the kind needed for a camera that may be as close as several feet. Good makeup people understand how the materials they use will photograph and how the proximity of the camera will represent their work.

These are just a few possibilities of what design can produce. A film can obviously go many different directions in terms of decor. The key is that it has to go somewhere. If low-budget films have a common failing, it is that they frequently lack a consistent approach to visual style. Often this is both a decor and a camera matter and is also largely an economic reality. The personnel and material for set design and decoration are frequently beyond the available resources. Low-budget films often get stuck in the locations that are available to them, shooting without the resources or the time to change things. Commercial features, as well as many other productions, spend great quantities of money to "own" their locations so they can change whatever they want to achieve the effect desired.

Organization on the Set

Once preproduction is concluded, a film moves into *principal shooting,* the concentrated shooting schedule of the scenes. When preparing a film, it seems like there are always things left undone prior to shooting. This is just the nature of the beast. Shooting can be seen as a series of tasks, replete with obstacles and rewards—all requiring a measured and thoughtful approach. It is almost impossible to anticipate all eventualities, but with experience comes the ability to visualize most potential problems and take preemptive steps. It is essential to put yourself in a good position. I always tell aspiring filmmakers that they can put themselves in a position where success is possible. Conversely, people can put themselves in a position where failure is not only possible, it is virtually guaranteed. Preproduction is where it all happens.

The preparation for shooting has become somewhat of a science. The following tools are useful in creating an order for shooting and determining all other practical aspects of daily activity on the set.

THE PRODUCTION BOARD

A key factor in creating an efficient approach to shooting is the *production board,* a representation of all the scenes and all the elements that the script requires—characters, props, vehicles and the like. **SEE 5-8** All the elements are listed down the vertical axis. The individual scenes themselves are listed or arranged on strips across the horizontal axis, with needed elements being checked in the column underneath the scene. The scenes are put in the order in which the production manager foresees shooting them. Scenes—and indeed entire films—are not shot in chronological order; they are shot in the order that allows the crew to be most efficient. Script pages are broken down into eighths for logging and shooting.

Most production managers today use computer software designed specifically for the purpose, but in the old days the production board was a huge chart kept by the PM in the production office. Each scene was on a long strip that was removed when the scene was completed. Whether on a wall or a computer, the production board dominates the film crew's efforts, being an overall flowchart detailing all the elements, both human and material, needed to make a specific film. It is an ever-present entity, the visual record of how the shooting is proceeding.

As suggested in chapter 4, the major purpose of the board is to assist the PM and the assistant director (AD) in organizing the most efficient approach to shooting an entire film and knowing at a glance what resources are needed for each scene. All the scenes to be shot at a specific location are grouped together, regardless of whether they occur close to each other in the narrative. As an example, both the beginning and concluding scenes from Jonathan Demme's *Something Wild* take place in and just outside the same New York City restaurant. In both scenes the shots are similar, with only the lighting and the actors' wardrobes changing. One can presume that both scenes were shot in the same time frame. When the material from the first scene was completed, the same setups—with lighting and wardrobe changes—from the final scene were then done. Everything is organized to be both cost efficient and logistically practical.

The production board starts as an apparently unwieldy mass of information. After each scene is completed, the corresponding strip is removed. As the film is shot, the board becomes smaller and smaller. The removal of the last strip usually occasions huge sighs of relief, wild partying, and submissions to exhaustion.

5-8

The production board comprises long, removable strips representing individual scenes across the horizontal axis; all the elements that the script requires are listed down the vertical axis

Scene	8	49	37	9	34	78
Day/Night	N	N	D	N	N	D
Interior/Exterior	I	I	i	I	I	I
Location/Studio	L	L	L	L	L	L
Number of Pages	1⅞	⅖	6⅜	1⅝	1⅛	⅞
Title: **THE WOK**	KITCHEN	KITCHEN	KITCHEN	THEATER	THEATER	THEATER
ANDREA MARTIN	X	X		X	X	
JOHN MARTIN	X		X	X	X	X
THEATER MANAGER				X	X	
PROJECTIONIST				X		X
CLEANING SUPPLIES	X		X			
WOK	X	X	X			
MONEY BELT W/BILLS				X		

STORYBOARDS AND ORGANIZATION

Storyboards are not only important conceptual tools but also valuable organizational tools. As a production board is used to organize an entire script, the storyboard (shot lists and other approaches work for this too) can be used to organize the crew's daily activities. Thus sections of the script that are to be shot from a specific setup can be grouped together and shot at the same time. The scene can then be organized so that setups are shot in a sequence that makes sense for all the departments, particularly the lighting crew. Relighting an area that has already been struck—that is, all the equipment taken down and repositioned for the next setups—can cause lighting continuity problems no matter how carefully the plan is reconstructed. Cost of talent and extras is also an issue. The setups can be sequenced so that time with talent is efficiently used and there is as little duplication of effort as possible.

The storyboard can thus be interrelated with the idea of the shot list to produce a snapshot of a day's work. In addition, when the frame and its contents are essentially a matter of public record, individual departments can anticipate almost any need. This is true of both preproduction and daily shooting. Many productions will post storyboard sheets in a prominent place, either in the production office or on the set, where the crew can consult them whenever needed. The camera department will know if specific camera mounts are needed; the lighting crew can be prepared to match color temperatures and respond to potential differences in the volumes of light if windows are in a shot of daytime interiors. Design and costume people can have everything prepared in advance. The props people can evaluate what is expected of them in terms of providing elements for each scene, and so on through the departments. The storyboard may not completely eliminate the need for consultation with responsible parties, but it does assist in individual initiative. The Coen brothers are a good example of a production team that posts the day's storyboards and are well regarded for their immaculately organized shoots. Their films reflect their careful and thoughtful approach.

Because the storyboard lays out how shots are supposed to be edited together sequentially, it is also of assistance to the script supervisor, who can be aware of which elements in the frame require attention. This happens primarily with novice directors, but nothing can be more frustrating for a script supervisor than being unable to understand the director's ideas about how a scene is supposed to cut together.

THE LINED SCRIPT

The *lined script* is a visual record of how a scene is being shot; it is the script supervisor's responsibility. Similar to one of the methods of working out coverage in the script, the script supervisor will draw a vertical line through the dialogue that is being covered from a specific setup. **SEE 5-9** If you were covering the first three lines of the script in the master, you would draw a line through those three lines of dialogue. If you were shooting everything except the first line in a medium shot from setup #2, a line would be drawn accordingly. If the last two lines were covered from setup #3, the appropriate line would be drawn. If you shot the fourth line in close-up, it would be marked as well. Different-colored pencils are used to denote the different types of shots. Scene numbers are also listed on the lined script, with camera roll and footage numbers often recorded as well. There are many other potential markings on this version of the script, but the general idea is to show what material has been covered from what angle.

The lined script is indispensable for keeping track of how much coverage is being done. The director and script supervisor can refer to it at any point to determine if the appropriate footage is being generated. As important as the lined script is on the set, it is also essential for the editorial staff. They use it to determine quickly if specific angles have been shot. For instance, if a close-up of a specific character would work well at a certain point in a scene, the lined script is first consulted to see if one was shot. If the close-up was shot, the scene number will appear on the lined script. The editor will then consult the camera reports to find exactly where the shot is on the many rolls of film.

PRODUCTION FORMS

Sophisticated recordkeeping is necessary both in the production office and on the set. Over the years the commercial film industry, and episodic television in particular, has developed production forms and notation sheets that help in the preparation

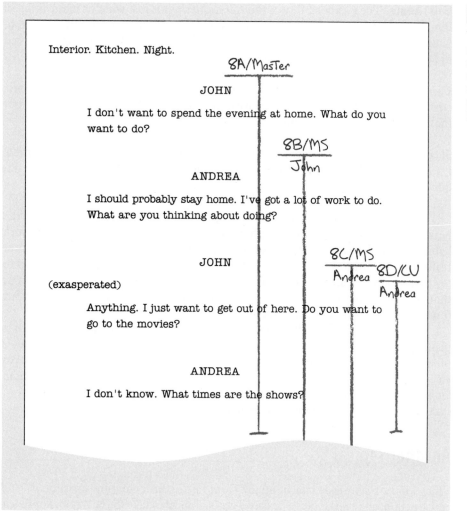

Interior. Kitchen. Night.

8A/Master

JOHN

I don't want to spend the evening at home. What do you
want to do?

8B/MS
John

ANDREA

I should probably stay home. I've got a lot of work to do.
What are you thinking about doing?

8C/MS
Andrea   8D/CU
                 Andrea

JOHN

(exasperated)

Anything. I just want to get out of here. Do you want to
go to the movies?

ANDREA

I don't know. What times are the shows?

and shooting of scenes. The phrase "verbal orders don't go" applies here. With the myriad elements that must be in the right place at the right time, all instructions must be in writing. As with storyboard sheets, the forms suggested herein are available commercially; there are software programs that can generate them as well. Although individual forms from different sources may vary somewhat in detail, they request the same basic information. Almost every department is expected to do some written recordkeeping, and only a few key forms are described here.

Budget forms Budgeting is essential to the creation of a workable shooting plan. A multitude of detailed forms list areas of potential cost. Many of these are nonissues for independents and students, though many costs are unavoidable, including those for raw stock, processing and printing, sound, finishing, and so on. Becoming familiar with the expenses that are easy to identify as well as those that are hidden will help avoid much painful recalculation down the road.

Script breakdown forms Prepared by the AD or PM, script breakdown forms precede the production board and represent all of an individual scene's needs on a single sheet. The form is generally a grid, with each square requesting information about specific needs, such as cast, extras, props, wardrobe, special effects, animals, and so on. A modified version is often used in actual production.

Call sheets   The responsibility of the AD, a *call sheet* is just what its name implies: It informs the talent of when they must be on the set and how much time is given to makeup, hair, and the like. It also details for crew members when they are supposed to be where, and what will be needed from them.

Continuity logs   These are kept by the script supervisor for records about specific elements in the frame. Some forms have an area for a rough sketch of the scene, but most require written information.

Script note forms   Also filled out by the script supervisor during shooting, these list all the technical details of the shots, including f-stops, filtering, lens length, duration of the shot, and so on.

Although the specific materials for organizing a shoot will be unfamiliar to the beginner, you should make every effort to establish and maintain organized work habits. The tools discussed in this section should provide guidance. It is difficult to realistically communicate the kinds of pressures you will find on the set. Suffice it to say that shooting a scene with a full crew is an intense experience. It may seem as though chaos is but a short step away. If you can keep chaos at arm's length, your time and efforts will be spent more productively.

Things will undoubtedly change on the set, no matter how carefully a shoot is planned. Unanticipated problems will require changes in some shots and render others impossible. This is particularly true for beginners, who lack the experience to visualize every eventuality. Crew members who can look at any shooting situation, anticipate problems, and deal with them in advance are greatly valued resources. Part of learning is understanding how to anticipate problems.

Another Typical Scene

What kind of synthesis can be made from all this information on shots, scene construction, and crews? It can be useful for beginners to take the backdoor approach to visualizing, organizing, and executing a scene: Start with a scene in a finished film and work back to a storyboard. This gives a sense of what choices have been made in camera positions. It can also clarify issues of the 180-degree rule and allow speculation on some practical organizational principles.

Breaking down a scene in this fashion produces a clear idea of what is occurring visually in relationship to the dialogue and action in the script. As always, the key words are *choice* and *strategy*. Creating overheads and storyboards facilitates planning the blocking of the scene, determining suitable setups, and apportioning the dialogue and actions accordingly. Reviewing the idea of elements is helpful. A scene consists of elements that the director must decide how to photograph, thus determining what should be emphasized at what point.

One straightforward and exceptionally effective scene from Jonathan Demme's *Something Wild* is a good example of this. Set in a diner, the scene involves the film's three main characters, Charlie (Jeff Daniels), Lulu (Melanie Griffith), and Ray (Ray Liotta). Charlie is attempting to get Lulu away from Ray, an ex-con on a crime spree. Charlie uses the presence of several police officers sitting nearby to intimidate Ray. The film is from a script by E. Max Frye.

As you read the transcription of the dialogue, think about breaking down the scene into elements. **SEE 5-10** Who are the key characters, and what objects and actions are important to the scene? What are the potential setups?

What would be considered the elements of this scene? There are clearly five: Lulu, Charlie, Ray, the waitress (Darlene), and the police officers. The scene is thus

5-10

Dialogue from the diner scene in *Something Wild*

90.   INTERIOR. DINER. NIGHT.   90.

RAY
Uh, let me have the "Rustler's Rhapsody."

DARLENE
"Rustler's Rhapsody."

Charles enters from behind Ray.

CHARLES
Just coffee for me . . . Darlene. You don't mind, do you, Ray?

LULU
Charlie, you gotta be outta your mind. You don't know what you're doing.

RAY
Charlie, you are one dumb son of a bitch. I'm almost starting to like you, Charlie.

DARLENE
(entering with coffee)
Here ya go.

CHARLES
Thanks, Darlene.
(to Ray)
I want Lulu.

RAY
Is that your name this week? Lulu?

LULU
Yes.

RAY
You know, Charlie, she's not going to be too happy driving around in a station wagon the rest of her life. You better think about that. You better ask yourself if you really want her.

CHARLES
I really want her.

RAY
Ahhhh.

LULU
Great.

RAY
Charlie, you gotta fight for a woman like this.

CHARLES
I don't have to fight you, Ray. I'm gonna take Lulu and we're gonna waltz right outta here and there's not a damn thing you can do to stop me.

RAY
Ooh. Rrrrrr. Ha, ha. Oh, Charlie, you are somethin'. You are somethin'.

CHARLES
Take a look over there. Go ahead. Evening, officer.

OFFICER
How's it goin'?

CHARLES
Ray, you're a convicted felon. You're in the possession of one, if not several, concealed weapons. You robbed a grocery store. You assaulted that poor kid with a gun. You left the state of Pennsylvania, which is gonna come as a surprise to your parole officer. And I'd be willing to wager that that Cadillac of yours sitting out in the parking lot, I bet it's hot.

LULU
Charlie!

CHARLES
Now it's you with something to lose.

RAY
Fuck you.

LULU
He's got you, Ray.

RAY
Fuck you too, Lulu.
The police officer is joined by two others.

CHARLES
Evening, officers.

OFFICER
How ya doin'?

CHARLES
Oh, good, pretty good. Thank you.
(to Ray)
Hand over the car keys. Come on, hand over the car keys.

LULU
Let's go.

RAY
You're going to regret this.

CHARLES
Well, life's full of regrets.

RAY
No. You are really going to regret this.

CHARLES
Now your wallet.

LULU
Charlie, come on.

RAY
You think you're pretty smart, don't you, Charlie.

CHARLES
Pretty smart. Well look, Ray, just to show you there are no hard feelings, this one's on me.
Charles waves the check at Ray. Charles and Lulu exit.

CHARLES
(to police)
Good night.

OFFICERS
Good night.

DARLENE
(giving Ray the check)
The gentleman said you'd take care of this.

RAY
That son of a bitch.

an interrelationship of these five elements. What are some potential setups? The entire action is presented from eight setups, at least until everything very significantly changes when Charlie and Lulu exit. The first setup is the master shot, the starting point of all conventional scene breakdown. There are two over-the-shoulder (OTS) shots, one of Ray over Lulu's shoulder and one of Lulu and Charlie over Ray's shoulder. There are three close-ups of the key people: Lulu, Ray, and Charlie. There is one setup for Darlene and one setup for the police officers. The two setups covering the exit are described later.

Note the overhead. **SEE 5-11** The positioning of the cameras for the close-ups (setups #3, #5, and #6) is slightly misleading, because the squashing of perspective and the out-of-focus background make it obvious that they were done using a longer lens, a telephoto, from roughly the positions of the OTS shots (setups #2 and #4). Even if they were done from precisely the same place as the OTS shots, the change of lens length marks them as different setups.

The scene is broken down in the following figure. **SEE 5-12** The ellipses (...) denote when a character's dialogue continues into the following shot. Pay attention to the way the shots break down in relation to the dialogue. How often are the reaction

5-11

Overhead of the diner scene

Setups

1   Master shot
2   OTS, Lulu to Ray
3   CU, Ray
4   OTS, Ray to Lulu and Charles
5   CU, Lulu
6   CU, Charles
7   MS, Darlene
8   LS, police officers

5-12

Breakdown of the diner scene

Dolly over

RAY
Uh, let me have the "Rustler's Rhapsody."

DARLENE
"Rustler's Rhapsody."

CHARLES
Just coffee for me, Darlene.

You don't mind, do you, Ray?

LULU
Charlie, you gotta be outta your mind. You don't know what you're doing.

RAY
Charlie, ...

... you are one dumb son of a bitch.

... I'm almost starting to like ...

... you, Charlie.

DARLENE
Here ya go.

CHARLES
Thanks, Darlene. I want Lulu.

RAY
Is that your name this week? Lulu?

LULU
Yes.

Breakdown of the diner scene *(continued)*

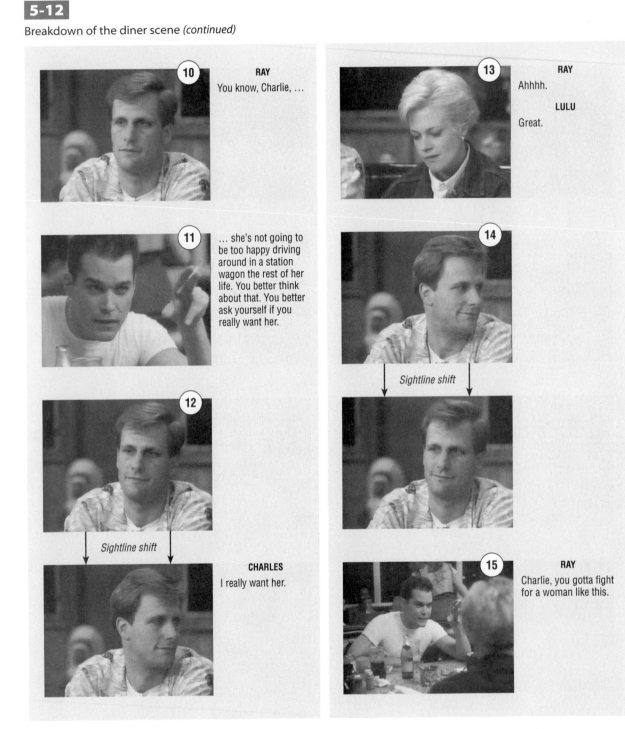

10
RAY
You know, Charlie, ...

11
... she's not going to be too happy driving around in a station wagon the rest of her life. You better think about that. You better ask yourself if you really want her.

12

Sightline shift

CHARLES
I really want her.

13
RAY
Ahhhh.
LULU
Great.

14

Sightline shift

15
RAY
Charlie, you gotta fight for a woman like this.

shots done without any dialogue? Is the 180-degree rule observed? How are the setups used to play the climax of the scene? Are the setups used in a logical way that reflects the shape of the scene?

As suggested, the master is used sparingly, three times to be exact (shots 1, 32, and 43). The first (1) does exactly what a classic master is supposed to do: present all the elements together. The police officer is shown seated as Charlie enters behind him. Then the camera dollies over to show Darlene taking dessert orders from Ray and Lulu.

5-12

Breakdown of the diner scene *(continued)*

16

CHARLES
I don't have to fight you, Ray. I'm gonna take Lulu and we're gonna waltz right outta here and there's not a damn thing you can do to stop me.

20

… Evening, officer.

OFFICER
How's it goin'?

17

RAY
Ooh. Rrrrrr. Ha ha. Oh, Charlie, you are somethin'. You are somethin'.

21

Sightline shift

18

CHARLES
Take a look over there …

19

… Go ahead …

22

CHARLES
Ray, you're a convicted felon. You're in the possession of one, if not several, concealed weapons. You robbed a grocery store. You assaulted that poor kid with a gun …

Sightline shift

23

… You left the state of Pennsylvania, which is gonna come as a surprise to your parole officer …

5-12

Breakdown of the diner scene *(continued)*

24 ... and I'd be willing to wager that that Cadillac of yours sitting out in the parking lot, I bet it's hot.

25 **LULU** Charlie!

26

27 **CHARLES** Now it's you with something to lose.

28 **RAY** Fuck you.

29 **LULU** He's got you, Ray.

30 **RAY** Fuck you too, Lulu.

31

After the initial master, the scene quickly moves in for the medium shots and close-ups. The first cuts are between the two OTS shots (setups #2 and #4). Close-ups are then used to present the basic elements at issue. Because the most intense part of the scene is yet to come, the cutting retreats back to mediums. Parameters of performance, such as the body language, are always key issues. One shot where Ray shakes his arms and hands to mock Charlie (17) clearly requires the medium shot. Although the logic of the scene may require an MS here anyway, it is clear that the MS is used to facilitate Ray Liotta's exceptional performance.

Breakdown of the diner scene *(continued)*

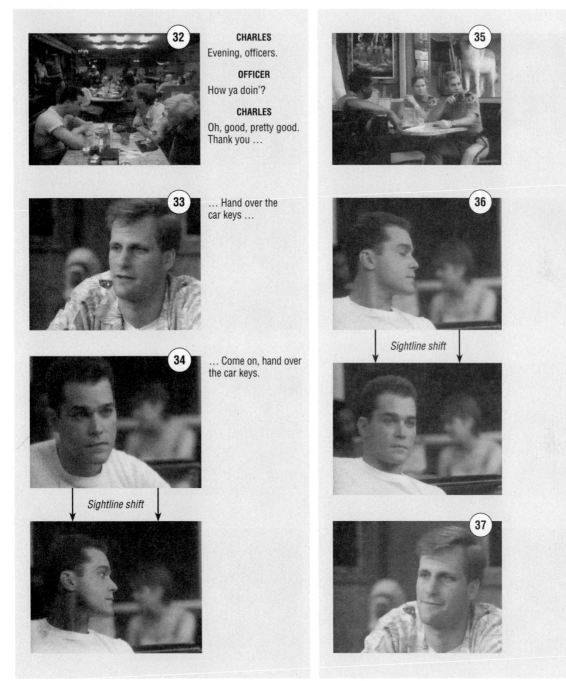

32

CHARLES
Evening, officers.

OFFICER
How ya doin'?

CHARLES
Oh, good, pretty good.
Thank you ...

33

... Hand over the
car keys ...

34

... Come on, hand over
the car keys.

Sightline shift

35

36

Sightline shift

37

The most intense part of this scene, the climax, is when Ray swears at Charlie and Lulu. As expected, it is played entirely in close-ups (21–31). Immediately after this the scene cuts to the master shot (32) in which Charlie makes verbal contact with the police officers. Used in the middle of a scene like this, the master shot can act as a release valve for tensions that have built up. Both the intensity of a scene and the closeness to the subjects can be such that we literally need to back off. Although the comic content of this shot is also a factor, the placement of the master makes one almost feel oneself breathe a sigh of relief.

5-12

Breakdown of the diner scene *(continued)*

LULU
Let's go.

RAY
You think you're pretty smart, don't you, Charlie.

CHARLES
Pretty smart ...

RAY
You're going to regret this.

CHARLES
Well, life's full of regrets.

RAY
No. You are really going to regret this.

... Well look, Ray, just to show you there are no hard feelings, this one's on me.

CHARLES
Now your wallet.

LULU
Charlie, come on.

CHARLES
Good night.

OFFICERS
Good night.

Breakdown of the diner scene *(continued)*

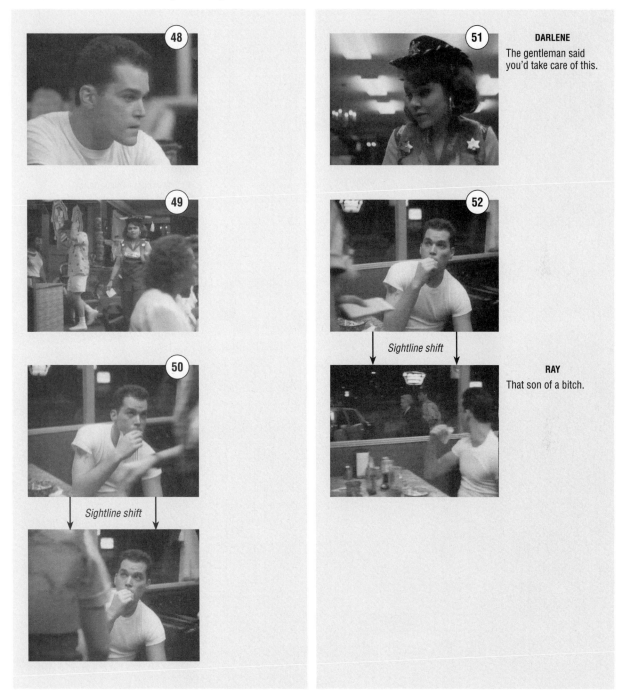

Despite this brief respite, the scene maintains its intensity. It returns to a sequence of close-ups for the exchange of the keys and wallet (33–42). As is so often the case, the master is also used to "bookend" the scene, although its final use (43) is somewhat before the end of the scene. As suggested, everything changes once Lulu and Charlie get up to leave (46). This requires two more camera positions. **SEE 5-13** Setup #9 is used just once (49) and is essentially a variation on the master shot. Setup #10 is used twice and has some significance in terms of the 180-degree rule.

Shooting the characters' exit requires two more setups

The final two setups are:

- Setup #9: Alternative master

- Setup #10: MS of Ray, with Lulu and Charlie running to the car in the background

The logic of a specific shooting plan is always open to argument, but the sequence in this case has clearly been considered carefully in terms of the way the setups are used to cover the action. The rightness of the camera positions is virtually inescapable.

THE LINE

What occurs in terms of the line (introduced in chapter 3) is interesting as well. For the bulk of the scene, the line clearly runs right through the table, and the camera is on the window side of the action. When Charlie and Lulu leave, the line switches from the window side to the restaurant side in the alternative master (49). Before this transition the only camera position on the far side of the action is the one for the police officers (setup #8), which is used twice before Charlie and Lulu's exit (20 and 35). On both occasions the employment of this setup is justified by Ray's sightline shift prior to its inclusion. Some editors might argue that the shot could be used without the sightline shift. The setup maintains the direction of the action and is lined up pointing in the same general direction as the other setups. The setup is used a third time (47) as Charlie and Lulu leave.

Shot 49, from setup #9, is the transition shot from one side of the line to the other. Then we can come back to shot 50 for the final interchange between Ray and Darlene. The original setup #7 of Darlene is used for this, although allowing her to pass in front of the camera in shots 50 and 52 constitutes a line cross. This could have been avoided by cutting before she passed in front of the camera, but the look of bewilderment on Ray's face would have been sacrificed. In this case editor Craig McKay and director Demme determined that the emotional content of the scene required keeping Ray's response, thus overshadowing any slight dislocation caused by the change of direction. Such are the compromises that are often made.

ORGANIZATIONAL CONSIDERATIONS

Although many considerations undoubtedly went into shooting this scene, the primary focus in the discussion here is on the sequence of shooting. For novices it is generally a good idea to shoot masters first, the most significant reason being that all issues of movement and continuity are ironed out at this stage. Understanding general continuity will allow all departments to anticipate the needs of the closer shots. In particular, the script supervisor can watch the scene and make mental and written notes about the details that will require matching. The positioning of all the bottles and plates on the table would require constant monitoring.

If indeed the master were shot first, all the material from setup #1 would be shot at once. Camera positions would not necessarily be shot in numerical order. Although discussion of the complexity of lighting is yet to come, it clearly is a major consideration when planning a sequence for shooting. It was not necessary to light the background for setup #2 for the master; thus setup #3 probably would be the next logical choice. You will often have to make some adjustments, but setup #3 is essentially already lighted. The shots would be filmed in the most logical order, again with lighting and efficiency with talent being the major determining factors.

Matching the lighting from setup to setup is another consideration. It is relatively easy for an experienced crew to match lighting when moving from the master to the close-ups. Going the other way—matching lighting from close-ups back to the master—is tricky. In the master the position of the camera and the wide field of view can present obstacles to placing instruments. A crack crew can easily overcome these problems, but master shots commonly require compromises in the lighting. It is essential to know what compromises are going to have to be made before lighting the closer material. Re-creating the lighting from a close-up with an instrument repositioned to shoot the master can consume important time on the set as well as produce uneven results.

There are numerous other considerations. In the scene just analyzed, the tables undoubtedly had to be moved away from the wall to create space for the camera. Indeed, many things changed in the final setups (#9 and particularly #10), and time devoted to relighting is a key consideration. The inside of the restaurant needed to be lighted for the initial eight setups. When the whole thing turned in the other direction, the exterior of the restaurant became an issue, both in terms of lighting and the control of elements in the parking lot. The last setup required an entire relight—a demanding albeit common occurrence. Shooting scripts or storyboards can be analyzed for all significant shooting complications and the appropriate response planned. Allowances for time, materials, and extra personnel can thus be made.

Another consideration is the scheduling of talent. The master shot usually requires the most bodies. Keeping and feeding extras is expensive, and the production office wants them cut loose as quickly as possible. The peripheral characters, the waitress and the police officers, also can be used in an efficient manner. For this reason all the shots requiring the most people are often shot at the beginning. Being able to dismiss the extras and bit players in a timely manner reinforces the importance of organizing the sequence of shooting. A 4-minute scene like this could easily have taken a day or two to shoot, and keeping all the extra bodies around for the whole time would waste precious resources. The AD needs to know the direction of all the shots in the scene, allowing him to identify which elements—characters, extras, and so on—are going to be necessary and for how long. There is nothing like coming to a setup late in a shooting day and realizing that the appropriate elements are no longer available.

This scene represents the classic approach to scene breakdown at its best. Camera setups are devised and the dialogue to be covered from each setup is determined. The scene is thus composed of an interrelationship of the different shots to emphasize the action and responses—the dramatic emphasis. Though other approaches can be considered, the clarity achieved here is undeniable. This straightforward example may lead some to believe that the conventional approach is somehow easy. Nothing could be farther from the truth. The difficulties of creating a seamless scene can be understood only by trying to create one yourself. It takes the skill of many different people to make a scene work.

Part II

The Camera

6

The Camera Body

Movement and Perception

In the late 1880s, Thomas Edison and W. L. K. Dickson produced what now constitutes the basic mechanism of the motion picture camera. The phenomenon that allows us to perceive a series of still images as a continuous representation of motion is based on the idea that the human eye will hold an image for a split second. For an example, look at a light bulb for a few seconds and then look away; the eye will hold the imprint of that light for a short period. When presented with a succession of images, each one making a momentary imprint, the eye blurs them into movement. The key to this process is that a person's view must be disrupted between each drawing or photograph. If not, all one will see is a complete blur.

Prior to the advent of motion pictures, inventors and tinkerers had perfected many contraptions that allowed people to perceive motion created from individual drawings of sequences of movement. Invented in the 1830s, the zoetrope is probably the most famous of these. **SEE 6-1** It was a simple drum on a turntable. The drum

The zoetrope, circa 1830, was an early example of simulating motion by viewing a series of individual drawings had vertical slits, spaced equally all around the drum. Individual drawings, each one representing a sequential point in a simple movement, were placed around the edges of the inside of the drum. When the drum was rotated, viewers would look through the slots at the pictures on the far side of the drum. They would see one picture, then their view would be disrupted by the exterior of the drum. The next slot would allow them to see the next picture, and so on. When the drum was rotated at the correct rate, viewers would see the pictures as a continuous movement.

These experiments quite naturally began to incorporate the relatively new technology of still photography. The most famous early experiments were by Eadweard Muybridge. The story goes that Leland Stanford, then governor of California, bet a friend that there were times in a horse's gallop when none of the animal's four feet was touching the ground. Stanford hired Muybridge to test this hypothesis. In 1878 Muybridge set up an ingenious testing ground in which he used still cameras with strings attached to their shutter releases. At brief intervals along a racetrack, he rigged a sequence of several dozen such cameras. As the horse ran by, the camera would take a picture of a discrete point of the horse's progress. When finished, Muybridge had a series of pictures, representing sequential points in the motion of a running horse. It was a simple matter to adapt these pictures to a zoetrope, and the result was a smooth representation of the horse's gallop—and Stanford's winning the bet. This is precisely what film is—a series of still photographs that, when presented in sequence, re-create movement. The only thing needed at that point was a more efficient way of capturing the image and a more sophisticated presentation device.

The technology to produce still photographs had existed since 1839, when Louis Jacques Mandé Daguerre introduced a device that could capture and transform light into a permanent image. The big step for motion pictures was to design both the equipment that could photograph a sequence of images and a medium on which those images could be recorded. Edison and Dickson were poised to provide a solution to the first requirement, and when George Eastman provided them with strip celluloid film their problems were solved. Despite many design variations, what they invented more than a hundred years ago remains the basic film mechanism. It is a relatively simple device, not unlike a sewing machine, and all filmmakers need a sophisticated understanding of how it works to get the desired images on film.

In the age of home video, many beginners have the expectation that the camera is just magically going to work. In film you find that it takes a measured and thoughtful approach to make the process work.

The Basic Mechanism

The fundamental mechanism that transports and exposes the film is made up of a small number of essential elements that are present in some form in virtually every camera. Their relatively simple interrelationship, what is called the camera's *action*, is the "how" of recording the images.

An illustration of a representative view of the interior of a camera is shown on the following page. **SEE 6-2** Each of the elements plays its own individual role. All cameras have a *film chamber*—the space in the camera where the unexposed film is stored. Many cameras employ a separate *magazine (mag)* as the film chamber. The design pictured here will have a *cover plate,* or *lid,* that closes over the film chamber.

The feed spool and take-up spool do what one would expect: The *feed spool* holds the unexposed film that you have bought from the manufacturer, referred to as *raw stock.* The *take-up spool* winds the film after it has been exposed. Both spools are mounted on *spindles,* the take-up being driven by the camera's motor. The feed spool turns as the film feeds off it. Some feed spools have a slight backward resistance—referred to as *torque*—that ensures even feeding into the mechanism.

6-2

All the parts shown here are important, but the real action occurs with the pull-down claw and shutter

The *sprocketed rollers* feed the film into and out of the area where each image is exposed. Each roller has sprocket teeth that correspond to the *pitch* (distance between sprocket holes) of the film; these rollers drive the film forward continuously. The two rollers are geared together so that they run at precisely the same speed: As the top roller is feeding the film in, the bottom roller is feeding it out simultaneously. This is key because the rollers keep a consistent amount of film in the gate area. When viewed from the front, the actual sprocket teeth are on the edge of the roller toward the body of the camera, away from the side you would be looking at.

Although this two-roller configuration is quite common, some camera designs employ a single sprocketed roller that does double-duty—one side of the roller feeds the film in as the other feeds it out. **SEE 6-3** The CP-16 (*CP* stands for *Cinema*

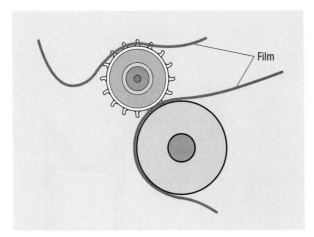

6-3

In a single-roller design, one side of the sprocketed roller feeds the film in as the other side feeds it out

Film

Products) and the Krasnagorsk are good examples of 16mm cameras with this approach.

Keepers do exactly what their name suggests: keep the film tight against the sprocketed roller. Their sole function is to ensure that the film does not slip away from the roller, which would throw off the whole system. They usually can and need to be pivoted out of the way for loading and cleaning. A spring-loaded pin (one that has a spring that pulls it back into position after it has been disengaged) locks them back in place. Forgetting to close the keepers can lead to camera jams and ruined film, although most cameras have safety features guarding against this mistake.

The *aperture*, usually referred to as the *gate*, is where each individual frame is exposed. Although the gate is a rather unassuming rectangular hole, it is a finely machined opening, and its care and maintenance are essential to producing a high-quality image. The *film plane* is not a mechanism, but is the point—the plane—where the light that has entered the lens strikes the emulsion of the film. It is the place toward which all efforts, hopes, and fears are directed. All issues of focus, focal length, exposure, and a host of others are resolved (or not) right here.

The *aperture plate*, also referred to as the *film guide*, is the polished metal plate that guides the film to the gate, where it is exposed. The **pressure plate** is usually mounted on spring-loaded pins and holds the film flat against the aperture plate. The film has to be held flat so the pull-down claw will engage properly. The pressure from the spring-loaded pins is also the main force that holds the film stable as it is being exposed, as well as flat against the gate for uniform focus. Film has a natural curl that would leave its edges closer to the lens than its center if not held flat. The pressure plate is removable to make cleaning the camera easier.

These parts of the mechanism are important, but the real action occurs with the pull-down claw and the shutter. The **pull-down claw** is the mechanism that advances each individual frame for exposure. **SEE 6-4** It is usually recessed in the body of the camera and, when rolling film, comes out and grabs each individual frame and pulls it down to be exposed. It then retracts, goes up and grabs the next frame, then pulls it down. This sequence, called **intermittent movement** because the frames are alternately moving and stationary as they rush past the gate, occurs continually; and in this manner every frame is pulled in front of the gate and exposed.

The shutter is the other key element. As stated, both the production and projection of the film image is based on disrupted vision. If there were nothing to block the light from the film as the pull-down claw advanced each frame, the image would blur because the film would be exposed while it was moving. The **shutter** is the necessary response to the action of the pull-down claw: It continuously rotates in front of the film, blocking the light while the film is moving, and allowing the light to reach the film for the brief moment that it is stationary in front of the gate.

6-4

The pull-down claw advances each frame of film for exposure

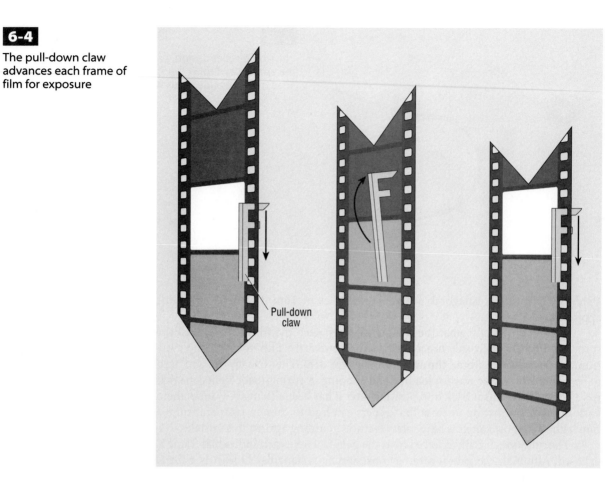

Pull-down claw

6-5

Many cameras employ a half-moon shutter, which is actually slightly less than 180 degrees of a circle

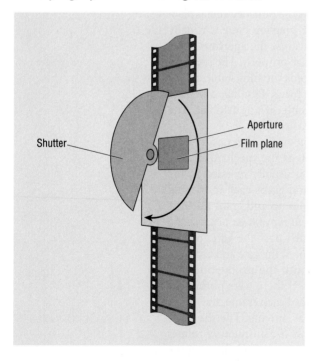

Shutter

Aperture

Film plane

Many cameras employ a half-disc-shaped shutter called a *half-moon shutter*. **SEE 6-5** In most designs they are actually slightly smaller than 180 degrees of a circle. Other shutter designs are discussed later in this chapter in the context of viewing systems.

This is how each frame is brought to the gate for exposure. The pull-down claw brings each frame to the gate, and the shutter blocks the light as the frame is being moved into place. As the claw is going up to get the next frame, each frame is exposed while it is stationary in front of the gate. All the other elements in the basic mechanism support this simple action.

The *Latham's loops* are an idiosyncrasy of the film stock. Named after their discoverer, they are not really part of the basic mechanism of the motion picture camera but are so essential to the way the image is formed that they warrant equal consideration. It is apparent that the basic mechanism employs two different types of motion. There is both the continuous motion of the sprocketed rollers and the intermittent movement of the pull-down claw. There clearly has to be someplace for these two movements to be reconciled. That place is in the loops. When loading film, you form a small loop with the film both above and below the gate. These flexible loops are where the give-and-take of the two movements occurs. If you run a "dummy load" with the lid open, you will see the film "chattering" (vibrating slightly) on the top and bottom.

With most cameras these loops are set at the start, and unless there is a malfunction or the camera gets rough treatment there should be little concern about losing the loop. High-end professional cameras have ways of checking the loops between shots, and you will see them being checked with relative frequency. These loops are crucial to achieving a usable image. Most everyone has seen a projector lose the film loop, whether during a classroom film presentation or at a commercial theater. When this happens the image starts to blur vertically. Most projectors have a loop restorer, a lever that pushes the film back into the correct position; if not, someone has to stop the projector and reset the loops.

When the loop is lost, the film becomes taut between one of the rollers and the pressure plate. **SEE 6-6** As the illustration suggests, the camera usually loses the loop on the bottom, with the excess film collecting at the top. When this happens the pull-down claw is no longer engaging with the sprocket holes—it is striking the film between sprockets. Rather than being driven by the intermittent movement of the claw, the film is being driven by the continuous movement of the sprocketed rollers. It is thus moving while it is being exposed. This is what creates the blurring effect, which is most noticeable in the bright areas of the image. Fluorescent lights, for example, will look like hanging bedsheets.

6-6

"Losing the loop" means that the film becomes taut between one of the rollers and the pressure plate

Pull-down claw does not engage

Losing the loop in the projector can be easily corrected, but its loss while shooting is disastrous. The image is exposed while the film is moving, and the resulting blur is not correctable. Reshooting or abandoning the material are the only options. Experimental filmmakers have occasionally used footage with a lost loop to good effect, most notably Bruce Baillie's *Castro Street* (1966). In most situations, however, it is undesirable.

Cameras do not lose the loop often, but when they do, the camera will usually sound different. Although it happens infrequently, you should nevertheless be constantly checking and guarding against it. The biggest culprit of lost loops is improper loading—one of the many reasons why learning proper loading technique is critical. Not closing the keepers is a common loading mistake that causes lost loops. Another cause can be the film's ***plastic memory:*** If the camera sits loaded and unused for an extended period (as little as half an hour), the film will conform to the shape in which it was left. When the camera is started again, that semi-rigid shape can cause the film to run through the mechanism poorly and lose the loop. A jar to the camera (which should always be avoided for obvious reasons) or flaws in the raw stock (which are extremely rare) can also create the problem. Camera malfunction, such as in the pull-down claw or the sprocketed rollers, can also be the cause. These would result from serious mechanical breakdowns and would occasion major repair costs.

Two other design options are part of the basic mechanism on many cameras. A registration pin and an inching knob are not absolutely necessary, but they are generally desirable. The purpose of a *registration pin* is to hold the film absolutely steady as it is being exposed. It is usually below the film gate and, like the pull-down claw, extends out and engages a sprocket hole.

In the explanation of the basic mechanism, it is apparent that nothing is holding the film in place when it is being exposed except the force of the pressure plate and the friction of the movement. The pull-down claw has retracted and is going up to grab the next frame. All cameras hold the image reasonably stable, but the registration pin guarantees perfect *registration*—that the frame will be absolutely stable in the gate. The pin extends from the body of the camera and engages the sprocket hole as each individual frame is being exposed. It retracts as the next frame is being pulled down. Perfect registration is essential in many applications, including animation, shooting for transfer to video, and when the film is going to be blown up to a larger frame size or projected a long distance.

An *inching knob* is used to manually move the basic mechanism backward or forward. It is usually found on the exterior of the camera, though occasionally it is inside the film chamber (a design that can be annoying). The knob is helpful in loading, because the mechanism can be advanced to ensure that the film is properly threaded (the pull-down claw and sprocket teeth properly engaged and the loops correct). It is particularly helpful in moving the shutter to enable you to see through the viewing system or check the gate for dirt and hair. The inching knob is also used to roll film with the plastic memory effect out of the sprocketed rollers, thus avoiding problems with the loop. Inching knobs are essential parts of projectors as well. Although both of these features are desirable, many fine cameras have neither. The Bolex, for example, can produce an exceptional image but has neither a registration pin nor an inching knob.

Most basic technical mistakes with the camera occur because of a lack of knowledge about the camera's inner workings. In the age of video, when many people just pop in a cartridge and expect things to work, producing a film image takes careful attention to detail. It begins to strike the aspiring filmmaker that the aspects of film that ought to be simple (such as getting a usable image) are difficult and those that ought to be hard (such as being an artist) are nearly impossible. As the mechanical age yields to the electronic age, there is nevertheless something irresistibly beautiful about the action of a well-designed camera. An understanding of the basic mechanism will serve both your ability to create images trouble-free and your awareness of film's possibilities. This appreciation not only enables you to know if a camera is malfunctioning, it also allows you to understand any camera with which you might have to work. Comprehending what is going on inside a camera is also critical to understanding what can and cannot be accomplished visually. The deceptively straightforward task of making sure the camera operates correctly will always require your careful attention.

FRAMES PER SECOND

Frames per second (fps), or the more general *frame rate,* refers to the number of individual frames being photographed each second. The professional frame rate is 24 fps, that is, 24 individual photographs are recorded per second. Many cameras come with several frame rates, with rates lower and higher than 24 used for fast- and slow-motion effects (see figure 6-18). The standard rate for projection equipment is 24 fps as well.

Prior to the introduction of sound in the 1920s, films were shot at 16 fps— the minimum number of frames that could reproduce normal motion without the flicker created by a slow-moving shutter. The change to 24 occurred with the advent of sound. Sixteen fps, or more frequently 18 fps, has remained the amateur standard, although there is not a lot of amateur film still being shot.

Motors

Camera motors can be divided into two useful categories: synchronous (sync) and wild. A *synchronous (sync) motor,* referred to as a *crystal* or a *DC servo-controlled motor,* is a speed-controlled motor that produces a virtually perfect 24 fps. This allows sync-sound filming—shooting in which the actual location sound is recorded in sync with the image. Sound for film is recorded separately on conventional or digital audio equipment, and precision speeds are necessary for the two to run in sync. (See chapter 11 for a further discussion of the synchronization of sound and picture.) A *wild motor,* on the other hand, will deviate slightly from the set frame rate. If set to run at 24 fps, the speed of a wild camera could vary a percentage point or two from a true 24 fps. Although this deviation would never be visible to the eye, the lack of precision makes later synchronization with sound virtually impossible. Wild cameras are used in situations where sound is not needed or, more common, when sound effects will be edited in later. They are used much more frequently than one might at first suspect.

Beyond this key distinction, there are two types of motors in common use: electric and spring-wound. Electric motors are the standard, but spring-wound types still see use in the 16mm format. Cameras with spring-wound motors are by definition wild cameras. Sync filming requires an electric motor, although not all battery-operated cameras have crystal motors. Electric motors generally run on rechargeable nickel-cadmium batteries, referred to as *nicads.* Individual cameras have different voltage requirements, usually somewhere between 8 and 20 volts.

Spring-wound motors are driven by a spring similar to that found in a mechanical clock. There is a hand crank on the side of the camera to manually wind the spring tight. The camera is driven by the spring's releasing its pent-up energy. Winds generally last about thirty seconds when filming normal motion. The camera has a "governed" motor that allows it to run at a constant speed—it does not slow down as the spring gets to the end of its wind.

The major advantages of spring-wound motors are their low cost and their ability to be used in situations in which electricity, either for camera operation or battery recharging, is either unavailable or impractical. Prior to the days of portable battery-operated cameras, spring-wound cameras were used to shoot most location documentaries, particularly combat footage and exploration footage. Unless preventive measures are taken, batteries perform poorly in the cold, making the spring designs particularly helpful in frigid climates. The drawbacks to the spring-wound motor are limitations on shot length, the constant rewinding, and the inability to run at a perfectly controlled speed.

Once you step into sync shooting, you enter a world where costs limit access, and personnel demands call for a larger crew (sound mixer, boom operator, and others). A bare-bones 16mm sync *camera package* (camera, lenses, magazines, batteries, battery chargers, tripod, and any other camera needs specific to the shoot) rents for roughly $500 to $600 a day. Access to this high-end equipment can be limited, particularly in university film programs. For this reason and many others, initial projects are usually shot with wild cameras, often spring-wound types. In this age of electronic everything, spring-wound cameras may appear old-fashioned, but they are still precision instruments that can produce stunning images. The filmmaker, not the motor, is the variable on whether or not the camera produces beautiful images. Although most everyone thinks in terms of dialogue scenes, the relatively high number of shots that do not require sync—having sound effects added later—is surprising. This said, battery-operated cameras are the standard for professional use.

Formats

The term *format* refers to the size of the film stock and the size of the image. There are two standard formats in general use: 35mm and 16mm. A third format, *Super 8,* is an amateur standard with some intriguing professional applications, but it has seen decreased use since the introduction of home video. Another format, Super 16, is an adaptation of the 16mm format. **SEE 6-7** There are a number of other formats (65mm, IMAX, Omnivision, and so on), but these have highly specialized applications and are prohibitively expensive for students and independents.

The bigger of the two standard formats is 35mm. It demands a substantial budget in terms of both the stock itself and the equipment used to shoot and edit it. A 16mm frame is roughly one-quarter the size of a 35mm frame. The frame's width-to-height relationship is called the **aspect ratio**. The 35mm film stocks have perforations on both sides of the film, referred to as **double perf**, or two row. The 16mm stocks are available in double perf as well as **single perf**, or *one row,* where sprocket holes are on only one side.

Beyond cost, the biggest difference between the formats is in image quality. The larger the frame, the more information contained and the more defined the

6-7

Film formats are distinctions based on the size of the film stock and the size of the image

35mm formats

Academy Aperture
1.33 : 1

American widescreen
1.85 : 1

Anamorphic 2:1 squeeze
2.35 : 1
(when projected)

16mm formats

Double perforated
1.33 : 1

Single perf with sound track
1.33 : 1

Super 16
1.66 : 1

8mm formats

Standard 8mm
1.33 : 1

Super 8
1.33 : 1

image. More definition aids in projectability and, of more importance recently, a higher-quality transfer to video. In a commercial theater, the projected image is as much as 300,000 times larger than the 35mm frame from which it originated. Because there is less information, a 16mm image will not stand that kind of expansion without significant image deterioration. Anything smaller would be a dim blur.

35MM

If you see a movie at a commercial theater, odds are that it was shot on *35mm* film. Music videos and commercials are also frequently shot on 35mm, then transferred to video for editing and finishing.

The 35mm stocks have four individual sprocket holes per frame. The high number allows for more-gentle handling of the film in cameras and projectors, sparing a single perforation from supporting the entire bulk and weight of the larger frame size. It is difficult to think in terms of the weight of an individual frame, but the film is so flexible and is being moved at such a high speed that it needs all the stability possible.

The aspect ratio for 35mm film is expressed as 1.33:1, meaning that the frame is four fields wide by three fields high. This is referred to as the *Academy Aperture*. The name derives from the standardized frame size and sound track configuration accepted by the Academy of Motion Picture Arts and Sciences shortly after the introduction of sound. The area to the left of the frame is for the sound track in final prints. This area also remains unused by the gate in the camera, though there are some applications in which the full frame is used.

In practice the Academy Aperture is frequently shot but rarely projected. It is usually masked in the projector to create widescreen. The masked image in *widescreen* has an aspect ratio of 1.85:1—almost two fields wide by one field high. This is the way most feature films are presented in commercial theaters. Clearly, much of the frame is lost when a film is shown on television.

Ratios larger than 1.85:1 are generally achieved with an *anamorphic* process. The film frame itself is the standard 35mm size (the image area is actually slightly larger than the Academy Aperture), but the anamorphic process uses a camera lens that "squeezes" the image so it appears to be stretched vertically. It is then "unsqueezed" in projection. The best-known anamorphic process, CinemaScope, has a projection aspect ratio of 2.35:1. When shown on television, title sequences are often left squeezed so that the sides of credits are not cut off, thus allowing the viewer to see this strange squeezed image.

Cameras for 35mm are large and expensive to rent and require substantial technical support (in terms of both crew and equipment). The use of 35mm is very difficult for low-budget independents and virtually impossible for students. The reality, unfortunately, is that it is difficult to get anything shown if it is not in 35mm. Few theaters of any size are equipped with 16mm projectors. Although much can be done in 16mm, the harsh reality is that 35mm is the format for people interested in extensive theatrical exhibition.

16MM

The *16mm* format is used in many independent film projects and most intermediate and advanced film production classes. This is the format that can support, in terms of equipment and technical resources, a level of production that students both need to learn and can afford. The term *afford* is used advisably, because it is still quite expensive.

The 16mm format was introduced in the 1920s and quickly became the amateur stock of choice. It took on greater significance with the rise of instructional filmmaking in the 1930s and 1940s and came to wide acceptance during World War

II, when the majority of combat footage was shot with 16mm cameras. It has developed into a full-blown professional format in the years since, though video has made a dent in its popularity.

The 16mm film stock has one sprocket hole per frame. The sprocket hole is right at the *frame line,* the hairline dividing one frame from another. The aspect ratio of 16mm is also 1.33:1, four fields wide by three fields high.

SUPER 16

Super 16 is an adaptation of the 16mm format. Many independent projects used to be shot in standard 16mm with the intention that there would be a blowup to 35mm for theatrical presentation. The drawback to this approach is that the dimensions of a 35mm widescreen frame are wider and shorter (1.85:1) than the 16mm frame. To transfer to 35mm, the top and bottom of the 16mm composition had to be eliminated to conform to the 35mm frame. Not only did this have to be considered by the person shooting the film when framing shots, it reduced the already small amount of information available to create the 35mm image.

Super 16 was introduced to counter this problem. Super 16 uses standard, single-perf 16mm stock and a modified 16mm camera. The area of the film that would be taken up by the second row of sprocket holes is used for additional image. This produces a composition with the same dimensions as widescreen 35mm, as well as substantially increases the information available for blowing up.

To shoot Super 16, a camera requires a wider-than-normal gate as well as a modified lens and viewing system. Most newer production cameras are designed for easy conversion to Super 16. Older cameras would require extensive retooling, an approach that generally is not cost-effective unless you foresee doing a substantial amount of work in Super 16. Even then, the adaptation may be questionable.

Beginning filmmakers need to keep in mind that there are only two reasons to shoot Super 16. The first is the aforementioned situation when a blowup to 35mm is planned. Shooting Super 16 to finish in conventional 16mm would be counterproductive. In conventional 16mm, the area of the second row of sprocket holes is eventually devoted to the sound track, meaning the elimination of an entire portion of the frame. Those beautifully balanced compositions might suddenly look as though something were missing. The second is that Super 16 is now receiving additional attention as a source of visuals for **high-definition television (HDTV),** or *Hi-Def,* which is very close to widescreen in format. In the long run, this may be the genesis of the majority of 16mm work.

Camera Loads

Raw stocks in 16mm can be purchased loaded in two different ways: on daylight spools and on cores. In 35mm, film is available only on core loads. Daylight spools and core loads each have advantages, although daylight spools are used more frequently on small projects, and core loads are the industry standard. Core loads are more complicated to use because they must be loaded in absolute darkness, usually in a **photographic darkroom bag,** often referred to as a *changing bag.*

DAYLIGHT SPOOLS

Daylight spools are so named because they allow the camera to be loaded in the light. They have two black metal flanges on a core with a hollow center. **SEE 6-8** The side flanges protect the film from accidental exposure.

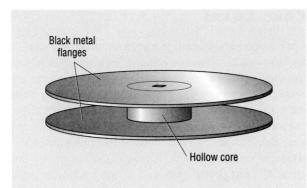

6-8

Daylight spools allow a camera to be loaded in lighted conditions

The flanges of a daylight spool are slightly farther apart than the actual width of the film to prevent the film from binding as it feeds off. So that light does not seep down into the center of the roll, the film is fed onto the spool with a reciprocal action. **SEE 6-9** One layer of film is fed against one flange of the daylight spool, then the film is shifted slightly to one side, and the next layer is fed against the other flange. The next layer is fed against the first flange, and so on. The outer layers of film prevent light from getting to the center of the roll in the loading process.

The 100-foot daylight spool, which runs for 2 minutes 40 seconds in normal filming for 16mm, is the most common for beginning projects. Daylight spools are generally used in smaller 16mm cameras, ones with the film chamber designed specifically for them. They are also handy when working in remote locations and when just one or two shots are needed. Also available are 400-foot daylight spools, which run just under 11 minutes in 16mm, but their use has diminished since video replaced film for shooting TV news. Television news photographers often had to change rolls on the fly, and daylight spools were more convenient. Their major drawback is that they are noisier in a magazine. Several cameras have felt-lined interiors to deaden the noise, an approach that would appear to deserve wider acceptance except for the difficulty of keeping the cloth clean.

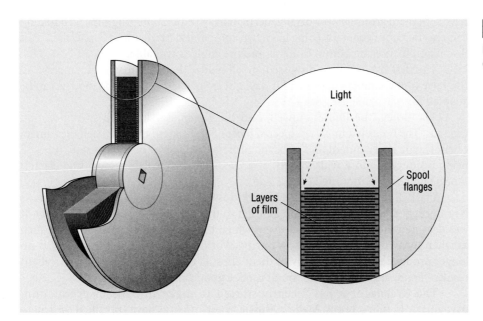

6-9

Reciprocally fed film on a daylight spool

6-10

Camera loads use 2-inch cores, which have no flanges, necessitating the use of a photographic darkroom bag

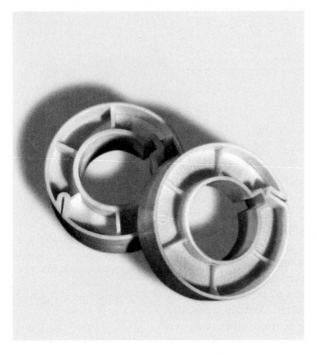

CORE LOADS

Core-loaded raw stock is the norm in professional film applications. A *core* is a circular plastic piece on which the film is wound. Unlike the daylight spool, there are no flanges to protect the film, meaning that all *core loads* must be loaded in changing bags. In 16mm the most common size is the 400-foot load; 1,200-foot loads are available but are practical only in highly controlled situations due to the bulk and extra weight of the attendant equipment. The 1,200-foot loads were once popular for formal interviewing situations, but so much of that type of application is now done on video that their use has diminished. Stock for 35mm is available in 400-foot and 1,000-foot loads, with the larger loads having more acceptance than in 16mm.

The cores themselves come in a variety of sizes and are also used extensively in the editing process. **SEE 6-10** Camera loads use 2-inch cores, whereas most editing applications use 3-inch cores or larger. The 3-inch cores limit the stress on the inner layers of film, which is particularly important for sound stock. Labs frequently wind processed film on 4-inch cores to eliminate as much stress as possible on the fragile emulsion.

Cameras

In terms of what is available, the range of camera types has consolidated considerably since the advent of video. Only a small number of companies have been able to weather the reduced demand. Many oddball cameras are no longer available due to age and peculiarity of design, but a number of 16mm cameras have either held on or flourished: Bolex, Scoopic, Aaton, Eclair, Arriflex, Krasnagorsk, and the Bell & Howell series. Some of these are no longer produced, but their durability and quality have kept them around and working, particularly in education programs. Production cameras in 35mm generally come from two companies: Arriflex and Panavision. This discussion focuses on 16mm cameras and the choices available.

The first five cameras discussed are all wild—that is, nonsync—cameras. All five have film chambers designed for daylight spools, although some models can be adapted for magazine use. **SEE 6-11**

The Bolex, the Bell & Howell, and the Krasnagorsk are all spring-wound cameras. The Bolex is a finely engineered piece of equipment that has been the camera of choice for independent and nonsync professional work for many years. It is still being produced, and a wide variety of accessories are available, including electric motors that can be mounted on the side.

The Bell & Howell is lovingly referred to as the "nail pounder," so named because it is so rugged people said it could be used to drive in tent stakes (do not try it). It was designed to withstand situations in which tender treatment was difficult, such as when thrown off landing barges during World War II. The Bell & Howell is no longer produced, although many of them are still available and providing excellent results. It was, and still is when found used, a good camera for beginners.

The Krasnagorsk has recently started to make inroads in production, particularly in film schools. Made in Russia, these cameras have ably filled the gap in inexpensive starter camera options for film students and beginners.

6-11

Nonsync cameras generally use daylight spools, although some can be adapted for mag use

The Bolex
Rex 5

The Bell & Howell
70-DL

The Krasnagorsk

The Arriflex S

The
Scoopic
MS

Both the Arriflex S (Arri S) and the Scoopic are battery operated. Some models of the Scoopic and all Arri S cameras can accept magazines. The Arri S is the only one of these cameras that has a registration pin. The Scoopic is specifically designed for easy handheld work and was used extensively in sports filming. Some models of Scoopics have motors that allow the camera to do sync sound, though it is generally too noisy and inflexible for critical applications. Neither the Arri S nor the Scoopic is still produced.

The five cameras in the group on the following page are all designed for sync-sound filming. **SEE 6-12** All of them are magazine-loading cameras with no room in the camera body for daylight spools. The first three are no longer being produced, though they are still common in rental and educational situations. The last two are state-of-the-art and are the two major production cameras currently in use.

The Eclair revolutionized the film industry in the early 1960s. The camera's light weight made it both portable and flexible enough to use in almost any situation, allowing it to go places a sync camera had never gone before. It and the Arriflex BL became the production cameras of the '60s and '70s; both have registration pins. Although the Eclair was a revolutionary handheld camera, it is a shoulder wrecker compared with the modern Aaton and the Arri SR. The Arri BL is considered a studio camera, with an extensive and bulky housing to make it noiseless.

Sync cameras are magazine loading and are used for sync-sound filming

The Eclair NPR

The Arriflex BL

The Arriflex 16SR 3

*Photo courtesy of
Arriflex Corporation*

The CP-16

The Aaton
ProdProfile 400

*Photo courtesy of
AbelCineTech, Inc.*

The CP-16, the most portable and lightweight of the older cameras, was designed for television news filming. It does not have a registration pin, though it is an excellent piece of equipment.

The Arri SR and the Aaton are both pin registered and adaptable to the Super 16 format. Arriflex cameras have been widely used since the 1930s; the Arri SR is a commonly available and frequently used system. The Aaton is less common in the United States but is considered the equal of the Arri SR. The newest models of the Aaton and the Arri SR have the capability to record *time code,* the rolling-clock reference used in video (see chapter 1). Aaton has also recently introduced the A Minima, a camera that shoots 200-foot rolls and emulates the compact quality and inexpensive operation of many video cameras.

Basic Threading Procedures

Although the basic theory is consistent, threading procedures vary slightly from one camera to the next. Some models are relatively easy to thread, whereas others require a modicum of understanding and skill. A number of wild cameras have an *automatic-threading mechanism* designed to feed the film unassisted. Most cameras, however, must be manually threaded. Wild cameras that employ daylight spools are covered here; tips for the more complicated magazines are discussed in chapter 10.

Finding a manual and following the instructions is the first step. Cameras often have either a printed diagram somewhere on their bodies or lines in the film chamber that indicate the threading path. These guides are indispensable, but the best way to learn about a camera is to be walked through it by someone with extensive experience. An hour or two with a person who really understands a camera can be an eye-opening experience on many counts. The following overview provides some basic tips.

All cameras are designed with as little excess space as possible in the film chambers. Space means bulk, and bulk means weight. There is precious little finger room, so keep the film chamber as free as possible, particularly by removing the take-up daylight spool.

On automatic-threading cameras, a small cutter in the film chamber is used to create an edge on the film. The film is fed into the top sprocketed roller as the camera is being run, the film thus feeding all the way through the mechanism. Automatic-threading cameras employ *loop setters*—small guards above and below the gate that create loops of the appropriate size and shape. The loop setters are closed for threading the film and open for shooting. Most cameras with this design have a release that automatically opens the loop setters when the cover plate is in place. Some older models have loop setters that must be opened manually, a step that if forgotten will result in ruined film. The Bolex and Scoopic are examples of cameras with automatic-threading mechanisms.

All other cameras must be threaded manually. This simply means opening the keepers and inserting the film, creating the loops, and threading the film in front of the pressure plate. Two major considerations are making sure that the loops are the correct size and that the sprocket holes of the film are engaged in the teeth of the rollers.

Making the loops just the right size is a requirement that may leave some people scratching their heads, but it should be clear on each individual camera. **SEE 6-13** The loops must not be so big that the top of the curve of film strikes the interior of the film chamber. Any contact brings with it the possibility of scratches on the film. Oversized loops may also cause poor registration, because the film is bouncing off the camera body as it is being exposed. The loops must not be so small, however, that they prevent the give-and-take between the continuous and intermittent movements.

Additionally, check to make sure that the sprocket holes are engaged in the teeth. This usually requires checking visually or gently pulling the film back and forth over the roller to ensure that it is engaged. Make sure the keepers are closed before proceeding.

Before putting on the cover plate, run the camera for two or three seconds to make sure all systems are working. Check the loops to ensure that they are both the correct size and holding their shape. Make sure the bottom daylight spool is taking up correctly. The take-up spool is usually the previous user's empty feed spool. Make sure it has not been pinched or otherwise damaged. If it has been pinched, the film will collect around the edges of the spool. Even if the film then seems to be falling onto the reel

6-13

Interior of a Bell & Howell with correctly set loops

after passing the pinched section, you will have problems later—the film will be loose on the take-up reel, and the full 100 feet will not fit onto it; the camera will jam toward the end of the reel. When you take off the cover plate, it will be like opening a jack-in-the-box—the "accordioned" film popping out of the camera because it had no place to go.

Beyond being threaded correctly in the mechanism, the other major consideration in loading a camera is that as little film be exposed to light as possible. As in 35mm still photography, manufacturers make the rolls a little longer than their stated length to allow for some spoilage during loading. Footage that is exposed to light in the loading process is referred to as *light struck,* and all efforts are made to minimize the amount of film subjected to this effect. Daylight spools can be loaded in bright daylight, though this should be done only if absolutely necessary, because you lose more film at the beginning.

Once you close the camera, use camera tape to cover all places where the camera body meets the cover plate. A 1-inch-wide opaque tape with an adhesive that does not leave a gummy residue, *camera tape* protects against *light leaks*—unwanted light striking the film, caused by any irregularities in the camera's tight-fitting junctions. Camera tape can be found at any film supply company or rental house.

Light leaks can be a problem with any camera but particularly with older models, where constant use has weakened latches or metal seams. Light leaks can be responsible for minor occasional flaws or completely destroyed film—clearly a problem to be avoided regardless of severity. Leaks are not common, but compulsory taping follows the old maxim: An ounce of prevention is worth a pound of cure. It is far better to expend a few cents' worth of tape than risk having an undetected problem ruin the film.

Gaffer's tape is the same material as camera tape, only it is 2 inches wide. These tapes look similar to common silver duct tape, but no substitutes should be used. Any other tape, particularly duct tape, will leave a gummy residue or tear off the camera's exterior covering. The residue is particularly destructive, because it attracts dirt that can eventually work its way into the camera. Gaffer's tape is a handy problem solver used by almost every member of a film crew.

Once the camera is closed and taped, it should be run for several seconds to get past the film that was light struck in the loading process. This can be done with the assistance of the *footage counter,* also called the *gas gauge,* an indicator that keeps track of how much film has been shot. Some cameras have rolling numbers similar to the odometer on a car; others have a simple tension bar that rests on the film inside the film chamber, driving a gauge on the body of the magazine or camera. On cameras using daylight spools, the counter will often have some room beneath the zero point (negative footage numbers) so the film can be run past the light-struck footage. This is called "running the camera to zero."

The following summary of the basic threading procedure may prove helpful:

1. Make sure the camera is wound or the battery attached.

2. If the camera has automatic threading, close the loop setters before threading the film.

3. On automatic-threading cameras, a small film cutter can usually be found just below the bottom loop setter in the film chamber. Use it to trim the front edge of the film. Insert the film in the top sprocketed roller with the trigger depressed—the camera running. When it feeds through to the bottom, stop the camera.

4. On manual-threading cameras, open the keepers and pressure plate and insert the film. Make sure the sprocket holes of the film are engaged with the teeth of the sprocketed rollers.

5. Set up the bottom daylight spool for take-up.

6. Make sure that the loops are set as they should be—not too big and not too small. This will require opening the loop setter on automatic-threading cameras.

7. Check that the take-up reel is taking up correctly. If a daylight spool is pinched, the camera will jam later.

8. Close and tape the camera. Run the camera to the zero point so that you get past all the light-struck film.

When *downloading*—unloading the film—greater care must be taken to avoid light-struck film. The reciprocal-feeding process described does not occur during take-up in the camera, and light can find its way deep into the spool, ruining many shots. Find a dark place or cover the camera with a heavy shirt. Do whatever you can to minimize contact with light. The last several shots on the roll will usually be ruined in downloading; if these are important to you, they can be saved by downloading in absolute darkness. You have only to take the reel out and get it into its packaging; this is not difficult to accomplish, because there is no unthreading involved. Finding a dark place may be the only obstacle. A friend tells the story of one shoot where he wanted to save every possible frame of the last shot on a roll. The only dark place he could find was the trunk of his car. His crew locked him in and he emerged in a few moments with the carefully preserved roll. He was quite pleased with his inventiveness until the police arrived with guns drawn, demanding that the assembled crew "let the guy out of the trunk." Seeing only the first part of the action, an onlooker had assumed that some Jimmy Cagney–style mayhem was about to occur.

Develop good camera habits from the start. Beginners often get rushed and forget important procedures, then cross their fingers and just hope the film turns out. Work toward eliminating luck as part of the equation. Shooting requires a measured and logical approach that takes all potential problems into consideration. Misthreading a camera is the most basic and destructive mistake that can be made.

Magazines

In the magazine (mag) design, the film chamber is separate from the camera. The magazine is loaded with film, then mounted on the camera. Core loads are used almost exclusively in magazines, although mags can be adapted to use daylight spools.

Again, core loads require the use of a photographic darkroom bag. There are two styles of magazines in general use: front-to-back and coaxial.

SINGLE AND DUAL COMPARTMENTS

The front-to-back style of magazine is probably the most familiar, with some mags having a single compartment and others having individual compartments for feed and take-up. Some versions of these, particularly older designs, resemble and are thus called "Mickey Mouse ears." The front-to-back approach has a front spindle that holds the feed roll and a rear spindle that holds the take-up. The film is fed out of the feed side and into the take-up side by means of a *lighttrap,* which guarantees that light will not penetrate the chamber. The front-to-back mag design has become less common in 16mm, although it is still used in a number of 35mm cameras.

In the front-to-back design, a loop of film is held out of the magazine to be threaded through the sprocketed rollers and gate area. The inside of the camera itself is a basic mechanism without room for daylight spools. The sprocketed rollers of the camera drag the film through rollers in the magazine's lighttrap. The drawback

6-14

The front-to-back magazine design employs a front chamber that holds the feed roll and a rear chamber that holds the take-up

CP-16 magazine

6-15

This modification of the front-to-back design employs sprocketed rollers in the lighttrap

Arri BL magazine

to this method is that it can take some time to thread the camera. The CP-16 employs this design. **SEE 6-14**

A modification of the front-to-back design employs sprocketed rollers in the lighttrap instead of simple rollers. The sprocketed rollers transport the film out of and back into the magazine. The mag takes more time to change in the changing bag, because the film must be threaded through both rollers, but the film has to be inserted only in front of the pressure plate in actual threading. The mag requires more attention, because the correct number of frames must be between the rollers to make the loops the right size. The Arriflex BL 16mm model is the best-known camera employing this configuration. **SEE 6-15**

There are two basic styles of magazine lids in the front-to-back design. One design hinges a front chamber and a rear chamber separately. In this style all that has to be done in the darkroom bag is get the film into the front chamber and fed through the lighttrap; lock the front compartment and you're done. The back can be set when you get out of the bag or when you are threading the camera. The CP-16 mag requires this approach.

The other type of mag has a single-hinged lid for the entire film chamber, with the feed and the take-up side by side. This of course means that both feed and take-up have to be threaded in the changing bag. If the film is not properly attached to the take-up core, the camera will jam quickly, because there will soon be no place for the film to go. Tape is never used to attach the film, because it attracts dirt and causes problems in the processing machines. You should put about an eighth-inch fold in the film that is slid into the core's slot. Threading this style of magazine can be somewhat intimidating at first, but it is easily mastered. The Arri BL magazine is a typical example of this design.

COAXIAL

Most of the newer generation of cameras, particularly in 16mm, uses the *coaxial* design with adjacent take-up and feed compartments. All the elements that transport the film to the gate (sprocketed rollers, keepers, pressure plate, room for loops) are in the magazine itself. The actual cameras themselves look quite odd because they comprise only a lens mount, a pull-down claw, a gate, and a viewing system attached to a motor. The main bulk of the camera comes when the magazine (and the lens) is attached. The Arriflex SR, the Aaton, and the older Eclair NPR are examples of 16mm cameras that use this design.

With the coaxial design, the film must be loaded and threaded through the magazine's first set of sprocketed rollers in the changing bag, but the rest can be done in the light of day. When you emerge from the bag, the film will be threaded out the front of the magazine on top of the pressure plate. It is then fed in at the bottom of the pressure plate to the bottom sprocketed roller. You will have to leave out enough film to form the loops; every camera has a specific number of frames that have to be left out. These frames are then pushed back into the magazine both above and below the pressure plate. The only nerve-racking aspect of this magazine is that the loops on some designs are hidden behind a facing plate, where you cannot see or test them.

The beauty of the coaxial design is that once loaded it is easy to change magazines. When a roll runs out, you pop off the magazine and pop on the next one. The change should take a second or two, whereas conventional magazines can take several minutes. Camera assistants are responsible for making sure there is always a fresh magazine at the ready.

Magazines and magazine loading with core loads are the standard industry approach. Daylight spools are handy for quick-and-dirty shooting or when you have just a few shots to get, but their drawbacks—noise and short length—generally exclude them from most professional applications. To facilitate fast changeovers, all camera packages should include two or more magazines, which should be numbered or otherwise identified in case problems show up when the film is processed.

Viewing Systems

The *viewing system* allows the cameraperson to view the image being filmed. Different makes of cameras employ different strategies to facilitate this, but two basic types are available: the rangefinder system and the reflex viewing system. With the rangefinder, the operator looks through a facsimile lens that is mounted on the side of the camera. In the reflex system, you are actually looking through the camera's lens while filming. Cameras with some kind of reflex viewing system are the industry standard.

RANGEFINDERS

Rangefinder viewing systems are found on older cameras, but there are enough of them still around to warrant a brief discussion. The biggest drawback to the rangefinder system is that the framing the operator sees is not exactly what is being filmed. This can result in minor framing errors when the subject is some distance from the camera, as well as to major ones, when the subject is close to the camera. This phenomenon is called *parallax*, and most rangefinder cameras have some method of parallax adjustment. A subject a long distance from the camera has enough room on either side that minor parallax differences are going to be relatively unnoticeable. When the subject is closer to the camera, these difficulties are increased.

The control for *parallax adjustment* is found around the eyepiece. It manipulates a hinge with which the back of the viewing system can be swiveled either away from or toward the body of the camera to make the center of the viewer image the same as the center of the film image. The control knob is calibrated with the same numbers as on a focus ring. If filming a subject 8 feet away, a parallax adjustment set to 8 feet will give the same center point for both images. This strategy is clearly useful for simple images, but it breaks down with complex images incorporating camera/subject movement and multiple focus points.

REFLEX VIEWING

Reflex viewing systems employ several different strategies for diverting light to the camera operator's eye. All reflex viewing, also called *through-the-lens (TTL) viewing*, systems must be engineered with the camera shutter in mind. Either there is something in front of the shutter that diverts the light, or the shutter itself is part of the viewing system. The Bolex employs a split-prism viewing system wherein a prism in front of the gate and shutter diverts a percentage of the light up through the viewing system. The rest of the light continues unhindered to the film plane. Split prisms are an excellent viewing strategy with one minor drawback: The light diverted to the viewfinder reduces the amount of light that is exposing the film. Though the amount of light diverted is not large, it is enough that it must be compensated for in exposure. In low-light situations where you need all the light you can get, the lost light can be a significant complication. It also means that the light available to the viewfinder is sometimes insufficient. Viewfinders can be dim, occasionally making the framing difficult.

A second viewing system has achieved wider acceptance. It was introduced by Arriflex in the 1930s and to this day the simplicity and logic of the design remains a thing of beauty. The design employs a *mirrored butterfly shutter*—the shutter has the shape of a butterfly—with *front-surfaced mirrors* for "wings." As opposed to the vertical design of conventional shutters, this shutter is set at a 45-degree angle to the film plane. As it rotates, the shutter alternately allows light to the film plane, or the mirrors block light to the film and send it to the viewing system, so there is no reduction of light in this system. **SEE 6-16** The shutter allows 100 percent of the light to reach the film plane in exposure, then 100 percent of the light is diverted to the viewing system.

A word of caution: Front-surfaced mirrors should be cleaned professionally. If you attempt to clean the mirror with a cloth or tissue, you may wipe off the mirror silver itself! Household mirrors are rear-surfaced mirrors: You look through glass to see your image. Minor distortion is not a problem in a household mirror, but in critical optics any distortion is unacceptable. With the mirror on the surface of the shutter, care must be taken that the surface is not damaged.

6-16

Viewing system with a rotating mirrored butterfly shutter, which alternately sends light to the film plane and whose mirrors send light to the viewing system

VIEWING SCREENS

As you look through the viewing system, you will see the viewing screen. **SEE 6-17** The screen is usually a piece of ground glass mounted just above where the light is diverted into the viewing system—adjacent to the butterfly shutter in that common design. The viewing screen, referred to as a *target,* has a series of markings that usually consist of crosshairs, the TV-safe frame, and the film frame itself. Newer cameras may also have the Super 16 frame as well. The *crosshairs* are right in the center and can be quite helpful in planning and executing movements. The *TV-safe frame* shows the boundaries that ensure appropriate framing when film is transferred to video, some of the edge areas of the film frame being lost in the transfer. Most professional cameras have some extra viewing room around the film frame so you can see elements that are approaching the frame.

DIOPTERS

All reflex viewing systems must be set to the operator's eye. This is achieved by setting the *diopter*—an adjustable glass element in the eyepiece. Every human eye is slightly different, and the diopter allows you to adjust the viewing system for the peculiarities of your eye to ensure as sharp an image as possible while shooting. Even two people with 20/20 vision need to set the diopter to the slight differences in their vision. When focusing to the eye—an approach that is more rare than one might first imagine—failure to adjust the diopter properly usually has serious consequences on focus quality.

   Although manuals for individual cameras should be followed to the letter, most 16mm and 35mm cameras employ similar methods for adjusting the diopter. The control for the diopter is found on or near the eyepiece, and diopters are set with the lens removed from the camera. The lens is a confusing factor, because you are not

6-17

The viewing screen usually displays crosshairs, the TV safe frame, and the film frame setting the lens to your eye, you are setting the viewing system to your eye. The lens is set to the film. The diopter will have a setscrew or locking ring for making adjustments. Most camera manufacturers recommend that you rotate the diopter until all the framing aids are crisp and sharp. This includes crosshairs and any boundaries for the frame. Once they are perfectly focused, lock the setscrew or ring.

Once the diopter is set, you do not need to touch it again. The viewing system is set to your eye, and the process is complete. The focus ring on the lens will be used to focus each individual shot (see figure 7-5). Occasionally, people get confused about this and will fiddle with the diopter during filming. This can be a recipe for disaster. Remember, you are setting the viewing system to your eye, not using it to focus on any one object.

The only caution on all of this is that the human eye can change during the course of a long day of shooting. Your eye can get fatigued and as it tires it actually changes shape. It is a good idea to check the diopter when you start to sense the strain of a long day.

Camera Options

Two important options that allow filmmakers to manipulate time are available on many cameras: variable frame rates and single framing.

VARIABLE FRAME RATES

As mentioned earlier, many cameras come with the capability to vary the frame rate. **SEE 6-18** Continuous running at frame rates other than 24 frames per second yields either slow-motion or fast-motion effects. Some cameras, including the Bolex and the Krasnagorsk, have a switch that gives a number of relatively common options. Other cameras, particularly certain Arriflex models, have a rheostat that lets you dial to the rate you want.

This may at first appear contradictory: Faster frame rates (36, 48, 64, et cetera) produce slow-motion shots, and slower frame rates (9, 12, 16, et cetera) produce fast motion. The key to understanding this is remembering that all projectors run at 24 fps. If you record 48 frames in 1 second and project that same piece at 24 fps, what took 1 second to shoot is going to take 2 seconds to project. Time is expanded, so 48 frames per second makes the action twice as long. Conversely, if you shoot at 12 fps, the material that is filmed in 2 seconds is presented in 1 second. In this case, the time is collapsed. **SEE 6-19**

Frame rate determines the number of frames photographed per second

There are two considerations you should be aware of when creating motion effects. The first is that you should never run a camera empty at speeds greater than 24 fps. The claw is designed to go out and engage a sprocket hole and it overreaches if there is no film in the camera. At high speeds the life of the mechanism can be significantly reduced. The second issue is that the basic mechanism, and thus the shutter, is running at a different speed when creating motion effects, and the film is receiving a different amount of light than at the 24 fps standard. Cameras with built-in exposure meters automatically compensate for this, but in most situations you need to know how to make the adjustments. Specific calculations are covered in chapter 15, but this should be kept in mind.

To create really dramatic slow-motion effects, a specialized camera is often necessary. General-use cameras that have variable frame rates usually go up to only 48 fps or at most 64. At 48 fps action is expanded to twice its natural length. For actions that take some time to unfold,

6-19

Shooting time versus projection time

such as human movements, 48 to 64 fps can create nicely stylized effects. For actions that take a brief time, this slowdown may be almost imperceptible. Students often ask how to achieve that lovely slow-motion ripple effect when a drop falls into water. It is useful to ask yourself how long this event takes in real time. A drop falling in water takes some fraction of a second. If you then double that time, it is still quite brief: The attempted slow-motion effect is barely noticeable.

The kind of effect that will make a speeding bullet visible takes a substantial number of frames per second. Both PhotoSonics and Arriflex make cameras capable of running up to 150 fps. Specialized cameras can shoot up to 10,000 fps. Some basic math indicates that what took one second to shoot at this rate takes almost seven minutes of projection time. High-speed cameras are used extensively in motion analysis, and this is one of the few areas in which video has not made inroads. NASA uses high-speed cameras to shoot a tremendous amount of footage of every takeoff. Construction and manufacturing companies also use them to analyze how products and structures resist stress. High-speed cameras can create many dramatic effects, though their use necessitates many technical considerations that are not immediately evident.

All filmmakers will quickly become conversant with all the multiples and divisors of 24. This is particularly true when editing. But whenever you need to determine how long a shot must be or how much screen time it is going to take, you can always calculate frames. Time becomes a physical length of film: A shot that is 72 frames long is going to take 3 seconds of screen time, and so on.

SINGLE FRAMING

Many cameras also come with a single-framing function, enabling you to shoot one frame at a time. One of the primary uses of this is, of course, *animation*—the technique that puts inanimate objects in motion. The most familiar form is the cartoon style of Walt Disney films and others of that ilk, an approach called *cel animation*. There are many other types, including clay animation, pixillation, cameraless animation, and computer animation.

The majority of animations, cel and otherwise, attempt to re-create the natural movements of characters and objects. In this approach one creates artwork that represents sequential points in movement. The movement of someone waving a hand would mean creating many points within that motion, from the hand at the character's side to points along the movement upward.

Animation is an immensely painstaking activity. Some basic math gives you a sense of this. If fluid movement is the goal, the maximum number of frames you can shoot of any single piece of artwork is two. If you shoot more, the movement will look staggered—it will not flow from one drawing to the next. If you are shooting 2 frames per drawing, 1 second of screen time takes 12 separate drawings. At 12 drawings for 1 second, a minute's worth of animation requires 720 drawings. A 90-minute film would need 64,800 drawings. The classic animations of the major studios were all done shooting 1 frame of film for each drawing. Just multiply all the previous figures by 2 if this approach is chosen. If all of this does not give you pause, you might have a future as an animator.

Camera Features

A number of other options are common on many cameras. The basics include the following.

Frame counter   These can be found on many wild cameras but only infrequently on sync cameras. Usually located close to the footage counter, the *frame counter* counts individual frames and is particularly helpful in such applications as animation. Usually, there is one dial that counts individual frames and another that keeps track of the frames in increments of 50 or 100. At normal running speeds, the frames fly by so fast that counting is useful only in such specialized situations as backwinding.

Backwinding   With *backwinding,* the basic mechanism of the camera can be driven backward with a hand crank. One can do a shot, back up, and make another pass over the same piece of film. This is useful for doing superimpositions, matte shots, and a variety of other effects. Multiple passes are possible, though modern multiple-exposure shots are usually done on separate pieces of film and later printed together on a single piece. Be aware that when backwinding you wind the film through the entire mechanism, including the shutter. The lens must be blocked or the film will be exposed while being backwound. At present the only commercially available 16mm camera with a backwinding feature is the Bolex.

Battery tester   Most cameras with electric motors have rudimentary battery-testing functions. Usually, a small scale with a pointer indicates whether there is adequate power. These scales are functional, but a handheld battery tester is much more useful. Many testers on the market have multiple functions, which can be helpful as well. Generally, one tests the voltage of the battery to see if it is at the level necessary for the camera to perform properly. There is further discussion on the care of batteries in the next section.

Lens turret An option on a small number of cameras, a *lens turret* is a moveable plate in front of the film gate with which you can rotate different lenses in front of the film, allowing you to switch lenses between shots. The Bolex and Arri S are examples of cameras with turret systems.

Filter slots and holders Many cameras have small *filter slots,* also called *filter holders,* either in the film chamber or on the exterior of the camera. The desired filter is mounted in a holder (a slide) which is then slid into a slot that positions it between the rear element of the lens and the film gate. Many cinematographers prefer filters that mount on the front of the lens, because rear filters affect the rear element–to–film plane relationship. Dirt or markings on rear filters are disastrous, as well as more difficult to control because they are unseen. Filter slots can also be used for opaque slides with patterns cut in them, such as a binocular-shaped cutout.

There are two cautions about the use of filter slots. First, if the filter slot is on the exterior of the camera, be sure that there is a dummy slide in the slot even if you are not using a filter. An empty slot allows a direct route to the film gate, and light will fog the film. Even if no filtering is being done, make sure a dummy slide is inserted. Both the Bolex and Scoopic have this design. Second, make sure that whoever used the camera before you did not leave an unwanted filter in the slide. An unwanted filter will add undesired color and change exposure. This should be checked, although the presence of a filter should be apparent when you clean the camera.

Variable shutters A small number of cameras come with a *variable shutter*—a means of changing the shutter's size. Variable-shutter controls most often make the shutter bigger, with smaller shutters not allowing time for the pull-down claw to advance each frame of film. The 180-degree shutter configuration is the size that gives optimum recording of natural movement. Shutters that are larger record such a small percentage of the action that movements do not blur from frame to frame. This causes a strobelike effect that can be interesting but is generally undesirable. It can be used to create fades, though they usually show the imperfections of moving the control by hand. Closing the variable shutter entirely is a good way of blocking light when backwinding the camera.

Tripod threading holes On the bottom of the camera body are one or more *tripod threading holes* that are used to attach the camera to the head. Distinctions involving their use are discussed later in this chapter in the section on tripods.

Cleaning and Care

Whoever coined the phrase "Cleanliness is next to godliness" must have been a filmmaker. It is absolutely crucial that the camera be clean. If it is not, the resulting footage may be jeopardized. Bright hopes are often dashed, and pocketbooks emptied, when film comes back from the lab scratched or otherwise ruined. It is clear that a few front-end preparations can deter a substantial percentage of disappointments. When film is ruined, the only remedy is reshooting. The cleanliness and care of the camera are among the numerous responsibilities of the *first assistant cameraperson (1st AC).*

CLEANING KIT

The 1st AC always carries a cleaning kit. Experienced ACs often have very sophisticated kits, but for people shooting their first films it is easy to put together a simple one. The following items are inexpensive and available at either a camera shop or a discount store:

Swabs   Many ACs use cotton swabs, although they have some very apparent drawbacks, the main one being that fibers on the tip can come off and work their way into the camera. In the past few years, swabs with sponge tips have been introduced and are in general use. They are substantially more expensive, however, and you may have to order them from a video supply catalog.

Alcohol   Denatured alcohol is preferable, although isopropyl will do in a pinch. Isopropyl alcohol has a lubricant that many ACs will warn you against, although I have never had a problem with it.

Orange stick   You can buy an orange stick for about a dollar at a camera store or pay seventy-nine cents for a half-dozen at a discount store. So named because they're made of the wood of an orange tree, they are used by manicurists to push back cuticles. For our purposes they are used to clean the gate; nothing else, unless designed by a camera's manufacturer, should be substituted.

Blower brush or camel-hair brush   Inexpensive blower brushes are available at camera stores and are simple rubber squeeze bulbs with a gentle-bristle brush attached where the air is blown out. Many ACs prefer a camel-hair brush, a better but more expensive option. Providing a very gentle bristle, most come in lipstick-style tubes in which the brush can be extended or withdrawn, an important feature, because it is essential that you never allow the bristles to get dirty. Touching them leaves skin oils that attract dust. Eventually, you will be brushing dirt into the camera. Brushes that get dirty are usually thrown away. If you have a simple blower brush, use the same care.

Lens-cleaning tissue and lens-cleaning fluid   Both lens-cleaning tissue and lens-cleaning fluid are available at any camera store and are necessary parts of any cleaning kit. They are produced by a number of different companies, but are very specific items, and no substitutes—such as facial tissue or a shirt sleeve—should be used. (Lens care is covered in chapter 7.)

Canned air   This is an optional item used to blow dust out of the camera body and magazines. Canned air used to contain chlorofluorocarbons (CFCs), which are listed as one of the major contaminants of the Earth's ozone layer, but many of the newer canned-air products do not. You may want to check the contents of specific canned-air products to determine if they are environmentally friendly. This is the most expensive element in the cleaning kit.

CLEANING METHOD

Cleaning techniques are specific to individual ACs, and there are probably those who would disagree with some of the following recommendations. But I have used these procedures enough, and have seen other ACs use them, to feel comfortable with their applications. You are free to work out your own methods, although there are some very important "don'ts" that are discussed as part of the process.

All pieces of the camera must be cleaned—from the lens, to the body, to the magazine. It would be silly to spend a half-hour making sure the body of the camera

6-20

Both types of film transport rollers have a recessed center so that the film touches them only at its edges

Sprocketed roller

Ordinary roller

is immaculate, then not clean the magazine. The film stock will just carry all the dirt from the magazine right into the body when you start filming.

The first step is to take the brush and dust out the camera completely; the canned air can also be used here. You will see many dust particles. Clean out what is visible and make every effort to get out anything else that may be in there. This applies to the magazines as well. Also clean the film chamber's cover plate or door in this manner, but do not open or remove the pressure plate.

The next step is to use the alcohol and swabs. Moisten the swab and clean all metal pieces with which the film is liable to come in contact. This does not include the pressure plate and the gate. Clean the rollers and keepers and anything else that the camera's specific design includes. Do not reinsert a dirty swab into the alcohol, as it will contaminate what remains in the bottle.

You will always encounter the two roller designs illustrated. **SEE 6-20** The sprocketed rollers are specifically designed to drive the film forward; all other rollers guide the film either from the feed or to the take-up. All cameras are designed so that the film's emulsion touches as few surfaces as possible. Any contact carries with it the possibility of scratching or abrading the film. All rollers, both sprocketed and ordinary, have a recessed center so that the film touches them only at its edges, in the area of the sprocket holes. Whenever you see either of these designs, the emulsion almost invariably goes toward it. Much of the rationale for camera and magazine design is made with protecting the film in mind.

As you are cleaning the camera, parts of the roller may be toward the keepers and thus inaccessible. In this case use the camera's inching knob to move the entire mechanism so you can access these areas. If the camera does not have an inching knob, it may have a single-framing capability that will allow you to move the mechanism in the increments necessary to get the whole assembly clean. In many cases not much more than the rollers and keepers need cleaning in this step.

Now for the pressure plate and gate area. The first step is to remove the pressure plate. With a clean, dry finger, just wipe the pressure plate. Then wipe the film guide. If the pull-down claw is extended, be careful not to jostle it unduly, as that can cause damage. Many ACs use a small chamois to wipe this area, but I have found wiping it with a finger to be perfectly adequate. Although skin oils attract dirt, this should be a relatively dirt-free environment.

The cleanliness of the gate is the chief goal of this step. Again, cameras are designed so that the film comes into contact with as few surfaces as possible, and this is the only place where contact is unavoidable, so cleanliness here is critical. The goal is to make sure there is no dust, hair, or any other offending presence in the gate. The call of "hair in the gate" (actually slivers of emulsion scraped off by the pull-down claw) is the bane of a film crew's existence. Everyone knows how distracting it can be when something gets in the projector gate at a theater. If you get one hair, it will soon be joined by brother and sister hairs. If this happens while shooting, the offending object is recorded for posterity. In addition, foreign matter anywhere in the camera, but particularly in the gate, can cause scratches.

◆ **RULE:** *Regarding cleaning the gate itself, do not clean it if you cannot see any dirt.*

Excessive cleaning will start to wear down the finely engineered edges of this critical area. Any dirt or hair that can cause a problem should be visible to the naked eye, although many ACs carry some type of magnification device for careful inspection. If there is dirt or hair in the gate, clean it immediately. The orange stick is used to clean the gate area, because it is a very soft wood. Do not use anything else, such as a toothpick or, worse, a paper clip. Anything hard can cause immediate damage to the aperture. If there is dirt or hair in the gate, use the stick to gently flick it off.

After this give the camera another quick brushing to get rid of any dirt that may have been dislodged in previous steps. It is impossible to get anything absolutely, guaranteeably clean, but the idea is to get the interior of the camera as clean as is humanly possible. This should take twenty to thirty minutes at the beginning of the day, and the camera should be checked frequently during shooting. Magazines are cleaned thoroughly every time they are reloaded. The film chamber is also cleaned as the camera is being reloaded.

The cleanliness of the gate is the most important consideration. All production cameras have a means of checking the gate between takes. Usually, the lens is removed and the inching knob is used to rotate the shutter out of the way. The AC can then see if there is anything in the gate, often with the aid of a flashlight and magnifying device. Many ACs check the gate with the lens still on the camera—using the lens as a magnifying glass—but this takes some experience to know what to look for.

Checking the gate is usually done immediately after the shooting from an individual setup has been concluded. No lights are struck and no actors excused. Nothing is changed until the 1st AC gives the go-ahead. If a substantial amount of material is being done from a single setup, the gate will be checked after each individual segment. If there is hair or dirt in the gate, all the preceding material will have to be reshot.

Canned air, blower brushes, and alcohol should not be used on anything to do with the gate or pressure plate. The air and blower brushes will just knock dirt into the shutter mechanism. Alcohol should not be used, because the interior of the gate is covered with an anti-reflectant coating that will eventually break down; pressure plates are generally covered with this material as well.

In many beginning courses, it is just you and your camera. Crew work and specific job responsibilities are yet to come. In this case remember that the cleanliness of the camera is your responsibility. Do not expect rental house or equipment room personnel to do your job for you, even though they should be giving you a clean and well-maintained camera. No matter whose hands you take the camera from, you should look it over and clean it before you shoot. The gate should be checked constantly, and the entire camera should be recleaned between rolls of film. Nothing strikes terror in the heart more than looking at your lab report and seeing those words: *hair in gate* or *scratches*. The notion of an ounce of prevention's being worth a pound of cure definitely applies here.

Check the loops to ensure that they are the correct size and shape. Use camera tape to ward off potential light leaks. Clean the camera and check the gate. Start developing good habits. With most camera problems, the only option is to reshoot—always a costly and dispiriting proposition.

6-21

Battery care and maintenance are essential to proper operation of the camera
The Cine 60 battery

BATTERIES

If you were to speak to every person who had ever shot with a motion picture or video camera, you would probably hear a battery-related horror story from each of them. Battery care and maintenance are essential to the proper operation of the camera. There is no feeling quite like having to scrap an expensive and preparation-heavy shoot right in the middle because of battery problems. **SEE 6-21**

Most batteries designed for film (or video) are the slow-charging type. They are usually plugged in during the evening and ready for use the next morning, although they need a long night's charge (twelve or more hours). Quick-charging batteries are made for some cameras, but the slow-charging models are generally more reliable and less expensive. The lengthy charging time does take preplanning so you do not get caught without power. The 1st AC, who is in charge of the batteries, will have at least one if not more backups. The number of magazines a battery will drive varies from camera to camera, but a fully charged battery should run at least four or five 400-foot magazines.

The key to long battery life is frequent, complete discharging. If a battery is not totally discharged over a period of time, it can develop *memory:* It will memorize the small amount of charge it needs to be topped off. When the battery is completely discharged after it has developed memory, it will recharge only the amount it has memorized, thus not giving its full potential. This problem is correctable, but the whole process significantly cuts down on the life of the battery. The way to avoid this problem is to make sure that the battery is fully discharged relatively frequently—once every week or so when in constant use.

Beyond the battery itself, most cameras employ a cable to hook the camera to the battery. This also requires care and attention. A general rule is to unplug the battery whenever the camera is not in use, even on relatively short delays between takes. The battery will discharge even if the camera is not running. Although this is standard procedure, it can cause quite a bit of wear and tear on the cable. When picking up the camera package, first make sure the cables are present—you will not shoot if you get out on location and they are not there; second, make sure they are working. As many student shoots close down over bad cables as over insufficient battery power.

Tripods

Creating steady shots, both moving and static, has been a goal since the experiments of the pioneer filmmakers. A handheld camera, though having a viable aesthetic of its own, does not offer adequate shot stability, thus necessitating the use of tripods or other related gear. This gear is referred to under the general category of *camera mounts,* or *camera support systems,* both umbrella terms that include tripods, dollies, cranes, the Steadicam, and many other specialized mounts.

A *tripod* is a three-legged camera support that is familiar to most readers. What is referred to as a tripod is actually two separate pieces: the *legs*—the actual tripod—and the *head.* The head is the mechanism on which you mount the camera and which has pan and tilt controls. The head-to-legs mount is usually a bowl design in which sits the rounded bottom of the head. A bolt and knob (usually a wing nut or similar design) extend from the bottom of the head for locking it in place. This knob-and-bolt arrangement plays a key role in leveling the tripod.

Tripods are a key part of the camera package for most smaller projects, even though their use on larger projects is not quite as common as it used to be. This is simply because the more versatile support systems, such as the new generation of relatively lightweight crab dollies, have become the standard. Rather than take down and reset the tripod, you can simply roll the camera to the next setup with a dolly. On films with a generous budget and a large camera/grip crew, the high rental cost, weight, and size of a dolly are easy obstacles to overcome. For smaller, inexperienced crews, the tripod is still the camera mount of choice.

LEGS

6-22

Standard legs are used for eye-level shots; baby legs are used for low shots

There are two common types of legs available: wooden legs and the newer metal legs. Wooden legs were the industry standard for many years, and though they still have many followers their use has become less prevalent. The metal legs have become popular because of their versatility and lightweight, sturdy design.

Wooden legs are designed so that one set of legs moves inside the other. A twist lock allows the user to set them at the desired height, as it does on some of the metal leg designs. This lock must be used to tighten the legs together. If the lock pushes the legs away from one another, damage can eventually result.

Wooden legs come in two different forms: standard legs and baby legs. **SEE 6-22** *Standard legs* are about 4 feet tall and extend from that height to around 7 feet. As their name implies, standard legs are used for shots that are done at a standard height (eye level or thereabouts). *Baby legs* are used for low shots. They are about 2 feet tall and can be extended to the lower end of the standard legs' range. To get lower than this, one needs to put the head on a *high hat,* which is basically a head mount with three feet. It stands about 6 inches tall and is also useful for mounting on tabletops and other surfaces. The head of the tripod is removable and is switched among these three types of legs, depending on the shot.

The wooden tripods do not have stops on the legs like many amateur and newer professional tripods, so the tripod will collapse spread-eagle on the floor if something is not used to hold the legs in place. For stability the legs require **spreaders,** also called *spiders* or *tri-downs.* The spreader is put on the floor and has three arms that extend to hold the tripod legs in position. The tripod legs have *spurs* (small pins at the base of the legs) that are put in the cups of the spreader. A large spring-loaded pin holds the legs in place. The spreader is an absolute necessity on smooth surfaces. If you are working on a rough surface, such as the ground or a carpet, the spurs dig in to hold the tripod steady. Most camera crews will use a spreader anyway, because it eliminates the possibility of someone's carelessly knocking out the legs.

The new metal legs are becoming more popular because they generally incorporate all three heights in their design. With wooden legs you have to bring three-leg systems (standard, baby, and high hat) and switch the head among them as the shot demands. This is not as big a hassle as some people make it seem, but it does complicate the task. But with the metal leg extensions sliding into each other, much greater height range can be achieved in a single leg. Metal legs stand about the height of baby legs, but can be extended to the highest range of standard legs. They usually have stops that allow the leg to be locked in the normal upright position, eliminating the need for a spreader. Many makes of tripods have stops that allow the legs to be spread out so they get the camera down to almost high hat level.

Heads

There are three basic types of heads: mechanical and friction heads, fluid heads, and gear heads. Fluid heads are generally preferred for initial efforts, although mechanical and friction heads also see substantial use. Gear heads are the industry standard for 35mm shooting. New fluid-effect heads are also making an impact on the amateur market and are discussed in the section on fluid heads.

The *head* is involved solely in pans and tilts. All heads have knobs for locking the pan and tilt, and many also have independent controls that regulate the amount of resistance in the movement. *Resistance* is the force against movement—a tightness that makes it more difficult to move the tripod head. At first this seems to be a contradiction. Why would anyone want something to be harder than it needs to be? Without this resistance, however, the operator tends to start over- or underpushing. If one is overpushing, the tendency is to respond by slowing down, and the move becomes uneven; underpushing produces the opposite result. When there is resistance to the movement, one can push more uniformly. The fineness of the pan and tilt fluid control plays a big part in the quality of the moves you are attempting to make.

Mechanical and friction heads Many people do not distinguish between mechanical heads and friction heads, but there are slight design differences that warrant separate treatment. *Mechanical heads* are both the most rudimentary and the most common type of tripod head. They are designed for still photography; people use them in film solely because of their availability. They are functional but are inadequate for finely defined movements. The movements of the pan and tilt are simply metal on metal. The tilt and pan are either locked or unlocked. There is no attempt made to cushion the move or create any resistance, because they are designed simply to get the camera from one position to another for still photographs.

Friction heads are close cousins to mechanical heads. They also have metal-on-metal interiors, although there is an effort to cushion movement, usually in the form of an internal swelling ring. Thus the pan and tilt controls will give some gradations of resistance between completely loosened and locked. Friction heads are a small step up from straight mechanical heads, although you have to fight for the smoothness of movement easily achieved on professional heads. They are an older design expressly produced to be an inexpensive alternative to fluid and gear heads, a role largely taken over by the new fluid-effect heads.

Fluid heads The fluid head will probably be the tripod of preference for the work you will be doing. *Fluid heads* actually employ a hydraulic fluid that is forced from chamber to chamber in the head. This is where you find the independent controls, labeled *pan fluid* and *tilt fluid,* that allow the user to regulate the firmness of resistance to movement.

Many newer tripods are being billed as having fluid-effect heads, and some of them are surprisingly good. The design of *fluid-effect heads* is similar to that of friction heads, but their moving parts are further cushioned with an enclosed viscous fluid that assists the metal-against-metal movement, facilitating smooth pan and tilt movements. They were designed to be a low-cost option that would produce results that were close to the more expensive true fluid heads. They seem to be quite useful with smaller cameras, though larger cameras still require a true fluid head or gear head.

Gear heads These are the standard in 35mm shooting. The pan and tilt of *gear heads* are controlled by hand cranks attached to gears. The operator turns the pan crank and the tilt crank to the desired positions. Resistance is not an issue, because the head is responding to the gears being cranked.

Gear heads yield exceptionally smooth movements, but one has to learn how to hand-crank both the tilt and the pan gears simultaneously. This can be tricky, though it is easily mastered by people with some coordination. Moves can also be preplanned—an assistant can put erasable marks on the head so it can be cranked to a specific position. Gear heads are heavy and bulky as well as expensive to rent, and they are largely intended for smooth moves with big cameras. They can certainly be used with smaller cameras, but fluid heads can often yield moves of equal quality.

Good movements can be made with inexpensive or poorly designed heads, but they certainly make the task much harder. On small projects you often have to use whatever tripod you can get your hands on. Such is the reality of the way you may have to work, but it is difficult to get the performance you want from tools that are inadequate or not designed for the purpose. You should get in the habit of doing everything possible to obtain the tools designed for the job, regardless of the dent it puts in your budget. Using equipment that makes the task harder can lead to hidden costs (lost time with location, talent, lighting, and, worst of all, inadequate results) that can be greater than anything expended on the front end.

Attaching the Camera

There are two types of threading on the screws used to attach a camera to a tripod head. The first is found on small and amateur cameras, and the second is the professional standard. The first screw type is a ¼-20 (quarter-twenty). Consumer video and small 16mm cameras have this type. The ¼ refers to the diameter of the screw; the 20 refers to the pitch of the screw threading. This is a common screw size available in any hardware store. With a few carpentry skills, you can use this knowledge to build many nifty camera supports. Be cautioned, however, that the screw used should not be deeper than the hole in the camera. The camera body often has circuitry above the hole. A thread that is too long can cause extensive—and expensive—damage.

The second type of camera screw is a ⅜-16. Again, this refers to the diameter of the screw and the thread pitch. This is the attaching screw for most larger 16mm and all 35mm cameras, used simply because the professional cameras are heavier. The ¼-20 screw is not strong enough to support the weight of the larger cameras.

Many smaller cameras have both sizes of screw holes, allowing them to be used on any tripod. Larger cameras often have a choice of two ⅜-16 holes, one toward the front of the camera, the other toward the back. This is to compensate for the weight of the lens you are using. If you are using a heavy lens, to keep the weight of the camera evenly distributed on the tripod you would use the front hole. The back hole is used with a lightweight lens.

Tripods and heads are rated for the maximum-weight camera that they can support. Never put a camera on a tripod and head not rated for its weight. If you do, with some effort you may still be able to create decent movements, but the arrangement will be an accident waiting to happen. The camera will be top-heavy and fall over with the least encouragement.

Occasionally, there is cause to adapt between the smaller threading and the larger hole. There are bushings available that will adapt a ⅜-inch camera-mounting hole to ¼-20 tripod threading. On smaller cameras that have only the ⅜-inch threading, such as older Bolexes, these can be quite useful. For safety reasons cameras bigger than the Bolex should not be adapted to the ¼-20 threading.

Older heads come with the attaching screw permanently mounted in the plate on which the camera rests. Newer head designs employ a *quick-release plate* that is detachable and screwed independently into the bottom of the camera. Plate and camera are then simply secured to the head. Particularly in documentary shooting, the quick release is quite handy for getting the camera off the tripod quickly if a new shot suddenly presents itself.

Caution: When attaching a camera to a head, whether with a quick-release plate or the traditional design, make certain the camera is properly attached before leaving it. Both the threads and the plates can appear to be attached without actually making a connection. If you step away, you may find the camera on the floor when you come back. Always test the connection by lifting the camera slightly; if the screw is properly threaded, the tripod will come with it.

LEVELING THE HEAD

Almost all tripod heads sold specifically for film or video work come with some means of leveling to ensure that the head is straight with the world. Most employ a *spirit level*—a small leveling bubble centered inside a circle—similar to that found on a carpenter's level. Some tripods have a knob and bolt on the underside of the head that are part of one leveling design called *ball joint leveling*, where turning the knob slightly clockwise loosens the head in the bowl. You can then position the head so that the leveling bubble is in the center of the circle. This is done with the camera on the head, because the weight of the camera may change the level slightly. This method is popular on 16mm tripods, whereas tripods for 35mm employ a variety of means. With some tripods you have to adjust the legs to achieve level, an approach that is annoying until you get used to it.

Leveling the head should become automatic. It is the first thing the AC does when moving to a new setup, even if there is a possibility that the camera position may still be changed. No effective evaluation of shot and composition can be done without a level tripod head. Shots can be set up that appear straight with the world, and a simple movement turns the world askew. When attaching the camera to the quick-release plate, be sure the camera is straight on the plate. If it is cockeyed, it will affect the alignment of the camera with the horizon. Even if the head is level, the shots will not look level, particularly when panning and, to a lesser extent, tilting.

CAMERA SAFETY CHECKLIST

☑ There is one essential rule of tripod safety: Never walk away from the camera without being 100 percent sure that the tilt is locked. If the tilt is not locked, the weight of the lens can cause the camera to tilt forward. As it moves it will gain momentum, and the lens can smash into a tripod leg, damaging or even ruining the lens. If the tripod itself is not secure, the whole system can fall over or the threading screw can shear off. In both cases the camera smashes to the floor. Some ACs never leave the camera for any reason. It is under their protection. If they absolutely must leave, they will get the 2nd AC to mind the camera until their return.

☑ The balance mechanisms on tripods are wonderful, but they can give camera personnel a false sense of security. With ball joint leveling, the head can be made level while the legs are uneven, leaving the whole system in a precarious position. Often the legs will have a leveling bubble as well and, although it is not necessary that it shows absolute level, the closer to level it is, the better.

☑ Set up the tripod so that one of the legs points in the same direction as the lens. As suggested, the greatest weight of a camera is usually toward the lens. If a camera falls over, it tends to fall lens first. With one leg pointed forward, the majority of the camera weight is supported.

☑ If a particular setup is the least bit insecure, use *sandbags* or other weights on the legs. The use of sandbags to secure light stands is fairly common, and several should be brought along for the camera. Sandbags can be used for *lockdowns*—situations in which the framing must be absolutely consistent from shot to shot, such as with superimpositions and matte shots.

☑ The camera must be secure at all times. One thing you can count on is that if you set up the camera so that some fool can knock it over, some fool will knock it over. This is a truth that extends to anything you rig on a set. There can be dozens of people wandering around a film set, and the odds are that at least one of them has no common sense around equipment. A top-of-the-line 16mm production camera with a good lens can easily cost $80,000 to $90,000. An improperly set tripod can be responsible for damage that either makes a rental company very unhappy or destroys your own investment. However much many of us enjoy building odd camera mounts and encourage students to experiment with same, the camera should never be put in jeopardy. It makes no sense to risk damage to the one tool that is indispensable in making films. Cameras can be repaired, but they often cannot be brought back to their original condition. After a careless crew member dropped it lens-first from a tripod, one camera was never again as quiet.

☑ Get set up and comfortable. Be sure that the tripod legs will not be in the way of any of your movements while executing the shots. Pans often require moving around the tripod, and anything blocking your way can affect the shot. Having to strain or stand on tiptoe to look through the eyepiece will affect your ability to execute the shot smoothly. Find something stable to stand on or reposition the tripod so you feel completely comfortable. Do not change the shot unnecessarily for your comfort—just find a way to make yourself comfortable.

Video and the Digital Domain

Although this text focuses primarily on film, some summary of the video world is appropriate, particularly the digital aspects. Video has essentially undergone three great transformations in its brief history. Occurring at roughly twenty-year intervals, each has had a significant impact on how the film world operates. The first great period, obviously, is the initial years—the "golden years" when television established itself as the dominant medium of public entertainment. The second started in the late 1970s, as analog video became portable and obviated the newsgathering and informational aspects of film. The third revolution is the ongoing digital one. Each of these transformations has impinged on the once-dominant world of film. The first forced Hollywood to find a way to be competitive with the highly attractive new medium. The second made film even more specialized, with film still providing the key impetus when image quality and complex design were critical issues—analog systems having profound limitations in many situations. Digital has changed all that.

ANALOG AND DIGITAL

The major distinction now is between analog and digital video. Many aspects of capture and exhibition remain similar, but there are some fundamental differences. As suggested, many film editors resisted editing on analog video, because it was very inflexible. Digital editing has largely broken down that resistance.

The terms *analog* and *digital* have very specific definitions regarding how information is encoded on a recording medium; it is easiest to understand the concepts with a simple example. A conventional typewriter (analog) and a word processor (digital) provide a good illustration of the difference. If the following sentence is typed on a sheet of paper (analog), the sentence occupies a specific amount of space on the page:

I could not anticipate all the problems.

If you decide to replace the phrase *could not anticipate* with the more informal *couldn't foresee,* you can use whatever erase function is available to eliminate the first phrase, but it is not possible to plug in *couldn't foresee* without there being extra space—the video parallel would be a blank space on the tape.

I could not anticipate all the problems.
I   all the problems.
I couldn't foresee   all the problems.

To eliminate the extra space, you would have to erase everything after the word *I* and retype the entire sentence from that point on. If you want to lengthen the sentence, say, replace *anticipate* with *possibly foresee,* the problem is even clearer. On a word processor, digital storage allows you to eliminate or change whatever you want while drawing all the succeeding information forward or pushing it back.

Linear and *nonlinear* are terms that get thrown around with some abandon and are sometimes mistaken as being the same as *analog* and *digital,* respectively. *Linear* simply means that information is stacked end to end in a line, film frames for instance; *nonlinear* means that the arrangement of information is fluid. Although there are similarities, everything that is analog is not by definition linear, and everything that is digital is not by definition nonlinear. Film is analog, yet its editing is nonlinear. Digital audio- and videotape record a digital signal, yet do so on a linear medium.

Conventional analog videotape is linear, with each shot laid end to end and filling up a specific amount of space on the tape. One cannot go into an edited tape to shorten or lengthen pieces. Different shots can be substituted, but only ones of the same length. As in the typewriter example, changing the length of a shot in the middle of an edited program would require reediting everything after that point. This was a significant shortcoming, particularly for editors trained in film, because it eliminated much of the flexibility in editing the image.

There has been great argument as to whether film is linear or analog. Its physical arrangement is clearly analog, because it is frames stacked in a linear order on the celluloid. And yet when you cut out one frame, the entire tail end of the film is brought forward that one frame in a manner consistent with digital encoding. Maybe a good compromise is to call film nonlinearlike. As such, it is infinitely flexible in its ability to move any one piece or pieces against others. Faced with the drawbacks of analog video editing in the initial years of the second video revolution, many editors continued to work in film because of its nonlinear capabilities. Any piece could be shortened or lengthened; all pieces could be moved against one another as desired.

Digital editing has brought video into the nonlinear world. A digital editing system is theoretically simplicity itself, working in a way not unlike a word processor. The ability to drag images and sounds to wherever you want with the click of a mouse, shortening and lengthening them as needed, is highly efficient. Though many film editors were frustrated by analog video, they rarely return to film once they enter the digital domain.

Digital brought video into the nonlinear world, and the many limitations of analog tape that made it so unattractive were overcome. The difference, however, still has to be considered. Even though you shot and edited digitally, will the project be output to an analog tape? If so, it cannot be projected digitally. And the projection of analog video has woeful shortcomings. With all its limitations, analog video is still in the picture.

The Video Image and the Video Camera

Most of the analog video cameras were comparable to a film camera in both dimension and weight, comprising a body and a lens. The major difference is that the film camera captures light photographically and a video camera turns the light into an electrical signal—the video signal—that is recorded on a magnetic tape in a manner analogous to sound recording. The internal workings of the film camera are impressive, yet they are essentially a nineteenth century technology. A video camera is a product of the electronic age.

Although the method of recording is different, the general designs remain the same or, more accurate, digital video mimics the attributes of analog video. The camera creates an electrical signal (the video signal) that is recorded as linear magnetic information in the case of analog video or as a sequence of 0's and 1's in the case of digital video.

The video signal itself has been around since the advent of television. In fact, the earliest broadcasts existed only as signals, with no method of recording. The first studio recorders were developed in the 1950s, and portable video became a dimly envisioned possibility in the mid-1960s, with the first half-inch reel-to-reel recorders. Video began transforming the entertainment industry in the late 1970s. Television news stations, which shot millions of feet of film per year and had in-house processing setups, quickly converted to the newer, cheaper, more immediate medium, and whatever primacy film had left was soon over.

The biggest initial difference between film and video is in what happens to the light. Rather than striking the film plane, in video the light strikes a *CCD (charge-coupled device)*, generally referred to as a chip. The *chip* is a flat board covered with thousands of light-sensitive pixels, which convert the light into a complex electrical signal. Most high-end video cameras have three chips, devoting one each to the primary colors of light—red, green, and blue *(RGB)*.

The technology to convert light into an electrical signal has been around for years and, in fact, is the basis of the most common approach to film sound. One of the most exciting aspects of the encoded electrical video signal is that it can be almost endlessly manipulated. The film image is in many ways written in stone. While there are complicated and potentially costly reprinting options, a film image is photographically imprinted and must be essentially changed manually from one print to the next. With the potential for electronic manipulation, the recorded video signal can be modified in many different ways both before it gets to the tape in initial recording and, particularly, as it is being edited in postproduction. As such it can be seen as a starting place for a complex and highly refined image. The ease of implementing optical effects and the increased creative possibilities have brought a new dimension to the process of creating a finished work.

Audio 1   Audio 2   Image

One scan line = one field   Two fields = one video frame   Control track

6-23

A typical half-inch videotape employs four separate tracks

Just as film is shot in frames per second, video is broken down into video frames per second; but whereas film frames are arranged consecutively down the celluloid, the video frame does not have such discrete boundaries. The video frame is recorded diagonally on the tape, with each frame composed of two diagonal lines—called fields—of information. Each *video field* represents every other horizontal line of visual information in the video image, and the fields are interlaced to create the image. Although the video frame is not a distinct entity viewable to the eye like the film frame is, the editor can examine a single video frame just as with film. Actually, when one still-frames a videotape one is generally looking at an individual field. Video runs at 29.97 frames per second, usually just stated as 30. As explained in chapter 1, this is referred to as the **NTSC** *(National Television System Committee)* signal. The recording method for video is similar to that of audio, but it requires much higher speeds to record a stable, usable image. Therefore, the record head rotates in the direction of tape travel to multiply the speed of the tape. This is referred to as **helical scan recording,** an approach that is used in both digital video and digital audio.

The standard consumer-grade half-inch videotape, VHS employs four separate tracks and is representative of the track configurations of most formats. The image track is in the center and takes up the largest portion of the tape. The audio is on two narrow tracks at the top of the tape. **SEE 6-23**

The bottom of the tape is reserved for the fourth track—the *control track*—which is recorded during shooting. Composed of a series of pulses, the control track and its emulators are central to the way video works. Much like in a crystal camera, the pulses are referenced in playback to reproduce perfect speed. Any imperfection in the control track will cause image breakup. There is 1 pulse per video frame, 30 *pulses per second (pps)*. In the editing process, the control track allows the easy identification and marking of video frames for determining the length of shots. On an *edit control unit (ECU)*—the main controller for analog video editing—the frames can be assigned a time reference in hours, minutes, seconds, and frames (e.g., 1:32:12:26). The pulses are thus critical for referencing frames, although the simple control track has a critical shortcoming in not providing a permanent address for individual frames. Time can be assigned to frames, but that changes whenever the counters are zeroed or the machines are turned off and on again.

TECHNICAL SPECIFICATIONS

Reading video specifications and technical manuals can be somewhat like tackling treatises on quantum physics (which to a certain extent they are). The complexity of much of the discussions of video technology is daunting. The following are a few basic technical considerations with which one should at least be familiar.

The first is the difference between interlaced video and progressive video. This is in essence the difference between the conventional television set and the computer monitor. Remembering that the video frame is composed of two individual fields of information in NTSC, in *interlaced video* each individual field is presented separately and then interlaced with its partner to form the image. This standard was arrived at in the early years of TV, because sequential presentation would have potentially overtaxed the available bandwidth. The progressive standard of the computer monitor presents the video information sequentially, as opposed to the even-odd approach of interlaced. For technical reasons *progressive video* is generally the preferred standard but not enough that it would be worth replacing the hundreds of millions of NTSC television sets in general use. The interlaced NTSC system is still the standard for TV in the United States and Canada, although HDTV employs progressive scanning, and many new digital production standards are progressive as well. The *p* of Sony's new 24p system that George Lucas is using stands for *progressive,* a not surprising fact in that it is a high-definition medium.

One other distinction of interlaced video is between composite video and component video. Composite video is the earlier of the two, and though many systems still incorporate this approach component video is the current preferred standard. The major difference is that *composite video* breaks the signal down into a relatively simple mix of RGB—red, green, and blue—components. *Component video* further breaks the signal down to these color components mixed with a luminance (brightness) component. Progressive video has a different approach altogether.

Although none of these technical distinctions are particularly pertinent to the average filmmaker, they do have a bearing on compression, a huge issue in both digital and analog video in terms of broadcast standards and overall quality. With the vast amount of information required to compose even a single frame of video, both storage and instantaneous retrieval become challenges. As most computer geeks know, *compression* is a way of reducing the amount of data by discarding information that appears redundant, such as that found in a blue sky. Both the color and luminance aspects of component video require compression. This gets into sampling and a host of other issues too complex for this brief discussion, but suffice it to say that component digital formats with 4:2:2 compression are the minimum standard for high-end feature and broadcast work. There are high-end digital formats that require no compression. Mini DV compresses the image so much that, while it still looks great to the eye, it can pose a great problem if you want to do color effects or computer-generated images (CGI).

EQUIPMENT AND FORMATS

There are essentially two approaches to video shooting and recording: with a video camera and a separate *VCR (videocassette recorder)* and with a *camcorder*—a combined camera and video recorder in one unit. The configuration of tracks on the videotape can be different from format to format; many formats mix some signals, whereas others have optional uses. All formats have at least two audio tracks, with some of the professional ones having room for more. In video there has also been a distinction between *consumer* gear, *industrial* gear—used for corporate and training videos and the like—and *commercial* gear—for the high end of the business.

Although a number of analog formats are still in use, with one significant exception digital video has completely supplanted analog as a commercial and industrial medium. Various formats still get minimal use—from Hi8 to 8mm video—but they no longer command significant market share or much in the way of commercial application. They are no longer significant players, but their small size paved the way for the micro digital cameras.

The most common video format is *VHS,* with the majority of consumer VCRs and camcorders using this standard half-inch format. VHS yields an acceptable image, particularly when playing back prerecorded movies and producing images for the home market.

Super VHS was introduced in the late 1980s and is a step up in image quality and stability from its predecessor. It is an industrial-quality medium, being used in schools and in-house business training. As a format it is under pressure from the lower-end digital formats.

Betacam is to a certain extent a relic of the past, but gets enough current use to warrant a brief mention. Beta was an early competitor for the consumer market that VHS came to dominate. It achieved a certain amount of use in the low-end professional world, and you occasionally run across it in a variety of situations.

Betacam SP, an improvement over Betacam, remains the only significant analog broadcast-quality professional standard for production. Beta SP camcorders are very common, particularly among television news departments. The *SP* stands for *superior performance.*

Three-quarter inch, or *U-matic,* was the most significant professional standard for the first ten years or so of the transformation to video of the newsgathering business. TV news was shot on three-quarter, although the equipment was eventually deemed too bulky and heavy for flexible location use, given the development of more lightweight gear. For some hard-to-fathom reason, it still receives extensive use as a playback medium. Probably because it has just been there for years, three-quarter still seems to be the presentation medium of choice in ad agencies and many postproduction facilities.

Digital videotape recording has made extensive inroads in both the high end and the low end of the video field and will continue to play a greater role in the future—if not eliminate analog gear altogether. The consumer and "prosumer" camcorders have not wiped out the old standby VHS, owing to its extensive use in the movie rental market and thus its compatibility with viewing home video. The size, versatility, and image quality of the new digital cameras, however, will continue to erode the VHS market share.

Mini DV was the result of a number of manufacturers getting together in 1993 to create a standard for digital consumer shooting and editing gear. Introduced in 1996, **Mini DV** is a stunning bit of electronic design in which a small camera can be interfaced with a desktop computer. It and its brethren are the most significant new players in recent years. Mini DV employs a very small cassette, roughly two inches by a little less than three inches, thus allowing a compact and lightweight camera. **SEE 6-24** This flexible format, like many other digital formats, continues to record its information in the same configuration on the tape as does analog video, but it's digitally encoded. Although Mini DV was designed as a consumer format, it has been robust enough to make the grade for some industrial-level work. Indeed manufacturers saw the possibilities in stepping up from Mini DV and introduced the next two formats: DVCPRO and DVCAM.

The initial upgrade from Mini DV, *DVCPRO* runs at a faster recording time that devotes more space and thus more information to each frame. DVCPRO allows the user to shoot two separate cassette sizes, with the

6-24

A DVCAM cassette and a Mini DV cassette

6-25

The Sony DSR-300A
DVCAM camcorder

tape compartment having channels to negotiate the different tapes. One of the cassettes is a little bigger than the Mini DV cassette, and the other is roughly three by five inches, about halfway between a Mini DV and a standard VHS cassette.

Introduced after DVCPRO and having made similar improvements to Mini DV, *DVCAM* has proved to be popular. **SEE 6-25** It too can play and record on two cassette sizes, but it can also record on Mini DV cassettes as well as a tape similar to the larger DVCPRO cassette. None of the cassettes, however, can be played on different mediums.

Between Mini DV and its bigger siblings, substantial commercial work is drifting toward these formats. The Mini DV family still requires extensive compression, however, and the feature film and network broadcast worlds work to the following higher standards.

Digital Betacam, referred to as *Digi Beta,* is the portable professional end of the digital world. Except in the highest strata of production, film transferred to video is mastered to Digi Beta.

D-1 was the initial version of the D series of formats, high-end recorders that are generally studio based and used for high-quality mastering of field tape and film transfers. Made by Sony, which has been a leader in high-end professional digital gear, it was followed in short order by D-2, D-3, and D-5—all coming from several manufacturers along with Sony: Panasonic, Hitachi, and Ampex. Of all these D-1 and D-5 have been the biggest players, although Sony continues development and is presently up to D-9, with D-10 and D-11 still on the drawing board.

Indeed the most talked-about new digital system is *24p.* It is a Sony product that is fast becoming the industry standard for shooting. A step up from the already excellent Digi Beta, many are claiming that 24p is the first format to get filmlike results from a video camera. In addition to Sony's major 24p camera, Panavision— the major provider of motion picture cameras to feature filmmakers—has a "Panavised" version, both of which are being used extensively in the field. Although American episodic TV held on and was shot on film for the initial twenty years of portable video, 24p is the format that is finally making some inroads into this previously closed-off world.

DVD (digital videodisc) is primarily a playback medium at this point, although authoring to DVD will become more prevalent. Capturing straight to disc as well as onto hard drives will receive extensive research energy over the coming years. There are a number of video cameras that capture straight to a hard drive, but they are not yet in widespread use.

A few other formats appear on occasion, such as Digital 8 and Digital S, but the preceding discussion covers the main players. In addition, there are a number of formats that are proprietary to either individual manufacturers or specific broadcaster's criteria, Panasonic's M1 system being a prime example. For the novice or industrial producer, Mini DV and DVCAM are presently the hottest properties.

USING A DIGITAL CAMERA

While much of what has been said in previous chapters applies to the general approach to shooting video, there are a few additional considerations. Choosing a digital camera should be done carefully. Cameras that interface with computers are marvels of digital/electronic design, but to achieve a consumer-friendly price they are frequently flawed by compromises in some of their image-gathering qualities. Cheap lenses are probably the biggest problem, with the search for a good one being critical. A colleague suggests the "rule of 5,000"; that is, if the camera costs less than $5,000, odds are that it does not have a very good lens.

Many of the new cameras are also flawed by their "automatic everything" approach. These features are designed to appeal to the consumer. Automatic focus and exposure are fine for the amateur but untenable for professional applications. Most cameras have manual overrides, whereby focus and exposure can be changed, but only in relation to undefined settings. When a lens is not calibrated in feet or meters, it is difficult to execute the thoughtful rack focuses that are common in feature films. In addition, when a lens is not calibrated in f-stops, it is difficult to establish light values that exist in relation to a certain exposure. Clearly, much videography is justifiably lit to the human eye in conjunction with the video monitor, but an understanding of how light relates to an exposure can be an advantage.

Sound is also a concern. Most video cameras, whether digital or analog, cheap or expensive, have excellent sound-recording specifications; they can record very high quality sound. That is not the problem. A large percentage of good audio recording depends on microphone placement (see chapter 11). Keep in mind that the built-in mics on most cameras will not produce the quality of sound needed for a project that you hope to get screened and distributed—largely because the mic is frequently too far from the subject. Most cameras have a jack for an external mic; consider using it and employing someone to monitor both mic placement and overall quality. You may want to put it through a mixer first—or even record it on a separate unit—but be sure that you understand the technical capabilities of the gear before going forward.

In a more global sense—and there will undoubtedly be some who strongly disagree with this assessment—one of the major problems with beginning video is that much of the initial shooting is undisciplined; that is, inexperienced shooters produce images that have no weight—no internal pacing or dramatic power. Video is so cheap and so immediate that it is easy to just turn on the camera without thinking about scene structure and the logic and clarity of shots. The great debate between Hollywood and independents (albeit perhaps a one-sided debate) is that the typical Hollywood image is so slick and expensively mounted that it is devoid of any intrinsic relationship with reality. Independents certainly have their points, but one can also think of spectacular images from Hollywood films that have profound emotional impact and dynamic power. There are Hollywood images that look like they are coated with a plastic layer of light and color, and there are also images in "indies" that are so devoid of engaging qualities as to render the projects visually uninteresting. Excellent films at any level are generally filled with remarkable images. How do *you* make remarkable images?

7

The Lens

THE camera *lens* **is the vehicle** that transfers light to the film. It can be as simple as a single piece of glass, called an *element,* or as complicated as multiple elements that can be moved in relation to one another.

The lens always includes three basic features that will be part of the decision-making process whenever you are shooting. On most lenses two of these features are in the form of moveable rings that have to be set for every shot: the focus ring and the *f*-stop ring. The third refers to the length—wide-angle, normal, or telephoto—of the lens, what is referred to as focal length. In a zoom lens, focal length is a variable as well and will also have a ring devoted to it.

The camera itself is based on the *camera obscura* phenomenon, observed when rays of light pass through a pinhole on a surface. The crossing rays create an upside-down representation of the world on the other side. A lens transmits the light in the same way only more efficiently, because the pinhole does not allow light through in sufficient quantity to create a workable exposure. When the film is later projected on a screen, the projector reverses the process. **SEE 7-1**

7-1

The camera obscura phenomenon projects an inverted image of the light entering through a tiny aperture

Focus

Light rays emanate from a point on a subject. They strike the surface of the lens and, as they travel through the lens and exit the rear element, are bent toward the film plane. After they pass out of the rear element, they converge and are represented as a point on the film plane. The illustration below shows a single-element lens, though virtually all lenses used for film or video are composed of multiple elements. **SEE 7-2** If this light comes from a subject at the distance for which you have set focus (point B), the light comes to a point right at the film plane. If the subject is at a different distance (A or C), the light comes to a point either in front of or behind the film plane.

Every shot you execute must be focused, and many shots (more than one would anticipate) may require shifts of focus to accommodate all of a scene's action. In a given composition, you have to choose a subject that you want to be in focus. You can focus on only one distance at a time. Everything in front of and behind that point is going to be out of focus to some degree. How much out of focus is dependent on depth of field, an issue that complicates any discussion of focus and which is explained fully later in this chapter.

In a simple lens, the *focus ring* controls the position of the front element of the lens in relation to the film plane. The front element is moved forward or backward as you turn the ring. As the front element moves, the points where the light rays converge change. **SEE 7-3** The focus ring gives a series of distances, from the closest focus point that the lens is able to achieve to infinity. **SEE 7-4** The universal symbol for infinity is ∞. A hatch mark against the focus ring is used to set the desired distance. If the subject is 8 feet away, you set the ring to 8 feet. **SEE 7-5** Focus rings are often marked in both feet and meters. Be sure you know which one you are using. Reading the meter indicator when you're thinking feet will obviously ruin many shots.

There are two methods of focusing. The first method works effectively only with cameras equipped with a reflex viewing system and a zoom lens. In this method the lens is focused to the eye as you look through it. To focus to your eye, you must have the *diopter* set properly. The first step is to zoom in all the way to

7-2

Single-element lens

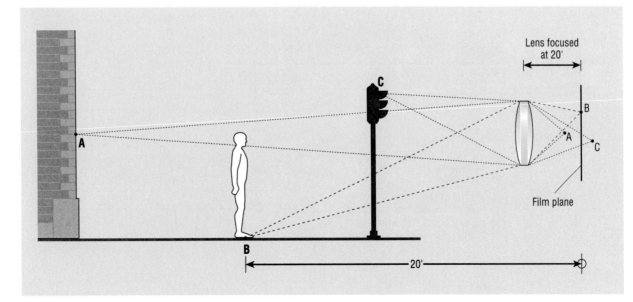

7-3

The streetlight resolves at the film plane when focused at 12 feet

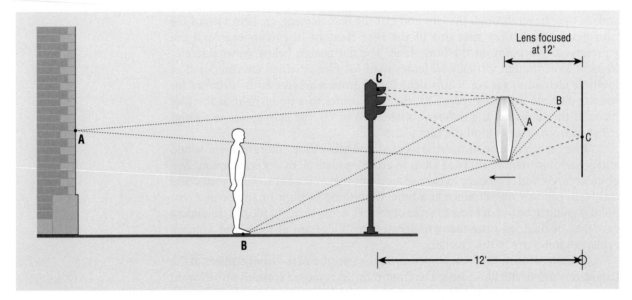

7-4

Subjects resolve at different points when the focus ring is shifted

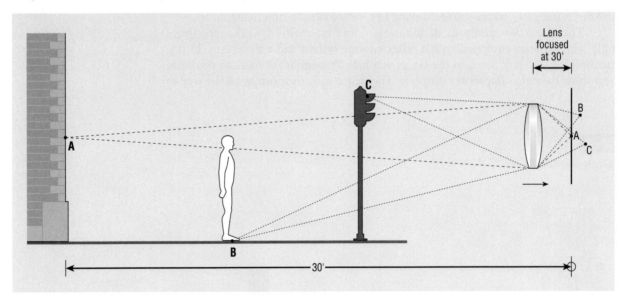

7-5

The focus ring controls the position of the front element of the lens in relation to the film plane the subject, gradations of focus being much more distinct with a telephoto lens. With most cameras you then rotate the focus ring until the subject is as sharp as possible. If you try to focus with a short lens or even a normal lens, you can rotate the focus ring a substantial distance without seeing a significant difference in the sharpness of the image.

The second method for setting focus is by using a tape measure. This might appear time-consuming and disruptive, but it is by far the preferred method. You simply measure from the camera to the subject and set the ring accordingly. It is virtually foolproof. You measure to the universal symbol for the film plane—not, as some might expect, to the front of the lens. This symbol can be found on the body of virtually every camera. **SEE 7-6**

Although some viewing systems can be difficult to use, the biggest culprit in focus problems is inattention to detail by the user. Not setting the diopter properly causes a substantial percentage of the problems, but the primary reason is simply inexactness of approach. When working by yourself or with small, inexperienced crews, it is easy to overlook many details. So many things demand attention, and there is constant pressure to keep the whole process moving forward. It will quickly become apparent that focus is one detail that can be overlooked only at the cost of your entire film. When even one piece of the puzzle is bad, it can be difficult to fit the whole thing together.

7-6

The universal symbol of the film plane is found on the body of virtually every camera

f-stop

The *f*-stop ring controls a small diaphragm in the lens, which regulates the amount of light reaching the film plane. **SEE 7-7** Its setting is determined by using a light meter. Discussion of the role of the *f*-stop in exposure dominates part IV of this text, and you will eventually come to see the *f*-stop as the starting point for any understanding of the creation of the motion picture image. How it interrelates or, more accurately, how you make it interrelate, with what is in front of the camera in terms of light is one of the dominant controls of the dramatic and expressive power of a film image.

Everyone has seen underexposed or overexposed film, and in its most simplistic sense the ***f-stop*** is used to obtain a usable exposure. If the *f*-stop is improperly set, the film will be over- or underexposed. The *f*-stop ring has a series of numbers. **SEE 7-8** Most lenses do not have numbers either as high or as low as are shown here, but these are the general parameters. Theoretically, the *f*-stops could go on to infinity.

The numbers can be somewhat confusing, because the smallest number represents the widest opening, or ***maximum aperture***, and the highest number represents the smallest opening, or ***minimum aperture***.

◆ **RULE:** *The lower the number (e.g., f/1), the larger the opening; the higher the number (e.g., f/22), the smaller the opening.*

7-7

The aperture in the lens regulates the amount of light reaching the film plane

| 1 | 1.4 | 2 | 2.8 | 4 | 5.6 | 8 | 11 | 16 | 22 | 32 | 45 | 64 |

7-8

The *f*-stop ring is used to set the *f*-stop for the desired exposure

7-9

Relative sizes of *f*-stops
correspond to the size of
the aperture

| *f*/1 | *f*/1.4 | *f*/2 | *f*/2.8 | *f*/4 | *f*/5.6 | *f*/8 | *f*/11 | *f*/16 | *f*/22 |

Thus, the lower *f*-stops let in more light, and the higher *f*-stops let in less light. Most lenses do not have anything numerically larger than *f*/22. There are also lenses with *f*-stops less than *f*/1—Stanley Kubrick used one to shoot in candlelight in *Barry Lyndon* (1975)—but they are so rare that *f*/1 serves as a sensible starting point.

Circles are used to represent approximate size relationships among the stops. **SEE 7-9** The actual size of any stop will depend on the focal length of the lens.

This more-light/less-light approach is invariably the way *f*-stops are presented, but it is somewhat of a backdoor tack. The goal in choosing an *f*-stop is often, though certainly not always, a clear and true-to-life picture. This is referred to as ***normal exposure.*** It takes a certain and reasonably consistent amount of light to produce a normal exposure, and the *f*-stop is used to transmit this light. In bright light the stop must be small so too much light does not reach the film. In low light the stop must be large.

The term ***lens speed*** refers to the maximum aperture—the widest the lens diaphragm will go. A lens with a maximum aperture of *f*/3.5 is considered a slow lens; a lens with a maximum aperture of *f*/1.8 is a fast lens. Due to the length of the lens and the construction of the lens barrel, telephoto lenses are almost always slower than wide-angle lenses. It makes sense that a short, squat lens would have a wider aperture than would a long, narrow one. If you want to use a telephoto lens in a low-light situation, you can almost surely anticipate some problems due to its slow speed. But with proper preparation, any situation of this nature can be handled.

It is recommended here that you bite the bullet and memorize the *f*-stops. They will be your constant companions if you have anything to do with ***technical camera***—everything concerning camera except calling different shots. If an aid to memorization is helpful, here is a useful mnemonic:

◆ **RULE:** *Every stop is a numerical double of the second previous stop, that is, 2.8 is twice 1.4, 8 is half of 16, and so on.* **SEE 7-10**

They cheat and round it off between 5.6 and 11. A second way is even more fun: All of these numbers, starting with 1, are multiples of the square root of 2 (1.4). Maybe if you are an idiot savant, this will be an acceptable method, but the point is made. Perhaps rote memorization is your preferred modus operandi.

As with the focus ring, there is a hatch mark by which to set the number. There is usually a ***detent,*** or a click stop, at each number. You can and frequently will use in-between settings, called half stops, quarter stops, and so on.

The numbers shown here are the true *f*-stops, referred to as *full stops,* and they represent specific points in the transmission of light. They are derived from a

7-10

Every stop is a numerical
double of the second
previous stop

| 1 | 1.4 | 2 | 2.8 | 4 | 5.6 | 8 | 11 | 16 | 22 | 32 |

mathematical formula that divides the focal length of the lens by the diameter of the diaphragm opening. Expressed as a formula, that is:

$$\frac{focal\ length}{diameter}$$

In terms of what you need to know to light a scene, this is not particularly earth-shattering information. It is important, though, to understand that *f*-stops have a mathematical derivation. In fact, everything becomes very mathematical once you start to light. You will occasionally see different numbers, but those are midpositions and are specific to the lens you are using.

This is a simplification, but in general the higher-numbered *f*-stops are used in bright-light situations, such as outdoors, and the lower-numbered *f*-stops in low-light situations, such as interiors. In essence you must determine the correct *f*-stop to get the exposure you want. It is worthwhile to think of the process of learning exposure technique as determining how to avoid major mistakes. At some basic level, mistakes result in under- or overexposure. The term *mistake* is used carefully, because you might ask if there are not times when we actually *want* over- or underexposure. If you have a shot of a person walking down a dark alley at night, the image would certainly incorporate many elements of underexposure. As we will come to see, virtually all film images have a wide range of volumes of light; an image without a range results in a shot that is flat and uninteresting. Eventually, you will come to see the task as controlling all the levels of exposure in what will often be a very complex image.

Thus the key to exposure is understanding the *f*-stop and how it relates, in terms of light, to what exists in front of the camera and what is happening at the film plane. Once lighting is added, what exists in front of the camera will eventually be something over which you have complete control. Once you fully understand *f*-stops, their use will appear somewhat easier; that said, however, the use of the *f*-stop will never be simple.

Focus and exposure are the two major areas in which beginning filmmakers consistently make technical mistakes. The key is to remember that both must be considered and addressed for every shot. In the first case, failure to do this will result in blurred and unusable images. In the second, over- and underexposure are the most immediate results, but an image that does not express what you want is the real downside.

Focal Length

The third feature of the lens is focal length, an issue that was approached from an aesthetic perspective in chapter 1. **Focal length** is usually expressed in millimeters (mm) and is the measurement from the optical center of a lens, which is usually in the front element, to the film plane. **SEE 7-11** A lens is referred to as a 25mm lens or a 75mm lens, for example, although the numbers should not be confused with the millimeters of the common formats. The focal length of a lens can generally be found on the barrel next to the front element. It is expressed as $f = n$, so $f = 25$ is a 25mm lens. Older American lenses often have focal lengths expressed in inches. Every inch is equal to 25mm, so a 2-inch lens is a 50mm lens, a 3-inch lens is a 75mm lens, and so on.

There are two major categories of lenses: prime and zoom. A **prime lens** is any fixed-focal-length lens; that is, it gives a fixed angle of view. Essentially, a prime lens is any nonzoom lens. Zoom lenses have many different focal lengths and are spoken of in terms of their range. For example, a lens having a range from 12mm to 120mm is referred to as a 12–120 lens. A sequence of numbers on the zoom ring indicate at what focal length the lens is set. **SEE 7-12**

7-11

Focal length is the distance from the optical center of a lens to the film plane

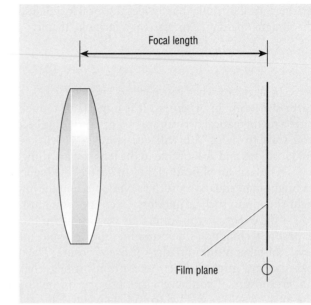

Lenses can be grouped into three different categories: wide-angle (short lens), normal, and telephoto (long lens). Wide-angle lenses make us appear farther from the object we are filming. Normal lenses do just what their name suggests: give a normal view of the scene. Telephoto lenses, like binoculars, make objects appear closer than they actually are. The zoom lens allows us to go uninterrupted from a wide shot to a close shot and vice versa.

The lens size required to achieve a specific distance effect varies with the size of the format being used. A smaller format requires a shorter lens to fill the smaller area of the frame. Many readers who have done 35mm still photography, one of the most common formats in still photography, know that a 50mm lens is generally considered a normal lens. This is true in motion picture cinematography as well. In 16mm a normal lens is roughly a 25mm lens. In Super 8 a normal lens is roughly

7-12

The zoom ring on a lens has a sequence of numbers that indicate focal length
Zoom ring on an Angénieux 12–120 lens

7-13

Focal lengths in different formats

	Wide-angle (short)	Normal	Telephoto (long)
Super 8	<12	12	>12
16mm	<16	16–25	>25
35mm	<50	50	>50

12mm. The pattern here is clear: As you halve the format size, you need roughly half the length to create the same effect. **SEE 7-13** The cutoff points here are rather arbitrary. Many people consider the 50mm lens the normal lens in the 35mm format; others consider normal somewhat less than 50.

Depth of Field

Depth of field refers to the distances down the field of the camera's view that remain in sharp focus. As stated, focus must be set one distance at a time. When you have chosen the focus point, everything in front of and behind that point is going to be out of focus to some extent. The focus at different distances is a matter of what is referred to as *acceptable sharpness*—the crispness or clarity of the detail of subjects or areas in an image. The range of distances before subjects become unacceptably soft—the depth of field—is dependent on several technical variables.

The overriding variable on depth of field is format size. The lenses used with larger formats have shallower depth-of-field characteristics than their counterparts in smaller formats. That is, if you use a lens that produces a normal perspective in the 35mm format (a 50mm lens) and a lens that produces normal perspective with a 16mm camera (25mm), the latter lens will produce more depth of field. Clearly, you would never choose a format based on depth-of-field concerns; usually, format is selected for such reasons as presentation, economics, and so on.

Beyond the choice of format size, the three variables of depth of field that are used while shooting are the same three found on lenses: f-stop, focal length, and focus point. There are two ways of determining the depth of field in a given situation: markings on the lens or printed depth-of-field tables. There are complex technical reasons for depth-of-field effects, but some general rules are presented here.

f-stop Higher f-stops yield greater depth-of-field characteristics—more will be in focus. Lower f-stops yield shallower depth-of-field characteristics—less will be in focus. If you are shooting at an $f/16$, you will have greater depth of field than if you shoot at an $f/2.8$. Do not take this to mean that you can arbitrarily set the f-stop to achieve greater or lesser depth of field. The f-stop is dependent on the lighting conditions under which you are shooting. If you were to get a reading of $f/5.6$ and decide to set the f-stop ring to $f/22$ to get more depth of field, the image would be completely underexposed. This may appear to make the f-stop an inflexible variable on depth of field, though in part IV we suggest how there can be room for changes.

Focal length Wide-angle (short) lenses yield greater depth of field. Telephoto (long) lenses yield shallower depth of field. This is why we said earlier that gradations of focus are more distinct with a long lens. If you are shooting with a 20mm lens, you will achieve greater depth-of-field characteristics than if you shoot with a 75mm lens. Again, filmmakers tend to choose lenses for the way they render space. If you are attempting to achieve specific focus effects, the depth-of-field characteristics of the lens clearly become part of the equation. You would not choose a 10mm lens if it defeated the way you envision the space; but filmmakers desiring a deep-focus effect generally shoot with a wide-angle lens. The film noir style of the 1940s and early 1950s incorporated tremendous depth within the image, and short lenses were clearly a central factor in the production of these films. A film such as Orson Welles's *Citizen Kane* employs the depth of field inherent in a wide-angle lens in conjunction with the lens's elongation effect to create its extraordinarily wide fields of focus.

Focus   Far focus settings yield greater depth of field. Close focus settings yield shallower depth of field. There is greater depth of field focused at 20 feet than if focused at 10 feet. Thus focus becomes more critical the closer the subject is to the camera. Focus is generally less of a variable than the previous two elements. If something needs to be in focus, you will frequently set focus to it. Focus is often manipulated, however, to create effect.

The depth of field—that is, how much of the image is in focus—is thus dependent on these three variables. Clearly, there are ways to minimize or maximize focus for effect. Factors that maximize focus are short lenses, high f-stops, and far focus points. Factors that minimize depth of field are long lenses, low f-stops, and close focus points.

DETERMINING DEPTH OF FIELD

There are two methods of determining depth of field for a given shot. The first is an option found on many prime lenses, which have hatch marks that give the parameters of depth of field. **SEE 7-14** There is a sequence of f-stop numbers on either side of the focus hatch mark. In this example, if you were shooting at an $f/4$ and focused at 8 feet, you could tell that everything from roughly 6 to 12 feet would be in focus; *roughly* is the key word here, because this method gives only general parameters. Many lenses use these markings, although there are different methods of indicating the boundaries. Bolex lenses, which usually have the name *Kern* or *Switar* on them, have a clever strategy that employs gold dots that appear as you close the aperture. Zoom lenses do not have these markings, because the focal length varies as you zoom, and thus no single chart would be correct.

The second method is far more common, mostly because of the inexact nature of the first method. *Depth-of-field tables* have a chart of the near and far parameters of focus for the common focal lengths. These tables generally list the depth of field down to inches. The *American Cinematographer Manual,* which is published by the **American Society of Cinematographers (ASC),** is generally used as a source for these tables, though they can be found elsewhere. The pocket-sized ASC manual is used constantly on the set.

Because lens length is a constant, there are tables devoted to specific lens lengths. You need a table for the format being used; the ASC manual has tables for 35mm and 16mm, but not Super 8. You might have to do some searching for a Super 8 table. If you are shooting 16mm and using a 35mm table, your results will be skewed. In 16mm the ASC manual has individual tables for 8, 9.5, 12, 16, 25, 35, 50, 85, 100, and 135mm lenses.

If you are shooting 16mm film with a 25mm lens, first you would look up the 25mm table. The tables have axes for both the focus and the f-stop. Tables are set up

7-14

The markings on the lens barrel give the depth-of-field parameters

7-15

Sample depth-of-field table

Lens focus	f/1	f/1.4	f/2	f/2.8	f/4	f/5.6	f/8	f/11	f/16	
50'	36' 80'			25' Infinity					7' Infinity	Near Far
25'	21' 1" 30' 8"									
15'						9' 3" 40'				
10'					7' 9" 14' 3"	7' 1" 17' 2"			4' 7" Infinity	
8'					6' 6" 10' 6"	6' 12'				
6'										
5'										
4'										
3'	2' 11" 3' ¾"									
2'	1' 11¾" 2' ½"			1' 11" 2' 1"					1' 7½" 2' 7½"	

somewhat like mileage tables in an atlas, where you can look down a column and across a row to see how far it is from Minneapolis to Indianapolis. The sample table includes only a few numbers but is representative of depth-of-field tables in general. **SEE 7-15**

If you are using a zoom lens, you can read the focal length off the zoom ring. If the ring setting falls between numbers, you should probably round up to the nearest focal length for which you find a table.

In looking at these numbers, notice that there is always more depth of field behind the focus point than in front of it. This has given rise to the *⅓-⅔ rule,* which states that one-third of the depth of field is in front of the focus point and two-thirds is behind. It does not always work quite this perfectly, but as a rule of thumb it is relatively close. Just remember that there is always more depth of field behind the focus point than in front of it.

The shallowest depth of field is always in the lower-left corner of the table. Factors that maximize depth of field are in the upper-right corner. Note, however, that the maximum depth of field is not actually in the farthest upper-right box; it is actually down the column where we are focused at 10 feet. Here everything from 4 feet 7 inches to infinity is in focus. This is because as we draw the focus point closer to the camera, we continue to include infinity in the depth of field. You can easily see this on the depth-of-field markings on the lens barrel. If you are shooting at an *f*/11 with focus set at infinity, the far end of depth of field will extend well past infinity. **SEE 7-16** You do not need to consult a philosopher to realize that the concept of "well past infinity" is absurd.

7-16

Depth of field and focusing at infinity

The point at which you are focused as close as you can be to the camera and still include infinity in the depth of field is called the *hyperfocal distance*. Each *f*-stop on each length lens has its own hyperfocal distance, because the depth of field expands and contracts with different *f*-stops. Hyperfocal distances are listed on most depth-of-field tables, and a knowledge of them can be handy, particularly in documentary work where many things may be happening spontaneously at different distances from the camera. Setting an arbitrary focus point for a specific depth of field, one that either includes or excludes objects in the frame, is a common practice.

DEPTH OF FIELD AND SETTING FOCUS

In pragmatic terms, you should determine the depth of field in virtually every shooting situation. Let's say that you are shooting a scene in which one person is in the foreground at 8 feet and another is in the background at 15 feet. **SEE 7-17A** You have determined—though this, of course, is not always the case—that you want both people in focus. A light meter reading determines that you will be shooting at an *f*/5.6.

7-17

Depth of field and setting focus

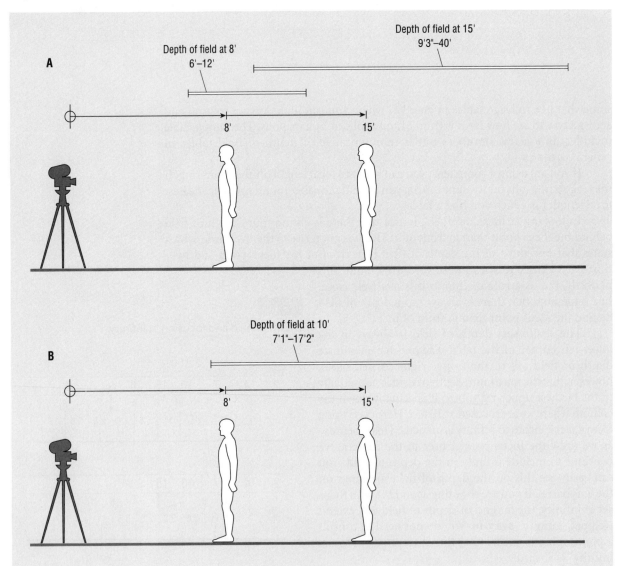

You consult the depth-of-field table and find that if you focus on the person in front, everything from 6 to 12 feet will be in focus. In this situation the second person would be out of focus. Conversely, when focused at 15 feet, the depth of field will be from 9 feet 3 inches to 40 feet, and focus will exclude the person in the foreground.

What would the options be if the goal were to have both figures in focus? As any clever person would be quick to point out, you can simply move the characters closer together. This is obviously a very reasonable approach, and many minor difficulties can be solved in this manner. That said, do not get in the habit of allowing technical limitations to determine the content of your compositions. If for some narrative or aesthetic reason you wanted the character positioning to remain as designed, what would be some other options? The first would be to shoot at a higher *f*-stop, but that would require more lights. This is a relatively common solution, though we will skip over it for now.

The easiest solution here would be to pick a focus point that included both people. Another look at the table determines that if focus is set at 10 feet, you will achieve the desired depth of field. **SEE 7-17B** In this case you would set focus at

7-17

Depth of field and setting focus *(continued)*

10 feet, and both subjects would be in focus. There may be no object in the image that is actually 10 feet away, but the focus setting is arbitrary to achieve a specific depth of field.

Conversely, there may be situations in which you do not want both subjects to be in focus. If a situation has subjects at 10 feet and 14 feet and you focus on the first figure, the depth of field includes the second figure as well. **SEE 7-17C** If you want the second figure out of focus, you would consult the table and find that focusing at 8 feet would reduce the depth of field to everything from 6 feet to 12 feet, thus achieving the desired effect. **SEE 7-17D**

So the focus point can be set arbitrarily to achieve specific effects. If you wanted the foreground figure out of focus, you could find a focus point that would achieve that effect. All of this must be done in consultation with a depth-of-field table or the hatch marks on the lens. Never arbitrarily shift a focus point without being very sure of the result.

As with everything, subject movement complicates these issues. In the first example, if the person in front moves toward the camera, a rack would be necessary to keep him or her in focus. That rack focus would certainly cause us to lose focus on the background person. If our goal was to keep both figures in focus, the only solution might be to bring in more light to achieve a higher *f*-stop. Consulting the table would tell us which *f*-stop we would need to create the effect.

The key concept is that focus points can be set arbitrarily to achieve specific depth-of-field effects. Just because a subject is at 8 feet does not mean you have to focus at 8 feet. As you set up your shots, you must always be concerned with what will and won't be in focus. As suggested, you do not automatically want everything to be in focus all the time, but you do want to be in control of what is and is not. Achieving the effects you want takes extensive reference to depth-of-field tables and complex manipulation of the focus point.

For beginners depth of field may seem to be more an effect that happens to you—one of those characteristics of the nature of lenses that buffets and batters you. But the more control you exert over the medium, the more you will be able to manipulate the variables to achieve the kinds of effects you desire. Often as a beginner you are forced to settle for the effect you can get; you do not have the resources to control the image that a larger project would have. If the background comes back out of focus, it may be because you did not have the lights or the lenses to achieve a different effect. This is largely unavoidable, though the long-term goal is to attain complete control.

NOTES ON DEPTH AND MOVEMENT

An issue that requires clarification is the difference between depth of field and the concept of depth. Students often confuse them, because both the terms and the issues are clearly interrelated. *Depth of field* is a technical consideration with highly defined parameters; it may be manipulated for aesthetic effect, but its determinants are technical. *Depth* is an aesthetic consideration in which you decide how you want your two-dimensional image to suggest space. If you want a decidedly three-dimensional feel to an image, you must consciously manipulate elements in front of the camera to suggest depth. Lighting is a factor. Placement of objects in the foreground and background is a factor as well. Depth of field is simply one more factor.

Movement is also affected by lens length. Wide-angle lenses are better for obtaining smooth handheld shots as well as complicated moves done on camera supports. The telephoto lens magnifies both the subject and any movement on the part of the cameraperson. Handheld shots done with very long lenses can be almost unwatchable when projected, even though no significant movement was detected while shooting. On the screen the image jumps all over—an effect that can cause symptoms similar to seasickness in the viewer. If you have to shoot some distance from the subject, such as when filming animals in a zoo, it can be difficult to use a wide-angle lens. A tripod is indispensable for this kind of filming. Normal lenses are simply in between the extremes of telephoto and wide-angle, in both focus and the ability to be handheld. If both normal perspective and deep focus are desired, a lens on the low end of normal may be required.

Prime Versus Zoom

Although less true now than ten or fifteen years ago, prime lenses are generally used more than zoom lenses, because they have better optical qualities. Zoom lenses are very complex, being composed of a number of elements. The more surfaces the light has to pass through, the more the light deteriorates. Prime lenses, because of their relative simplicity, generally give sharper images. This said, it should be noted that zoom lenses have been steadily improving, and some of the new zooms are billed as being the optical equals of their prime brethren. Cinematographers seem to be split pretty evenly on this issue. When you are going to be zooming, only a zoom lens will do. When the shot is static or if the camera is doing the movement, the prime lens is still the most common choice.

Cinematographers sometimes prefer a zoom lens because it gives them more compositional flexibility. If they want a slightly closer shot, they can just zoom in and not have to go through the time-consuming process of moving and releveling the camera. This also can be handy in moving from medium shots to close-ups without having to change the setup, although there are some pitfalls when you do this. The biggest concern is how the two lens lengths represent space. In the medium shot, a wall may appear to be several feet behind a subject, whereas in the close-up, when zoomed in to a longer focal length, it can appear to be just off the subject's shoulder. It can be disconcerting to have shots with differently represented backgrounds included in the same scene. Some cinematographers, usually with director input, will change the setup to maintain consistent spatial relationships. How this is handled will be your decision, and you will no doubt see scenes that approach it both ways.

A further deterrent to the use of zooms is that rack focuses executed on zoom lenses have a slight zooming effect. The moving front element of the rack focus does the same thing as the moving element of the zoom, only to a lesser extent; this is called *breathing*. It is difficult to see as the shot is being executed, but the effect can be quite disconcerting if it is not desired. Some of the newer zoom lenses have corrected this problem, but these are very expensive and may be out of reach of novice filmmakers.

Zoom lenses can be very attractive to many beginners, however; nowhere can you push or turn anything and get such immediate results. But because of this, they tend to be overused. Infatuated with this minor but gratifying feature, students will zoom in and out and in and out ad nauseam. I discourage beginners from doing more than a couple of zooms in their first films, and those only to get it out of their systems. When you start looking for them in films, you will be surprised by how few you see. Very few directors use them intelligently, Robert Altman and Sergio Leone being notable exceptions.

Lens Mounts

Lens mount refers to the method by which the lens is attached to the camera. As with many situations in which manufacturers are competing for markets, lens mounts are not standardized. Arriflex has one mount, Bolex uses *C-mount* lenses, and the

CP-16 has a different mount altogether. Both the Arri and the CP mounts are called *bayonet mounts*. The part of the lens that is inserted into the camera is called the *flange*. C-mount lenses have threaded flanges, and attaching them is a simple matter of screwing the lens in. Bayonet mounts have an extended pin that interlocks with the lens. Some lenses can be adapted to other makes of cameras, whereas others cannot be. For example, there is an adapter available that allows some Arriflex lenses to be used on the CP-16 but not vice versa. The relationship of the rear element of the lens to the body of the camera is just too different to be matched.

The area where the flange meets the camera is crucial. There is virtually no room for error in the flange-to-camera relationship, because it will affect the highly critical distance between the rear element and the film plane. If a lens is improperly mounted—even slightly—whatever film is shot will most likely be out of focus. This leads to one of the fundamental rules of camera care:

◆ **RULE:** *Never pick up a camera by its lens.*

This puts undue stress on the flange area and will eventually cause the lens to be loose in its mount, leading to rear element–to–film plane difficulties.

Many lenses, particularly zooms, are so heavy that they could put undue stress on the camera's lens mount. These lenses generally have a *lens support system*, consisting of rods that extend from the body of the camera, to support the weight of the lens. This is a very common strategy in 35mm shooting. A lens that is too heavy may damage the lens mount if not properly supported.

When deciding on lenses, make sure you have an appropriate match of lens and camera. When you are using equipment from a rental house, they will know the appropriate lenses, even though it is still your responsibility to make sure everything works together. Low-budget filmmakers often get a special lens from a friend of a friend, and the camera from some other source altogether. This is where you can run into trouble. Be sure the pieces match. Shoot a test roll if you can.

The lens should not be mounted on the camera when it is being transported. Again, the flange area is critical, and any shocks to the camera while the lens is mounted can jar the lens position. A bumpy ride in a car might cause significant focus problems. The lens should be packed in a material that will absorb as many shocks as possible.

Front-Filters and Matte Boxes

Virtually all lenses have some method of front-mounting filters. Most *front-filters* for 16mm lenses are round, thin glass pieces that can be mounted in rings that screw into the front of the lens. **SEE 7-18** Several lenses use rectangular filters that are mounted in a holder that attaches to the front of the lens, an approach more common in 35mm. *Series 9 filters* (*series* refers to a size) and their attendant ring adapters are the most common in 16mm, particularly for zoom lenses. These rings are designed to screw into each other so a director of photography (DP) can sandwich as many filters together as desired. The more surfaces the light passes through, however, the more its quality degrades. When multiple filter effects are needed, DPs generally prefer single filters that combine effects or will sandwich no more than two at a time.

A *matte box* is an accordion-like bellows attachment that is mounted on the front of the lens. **SEE 7-19** It can be used to mount filters or to shade the lens from direct light. A *sunshade* is also used for this purpose. The matte box was originally designed to create shots

Most front-filters for 16mm are round, thin glass discs mounted in rings that screw into the front of the lens
Series 9 filters and adapter rings

7-19

A matte box is an accordion-like bellows attachment mounted on the front of the lens
Aaton XTR *prod* with matte box

that matte out (block light from) certain areas of the frame. The mattes are generally made out of heavy cardboard or metal and are inserted in the front of the matte box. They can be used to create a variety of patterns (keyholes, binoculars, question marks, and such) or, in conjunction with a camera's backwinding function, to make multiple passes on the film, blocking out areas intended for other information in later passes. The most common example of this is the split-screen effect, in which you see two separate images side by side on the screen. You block off one side of the lens on one pass and then block off the other side on the next pass. As attractive as this feature might appear, this type of matting is done infrequently. Most matte shots are now done with blue screen mattes or on optical printers.

Care and Maintenance

All modern lenses have a purplish antireflectant coating. This coating reduces stray light bouncing around in the lens—a phenomenon that reduces *contrast,* the play between lights and darks in a photographic image. If a lens is cleaned unnecessarily, that coating will eventually wear down. Clean a lens only if there is some noticeable mark, such as a smudge or fingerprint—then clean the lens immediately. The oil from your finger can etch a permanent pattern in the antireflectant coating if it is left for any significant amount of time.

◆ **RULE:** *If a lens is not dirty, don't clean it. If it is dirty, clean it immediately.*

When you do have to clean a lens, use only the materials specifically designed for the purpose: commercially produced lens-cleaning tissue and lens-cleaning fluid. The tissue should be used first, the drops only as a last resort. If there is substantial dust or grit on the lens, clean it off with a camel-hair brush before using tissue; otherwise, the dirt can get into the paper and scratch the coating and possibly the lens itself. I roll up the tissue like a cigarette, then swirl the end around the mark until it's gone. If this doesn't get rid of the mark, then, and only then, use the lens-cleaning fluid in conjunction with the tissue.

When you have to use the fluid, put a drop on the center of the lens and use the tissue as just described. This should get rid of most anything. Be careful that the fluid does not run down into the area where the glass meets the barrel of the lens. All lenses are cemented into position, and the fluid, if not used carefully, will eventually start to break down that cement. If the cement gets broken down, any shock to the lens could cause the elements to shift. The distance between the elements and the film plane are precisely engineered, so movement of even a fraction of a millimeter will seriously degrade the image. All shocks to the lens should be minimized, but transportation is the biggest culprit; excessive heat can also weaken the cement and cause problems.

These recommendations also apply to filters, and their care is a significant issue. It would be foolish to spend half an hour cleaning a lens only to put a dirty filter in front of it. If anything, you will see the AC spending more time with filters than with the lens itself.

There is substantial disagreement about the role of dust on the lens and filters. Some people claim it reduces contrast; others say that a modest amount has no significant effect, because it could not conceivably be in the range of focus. It is virtually impossible to eliminate all dust, but cleaning is called for if there is a substantial amount of it. The camel-hair brush is the tool of choice for this job.

As important as the front element of a lens is, always check the rear element as well. Given that the lens is removed frequently either to check the gate for hair or to mount a new lens, dust and marks can be a factor here as well. In fact, something on the rear element degrades the image more dramatically than do front-element marks. The distance between this rear element and the film plane is absolutely crucial to the quality of the image. Anything that may degrade the quality of the light must be avoided at all costs, so be sure to check both ends of the lens.

The flanges of both the lens and the mount on the camera should be cleaned as well. If a piece of dirt or grit gets lodged between the lens and the camera, it can actually change the distance between the rear element of the lens and the film plane. Again, even the slightest shift can jeopardize the sharpness of the image. Alcohol and a swab are the accepted materials for cleaning these critical areas.

Don't make the mistake of cleaning a lens with alcohol and swabs, even though they're part of a standard cleaning kit. This would make the antireflectant coating look like the swirls on a poorly cleaned window. It is extremely important to use the appropriate materials on the appropriate parts. Do not use facial tissue. Do not use a corner of your shirt sleeve. Do not attempt to blow the dust off with your breath; no matter how hard you try to avoid it, you will get spit on the lens. Watch how ACs take care of their lenses, and develop your own good habits from the start.

Any discussion of lenses can get quite complicated. Optics is a highly developed science, and lenses are extensively researched and tested. You will eventually hear such terms as *astigmatic aberrations, coma,* and *longitudinal chromatic aberrations,* as well as an endless list of technical reasons why what's in front of the camera never arrives at the film plane in perfect shape. To avoid these problems, remember that any lens is an amalgamation of compromises. The manufacturer had to give up one thing to get something else. Older zoom lenses in particular can sacrifice quite a bit of sharpness to get longer zoom ranges. The molded-plastic lenses in cheap cameras give up just about everything. These kinds of optics just will not do for motion pictures. If you start with an impoverished image, there may not be much left by the time it has been projected 90 feet.

Still, there are lenses that yield beautiful results and, with proper use and care, will serve your needs for many years. Cinematographers tend to latch on to specific lenses and go to great lengths to hold on to them and care for them. Start thinking about how you want a lens to perform and which lenses live up to your standards.

8

Film Stocks, Processing, and Video Transfer and Capture

FILM stocks are distinguished by a number of key factors. These include the stock's general construction; the exposure index, which rates the film's responsiveness to light; the color balance, which is the way the stock responds to different colors of light; and the latitude, the range of lighting values within which a film stock will produce a usable exposure. Although latitude is important in choosing a film stock, it is intrinsic to discussions of lighting and is covered in part IV. All other elements are primary factors in choosing a film stock.

Construction of the Film Stock

Motion picture film is a strip of celluloid covered with a light-sensitive emulsion. It has *sprocket holes*, also called *perforations*, which facilitate the movement and thus the exposure of the film. The construction of color film can be quite complex, but black-and-white film is relatively simple. There are several layers of coatings and adhesives, but black-and-white film is essentially made up of three basic elements: emulsion, base, and antihalation backing. **SEE 8-1** Film that has not yet been exposed is referred to as *raw stock*.

The *emulsion* is a solution of *silver halide crystals* suspended in a gelatin bath. When these silver halides are struck by light—that is, exposed—they change their properties. They further change their properties when subjected to chemical developers. In the case of negative film, the exposed halides harden and become opaque. In reversal film, the film is bleached or reexposed to reverse the areas that would be opaque in a negative. Either way, the film is barely touched by the light as it leaves an imprint. The analogy of a fingerprint can be invoked here. The chemical processing brings out the latent qualities of this "fingerprint." The emulsion side of unexposed film is a neutral color, usually tan or light green.

If the silver halide crystals are large, they can be discernible to the viewer as shimmering building blocks of the image, called **grain**. Grain is similar to *pixels* (short for *picture elements*) on a video screen. The

8-1

Black-and-white film stock is composed of emulsion, base, and antihalation backing

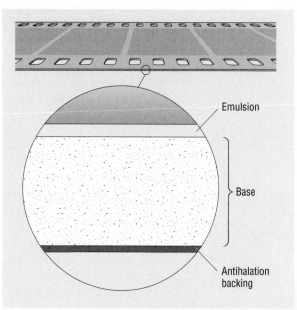

Emulsion

Base

Antihalation backing

159

smaller the grain and the smaller the pixel, the less likely a viewer is to notice that the image is made up of small dots. In the majority of commercial films, substantial effort is devoted to making grain as unnoticeable as possible. Grain is used to good effect in many films with a highly expressive image, calling attention to the construction of the photographic image and enhancing its abstract qualities.

The *base* is the celluloid medium on which the emulsion is laid. The opposite side of the film, the *antihalation backing,* is a dark and shiny coating that minimizes reflections that can cause bright areas to bleed into adjacent parts of the frame. In the early days of still photography, there was no antihalation backing, and the camera operators, under a light-tight hood, actually looked through the base of the film as they were filming. Before the development of modern viewing systems, this was the way photographers checked composition. The antihalation backing is completely removed in the developing process.

Color film stocks have a much more complicated construction. Although there are a number of different processes, the industry-standard color negative stocks are probably the best example. They work on the principle of separating the colors into three different layers of emulsion, with dye couplers and interlayer filters incorporated into the design. Each layer is sensitive to one segment of the color spectrum, although it does not break down simply into the three primary colors of light: red, green, and blue (referred to as *RGB*). The top layer records the blue record, the next layer the blue and green record, and the final layer the blue and red. The base and antihalation backing are the same. There are other designs, but this one is fairly typical.

NEGATIVE AND REVERSAL

Raw stock comes in two forms: negative and reversal. Most readers are familiar with *negative film,* which has all the lights and darks reversed from how they are normally perceived. *Reversal film* is the opposite: All colors and shades are rendered normally, photographic slides being a common example.

Negative stock cannot be used as a primary projection medium but must be printed onto a second piece of film that is a frame-for-frame replication of the *original*—the film that actually ran through the camera when shooting. These duplicate prints are called *workprints* and are made by a motion picture processing laboratory—the *lab*. As the term *workprint* suggests, one does all the work of editing with these prints. Due to fears of damaging the fragile emulsion, the original is touched only when absolutely necessary. Except in a few limited applications, the original is never projected. A film's original exists as a medium used to produce either the workprint or the final product, a *projection print*. Many large projects also employ intermediate prints.

Negative stock is the professional standard. It generally yields an image with tighter grain structure and is responsive to a wider range of light values. With reversal film, the reversing process is another level of manipulation. The reversed original in a sense becomes the second generation of the negative, a *generation* being the number of copies away from the original. A workprint is one generation from the original, and thus a second-generation print. A print of a print would be a third generation. The farther one gets from the original, the more the quality degrades, which is why so many versions of early films have lost much of their original visual grandeur. In this process grain increases and contrast decreases. Negative film stock also provides a higher-quality transfer to video, further cementing its dominant position. Virtually all commercial features are shot on negative film.

Negative stock's being the standard has led to some confusion in terminology. In the press and trade journals, the camera original produced on location is often referred to as the negative, leading one to think that *negative* and *original* are synonymous terms. But if one shoots *reversal* film, the piece of film that ran through the camera is an original as well. The term *original* simply refers to the film run through the camera during shooting. Even when the original is on reversal, which can be projected without a print, workprints are made when protecting the original is desired.

Exposure Index

Exposure index (EI) rates how sensitive a film stock is to light, what is referred to as *film speed.* Different sources may refer to this as *ASA* (for American Standards Association) or *ISO* (for International Standards Organization), but they are just different names for the same thing. Under whatever name, EI is a somewhat arbitrary number that is found on the film's packaging. This number will be set on the light meter and is the sole variable in the conversion of an amount of light in front of the camera to the corresponding *f*-stop. How the film stock responds to different volumes of light depends solely on how the manufacturer (Kodak and Fuji being the primary ones) has designed and produced the stock.

◆ **RULE:** *The lower the EI number, the less sensitive the film is to light; the higher the EI, the more sensitive the film is to light.*

The most significant difference in the construction of different film stocks is the size of the silver halides and how closely they are packed together, which determines the film's sensitivity to light. Film stocks with large, loosely packed silver halide crystals respond better to low volumes of light. Film stocks with smaller crystals and tighter construction require more light to expose them. A film stock with a low EI, such as Kodak Plus-X black-and-white reversal film (EI 40), is less sensitive to light; thus you need a greater amount of light to expose it. Plus-X would therefore be easier to use in a high-light situation, such as outdoors in sunlight. A film stock with a higher EI, such as Kodak Ektachrome Color Negative 7279 (EI 500), is more sensitive to light; less light is required to expose it, thus making it easier to use in low-light situations, such as indoors.

At least in the early stages, you will probably want to determine your film stock by the lighting conditions in which you are going to shoot. Most beginners will make this simple distinction: When shooting outdoors, use a stock with a lower EI; when shooting indoors, use a stock with a higher EI. This is not a bad way to start out, but be aware that most film professionals do not choose their film stocks on this basis. If someone is shooting indoors but wants the look of Plus-X, he will just light the set so he can shoot with Plus-X. This idea of the *look* of a film stock is quite complicated, but it mostly has to do with issues of grain, color separation, and how stocks respond to under- and overexposure.

For now you should probably use the manufacturer's recommendation on the film's packaging, which will say that the stock has an EI of 50 or 320 or whatever. There will be a place to set the number on your light meter, and this should be done immediately. Once you have decided on a film stock and have set its EI on the light meter, the EI becomes a constant.

Color Balance

All types of light sources have their own color qualities. Daylight is generally somewhere close to white. Tungsten light, which includes the majority of indoor illumination and most motion picture lighting instruments, is reddish-orange (referred to here as *amber*). Fluorescent light is, unfortunately, green.

The film stock and our eyes respond to the color of these light sources differently. When we are under tungsten light, do we perceive it as amber? When we are under fluorescent light, do we perceive it as green? If you look carefully, you actually will perceive these colors. In reality, though, you probably don't pay much attention and average everything as a relatively even color—white. The film, of course, does see the difference. If a light source is amber, amber is the light reaching the film plane. *Color balance* refers to the way that color film stocks are designed for different types of light sources. If you are shooting in amber light (tungsten), the film stock must be appropriately balanced so we see that light as white.

The distinct color of a given source is rated by its *color temperature.* Color temperature is measured in degrees *Kelvin (K),* which refers to the temperature at which a black-bodied object—a surface that does not reflect light—changes color as it is heated. Most people have seen films on making steel and know that as metal is heated it changes color; first amber, then yellow, then white, and finally blue. The temperature at which the black object turns a specific color is arbitrarily assigned to the color of a light source. *Tungsten (T)* lamps rated for motion picture photography are 3,200° Kelvin. They produce the same color as a black-bodied surface when heated to 3,200°. *Daylight (D),* or photographic white, is 5,500° K. Other light sources will fall in the scale at different points. Standard household tungsten bulbs (40-watt, 60-watt, et cetera) are less, say 2,800° K or 2,900° K. Fluorescent light, lacking a true color temperature, is about 3,800° K. An overcast day will actually be blue and can range from just above 8,000° K to 20,000° K.

Tungsten and daylight color temperature are the two that are most important to photography (T = 3,200° K, D = 5,500° K). All color film stocks (color temperature is not an issue when shooting with black-and-white) will be balanced to one of these two. Shooting under the wrong light with the wrong film will yield strange results. Many have probably seen this in personal still photographs. If you shoot with daylight film under tungsten light, the film will come back with an orange cast. If tungsten-balanced film is shot in daylight, the film will come back with a blue cast.

So what is going on when you shoot under tungsten light with a film stock balanced for tungsten light? The color of the light is amber, but you want the film to read it as white or normal. The manufacturer has simply made the red layer of the film less sensitive than the green and blue layers. There is physically less emulsion that responds to the red area of the spectrum. Being less responsive to the red spectrum area, the film stock will take amber light and read it as white light. **SEE 8-2** Daylight stock is simply balanced to see white light as white.

The practical application of this seems simple: Just shoot with the right stock in the right situation. Of course, nothing is ever that simple. The first problem arises when you have to move from a tungsten situation to a daylight situation. Switching rolls can be time-consuming and require too much handling of the film, so a method was devised to use a stock balanced for one source under the other source. That is, there had to be a way to use either a film stock balanced for daylight under tungsten light or a film stock balanced for tungsten light in daylight.

For a variety of reasons, mostly having to do with versatility, the latter approach (choosing tungsten film and adapting it to daylight) is prevalent. To use tungsten film stock in a daylight situation, the adjustment is quite simple. Simply use an 85 filter, which is amber colored. **SEE 8-3** The 85 filter takes the white light of daylight and adds an amber component to it. The tungsten-balanced film, which reads amber light as white light, then renders that light as white. To state it another way, the 85 filter turns the white daylight amber, and the tungsten-balanced film stock then reads it as white.

Why bother going through all this? one might reasonably ask. It is because the opposite translation has tremendous drawbacks. Shooting daylight-balanced film stock under tungsten light requires the use of a deep-blue 80a filter. All filters will reduce the amount of light reaching the film plane. The 80a filter cuts out two and two-thirds stops of light, whereas the 85 cuts out just two-thirds of a stop.

8-2

The red layer of tungsten-balanced film is less sensitive than the green and blue layers, hence it is less responsive to the red spectrum

8-3

Using an 85 filter when shooting tungsten-balanced film in daylight turns the white light red, which the film then reads as white

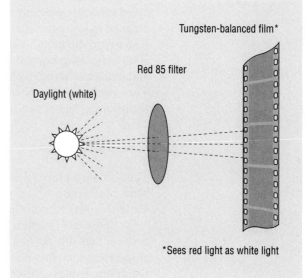

The problem becomes apparent in almost any situation in which you try to take a daylight stock into a tungsten situation, a circumstance in which you are usually going from a bright area (outside) to a darker area (inside). If you lose two and two-thirds stops of light to begin with, you may not have enough light to get an exposure. Add to this the probability that you started with a pretty low EI stock, needed for exteriors, and you can see how untenable the situation is.

The 85 filter makes much more sense because of its versatility. For that reason a majority of color film stocks, particularly those designed primarily for professional use, are balanced for tungsten light. For several years 16mm daylight-balanced color negative film stocks were not available from the most prominent manufacturers. This lack has been rectified, but tungsten-balanced film still dominates the field.

Most manufacturers recommend a different EI that automatically adjusts for the two-thirds of a stop lost by using an 85 filter. On the film's packaging, you will find one EI for tungsten light (T) and one EI for daylight (D). After the daylight EI, it will always say "with 85 filter." The daylight number is always lower than the tungsten number, and the "with 85 filter" is the reason why. The manufacturer is simply compensating for the lost light in the EI.

To make the correction from tungsten to daylight, glass front-filters can be mounted on the lens. Virtually all lenses have ring adapters that screw into the lens. Rather than use the front-filter method, some cameras have a filter slot directly in front of the film plane in which you can insert a small piece of *gel*, a colored, cellophane-like material that changes the color or quality of the light.

This is all still relatively uncomplicated. If you are outdoors shooting with a tungsten-balanced stock, you use the 85 filter. If you are indoors shooting in tungsten light, you do not. This issue would appear destined for the minor-details department, except that complexity is added when you encounter a mix of several sources with different color temperatures. Lighting crews spend a substantial amount of time on this, and it is an issue that eventually will have you jumping through hoops, too. (See chapter 15 for further discussion.)

Raw Stocks

As stated, film that has not been exposed to light is called *raw stock*. For beginning cinematographers the primary factor in the choice of a raw stock is usually the film's speed—the EI, or number that rates how sensitive a film stock is to light. Lower-speed stocks are generally more suitable for high-light conditions; higher-speed stocks are used in low-light situations. Lower-speed stocks have tighter grain structure and better reproduction of blacks than do higher-speed stocks, although the latter have shown dramatic improvement in recent years. Filmmakers with limited resources and smaller lights often choose the stocks with higher EIs, because of their versatility when working with low volumes of light and the greater depth of field achieved with the resulting higher f-stops.

COLOR STOCKS

The bulk of commercial work is done in color and is shot predominantly on negative. Most black-and-white shooting is done on reversal, although negative should be seriously considered for advanced projects.

Color reversal film stocks were very popular prior to the advent of video, because they did not require printing to be viewed. Applications where scratches and permanency were not major issues, such as television news and amateur sporting events, used miles of reversal film, because the film could be slapped onto a projector or telecine and shown as frequently as needed. Then it could be put on a shelf, or in a garbage can, never to be seen again. Once this "shoot and show" function was taken over by video, the higher quality of negative stocks ensured that they would become the standard for professional work, at least in color. There are a few color reversal stocks, but both lower image quality and inadequate lab support make them less desirable. The world has become a negative place, at least for color film.

There are presently two major producers of color film stock: Kodak and Fuji. Kodak remains the dominant producer, although Fuji has initiated aggressive marketing strategies. Check with the manufacturers about student discounts. Each manufacturer's film stocks have a slightly different look, both boasting excellent color rendition, tight grain structure, and good reproduction of dark areas in the frame. The best way to learn about the characteristics of individual stocks is to shoot the film and talk to labs and DPs who have dealt with the specific stocks.

The film stocks that these manufacturers produce change according to technological developments driven by the demands of the industry. Any list of stocks will eventually become out of date, although there are some considerations that remain constant. Film stocks are usually referred to by their numbers, for example, Kodak 7248 or Fuji F-500. Although 35mm has a more significant share of the market, the following discussion focuses on the 16mm stocks frequently used by students and independents. Most 16mm stocks have 35mm equivalents.

The chart at right shows the stocks designed for tungsten (T) that are available as of this writing. **SEE 8-4** All stocks come with two EIs, the lower rating for daylight (D) reflecting the compensation for the light lost when using the 85 filter.

The most surprising recent trend in film stocks has been the resurgence of daylight-balanced negative film stocks. Selection was very limited for many years, but demand has evidently convinced manufacturers that there is a market for it. In fact, Fuji even discontinued its low-rated tungsten stock, F-64, which was commonly used by filmmakers outdoors with the 85 filter. Higher-EI stocks had tight enough grain structure, and the daylight stocks were eliminating that use. Both Kodak and Fuji offer daylight-balanced stocks, both having one low-speed and one high-speed version. **SEE 8-5** The manufacturers generally do not list tungsten ratings on daylight film stocks, the 80a filter reducing the EIs to the extent (two and two-thirds stops)

	Kodak			Fuji	
	EXR Stock	Vision Stock	EI	Film Stock	EI
Low Speed	7248		100 (T) 64 (D)		
Midrange Speed	7293	7274	200 (T) 125 (D)	F-125	125 (T) 80 (D)
		7277	320 (T) 200 (D)	F-250	250 (T) 160 (D)
High Speed		7279	500 (T) 320 (D)	F-500	500 (T) 320 (D)
		7289	800 (T) 500 (D)		

8-4

Available tungsten-balanced stocks, including Kodak's Vision camera films

	Kodak		Fuji	
	Film Stock	EI	Film Stock	EI
Low Speed	7245	50 (D)	F-64D	64 (D)
High Speed	7246	250 (D)	F-250D	250 (D)

8-5

Available daylight-balanced stocks

that the stocks become harder to use. The higher-speed stocks are actually very difficult to use in bright exteriors, because the high EIs yield higher *f*-stops than many lenses have. They are primarily designed for arena and stadium shooting, where there are usually lights producing 5,500° Kelvin light or thereabout.

Kodak and Fuji also offer color reversal stocks. Fuji offers one high-speed stock. Kodak offers a total of four: a low-speed and a high-speed stock for both tungsten and daylight.

BLACK-AND-WHITE STOCKS

The preference for raw stock is the opposite in black-and-white, with reversal being the prevalent choice. Although a few notable exceptions come to mind, such as Spike Lee's *She's Gotta Have It* (1986), Steven Spielberg's *Schindler's List* (1993), and Martin Scorsese's *Raging Bull* (1980), the majority of black-and-white shot is on nonprofessional projects. This includes early student exercises and producers who have not switched over to video, such as at high schools that do not have adequate stadium lighting to support video. Thus, reversal is dominant and more plentiful than negative, and filmmakers will have an easier time finding competent processing. If the final product is going to be a film print or high-end transfer to video, however, negative should be carefully considered. You may have to do some modest searching for both the stock and high-quality laboratory services, but if image clarity is a goal, negative is the better choice.

	Kodak				Ilford	
	Negative		**Reversal**		**Negative**	
	Film Stock	**EI**	**Film Stock**	**EI**	**Film Stock**	**EI**
Low Speed	Plus-X	64 (T)	Plus-X	40 (T)	FP4	100 (T)
		80 (D)		50 (D)		125 (D)
High Speed	Double-X	200 (T)	Tri-X	160 (T)	HP5	200 (T)
		250 (D)		200 (D)		400 (D)

Kodak and Ilford are the only manufacturers producing black-and-white film. Each has two negative film stocks, and Kodak has two reversal film stocks. Black-and-white film stocks list an EI for both tungsten and daylight, the tungsten rating being lower. This, of course, has nothing to do with color temperature. Black-and-white film is less sensitive to the red area of the spectrum, and thus with the lower EI the manufacturer is recommending slightly more exposure under tungsten light. Black-and-white generally costs about two-thirds what color costs. **SEE 8-6**

Product catalogs list several other choices you need to make. One is whether to buy the film on core loads or daylight spools. This depends largely on the camera you are using and, to a lesser extent, the size of the shoot. Smaller cameras generally require 100-foot daylight spools. Although magazines can run daylight spools, 400-foot core loads are the professional standard for magazine-loading cameras. 35mm is available in 1,000-foot loads. Another choice in 16mm is between single- or double-perf film. Again, most producers shoot double-perf, because it is more versatile in editing, although single-perf is perfectly adequate for most applications.

Product brochures list catalog numbers and all ordering information. The film business being what it is, manufacturers are wary of sending stock without 100 percent guarantee of payment. Establish credit if possible or be ready to pay up-front. Personal checks generally must clear before shipments will be made. Credit cards open most doors.

Processing

Motion picture film has to be taken to a professional processing lab. Although the services required of a lab can become quite complex, initial services on a film usually consist of processing the original and making a workprint. Unlike still photography, where a short piece of film is loaded onto a small reel to be developed, motion picture film processing requires large tanks to accommodate the longer camera loads. The film is moved on rollers and literally dragged through the processing chemicals. This ensures that layers of film do not become sandwiched together, which would impede the chemical process.

Today finding the processing services you need may mean dealing with a number of far-flung labs. As with any other business, labs specialize, and students and independents outside of major urban centers may have to do some searching. Lab services are generally expressed in cents per foot. Processing might cost ten cents per foot, for example. Although the figures look small on paper, they add up quickly enough. A number of labs have student pricing, a boon to any on-the-edge producer. You might find one lab that charges forty-five cents per foot for processing and workprinting and another that charges twenty-five. The difference between these two prices may not amount to much for a commercial project, but for a student it can be a significant sum.

PRINTING

The processed original is then loaded on a *printer* to make the workprint. A piece of raw stock is sandwiched with the original, and the workprint is thus a frame-for-frame *contact print*. **SEE 8-7** Printers have one high-wattage bulb that shoots a single piece of bright light toward the film gate. In the path to the gate, there is an upper and a lower level of filters and front-surfaced mirrors, each positioned at a 45-degree angle. The upper level separates the light into its three primary colors—red, green, and blue. The now three separate paths of light have a shutterlike device that can be opened and closed to individually control the volume of each color in the print. These valves are generically referred to as the *printer lights*, and their role throughout the entire photographic process is essential. The path of the light generally resembles the illustration. **SEE 8-8**

  The first filter on the top row diverts all red light down through the light valve. It allows all the blue and green light to pass through to a second filter, which diverts the green light down to its own light valve. A front-surfaced mirror diverts the remaining blue light to a third valve that controls its volume. The bottom row recombines the three lights to expose the film at the printer gate. The intensity of the three primary colors of light in the printer can thus be adjusted to achieve an effect the DP is trying to obtain or to compensate for any mistakes in exposure or

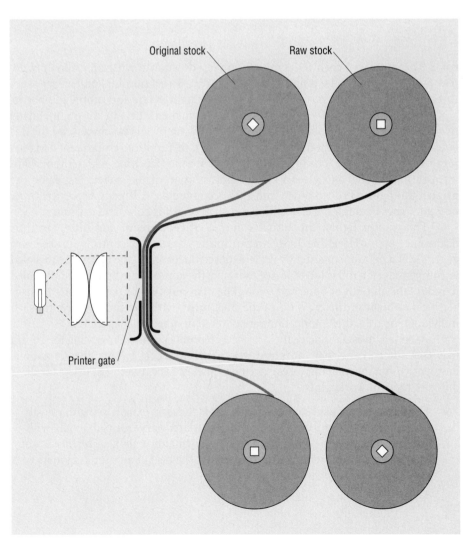

Original stock

Raw stock

Printer gate

8-7

Making a contact print involves sandwiching the processed film with a piece of raw stock

Path of light in film printing

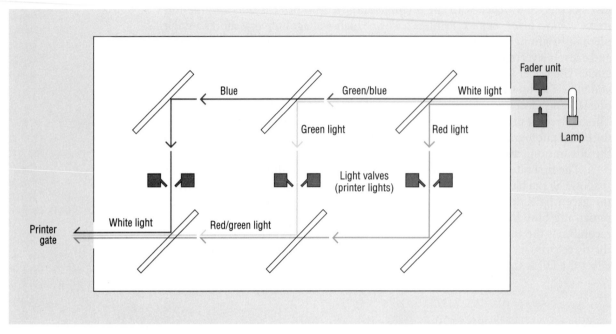

color. The control of each RGB color is broken down into what are called *printer points* on the printer. The points run from 0 to 50, with a nominal perfect exposure theoretically being right in the middle, with less light below and more light above.

If desired, prior to workprinting the original can be put on an analyzing machine, where overall color and exposure is evaluated. The machine used for this is generally a *Hazeltine,* though other companies have produced equipment designed for this purpose as well. The original is loaded into the Hazeltine, which shoots light through the original and gives a video representation of the image. Just as on the printer, this light is broken down into RGB components. A lab employee, the *timer* or *grader,* goes through the entire film and analyzes it for color and exposure.

The printer lights, the actual volumes of red, green, and blue, are thus determined on the Hazeltine. In the workprinting phase, these controls are used very generally. If a roll was consistently underexposed on location, the lights can be dialed to compensate; if a roll is too blue, for example, the appropriate light could be dialed to reduce the amount of blue, and so on. The manipulation of these printer lights is a critical element in the creation of the final print, with the timer analyzing each individual shot. Further applications are covered in detail in chapter 18.

As stated, most labs price their services in cents per foot. Processing for 16mm may cost fifteen cents per foot, and workprint may cost twenty-five. It sounds inexpensive, but the total increases extremely quickly. Labs usually list prices for three different types of workprints:

- **One light.** Also called *standard light,* this is the least expensive, with the lab using its accepted norm in the printer. Standards vary from lab to lab, with temperatures and processing times being the major variable. The film is not analyzed on the Hazeltine. This is often not the best choice for beginners, who may have exposure difficulties.

- **Best light.** This is more expensive and indicates that the timer will look through the negative and choose the best light for the entire roll. This is often the best approach for newcomers, who are learning the complexities of exposing and processing film.

- **Timed.** This indicates that the timer checks the original and determines the best printer light for each individual shot. This is a very expensive option and is used only infrequently, even for projects that might potentially have the budget to support it.

Communication about such issues should be as clear and unambiguous as possible. Mistakes are costly and could jeopardize the integrity of the exposed film itself. Other information that needs to be communicated to the lab is covered in chapter 10.

There are fewer motion picture laboratories today than there were twenty years ago, and finding the right one will take some research. The video revolution has reduced the demand for processing and, particularly, workprinting. This loss of business eliminated most of the labs that processed limited amounts of film, particularly in small urban areas. Only labs in the largest and most film-active American cities have been able to stay in business. Start collecting lab brochures and price lists to determine which ones provide the services you need at a price that is acceptable. As labs become more dependent on big jobs from commercials and feature films, finding high-quality processing and reliable service is becoming increasingly difficult for students and independents, a reality sadly complicated by irresponsible independents who fail to pay bills. Despite this, there are still many labs that wisely see newcomers as the future of the business. Try to talk to film teachers or independent filmmakers in your area to find out which labs have provided good service in the past.

Working with labs is one of the realities of the field, although jury-rigged processing can be done to create extraordinary effects. It is said that the North Vietnamese processed their propaganda films in garbage cans during the Vietnam War. The product was rough, but if anything the undiluted roughness added to the persuasiveness of the footage. One of the most beautiful student films I have ever seen was self-processed, with the sandwiching causing the sprocket patterns on the unprocessed layers to swirl in abstract designs. The approach is not useful, however, unless you are willing to accept the attendant effects.

EDGE NUMBERS

The workprint is used for all the hard work of editing, maintaining the pristine original as a later source for the production of prints of the finished film. The original is "conformed" to what the editor has done in the edited workprint. This process of matching the original to the workprint is generally done by a contracted professional called a *negative cutter* (see part V for a complete discussion of this part of the process). Clearly, reference points are needed between the workprint and the original. *Edge numbers,* also referred to by Kodak as *key numbers,* are latent information that each manufacturer photographically imprints between the sprocket holes on all raw film stocks. As the image is processed, the numbers develop as well and are printed through to the workprint, serving as critical guideposts for conforming the original film to the edited workprint.

Edge numbers come every twenty frames (6 inches) in 16mm and every sixteen frames (1 foot) in 35mm. **SEE 8-9** There are actually three sets of information. The

Edge numbers are used primarily as guideposts for conforming the original to the edited workprint

Zero frame

first set of letters and numbers (kM63 in figure 8-9) refer to the date produced and the emulsion batch. The other two sets (0646 and 6104) are part of a sequence of ascending numbers that go from the head of the film to the tail. The frame that is 20 frames toward the tail would be identified as 0646, 6105. Twenty frames farther on would be 0646, 6106, et cetera. Kodak is presently identifying what is referred to as the *zero frame,* the frame on which the counting of each sequence of 20 frames starts, by a small dot above the *K* (for Kodak) in the first set (kM63 in figure 8-9). On Fuji stock it is similarly placed above an *F*. The zero frame is important for the negative cutter in counting frames for matching the original and it has become even more important in preparing for a transfer to video.

The newest wrinkle in the edge number picture is the introduction of magnetic bar coding, called Keycode™ by Kodak and Mr. Code™ by Fuji, mostly used for referencing between videotape and film. Along with the still-present edge numbers, the bar codes are located between the sprocket holes and provide an electronic output of the corresponding edge numbers. The bar-coded edge numbers can be referenced with videotape in the process of transferring the film to video. Once a video edit is completed, the bar codes can be translated back to edge numbers and a film print can be made. This system sounds great in theory but has a number of pitfalls that are explored later. The bar codes can also be referenced for externally produced information mostly having to do with synchronizing sound.

VIEWING DAILIES

There is nothing quite so exhilarating as watching *dailies,* which is the footage from the previous day's work. All the painstaking effort that went into execution has a concrete representation in the final product. Viewing dailies, also called *rushes,* can be a tension-inducing experience as well. This is where you see any unpleasant surprises that were not anticipated during the shoot. With experience you should be able to avert any outright disasters, but there are almost always things that you wish were better.

Dailies should be watched with a critical eye from several perspectives. The first time through, thoroughly check the condition of the workprint and, by extension, the original. If there are flaws or damage, they should be identified and addressed at this stage. If you do not find the problem on the workprint, have the lab check the original. Damaged or dirty film is generally discarded and the material reshot, so be completely conversant with any flaws and identify their source immediately. If the problem is caused by the camera, early identification may avert further damage. In addition, the more the film is handled in editing, the more it will show stress. If you notice damage later in editing, you may wonder at what stage it occurred if the film is not checked at the start.

Video Applications

In many of its functions, the video camera is, of course, similar to the film camera. It has a focus ring, some form of exposure control, and a lens with something akin to a focal length—usually a zoom lens. Video equipment must address the same technical issues, yet filmmakers are often frustrated by the lack of clearly defined technical parameters in video. Issues that are reasonably concrete in film, particularly EI, depth of field, and exposure, become somewhat more slippery. All three of these issues are in some way dependent on the construction of the chip for individual video cameras, not necessarily on the technical quantification of light as they are in film.

Videotape does not have an EI as such, with sensitivity to light based not on the formulation of the tape in a way similar to the construction of the film emulsion, but rather on the number and design of pixels. Short for picture elements, pixels are the imaging sensing devices on the video camera's chip that translate the light it receives into an electrical signal. Theoretically, each model of video camera creates its own EI, with most newer cameras responding well in extremely low light situations. It is generally agreed that the EI for video is somewhere in the neighborhood of 200 to 320, but one needs to become familiar with how specific cameras perform under different lighting conditions. In terms of exposure, there is still a diaphragm in the video camera lens that could be, and occasionally is, calibrated in f-stops. The volume of light the lens transmits is the same, but the camera's response to that light varies on a camera-to-camera basis, again based on the design of the chip.

So video camera lenses have a focal length and an f-stop that are based on mathematical formulations just as in film. Despite this, depth of field and exposure are not generally taken into account in a similar fashion. In video as in film, depth of field is dependent on the size of the format being used—in video's case, the chip size. Wide-angle, normal, and telephoto focal lengths can be identified for each chip size, although video manuals rarely list depth-of-field charts, because there is not usually a specific f-stop and videographers tend to chart depth of field and focus effects by eye as the shots are being set up. This is a perfectly acceptable method except that it does hamper the ability to plan for focus effects in advance. For those who have a hard time abandoning the film approach, the three chip sizes roughly translate to the three basic film formats: A Super 8 chart is close to a one-third-inch chip, a 16mm chart can be used for a half-inch chip, and 35mm converts to two-thirds inch. That these are only rough equivalents should be emphasized. Depending on a film depth-of-field chart for precise focus parameters for video would be a mistake.

Although these issues can be frustrating, the method of handling color temperature is substantially easier in video. Color temperature is addressed in depth in chapter 15, but suffice it to say that, unlike photographic mediums, the video signal can be trimmed electronically to conform to virtually any color source—to see almost any color source as white; this is referred to as *white balance*. White balancing is done by holding a white card in front of the camera. Under tungsten light, for example, the white card will reflect the light's amber color. The camera will see this and adjust the levels of individual colors (RGB) until it sees the card as white. Thus everything shot under the tungsten light will read the light as white. This eliminates the need for color balance filters, particularly film's omnipresent 85 filter.

The 85 is not really a significant burden, but more-difficult lighting situations—fluorescent, mercury vapor, and so on—can be easily addressed in video. This brief discussion may appear to simplify the entire issue of color temperature, but it actually omits only a modest number of basic differences. One must still consider the more significant issue of matching color sources in front of the camera to each other, which is explored in detail in chapter 15.

Film-to-Video Transfer and Digital Editing

It is at this point that the divergence occurs between the old-fashioned—but virtually bulletproof—world of the conventional film edit and the bright new—but occasionally treacherous—world of digital *nonlinear editing (NLE)*. The video-editing world has largely abandoned the old, inflexible practice of analog video editing in favor of cutting digitized video on computer. The film world has, by necessity, kept up. The interface between the two mediums—and they are distinctly different—has been both very productive and very challenging.

The starting point is to transfer the film to video, with either analog or, preferably, digital video being the standard entrance point into the computer. Operating under the assumption that a film print is the final destination, there are two primary considerations when transferring. The first is to create the information that will eventually provide the negative cutter with edge numbers by which to conform the original film. The second is to maintain synchronization of the sound with the film. As we shall see, making both of these happen can be a daunting task.

THE BIG QUESTION

To pose again the initial question from chapter 1: Do you want your end product to be a film or a videotape? First, do not confuse the two. A film is a film and a videotape is a videotape. Each has its advantages and disadvantages, but one is not the other. Having shot your project on film, do you need to have a finished film? This is largely a question of exhibition and audience, although budgets are a major consideration as well. A film is meant to be projected on a theatrical screen and, although digital projection is slowly becoming a viable alternative, a videotape is generally destined for television. As of this writing, having only a videotape will limit exhibition possibilities. The following discussion should not be taken as the gospel of exhibition alternatives, but the general feeling remains that having a film in hand puts one in a better position. The Sundance Film Festival notwithstanding, most festivals and all theaters still project motion picture film. Many people who screen projects for festival inclusion will be more than happy to tell you that if they put out a call for video projects, they will get a thousand entries of which only a handful are possibilities. If they put out a call for projects that have a final film print, they will get a hundred or so entries, a third of which are worthy of careful consideration. No festival screening committee has time to sort through a thousand submissions. If the submitted project has been successful elsewhere, that might carry some weight. If a distributor has enough faith in a project to transfer it to film, that might really mean something.

Certainly, transferring to film from a finished videotape must be factored in here. The list of films employing this method continues to grow. And yet, as an independent, is it really an alternative? Even with a finished video product in hand, what distributor is going to want to put in the $70,000 to $100,000 to bump it over to film? It *has* happened—*The Blair Witch Project* (Eduardo Sanchez and Daniel Myrick, 1999) probably being the best example—but can you realistically count on this? This text's unapologetic bias toward film notwithstanding, the odds are not with you.

Barring transfer from video to film, if the decision is to have a finished film, you are faced with yet another question: Should you edit on film or edit in a digital environment and return to film for a print? Once again, this is a difficult decision. Film editing is hard, slow, painstaking work. NLE is popularly seen as being sexy, inexpensive, easy, fast, and what everybody is doing. Yes, it is sexy. No, it is doubtful that it will be any cheaper. In many ways and for many functions, it is easier. It is probably not any faster than other methods. And, yes, everybody is doing it—if they are finishing on tape. NLE is certainly used by a high percentage of people finishing on film, but the overwhelming number of projects finishing on videotape skews perceptions. And the expense is rarely part of the factoring. There are credible arguments for both film editing and NLE—as well as for some hybrid of the two.

If NLE is the final decision, life gets decidedly more complicated. *Matchback*—the creation of the information needed to return from a digital edit to the camera original negative—requires a set of operating principles that require careful consideration. Speed and frame rate conversions are the chief villains here, with the intrinsic differences between film and video creating as many challenges as film editing. The challenges may be different, but they are every bit as demanding.

A substantial part of the battle is won or lost with the initial transfer from film to videotape. Suffice it to say that if you do not get the project started correctly, matchback information will be flawed all the way down the line, and the end product will be riddled with unacceptable errors that are very expensive to correct. Technical aspects of the film finishing process are complex and require comprehension before exploring matchback. Therefore the bulk of the information on matchback here is given in the context of editing in part V. What follows are a few of the initial concepts, procedures, and complexities involved in returning to film. Frankly, there is much in the digital realm that requires extensive technical study and which is really not feasible to present in this context. The object here and in later chapters is to make you aware of potential problems so that you can ask the right questions when you start working with the lab personnel and technicians who will be involved in the process. The following discussion may at times make this whole matchback relationship appear to be untenable, but many filmmakers are making it work even on very small budgets.

The bottom line for choosing a film finish or a video finish boils down to whether you want to project a motion picture or exhibit a videotape. Before committing, carefully think out your options here—with potential audience and what kind of exhibition you can honestly expect your piece to receive being major considerations. Dealing with edge numbers, frame rates, slowdowns, color accuracy, and a host of other issues will become your lot in life.

THE TELECINE

There are a number of ways to transfer film to video, from the relatively inexpensive methods to those that can make film costs look reasonable. Unless you are after some specialized visual goal, color negative film is shot on location with the image being reversed in the transferring process. There are essentially two practical ways of transferring film to video. The *flying spot scanner* approach, employed on the majority of professional transfer machines, uses a strong piece of light that is shot through the film; it rapidly scans each frame, separating out the RGB components to create the video image. The second method employs a *charge-coupled device (CCD)* arrangement, with light shot through the film striking a chip with thousands of light-sensitive pixels. The receptacle here is relatively similar to the configuration in a typical video camera, with the high-end systems also separating the light into RGB components. Both methods scan the image horizontally, with telecines scanning in 525 lines of information in NTSC product and 625 lines in *PAL,* the European standard.

The crudest CCD systems essentially shoot a video camera into a film projector with a five-bladed shutter—a common approach for consumer transfers. These are not very costly and are unacceptable by professional standards. Typically, professional telecine sessions cost in the neighborhood of $500 per hour, with the most in-demand southern California and New York houses commanding substantially more. The telecine is operated by the video *colorist,* a role akin to that of the timer in a chemical lab. A telecine session can be either supervised or unsupervised, meaning that the colorist can do either an equivalent of a "best light" workprint or a "timed" workprint. In an *unsupervised transfer,* the colorist will create global settings for the transfer, then sit back and monitor the tape. In a *supervised transfer,* the colorist will do *scene correction,* stopping and analyzing every scene for color and exposure. Just as with the film contact printer, the colorist will have full control over RGB characteristics as well as a host of other "sweetening" options. Possibilities for image manipulation here abound, although if the project is returning to the film negative for a final print, you'll need to know if the effects can be duplicated in the printing process.

Although supervised sessions are usually only slightly more expensive on a facility's rate sheet, the critical difference is how much footage can be transferred per hour. Supervised transfer may logically go through about 400 feet per hour, whereas unsupervised might go as high as 1,200 feet. Many facilities offer good discounts for students, and the customer can often attend, if willing to pay a little extra—they (we) by nature can slow things down.

Observant readers will realize that a supervised workprint is akin to the rarely requested timed workprint; however, the video that the colorist creates will in many cases be the source for the final product and require very little extra attention during the project's completion. With a conventional film finish, on the other hand, all correction will happen in the very last stages. It is matter of putting the attention (and dollars) in at the very beginning rather than in the final stages. Many projects will require this high-quality initial transfer, but such is not always the case. It is not uncommon to edit with a lower-quality video copy, with the intention of returning to the original to finish. In this case returning to the original may indicate a high-quality transfer that was done earlier, or going all the way back to the film negative itself for scene-by-scene transfers. In the latter case, a negative cutter would pull the indicated shots from "flash to flash"—from the flash frame at the beginning to the flash frame at the end. Another method is to have the telecine operator role to the indicated takes and do a corrected transfer of just the needed material. In both instances the entire project can be rebuilt with high-quality elements. When working with a low-res version, one is working with something akin to a video workprint. In both cases it is necessary to know the endgame before you blindly choose a transfer method.

Understanding what happens on the telecine is of paramount importance in making sure that matchback to the original film will be possible. Part of the present problem is that there are very few people who truly understand all the issues pertaining to matchback. Misinformation or inadequate information abounds, particularly among video-trained postproduction personnel who finish within a digital environment and do not have to deal with the complex film stuff. When you start talking to filmmakers and lab personnel, you will hear legions of horror stories about films coming back with the sound out of sync or with the wrong shots inserted. The past few years have seen a painful process of working out the bugs. We are at last approaching the bulletproof nature of the conventional film finish, but there are still many problematic occurrences, and there are not many "happy accidents" here. A number of photographic considerations are handled in later chapters; the following is a brief overview of the many issues that must be considered.

Basic Definitions

To better understand the relationship between film and video, it is important to understand the key considerations when going to the telecine. There is a whole laundry list of concerns.

BROADCAST QUALITY

Broadcast quality refers to the incorporation of a video image that meets certain emission standards. In a manual, equipment fulfilling this requirement is listed as meeting *RS-170A standards*. Although these standards are based on objective technical specifications, including signal-to-noise ratio, resolution, and color accuracy, among others, just what constitutes a broadcast-quality signal can be a matter of some disagreement. The problem is that most professional equipment exceeds the established standards to the extent that many people in the field subjectively establish higher standards. Although a hard-and-fast definition of broadcast quality is elusive, amateur video is not generally considered of sufficient quality to gain wide use. There are, of course, the home-video-clip TV shows, and the lower-image quality of the submitted clips clearly demonstrates the differences.

OFF-LINE AND ON-LINE

With the many new powerful NLE systems and consumer computers with massive hard drives, off-line and on-line are becoming less of an issue but still warrant attention. The distinction between off-line and on-line concerns the working methods in finishing a project. An *off-line editing system* is used to make all the basic editorial decisions; an *on-line editing system* is used to finish the project, with broadcast quality being one major issue. Going back to an earlier discussion, off-line systems employ a lower-quality image—a video workprint or low-resolution digitized version. Off-line editing systems are less sophisticated, often lacking the hardware and software designed to manipulate the image and create optical effects. Their primary advantage is that they provide a low-cost place for the time-consuming process of making editorial decisions. They also require less space on the computer, allowing the editor to store more material from which to choose or to work on bigger segments. Thus the intention is to return to a higher-quality image and finish on a more sophisticated system—an on-line system. Many production companies have on-line facilities but, more often than not, finishing means going to an expensive professional studio. Working off-line saves the time with the expensive gear for when many of the decisions have already been made.

Though the idea of not working on a finished product may seem peculiar, it is worthwhile to remember that film editing is essentially an off-line process. You are editing a workprint that must be taken to a lab to create a finished product.

RESOLUTION AND STORAGE

This brings up another key consideration which is how, and at what resolution, you want the material captured. *Resolution* refers to the number of pixels devoted to each individual image. The software you are using will have a number of choices as to the rate at which the video image can be transferred; 640×480 is the typical resolution for broadcast quality. The resolution at which you digitize has implications for both off-line/on-line editing and information storage—issues that pertain to finishing on either film or video.

Many NLE system manufacturers promote their products as being able to do an on-line edit of your project. This is indeed the case, but the question is whether you have enough storage to hold the project at the resolution required for a broadcast-quality finish. The general rule is that at the highest resolution, 4 minutes of video requires about 1 gigabyte. All the footage required for a feature would obviously require an enormous amount of storage. The solution is often to capture at a lower resolution and return to a higher-quality image in either an on-line video environment or with film.

If you can cut on-line from the very start, this clearly can avoid a time-consuming on-line finish later. But cutting on-line is expensive, and storage is an issue. Typically, commercials can work-on line because they start with a reasonably small amount of footage. A typical feature, uncomplicated by extensive digital effects and digitized at a moderate resolution, requires somewhere in the neighborhood of 60 to 100 gigabytes of storage. The only problem with working with a lower-resolution image is that the editing team can sometimes lose track of the quality of the shots. This has been a major consideration in the feature world and has been addressed in ways that are explored later in this text.

TIME CODE

As explained in chapter 1, *time code* is simply a perfect-time rolling clock that is recorded on a track on the videotape. Designed to address the failings of the basic control track, time code reads in hours, minutes, seconds, and frames. You can base this rolling clock on the hour of the day, determine an individual start point for each tape, or have new start points for whatever you choose while shooting on location. The advantage of time code is that when a frame is identified, it can be returned to at any point during editing. Unless removed for some reason, the numbers are consistent throughout the life of the tape. If time code has not been recorded during shooting, it can be introduced by *striping* the video—recording externally produced though equally functional reference times. The application and use of time code is a constant presence during shooting and particularly in the editing room.

THREE:TWO PULL-DOWN

The first significant complication to be addressed is the conversion from the 24 frames of film to the 30 frames of video. Film frames must be converted to distinct video frames, and the numbers simply do not add up. The strategy that has become the industry standard to resolve this difference incorporates a change in the fields, not in the frames—what is called *three:two pull-down*. The strategy is for the telecine to print a third field of every second film frame, thus alternately printing two video fields of one film frame and then three fields of the next film frame, hence the name. **SEE 8-10** In this fashion 60 video fields becomes divisible by the 24 frames of film: 12 film frames are printed twice for 24; the other 12 frames are printed three times each for 36; 24 plus 36 equals 60.

The irregular duplication of fields is generally not visible to the eye. The problems occur when attempting matchback to film. In film one-sixth of a second is divided into 4 frames, whereas in video one-sixth of a second is 5 frames. The videotape thus has a frame that does not correspond to any film frame. We could potentially make the cut on that frame in the video edit and, when we go back to the film, find that there is no corresponding frame. We could move our cut to the next frame, but the whole thing plays havoc with timing. In addition, any frame of video that corresponds to a film frame (two field or three field) represents a different fraction of a second than a film frame. Systems have found ways to resolve these issues, but not without some dramatic jumping through hoops.

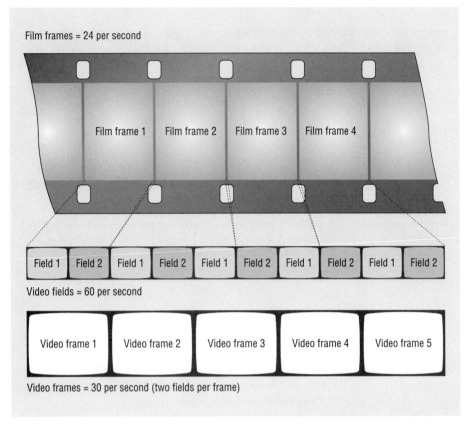

8-10

In three:two pull-down, four film frames are converted into five video frames

A, B, C, AND D FRAMES

As suggested, the great complication of three:two pull-down is that it creates information that does not correspond directly to the film frames. Fields unfortunately only complicate this issue. If not addressed in setup, the telecine does not necessarily start printing on a first field of a frame on the videotape. The first frame transferred from a film roll could land on a second and first field, respectively, causing further confusion as to its relationship to its sister or brother film frame. With some film frames occupying three fields as opposed to two, the confusion multiplies. To sort this out when transferring from film, video frames are referred to by the type of frame they are in terms of their relationship to the fields. They are designated as either *A, B, C, or D frames*. The A frame is two video fields, starting on a first field. The B frame also starts on a first field, but is three fields long. The C frame starts on a second field and is two frames long; and the D frame also starts on a second field and is three frames long. **SEE 8-11** As suggested, if the telecine is started randomly, the first film frame could potentially fall on the second field of one video frame and the first field of the next, making it a C frame, or it could also be three fields long, making it a D frame.

Suffice it to say that as troublesome as this conversion appears, the whole system will be unacceptably flawed if the transfer is not done correctly. It is critical that the first frame of film on a roll—or, more accurate, what we designate as the first frame of film—have a direct relationship with a video frame. The only frame where this is the case is the A frame, so the telecine must start on a designated first film frame and transfer to an A frame of video. To prefigure ensuing discussions, the solution to this has been to put a hole punch in the frame with the first legible edge number on the film roll. Legibility is crucial, because the light-struck portion at the beginning of a roll may obliterate some numbers, causing them to be unreadable by the telecine.

Types of converted film frames are identified as A, B, C, or D frames

Film frame 1   Film frame 2   Film frame 3   Film frame 4

A   **B**   **C**   **D**

| Field 1 | Field 2 | Field 1 | Field 2 | Field 1 | Field 2 | Field 1 | Field 2 | Field 1 | Field 2 |

Two fields starting with field 1   Three fields starting with field 1   Two fields starting with field 2   Three fields starting with field 2

The punched frame allows the telecine operator to start the transfer in a way that will make these critical relationships understandable later. Check with your telecine operator to make sure that you fully understand these issues.

PULL-UP/PULL-DOWN

Not only does the frame conversion have to be reconciled, but there are speed issues as well. This has caused many otherwise strong-minded people, from the innocent neophyte to the most seasoned technician, to want to pull their hair out. The speed conversion issue is referred to as *pull-up* and *pull-down,* and it is not to be confused with three:two pull-down, as it is a completely different, albeit related, concern.

As stated earlier, though we refer to video as running at 30 frames per second, it actually runs at 29.97 fps—although in its initial black-and-white days it was recorded at a true 30 fps. The story goes (and this may be more media mythology than video vérité) that when color came in, the technicians found that the technical character of the color video signal caused an unwanted artifact in video playback. Some anonymous technician, whose memory shall live in infamy, experimented and found that if he slowed the tape slightly (0.1 percent to be exact) the problem disappeared. At that point video speed became 29.97 fps.

Herein lies the source of the great quandary. When film is transferred to video, it is slowed down by 0.1 percent. Clearly, the change in motion is not visible to the eye, but the slowdown can have many repercussions and is most problematic in the synchronization of sound, which is recorded separately on location. One-tenth of 1 percent does not sound like a great amount, but it can add up over the course of a longer show, to the extent that the project will be substantially out of sync. It amounts to 1.8 frames per minute (a problem, but not a show-wrecker) and thus 18 frames every 10 minutes (almost a full second out of sync and obviously unacceptable). The solution is to slow down the sound by that same 0.1 percent when it is either transferred to video or digitized from its original source; hence *pull-down.* When it is later returned to film, the sound must be speeded back up; hence *pull-up.*

Postproduction facilities that are experienced with matchback are very familiar with this issue, but you must make sure that everyone down the line understands both what the final and intermediate destinations are. Failure to address this at any step will result in sound drifting unacceptably out of sync. You must also understand how the playback of the primary sound format (such as DAT, quarter-inch, or cassette) is going to be manipulated to facilitate the slowdown. Most newer recorders, particularly those with time-code capabilities, are set up for this, but there are some, particularly older gear, with which your audio may require expensive manipulation in postproduction.

When you start interfacing film and video, you get into a conflict between a world of whole numbers (film) and a world of fractions (video). The bottom line is that you have to keep track of which environment is film and which is NTSC. When you exit the film world—that is, transfer film to video—you enter NTSC. Everything drops down by 0.1 percent, with the synchronization of sound being the critical consideration. When you reenter the film world, everything must be sped up again. Every time you go back and forth, pull-up/pull-down must be addressed.

FORMATS

The last decision is to what *format* you want to transfer. Again, this is the usual set of suspects (Mini DV, DVCPRO, DVCAM, Digi Beta, three-quarter-inch) but as always you need to think about the end product. For the amateur and beginning professional, it probably makes most sense to use the Mini DV format.

FLEX FILES AND ORGANIZATION

A *flex file* is a data/text file employed on multiple platforms that interrelates the edge numbers of film with the time code of the transferred videotape. This is input either manually or electronically at the telecine stage. Obviously this data encoding must be done properly or everything down the road will be flawed. The lab should give the flex files to you on a floppy disk, and they should be referenced against the edited project in the finishing process. Not all software supports the flex file concept, but a recordkeeping feature is critical to the telecine process.

The flex files and similar approaches are critical, yet there still needs to be an overarching organizational scheme to keep the project manageable. A number of NLE programs include proprietary organizational features to keep track of edge numbers, time-code numbers, and the many other pieces of information that are of concern. Film Logic™ by Focal Point Systems Inc., which was recently acquired by Macintosh, is a typical example of such a program. It will undoubtedly be the proprietary product for Final Cut Pro (FCP). It manages the flex files and electronically monitors all relationships among numbering systems. It also keeps track of the *edit decision lists (EDLs)*, and when the appropriate time comes will easily produce a list of edge numbers for the negative cutter.

In summary, both three:two pull-down and pull-up/pull-down require that you carefully control all issues of frames and sync if you wish to go back to film. This must be done in the initial transfer. Once transferred, different NLE systems have devised strategies to further address these complications. Some of the specifics are addressed in part V of this text. Once you enter the video world—that is, transfer your film to video—you are there for good if you have not created the appropriate information in the telecine process. Unless you do a very expensive video-to-film transfer or go back upstream to redo an expensive transfer, you will be trapped forever in the confines of the video world.

Capturing Video

Capture is the term used for getting your media into a computer. Novices often blanche at all the preparation that has to occur before a film edit, but capture and its attendant requirements can be equally time-consuming. Occasionally, you will see the capture process referred to as *digitizing,* but digitizing is necessary only when the source is an analog videotape, say, a VHS tape or any other conventional tape format. *Digitizing* an analog source can be accomplished either by transferring the material to a digital camera or VCR or by employing specific hardware. Sony makes a popular product that can digitize the signal as it goes into the computer. If your source is already digital—from Mini DV, DVCPRO, Digi Beta, or whatever—it simply needs to be captured. With the appropriate hardware, most NLE software can capture from any video medium, but it is probably most convenient to capture from a signal that is already digital.

There are a number of ways to capture, but the most common is to use an *external video device* that is controlled by your computer and the NLE software. Referred to as *deck control,* the system employs the VCR function on a camera or a standard VCR designed for the purpose. The source deck essentially becomes peripheral, with the standard functions of the deck (*play, pause, fast-forward,* and so on) taken over by the appropriate windows in the software. On newer computers, whether on Macintosh or PC, the data is transferred from the camera to the computer via *FireWire.* The typical home desktop situation will employ the camera as the external video device for maximum efficiency. **SEE 8-12** Most newer computers come "media ready," but some may require a media card to interface the interlaced video of an NTSC source to the progressive scan of the computer.

As detailed in previous sections, the first step is to have your film transferred to video. The resulting tape is loaded into the deck used in your desktop setup. Capture is generally a function in one of the menus in the NLE software. In Final

8-12

Rear view of the Sony VX-1000 in VCR mode and with FireWire attached

8-13

The Log and Capture window in Final Cut Pro

Cut Pro, it is referred to as Log and Capture, indicating the importance of both getting media into the computer and properly organizing it. You will find that scrupulous organization is of paramount importance, maybe even more so than in film editing. The Log and Capture window will open, and you will be presented with a variety of options. **SEE 8-13**

Under Capture Settings in Final Cut Pro, you select the media you want to input. The choices are generally between capturing video and audio together, video by itself, or audio by itself. The first option would typically be for material that originated on video, because picture and sound are together on the tape. Because sound and picture are recorded separately on a film shoot, capturing the two together is not usually an option. Once captured individually, sound and picture must then be synced up just as in the conventional film approach. This said, many telecine facilities offer the service of syncing up the location audio during the telecine process and, if you had chosen this rather expensive option, you may be capturing them together. Still, the individual capture functions are used extensively for *MOS* footage (footage without sound) and nonproduction sound such as music, effects, and narration. Farther down in audio settings, there will be a choice of how to input the sound. Most NLE timelines open with two initial tracks of audio, and most software makers recommend that you capture the audio to both tracks to ensure stability. Generally, the choices are to input the sound in stereo, left channel only, right channel only, or both—the last one being the manufacturer's recommendation.

Some software will have this option elsewhere, but in many the capture window will also have a setting for the desired resolution.

When you select Log and Capture from the FCP menu, a screen will appear with a *play* function and markers for in- and out-points. Shots, called *clips* in most NLE software, are generally captured individually rather than in sequences or groups. Sound is typically handled in a similar fashion. One simply *scrubs*—moves slowly frame by frame—to the first frame of the shot and clicks the in-marker, then scrubs to the last frame of the shot and clicks the out-marker. It is usually a good idea to capture the entire shot rather than attempt to be discriminating and capture just the part of the shots you think you are going to use. First, as the editing progresses your ideas may change about what you need and, second, there is a general rule in editing to not mix editorial stages. Mixing functions will draw already tedious start-up processes to unbearable lengths.

8-14

The dialog box for logging clips in Final Cut Pro

Once you have marked the in- and out-points, the capture window offers a logging function. **SEE 8-14** This gives you a place to identify the clip, establish its location on tape rolls, and register any pertinent information. Slating shots is covered in depth in chapter 10; suffice it to say here that a numbering system is created while shooting and these numbers should supply the needed information in the logging part of the capture process. Staying organized in a film edit is extremely important, but the editor in NLE is hopelessly lost without it. With film there are pieces to refer to and search for; with NLE all you have is a bunch of icons and what is written down, and if the text is flawed or incomplete you will find yourself spending more time searching data files than editing.

Once the clip is logged in FCP, an icon with a diagonal red line through it appears in the *bin*—the window where unedited clips are stored. This means that the clip has been identified, logged, but not yet actually captured. There are three different methods of capturing, all essentially duplicated in most other NLE software. The choices are: Clip, Now, and Batch. *Clip* is for capturing individual shots and/or sounds; *Now* is for capturing on the fly; *Batch* is for capturing a number of previously logged clips. Now, of course, precludes previous logging and is for capturing a bunch of material quickly. It is often good for finessing in material that does not have appropriate time code. **Batch capture** is for when you have logged a number of clips and want to bring them in in one process. Batch is the preferred method, with the editor logging quite a few clips, then allowing the software to do the rest.

Once you have logged a number of clips, you click Batch capture. The software prompts you for verification, then, when you click OK, the capture process begins. The software instructs the camera or VCR to back up and cue at the first shot logged; that shot is then captured, and the camera will cue up the second clip, and so on. The same process occurs for sound.

Once you have everything in the computer, editing can proceed. Of course, you may have to do some syncing up (see chapter 17), but otherwise you are set to go.

Part III

Shooting

9

Composition

As in painting and graphic design, *composition* in film refers to the arrangement of shapes, volumes, and forms within an artistic frame. It is a key—possibly *the* key— element in a film's overall visual design. There are many films in which the composition is formulaic and uninspired. More often than not the composition is thoughtful and workmanlike. On a few celebrated occasions, the composition is inspired, taking the film into that rare arena of visual poetry. Whether or not it reaches this lofty status, effective composition is rarely noticed. There are, however, poorly composed films that leave the viewer unsatisfied, with the uncomfortable feeling that something is amiss—that the film is creating a world that is not only out of balance but also lacks internal cohesion.

Whereas a painter has the ability to thoughtfully predetermine the positioning of elements in a composition, the filmmaker has a more complicated task. This, of course, is because of the added dimension of movement. The key to composition for the film frame is the awareness that composition is dynamic, always in flux, ever changing. Whether you are dealing with camera movement, subject movement, or both, the elements in the frame will almost always be changing position, and you have to think out each composition in terms of what is occurring at all times. You can start out with a perfectly balanced frame, and one small movement by a character—something as simple as shifting body weight—can make the composition fall apart, the frame becoming completely unbalanced. Thus, the person shooting has to plan a response to the movement of both the subject being filmed and the camera itself.

The Director of Photography

Effective filming can be done by a single person with a camera or by a full-scale feature crew. Whether working on your own or with a crew, the creativity and care needed for effective shooting remains consistent. The *director of photography (DP)* has two primary responsibilities: composition and lighting. There are also many unstated expectations. Primary among these is the ability to evaluate whether the individual shots work within the greater context of the film. This can range from simply making sure the shots look good, to making sure that they have the appropriate pace and dynamic visual energy, to—most important—evaluating on a shot-by-shot basis whether the shots will cut together. A DP with experience in the editing room brings a valuable perspective to the process.

When you view a film, you are looking at someone's (the DP's) conscious approach to composition. He or she has had to *line up the shots*—that is, look at what is in front of the camera and decide how to arrange it in relation to the boundaries of the film frame. Beginners quickly learn that there is a big difference between looking through a camera and shooting. Anyone can look through a camera, but it takes a creative eye to produce framings that are both consistently dynamic and part of a cohesive vision of the whole.

The DP's role is obviously central. Many beginners venture into filmmaking with an innocently formed intent to become a DP. Indeed, there is a certain romance to the camera. It sits at the center of attention on a set, almost like a throne, with its minions scurrying about, ministering to its needs. Once you learn a little about the camera, however, you realize that a DP has to be part mathematician, part magician, and part personnel manager. It soon becomes clear that people have very high expectations of you. Beyond serviceable composition, the unwritten expectation is that you will bring life and animation to the subject—even if that subject is somewhat less than spellbinding on its own. I know DPs who cannot sleep the night before big shoots, with butterflies created by the tension associated with high expectations. There is no substitute for getting it right, and there are hundreds of things that will conspire against the easy execution of even the simplest shots.

The Frame

Beyond content issues that can be analyzed on an interpretative level, the formal elements of a *frame* demand equal consideration. The term *formal* refers to the choices one makes beyond the narrative structure of a film—the lighting, the camera angles, employment of movement, and all the other resources discussed in the menu in chapter 3. In a sense, *structure* is the straight line of the narrative, and *form* is the variation in the presentation of details from that line. When Jim Jarmusch uses single takes to cover scenes in *Stranger Than Paradise* (1984), the scenes themselves and their order are the structural elements and the single take is the formal approach. When cinematographer Haskell Wexler pre-exposes film to create a milky, old-feeling image in Hal Ashby's film biography of Woody Guthrie, *Bound for Glory* (1976), that is a formal approach. Mira Nair's *Mississippi Masala* (1992) is suffused with red, creating a visual analogy for the ease and warmth with which the people live. Color, shape, the play between light and dark, the texture of the image, the dynamics of movement, and a host of other formal elements—all add immeasurably to the impact of an image. More than simply establishing atmosphere or mood, formal elements shape the way we perceive characters and events.

Composition should never be looked at schematically or as being dominated by any unbreakable rules. There are, however, a number of commonly accepted principles that need to be considered. Examples that illustrate these principles could go on forever, as could examples of exceptions—compositions that play against accepted conventions. The goal here is to put forth a few straightforward ideas that can serve as an impetus for further exploration on your own.

BALANCE AND THE FRAME, AND THE RULE OF THIRDS

The dominant compositional principle, the ***rule of thirds,*** is a guideline for creating a balanced frame, by drawing four lines that divide the frame into thirds horizontally and vertically. **SEE 9-1** Areas and objects of visual interest are then put on these lines to balance the composition.

The rule of thirds is a guideline for creating a balanced frame

A typical rule-of-thirds framing
Terrence Malick's *Badlands*

Balance is a key to and a natural component of composition. Both human perception and movement are dependent on a sense of equilibrium. Observation has shown that human beings want literally to have both feet on the ground when either confronting visual phenomena or moving through them.[1] The human eye—actually, the processes of the mind—relentlessly attempts to impose balance on natural phenomena. The mind can find balance in triangles, abstracting a center point or finding an axis that balances the weight of the form. Rectangles and squares immediately suggest their own internal balance. Trapezoids and a number of other shapes lend themselves to similar treatment.

Other shapes announce balance less openly but still lend themselves to the eye's desire for equilibrium. Circles have no immediate balance, and yet the eye will be drawn to the center, create an axis, and thus suggest balance. Even completely free-form shapes will often have some center of balance. Forms that do not suggest balance are said to have stress, which is discussed in the next section.

Just as the eye looks for order in abstract shapes, it desires to impose order on an artistic frame—a composition. The rule of thirds simply gives artistic form to this natural human ability to create balance. Whereas balance in painting and still photography is at least superficially straightforward, balance in film is complicated by movement. Many framings that look unstable by themselves are balanced by movement. Still, some relatively straightforward examples can be shown. Terrence Malick's *Badlands* is an engagingly visual film. One scene, roughly halfway into the film, has Kit (Martin Sheen) aimlessly walking across the plains. **SEE 9-2** The horizon is on the bottom thirds line, with the moon in the upper left, balancing Kit on the right.

Fritz Lang's *Scarlet Street* (1945, Milton Krasner, DP) has a wealth of examples of classic balanced compositions. One scene has a group of reporters questioning the main character during a train ride. **SEE 9-3** The balancing of the three faces, the two characters on the vertical thirds lines, and the hands with the cards is a classic balanced composition and also a common strategy for handling a shot with three people.

It may be difficult for the experimental part of our nature to admit, but the rule of thirds is the basis for much film composition. Its application can be so conventional and lead to so much predictable composition that one almost wishes there might be another starting point. The rule of thirds is a natural reflection of human perceptual experience, however, and must be given careful consideration. If you were to take four strips of film tape and put them on your television set according

1. Much of the experimentation regarding the psychological ordering of perceptual experience has been done from the perspective of Gestalt psychology. Donis A Dondis's *A Primer for Visual Literacy* (Cambridge, Mass.: MIT Press, 1974) and the work of Rudolph Arnheim are excellent sources for those interested in the studies of perceptual experience.

to the thirds lines, the results would be stunning. You could marvel at the power of a simple straightforward composition or agonize over the depressing sameness of it all. Whether you are looking at a routine television show, a studio-age Hollywood film, or the most on-the-edge narrative piece, the lines would almost invariably intersect obvious areas of interest within the compositions. Although one may want to venture past this fundamental principle, the rule of thirds remains a starting place.

9-3

This classic balanced composition is a common strategy for handling shots with three characters
Fritz Lang's *Scarlet Street*

An acquaintance of mine sniffed when I mentioned that I teach students the rule of thirds. "A recipe for boring composition," he intoned. Despite the snootiness of the comment, there is a certain amount of truth there. Composition should be arresting and dynamic rather than formulaic and conventional. The past one hundred–plus years of modern painting have been a direct reaction against conventions dating to the ancient Greeks and further formalized during the Renaissance. And yet one has to learn how to draw a straight line before one can draw anything else. The notion that "anything goes" can be an even more disastrous recipe for composition. There is a big difference between composition that is new and challenging and composition that comes out of nowhere and is bad. Like it or not, a high percentage of the composition you see derives from some form of the rule of thirds.

GENERAL DESIGN CHARACTERISTICS

Working DPs frequently invoke the names of great artists when discussing their approach to specific films. With the goal of creating rich, complex, and subtle images, a study of the historical development of the graphic arts—painting, graphic design, and photography—provides valuable schooling for the inexperienced cinematographer. A knowledge of the breadth of approaches to the arrangement of elements in a composition, the handling of line and shape, the shaping and direction of light, and the incorporation of content elements to produce meaning informs the framing and arrangement of any image.

Student images are frequently criticized for concentrating on foreground elements (the subject) to the exclusion of a shot's background—an idea that is more complex than simply what is behind the subject. It is that extra information, that detail, that gives an image its context and character. This does not mean that cinematographers need to be imitative of specific works, nor should their work become static and arty. Just as there are books of painting and still photography designed for the coffee table, there can be coffee-table movies. But the sense that a composition can have a "painterly" quality is a key first step in moving toward a necessarily complex approach to the image.

A short list of conventional design characteristics will necessarily leave many things out. Images dominated by horizontals tend to be restful and suggest stability. Verticals suggest strength and power. As might be suspected, diagonals tend to suggest imbalance, although when employed in highly structured arrangements, diagonals can create powerful images as well. The German expressionists, in their fascination with heroic myth, created paintings and films with dominant vertical elements. Leni Riefenstahl's famous and notorious *Triumph of the Will* (1935), an ode to Adolf Hitler and the Nazi Party, is an excellent example of a film that uses vertical and diagonal compositional elements to suggest strength and power.

9-4

Costume and arrangement of peripheral characters
direct viewer attention
Milos Forman's *Amadeus*

Color is a key element in creating associations and tone. Blue is considered a cool color, both emotionally and physically. Red is hotter, suggesting warmer emotional content. Browns and greens are earth tones, suggesting naturalness and security. Lushness and brightness play a significant role in the texture of an image, as do muted and desaturated tones.

Compositions can also be arranged to direct viewer attention to specific parts of the frame. This can be done with lighting, arrangement of shapes, and design elements such as costume and makeup. Pools of light can be used to direct attention to specific areas. An example of two of these elements can be found in Milos Forman's *Amadeus* (Miroslav Ondricek, DP). **SEE 9-4** As Salieri hears Mozart conduct a recital for the first time, he advances through the audience in awe. The composition is designed to direct our eye to Salieri. The dark costume makes him stand out from the other concert-goers, and the arrangement of peripheral characters creates lines that, when followed, lead the eye straight to Salieri.

COMPOSITION AND CONTENT

The foremost consideration in composing for film is that the image should be a meaning-producing instrument. This is difficult both to accomplish and to discuss. The concept of images producing meaning has long been analyzed in painting, graphic design, and photography, but no single discussion could ever be definitive. This is as it should be, the potential for any artistic expression being unlimited. It is not simply what is in the frame that creates meaning; it is also the way the subject is framed, arranged, and lighted, using all the resources discussed in other chapters.

On a purely content level, a few typical examples will be helpful. Terrence Malick's *Days of Heaven* (1978, Nestor Almendros, DP) recounts a romance between a poor migrant worker (Brooke Adams) and a wealthy young farmer (Sam Shepard). Many of the film's images are dominated by the farmer's house, an impressive but isolated structure (based on a painting by Edward Hopper) designed to suggest some of the same emotional qualities in its owner. Frequently, the house is framed in the background of the migrants' activities, serving as a constant reminder of both the workers' reduced circumstances and the vast gap between them and the owner. One particularly telling sequence has the Brooke Adams character surprising the farmer as he sits in the tall grass, watching the sunset. As the two characters speak, the farmer's opulent home in the background dominates the space between them. **SEE 9-5** The visual arrangement of the shot itself suggests the relationship—the chasm—between the two characters. The house—and all it represents—will always separate them, no matter what events occur later in their relationship. What might appear to be an innocent encounter is literally overshadowed by this dominating symbol of class distinction.

Ivan Passer's *Cutter's Way* (1981, Jordan Cronenweth, DP) provides a similar example. The story involves several friends living on the fringes of society, who suspect a rich man of committing a murder. At one point two characters go sailing to escape the mounting tension. **SEE 9-6** As their boat plies the waves, an oil rig dominates the background of virtually every shot. As a symbol the open sea generally suggests freedom and openness, a place where people can escape the ever-present demands of a complicated social existence; but here the placement of the oil rig continually reminds us otherwise. It is omnipresent. The employment of *visual subtext*—

9-5

Visual arrangement of elements symbolize the relationship of the characters
Terrence Malick's *Days of Heaven*

9-6

Visual subtext is meaningful information not present in the narrative but implicit in the visual presentation
Ivan Passer's *Cutter's Way*

information not present in the content and structure of the narrative but implicit in the visual presentation—is crucial in creating a complex image.

COMPOSITION AND STRESS

Whereas many shapes suggest internal balance, there are others that cannot resolve their imbalance. These shapes and arrangements are said to have compositional *stress*, also referred to as *tension*. Sometimes stress can be resolved by either implied or actual elements moving in the frame. Other times that stress is purposefully unresolved, creating an artwork that challenges conventional formal interpretation.

Although most American films of the studio age relied on balanced compositions, *film noir* was the first style in commercial features to exploit compositional stress significantly to give a sense of a world in which something was catastrophically wrong. Joseph H. Lewis's *Gun Crazy* (1949, Russell Harlan, DP)—a classic independent, low-budget film noir—has many images that lack conventional balance. The film chronicles a couple's fascination with guns. Their eventual descent into criminality ends with the couple (Peggy Cummins and John Dahl) fleeing the police by car. In this final scene, the characters' mental strain has a reciprocal representation in the imbalance of the composition. **SEE 9-7**

Although the impetus for the film noir sensibility faltered in the 1950s, the importance of compositional stress was rediscovered by cinematographers of the '60s and '70s, a sensibility continued in the films of David Lynch and others. Bernardo Bertolucci's *The Conformist* (1971, Vittorio Storaro, DP), a film that extensively influenced visual style of the period, has many intriguing examples of unbalanced compositions. An early scene in a radio station sets the visual tone, with a stark composition of the film's protagonist (Jean-Louis

9-7

Compositional stress gives a sense of a world in which something is very wrong
Joseph H. Lewis's *Gun Crazy*

Stark, unbalanced compositions can reflect ambiguous content
Bernardo Bertolucci's *The Conformist*

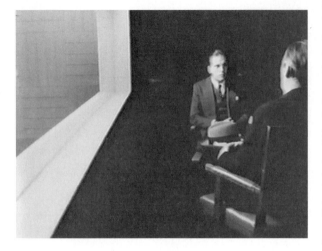

9-9

Compositional stress caused by elements with disproportional weight
Jean-Louis Trintignant in *The Conformist*

Trintignant) having a conversation that is as ambiguous as the composition. **SEE 9-8**

Another famous composition from *The Conformist* demonstrates a different kind of imbalance. **SEE 9-9** The lines of the image are very symmetrical, yet the face has too much weight to balance the other elements in the frame. In this case there is almost a rule of thirds–like division and yet the weight given individual elements creates a very unbalanced image.

Compositional stress often creates the expectation of resolution. When a space is left open, the expectation is created that it will be filled. An example of this is a shot of an individual sitting at a bar. If the empty bar stool next to the person is included in the shot, the expectation is created that the seat will be filled. If the shot is more conventionally balanced, someone *forcing* his way into the composition might be perceived as intrusive.

Horror films take particular advantage of this tension. Space is used to create the expectation on the part of the audience that something, usually bad, is going to happen. The open door behind the unsuspecting character is going to be filled by whatever representation of our inner fears the film is exploiting. Our expectations can be either fulfilled or frustrated. John Carpenter's *Halloween* (1978) has several situations in which the viewer is aware that the killer is near. Characters oblivious to the danger are shown in shots that have space left for the killer to enter. But the film purposefully increases tension—keeps us on the edge of our seats—by not delivering. When we get the relief of a more conventionally balanced composition, apparently signaling the passing of danger, Carpenter increases the shock by having the killer appear, violating the equilibrium.

STRESS AND PHOTOGRAPHIC FACTORS

Images can achieve stress through methods other than simple compositional imbalance. For example, elements specific to photography can be employed to create tension. Leaving elements out of focus can create confusion and frustration, particularly when the image is designed to make us want to see the subject. Distorting lenses can be a contributing factor as well, showing objects that are out of proportion in relation to the size of other elements in the frame.

Wide-angle lenses are frequently employed to create this type of stress. The bending of foreground elements mixed with the elongation, making background images appear smaller, can create exaggerated effects. The couple from *Gun Crazy* is often presented in shots that fragment their presence between the foreground and the background. **SEE 9-10** This is an issue of *scale*—the size of objects in relation to one another. Although it might be argued that these shots have some internal balance, the distortion of relationships definitely adds an element of stress.

Also from *Gun Crazy,* the companion shot to figure 9-7 is a good example of distortions of scale. **SEE 9-11** The steering wheel is so distorted in relationship to

9-10

Use of wide-angle lens to create stress

Peggy Cummins and John Dahl in *Gun Crazy*

9-11

Use of distortions of scale to create stress

John Dahl in *Gun Crazy*

the face that, despite some internal balance, compositional stress is clearly an issue. Long lenses too can create a confining and distorting perspective. The prelude to one of the key musical sequences in Bob Fosse's *Cabaret* (1972) has an excellent example of this. **SEE 9-12** The song "Tomorrow Belongs to Me" is set in a beautiful alpine beer garden. The establishment of this setting, however, which conventionally might be shot with a wide-angle or normal lens to give a complete view, is shot entirely with a long lens. The subtle claustrophobia—the lack of expected openness—creates apprehension that is borne out when the deceptively bucolic atmosphere turns menacing as it evolves into a pro-Nazi songfest. In Jane Campion's *The Piano* (1993), the long lens is a factor in the scene where Ada's note to Baines (played by Holly Hunter and Harvy Keitel) falls into the wrong hands—a prelude to the film's violent action. **SEE 9-13** Filmed along a fence line in the hills, the squashed and angular compositions are so distorted that the scene is invested with an undertone foreshadowing the impending conflict.

9-12

The long lens can create a mood of claustrophobia and apprehension

Bob Fosse's *Cabaret*

9-13

The squashed and angular composition foreshadows impending conflict

Jane Campion's *The Piano*

Lining Up the Shots

As stated, lining up the shots consists of looking at what is in front of the camera and deciding how to arrange it in relation to the boundaries of the film frame. This conscious approach to composition is the responsibility of the director of photography.

HEADROOM AND EYEROOM

The predominant content element in most shots in narrative films is most frequently one or more people. When a person is the focus of compositional interest, where is the viewer's eye drawn? Usually to the eyes. When people are composed on film, the eyes are almost always on the top thirds line. **SEE 9-14** If the eyes are lower, you will probably have problems with *headroom*—the amount of space above the head. Too much headroom tends to diminish the subject. **SEE 9-15** This example obviously overstates the effect; less exaggerated effects diminish to a lesser degree.

Individual cinematographers handle headroom differently, but generally keep the top of the head close to the top of the frame. Headroom is more critical in close shots; close-ups with an inordinate amount of headroom definitely diminish the subject. A little more headroom can be allowed in longer shots, although putting the eyes below the top thirds line can produce disagreeable results. Some cinematographers maintain that you can err on the side of too little headroom as well. Cropping that is too tight can make a character look constrained, as if in a room with a low ceiling.

Eyeroom, or *looking room,* refers to the practice of giving characters space in the direction they are looking. A character looking frame-right would be composed around the left thirds line and vice versa. If a character is not given eyeroom, the shot will feel confined, as if sight is somehow limited or the character's face is pressed up against something.

Many cameras have viewing systems with crosshairs or ground-glass centers. Beginners occasionally mistake these for compositional aids, thinking that they are supposed to put the crosshairs right between the subject's eyes. I like to call this the "assassination theory of composition." I once saw this theory applied in a videotape of a man giving a very powerful speech. It was shot by an obviously inexperienced

9-14

People are almost always composed with the eyes on the top thirds line

9-15

Too much headroom diminishes the subject

camera operator, who consistently kept the speaker's eyes right in the center of the frame. Given the limited options of taping a speech from a fixed camera position, the operator did about the only thing one can do: zoom in and zoom out. When the lens was zoomed in, the effect was bad, though not entirely unacceptable. But when the lens was zoomed out, the cavernous space above the speaker's head made him appear tiny and unimpressive, completely subverting his powerful oration.

CLEANING THE IMAGE

It is usually necessary to "clean" the image of any elements that draw the viewer's attention to undesired parts of the frame or that make for an odd visual presentation. In the first case, this refers to objects that either are an unwarranted distraction or are hovering around the edges of the frame. If an object, say, a chair leg, is barely protruding into the frame, it will draw attention to itself. The viewer's eye will unconsciously search it to see what it is. The more difficult it is to read, the bigger the distraction and the more it will disrupt the frame. The solution is to position the object entirely outside the frame or enough in the frame that the viewer can unconsciously recognize it without effort. The longer an image is held, the more the viewer will search the frame. If the viewer's attention is held by an element in the frame that is confusing, it can detract from simple involvement.

Josef von Sternberg, one of the greatest of all visual directors, once stated that when presented with a shot of a character seated in a chair, he would be sure that all four chair legs were in the shot. His assumption was that the chair would appear to be on the verge of collapse if proper support were not evident. Although this may show a lack of faith in the viewer's ability to understand images, the point is nevertheless made. That which an image needs, it must have. That which an image does not need should be eliminated.

The latter case refers to background and, to a lesser extent, foreground, elements that are peculiarly positioned, such as telephone poles coming out of people's heads, and light switches, household plugs, and similar objects that because of their positioning appear attached to the body. Mel Stuart's *Willie Wonka and the Chocolate Factory* (1971) has an effective parody of the problem. **SEE 9-16** A television reporter is framed in such a way that the antlers of a trophy in the background appear to be coming out of his head. Although this example is a good gag, it can create peculiar effects when not desired. My favorite example is a student who unknowingly positioned a distant highway on a level with the ears of an interview subject. Cars entering one side of the subject's head and exiting the other side, though hilarious, completely destroyed the credibility of the shot.

9-16

Distracting background image creates peculiar effect

Mel Stuart's *Willie Wonka and the Chocolate Factory*

9-17

This example of cheating in positioning the characters defies logic but often goes unnoticed by the viewer
Alfred Hitchcock's *The Man Who Knew Too Much*

CHEATING

Shifting elements in the composition to balance the frame, thus improving an otherwise problematic shot, is called *cheating*. Most cheats are relatively simple: Moving items on a table, shifting furniture, or relocating artwork on a wall is frequently enough to fix an untenable frame. Continuity is a key concern when cheating, although experience helps in understanding what you can get away with.

Cheating applies to the positioning of characters as well. If a character is blocked in a specific way for one angle, there may be a difficult background element that creates a problem—say, a door frame or light switch—in another angle. To eliminate the problem, simply move the actor in the appropriate direction either to cover up the offending object or to allow recomposition to exclude it.

Alfred Hitchcock, who seemed to delight in these simple manipulations, did a cheat in *The Man Who Knew Too Much* (1956, Robert Burks, DP) that defies logic, but which still goes largely unnoticed by the audience. The scene involves two couples sitting across from each other at a table. **SEE 9-17** Although both couples are shoulder to shoulder when facing the camera, they are several feet apart in their respective reverses. Shooting a conversation like this is always a challenge due to questions of the line and shifting perspective. This example represents an adventurous solution, one that may have left a less prestigious director making explanations to studio chiefs.

Directors of photography are always adjusting things, fussing with the set, and rearranging props to get the perfect composition. With an eye to the camera, a camera operator's asking a props person or set dresser to slide things a little bit one way or the other is common. Sloppiness is acceptable only in a few specific applications, and DPs will generally work hard to achieve an image that is clean and not confusing.

MOVEMENT AND ANTICIPATORY CAMERA

As suggested in chapter 2, much of the camera movement in film is not noticed by the viewer. It is movement that responds to—or, more accurate—anticipates subject movement. *Anticipatory camera*—an approach to cinematography that is particularly associated with classic Hollywood cinema—is structured, highly choreographed camerawork that leads rather than follows movement, making adjustments for the movement of characters in the frame or the entrances of others. Not all camerawork is this formal, but the approach so dominates cinematography that it influences the way one thinks about shooting.

Thus, the DP must respond intelligently to shifting elements within the frame. A common example is a two-shot in which one of the characters exits. The initial frame can be balanced for two people, but that balance falls apart once one person leaves. The solution is to pan slightly in the appropriate direction to rebalance the frame. Whenever there is movement in the frame, the DP is confronted with a question: What should be done to compensate for the movement? Generally, failure to adjust results in poor framing.

Just as performance is rehearsed, camerawork is rehearsed as well. During the final blocking of the scene in rehearsals, the actor's movements should become consistent, and a plan for shooting can be devised and rehearsed. If the actor shifts her weight or turns to face a new direction, the responding movement of the camera can be perfectly timed to anticipate that action. If the actor is going through a bigger movement, the camera can accommodate it by drifting or moving boldly in the appropriate direction. The key is rehearsal so that the camera operator knows the movement and has a planned response.

The concluding scenes of Fritz Lang's *Scarlet Street* have many excellent examples of camera movement used to create a balanced composition and anticipate movement. In one scene, where the main character, Christopher Cross (Edward G. Robinson), is overwhelmed with guilt, he begins hearing the voices of the people whose deaths he has caused. In one shot he tears away the canopy on his bed to find the source of the voices. The camera starts with a balanced composition of the bed sheets shielded by a canopy. **SEE 9-18A** In an exceedingly subtle move that is a perfect demonstration of this concept, a quick tilt is done to create room for Chris as he enters the frame. **SEE 9-18B** The camera does not react *after* Chris enters the shot; it starts the movement just before he enters the frame and is finished by the time he reaches his final position. On the surface a move like this appears to be almost inconsequential, but it is with responses such as this that camerawork achieves much of its subtlety and fluidity.

Broader movements benefit from thoughtful planning as well. A shot following the one just described leads Chris through a complex movement. The shot starts with Chris seated on the bed. **SEE 9-18C** The camera starts to dolly out to give Chris

9-18

Using camera movement to create balance and anticipate subject movement
Edward G. Robinson in *Scarlet Street*

Using camera movement to create balance and anticipate subject movement *(continued)*
Edward G. Robinson in *Scarlet Street*

room to stand. **SEE 9-18D** Before he stands, Chris looks frame-left. **SEE 9-18E** The camera anticipates this by drifting left to create eyeroom, also anticipating the direction Chris will go when he rises from the bed. The camera does not give full headroom for Chris's final position when standing, as that would create too much headroom while he is still on the bed. The top of the frame is completed in a tilt timed to his rising. **SEE 9-18F** The camera then continues to drift frame-left as Chris advances through the room. **SEE 9-18G** Both camera movement and character movement are then perfectly timed for an ending composition, allowing room for a striking shadow of Chris as he points to something. **SEE 9-18H**

Anticipatory camera movements are the result of choices that must be made constantly while preparing each shot, working out strategies for covering the action in front of the camera. A camera operator must respond to all subject movement. Failure to do so results in compositions that may begin well but which wind up out of balance.

On a set there is constant dialogue among the director, the DP, the camera operator, and the talent regarding the inclusion and arrangement of elements within the frame. Although most movements of this nature are planned in advance, the camera operator should be ready for minor adjustments. The biggest mistake novice camera operators make is to find a good beginning composition and then lock down the tilt and pan, as if this is the framing the world should have forever. The camera operator generally wants to have the tilt and pan unlocked (usually both on tight fluid) to respond to subject movement.

Planning and executing movements that are assured and decisive is an important goal for a beginning cinematographer. You can always tell when a cinematographer has not quite decided what to do in a specific situation. There is a tentative quality to the movements that betrays the operator's lack of confidence. Part of maturing as a camera operator is building confidence in your judgment and showing conviction in the effects you are trying to accomplish.

MOVEMENT AND COMPOSITIONAL BALANCE

Frequently, camera movement is necessary to create balance in a composition that has been disrupted by or simply needs to follow the action. DPs will often use elements in the foreground or background to balance compositions. As characters move, however, these balancing elements can become liabilities unless appropriately managed.

The opening of the previously discussed scene from *Scarlet Street* has Chris entering his rented room. Elements on a table in the foreground are used to create balance as he walks through the room. As he comes in, he is balanced by a bottle frame-right and a wall light fixture frame-left. **SEE 9-19A** As he moves across the room toward a window, the camera dollies left while panning right. **SEE 9-19B** In the resulting composition, Chris is balanced by a coffee pot and cup at frame-left and the window at frame-right. **SEE 9-19C** Balance is a key goal here, but these elements are also used to create a sense of depth in the image. Why the dolly? Could a pan have been done instead? Although this movement may have been a feature of a grand plan on Lang's part (as befits the main character's name, there is much crossing imagery in the film), it also could have been just one of those things that was worked out on the set. Within the confines of the set, a pan may not have created the final composition that Lang and DP Milton Krasner felt was appropriate.

SUBJECT MOVEMENT TOWARD OR AWAY FROM THE CAMERA

A subject moving toward or away from the camera almost always requires some adjustment. If the composition is correct at the beginning of the shot, a character would move out of the top of the composition as he approaches the camera if no correction is made. **SEE 9-20** A tilt is usually in order, often with a pan incorporated for any horizontal changes. The key to executing a good move is to find some aspect of the composition that is going to remain relatively stable; in this case, keeping the appropriate headroom would be a key issue.

The previously mentioned shot from *Amadeus* concludes with a stunned Salieri approaching the camera. **SEE 9-21A** As Salieri comes closer, the camera is subtly and fluidly tilted to give the appropriate headroom for the new composition. The timing is immaculate, with the headroom

9-19

Using camera movement and foreground and background elements for compositional balance
Fritz Lang's *Scarlet Street*

A

B

← Dolly

C

9-20

A character approaching the camera moves out of the top of the composition, necessitating a tilt

9-21

Tilting to give appropriate headroom as the subject approaches the camera
F. Murray Abraham in *Amadeus*

kept perfectly even throughout the move. By the end the camera is at a low angle that exaggerates Salieri's features and diminishes the peripheral characters in the background. **SEE 9-21B** Movement like this requires rack focusing as well.

CAMERA MOVEMENT TOWARD OR AWAY FROM A SUBJECT

The same principles apply to dollies and zooms toward and away from a subject as with subject movement. A tilt is almost always necessary, and often a pan as well. **SEE 9-22** Despite the aesthetic differences between a dolly and a zoom, when considering compositional adjustments made necessary by their use they become virtually synonymous.

9-22

A dolly or zoom toward a subject usually requires a tilt

MOVEMENT TO CREATE SPACE

Moving the camera to create room for a character's entering the frame is a common approach. Director Nicholas Ray has garnered recognition for the fluid and thoughtful use of the camera in his films. Ray's *In a Lonely Place* (1950, Burnett Guffey, DP) has many examples of the camera's being used to accommodate character entrances and exits. A typical shot features a literary agent (Art Smith) being joined by the main female lead, Laurel (Virginia Graham). Again, timing is everything. The camera starts with a composition of the agent. **SEE 9-23A** The composition starts to drift right and slightly up to anticipate Laurel's entrance. When she enters the frame, the composition is completing as she reaches her final position. **SEE 9-23B**

9-23

Gradually moving the camera to accommodate a subject's entering the frame
Nicholas Ray's *In a Lonely Place*

Using character movement to fill compositional voids
Fritz Lang's *Scarlet Street*

CHARACTER MOVEMENT TO BALANCE COMPOSITION

Having a character move to fill a compositional void is also a very common approach. Rather than plan some extensive and time-consuming camera move, simply have the talent move to positions that fill out the composition. *Scarlet Street* has an excellent, though almost comically transparent, example of this. The scene immediately following the previous example involves two police officers rousting the now derelict main character from a park bench. **SEE 9-24A** The entire scene is done in a single take and, though many viewers might not notice it, incorporates significant camera movement. This sequence of three frames illustrates how characters can be regrouped after they are set in motion.

The shorter officer in the foreground does all the talking, while the taller officer is essentially a shill to be played off of. As Chris starts to get off the bench, the first officer steps toward him, disrupting the balance of the frame. **SEE 9-24B** The second officer steps frame-left—into the empty space—to reestablish balance. **SEE 9-24C** It is clear from its stiffness that this movement is done at someone's direction and is solely intended to rebalance composition.

Such movements are the subject of much discussion on the set. The DP often has to ask the talent to move to specific positions to be in proper composition. Again, this is what marks are for. If beginning film actors share a common shortcoming, it is in neither understanding nor accommodating the requirements of composition. Occasionally, directors have to take young performers (particularly stage-trained ones) aside and explain "the rules of the road." Shots are effective only if certain principles are considered while shooting.

MOVEMENT AND MEANING

We have mainly been detailing the practical considerations of movement, but many thematic issues are dependent on movement as well, incorporating the creation of space for meaning. The end of the park bench shot from *Scarlet Street* provides an example of both: the creation of emotional space intermingled with a pragmatic use of movement. After the police have rousted Chris, he shuffles off behind them. **SEE 9-25** The camera drifts left to allow him space to leave. Not only is this a practical necessity, it also allows Chris to disappear miserably into the distance.

One final note: Although camera operators are given rehearsals for complicated moves, they are usually expected to handle simple ones on their own. It may be considerate to allow beginning DPs several practices, but this may not be the case in much standard production.

Creating emotional space with a pragmatic use of movement
Fritz Lang's Scarlet Street

Practical Considerations

As always, practical considerations shape many of the decisions made about shooting. Whatever is planned will have complications, and being able to readjust effectively is essential.

COMPOSITION AND COMPROMISE

Composition often requires compromise. That is, either to avoid some bothersome element or to integrate a difficult camera move, a framing that is less than perfect has to be made. The camera might have to be tilted down to avoid a hanging light in a tight location. The camera might have to be panned in one direction or the other to avoid an undesired background element. How do you respond when there is a substantial difference in the heights of the characters, or if one character is seated and the other is standing? Do you tilt up to make room for a character entering the frame, or start with too much headroom and let the character fill it?

The previously discussed shot from Nicholas Ray's *In a Lonely Place* is a good example of a typical compromise (figure 9-23). The initial framing of this shot is easy to criticize as being too loose, having unnecessary headroom in particular. The logic of the composition, however, is made apparent when the second character enters. The move to the final composition would have been too extreme—the tilt would have covered too much distance too quickly—if the first framing had been tighter. The movement would not have been fluid, particularly when matching movement from other shots. As in this example, framings occasionally have to be left loose to incorporate some other element entering or exiting the frame. In this case the first composition is left loose to facilitate a subtle move to the second, tighter composition.

Often, such compromises have to do with avoiding undesired elements in the foreground or background. If there are television antennas on the homes in a period piece, framing will have to be adjusted so that they are not in the shots. If a room has a low ceiling, high camera angles may have to be used to avoid light fixtures or microphone booms. There are myriad obstacles that make slight changes in shots necessary.

Compromises are a necessity in situations in which achieving complete control of all the elements is impossible. (This notion is explored further in a variety of contexts.) On amply budgeted films, a great deal of time and money goes into securing shooting spaces that can be manipulated according to the needs of filmmakers. The production likes to "own the location." If something is posing a problem, it will simply be eliminated. This can include a wide range of obstacles, many of them beyond the question of compositional challenges—from television antennas to unattractive paint jobs to bothersome people. Without the money or time to change things, independents and students wind up shooting, in some cases literally, around obstacles. It is often a matter of what you are willing to give up compositionally to create something that is workable.

CAMERA AND PERFORMANCE

The dialogue between the DP and the talent is critical, although in many cases it is funneled through the director or AD. The talent often has specific expectations of the DP, and the DP always needs the performers to respond to compositional requirements. Communication is constant and is essential to the visual shape of a film.

One expectation is that the DP must make the talent look good. There are legendary stories of actors who insisted that they be filmed and lighted in very specific ways. Although one might prefer not to be a slave to some cultural beauty stereotype, one must recognize that there are indeed angles on performers that do not do them justice. A certain amount of cinematography is still based on the old glamour approach of the studio age. Making sure that all the elements display the talent at their best can affect a wide range of decisions. Determining which side of the line from which to film based on the actor's better side is a typical example.

Performers' movements must be integrated into the needs of a balanced frame. Usually, this is a matter of setting up marks for the talent to hit as they move through a scene, the approach representing a tightly choreographed interplay between camera and subject. A good example of this is when the director wants a moving subject in a close-up, in which case the DP has to make the performer move within tightly controlled parameters. The DP will draw a frame in the air that will give the boundaries of a performer's possible movements: "If you move too far this way, you will be out of composition. If you go too far that way..."

One potential concern is that if the space is too defined, actors can become so absorbed in the mechanical aspects of their movements that the performance gets lost. Being able to work within the technical demands of the medium, however, depends on the ability and professionalism of the actor. Alfred Hitchcock's *Notorious* (Ted Tetzlaff, DP) has many shots of characters in movement that are so tight that it clearly took much communication among talent, DP, and director to achieve the desired stability of composition. Shots of Alicia nervously pacing in the midst of a party as Dev plans a search for clues in the wine cellar are particularly good examples of moving shots that are very tightly controlled. One can clearly visualize the DP indicating the boundaries—imaginary lines of a frame drawn in the air—of her movement. This tight control is very purposeful in emphasizing the tension Alicia feels while trying to aid Dev's clandestine activities. To allow a wider frame for greater freedom of movement would have diluted the claustrophobic effect. Despite the constraints, Bergman's performance is one of the most luminescent in film. Every emotional shading shines within the tightly controlled technique that displays it. Considering all the technical adjustments that must have been transpiring, Bergman maintained focus on the smallest elements of her performance.

Still, inexperienced performers may have difficulties keeping compositional considerations from affecting their performance. Some actors may rebel at the tightly controlled parameters. Being sensitive to the performers' concerns is a necessity, but being firm about the demands of the medium is also important. Talent who cannot hit marks or understand abstract parameters will be the source of sloppy compositions.

Informal Camera Styles

The classic approach to camerawork is one more convention to be questioned and tested. The 1960s and 1970s saw a movement toward a more informal image in films—a movement that had its genesis in post–World War II Italian film and the French New Wave of the '50s and '60s. In films ranging from the work of Robert Altman and John Cassavetes to that of a new generation of experimental and documentary filmmakers, there was an attempt to create an image that was more spontaneous than the highly choreographed Hollywood prototype.

In such films as *Faces* (1968) and *Husbands* (1970), Cassavetes was a true innovator. The most striking feature of these films is their improvisational tone. The majority of the scenes were shot handheld, and one gets a sense that the camera operator was given the camera and told to do the best he could, not knowing what was going to happen next. The films have an almost documentary shooting approach, the camera being used to film a narrative with improvised elements.

The handheld camera can create less structured and less static imagery, but informal imagery and the handheld camera are not synonymous. Robert Altman's early masterworks *McCabe and Mrs. Miller* (1971) and *The Long Goodbye* have images and sequences of shots that were largely undreamed of prior to these films. Altman and his cinematographer, Vilmos Zsigmond, specifically planned for the camera to be always moving in *The Long Goodbye*. The actors were also allowed great freedom, making the compositions feel less arranged. After his work in *The Long Goodbye*, actor Sterling Hayden remarked how much he enjoyed the freedom this approach allowed the actor. He was not constantly annoyed by having to hit the marks that are required in a more structured approach.

The style of films like these can be quite engaging, though it never gained wide acceptance by audiences. Jean-Luc Godard was systematic in his theoretical and filmic assaults on the shackles of the old, highly choreographed style. In the United States, Dennis Hopper's *Easy Rider* (1969) was a key work in paving the way toward a less structured approach. Gordon Willis's shooting in Francis Ford Coppola's *The Godfather II* (1974), however, and John Alonzo's in Roman Polanski's *Chinatown* (1974), among others, marked a return to formal, structured imagery. The impulse remains, but the revolutionary fervor has diminished. With his ability to integrate both formal and informal styles, Martin Scorsese is one of the few directors to incorporate this style effectively over the long term.

Notes and Suggestions

One critical thing to remember is that there is a big difference between just looking through the camera and "shooting." Anyone can look through a camera. Shooting is an art. Many young camera operators bring to shooting too much of their experience of viewing film. When looking at a shot, the eye is generally drawn to a specific area of the frame, and awareness of the rest of the frame is limited. If it is a shot of a person, the viewer's eyes are generally drawn to those of the performer. In a classroom exercise several years ago, I asked a student camera operator for an MS of an actor. A crew member hit the slate that marks each scene and stepped to the side. I thought he was standing too close to the actor for the composition I had called. I assumed the camera operator was doing the right thing. When we got the film back, there was the guy with the slate, standing a few feet away, smiling and enjoying the performance. Everyone ribbed him mercilessly until I pointed out that this was really the operator's responsibility. The camera operator was shooting like a movie viewer.

He zeroed in on the performer's eyes, completely unaware of the rest of the frame. He was watching content when he should have been watching form. A camera operator needs a whole-frame awareness when shooting film.

A good DP is going to find a way to make the composition arresting and interesting at all times. It is not a matter of coming up with a decent composition occasionally. If you set up a camera on a busy street, a decent composition will wander by every once in a while. But this is not filmmaking. The tension between the edges of the frame and its contents is of paramount importance. There must be a symbiotic relationship between the contents of the frame and the "rightness" of their arrangement.

Again, the primary responsibility is an awareness of whether what is being shot will cut together. It is clearly the director's responsibility to make sure that what is shot works, but the DP monitors exactly what the pieces will be and should be able to extrapolate to an edited finished product. Many students have heard the famous story of Orson Welles's encounter with a balky DP. While shooting a scene, the DP was constantly interjecting his opinion about what shots would cut and arguing about shots he felt would not cut. In exasperation Welles told him that they were filming a dream sequence. By Welles's account the DP was putty in his hands from that moment on. Whether or not this story is true (anyone familiar with the day-to-day practical aspects of production would have to be dubious), it is repeated too frequently by people who do not have the experience and, potentially, vision that Welles had. The knowledge that a good DP has about cutting should be seen as an asset, not a source for confrontation. There will always be technical people who are overbearing and overly schematic in their approach. But an equal number of directors should be listening when they are about to make a mistake. As suggested, a DP with some editing room experience is often a real ally.

10

Procedures and Equipment

THE execution of the setup is a complex process of confronting and solving the many problems that will inevitably arise. Many concerns regarding the overall quality and character of the image have to be resolved before the camera can roll. This chapter delineates some of the necessary considerations for individual setups.

The *setup*—the basic component of a film's production, that is, each individual camera position, placement, angle—generally represents hours of preparation, which includes the devotion of extensive resources, both human and monetary. Conventional theatrical films usually evaluate a day's work by the number of script pages completed, but they also evaluate their efficiency in terms of number of setups executed. A feature film crew that averages twelve to fifteen setups a day will generally be considered acceptably efficient. Episodic television crews must work much faster. Given the small number of shots and the intense expectations invested in each of them, crews shooting television commercials often work much more slowly. Independents, due to restricted budgets and limited time with locations and talent, often have to average twice as many setups per day as a standard feature.

Just as a day's work can be measured in terms of setups, an entire film can be similarly measured. Films with slow, contemplative editing might average somewhere around 800 setups for the entire film. An action film with fast-paced editing can easily have double that number. Robert Rodriguez's *El Mariachi* reportedly had almost 3,500 setups, an extraordinary number given the film's minuscule budget. Woody Allen's *Annie Hall* employs slightly fewer than 400 individual shots in its final form. Although Allen reportedly shot much more material setups than this, the figure illustrates much about his working method. Some of the film's most famous scenes—the film critic in the ticket line, Alvy and Annie chasing lobsters in the kitchen—are done in single, extended shots. Jim Jarmusch's *Stranger Than Paradise,* in which every scene is done from a single camera position with no cuts, consists of roughly 70 setups.

The Take

Scenes—the basic unit of a script—are broken down into *shots,* which translate to setups for shooting. These setups are numbered so they can be marked and logged. Each setup is then covered in *takes*—the number of attempts at each shot needed to produce at least several usable versions.

The Slate

The *slate* is used for organization in shooting, easy identification of the shots in editing, and, most critical, matching location sound and picture. It consists of a board for writing pertinent information and a striped bar across the top that is slapped at the beginning of every sound take. **SEE 10-1**

There are two common methods of numbering scenes on the slate. The first is to number all shots sequentially from the first day of shooting. Slate numbers would run from #1 for the first shot on the first day of filming to the last shot on the last day, the final number depending on how many individual setups the film had. This method is perfectly acceptable, although it can become difficult to manage for those inexperienced with dealing with many days of shooting. The second method is to use the scene numbers as listed in the shooting script combined with letters designating the position of the shot within the scene, probably a more logical system for novices. The opening master for scene #80 might be listed as #80A. A close-up in the middle of the scene might be #80F. The closing master might be #80R. Whatever the numbering method used, the shot is identified by both scene and take when the clapper/loader (2nd AC) marks each scene. "Scene 80C, take 5" would denote the fifth take of scene #80C in the shooting script.

The science of slates and slating has advanced dramatically in recent years. Time code slates are common, with LEDs providing a constant, rolling readout of time. Tie-tack or lapel slates are also popular. Worn by the sound person, they emit a light when a button is pressed, with a matching tone being sent to the recorder. The camera operator must pan to the sound person to photograph the light. The old-fashioned slap-style slate, however, remains in wide use.

10-1

The slate is used for organization in shooting, easy identification of shots, and matching production sound and picture

Executing the Shots

The sequence of events to initiate a shot may vary slightly from set to set but is usually something like the following. The director, or the AD on most sets, will call for sound. The sound recorder is started and, upon seeing the appropriate speed indicator on the recorder, the recordist will yell out, "Speed." The director will then call for camera. The 1st AC hits the trigger and will call out, "Rolling," once the speed indicator flashes (a red light on many cameras). The director will then call for the slate. The person with the slate, the clapper/loader, will call out the numbers and hit the slate. The director will then call for action. Each scene ends with a "Cut" from the director.

The sequence is a set of calls and responses:

Sound: *Speed*

Camera: *Rolling*

Mark it: *Scene 1, take 1, hit of slate*

Action:

Cut.

Hollywood tradition dictates that the scene and take numbers be said before hitting the slate, but it is recommended here that this information be stated *after* the hit. This approach is slightly unorthodox, but it makes syncing sound and image a little easier for the novice. On commercial shoots this sequence will be preceded by the AD requesting to be "put on the light and bell"—a visual and audio cueing device that tells the crew that the camera will be rolling and to be quiet until it is shut off.

Marking a scene appears to be a straightforward matter, but a number of factors must be considered to make sure that the appropriate people can see the slate. The entire slate should be recorded, but the hit of the bars is the crucial piece of information. This is what the editorial staff needs to match sound and picture. All the issues that are important to the shot itself are essential here: exposure, clarity, focus, framing, and so on.

If the scene is low-key, the slate could potentially be held in an area too dark for adequate exposure. In this situation the gaffer will set up a slate light, the sole purpose of which is to illuminate the slate as the scene is being marked. The light is switched off before action is called.

Having the slate numbers large enough to be read is also an issue. The general rule is to keep the slate 1 foot from the camera for every 10 millimeters of lens length; thus the slate should be 5 feet from the camera for a 50mm lens, and so on. When the action is some distance from the camera, this can lead to focus issues, usually resolved by having the AC rack focus from the slate to the action after the scene is marked.

The bars at the top of the slate are again most important. This is usually a simple matter, but mistakes can be made in tight close-ups or when "running and gunning"—shooting quickly due to lack of time or because of involvement in a spontaneous event. In the first case, this may require a pan or zoom from the slate to the subject after the scene is marked, often requiring a rack focus in the process. In the second case, taking a few seconds to get the slate right will prevent headaches for the editors. Whatever is necessary, the bars must be visible.

The clapper/loader should be in position, ready to hit the slate when the camera is rolling, because trying to find the correct position while the camera is running wastes precious film. The camera operator uses hand signals to guide the clapper/loader into position before the take starts, spoken directions being superfluous for two people facing each other. Once the scene is marked, the clapper/loader should know where to go and get there quickly. When exiting, avoid casting a shadow on the scene or walking in front of the camera, as well as making excessive noise while moving.

Some shots require different methods of slating. Because the slap of the bars can be disconcerting for inexperienced talent, particularly documentary subjects and children, the ***tail slate*** is done at the end of the shot. Sometimes it is simply more convenient. The clapper/loader inserts the slate at the end of the shot and marks it there. The slate is held upside down and the bar is slapped up to denote the tail position.

SYNC AND MOS

All shots are done either *sync*—with sound—or *MOS*—without sound. The legend for the term *MOS* is that, shortly after the introduction of sound, a German director replying to a question about mic placement said something to the effect of, "Oh, no, vee do dis vone *mitt out sound*." Thus *MOS* became the acronym for shots that are done without the sound recorder rolling. A surprisingly high percentage of shots can be done MOS, from reaction shots to action shots that will have sound added later. Feature productions often roll sound on virtually everything, however, because it is easy to do and makes syncing less complicated.

MOS shots are slated similarly to other shots except that the bars on the slate are not hit. The clapper/loader will simply insert the slate, and the 1st AC will "squeeze off" a few frames of it. The shot will then be initiated with a simple "Roll camera" and "Action."

CAMERA REPORTS

The *camera report,* or *log,* provides a daily chronology of shooting. It is indispensable as a record of all the shooting activity on the set but is most valuable in keeping the many rolls of film organized during editing. The 2nd AC is usually responsible for filling it out after every take.

Blank camera report forms are available from commercial sources, but you can work up a simple camera report quite easily by simply providing places for the key information. **SEE 10-2**

The main headings are used to list the particulars of the shoot. Manufacturer and stock numbers are written in the middle. Emulsion numbers are taken from the label on the raw stock. The magazine's number is recorded here so any problems (scratches, light leaks, and the like) can be traced later. The first two columns are for the scene and take numbers. These come from the shooting script or storyboard and are provided by the script supervisor. They are also replicated in the lined script.

Beginning and ending footage is recorded to keep track of where specific shots are located on the rolls. Barring any camera runs for testing, the ending footage number is transposed to the beginning footage for the next take. Beginning and ending footage are important for *spot printing,* a common practice on feature films, in which the desired takes are circled on the camera report for later identification and printing.

Remarks generally pertain to the quality of the take, noting deviations from other takes—different positioning of performer, different line readings, slightly different camera strategies, and so on. The notation *NG* (no good) obviously designates spoiled takes.

The sound mixer keeps a *sound log* as well, with all the same information as the camera report except beginning and ending footage. Some form of designation for all camera and sound rolls is very important. At the beginning of a project, the

10-2

A basic camera report form should include all the key information

Date		Scene #		Title			
Film stock		Emulsion #		Director			
Processing instructions				Camera			
Scene	Take	Remarks	MOS/sync	Begin footage	End footage	Camera roll	Sound roll

1st AC and sound mixer will start a numbering system, usually numbering rolls sequentially from the first day. The camera roll number is written on camera tape and is kept both on the film's packaging and on the magazine itself. This helps the 1st AC keep the rolls organized for appropriate marking for the lab.

As suggested, camera reports are important for keeping track of rolls in the editing room. If the editor wants to try another take of a shot, the assistant editor can consult the camera report, determine the appropriate roll, see if it was printed (if applicable), and find it among all the *outtakes* (the unused shots). Beginning and ending footage are important here as well for determining exact locations on the rolls. Similar logging of sound rolls allows for easy location of desired takes.

The camera report is also used to keep track of the camera's performance. The AC will indicate in the remarks column when the gate was last checked and if problems were found, irregularities on the camera's part such as excessive noise, and any other problems that may have been noticed.

The Camera Assistant

Many of the 1st AC's duties are covered in earlier chapters, but there are several other considerations essential to producing a clean product as well as general efficiency on the set. Although this section details advanced production practices and magazine-loading cameras, ambitious learners will want to take them into account from the start.

CAMERA PREPARATION

The AC's first responsibility is to pick up the camera package and get it ready for use. Whether picking up a camera from a friend, a school equipment room, or a rental house, it is imperative that you check to make sure the camera package has everything you require. Failure to have necessary pieces or to check key features can result in canceled shoots or, worse in its own way, unpleasant surprises when you get the film back.

In addition, practice the threading procedure many times before attempting to load that precious celluloid gold (this is the 2nd AC's responsibility). Use a *dummy load*—a ruined roll of raw stock; labs, schools, and rental houses are potential sources. Become completely conversant with the camera's loading procedures as you practice. Mistakes in threading account for more ruined footage than any other single cause.

MAGAZINES AND LOADING

Each camera has its own unique magazine design and threading pattern. A knowledge of the basic mechanism should make every camera an open book to you, although one should never be arrogant when learning a camera. Finding either a manual or a person to walk you through loading is, again, the best approach.

Because all cameras have at least slight differences, it is impossible to give specific loading instructions. Despite this, a few general principles will be helpful.

☑ When working with core loads, a *photographic darkroom bag*—the *changing bag*—is used to load the film. Using the bag can be disconcerting at first. Become familiar with what is supposed to happen in the bag and how to respond to any problems that arise. Individual magazines have their own idiosyncrasies: The lighttrap might be very tight on one magazine; the counter arm may not be locking out of the way on another. Learn to anticipate all difficulties.

☑ Once you feel completely comfortable with threading procedures from practicing in the light of day, you are ready to use the bag. The traditional changing bag is black and rectangular, although a tent-shaped bag, which keeps the folds of material off your hands and is quite popular with ACs, is available. Changing bags have two compartments, each with a separate zipper, to make sure no light gets in. The bag has two armholes with elastic that makes the sleeves tight against your arms. Once the film is out of its packaging, you cannot remove your arms from the holes without risking ruining the film. If you have to get out of the bag, put the film back in its packaging or in a closed and locked magazine.

☑ Core-loaded film comes packaged in a metal can. Inside the can a black plastic bag acts as an inner layer of protection from light. This plastic bag is not designed to protect the film outside the can, and *a can should never be opened outside of the changing bag*. A piece of blue tape secures the unexposed roll. After loading the magazine, save the can and plastic bag for downloading the exposed film. The piece of tape that secures the roll should be carefully preserved inside the bag; make sure that it is not left in the magazine, where it could cause a camera jam. Bring extra cans with black bags for *recanning* (repackaging) the **short ends**—the film that remains in the magazine at the end of the day or when a change to different film stock occurs.

☑ In the changing bag, feed the film through the lighttrap before you mount the load on the spindle. Once this is done, close the film compartment and lock it shut. Most magazines need only the feed side set up in total darkness, so the mag can be removed from the bag and the take-up finished in the light. Tape the feed side of the mag immediately after removing it from the bag.

☑ Thread the camera. Always test the threading with the inching knob, then run the camera to make sure the loops remain consistent. If the camera's design allows it, run the camera to make sure that the take-up core is operating correctly.

☑ When you are threading the camera, the emulsion must be facing the front. Although this is obvious, it seems like just about everyone makes this mistake once in their career. If the antihalation backing is toward the front of the camera, something has been done wrong.

☑ The diameter of the hole in the center of a core is larger than that of a daylight spool. The spindles in the magazine require *core adapters* to make up the difference. Core adapters mount and lock onto the spindles—and they can be accidentally removed when downloading and sent off to the lab. Be sure the magazine has all its core adapters when you take the camera on location. You won't be able to shoot if one is missing and you are unable to cannibalize one from another magazine. Sometimes the smallest things can bring a shoot to a standstill. You will also need a core for take-up. Be sure to bring extra cores, as you may have to download unfinished rolls. The extras will be needed when you reload a new magazine. Use only 2-inch cores, because larger ones do not allow room for take-up of the entire 400 feet of film.

Become completely familiar with as many cameras and magazines as possible. A person who knows cameras and can load them quickly, accurately, and cleanly has some very marketable skills. Many entry-level positions in film are on the camera crew, which is a good way to get some experience on the set. It can also pay bills as you pursue other interests. You may have to work into it slowly, because no one is going to be hired to load magazines without proven ability. Loading appears to be a small cog in the system, but it is far too critical a cog to be left to someone with limited knowledge. I knew an aspiring AC who scratched several thousand feet of film on a project, because he did not know a specific loading peculiarity of one camera. He had a hard time finding work for quite some time thereafter. Know your camera.

RACKING FOCUS

As with so much else, racking focus is something that is worked out and rehearsed in advance. As explained in chapter 2, in a **rack focus** the AC stands by the camera and physically rotates the focus ring as the shot is being executed. To set up a rack focus, you need a roll of **film tape** (also called *white paper tape*—a narrow tape that does not leave a residue), a permanent marker, and some gaffer's tape. Film tape is available at motion picture supply stores, and no substitute should be used. You put the film tape on the barrel of the lens. The gaffer's tape is used to mark the talent's position on the floor.

Using a character moving toward the camera as an example, the AC has to ascertain and mark on the floor the talent's position at the beginning and end of her move. **SEE 10-3** If it is a long move, the AC also measures and marks on the floor several arbitrary points in between. A piece of film tape is placed on the movable part of the focus ring, across from the hatch mark. If distances of 15, 10, 8, 6, and 5 feet have been measured, a mark is put on the film tape at the appropriate distances. These marks will be lined up with the hatch mark by turning the focus ring as the shot is being executed. **SEE 10-4** During performance and camera rehearsals, the AC will practice the focus move as well, hitting the specific focus points as the talent hits the corresponding marks on the floor.

Marks are used in dolly movements as well. **SEE 10-5** Though dolly moves can incorporate both subject and camera movement, we will use the example of the camera moving in on a stationary subject. Rather than measure to points in the subject's movement, the AC bases the measurements on the distance from the subject to the dolly. The measurements are the same as in the previous example (15, 10, 8, 6, and 5 feet), so these distances are marked on the floor with gaffer's tape along the path of the dolly. As the dolly shot is being executed, the AC will rack focus to the appropriate distance as the dolly passes the marks on the floor.

Good ACs become very sensitive to how to move the focus ring and keep the subject in focus, though even they make occasional mistakes. Actually, some of the great shots with rack focuses, such as the crane shot in Alfred Hitchcock's *Notorious*, drift slightly out of focus toward the ends of their movements. It just shows that it was made by human hands.

10-3

When a character will be moving toward the camera, the AC marks the talent's beginning and ending positions, as well as several positions in between

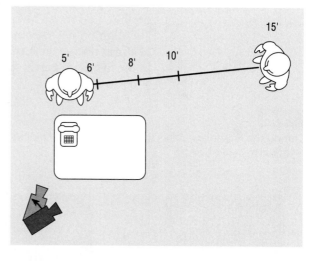

10-4

Marks on film tape corresponding to measurements on the floor are aligned with the focus hatch mark as the rack focus is being executed

10-5

When marking dolly movements, the AC bases the measurements on the distance from the subject to the dolly

RACKING FOCUS AND DEPTH OF FIELD

The 1st AC must be aware that the depth of field changes when racking focus. As the focus point shifts farther from or closer to the camera, the depth of field also shifts. If a character moves from 10 feet to 5 feet from the camera, the depth of field changes as you do the attendant focus rack.

The example from Mike Nichols's *The Graduate* discussed in chapter 2 illustrates this point. Dustin Hoffman's long run toward the camera clearly incorporates a substantial rack. **SEE 10-6** While the 1st AC is racking focus, the depth of field travels toward the camera, becoming increasingly shallow. Focus your attention on an object in the background as you watch the shot. By the time Hoffman reaches the turn, the background is completely out of focus. The numbers in the figure are purely speculative.

10-6

During the rack focus in this scene, the depth of field becomes increasingly shallow
Mike Nichols's *The Graduate*

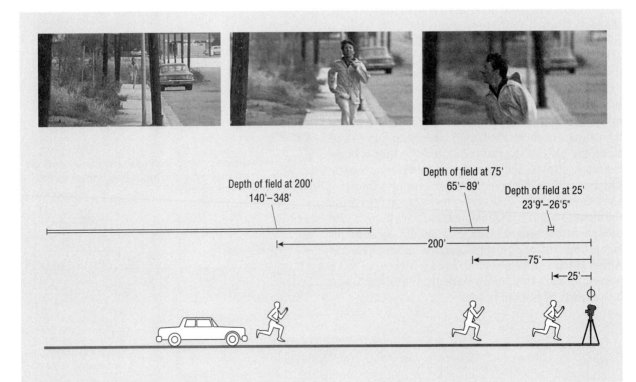

You will notice that objects, the car in particular, go soft slowly at first. As Hoffman approaches the turn, the rate at which the car becomes soft increases. By the time the camera pans, the car is a completely abstract shape. In the final position, we are dealing with at least two elements that are minimizing depth of field: long focal length and close focus. Because it was a sunny day, one can presume a high f-stop, bringing to mind the potential problems of doing a similar shot in low light. Significantly, when the zoom out is executed, we suddenly see all the elements that maximize depth of field. The shot now incorporates a wide-angle lens, a high f-stop, and, one would presume, a relatively far focus point.

Although this event may not be noticed by the average viewer and cannot be categorized as any kind of aesthetic effect, it clearly must be considered while shooting. You can tell that it is a technical by-product of attempting to achieve another effect.

A Note on Movement and Efficiency

Intricate moving shots are very attractive to first-time directors. Both the time devoted to them on the set and the internal pacing of the shots themselves, however, pose significant challenges. Movement is essential to a film, but specific camera moves need to be weighed in terms of their value in the script versus the time it takes to execute them.

Activity on the set slows down whenever you start moving the camera, particularly with inexperienced crews. Focus marks must be set, dolly track may need to be laid, and the movements have to be practiced. The talent must be thoroughly drilled on what the boundaries of their movements are. Lights and the microphone boom have to be carefully considered so they are not in the shot.

Timing and pacing of the shot are also critical. What is on screen should always be interesting visually. If it takes too long to move from one key composition to the next, the "travel time" will slow the pace of the finished product: Material that should logically occupy a few seconds of screen time occupies double or triple that. Editing allows you to condense time, eliminating the less interesting aspects of getting a subject from here to there. If the camera covers action that would otherwise be eliminated, the viewer is forced to watch action that is not germane. Many carefully planned and painstakingly executed moving shots wind up being cut into pieces in the editing room, because their dead spots kill the pace of the film.

The flip side of both of these drawbacks is that if you do not move the camera, the film will usually be flat and static. Also be aware that movement is the lifeblood of the actors' performance. Deprived of the ability to move, performers can become stilted and unnatural. It is one of the great paradoxes that the movement that is so essential to the performer is a complicating factor for inexperienced camera crews.

The beauty of movement is that you can cover significant portions of the script in a single shot. The 8-minute opening shot from Robert Altman's *The Player* presumably covers action for about eight pages of script, potentially taking dozens of setups to cover. Despite this, be careful of movements that are peripheral and slow you down. With inexperienced crews, time-consuming moves that do not cover at least a modicum of script can kill a shoot.

One novice director had to film a scene in which one detail was a boy getting up to answer the phone. The phone was in the foreground of the shot, and the boy was in the background. To recompose for the movement, the director decided to dolly right and pedestal up. The crew, all beginners as well, got the dolly set up and practiced the move without the camera. Then they measured for focus and planned the pedestal. At the end of the dolly, they found that the camera saw part of the room that had not yet been lighted. Three hours after starting, they had a few usable takes. After the shot was finished, I took the director aside and pointed out that he had spent almost half a day shooting one-eighth of a script page. At that rate his 10-minute film would take forty days to shoot. Weigh carefully whether the material in the script warrants the kind of time devoted to the proposed shot.

This is one of the fundamental albeit subtle differences between commercial features and low-budget independents. The previous example might take a professional crew about an hour to work out and so may have been worth the time devoted to it. Independents are often stuck in the position of accomplishing more script pages with a less experienced crew, a primary reason why independent films do not have the production values that commercial features enjoy.

LENS FLARES

The 1st AC also needs to check for *lens flares,* which are produced by light shining directly into the lens, causing either washed-out areas or multifaceted patterns on the image. Backlights and the sun are particularly notorious for causing flare problems. Flares can be seen as small points of light, called *kicks* or *hits,* on the front element of the lens. The effect can sometimes be seen by the camera operator, but just as often it will not be visible when looking through the viewing system. Thus, potential problems are identified by standing right in front of the camera and looking straight "down the throat" of the lens. Flares are tricky, because not all kicks cause a problem.

The AC is responsible for checking the front of the lens. If a problem is seen, something must be set up to block the offending light source from hitting the lens. Identifying which instrument is causing the problem can be tricky, with turning off or blocking the suspected culprit being the best method. While the offending ray of light can occasionally be cut at the instrument, the flare is usually blocked by a *flag,* a rectangular piece of black material, on a stand at the camera. This is the AC's call, and a grip sets it.

Moving shots present more-complex problems. Flares might be eliminated at the beginning position but then appear at a later point in the camera's movement. This requires at least one *run-through* in which the AC walks in front of the camera, watching for problems. Obviously, a stationary flag on a stand is useless in this situation. A *French flag,* a small flag on an articulated arm that mounts on the camera, is particularly helpful with these kinds of flares, as is a matte box or sunshade.

The multifaceted patterns caused by flares from the sun are occasionally incorporated into shots as stylized effects. Most flares, however, are unacceptable and require some effort to eliminate them on the set. The AC does this as a matter of course, disrupting the set as little as possible in the process.

SCRATCH TESTS

Scratched film is a significant problem, particularly when working with older cameras. It is usually caused by dirt, improper loading, or a problem with the camera. Whenever possible, the AC breaks off the first few feet of film that are run through the camera while loading is being checked. Left on a core, the piece is labeled with the camera roll number and stored for future reference. If there is any scratching, the scratch test can be processed to see if it was a camera problem or a problem caused by the lab.

LAB INSTRUCTIONS

The 2nd AC is also responsible for marking all the film cans and shipping them to the lab. The film is often either shipped to a distant lab or left in a late-night drop-off box, so marking the cans accurately is essential to avoiding misunderstandings at the lab. Even if the AC drops off the film in person, verbal instructions need written reinforcement. Mistakes in communication can have disastrous results and are almost always the filmmaker's fault for giving poor or inadequate instructions. The film cans should be labeled with the following information:

- **Production title and camera roll number.** These are necessary for keeping footage organized in editing.

- **Production company and billing information.** The lab likes to know who is going to pay. Advance payment is generally required from customers who do not have a credit history with the lab.

- **Stock number.** Even if the film is in its original packaging, write the stock numbers in prominent places. Leave no room for error.

- **Footage.** Write down the amount of footage in each can. Shooting less than a full roll is common, and the lab needs to know approximate totals to plan its processing runs.

- **Printing and processing instructions.** Identify the type of workprint desired—standard or best light are the two common choices (see chapter 8). Beyond that, the lab needs to be alerted to any specific requirements such as force processing or any of the other "tortures" covered in chapter 15. This may require a separate sheet if there are complex instructions. The AC often turns in a copy of the camera report that lists any desired lab manipulations and any spot printing to be done. Be sure that these instructions are explicit, making the lab aware of any special effect—such as color, exposure, and so on—done on the film.

- **Phone number.** If there are any questions about exposure or printing instructions, the lab may need to get in touch with you on short notice to facilitate a quick turnaround on the job. You will want to answer any questions they have.

The rolls should be marked clearly and the instructions unambiguous. An AC on one shoot was labeling two rolls of film that were being pushed one stop for effect. He carefully labeled the two cans, put them on top of two other cans that were to be processed normally, and taped them all together to ship to the lab. The lab saw the labeling on the top two cans and force-processed all four cans. The film was not completely ruined, because exposure was well within the latitude of the film, but there were heated denunciations of the lab among crew members when the news of the error arrived. In a private moment afterward, however, the DP castigated the AC for packaging the film in a way that left the potential for misunderstanding. Clarity is absolutely essential in all communications with the lab.

Equipment

Having the necessary equipment on location is essential. Forgetting important pieces of equipment can slow down or, in extreme cases, even terminate shoots. Always delineate who is responsible for bringing what. I have seen inexperienced crews arriving on location missing everything from tripods to the film itself, because everyone thought someone else was going to bring it. On professional crews this virtually never happens, because responsibility has been delegated in very clear channels: The AC always brings the tripod; the key grip handles anything to do with dollies; and the gaffer is responsible for obtaining the necessary gear to rig the lights.

EQUIPMENT CHECKLIST

The time to be focused on equipment needs is when you are preparing for and picking up the gear at the equipment room or rental house. Know what you need, check that it works, and be sure you leave with it in hand.

The lists shown in the following figure include the equipment often available at schools and media arts centers. **SEE 10-7** An experienced AC or gaffer could list dozens of other useful items. Some things, such as cleaning and repair kits, a beginning professional may want to start acquiring. Every experienced crew member seems to have accumulated several cases of tools that are commonly used for specific jobs. Lighting and sound gear are clarified in their corresponding chapters.

Do not hesitate to think big in terms of obtaining equipment, but be prepared to make do with what you can get. Rental houses are often beyond the means of noncommercial producers. Still, the fact that your primary time with busy talent is often on weekends may be in your favor. This is the rental houses' slow time, when much of their gear is sitting on the shelf. Get to know people at the rental houses and try to impress them with your knowledge and responsibility. If you make the right impression, rental houses will on occasion cut deals, particularly if you are working on the weekend. On the other hand, if they perceive you as someone who neither understands nor is concerned with the care of equipment, they will do anything to avoid letting you use their gear.

10-7

These checklists include equipment essential for a location shoot

Camera package
- ☐ Camera
- ☐ Lens and lens cap
- ☐ Film
- ☐ 2 to 3 magazines
- ☐ Core adapters
- ☐ Cores
- ☐ 85 filter
- ☐ Neutral density filters, 0.3, 0.6, and 0.9
- ☐ Proper filter ring adapters
- ☐ Sunshade
- ☐ Batteries (check for charge)
- ☐ Battery cables (plus backup)
- ☐ Changing bag
- ☐ Extra 400' cans (with black plastic bags)
- ☐ Camera tape and film tape
- ☐ Slate
- ☐ Tape measure
- ☐ Light meters
  - ☐ High slide
  - ☐ Incident disc
  - ☐ Reflective disc
  - ☐ Flat disc
- ☐ Chip chart
- ☐ Pens and permanent markers
- ☐ Log sheets and clipboard
- ☐ *American Cinematographer* manual

Tripods
- ☐ Head and legs
- ☐ Tri-downs
- ☐ Quick release
- ☐ Bushing for mount adapters

Lighting
- ☐ Complete kits—barn doors and stands
- ☐ Extra bulbs for each light
- ☐ Extension cords
- ☐ Cheaters
- ☐ Clothes pins
- ☐ C-stands and arms
- ☐ Modifying materials
- ☐ Blue gel
- ☐ Gaffer's clamps
- ☐ Gaffer's tape
- ☐ Electrician's tape
- ☐ Practical bulbs
- ☐ Shims
- ☐ Leather gloves
- ☐ Gel cutter
- ☐ Electrical tester
- ☐ Rope
- ☐ Sandbags
- ☐ Spare fuses (if applicable)

Repair kits *(camera and sound)*
- ☐ Pocketknife
- ☐ Flashlight
- ☐ Flat- and Phillips-head screwdrivers
- ☐ Jeweler's screwdrivers
- ☐ Solder and iron
- ☐ Scissors
- ☐ Set of Allen wrenches
- ☐ Battery tester with ohms meter
- ☐ Needle-nose pliers
- ☐ Wire cutters and strippers
- ☐ Tweezers
- ☐ Electrician's tape

Sound
- ☐ Recorder and supplies
  - ☐ Audiotape
  - ☐ Spindle locks
  - ☐ Crystal plugs
  - ☐ Extra take-up reels
- ☐ Microphones (plus backups)
- ☐ Mic cords (plus backups for every mic)
- ☐ Boom
- ☐ Shock mount (with adapter)
- ☐ Wind zeppelin
- ☐ 2 headphones (monaural)
- ☐ Y adapter for above
- ☐ Headphone extension cord
- ☐ Log sheets and clipboard
- ☐ Extra batteries
- ☐ Gaffer's tape

Cleaning kits
- ☐ Lens-cleaning tissue and fluid
- ☐ Denatured alcohol
- ☐ Cotton swabs
- ☐ Compressed air
- ☐ Camel-hair brush
- ☐ Orange stick
- ☐ Small flashlight

Miscellaneous
- ☐ Pens and pencils
- ☐ Permanent markers
- ☐ Notebooks
- ☐ Polaroid camera and film
- ☐ First-aid kit

11
Sound

SERIOUS consideration of sound often gets postponed to the end of the film-making process. Students usually do not get to the subject until later in their academic careers, and independents often lack the resources or support staff to give it consistent attention from the beginning of a project. Even many professionals often give it little attention until late in the editing phase. No matter how strong the visuals, sound is a critical component of any film and is often one of the glaring weaknesses in student and independent projects. Alfred Hitchcock is often referred to as one of the great visual directors, yet his films could never effectively be played without sound. Small segments of his films, such as the museum and cemetery scenes from *Vertigo* or the cornfield sequence from *North by Northwest* (1959), work without words. These scenes, however, are still highly dependent on music to achieve their effects. And there are certainly equal stretches in his films that are dialogue driven. The often-observed fact that many works, particularly episodic television programs and soap operas, can be followed just as easily with your back turned to the picture may speak to a weakness in conception. But there are also few films that can be equally powerful with their sound shut off. Even the pre-1927 "silent" films had titles and were designed for and always had musical accompaniment.

Just as with the picture, the controlling factor in recording sound for later use is determining and producing what the editors need in order to cut the sound tracks. Nothing is more instructive in grasping recording mistakes than trying to cut sound that is inadequate in quality, insufficient in length, or conceptually flawed in terms of continuity. As with so much else, understanding the hows and whys of generating material that meets the needs of the editing room is the goal of learning good audio-recording technique.

Toward a Final Sound Track

During production sound and image are recorded separately, and synchronization between the two is critical. There are a number of approaches to recording location sound for film, but in commercial production two formats are dominant: speed-controlled conventional audiotape and the relatively new DAT (digital audiotape) recorders. If the project is going to be edited on film, the sound recorded on location as well as sound effects and music are then transferred to *magnetic film stock*. Called *mag stock*, it has sprocket holes of the same size and pitch as film and is covered with the same magnetized oxide coating that standard cassette and quarter-inch audiotapes have. This is the medium of sound editing in conventional film. If the edit will be performed on a computer, the sound is digitized and input into a *nonlinear editing (NLE)* system.

During the editing process, the editor creates multiple tracks of edited sound, layering effects on top of one another to create the complexity of sound desired. In film these are called *mixtracks,* and in NLE sound is input to tracks on a *timeline.* If you foresee needing the sound of a dog barking mixed with trains rumbling by in the distance, you would never record the two sounds together. *Premixed sound—* sound that is already combined on one piece of film—is generally too inflexible for the elastic demands of the editing process. If sound is premixed, the timing of the audio elements tends to dominate how you cut the visuals to match, an approach that usually compromises optimum picture efficiency. You would record the train and the barking dog separately; they then can be moved against each other on separate tracks as well as against the picture. You want to be able to move any piece of sound against other sound to facilitate optimal positioning.

All these separate tracks are eventually mixed down to produce the final *sound track* for the film. In the conventional film approach, the edited film and mixtracks are taken to a commercial *audio mixing* facility, where each individual mixtrack is assigned to a channel on a studio mixing console. In NLE sound can be mixed internally on many systems or taken to a commercial facility if desired. It is at this stage that the loudness of each individual sound in the final sound track is set with a volume *fader.* In addition, each channel has, or can be patched into, various signal processors—equalization, reverb, echo, delay, and so on—that offer many opportunities to manipulate the quality and character of the sound. If the original recordings are of sufficient quality, these options can create virtually any desired effect in the sound. For this reason *the goal in initial recording is to record every sound at the optimal quality, no matter what it is supposed to sound like in the final film.*

To a certain extent, you do what works to create the desired sound. If you find a multilayered piece of sound that suits your needs, you would never hesitate to use it. But if any effect needs to be manipulated against another, that is, needs to change positions against other sound, it must be recorded and transferred to the appropriate medium as a separate entity. Thus it is imperative to collect sounds individually and to have each one be as clean as possible, meaning that it is optimally recorded and free of interfering recording-system and background noise.

APPLICATIONS

There are two distinct approaches to collecting sound for films: sync and nonsync. *Sync sound* is recorded as the camera is rolling on location or on the soundstage; it is also referred to as *production sound* and is generally, though not exclusively, dialogue. *Nonsync sound* is recorded at other times, ranging from effects that the location mixer collects, to effects recorded later in a sound studio, to library effects, to music that was prerecorded or specifically designed for the film. *Nonsync sound* appears to be a misnomer, because eventually all sound is precisely positioned against the picture and ultimately is in sync.

A distinction is often made between recording production sound in a studio and on location. As with virtually everything else, doing sound is much simpler in the studio, although the recording crew may have to contend with some of the contraptions (such as fog machines and fans) that are required for the picture, as well as with their operators. Locations can occasionally be a real nightmare. With the goal being clean dialogue and effects, responding to horrible acoustics, passing airplanes, traffic noise, air conditioners, heating systems, and a host of other complicating factors can make recording on location a formidable challenge. A measure of a good *sound mixer*—the person running the recorder and the head of the sound crew—may well be the ability to deal with difficult situations.

Due to considerations like this, the production sound is often replaced in postproduction editing, particularly on features and episodic television shows. *Postdubbing*—rerecording the dialogue and replacing it later—is a relatively frequent reality, although it takes a healthy budget to support the needed studio time and additional time with talent. Independents and students should be encouraged to get it right on location, even though they often have limited control over locations precisely because they have limited funds.

Single- and Double-System Sound

Single and *double system* refer to methods of achieving sync sound. For a generation brought up on confrontational video journalism, the notion that achieving lip and picture synchronization requires some effort may catch many off guard. Sound became a viable commercial entity in film only in the late 1920s. Any student of film history knows that the early sync-sound cameras were very big, requiring their own soundproof closets. These early limitations were actually overcome quite quickly, although the cameras and sound gear used to make feature films during the early years were far from portable.

Outside of instructional filmmaking, sync-sound equipment did not come into the hands of non-Hollywood filmmakers until the early 1960s, with the introduction of lightweight, portable sound and camera equipment. Just as video has created its own revolution, the introduction of the lightweight *crystal camera* and portable sound recorders also revolutionized the way films were made. These developments, along with more-light-sensitive film stocks, allowed makers to film in almost any situation.

It would seem at first that the most sensible solution to the problem of how to incorporate sound would be to put the sound along the edge of the film. Though it has drawbacks, this is indeed one approach. With the **single-system sound** method, film chambers are outfitted with a record head, and the microphone is connected directly to the camera; the sound is then recorded on a magnetic stripe along the edge of the film. **SEE 11-1** Rather than the standard double-perf configuration, single-perf film is used, with the area normally devoted to the second set of perfs taken up by the sound. Called *striped film,* it is available from several manufacturers.

The most significant drawback to this approach has to do with the different types of movement needed to both record and reproduce the two media. The film image requires intermittent movement at the gate and, as everyone knows, sound must move continuously across the heads. The two movements cannot be recorded at the same pace, so the record head has to be displaced from the gate. **SEE 11-2** The sound is displaced by 28 frames, reconciling the two types of movements. Projectors, and thus the presentation of the final film, also employ this displacement.

11-1

In single-system sound, audio is recorded on a magnetic stripe along the edge of the film

Magnetic stripe

Because the movement of the film image must be intermittent and that of the sound must be continuous, the record head is positioned below the gate area and controlled by the sprocketed rollers

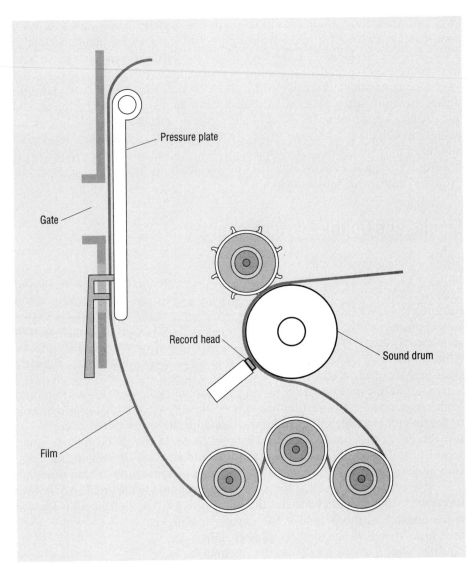

Although fine for recording and projecting, this is untenable for editing. If you cut the picture at a particular frame, you affect a different part of the sound track. Thus, critical editing is impossible with single-system sound. In addition, adding sound such as music or effects to a film is impossible, because the recorded sound occupies the entire track. The whole system is too inflexible for anything but the crudest editing.

These drawbacks are why double-system sound is the accepted method. In the *double-system sound* approach, the camera and sound recorder are separate entities. The problem lies in synchronizing the two media. When you set a wild camera at 24 fps, it does not run at precisely 24 fps—it will run at some percentage above or below 24, with no visible difference in the reproduction of movement until you get three or four frames away. When you set a conventional tape recorder to 7½ inches per second, it will have some fluctuation as well. When you add in the variable of inexact projectors and sound playback systems, the possibility of sound and image playing back at the same rate is statistically improbable.

In the days when television news was shot on film, a receding memory at best, single-system sound was very common. The film was shot for immediate broadcast, with no intention of editing. This approach was also quite popular with consumer Super 8 cameras. Single-system sound is no longer used extensively, although it has made somewhat of a comeback as a portable medium when the intention is to transfer to and finish on video.

Synchronization

Crystal cameras are the image part of the solution to synchronization, because they run at precisely 24 fps—precise at least to the extent that their fluctuations amount to at most a 1-frame variance every ten or so minutes. This was accomplished by outfitting the camera with a crystal oscillator that produces a perfect tone. This tone is then referenced against a variable tone that is produced by and dependent on the speed of the camera's motor. When the two tones match, the camera is running at 24 fps.

When this technology was introduced in the late 1950s, finding a tape recorder that could interlock with the camera was problematic. There is no such thing as a crystal tape recorder, at least in terms of conventional magnetic audiotape. Tape recorders cannot run a precise amount of tape across the sound heads because of capstan slippage and tape stretch; if the tape stretches, it would run a different amount of tape past the head. The solution was to design a recorder with a crystal oscillator that, like the one in the camera, produces a perfect tone. This tone is recorded on a small area of the tape, usually down the center. When these production sound tapes are brought back into the studio, the recorded tone is played back and *slaved* to the 60-cycle tone in standard 120-volt electrical current. The mag stock recorder is also slaved to this tone, and thus a real-time transfer is achieved. In editing, the slate is used to match picture and sound manually.

This slaved-tone approach was the standard for many years. It is still a key player, but video technologies, and eventually DAT, have introduced other methods of producing speeds that are perfect or can be duplicated. Actually, with the appropriate sideboard equipment any stereo recorder, whether cassette or quarter-inch, can be a sync recorder. A tone from a separate oscillator can be recorded onto one of the two stereo tracks, with the mono microphone signal being recorded on the other track. With the appropriate equipment, this tone is used to produce a sync transfer. The ever-increasing quality of professional cassette recorders has made this a popular modification.

The ability to produce time code has become a critical feature for sync recorders. Time code plays a significant role in slating, syncing, and identifying frames and is also critical in pull-up/pull-down to the 0.1 percent slowdown of 29.97 (see chapter 8). If a recording has time code, it can be slowed by manipulating the tape's internal clock. If a recording does not have time code, other steps need to be taken. On a digital machine, either the principal recording must be geared to 29.97, or playback for transfer must be on a machine that is internally switchable to the 0.1 percent slowdown. If an analog tape has been made, an expensive piece of sideboard gear is needed for the slowdown. Be sure to check with postproduction personnel about this.

Original recording on a sync recorder is not essential for effects and music. They are generally fitted to the picture, and production sound is the only thing that must be sync. Even so, recording everything sync, particularly music, can avoid potential difficulties in postproduction. Many people will transfer music to a sync recorder first, because it provides a sync transfer that can be duplicated. This approach pays off if more than one copy is needed or if the mag stock being used in a film edit must be replaced due to damage.

The Character of Sound

Extensive knowledge of sound and its reproduction is not necessary to make simple recordings, but the more complex the challenge, the more a lack of knowledge will cause inadequate sound. Therefore, some basics about the character and recording of sound are presented here.

Sound emanates from a source and becomes the vibration of elements in a transmission medium, usually molecules in the air. *Sound* is air molecules compressing and separating, generally represented as a wave. **SEE 11-3**

The frequency with which the signal fluctuates above and below normal air pressure is called *cycles per second (cps)* or, more common, hertz. *Hertz (Hz)* represents the *pitch* of the sound, that is, whether it is a low, midrange, or high tone. Sounds with rapid rates of fluctuation are higher, such as a soprano singer or a flute. Sounds with slow rates of frequency are low, such as a bass singer or a tuba.

Frequency range refers to the spectrum of audible and inaudible sound, represented in hertz. The average adult human ear hears from roughly 20 to 16,000 Hz. Sound exists above and below these parameters but it is inaudible. The distance of variance from normal air pressure represents *amplitude*—or the strength of the signal: The more the air is disturbed, the louder the sound.

Musical notes are at specific frequencies measured in hertz, with the audible spectrum easily divisible into octaves. Middle C is about 260 Hz. Someone singing bass would be in a range roughly from 60 to 200 Hz; a soprano would be around 2,000 to 3,500 Hz. Despite the general accuracy of these last two statements, wherever in the audible spectrum a particular human voice is, that voice has elements of other frequencies in it. Even if a person has a very low voice, that voice includes elements of high frequencies. Conversely, a high voice has elements of low frequencies. This is true of all sound, from distant thunder to the piccolo. When one starts manipulating sound with equalizers and other signal processors, this becomes a significant consideration.

Frequency response refers to how evenly and completely a specific recorder or playback format reproduces the audible range. High-quality recorders reproduce almost the entire spectrum of human hearing. Consumer recorders may record only within a relatively narrow range. Some recorders have poor low-frequency reproduction, whereas others fail on the high end. A recorder's frequency response can be checked in the machine's "specs," a list of its technical specifications. Find a recorder that reproduces as much of the sound spectrum as possible.

Frequency response is based on technical considerations, most notably quality of electronic circuitry, tape speed, and area on the tape devoted to the signal. Quality of audiotape is also a contributing factor. Due to the nature of photographic reproduction, sound on 16mm films is notoriously poor—reproducing the range of frequencies from about 70 to 7,000 Hz. Sound for 35mm is significantly better, because it is running at a faster rate and has a larger area devoted to it.

The following terms and concepts are necessary to understanding some of the fundamentals of sound.

11-3

A sound wave is a representation of compressing and separating air molecules

Decibels   A *decibel (dB)* is an increment of measurement of the amplitude, or loudness, of sound. Decibels are logarithmically based and defy any simple explanation. Suffice it to say that most recorders represent decibels either as a unit of amplitude in the recording of an audio signal or as a percentage or increment away from an optimal recording.

Mixing   There are generally two types of mixers available: the previously mentioned studio mixing console and the field mixer. A studio console is a large board with a varying number of channels for individual signals. A *field mixer,* also called a *mic mixer,* is a simple unit with a small number of mic inputs and, on some models, a few signal-processing options. A field mixer is not a requirement for location recording, but one is used when a particular setup requires more than the standard two mic inputs on most professional recorders. A field mixer converts the *mic signal*—the electric current—to a *line signal,* which is then fed to the recorder.

Signal processing   The idea that an audio signal can be changed and shaped is important. When dealing with sound coming from a microphone, you are faced with an electrical, or possibly digital, signal that can be altered as desired. Signal processors such as equalizers are frequently used to "clean" or "brighten" sound that was recorded in less than optimal conditions. Other signal processors, such as reverb units and echo chambers, can add specific character to sound.

Signal path   The route an audio signal travels—the *signal path*—is important to understand, both for troubleshooting and for determining what processes the signal is going through. The microphone converts sound into an electrical signal that is directed by the mic cord toward the record head. The signal goes into a mic input on the recorder, where the weak microphone signal is boosted by a *preamp.* In a simple recording system, the signal is then fed to the record head. In a complex recording system, the signal may be routed through a number of internal circuits.

Virtually all audio equipment—recorders, mixers, signal processors, and so on—come equipped with *line inputs* and *outputs.* The audio signal can be routed through a *line out* of one machine to the *line in* of another. You might choose to route the signal through a variety of sideboard signal processors. If you send it to an equalizer, it has to come out again. If you send it to a field mixer, you should be able to find out where it is and how to send it where it needs to go. With some basic knowledge of how signals travel, you should be able to route a signal wherever you want.

As a sound person, you should also be able to follow the often labyrinthine path of virtually any signal in any setup, including the path of a video signal. When the path of the audio signal for a specific setup is understood, the various things that affect the signal become less mysterious. There are also many points in the chain where the signal can get waylaid, and understanding the concept of how a path works can be helpful in audio troubleshooting, a skill all too frequently needed on the set.

Ambience   The quality and character of the underlying sound in any given location is called *ambience.* The *acoustics*—or total effect of sound—of any space give the sound a distinct character, whether it is the muted sound in a plush bedroom, an echo-filled school gymnasium, or the cavernous sound of Grand Central Station. This ambience colors the dialogue and effects you are recording as well and will have a specific character in even the briefest silent stretches in a scene. Even if there is no discernible audio occurring, every space has distinct acoustic characteristics. One generally attempts to exclude as much ambient sound as possible. Ambience is distinguished from *background noise,* such as distant traffic, heaters, fans, and similar interfering sources—all of which must also be addressed (both concerns are discussed later in this chapter).

Generation The term *generation* refers to the "family tree" of an image or piece of sound. In the context of sound, it relates to how the quality of recorded sound deteriorates as it is transferred from the original to various levels of copies. Successive dubs eventually degrade noticeably from the original. Recorded sound has to go through a number of generations to get to a final product. Although sound holds up well through this process, this is another reason why the original recording must be as high quality as possible. Sound degradation through dubbing has been a difficulty in conventional audiotape recording, but one of the major benefits of digital reproduction is that the number of generations is not an issue.

Sync Recorders

The situation with sync recorders has shifted somewhat in the past ten or fifteen years, with digital technologies again having an impact. Beyond the critical requirement of recording sound that can be synced with picture, a key to recording high-quality sound is to have as strong a technical system as possible. As important as such things as mic position are, the recording equipment must be equal to the task. Do not use an inexpensive consumer recorder or, more important, an inferior microphone. The sound will be only as good as the weakest link in the chain. You can go almost anywhere with a good strong signal, but a weak or inferior signal leaves you with limited options. Although there are methods for improving signals, a poor signal generally gets worse as it undergoes the necessary generations for transferring and mixing.

Nagra

The most familiar analog machine with the ability to record sync sound is the *Nagra*. **SEE 11-4** Although Nagra is a product name, this quarter-inch reel-to-reel recorder has been so central to the development of portable sync-sound filmmaking that it has become virtually synonymous with sync sound. Lightweight and portable, the Nagra is designed to be either carried on the shoulder or set up in convenient spots on location.

Magnetic recording tapes are composed of a magnetic oxide solution applied to a polyester or acetate backing. The electrical signal created by the microphone is

11-4

The Nagra recorder has become virtually synonymous with sync-sound recording
The Nagra 4.2 recorder

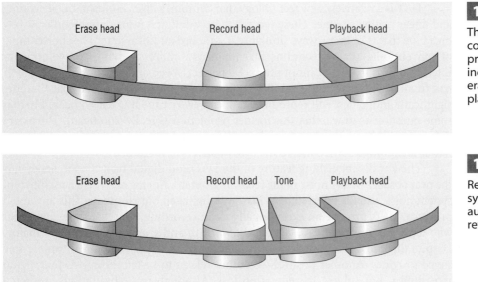

11-5

The conventional head configuration on a professional recorder includes three heads: erase, record, and playback

11-6

Recorders designed for sync sound have a fourth audio head that lays the reference tone

arranged as patterns in the magnetic oxide at the record head. The conventional head configuration on a professional recorder includes an erase head, a record head, and a playback head. **SEE 11-5** Most consumer cassette recorders combine the record and playback heads in a single head. Recorders designed for sync sound, such as the Nagra, have a fourth audio head that lays the tone needed to generate the reference on the tape for synchronization. **SEE 11-6**

DAT

Although the Nagra held a virtual but benign stranglehold on the sync world for more than thirty years, it is now seeing increased competition from *digital audiotape (DAT)* recorders. DATs have won substantial acceptance because of their almost nonexistent noise floor and their ability to interface with other digital systems. DATs are available both with and without time code capabilities, with time code DATs being substantially more expensive. Excellent DAT machines are made by Fostex, Sony, and Tascam. **SEE 11-7**

11-7

The Tascam DA-P1 DAT recorder

DAT is a relatively new technology that combines digital information encoding and linear analog storage. These recorders record digital information consecutively on a tape that is in many ways similar to a standard audiocassette. The shortcoming of conventional analog recording that the Nagra addressed with its revolutionary internal tone is that you cannot produce a perfect-speed analog recording. The DAT has finally overcome that inability: It is a perfect-speed recorder that, barring significant anomalies, will reproduce its speed every time it is played back. There is some question as to whether this former problem was really significant. The Nagra did, and still does, its job extremely well, but the analog world is fading fast and newer technologies will come to the fore by sheer momentum.

The key distinguishing feature of the DAT, and digital recording in general, is the near absence of any noise in the recording system. Analog recorders have inherent system noise, usually referred to as *hiss,* and digital all but eliminates this unwanted presence. DATs provide an exceptionally clean recording, however there are critics who have said it is *too* clean, lacking the warmth and ambient character of analog. Despite this most sound mixers have opted for the security that a less trouble-free signal provides. Another positive—one that relates to system noise—is that digital recording is not subject to generation loss. Although some limitations are being discovered, digital information can be copied many times without degradation of the signal. This is a particularly good feature because, as stated, sound is rerecorded a number of times in postproduction. DAT has also won wide acceptance because it is one more digital component in an increasingly digital postproduction landscape.

The downside of DAT recorders has been their tendency to respond poorly to climate extremes and other environmental factors. Extreme humidity has been known to render machines inoperable, and dust, cold, and heat have been problems as well. The newer DATs have addressed some of these shortcomings, but reliability remains an issue.

Beyond sync recording there is usually an extensive campaign for recording effects and music. This can be as simple as someone recording a local band or whipping up funky effects in the kitchen with a cassette recorder and mic, or it can be highly sophisticated audio studios recording a full orchestra or producing complex effects in a Foley studio. This phase can also involve narration sessions and the replacement of bad or inadequate dialogue. (See chapter 17 for a discussion of effects creation and automated dialogue replacement.)

11-8

An omnidirectional microphone picks up sound in a spherical pattern

Microphones

Microphones are classed by their *pickup,* or *polar pattern,* which refers to how a mic picks up sound from different directions in relationship to where the mic is pointing. The two types of mics that are generally available to students are omnidirectional and cardioid.

Omnidirectional mics pick up sound in a spherical pattern, that is, equally in all directions. **SEE 11-8** This approach is not particularly useful because of the more focused recordings required for sound in motion pictures. These mics do, however, have occasional applications. They can be useful for picking up the general sound, the ambience, of a scene or location. When held close to the mouth, they can also be used for voice in a reporting or interview situation. The ElectroVoice (EV) 635a is a typical example of an exceptionally durable omnidirectional mic used in field recording.

Cardioid, or *unidirectional*, mics pick up sound in a heart-shaped pattern, hence the name. They pick up sources in front of the microphone to the general exclusion of sources behind. **SEE 11-9** In the familiar "shotgun" variation, cardioids are designed to pick up sound in a narrow angle. Because of the need to focus on specific sound, these short cardioids *(short shotguns)* and supercardioids *(super shotguns)* tend to be the mics of choice for location recording. **SEE 11-10** Sennheiser, AKG, and a number of other companies make high-quality shotguns that are in common use.

Many different types of microphones are used in film production, but mics with narrow pickup patterns have obvious advantages. Traditional voice mics, such as the ones used by rock bands, are not suitable for film applications. They are meant to be put close to the mouth, which is unfeasible in most filming situations. The long shotguns, though physically impressive, are usually too much for interiors, their weight and size making them difficult to use in the often tight quarters of locations. Using a short shotgun indoors and a long shotgun outdoors is a common approach.

Shotgun mics are also used because their narrow pickup pattern excludes some amount of unwanted ambience or background noise. This has led to certain misunderstandings, however. Just because a sound originates from behind a microphone does not mean that it does not exist in some form in front of the mic. Sound is like water—or light for that matter: It flows into any area it is not completely blocked out of. If a sound is emanating from behind a microphone position, elements of it will be recorded no matter how dissipated. Shotgun mics do not eliminate unwanted sound, they simply lessen the impact.

Lavalier mics (lavs) are small clip-on mics that are frequently used for interviews, although they have a wide variety of applications in film. Lavs are not truly a class of mics, as they can be omnidirectional or cardioid, although most of them pick up in a cardioid pattern. One complication of using lavs in many film applications is that they have to be hidden. Many filmmakers leave them in plain sight in interview or documentary situations, but they must be concealed in other circumstances. This can lead to problems of muffling and the rustling of clothes.

Wireless mics, also called *radio mics*, have become increasingly popular in recent years. This mic is usually a lavalier plugged into a radio transmitter, which is clipped onto the back of the performer's waistband, taped to the body, or placed in a pocket. The radio signal is sent to a receiver that feeds it to the recorder, usually into a mic input. These mics can be handy for long shots where effective conventional miking is impossible or when the subjects are moving through tightly confined spaces.

11-9

Unidirectional, or cardioid, mics pick up sound in a heart-shaped pattern

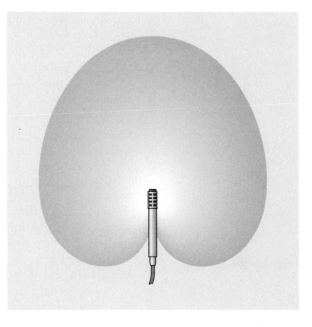

11-10

Mics with narrow pickup patterns, such as super-cardioids, have obvious advantages in film production

Radio mics are useful for many applications, but their convenience must be balanced against their recording capabilities. The quality of the signal they produce is arguably lower than that produced by a conventional mic, mostly because of muffling and clothes rustle. Their use is also complicated by the interference of other radio signals. Many locations are so saturated with radio frequencies (RFs) that other signals, such as radio stations, CBs, and cordless phones, can get thrown into the mix. The higher-end mics have many of the bugs worked out, but the rental costs of these may be beyond the means of many independents and students.

Though there are a number of other approaches, dynamic and condenser microphones are the two most common types found in schools and arts centers. In a *dynamic mic*, the current—the mic signal—is produced by air movement within a magnetic field. The moving air created by sound hits a membrane in the head of the mic, and the resulting vibration generates the signal. *Condenser mics*, also called *capacitor mics*, require a source of power, usually a battery, that supplies the microphone head with a consistent electrical signal. In this case the consistent electrical signal is altered by the movement of air against a similar membrane.

A common method of powering condenser mics, as well as several other types, is the phantom powering system. *Phantom mics* are powered by the batteries in the recorder rather than an internal battery. In many applications mic cords have to be specially wired with the polarity reversed for the current to reach the mic. The phantom design is one you will encounter frequently.

Sound people tend to find a small number of mics with which they are comfortable and they can be very opinionated, with arguments about what constitutes the best mic getting emotional and vehement. You need to get past the hype to pick the right mic for a given situation. Try out as many mics as you can. Listen to mics side by side to get a sense of which one produces the cleanest and highest-quality signal. Remember that the recording chain is only as strong as its weakest link, and a good microphone is essential to a high-quality recording.

AUDIO CONNECTORS AND MICROPHONE CORDS

There are four basic types of audio connectors used in the United States: quarter-inch, mini, RCA, and XLR. You will occasionally find others, such as the banana plug, but they are generally associated with foreign-made, mostly European, equipment or specific brands. Japanese and American recorders tend to conform to the same standards.

Audio connectors and cords are all based on a simple connection. Most connectors have simple positive-to-positive and negative-to-negative contacts. On the standard plug-style connector, the tip of the pin is the positive, or "hot," contact and the shaft is the negative, or ground, contact. **SEE 11-11** Microphone cords are equally straightforward. A simple cable has a single conductor surrounded by *shielding*—a metal mesh that encases the conductors for the length of the cable. The single conductor is connected from one hot contact to the other, and the shield is used to connect the grounds. All connections are soldered. The plug end of a connector is traditionally referred to as the male end, and the input end is referred to as female. Though some may find this usage of language peculiar or uncomfortable, it nevertheless remains the terminology of choice among audio people.

There are two types of audio inputs in general use in filmmaking applications: microphone and line. Mic inputs, of course, accept the signal from the mic. A line signal is of higher voltage and is exchanged either internally or between two machines. All the connections among recorders, mixers, and signal processors are line connections.

Mic and line connections are differentiated by the voltage level of their signal. Inputs are rated by their *impedance,* which refers to the designed resistance to voltage in the line. Low-impedance microphones and thus inputs are standard. Line inputs

All audio connectors and cords are based on a simple negative/positive connection

Quarter-inch phone plug
Conductor in tip carries positive signal, shielded by negative current in shaft

− +

Mini plug
Monaural shown— stereo version *(right)* often used for small personal headphones

RCA plug
Commonly used in pairs to connect home stereo equipment

Banana plug
Used more frequently in Europe

Stereo connectors
Note ring near tip to carry extra channel for stereo

XLR or Canon jack
"Female" connector

XLR or Canon plug
"Male" connector

are generally high impedance. Mic and line connections are not interchangeable. You cannot plug a mic into a line input, or vice versa, unless you use an impedance transformer. These are usually available for circumstances in which gear does not have the output or input needed. In filmmaking applications, however, most inputs are used for the purpose for which they were designed. The only other signal impedance of interest is with speaker connections.

Quarter-inch, or phone, plug The durable and heavy *quarter-inch plug* receives extensive use as both a mic connection and a line connection. Professional headphones are also usually equipped with a quarter-inch plug, also called a *phone* *plug.* The input requires quite a bit of dedicated space in the interior of the record deck, a possible reason why phone plugs are not as popular as they might be in consumer equipment.

Mini plug   A *mini plug* looks like a smaller version of the quarter-inch plug. It is generally used as a microphone input on consumer cassette recorders and video cameras. Its major drawback is that it is not very durable, particularly on the input end, which is on the recorder or camera. The mini plug is also prone to being accidentally pulled out of the recorder. It is also a common headphone jack, though rarely found on professional equipment.

RCA plug   The *RCA plug* is used almost exclusively as a line connection and is probably the most common type. It is found on everything from consumer stereos to VCRs. The center pin is the positive connection, and the sleeve is the negative connection. The sleeve also allows for a tight fit on the line input.

XLR or Canon   The *XLR plug* has a three-pin configuration and is the standard mic connection on most professional equipment. Also known as the *Canon plug,* it is used for line connections in high-end studio gear as well. The XLR is the norm because the three-pin configuration incorporates a second conductor to connect the grounds and uses the shield to protect the signal from electronic interference. The hot contact carries the signal, and the ground carries its opposite.

Banana plugs   These are used more frequently on European-produced equipment, particularly the Nagra. In a *banana plug,* the two leads are separated out into individual plugs. The plug has a flexible sleeve that constricts when inserted into the line input, thus holding it in place. The banana configuration is one of the key connectors used with the Nagra, although it does not show up that frequently on other equipment.

There are a number of other specialized pins, Tuchel pins and DIN pins to name two. *Tuchel pins* are used with the Nagra and often come with a threaded sleeve—a loose-fitting sleeve on the connector that screws into the body of the recorder. The *DIN pin* is a European connector found on older equipment, including the Uher recorder, which was used extensively in sync recording.

Adapters convert one type of plug to another, from a male mini to a female RCA, for instance. Anticipating all needs is always the goal, and having a good selection of adapters on hand can get you out of many tight situations.

Stereo and monaural (mono) are also important issues. The separate channel configuration of *stereo,* which consists of two separately recorded tracks on the same tape played back simultaneously, has become such a standard in home audio systems that the old single-signal mono has almost been forgotten by consumers. Until recently, recorders designed for films recorded in *mono,* because all individual sounds are treated separately in editing and the final product is usually mono. Advanced theatrical sound systems and transfers to video have complicated this issue, but sound for film is still frequently recorded in mono. Given that so much audio equipment is set up for stereo, this can cause problems in matching equipment so that the signal is both transferred and monitored properly.

In line connections the stereo signal is handled by two separate conductors, particularly the familiar, paired *stereo RCA* cords. There are single cords designed to carry the stereo signal, particularly quarter-inch and mini headphone plugs. As with a mono connector, the tip carries one channel; the shaft of the connector has a band just below the tip which is the contact for the second channel. The stereo cable has a separate conductor connected to this second contact. Stereo headphones plugged into a mono headphone jack will produce sound in only one ear. Adapters that convert the mono signal so that it can be heard on stereo headphones are handy to have when different pieces of equipment are being used.

Stereo recorders have seen increased use in professional production in recent years, because there is a growing feeling that a stereo recording allows more options in editing. The mono system remains an adequate approach, although a wide release on video requires a stereo signal. If stereo separation is an issue, it can always be part of the audio design in the final mixdown. Nagra produced both a stereo and a mono model, and many schools have the older, traditional mono machines.

RECORDER FEATURES AND ACCESSORIES

Sound recorders come with a variety of features, all designed to aid the sound person in creating the highest-quality recording possible while on the set. Although these features aid in controlling and manipulating the technical quality of the audio signal, your ear should be the final arbiter of the sound. You can make everything look fine on the recorder's displays, but if the mic is too far away, the result will be inadequate sound. If it doesn't sound good to your ear, it won't sound good when you try to plug it into your film. The same is true of the ear as is of the eye in lighting: Just because it sounds good to the ear does not mean that you are getting the best recording possible. It has to be happening with both the ears and the displays. Being sensitive as well as attentive to the evaluative tools is one mark of a good sound person.

Running speeds Most professional recorders give a number of options for *running speed*, measured in *inches per second (ips)*. A typical professional quarter-inch recorder might offer speeds of 3¾, 7½, and 15 ips. Cassette players run at 1⅞ ips, with many professional decks offering a higher speed as an option. Higher running speeds produce higher-quality sound. The major reason for this is that a higher speed devotes more magnetic material to the sound per second. Another major consideration is consistent speed and stable transport across the head. Slower recording speeds are harder to keep constant; the tape tends to wobble on the heads, causing "wow" and "flutter."

Most recording is done at 7½ ips for dialogue scenes. The 15 ips speed runs through tape at high rates, but the extra speed does not translate to higher-quality sound in terms of the human voice. The difference, however, between 7½ and 3¾ is substantial, so the slower speed is rarely used. For the most part, the slow speed is present on professional recorders to facilitate disposable recordings that are not film related—recordings of meetings and similar events that may not even be saved, much less used in a final product. Music is usually recorded at 15 ips, as the reproduction of extended tones and notes requires the highest quality possible. Sound effects are usually recorded at 7½ ips, although they are the least needy in terms of perfect reproduction.

Mic inputs Professional recorders generally employ the XLR plug. Occasionally, you will find a professional deck with quarter-inch inputs. Stereo machines have separate mic inputs, with each mic signal being fed to its own individual track. The older mono Nagras also have two mic inputs, with the signal being mixed internally. Some recorders have switchable mic inputs that can change to other impedances or microphone-powering methods.

Line inputs and outputs Line connections are an important feature on any recorder. When recording subjects that are being amplified or that require multiple mics, such as a rock band or someone speaking at a meeting, it is preferable to patch

The VU meter shows
the level of the audio
signal being fed to the
record head
Stereo VU meters on a Sony
TC-D5M cassette recorder

into the sound system being used. This should give good, clean sound, avoiding the acoustic effects of the amplified signal.

Record level adjustments   Recorders generally have twist knobs to control the record level of the sound. These are called *potentiometers (pots)* or *gain controls*. A *fader* is the sliding control found on most mixing consoles. Stereo machines have a pot for each channel, as does the mono Nagra.

VU meter   The *VU (volume unit) meter* monitors the level of the audio signal being fed to the record head. It is the familiar scale on the front of all but the most rudimentary recording machines. **SEE 11-12** The microphone turns sound into electrical energy, which triggers the needle on the VU meter. The needle registers the high-amplitude points—the peak—and low-amplitude points of the audio signal as it is expressed in the electrical current. *Zero VU (0 VU)* is often presented as the point the signal should not exceed to avoid distortion, although this is not a completely accurate assertion. VU meters are imperfect tools, because they are peak-averaging meters; they do not show all the high points of the recorded signal, but only an average, so that they are in position to respond to the next signal. This has led designers to leave *headroom* in the meters, that is, room above 0 VU where the recorder still reproduces an undistorted signal. Although there are different theories for recording various sounds, suffice it to say that professional sound people frequently record certain sounds substantially above 0 VU.

Peak program meter   The *peak program meter (PPM)* is generally considered an improvement over the VU meter. It is featured on many high-end machines, most notably the Nagra, on which it is referred to as a *modulometer*. The *ballistics* of its needle are delicate enough to respond to all fluctuations in volume, giving an accurate reading of the signal at all times. Modulometers do not have a 0 VU point as do standard VU meters; they have instead a 0 dB point that displays how far off the nominal distortion point you are. Unlike 0 VU, the 0 dB point on a modulometer is the effective limit past which distortion occurs. An occasional swing over 0 on a modulometer may be acceptable because, given that distortion is not an absolute concept, there may still be slight headroom. Sound mixers generally keep the signal around the middle of the meter.

Although zero on either meter represents an important point in the consideration of distortion, it also represents an important qualitative measure. It is roughly the point at which the recorded signal best covers the inherent noise of the recording system. Many beginning sound mixers are so terrified by 0 VU on the meter that they tend to underrecord the signal, assuming that anything is better than the dreaded distortion. If the recorded signal is too low, the sound may be overwhelmed by what is called the *noise floor* of the recorder and can eventually become unintelligible. Although the effect of system noise on the tape may not be immediately audible, sound has to go through a number of generations to reach a final sound track; any hiss on the tape will be magnified in this process. Underrecording is actually worse than having the signal occasionally go above peak levels, with slight distortion on a peak often not a problem, because it can replicate how we hear loud sounds.

Effective recording can be done with either the VU meter or the PPM, although the latter gives a more accurate depiction of the sound. The key is to know the capabilities of each.

11-13

A typical LED meter display on a DAT recorder

DAT LED meters DATs too have peak meters for monitoring volume levels. A digital display has ascending vertical bars representing the fluctuations of record levels. **SEE 11-13** The major difference with these meters is that, although there is substantial wiggle room with a VU meter and a little less with a PPM, zero on a DAT meter represents an absolute threshold. If the meter peaks above zero, rather than distorting, the signal simply collapses. The mixer must be exceedingly careful to avoid zero. Fortunately, the character of the recorded signal on a DAT assists in accomplishing this. With virtually no system noise, there is nothing inherent in the recording to cover up. With a conventional recorder, consciously underrecording to avoid distortion can have dire consequences in the form of more noise in the system. With the DAT, however, you can underrecord with the knowledge that it should not negatively affect the final product. General practice is to keep the recording around −12 on the meter.

Most of these meters also have a very useful *peak-hold* feature. A series of unconnected vertical bars gives a representation of the most recent peak and holds in that position for a few seconds. If you are surprised by a sound or look away for a second, you can look back and tell immediately if the peak is going to present a problem. There is also a *margin* feature that can be quite useful—in some ways more so than even the peak reading level meter. It tells you exactly how close in decibels the signal has come to absolute 0 and holds that value as long as needed. This ensures that short-duration level peaks are not missed. By monitoring the margin readout, you can set overall levels so that you always have a margin of safety below absolute 0 for peaks. Later in postproduction the level of the entire recording can be brought up to just under absolute 0 in a process called *normalization*.

Tape/direct Most professional recorders offer a choice of how to monitor the sound as it is being recorded. Recorders with separate record and playback heads have a *tape/direct switch* that allows you to toggle between monitoring the sound as it comes to the record head (direct, which is labeled *source* or *input* on some machines) or off the playback head *(tape)*. When monitoring in the *tape* position, the sound is recorded at the record head, then played back next to it at the playback head. Because of this you will hear a slight delay between the actual live sound and the playback sound, which can be quite disconcerting for beginning mixers. But, because there can be some difference between the microphone signal and the signal that is actually recorded, many mixers monitor in the *tape* position. They get accustomed to the delay and can feel confident in the quality of the final product. On a more mundane level, it also lets you know when you are out of tape. This is handy when you are on the move, working on documentaries or in difficult locations.

Headphones Be sure to obtain a pair of headphones that gives a complete representation of sound and that isolates any confusing external noise. This means getting the padded, cup-shaped isolation headphones rather than cheaper pad or flat consumer models. Do not hesitate to pay for a high-quality set. There are few things more foolish than using a $15 pair of headphones to monitor the recording of critically important sound on a $10,000 tape recorder.

Use headphones for all film applications, whether recording key production sound or seemingly innocuous background effects. The internal speakers on most production recorders, including the Nagra, are not of sufficient quality to monitor sound, and you probably won't have the time to go back and listen to something you have just recorded anyway. Without headphones there is no effective way to detect minor flaws in the recording.

Two pairs of headphones are needed for the sound crew: one for the person recording and one for the person handling the mic. A simple Y adapter that splits the signal at the headphone jack is generally used, although you have to be careful that the signal fed to the headphones is not adversely affected.

Headphone volume controls and headphone jacks These are relatively straightforward parts of the recorder but warrant a few comments. While recording on a set, be careful not to overcrank the headphone volume. The sound can bleed through and disturb the recording, particularly if you are monitoring in the *tape* position with the delay. This extra sound may render location recordings unusable; even if the bleed-through is quiet enough that it is not recorded, it may be disconcerting to the talent. Set the volume to a level that is both comfortable for you and an accurate reflection of the sound, without being audible to other people on the set.

When organizing the equipment for a shoot, check to see if you need stereo or mono headphones. Mismatched headphones and recorders will leave you with sound in only one ear and may cause volume-level problems. Adapters are available to convert a mono output signal to stereo headphones, and having a few on hand is helpful if you need to plug into various pieces of equipment.

Automatic gain control The *automatic gain control (AGC)* reads the signal being fed to the record head and automatically adjusts the record level appropriately. Referred to as the *automatic level control (ALC)* on the Nagra, it is available on many recorders, although it generally gives disagreeable results. The drawback is that AGCs tend to overrespond to peak and low signals, with frequent wide and seemingly uncontrolled swings of the record level, particularly with complex sound. The result can have a mechanical sound to it. It is somewhat like automatic exposure on a camera; you want to control the record levels just as you want to control the exposure. A number of high-end recorders have very sophisticated AGC features that anticipate these difficulties and minimize negative side effects. Even so, they are not used extensively. A good AGC feature can be useful in documentary situations, when you are working with a small crew and may have to leave the recorder unattended or cannot keep your eyes on the meter (a situation that generally should be avoided).

Limiters A *limiter* adjusts peak signals that are liable to be distorted. It is used while manually setting the record level and kicks in during the occasional peaks that you cannot anticipate or respond to adequately. It is something like a cap that will not allow the signal to be recorded above a certain level, usually 0 VU or 0 on the PPM. If used carelessly, it can lend the same mechanically manipulated quality to a recording as the AGC. When the levels are being carefully monitored, however, it can knock the top out of a signal that would otherwise be distorted.

Equalizers An *equalizer* is commonly used to manipulate the quality of sound, cutting or boosting it at specific frequencies. Equalizers are used either to clean up sound that has unwanted elements or to add brightness or character to the production sound. Though the goal is to record perfect production sound, conditions often prevent this. Equalization can add dimension to the sound that was impossible to obtain in the location recordings, although there are limits to what can be done.

An equalizer consists of controls that either boost or cut the amplitude of frequencies at specific pitches. The equalizer divides the sound into *bands,* each of which centers on a specific frequency that is controlled by either a fader or a pot. **SEE 11-14** The unit portrayed in the figure equalizes the sound at twenty-seven different frequencies. Just as with the spectrum of audible sound, equalizers can be, and frequently are, broken down into octaves.

Though the faders control amplitude at a specific frequency, those on either side of the selected frequency are also affected. Equalizers with more bands offer finer discriminations in affecting individual sounds and are generally more useful in film as well as most other audio applications. The equalizer shown in figure 11-14 separates the audible spectrum into many increments. Each band thus controls a narrow range of frequencies, having a relatively small effect on adjacent frequencies. Equalizers that separate the sound into a small number of bands affect an often unacceptably wide range of adjacent frequencies at each band.

Equalization is an important tool in transferring production sound to mag stock and in the mixing stages of a film. Equalizers are occasionally brought on location, but even then it is a good idea to save most signal processing for postproduction. If you have an unwanted low-frequency sound, traffic rumble in the background, for instance, you could equalize certain low frequencies and limit or eliminate the sound. If there was an unavoidable high-pitched hum from fluorescent lights, you might be able to make it less objectionable by equalizing some high frequencies. These problems, however, can be partially or completely eliminated

An equalizer divides sound into bands, each of which centers on a specific frequency in the transfer and then further addressed at the mix if necessary. Conditions on the set are generally not optimal for effectively monitoring sound, and thus it is difficult to be consistent with how the sound is manipulated. Like a DP's eyes, a sound person's ears can change over the course of a long day.

Slavishly attempting to create the desired audio effect in the original recording is one of the biggest mistakes a mixer can make. A certain amount of this is all right, but the mixer must first and foremost produce a usable recording. If you want someone to be speaking from the other side of a closed door, the sound should be recorded clean. If the sound is recorded through the door, it may not be intelligible by the time it gets to the final sound track. As suggested at the beginning of this chapter, if the recorded sound is good, you can go almost anywhere with it, making extensive adjustments in the mixing process. But if the recorded sound is poor, the ability to manipulate it will be severely limited.

Unaltered sound can be disconcerting for uninitiated viewers of the dailies and rough cuts, so sound mixers occasionally find themselves recording sound "for the dailies." This approach reflects an understandable fear of those unfamiliar with the process, often clients or potential funders. A friend tells the story of being called on the carpet by an inexperienced producer and client "to explain himself" for a clean recording of a sound that would be manipulated later. When he launched into a lengthy technical explanation, he was cut off and told to do better next time. Most people on the production team do, however, understand the technical requirements of sound.

Filters   The term *filter* has several connotations. The controls on equalizers are often referred to as filters, although they are used primarily for controlling the amplitude at desired frequencies. When spoken of outside of this usage, **filters** refer to options on the audio recorder that affect a wide range of frequencies above or below a certain point. Recorders often come with a few filtering options. The following are common choices, each cutting out a certain range of frequencies. Where exactly they start cutting the signal is dependent on how the individual filter is set by the manufacturer.

- *High-pass filters* filter out low frequencies, allowing high frequencies to pass through to the tape.

- *Low-pass filters* do the opposite, allowing low frequencies to pass while cutting high frequencies.

- *Low-frequency attenuators (LFAs)* cut low-frequency signals, *attenuation* being a common technical term for cutting.

- *High-frequency attenuators (HFAs)* cut the sound above a preset level.

Most location sound mixers do not do much filtering while recording sync takes. Filters affect quite a bit of the audio signal, changing the character of a wide range of sounds. They tend to be coarse controls, used as broad remedies for big consistent problems in the sound, such as traffic, fans, heating systems, and the like, that cannot be addressed by other means. If, however, you can get to the source of the sound and shut it off, that is far preferable to filtering.

To a certain extent, the acquisition format is somewhat irrelevant. The critical factor is obtaining a recording that both fulfills technical specifications and is free of unwanted additional sound. Beyond these two considerations, the critical arbiter is your ears. Does it sound good and does it sound like something we want on a soundtrack?

The Production Sound Crew

The sound crew has one of the more frustrating jobs on a film set, because sound is rarely afforded the attention that camera and lighting receive. Because so many fellow crew members are devoted to the picture—camera crew, gaffer and grip crews, design people, makeup, script supervisor, and so on—the sound crew can feel substantially outnumbered and overwhelmed by picture people. There is a saying in the business: "An hour for picture, a minute for sound"—an accurate assessment of the weight given each endeavor in shooting a film. Because of this attitude, the sound crew may occasionally have to assert the importance of their endeavors in the general scheme of things.

Although this lack of acknowledgment can be exasperating for the sound crew, there is a certain amount of justification for it. If the sound recorded on location is not good, there are a number of viable remedies. If you do not get the picture, however, you have nothing. As suggested, location dialogue recording is often done with the knowledge that it will be replaced. Many sound effects are also done in postproduction. Despite all this everything should be done to get high-quality location sound, particularly for filmmakers with small budgets. When working with limited resources, dealing with inadequate sound can be an expensive, messy, and time-consuming process. Whenever you find yourself saying, "I can get that sound later," it will usually prove easier to get it right then and there.

The sound crew is usually asked to do its job without disrupting the set. As shots are set up, the sound crew cannot expect the lighting crew to arrange the instruments in a way that facilitates sound work, nor should it. If lighting, usually from above, makes it virtually impossible to use a microphone boom, the sound crew may have to try a different approach to miking. All this does not mean, however, that the sound crew should not be assertive when elements are conspiring to make recording high-quality sound next to impossible. There is a certain "deal with it" attitude on the part of many picture people that occasionally requires some forceful behavior modification.

The sound crew is generally composed of two people: the previously mentioned sound mixer and the boom operator. On larger commercial productions, the sound crew may have the luxury of a third person, who is generally listed in the credits as a cable puller. The *cable puller* helps with setup, keeps the mic cords out of the way during the shot, and often takes care of the *sound log*—the log of the daily activity of the sound crew.

The *sound mixer* has four primary responsibilities: determining microphone positions for the best sound reproduction, addressing any excess noise that is interfering, determining how best to work with the acoustics of the shooting space, and monitoring audio levels for optimal recording. At the direction of the mixer, the *boom operator* generally handholds the mic on a boom above the heads of the talent. If characters are moving or if there is more than one person being recorded, the boom operator may have to incorporate substantial mic movement during a shot. As one might suspect, booming can be physically demanding, requiring stamina and good upper-body strength. The physical stress is somewhat mitigated by the boom's needing to be in position only for the generally short duration of the individual takes. The mic cord should be cradled gently in the hands, making sure that cable noise does not become a problem.

It is the sound mixer's responsibility to formulate a miking strategy for each shot. The three keys to successful miking are the same as those to establishing a successful restaurant: location, location, and location. Get the microphone as close to the subject as possible. Given the complexity of many shots, this can be quite tricky. If the subject is too far from the mic, the mixer has to crank the record level, and when the mixer has to crank the volume, the acoustics of the space and unwanted extraneous noise become stronger elements. The closer the mic is, the more the recording can be focused on the subject.

The assistant director lets the mixer know what the next shot is going to be and what setups are being considered for the near future. As the scene is being blocked for the camera, the mixer should determine where the boom operator can stand and what mic movement will be needed. An experienced boom operator will have worthwhile input into this planning. Essentially, the mixer observes the entire shot and designs the miking so that the subject is always optimally recorded.

The boom operator needs to be aware of two problems of which he or she may be the source: casting boom shadows on the scene and allowing the boom to drop into the frame. The sound crew should handle as much of this as possible, but these concerns frequently require consultation with the camera crew.

Boom shadows in a shot are unacceptable, and their presence demands that alternative miking positions be found. In conjunction with the mixer, the boom operator should pay attention to the lighting of a scene to find the "path of least resistance" to the subject—that is, where the boom can be positioned without casting shadows. Frequently, the boom operator's best path is to come in from around the fill light. This keeps the mic out of the path of the key light, staying near the softest and most diffuse light. (The types of lighting instruments and their uses are discussed in chapter 12.)

The boom will always cast some shadows, and it is the camera operator who will identify which ones are in the shot and which ones fall harmlessly outside the frame. But be aware that there are many elements in the frame that demand the camera operator's attention; subtle shadows may be missed. If concerned about a shadow, the boom operator should tell the camera operator, who will check the shot or do an entire *walk-through,* an initial rehearsal in which the technical personnel and the actors walk slowly through a shot to identify potential problems, in this case looking specifically for errant shadows.

Boom mics dropping into the frame were a staple on old late-night talk shows but are unacceptable in film applications. With the goal being to get the mic as close to the subject as possible, the boom operator must know exactly where the top of the frame is and have the mic hover just above it. Knowing some basic compositional principles helps in this regard. Individual DPs generally have consistent approaches to headroom. If you know what that approach is, you should be able to determine boom position without too much consultation. Inexperienced boom operators may be tempted to hold the boom so high that it could not possibly be in the shot. This mistake amplifies room ambience and compromises the quality of the sound. Simply find out what the limits of the frame are and stay just outside of them. In my booming days, I became so familiar with one DP's shooting style that we rarely spoke to each other on the set except to determine where to go to relax after the shoot.

In the final analysis, it is the camera operator's responsibility to identify both boom shadows and encroaching mics in the shot. It is the boom operator's responsibility to eliminate them. Both concerns are complicated by the shifting frame and the necessity to follow moving subjects with the boom. The shot has to be checked from beginning to end to ascertain that the boom is not presenting a problem anywhere. The camera crew will of course expect minimal interference from the boom operator, but to achieve sound quality that is as high as possible, the sound crew should be assertive if the need arises.

Riding gain means shifting the record level during each take to respond to changing audio levels

The meter and needle on the Nagra

Riding Gain

Shifting the record level during each recorded take to respond to changing levels of sound is known as *riding gain*. Whether the sound is an actor's voice or an effect, its volume within a shot will most likely change. The mixer must constantly adjust the potentiometer (pot) to keep the meter's needle as close to the appropriate record level as possible. **SEE 11-15** The mixer's attention should be completely devoted to the meter during takes. If you can see a mixer's eyes during rehearsals or takes, he or she may not be doing the job properly. By constantly adjusting the pot, the mixer is able to obtain an optimum recording at all times.

Just as there are rehearsals for the actors and the camera, recording of the sound needs practice as well. After getting a description of the shot from the AD, the mixer uses the first walk-throughs to ascertain what is occurring in the sound. In conjunction with the mixer, the boom operator develops a plan for booming the scene and then must be ready for the rehearsals. Just as the mixer has a plan for miking each setup, he or she must formulate a strategy for riding gain as well. During rehearsals the mixer should practice all the movements of the pot. By the time shooting starts, the mixer should have all adjustments finalized and be able to anticipate all fluctuations in amplitude. Obviously, there can be differences in individual performances by the talent, but the mixer should be able to keep the meter within accepted tolerances.

Most volume adjustments require only small movements of the pot, but occasionally there are times when a more dramatic response is needed. I was once recording an actor who whispered a line and then broke into a loud laugh. Even though I could get quite close with the mic, I had to turn the pot up almost all the way to obtain a usable recording of the whisper. When the loud laugh came, I had to turn the pot almost 180 degrees to get an undistorted signal. After several rehearsals, I had a sense of the actor's timing and was able to shift the pot at the right moment. The boom operator helped me by moving the mic slightly away from the actor just before the laugh came, although this response to a louder sound is not always the best one.

The approach to riding gain is very similar to that of anticipatory camera, except that the boundaries are less distinct. There is no frame line to watch through the viewfinder; the representations of the needle are the only guide—one that can start to feel quite abstract even though it represents something very real. Just as the camera leads subject movement, the recording of the audio should lead the fluctuating levels of sound. As with many elements, proper audio recording goes largely unnoticed; the listener recognizes that the sound recording has not been done properly only when there is a glaring error or something is unintelligible.

Keep in mind that the goal is always an optimum recording. Fear of distortion, again, often causes beginning mixers to mistakenly underrecord. Always keep the needle as close to zero as possible for all dialogue and effects. Occasional peaks above zero will not render the recording unusable, and a good limiter will soften any potential distortion. Although the needles and meters give an accurate depiction of the technical quality of the signal, your ear should be the final arbiter of the sound. If it does not sound good on location, it will not sound good when the editor starts trying to incorporate it into the film.

The biggest challenge in recording sync sound in conventional filming situations is the issue that has complicated so much of the task: continuity. Producing a clean signal clearly serves the requirements of continuity, and a "dirty" signal causes problems. Beyond that, if mic positions are wildly different or record levels fluctuate, consistency will suffer and production sound may prove uncuttable. Ensuring that the pieces are going to cut together becomes the determining factor.

Recording a Scene

As with everything else in film production, creating usable sound for a scene takes careful preparation and a measured and thoughtful approach. There are many things that complicate what appears to be, but of course isn't, a simple task.

COMPLICATING FACTORS

Effective recording of a scene requires an understanding of how all the individual elements of sound are going to interlock. With the exception of perspective and phasing, the following discussion outlines problems associated specifically with location filming, the controlled atmosphere of studio shooting eliminating many of these potential headaches.

Ambience   The sound crew is concerned with ambience in two different ways. The mixer generally wants to exclude as much ambience as possible in the original recording. The less ambience present in a take, the less likely it is to interfere with consistency. Ambience can always be added, but it is problematic to take out. The second concern is that even though we have attempted to eliminate as much ambience as possible, the editors need some recorded ambient sound to cover silent or empty spots in the sound track. As suggested, every place in which you shoot will have its own distinct sound characteristics. Just as darkness is not the absence of light, silence is not a total absence of sound. Any gaps in the dialogue tracks—and there will always be some—must therefore be covered by recorded silence matching the ambience level that is under the dialogue. Variously called *presence* or *room tone*, several minutes of uninterrupted silence should be recorded by the sound mixer in each location.

Background noise Of even greater concern is background noise, which often causes substantial problems with the consistency of sound in editing. Problematic background interference is relatively common on location and must be found and eliminated. Sometimes this simply requires locating the source and shutting it off. Other problems may cause lengthy delays while the source gets out of hearing range. Some unsolvable problems may force replacement of the dialogue during postproduction.

Air-conditioning and heating systems frequently cause problems, as do fluorescent lights, which make a highly undesirable hum—another reason to avoid shooting under them. Shooting in a restaurant or a kitchen necessitates turning off refrigerators and other noisy appliances. Noisy neighbors may need to be quieted, and the guy mowing his lawn down the street may need some incentive to postpone the job.

More-permanent problems can impose even greater demands. Shooting near heavy traffic areas or airport approaches can ruin sound takes and cause lengthy delays. As a sound such as an airplane recedes, the mixer lets the crew know that the sound has diminished enough to try a take. Given the odd path that reflected sound can often take, this can be a risky proposition. Such circumstances can turn four-hour shoots into eight-hour nightmares. As suggested, postdubbing sound may be a foregone conclusion when working in completely untenable locations.

Camera noise This can also be problematic, particularly when working with older cameras. The new generation of sync cameras, such as the Aaton and the Arri SR, generally do not pose a problem, although in the pin-drop quiet of a set even they can be picked up on a sensitive microphone. *Camera noise* can be muted with a *barney*, a padded slip-on hood designed for a specific camera. In the absence of a barney, sound can be reduced by *blimping* the camera—wrapping it with a heavy jacket or something similar. Unfortunately, the camera lens tends to act like a megaphone for camera noise, shooting it right out in front of the camera which, as luck would have it, just happens to be right where the subject you are recording is. Although my suggestion of putting a sock over the lens has always fallen on deaf ears, the glass filters used to protect the front element of the lens can help with sound problems as well.

If the camera is noisy, it must be recorded with the space's ambience. Recording room tone without the camera noise is meaningless if camera noise is contributing significantly to the sound in a space. And it must be recorded with the camera loaded, because a camera running empty does not sound the same. Some camera crews will go so far as to bring dummy loads in anticipation of camera noise. Barring this, recording sound during shots that do not require sync sound can be a good source for this sound. The editor can then make the offending source consistent rather than having it irritatingly drop in and out.

Wind noise This is a slightly different type of unwanted sound that is frequently problematic. Wind is similar to sound in that it is moving molecules in the air. If not taken into account, *wind noise* can play havoc with microphones, causing such a strong signal to be fed to the recorder that distortion is unavoidable. A *wind zeppelin*, also called a *wind shield*, has a baffle design that cuts much of the interference from wind. **SEE 11-16** Many zeppelins have an additional *windsock* that fits around the exterior for high-wind situations. Moving air in interiors can be an issue as well, mostly through air-passage systems associated with heating or air-conditioning. Using a zeppelin or a simple slip-on foam wind shield to protect against moving air is common. Be particularly careful of wind noise in spontaneous shooting situations,

11-16

A wind zeppelin, or wind shield, has a baffle design that cuts much of the interference from wind

Rycote™ wind zeppelin

documentary shoots for instance, where you cannot monitor the recorder's meter. In the *direct* position, the distortion caused by wind noise will often go unheard, although it does show on the meter. When wind is an issue, be sure to monitor in the *tape* position, hearing the actual signal that has been recorded.

Acoustics   As stated earlier, *acoustics* refers to the way sound travels in a given space and particularly to how it reflects off surfaces before arriving at the microphone or ear.   **SEE 11-17** It is one of the greatest challenges to the sound crew. Spaces are frequently referred to as being either "live" or "dead." A *live space* has many hard surfaces off which the sound bounces. The sound thus comes to the microphone at different rates and from many different directions. Although the sounds reaching the mic are only milliseconds apart, this accounts for sound that has a boomy, echolike character. Gymnasiums and museums are classic examples of live spaces, as are bathrooms and tiled kitchens. *Dead spaces* usually have many absorbent surfaces, such as plush couches, draperies, and, particularly, carpets. This substantially reduces the reflected sound arriving at the microphone.

11-17

Working with acoustics is one of the greatest challenges to the sound crew

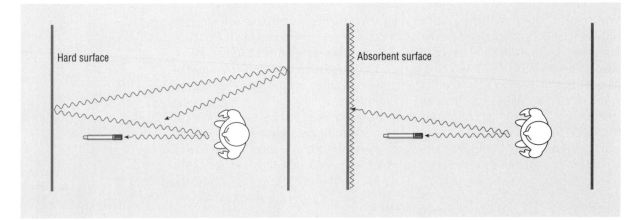

In most instances, the mixer wants the space to be relatively dead. Like ambience, some liveness can always be put back into a recording but it cannot be effectively taken out. To this end acoustic characteristics can be altered. The sound mixer hangs sound blankets or other acoustic material to deaden live spaces. Hang them on stands and put up as many as possible; if you have only a few, putting them directly in front of the speaker is the most effective position. Hardwood floors are notoriously difficult surfaces. If the floor is not in camera view, laying down blankets or spare carpet can be effective. Miking as tightly as possible is also important. The resultant lower record level will lessen the recording of the lower-amplitude reflected sound.

Sound perspective   The way we expect to experience sound at specific proxemic positions is known as *sound perspective*. In a close-up the viewer expects to be very near to the sound. When a character is in a long shot, the expectation is that the voice will sound more distant and the ambient sound of the location will be a more significant factor. The voice of an actor speaking from the other side of a door will have a specific character.

   The key is to remember that the sound should always be recorded cleanly, whatever the perspective characteristics desired for the final product. Excessive distance from the mic may produce an unusable recording. Having some perspective in a recording, however, is unavoidable and is not necessarily negative. Long shots often have more headroom than close-ups, and, barring using wireless mics, getting a mic the same distance away as the close-ups may not be possible. Just plan to get the mic as close as you can, and slight differences in perspective will probably be acceptable.

Phasing   The complex phenomenon in which specific frequencies are canceled out and thus not recorded is known as *phasing*. It can affect sound waves before they strike the microphone or, when using more than one mic, the electrical signal as it passes through the recorder's circuitry. In the first case, when a sound wave is met by a wave of the opposite shape, they balance out movement in the air pressure, thus negating each other. This kind of phasing, from the source to the microphone, is uncommon in most film recording and is difficult to control anyway. The second case, phasing in the electrical signal, occurs when signals from separate microphones meet in the recorder's circuitry and cancel each other out. This is dependent on how mics are positioned in relation to each other. Though there can be a sophisticated science to phasing, trying the mics in different positions is a solution whenever a problem is heard.

   Phasing is one reason why mixers try to use a single microphone whenever possible. Using two microphones with similar pickup patterns, particularly the shotguns, can create some of the most baffling phasing effects. Phasing is not always a bad thing: Highly skilled sound technicians can position microphones to set certain frequencies, such as those associated with ambient traffic sounds, "out of phase." For the beginner, however, phasing is generally a negative factor, eliminating important frequencies that can dramatically alter the character of the sound. With the goal being consistency, anything that changes the character of the sound poses a problem.

Any one of these concerns can cause major headaches when trying to produce usable production sound, so potential problems must be addressed before effective recording can occur. The need to cope with unwanted sound is the common thread. As the film is being edited, the presence of unwanted sound in itself is not so much the problem; rather, it is the inconsistency of that sound. The variety of different mic positions and record levels employed will mean that ambience, background noise, and camera noise will sound different from one setup to the next. Listeners may accept some background noise, but when its amplitude and character jump at every cut, it becomes very unnatural and noticeable. Many of these problems can be covered by music or some other consistent effect, but when music or effects are employed to cover things rather than to follow some internal logic in the script, they can be a distraction as well.

SYNC RECORDING

Like the other departments, the sound crew must be prepared for all eventualities. Although not always afforded the luxury, the mixer can evaluate a location and plan out an approach that will ensure optimal sound. If this preparation is possible, the mixer should be able to deal with acoustical problems, quickly identify and eliminate unwanted sound, and determine a strategy for miking the scene. And though there are as many miking strategies as there are setups, a few common approaches should give direction.

Again, the primary goal in sync-sound recording for motion pictures is to get the microphone in the optimum position for recording the source. In practice this presents many complications and obstacles. The more complicated the shot, the more difficult the boom operator's job is. As suggested, the sound crew will mic each setup with a single mic on a boom whenever possible. Avoiding phasing is a major reason for this, but a single high-quality mic simply produces a cleaner, less complicated signal. The mixer will try to employ just one mic for entire scenes as well. Using mics from different manufacturers or with different pickup patterns to record different setups in the same scene can cause consistency problems. If another mic needs to be incorporated, it is generally done with the first mic kept slightly open to give the sound the same character as the rest of the scene.

Booming from above is preferred. It gives the cleanest, most natural sound and, with the mic pointed down, excludes excessive noise from the background of the shot. Booming from below is an alternative when lighting or location interference force it, but this position usually amplifies bass frequencies. *Plant mics,* which are camouflaged or "planted" in the shot, can be useful; wireless mics are also occasionally employed.

Barring difficulties with unwanted sound, booming and recording a single, stationary subject is relatively simple. Just as the camera operator needs to adjust for body position, the boom operator must be prepared for the minor movements conducive to a fluid performance. The boom should be held above the talent's head, and the mic brought in as close to the mouth as possible. To avoid clicking and swallowing sounds, the mic should be pointed several inches in front of the talent's mouth rather than straight on. Sound flows out of the mouth, and the mixer should receive a good strong signal no matter how loud the talent's delivery.

When movements or multiple characters are introduced, the challenge increases. If characters are in close proximity to each other, pivoting and swinging the mic back and forth between them for each line of dialogue is usually the best approach. **SEE 11-18** To facilitate movement the mic is cradled in a *shock mount*, a suspension system that absorbs any moderate shaking of or shocks to the boom. Even with a shock mount, move the mic gently to reduce excessive rattling of the mic and thus the likelihood of producing unacceptable sound. Be careful of windlike noises as well. If the mic has to be swung so fast that it creates noise, a different miking arrangement should be tried. A wind shield may help with quick movements, but there are limits to how fast you can go. The mic cable must be gripped so it does not rattle against the boom, but neither should it be tightly stretched across the boom. It should be loosely wrapped around the boom, but not so loose that it flaps around.

When characters are separated by some distance—which, oddly enough, does not occur that frequently—it may be necessary to use two mics. Using shotgun mics together is generally a mistake (due to phasing), so two booms would not be

11-18

Pivoting a single mic back and forth between two characters is usually the best approach

employed. Putting one character on the boom and the other on a plant mic is one viable solution. Hide the plant mic where it can pick up the needed dialogue. *Boundary layer microphones (BLMs)* are small, flat mics that can be set on a piece of furniture or taped to the ceiling. Although BLMs are quite expensive, they are expressly designed for this purpose. High-end versions have interchangeable mic heads that control the shape and direction of the pickup pattern. In lieu of a BLM, a simple lavalier planted at a specific location on the set can accomplish roughly the same thing.

Subject movement requires the boom to follow or, more accurate, lead the subject through a space. **SEE 11-19** Just as with anticipatory camera, boom operators use the rehearsals to monitor subject movement and find a way to always have the mic in front of the performer(s). Except for minor adjustments, as a boom operator you should never react to anything that happens; you should always lead the movement. You may be able to mic small movements from a single position by simply extending your arms. Larger movements require that you move along with the situation. When a character moves from one position to another, you have to lead the subject from the first point to the next. This is easiest when you can incorporate a swing of the boom with your own small movement. To maintain the correct mic position, you must keep your eyes on the performers as the shots are being executed. Given the "grip jungles" that are often created, planning your footing so you don't trip or run into things is a necessity. In walk-throughs, as a boom operator you must quickly determine where you are going and how to get there.

If the movement is broader, for instance characters moving in front of a dollying camera, you will have to

11-19

Subject movement requires the boom to lead the subject through a space

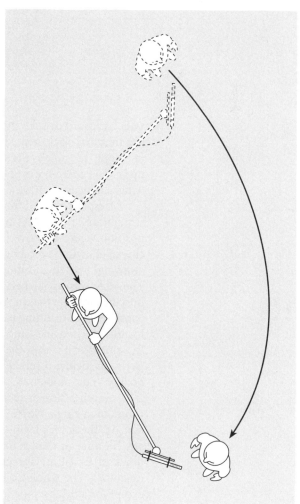

11-20

For broad movements, such as characters moving in front of a dollying camera, the boom operator has to walk backward or sideways when leading

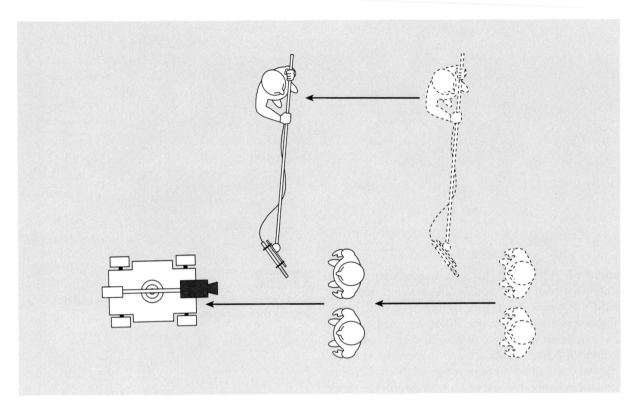

walk backward or sideways when leading. **SEE 11-20** Cabling can be tricky on shots like this: The slack created during the move can trip you. A cable puller is in charge of coiling the cable as the shot is being executed, making sure that no one gets fouled up in the excess. Barring that, the mixer may have to pull the cable with one hand while riding gain with the other.

Despite the need for some fancy footwork, these movements are still relatively straightforward. Talent movement, however, can occasionally put the actor in a position where effective booming is impossible. One scene I mixed began with a character saying several lines of dialogue in a standard medium shot. He then turned away and started shouting while pounding his fists on a table, venting his anger. The table was up against a window, and the shouted lines were delivered directly into the tabletop, making booming impossible. My solution was to hide a lav on the windowsill, positioning it so it was pointing directly at the actor's mouth. The boom handled the first lines, and the lav, with the pot turned very low, handled the shouting. In a situation like this, the pot for the boom is turned down as the lav is brought up. In this particular case, the boom mic was left partially open to maintain a consistent quality in the ambience.

Another similar example was a scene I boomed that took place in a hospital room, involving a woman talking to her ailing husband. **SEE 11-21** To portray the tension, the actor playing the wife wanted to have full freedom to pace around the set. The director wanted to shoot the entire three-minute scene in master (an irritating quirk of first-time directors that places heavy physical demands on the boom operator). The whole scene could be boomed with some movement on my part, except for a brief segment in which the actor nervously fiddled with a plant as she

11-21

In cases of complicated movement, a subject may need multiple mic setups

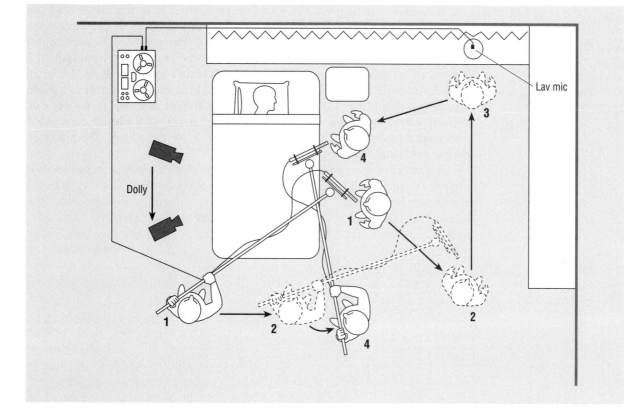

spoke. With the woman's back to the mic and her face virtually buried in the plant, the boom was unable to pick up her dialogue. We ran a lav under a window curtain and pushed it right up the middle of the plant. The actor was told not to be too rough with the plant, and her lines were picked up perfectly.

These are just a few representative examples. Many setups are easy to boom; others will test your skills. Recording and miking is about anticipation and problem solving. The sound mixer has to determine the best way to mic a scene and then practice the best way to record it. The mixer is generally not as vocal as the DP, but will on occasion have to speak up. If, for instance, the latch sound from a door closing is interfering with a line, be sure the door is muffled in some way. If the door's hinges are squeaking, have them oiled. If an actor's shoes are making too much noise on a hard floor, have the shoes removed or lay down a blanket. Anything causing a problem with the sound must be addressed.

AUTOMATED DIALOGUE REPLACEMENT

Once referred to as *looping, **automated dialogue replacement (ADR)** is a method of creating and replacing dialogue in postproduction. This is done when recording high-quality production sound is not possible, when a better reading is desired from the actor, or when script deficiencies can be cured by a choicely added line. The shot or shots that need this treatment are cut (digitally these days) into a loop with a set of visual cues. The actor sits in a soundproof booth, with the loop projected on a screen. The actor has a set of headphones that play back the original sound preceded by three short tones that correspond to the visual cues. With these cues, the actor can anticipate the visual and time the reading of the lines to the film. The actor does as many readings of the line as the director of the session feels are necessary. Each reading is dropped onto a synced tape, and the editor can later choose the desired take.

If ADR is not feasible, the sound mixer should have the talent read the dialogue in a quiet place. The director may want to be present to ensure that the delivery conforms to expectations. The editor will later position this new sound against the appropriate visuals. Although this is the hard way to approach it, a talented editor can generally make it work. Whether using ADR or the latter method, recording a *scratch track*—a conventional sync track that serves as a guide in editing—should be done on location. This means that the mixer records normally, even though the result will not be used in the final film. It is recorded to serve as a guide for the actor in postdubbing or for the editor, who positions specific words and effects against the picture.

A number of years ago, I worked on a film in which a lovely spontaneous shot happened during a lull in shooting. In the film's story, a young boy was stranded on a broken Ferris wheel. As we were in one of the often unavoidable delays, the AC asked the boy if he knew any songs, and he launched into "Help Me Rhonda"— the Beach Boys standard. The boy was much too far from my mic to get any usable sound, but I recorded it anyway, knowing it would be useful. I later took the boy aside and had him sing the song into the microphone. The editor was able to use the scratch track as a guide to matching the words recorded later to the visuals recorded on location.

All this said, it is important to get high-quality production sound, particularly when working on independent or student projects. Replacing dialogue is expensive and can be difficult for novice talent. The experience of being in an ADR booth can be somewhat akin to spending a day in a sensory deprivation tank. There is no input except seeing and hearing the same lines repeated over and over. When the actor starts having out-of-body experiences à la *Altered States,* you know that that is all you are going to get done that day. Recording usable production sound at the outset reduces costs and hassles in the editorial process.

Sound Effects

Although *sound effects (SFX)* often go virtually unnoticed by the viewer, most films would seem empty without them. Their frequency and employment is, of course, up to the postproduction team. Some situations require sparse, minimal sound, whereas others demand highly dense and layered sound. Hampered by limited time and experience in editing rooms, sound-effects studios, and mixing houses, student and independent films often have sound that is thin, particularly when compared with the dominant trend of lush sound tracks in commercial feature films. Of course individual films call for different approaches, but creating sound that is full and logical is usually the goal.

On location, mics are usually positioned to record dialogue, often leaving sync effects, such as doors opening, footsteps, and so on, dull or indifferently recorded. Recording quality aside, the real sound of things is often not as vital and dynamic as one might at first assume, so there is need for some dramatic heightening in postproduction. Replacing effects recorded on location is common, with going into the sound studio to improve something almost the norm. In addition, virtually all off-screen effects—those that are not generated by some action in the shot—are recorded later and positioned by the editor in the appropriate place against the visuals.

RECORDING EFFECTS ON LOCATION

On large commercial projects, the producers may be planning a sophisticated sound-effects campaign, and the need for the mixer to consider sound effects on location may be limited. On smaller films, on the other hand, it is sensible to get the effects then and there, when all the elements needed to produce the sound are assembled. Planning to record effects later or using sounds from an effects library are perfectly good approaches if the resources and personnel are there to do the work. But when resources are limited, creating sound in postproduction can be a difficult process. In addition, acquiring sounds from effects libraries can require extensive searching, and once found they often lack authenticity.

The sound mixer should be familiar enough with the script to anticipate needed effects and, as shooting proceeds, make a list of everything required. The sound crew is rarely afforded the luxury of stopping the whole production to collect sound. Some effects can be recorded during a lull in the shooting, just after a shot as the camera crew is checking the gate, or after the day's shooting has wrapped. I once worked on a film that was set in the 1840s, with shooting plagued by the sounds of a nearby modern urban center. All kinds of effects, from ax chops to footsteps in the forest, were on my list. We simply set our alarms for three in the morning and went out and got all we needed while the city slept. To go back later and re-create these effects would have meant the investment of substantial time, as well as creating the potential for delays in the editing process.

FOLEY

The *Foley* room is similar to the ADR room, but with more space for the active process of creating effects. The activities of the Foley room surely resemble those of crews for the old radio programs, a variety of voice artists and sound-effects people banging garbage can lids and running in place. The Foley room has numerous materials and objects for creating different sounds, from creaking doors to broken glass to squeaky chairs. It is also outfitted with a variety of surfaces on which to re-create footsteps, such as on carpet, gravel, tile, and so on. The Foley artists watch the projected picture and create an appropriate effect at the precise moment. What they produce is recorded on a synced tape that is easily dropped into the film. They also have access to a variety of prerecorded effects, which can be tested against the projected picture.

Although commercial films may achieve effects through Foley, many filmmakers simply go out and create the needed effects. In the absence of a soundproof booth, it may be hard to find a quiet place to do the effects. Again, recording effects at three in the morning when passing traffic is limited is not a bad approach. It is amazing what tasty effects you can whip up in your kitchen late at night.

The sound-effects campaign in independent and student films is often neglected and left for last. In many situations someone, often the editor or an assistant, goes out with a recorder and tries to drum up a few quick effects. It is no surprise that these effects are often inadequate. Get someone who understands the requirements involved in successfully creating and competently recording sound effects. If you are in a city with an active professional filmmaking community, you may find a Foley artist who will cut you a deal. The services of a competent professional could mean the difference between effects that sound bland and fake and effects that add flavor and character to your film. Just like the backgrounds of shots, this underlayer of sound often constitutes the difference between a one-note, single-dimension film and a rich and complex work.

Sound Transfers

In a conventional film edit, the sound is transferred to magnetic stock. The path for sound in an NLE edit is covered in part V. Recording to mag stock is a specialized process that can be done only with the appropriate equipment. This transfer is usually made at a professional facility, often the same one that will do the final audio mixdown. The mag stock recorder is set up like the camera, a set of sprocketed rollers feeding the mag stock across the record head just like the film and the gate, minus the pull-down claw. **SEE 11-22**

An audio signal from any source can be transferred to the mag stock. Cassette, quarter-inch, DAT, or compact disc are the common source media, although any equipment with an audio line output, from a video deck to a synthesizer, could be used. Record original narration, effects, and music on audiotape first rather than straight onto the mag stock.

All sounds are transferred individually to the magnetic stock. Transferring everything except the clearly unusable recorded sound is standard procedure. This leaves the selection of individual sounds to the editor. Although it means transferring quite a bit of material, the selection process is done only once rather than twice.

Again, the transfer is often a good time to do some initial manipulation of the sound. Equalization may reduce or eliminate some significant problems. The goal is to eliminate as much as you can here, with the final mixdown being another place to address problems. Though unwanted sound should be addressed on location, the transfer houses and mixing personnel can do some amazing things. A huge generator at a carnival once caused me major headaches. I recorded the generator by itself for a minute, and from this the transfer house was able to isolate the frequencies and eliminate most of the noise. Transfer house personnel must be alerted to problems in the production sound. This is done on a sound report and by clearly marking the tape's packaging.

There are, of course, limits. Sound people occasionally get into the bad habit of depending on postproduction equalization to eliminate blemishes that may be

11-22

The mag stock recorder is set up like the camera, a set of sprocketed rollers feeding the mag stock across the record head—just like the film and gate

Moviola/Magnasync mag stock recorder

addressable during recording. If the offending sound is too loud or covers too wide a range of frequencies, equalization may be a small bandage on a big wound. When you equalize at a specific frequency, you affect not only the desired sound, but all other similar sounds as well. If you have an actor with a particularly deep voice, for example, equalizing low frequencies to eliminate traffic ambience may create an unwanted change in the voice. Remember also that a wide range of frequencies exists in some form in any sound, and excessive equalization will change the character of a sound even when you are working on entirely different frequencies. Bass voices devoid of high frequencies may turn muddy and unintelligible. High sounds are less affected by the absence of low frequencies, although voices can sound tinny and shrill.

Many schools and media arts centers have individual transfer machines, which can save substantially on transfer charges. Be aware, however, that most of these machines cannot be serviced and maintained at a level comparable to those at a professional facility. With sound that requires the best reproduction possible, dialogue and music in particular, it is generally better to spend the money for a professional transfer.

Cleaning and Repair

Cleanliness is as crucial in sound as it is in other realms. The biggest concern is keeping the record head and the other heads clean. There are commercial cleaning solutions that can be applied with a cotton swab. This should be done before shooting every day, and maybe once more on a busy day. These solutions should not be applied to the rubber capstan roller, as they will eventually dry the rubber out.

Demagnetizing the heads should also be done frequently. The constant tape movement can make the record head develop a magnetic charge that must be removed with a commercial demagnetizer. The recorder must be turned off and the tape removed during this process. The demagnetizer is turned on several feet from the recorder and brought in to the heads without touching them. It is then pulled away from the recorder and turned off when it is at least four or five feet away.

Mic cables must also be kept clean, and connections must have integrity. Dust on dirty mic cables can actually build an electric charge that can disturb the signal. Connections are equally important. Being able to troubleshoot audio takes a basic knowledge of signal paths. The theory behind a mic cable is quite simple. The cable can be checked with a *multimeter*, an inexpensive meter that tests batteries, as well as having other useful functions. Using the meter function for testing *ohms*—the unit of measure of the resistance to a signal passing through a line—you can check for resistance and thus whether you have a connection. This function can be used to check virtually any electric or electronic connection. When touched together, the ground and hot leads from the multimeter give a reading on the display, indicating you have completed a circuit. To test any other circuit, you simply put the connection to be tested in sequence with the ground and hot leads off the multimeter. Touch one tester lead to the hot lead on one end of the audio plug, then touch the other tester lead to the hot lead on the other end of the cable—from the tip of one quarter-inch plug to the tip of the other end, for instance. You can find adequate multimeters for around twenty dollars, although good ones cost four to five times that much.

It is not uncommon to set up the recorder on location and get no signal on the meters, particularly when you are just learning the vagaries of sound. Being able to follow and test the logic of the signal path will help you go into the chain and identify the problem. A kit with jeweler's screwdrivers, a soldering iron, and solder is useful if a connection has gone bad. Always bring extra cords for quick testing and replacement.

Part IV
Lighting and Exposure

12

Concepts and Equipment

The Importance of Lighting

One shock for aspiring filmmakers is the high percentage of films that make extensive use of artificial light for both interior and exterior shooting. The necessity for interior lighting surprises no one, but the number of lights and the complexity of their implementation often does. Beautiful exterior light—natural light—has always been found by still photographers, but it occurs too unpredictably and changes too rapidly to be a good ally of filmmakers. On his film *Ran* (1985), it is said that director Akira Kurosawa kept a cast of thousands standing by for several hours, waiting for just the right cloud formation. Most filmmakers do not have that luxury. Because the light in any situation may not exist in the volume or with the highlights desired, a filmmaker must know how to evaluate existing lighting situations and become completely conversant in the uses of artificial light.

Just as a painter starts with a blank canvas, a filmmaker starts with an unlit space. Light is the filmmaker's brush and palette. Phrases such as "painting with light" or the "painterly qualities" of light suggest the power of light, dark, and color to establish mood, suggest psychological states, and communicate the tactile qualities of observed objects. *Lighting* can accomplish much more than this, but it is nevertheless a key building block of the photographic image.

Despite the fundamental importance of light and lighting, industry professionals often express frustration with the poor preparation students receive in the area of lighting, a distressing situation given that many entry-level positions are on lighting crews. Although there are a number of reasons for this, the major one is that students cannot possibly duplicate the Hollywood model for lighting. Limited in financial resources, schools cannot afford the sophisticated equipment that makers of features and commercials use daily. Even if the equipment were available, the complexity of setup would stymie even the most ambitious student. Achieving the production values of commercial features requires a commitment of time, equipment, personnel, and access to locations beyond the means of any individual, particularly an inexperienced one.

The last reason is probably the most decisive. Although the story and content elements will always be the hardest parts of making a film, a mastery of lighting and exposure is one of the most difficult things for students at all levels to achieve. The novice lighting person is going to make many mistakes. Without knowing a few tricks of the trade, it is hard to get the lights to create the effects that one wants and sees achieved so apparently easily in other films. There are many technical specifications to learn. The equipment is heavy and bulky and, without strong and compassionate friends, it can be a struggle just getting it from here to there.

The key to this is control. Every beginner sweats through that seemingly interminable period between turning the film into the processing lab and getting it back, vexed by the question: Is the film going to turn out the way I want? What this chapter addresses, and what you will have as a long-term goal, is the elimination of that query. Lighting is presented here in a systematic way that, albeit technical, does not intimidate the reader. Before beginners can usefully move to advanced technical lighting manuals, they must understand some key concepts clearly and unambiguously.

The following is a simple, step-by-step introduction to how to think about lighting. That is not the same as teaching you how to light. The only way to learn that is by actually doing it. There are no quick fixes, no way to be there without the process of getting there. The getting there part not only is what teaches you the craft of lighting but also is central to the process of maturing as a creative individual. And, besides, getting there is all the fun.

Basic Three-Point Lighting

This basic lighting setup is so fundamental that people have a tendency, when it is first presented to them, to dismiss it as too simplistic. The ***three-point setup*** is the textbook approach to figure (character) lighting, comprising a key light, a fill light, and a backlight, and most everyone knows that lighting is generally more complicated than this. To some very small degree, they are right. Most lighting is far more complicated, with many more lights used than in the three-point setup. But it is still the starting point for most lighting. Whatever else you are doing, you almost always have to consider these points, particularly the first two. **SEE 12-1**

KEY LIGHT

The ***key light*** is usually the major source of illumination. It is generally, though certainly not always, a hard beam of light that casts harsh shadows. It will create a deep nose shadow on the side of the face away from the light. The rest of that side of the face will be dark. It is usually the main source of light in a shot. The viewer identifies it, though probably unconsciously, as the direction from which the light is coming. When we are outside during the day, the key light is, of course, the sun. At night it might be the moon or some artificial source. Indoors it may be a window, a lamp, or a ceiling fixture. You can think of the key light as the "source" light or the "main" light, but it is usually referred to as the "key." Some lighting people prefer the term *point source*. The key light is frequently, though not always, the light that is used to determine the *f*-stop.

FILL LIGHT

The ***fill light*** is generally on the opposite side of the camera from the key light; it is generally softer than the key and, as its name suggests, it "fills in" the harshness

12-1

The basic three-point setup is the textbook, but logical, approach to lighting.

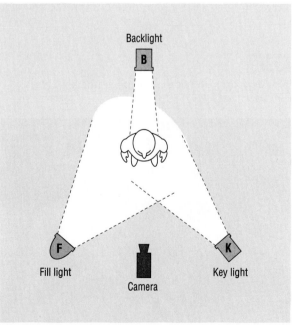

of the shadows created by the key. To a large extent, the intensity of the fill light in relationship to the key light controls the dramatic quality of the shadows. If the fill is close to the key in intensity, the shadows will be soft. If the fill is much lower than the key, the shadows will be deeper.

BACKLIGHT

The *backlight* is generally above and behind the subject, shining down and hitting the subject on the back of the head. Its use can be more general than this, hitting a more substantial part of the body. In recent years, though, the term has come to identify what used to be called a "hair" light. It provides texture and definition to the hair and also helps separate the subject from the background. The lack of a backlight will often leave the subject's hair shapeless and looking like a single mass sticking straight up out of the head. The backlight is often considered the least essential of the three points. Its presence is open to a certain amount of debate, as it is often difficult to determine what its source is.

If you think about it, these three points of light, particularly the first two, are very logical and are going to exist in some form in most images. All light has a source, and we can think of that source as the key light. A cinematographer friend likes to use the example of "sun and sand." Sunlight hits a person and casts harsh shadows on the side away from it. This light continues through to the sand, which reflects the light back to fill in the harsh shadows created by the sun. The same is true indoors. The source light's reflection off of other surfaces in the room, such as the walls and ceiling, fills in the side away from the source. Generally, we refer to this bounced or reflected light as *ambient light*. Not only does the key light have a source (it *is* the source), but the fill light also has a source that can be identified.

This is where the backlight becomes somewhat controversial: There is often no identifiable source for it. Many people who light for film like to think of a light's source in terms of there being some *justification* for a light hitting a subject from a specific direction. Sometimes DPs are every bit as careful about establishing where the source of light is as directors are in establishing the spatial characteristics of the scene. There are DPs who will not use backlights for this reason. For the many who do, however, the major justification is photographic. Without it the hair can look characterless and flat. This idea of justification is a significant one and is discussed further in this and subsequent chapters.

It was stated that one of the controls of the dramatic quality of an image is how intense the fill light is in relationship to the key light. But why is it necessary to have a key side and a fill side? It is essential to have a shaded side of the face (or object), because it aids the perception of depth in an image. The film image is two-dimensional, and achieving a sense of three-dimensionality requires some work. If the key light and the fill light are even in intensity, facial features will be flattened—the nose will appear to be pushed flat against the face.

Using a key and a fill does not necessarily mean that one side of the face must be in shadow. In several scenes of Ivan Passer's *Cutter's Way*, cinematographer Jordan Cronenweth essentially exposed for the traditional fill side, allowing the key side to overexpose dramatically. **SEE 12-2** The effect is the same, but with the bright side being responsible for dimensionality.

Exposing for the fill side overexposes the key side
Ivan Passer's *Cutter's Way*

Eventually, you may not even think about lighting in terms of these discrete points, but the key/fill/backlight system will remain central to the process of lighting. The three-point setup is so basic that people tend to either be too dogmatic with their application or disregard them altogether. The latter is by far the greater sin. Invariably, I get at least one student per semester who wants to skip over this dry, textbook stuff and get on to the exciting business. Get out the fog machines! It is somewhat like jumping into trigonometry before learning how to add. You must have a starting point, and the three-point system is just that, in terms of learning not only how to light but also how to approach many of the other elements in the scene.

The key/fill concept works because, just as in daily life, there has to be some source of light. This does not mean that there is just one source or just one key light; there may be many. There may not be just one fill—there may be two or twenty. There may not be a backlight as we have defined it. There may be a light used for that function as well as others. But these basic lights are going to exist. All of them will not necessarily be on every shot, but the concepts are nevertheless fundamental.

I once worked on a film in which a group of characters walked down a carnival midway at night. What would be the source of light? Obviously, there was more than one. As they passed every hotdog stand and ring toss parlor, we created some kind of light to expose them the way we wanted. Sometimes the light from the hotdog stand was filling while the ring toss keyed. Occasionally, the characters passed through a darkened area. And this was only the starting point.

When you approach the lighting of a shot, you generally have something in the frame that you consider most important. Often you want that subject, let's say it's a person, to be normally exposed—and if you do not want the person normally exposed, the same reasoning applies. The amount of light you have on the person you want normally exposed is then going to become the dominant light value. Thinking of the key light as being this dominant value helps us plot out all the other values.

In other words, once you have set the key, you have established the value for which you are exposing the scene. If you key someone to an $f/5.6$ and want that person normally exposed, you are going to shoot at an $f/5.6$. This may seem like backward logic, but once the f-stop has been determined, you can decide where you want all the other values. If you have another area or object that you want normally exposed, you will light that to the established value, and so on. Once you figure out what you want normally exposed, all the other values will fall in line. How do you want to fill it? What do you do for backlight?

High-key and Low-key

The terms *high-key* and *low-key* refer to types of lighting (not to the position of the key light) and have standard definitions that you should know.

HIGH-KEY

Even, fairly flat lighting is known as **high-key** lighting. One could call it nonjudgmental lighting. There is little contrast between the darks and the lights in the image, a large part of which exists within a fairly neutral range. Writers on film usually associate high-key lighting with musicals and comedies. It is used when we do not want the quality of the light to dominate what is occurring in the image or to imply judgments that are not associated with the subject. In other words, we do not want the lighting to contradict what the image is doing. Some might call this lighting Rockwellian, because it gives an even sense of well-being and normalcy, like the works of the American painter Norman Rockwell.

12-3

The contrast between light and dark in a typical low-key image

Orson Welles's *Touch of Evil*

12-4

Stretching the conventions of lighting

Alfred Hitchcock's *Shadow of a Doubt*

LOW-KEY

The opposite of high-key, **low-key** lighting is moody and atmospheric and might be considered judgmental. There is contrast within the image and therefore a significant play between the lights and the darks. **SEE 12-3** Low-key lighting is often associated with horror films, mysteries, psychological dramas, and crime stories. The German filmmakers of the 1920s were pioneers in their experiments with the expressive qualities of light in film. Certainly, the apex of low-key lighting in American film came in the 1940s and 1950s with a group of films called *film noir* (discussed in the following section).

Again, these are basic definitions. They are the conventions, and their use has become somewhat clichéd, from the moody lighting of Dracula's castle to the sunny atmosphere of a romantic comedy. Still, at least in terms of conventional narrative films, high-key and low-key are the choices, and nearly all variations at least recognize these limits. More-adventurous directors will stretch the conventions—witness many of the family scenes from Alfred Hitchcock's *Shadow of a Doubt* (1943). The high-key images of uncomplicated small-town life are undermined by the viewer's—and eventually one of the character's—knowledge that the beloved Uncle Charlie (Joseph Cotten) is a killer. One scene that takes place on the family's sunny front porch could be an image from any Norman Rockwell tableau. **SEE 12-4** In Hitchcock's hands the scene is invested with a dark undertone. The parameters of the conventions are being played with. It is not so much whether the conventions exist as what you do within them and how you manipulate them.

European cinematographers tend to break down light into three distinct categories, rather than the two that Americans use. Low-key remains the same, but what Americans call high-key is referred to as *normal-key*. When Europeans use the term *high-key*, they are referring to overly bright, termed *overexposed*, images. Ingmar Bergman's *Persona* (1966) uses this approach to great effect. Virtually the entire film is shot slightly overexposed. This **overexposure** gives the film a very unrealistic tone, and the characters, as well as the audience, always seem to be squinting, almost overwhelmed by the act of trying to see. The final sequences of Stanley Kubrick's *2001: A Space Odyssey* (1968), in which the aged astronaut wanders around his brightly lit living quarters, is another example of a very expressive use of an overexposed image. The last shot of Oliver Stone's *Platoon* (1986), in which the main character is lost in the sun as the helicopter flies away, is also a good example.

Given American filmmaking's fascination with realism, overexposure has not found wide acceptance. On the other hand, **underexposure**, dark areas in the shot, replicates common perceptual experience and is frequently employed. Overexposure does not mimic routine perceptual experience, an exception being the painful adjustment to strong light after emerging from a dark space (such as a theater). As such, the strongest association with overexposure is probably pain, so its exclusion is probably understandable if not entirely justified.

In discussing low-key and high-key lighting, we in some sense return to the key/fill relationship. Intensity of the fill light in relationship to the key light goes a long way toward determining the general character of the image. If the fill is close to the key in intensity, the shadows will be light and the shot will be high-key. If the fill is much less intense than the key, the shadows will be darker and thus the shot more low-key. The distinction suffers somewhat because key and fill are generally discussed in relationship to figure lighting, whereas high-key and low-key are used in terms of the whole image. Nevertheless, the relationship of all light values, particularly the fill, to the dominant value is a factor in determining the overall character of the image.

Lighting Styles

Lighting styles are difficult to categorize. The possibilities are so limitless that even within a single film there may be many different approaches. Certainly, such terms as *high-key* and *low-key* are helpful. Terms like *texture* and *mood* may also apply. Depth and dimensionality play a role in a film's overall approach to the subject it is covering. Lighting can also be used to direct viewer attention to bright areas of the frame and focus it on specific parts of the image.

The most significant trend in lighting has probably been *film noir,* a style that advanced the use of an expressive image in American films. Noticing a trend in the films that flooded their screens just after World War II, the French coined the term *film noir,* roughly translated as "dark film," to describe a body of films that were very dark and pessimistic in both their content and their low-key look. **SEE 12-5** These films created a claustrophobic, nightmarish universe filled with guilt, hysteria, and moral ambiguity. Film noir's use of dark and foreboding visuals and stark, unorthodox compositions put Hollywood film in the same arena, albeit belatedly, with many of the radical formal concerns of modern art.

Highly influenced by the detective fiction of Dashiell Hammett, Raymond Chandler, and James M. Cain, film noir has been identified as a style and trend that appears in a wide variety of genres. In films ranging from Michael Curtiz's *Mildred Pierce* (1945) to Joseph H. Lewis's *The Big Combo* (1955), noir represents Hollywood's first extensive experimentation with an expressive image. What was being expressed was much stronger on a visual level than the stories, which were still bound to a certain extent by the Hollywood tradition of the happy ending. The grim visual and moral world they created largely negated any neat narrative closure or cheerful conclusion.

Film noir is possibly the most chronicled of Hollywood's stylistic and thematic trends. It has also

12-5

Classic film noir created a dark, claustrophobic visual environment
Edward Dmytryk's *Crossfire* (1947)

Modern film noir color cinematography
Jack Nicholson in *The Postman Always Rings Twice*

been of great interest to modern cinematographers, particularly after a period of generally bland productions in the 1950s and early 1960s. Many American and international cinematographers have been greatly influenced by noir stylistics, because the approach allowed them to do their most challenging work. The image in classic Hollywood film prior to noir, in its own way a high point in the art of cinematography, was still generally a vehicle for performance, setting, and action. In film noir the image became such an integral and expressive part of the presentation that it often overpowered content elements. The interest in noir and the expressive image on the part of a new generation of cinematographers produced what might be called the "great age of modern cinematography," a period in films that stretched from roughly the late 1960s to the early 1980s.

Bernardo Bertolucci's *The Conformist* has examples of some of the most adventurous images in color cinematography. The film's dark tone gives a nightmarish visual representation of fascist Italy in the late 1930s. Cinematographer Gordon Willis was responsible for great modernizations of noir stylistics, particularly in Alan Pakula's *Klute* (1971) and Francis Ford Coppola's *The Godfather* films.

Sven Nykvist's cinematography for Bob Rafelson's *The Postman Always Rings Twice* (1981) has many exceptional examples of noir color cinematography. **SEE 12-6** Although many have considered the film a disappointment on a content level, it is probably one of the greatest explorations of modern film noir stylistics.

This trend toward modern noir interpretations seems to have been followed by an equal interest in color and design, as represented in such films as Ridley Scott's *Blade Runner* (1982) and television shows like "Miami Vice." The pursuit of an expressive image remains consistent and fuels much of the work of the lighting crew and the DP. The light that you create will always be an important factor in defining the content and the character of the image.

Types of Lighting Instruments

A tour of a lighting equipment rental company would probably leave you struck by the size and variety of lights available. In the industry lights are called *instruments*, to distinguish equipment that produces light from the light itself. Although there are many specialized instruments, only a few need be known from the outset. Generally speaking, lighting instruments are either focusable spots or floodlights, a distinction that parallels the difference between two *types* of light: specular and diffused. Focusable spots and floodlights have characteristics that make them useful for establishing key and fill. Key light has been defined as a strong beam of light casting harsh shadows, and fill light as a soft piece of light brought in to fill those shadows. Focusable spots are frequently used as key lights, and softlights as fill lights, but these are traditional roles, not hard-and-fast rules. There are many situations in which a filmmaker might use a softlight as a key, because that is the quality of light desired. So, although the key/fill distinction between spots and floods is useful, remember that it is not ironclad.

Specular light is direct light and is produced by focusable spots. The best example of specular light is the sun. Light rays from the sun are parallel, and on a clear, bright day they create harsh shadows with well-defined edges. *Diffused light*, on the other hand, is light that has passed through a medium, such as clouds, or that has reflected off a textured surface. It is indirect and is produced by floodlights. Some hard surfaces, of course, do not diffuse light. If the light hits a uniformly smooth and reflectant surface, such as a mirror, it will remain specular. If the surface is rough or absorbent, the light will be diffused.

The DP is responsible for determining the type, size, and quantity of lights needed. In this, he or she is assisted by the *gaffer,* a key crew member who heads the lighting crew and is responsible for the technical implementation of the lighting plan.

The following discussion outlines the types of lights available to most small projects. Again, if you go to a rental house you will see a number of other types as well. As your projects become more sophisticated, you will use more specialized lights, although most of them are either so specialized or so big that you will not have access to them while you are learning the field. The bigger lights usually have substantial electrical power requirements, requiring a trained electrician and/or a powerful generator.

FOCUSABLE SPOTS

There are two types of *focusable spots:* open-faced and lensed. Lensed instruments have a glass lens through which light passes; open-faced instruments do not. Focusable spots of both types have a single bulb called a *lamp,* which is usually seated in a ceramic base. The lamp and its base are mounted in a spherical reflector coated with a polished silver material. Most open-faced and lensed focusable spots come with *barn doors,* adjustable black metal doors that are mounted on the front of the instrument. They are used to cut and shape the light as well as eliminate unwanted *spill,* a term you will hear quite frequently which refers to excess light from an instrument.

Both open-faced and lensed focusable spots are called focusable because the operator has the ability to *spot* and *flood* the light's beam. In spot position, the energy of the lamp is focused in the center of the beam, where it is narrow, intense, and hard. Away from that intense center, the volume of light drops off very rapidly. This drop in intensity, from either the center of the beam or the instrument itself, is called *falloff.* In flood position, the energy of the lamp is spread out more evenly; it is wider, not quite so intense, and softer than in spot, so the falloff is considerably slower. A knob on the instrument, usually on the back, controls the movement of the ceramic base and lamp against the reflector. Turning the knob back and forth controls whether the light is spotted in or flooded out. As the lamp moves away from the reflector, the instrument floods out. As it moves closer to the reflector, it is spotted in. A small number of instruments employ the opposite strategy, and in some designs both the lamp and the reflector move. **SEE 12-7**

Spot and flood are important ways of manipulating both the quality and volume of light from a focusable spot.

Open-faced focusable spots *Open-faced focusable spots* are characterized by a bare lamp with no lens. **SEE 12-8** The light they produce is a little more difficult to control than that from a lensed instrument. Open-faced instruments create a big, hard, fairly general beam of light and are often used when precise manipulation of light is not critical. They are difficult to use, however, when the goal is to cut out part of the light for a shadowy or low-key effect. In such cases open-faced spots require a great deal of work for the desired effects.

12-7

Basic mechanics of lighting instruments

12-8

Open-faced instruments produce a big, hard, fairly general beam

A minor drawback of the open-faced design is that direct light from the lamp mixes with light bouncing from the smooth, hard reflector. **SEE 12-9** Light thus hits the subject from several different directions, creating shadows that are not hard enough for some applications. A subject lit by an open-faced instrument has a harsh shadow mixed with less distinct shadows caused by light from the reflector. Light appears to bend and wrap around objects, though it actually does not. Open-faced

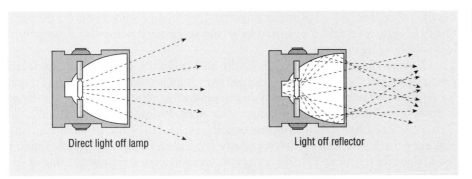

12-9

Reflector causes light to come from multiple directions, creating indistinct edges to the shadows

Direct light off lamp · Light off reflector

instruments produce harsh shadows, but without the hard edges associated with light from a single source.

On the other hand, open-faced spots are less expensive than lensed instruments, both in original outlay and in continued operation (the lamps are less expensive). The weight of the glass lens and the attendant instrument housing of lensed lights means that they are heavier and need sturdier stands. Open-faced spots are generally more compact, and a number of companies make very good lightweight, portable kits. These kits are used in many schools, particularly in beginning and intermediate classes.

Lensed focusable spots *Lensed focusable spots* are generally more desirable than open-faced instruments because they are easier to manipulate. The most popular type of lensed instrument has a *Fresnel* (pronounced "fre-NEL") lens, which employs concentric rings of glass. **SEE 12-10** The Fresnel spot is named for the

12-10

The most popular lensed focusable spots use a Fresnel lens, named for its inventor

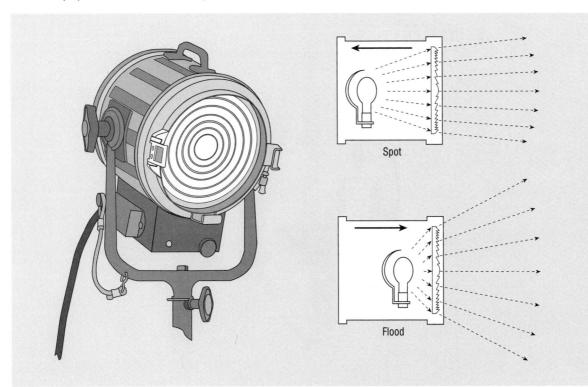

Spot

Flood

inventor of its lens, French physicist Augustin-Jean Fresnel, who supported the wave theory of light, investigated polarized light, and originally developed the compound lens for use in lighthouses.

Lensed lights have the same bulb and reflector design as open-faced instruments, but the lens redirects the light into a single specular beam. The Fresnel lens eliminates the multiple sources and the indistinct shadows of the open-faced instruments, allowing easier manipulation for hard shadow effects (fast falloff).

Whereas open-faced kits are usually satisfactory for general lighting requirements, lensed instruments are relatively inexpensive to rent, and obtaining a few of them for the more discriminating effects can be a good approach, using open-faced instruments to light peripheral areas if necessary.

FLOODLIGHTS

Floodlights, so called because they produce diffused, indirect light, are of three basic types: scoops, broads, and softlights. Scoops and broads have limited uses in filmmaking, whereas the softlight is popular and can be used very effectively in location shooting. One important characteristic of floodlights is that they create indistinct shadows or no shadows at all.

Scoops Big instruments with large parabolic reflectors, *scoops* have a single bare lamp but present so much reflecting surface that the light emitted has no single source. **SEE 12-11** Scoops produce a big, general piece of light that is difficult to control. Because they are large, heavy, and difficult to manipulate, they are not very popular in location film production, but they are often quite useful as permanently mounted lights, especially in studios.

Broads Broad lights are somewhat more common than scoops in film production. *Broads* are characterized by a long, bare, cylindrical lamp seated in a shallow reflector. **SEE 12-12** Although this design would seem to produce direct light, broads

12-11

Scoop lights incorporate such a large reflecting surface that the emitted light has no single source

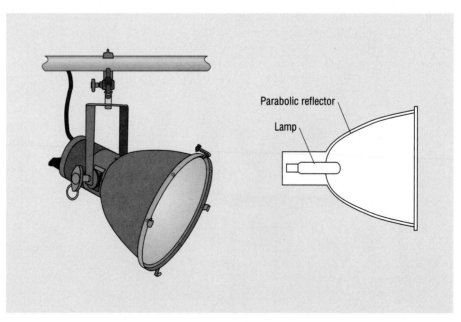

actually create diffused light, because the filament is long, creating many sources. Focusable spots, in contrast, have a pear-shaped lamp with a single filament, creating a single source. Many broad lights diffuse their light further with a frosted glass lamp or a textured reflector.

Of all the lights, the broad is probably the least controllable—it just creates a large, diffuse piece of light. Yet it is more popular than the scoop because of its small size—usually less than a foot long—and because it can be shot into a variety of reflectant surfaces. Used in that way, a broad light can create a nice general fill for a shot. Broads are much better for bouncing than are focusable spots, because they distribute their heat across the length of the lamp. Focusable spots concentrate their light and heat in the center of the beam, and if the instrument is spotted in all the way, materials can actually catch fire. By comparison, the broad has proved itself very effective and safe in shooting into a variety of materials.

Softlights By far the most popular of the floodlights for filmmaking applications, the compact size and portability of softlights make them ideal for location work. *Softlights* are similar to broads in the design of the lamp housing—a long, cylindrical lamp mounted in a shallow reflector—but, unlike a broad, the lamp of the softlight is hidden from view in the base and it shoots light from below into a spherical white or silver reflector, called a *shell*. **SEE 12-13**

Light from the softlight comes from reflections off the shell and is very diffused. Softlights produce an even, soft, almost shadowless light, which can be handy when trying to avoid the multiple shadows that plague lighting crews.

12-12

Broad lights produce a large, fairly diffuse light

Barn doors

12-13

Softlights emit a very soft and even, almost shadowless light

Shell

Spherical reflector

Lamp housing

Other Types of Sources

Three other light sources—ellipsoidal spots, practicals, and reflectors—are not as common as focusable spots and floodlights but can prove quite useful.

ELLIPSOIDAL SPOTS

Commonly referred to as *lekos, ellipsoidal spots* are barrel shaped and are often, though not always, equipped with Fresnel lenses. Due to their lamp housing and reflector design, ellipsoidal spots produce hard, specular light, creating highly defined shadows. **SEE 12-14** Even Fresnel instruments create shadows with slightly diffused edges, but the leko allows virtually no diffusion. Lekos are difficult to use on foreground subjects, however, because the light they produce is hard and unattractive, at least for people or objects of interest.

Lekos are generally used to create hard-edged lighting effects, particularly patterns and designs on backgrounds, such as prison bars and venetian blinds. To accomplish this there is a slot just behind the shutter for inserting plates with cutout designs. With filters in the pattern slot, lekos can also produce color effects. Ellipsoidal spots get more use in television studios and traditional stage productions than in film, but there are many applications for them on location.

PRACTICALS

Resembling standard light bulbs in shape and function, *practicals* are bigger and more powerful than their household counterparts. There are several types of practicals, but most are in the 250-watt to 500-watt range, with the bigger ones usually the bell-shaped photoflood type.

Practicals are screwed into standard household sockets, such as table and floor lamps and ceiling fixtures, and are used to duplicate the light emitted, for example, by a typical living room lamp or other ordinary fixture. Practicals are necessary because household bulbs burn redder than do standard motion picture lights; without them, matching the color of other instruments would be problematic. (See the discussion of color temperature in chapter 8.)

12-14

Ellipsoidal spotlights (lekos) produce hard, specular light and highly defined shadows

Reflector boards are two-sided, to provide both hard and soft light

Hard side (smooth surface)   Soft side (textured surface)

Although they are most often used in lamps, practicals are also handy for screwing into fixtures outside the frame for general fill in a scene. If there is a ceiling fixture in a room, a DP can screw a practical into it to give a certain level of light in the room. They can be employed for a variety of purposes, particularly in location shooting.

REFLECTORS

Not instruments per se, *reflectors* are used frequently, especially in exteriors. The most sophisticated are called *reflector boards,* which pivot in a U-shaped holder. **SEE 12-15** One side of the board is a hard surface that reflects specular light; the flip side is often divided into sections or is textured to provide a softer fill.

Reflectors are most often used to reflect sunlight into shadows when shooting outside. They are particularly handy for producing fill light for characters, especially when the actors are walking through shaded areas. Small reflectors are popular for many situations, and there are some very large ones generally used on bigger projects.

There are other types of reflectors, including handheld boards. *Foam core,* a material used in picture framing, is one of the most popular inexpensive "bounce boards." On location it is common to see a grip following a scene with a board in hand; light coming from the board punches up the characters just a little bit. Reflectors can be very handy for saving the time and bother of setting up an electric instrument to accomplish a simple fill effect.

Light Meters

There are two approaches to light measurement: one measuring incident light and the other measuring reflective light. In measuring ***incident light***—light that falls on a subject—a light meter is held at the subject and pointed toward the camera. From this position the meter determines how much light is on the subject. In measuring *reflective light*—light that is bounced off the illuminated subject—the opposite approach is taken. In its most simple application, the meter is held at the camera to determine how much light is being reflected from the subject back to the camera lens.

Many cameras have light meters built into the viewing system; these internal meters are called *through-the-lens (TTL)* metering systems and they read reflective light. As we will see, TTL metering systems have shortcomings that make them of limited use to film professionals. *Reflective-light meters* in general have limited applications although, if understood correctly, they can give more-detailed information than can *incident-light meters*. In film production, the incident meter, however, tends to be preferred more for reasons of working style than for any inherent inadequacies of the reflective meter. A *spot meter*, a type of reflective meter that measures light in a very narrow angle, can be particularly useful and is used extensively on sets.

Except for the TTL systems, light meters are handheld and can usually measure either reflective or incident light. Meters typically come with both a white bulb for reading incident light and an interchangeable flat grid for reading reflective light. You insert either the bulb or the grid, depending on which kind of light you need to measure.

The Sekonic L-398, shown here with the hemispheric incident bulb, is a light meter commonly used by beginners. **SEE 12-16** Other makes have similar displays and, although occasionally employing different strategies, are used in the same ways. The hemisphere measures light in a 180-degree radius, the bulb simulating the shape of a human face. Many light meters, the Sekonic included, also have a white, flat incident disc for measuring individual light sources. Though I encourage people to measure the light produced by individual instruments, I rarely use the flat disc, preferring to turn off the offending source or shade the bulb from it.

The scale in the middle of the light meter displays the measurement of the amount of light present in the scene. The button in the center of the dial activates the needle, which renders the amount of light in foot-candles. The term *foot-candle (FC)* refers to the amount of light that falls 1 foot in any direction from a candle. A foot-candle is a standard unit of measure, like an ounce, a pound, a foot, or a mile, measuring a volume of light. If the light meter reads 20 fc, it means there is twenty times the amount of light as can be found 1 foot from a candle. People sometimes have a hard time grasping the fact that light is measurable, but measuring the light in a room and finding 20 foot-candles is just as certain and objective as measuring the width of the room and finding it to be 12 feet across. It is certain and objective at least once you understand the complexities of using the light meter.

Many readers are undoubtedly aware that most newer light meters display their information in digital readouts (usually in *f*-stops), rather then with the moving needle and foot-candles of the Sekonic shown here. Although digital-display meters are very attractive for beginners, an understanding of foot-candles is critical to an integrated comprehension of the fundamentals of lighting. Only the most expensive digital meters can display in foot-candles. Though analog can appear old-fashioned and clunky, learning foot-candles is recommended, because you will eventually be

12-16

The Sekonic L-398 is a typical, analog-display light meter

Bulb or grid (bulb shown)

Foot-candle readings

Needle

Activating button

INCIDENT LIGHT

required to know them and it helps you think about light in terms of shifting volumes. It is quite instructive to watch the needle physically respond to different amounts of light. Once you understand them, reading in foot-candles will be unnecessary, and you will find that most crews communicate in *f*-stops (or, actually, in *t*-stops, which are discussed in chapter 13).

SHUTTER SPEED

Shutter speed refers to how long each individual frame of film is being exposed to light. It is referred to in terms of fractions of seconds, say, $\frac{1}{30}$, $\frac{1}{500}$, and so on. Those with experience in still photography know that shutter speed, along with the *f*-stop, is a major control of how an image is exposed. In film, shutter speed is not so critical a variable, because, unless you are going for some specialized motion effect, it is a constant, dependent on the number of frames per second at which you are running. Shutter speed is calculated by a straightforward formula:

$$\frac{1}{2 \times fps}$$

This is simple common sense. If the camera is running at 24 fps, how much attention is each individual frame of film getting? Each frame has $\frac{1}{24}$ of a second devoted to it, but it is actually being exposed only half that time—the other half of the time the light is being blocked by the rotation of the half-moon shutter—so it is being exposed for one-half of $\frac{1}{24}$ of a second. **SEE 12-17** The actual shutter speed would be $\frac{1}{48}$ second, usually rounded off to $\frac{1}{50}$. Whatever fps you have chosen for the camera, the frame is getting light half the time of its possible exposure. Shutter speed becomes an issue only when you change running speeds (that is, frames per second) for slow- or fast-motion effects. If you change speeds, you have to make the necessary adjustments. (See the discussion of slow motion and fast motion in chapter 15.)

The variable that is not addressed in this simple formula is the size of the shutter. Most shutters are the half-moon configuration or close to it (most are actually a little smaller). But if for some reason you need to use a different-size shutter, which is very rare, you have to know the complex formula:

$$\frac{Degrees\ of\ shutter}{360\ (total\ degrees\ in\ a\ circle)} \times \frac{1}{fps}$$

If the camera shutter has the half-moon configuration, which is 180 degrees of the circle, the first part of the formula will simply reduce to one-half (180 / 360). With a normal shutter, the formula is always going to be simple—one over two times the fps. Again, the only time you need the complex formula is when you are dealing with a shutter that is not the standard half-moon configuration.

On still-photography cameras, the shutter speed is variable, and not having a variable shutter speed can be a real shock for people with a photography background. I often use Kodak Tri-X black-and-white film for outdoor still photography. Because it has such a high exposure index (EI), I can shoot at a high

12-17

The shutter allows light to reach the film plane during half its rotation

Film gate

Shutter

shutter speed and a high *f*-stop; that would stop fast-moving action and give tremendous depth of field. In motion picture photography, you just cannot do that. Without substantial filtering, a stock with an EI like Tri-X (400 in still photography) would be unusable on a bright, sunny day. Without the ability to get less light from the shutter speed, you would get an *f*-stop higher than anything on the lens. It makes for a whole new set of considerations.

THE COMPUTER

The first function of a light meter is to measure the amount of light in an area. The second function is to translate the foot-candle readings into an *f*-stop, usually one that will produce a normally exposed image. The dials on the bottom of the light meter are used to set the EI, the shutter speed, and, eventually, to determine the *f*-stop. Some manufacturers call this the light meter's *computer,* used to compute the *f*-stop.

The EI is the first thing to set on the light meter. The meter usually has a window that displays the range of EI numbers, and you simply dial to the number that the manufacturer recommends. **SEE 12-18**

Light meters are also used by still photographers and thus have a scale with the full range of shutter speeds. Because shutter speed is determined by frames per second in motion picture photography, a small scale with fps numbers, generally called the *cine scale,* will be interrelated with the still-photography numbers. The numbers pictured here are fps rates commonly used in filmmaking. **SEE 12-19**

To find the *f*-stop, the computer will have a moving scale to set the foot-candle reading that the light meter has given. As this is set, the cine scale moves against the *f*-stop scale. Once set, the *f*-stop that will produce normal exposure for that foot-candle value is displayed directly below the fps. **SEE 12-20**

Although this gives simple *f*-stops, the process of metering and determining *f*-stops is far more complicated than this. The goal, which is developed in the following chapters, is to be able to evaluate and control a complex image that has a wide range of lights and darks.

The film stock's EI is the first thing to set on a light meter

12-19

The cine scale gives the fps rates commonly used in filmmaking

CINE		8	12	18	24	36	48	72	96	
2		2.8		4		5.6		8	11	16	22

12-20

To find the *f*-stop, set the foot-candle reading; the cine scale moves against the *f*-stop scale to yield the value for a normal exposure

Manipulation of Lights

Manipulating the lights means changing the volume, the pattern, or the quality of the light to suit your purposes. A common example of a situation in which you might want to manipulate the light is when you want to soften or diffuse a hard light without going all the way to a softlight. Another case is when you want the light to have a different feel, say, warmer or multifaceted. The most common situation is when you simply have too much or too little light to achieve the desired effect.

The primary way to manipulate light is in your initial choice of instruments. You will be working with the two basic types—focusable spots and floodlights—which produce two different kinds of light—direct and indirect, respectively. Once you have the instruments, you still will be constantly changing or adjusting them to create the exact effect you want. Taking an example of an instrument that is producing too much light for a scene is a good starting point.

PROBLEM

Let's say you set up an instrument and get a reading of 160 fc, but you want 40 fc. (Potential reasons for desiring specific volumes of light are covered in chapter 13.) In this case you want to *back off* the light, that is, make it less intense. How would you deal with this situation?

There are many options and materials you can use to manipulate the instruments. Seven potential solutions are given here, but there are many others. The first three solutions are probably the most common; the last four can create a variety of side effects, the severity of which is discussed. If you want to *bring in* a light rather than back it off, simply do the reverse of what is suggested. Either way, this process of changing the shape, quality, or intensity of the light an instrument produces is called *trimming* the instrument. Trimming can be much more complex than simply backing off and bringing in, but these terms are a good starting point.

SOLUTIONS

Move the light back   This is straightforward. Have an assistant stand at the subject with a light meter, keeping the activating button depressed. As the instrument is moved back, the needle will respond to the lower volume of light. Just move the instrument back until you achieve the desired foot-candle value. This is most easily accomplished with an assistant, as are most things in lighting. If you try to do it alone, you will find yourself running back and forth from light source to subject—a physically wearing and unnecessarily time-consuming proposition.

Flood out the light   If you are using a focusable spot, it will have a spot/flood capability. In spot, the greatest amount of light is concentrated in the center. When you flood the light out, you widen the beam and, consequently, have less light in the center. Keep the activating button depressed as you flood the light out, and the meter will tell precisely how much the light falls off. Just flood it until you get the reading you want.

Use modifying material in front of the light   Modifying materials come in many forms and work in various ways, from simply cutting down the amount of light to significantly altering its quality, which most manufacturers call *redistributing* the light. Clothespins are used to attach materials to the barn doors; such materials can be used to cover all or part of the light. Commonly used modifying materials include the following:

■ **Scrims**   Made from a metal screenlike material, scrims cut down the amount of light without significantly diffusing it. Usually, these are designed for a specific make of instrument and slip into a holder between the barn doors and the lamp itself.

■ **Nets**   This material looks like mosquito netting. Nets are similar to scrims, and sometimes the terms are used interchangeably. Constructed like silks, nets are also used on C-stands.   **SEE 12-21**   They come in different shapes and sizes that have exotic names, such as "fingers" and "dots."

■ **Silk**   A white artificial material that resembles its namesake, silk cuts down the volume of light and strongly diffuses it. Coming in a variety of sizes, silks have metal frames and are usually set in front of the instrument on a *C-stand (Century stand),*

12-21

A C-stand rigged with a net, used to cut down the volume of light one of the key pieces of equipment used for setting things in front of lights. Silks made out of *real* silk are available but are very expensive and require careful handling.

■ **Spun**   This is an artificial spun glass–like material. Spun is one of the most popular modifying materials for beginners; it cuts down the light as well as diffuses it.

■ **Frost and tough-white diffusion**   These are milky-looking diffusion *gels* (a cellophane-like material). The use of 216 (one of the tough whites) is very common. Both 216 and frost are popular ways of softening and giving a warm feel to the lights.

■ **Opal diffuser**   This type of diffusion softens the light and is also quite popular. An opal diffuser is similar to frost but gives a slightly harder feel to the light, as though it were broken down into the facets of an opal gem.

■ **Rolux**   Denser than opal, this material cuts down the light tremendously and can make the light source very indistinct. This is effective when you want an unlit feel to the image. Because it cuts the volume so dramatically, it is used mostly on larger lights.

■ **Shower curtain**   This material, which looks similar to its namesake, is less dense than Rolux but affords the same soft feel.

■ **Tracing paper**   Also called *trace,* tracing paper is used for many purposes, but particularly on backlights to diminish the harsh quality of the shadows they create.

■ **Flags**   Made of black opaque material, flags are similar in design to silks and nets. Flags are not true modifying materials because they *cut,* or block, the light from individual instruments. Nevertheless, they are used in much the same way as many of the other materials, and their role in manipulating light is significant. Like nets, flags come in a variety of shapes and sizes that have names such as "cutters" and "solids."

■ **Cookies**   Short for *cukaloris,* cookies are similar to flags, but with cutout designs that break up the light. A cookie, also called a *kook,* is generally used to lend texture to a background. They are difficult to use on foreground subjects, because shadows from their cut-outs would be noticeable, but they are very effective in breaking up flat and uninteresting light in other areas of the frame. Like flags, cookies are not true modifying materials but, again like flags, are used in enough situations to warrant a mention here.

Change the wattage of the lamp   Within the limitations of the manufacturer's recommendations, almost all lighting instruments will accept different wattages of lamps. Lamps with lower wattage produce less light. This strategy is less attractive to many users, because taking apart hot lights on location consumes valuable time and can be dangerous. It is better to think about this in planning a lighting setup. A competent gaffer will think out what kind of space the crew is working in and plan in advance the lamp sizes needed. It is not unheard of to switch lamps on location, but efficient use of time advises that such decisions be made earlier rather than later.

Bounce the light   This is a possible solution, but it carries its own liabilities in that the quality of the light is so different from what you started with that it significantly changes the shot. That said, there are many surfaces that serve as good vehicles for bouncing, from white walls and ceilings to specially designed aluminum reflectors; one of the most popular is foam core. The practice of bouncing light is very common, but more as a source than a modification. If your goal is to modify a light from 640 fc to 320 fc, bouncing the light could create a more radical change than you want in terms of both volume and quality.

Use a neutral density filter   A gray gel that cuts down the amount of light passing through it, a *neutral density (ND) filter* does not change any color quality, nor does it diffuse the light—it just cuts the amount of light from the instrument. ND is available in filters rated at 0.1, 0.2, 0.3, and so on; each tenth represents one-third of an f-stop. Thus, a 0.3 equals one stop, a 0.6 equals two stops, and a 0.9 equals three stops. Usually, people just drop the point, so a 0.3 filter is called an "ND3."

Although a few professionals use ND on lights, it is much less useful than may first appear. One general rule of lighting is that the more you put on an instrument, the harder it is to use other modifying materials on it. Neutral density can be cumbersome, and its use on or in front of an instrument is infrequent. ND does have many other important applications, however, such as in window gels (see figure 15-12) and as front filters on lenses.

Focus the light so the subject is off center   By closing the barn doors or panning the light, you can position it so that the subject is not in the center of the beam. This is often the first thing people want to try, yet it is the least viable solution of all. In both cases, a lower reading is produced by narrowing or changing the point where the light shines. Most often the subject simply looks unlit, as if the light is shooting past it or it is sitting outside the beam. This is the kind of effect that calls attention to lighting and can appear to be very artificial.

Another technology that is available is theatrical *dimmers*. Though they may seem useful for backing off lights, their application in film is somewhat limited. The big problem with dimming is that when voltage to the instrument is reduced, the color of the light—the color temperature—changes. On occasion, filmmakers use instruments on dimmers very successfully to create peripheral light, that is, light on the background. But if dimmered light is used on foreground figures, particularly people, unwelcome effects may result. You need to know your way around color temperature to work with dimmers effectively.

Many modifying materials discussed here were developed specifically for film to replicate what can be achieved quite easily on stage with theatrical dimmers. In film, because you generally need consistent color temperature, you have to put something on the light to reduce the foot-candles rather than simply reduce the voltage to the instrument.

These are some of the main options available for manipulating light. Once you get the instruments up, the object is to adjust them until you get the values and quality of light you want. Keep working with the instruments and the materials. Experience will be your best teacher.

13

Exposure and Latitude

Exposure Index, Foot-candles, and *f*-stops

Although there are a number of considerations in choosing a film stock, *exposure index (EI)*—the rating of film's sensitivity to light—is often the determining factor for beginners and those with limited resources. It harkens back to the key distinction made earlier: Use a film stock with a high EI when filming in low light and, conversely, a stock with a low EI in high light. Given their ability to manipulate light in almost any way imaginable, however, experienced DPs can use whatever film stock they want and simply light for it.

The key variable in the relationship between a given amount of foot-candles and an *f*-stop is the EI of the film stock that was chosen. Once the film stock is determined and the EI on the light meter has been set, the translation of specific foot-candle readings to *f*-stops becomes automatic. With this in mind, a chart can give the foot-candle–to–*f*-stop relationship for a number of potential film stocks. **SEE 13-1** These exposures are the manufacturers' recommendations, all made with normal exposure as the stated goal. There are, of course, other possible EIs.

Foot-candles	EI				
	32	**100**	**125**	**250**	**500**
5				*f*/1	*f*/1.4
10			*f*/1	*f*/1.4	*f*/2
20		*f*/1/1.4	*f*/1.4	*f*/2	*f*/2.8
40	*f*/1	*f*/1.4/2	*f*/2	*f*/2.8	*f*/4
80	*f*/1.4	*f*/2/2.8	*f*/2.8	*f*/4	*f*/5.6
160	*f*/2	*f*/2.8/4	*f*/4	*f*/5.6	*f*/8
320	*f*/2.8	*f*/4/5.6	*f*/5.6	*f*/8	*f*/11
640	*f*/4	*f*/5.6/8	*f*/8	*f*/11	*f*/16
1,280	*f*/5.6	*f*/8/11	*f*/11	*f*/16	*f*/22
2,560	*f*/8	*f*/11/16	*f*/16	*f*/22	*f*/32

13-1

The foot-candle–to–*f*-stop relationship for potential film stocks

If you are shooting with a film stock that has an EI of 500 and your light meter gives a reading of 320 fc, you would shoot at $f/11$ to produce normal exposure. If you are shooting with 100 EI film and get a reading of 160 fc, an $f/2.8/4$ would produce normal exposure; that is read as "2.8 slash 4," and you set the f-stop ring between those two stops.

◆ **RULE:** *A film stock with a low EI will yield one f-stop, lower numerically (say, $f/2.8$), whereas a film stock with a higher EI will yield another f-stop, higher numerically (say, $f/5.6$).*

As suggested, you should probably use the manufacturer's recommended EI, although you will eventually discover that this number is not written in stone. DPs often rate the film stock differently, because they know they will achieve a specific effect if they do. If you rate a film stock higher or lower numerically, you are just building in a consistent level of over- or underexposure. There are limits, of course.

Using the Light Meter

The choice between an incident- and a reflective-light meter represents different approaches to metering a scene. Each approach has its own advantages and disadvantages. For film applications, however, the incident meter is far more useful than the reflective meter.

A hypothetical situation with a person standing in front of a window can illustrate the difference between the two types of meters. Outside the window in the background, there is a street awash in sunlight and a building in the shade. Inside the room on the table there is a lamp that is turned on. The room itself is not receiving any direct sunlight, but the left side, that is, the person's back and the bookcase, is receiving strong ambient light. **SEE 13-2**

13-2

A wide range of light values in a given scene necessitates the use of an incident-light meter

Given the assumptions of the situation, you should see an immediate problem: There is a wide range of light values in this scene, with a relatively dark subject against a brilliant background. Because the *reflective-light meter* can be pointed only at the scene as a whole for an average, its readings will not indicate the various amounts of light in different parts of the scene. If you shoot at the *f*-stop suggested by the meter, whatever is lit to that value will expose correctly, but everything else will come in at different and potentially unacceptable exposures.

So the problem is not how much light is present in the scene as a whole, but how much light is on each subject or area. Furthermore, as subjects move in a composition, they also move through exposure. Does the subject get too dark over here? Is the backlight more than we want over there? These questions suggest why the incident light meter becomes not only the tool of choice but the tool of necessity.

With the *incident-light meter,* as suggested earlier, you can go through a scene and measure the light in specific areas. The meter can indicate precisely how the light is increasing or falling off. If you walk through the scene with the activating button depressed, you will actually be able to see, as the needle responds, where the light is above or below the desired amount. Steps can then be taken to compensate.

Although a few cameras offer through-the-lens (TTL) reflective-light meters with an automatic exposure option—the camera automatically sets the *f*-stop for the user—few if any professional camerapeople use it. Automatic reflective meters are too random in evaluating the information they collect. They may work for basic still photography, but do not perform to the exacting standards necessary in most filmmaking applications. Automatic exposure meters do have their uses, particularly in documentary filmmaking, but their value is limited and they should not be used beyond formative efforts.

The example of the person in front of the window provides an instance where training in the use of light meters pays off. To show some simple metering techniques, consider the previous example but eliminate the window. The image is by no means simple, however. Even here it is easy to make some basic mistakes. Again, the lamp is turned on. **SEE 13-3**

With the incident-light meter, you measure how much light there is in any one spot. Remembering what has been said about the key and fill, go to the person and

13-3

A single source may not provide the light levels required for a usable exposure

13-4

To take readings on the key and fill sides of the subject's face, point the meter in the direction you want to measure

13-5

Light levels are measured by moving the meter through the scene

take individual readings on each side of his face. **SEE 13-4** The side toward the lamp is going to be the key side, and the side away from the lamp is going to be the fill side. With the activating button depressed, move the meter around; let's say that the readings shown in the figure are found. In this case point the meter toward the source rather than toward the camera as was suggested earlier. Generally, when trying to find out what a specific instrument is accomplishing, point the meter right at the source.

As suspected, the reading on the fill side is very low, because it is getting no direct light. When you measure an individual instrument as you have measured the fill here, you have to be careful that the reading is not being skewed by another instrument. Sometimes just blocking the offending source with your hand or a card is all it takes to eliminate the problem. In many situations you can just turn off the instruments that you don't want confusing the reading. Because the lamp is the sole source in this instance, you will not be able to do that here.

The readings around the lamp are also significant. **SEE 13-5** You do a general reading and find 320 fc right under the lamp. Let's say you find 640 fc halfway between the lampshade and the table. The light is stronger as you move toward the lamp and weaker as you move away.

Going back to the foot-candle chart in figure 13-1, translate these readings into *f*-stops. If you are shooting with a film stock with an EI of 500, the reading at the top of the lamp base (1,280 fc) translates to an *f*/22. That is, if you shoot at an *f*/22, the top part of the lamp base will be normally exposed. The 320 fc on the table translates to an *f*/11, which would give normal exposure there. It is literally an *f*/22 at the top of the lamp base and an *f*/11 on the table.

It is important to note that this is not an evaluative process at this point; it is a measurement process. It does take experience and skill to do it correctly, but once you are aware of the pitfalls, this is essentially no different than checking the dipstick of your car or weighing yourself on a bathroom scale. If there is *x* amount of light in an area, there is *x* amount of light. That does not mean it will not or cannot change; it just means that at the time the measurement is taken, there is *x* amount of light. Once you get these readings, you are faced with some decisions.

The ability to evaluate, of course, precedes the ability to control, or manipulate, the light. Clearly, if you can find out what a specific light source is reading, you can also introduce an artificial light source and manipulate it to a specific value.

A cinematographer friend tells the story of a mistake he made on one of his first big jobs—lighting a convention hall for a political figure whose speech was getting network coverage. The advance men told him they wanted the hall lit to an *f*/5.6.

13-6

Anything less than the plateau level (an *f*/5.6 in this case) can be thought of as a valley, and areas falling into a valley will be underexposed

13-7

Additional instruments can illuminate the valleys, bringing those areas up to the appropriate level

With an incident meter as a guide, one can go through and manipulate the lights to an even *f*/5.6. The cinematographer went into the huge convention hall and proceeded to light the podium. On the evening of the speech, two Secret Service types showed up, took one look at the hall, and, in unison, reached inside their trenchcoats. Suddenly, the cinematographer had visions of his career coming to an abrupt and violent end, but rather than producing the anticipated instruments of destruction, the agents produced . . . light meters.

The two men then proceeded to go through the entire hall, reading all the light values. Aha, a 2.8 here. Here we drop all the way down to an *f*/2. The cinematographer was mortified but immediately realized the misunderstanding. They had wanted an even *f*/5.6 throughout the entire hall, and he had left areas at less than that. In a sense the *f*/5.6 was the plateau he was supposed to achieve, and anything less was a valley. And by falling into the valley, the shots would fall into underexposure. **SEE 13-6**

My friend lived to light again, but with more instruments he could have easily accomplished what was wanted of him. With the incident meter, he could determine where the exposure dropped below an *f*/5.6 and set up additional instruments to bring those areas up to the appropriate level. **SEE 13-7** He could literally fill in the holes. In the areas where he found an *f*/4, he needed a relatively small amount of light. Where he found a large area lit to an *f*/2, he would have to bring in a number of instruments.

You will rarely want lighting that is this even. This is television news lighting— what's referred to as *illumination*. The point is that you need to go through any scene and determine all the lighting values present. Second, and of much greater importance, the incident meter is your best guide for manipulating the instruments to achieve the levels of exposure desired. A conventional reflective-light meter can give only an average of a complex situation, but an incident-light meter allows you to check every source and determine how much light is there.

The incident meter allows you to be reasonably precise. It gives you more control not only in evaluating, but eventually in manipulating the values that will create the dramatic quality of your images.

HALVING AND DOUBLING

So far, the light meter readings used in the illustrations have been either halves or doubles of each other. This has been deliberate to illustrate another important concept:

◆ **RULE:** *Virtually everything to do with the measurement and transmission of light is based on halves and doubles.*

The reason why the numbers that have been presented are the f-stops is because each one represents the discrete and identifiable point at which the light halves or doubles from the previous stop.

Reciprocally, every doubling or halving of foot-candles represents a one–f-stop change. If you get a foot-candle reading in a specific area and then find either half as much or twice as much light in another, there is a one–f-stop difference between those two areas. This means that there is a one–f-stop difference between the 320 fc of the table and the 640 fc halfway to the lampshade. There is a two–f-stop difference between the 20 fc of the key side of the face and the 5 fc of the fill side.

The concept of halving and doubling pertains not only to the light in front of the camera, but also to the f-stops. Assuming a consistent amount of light in front of the camera, every sequential change from one f-stop to another represents a halving or a doubling of the amount of light reaching the film plane. Thus, if you are shooting at an $f/4$ and change to an $f/5.6$, half as much light is reaching the film plane as before. If you change to an $f/2.8$ from an $f/4$, twice as much light is reaching the film plane.

As you may have noticed from figure 13-1, this doubling and halving also includes the EI.

◆ **RULE:** *Every halving or doubling of EI represents a one–f-stop difference.*

If you are shooting with an EI 160 film stock and getting an $f/5.6$, what would happen to the f-stop if you reloaded (and DPs do not make arbitrary changes like this) with a film stock that has an EI of 320? You could, theoretically, reset the f-stop without remetering. What would the new stop be? Would you *open up*, that is, choose a lower-numbered f-stop? Or would you *close down*, that is, choose a higher-numbered f-stop?

Because the EI is going up numerically and the film stock is more sensitive to light, you need less light to expose it. You would close down to an $f/8$. If you were to change to a film stock with an EI of 80, you would do the opposite: The film stock is less sensitive to light, so you need more light to expose it; you would open up to an $f/4$. In both examples you need to either double or halve the volume of light provided by the f-stop to produce a normal exposure.

Halving and doubling the light may sound drastic, but it is actually a relatively small change in terms of the image. The primary goal at the outset is to achieve a usable image, and a deviation of one f-stop is relatively minor. It is a noticeable change, however, and the difference can be significant when shooting scenes where matching the lighting from one shot to the next becomes an issue.

How this relates to the concept of normal exposure is explored in succeeding sections, but you can see that already you are presented with a choice. When there are so many *f*-stop values present in the scene, how do you expose the image? Or, more to the point, what foot-candle value do you choose to expose for in this, or any, complex image? Although the rule of halves and doubles may seem like a trivial detail at this point, it is crucial to remember it when evaluating the different exposure levels in any image.

The Central Confusion

Up to this point, we have referred to light and *f*-stops in two different senses. Earlier it was shown that higher *f*-stops on the camera mean less light reaching the film plane. But higher *f*-stops also mean *more* light—it being *f*/22 closer to the lamp and *f*/11 farther away. This is what I like to call the "central confusion," and the fact that we use the term *f-stop* in two different ways must be clearly understood before proceeding to advanced lighting techniques.

Put simply, the term *f-stop* is used to refer to *both the light in front of the camera and the actual setting on the aperture ring.* It is used to refer to light in two different places: at the subject and in the camera. Up to this point, we have measured the light in front of the camera in foot-candles. So far so good. But once we have the EI, we can convert our readings into *f*-stops. So, for example, if we get a reading of *f*/8 at A and then go to B and get an *f*/11, which area has the most light? B must have more light, because we need to use a smaller diaphragm opening to get a normal exposure. Areas with greater volumes of light require smaller openings, that is, higher *f*-stops. Areas with smaller amounts of light require wider openings, that is, lower *f*-stops.

Of course, *f*-stop also refers to the diaphragm on the lens. If we get a reading of *f*/8 at the subject and set the lens to an *f*/11, less light is going to reach the film plane than if we set the diaphragm to an *f*/8. Smaller openings allow less light to reach the film plane and are the appropriate response to greater volumes of light.

We have, then, two different ways of talking about the same thing. One is the amount of light at the point of metering. The other is the amount of light reaching the film plane. Getting a reading of *f*/2.8 at a subject by definition means that there is a small amount of light there; that same *f*/2.8 on the camera means more light reaching the film plane than with a higher *f*-stop. Conversely, getting a reading of *f*/11 at a subject means there is a large amount of light there; that same *f*/11 means less light reaching the film plane than with, say, an *f*/2.8.

These less-and-more distinctions may baffle you for a while. It can be quite confusing to hear people talking in *f*-stops all the time on the set. Until you learn the language, listening to people speaking in *f*-stops can be just like listening to people conversing in an unfamiliar tongue. But the language of light is a fundamental part of filmmaking, and the sooner it is understood, the sooner you'll be able to communicate with the rest of the crew.

Evaluating Existing Light

Now the big question: How do you determine your *f*-stop? The answer is not necessarily an easy one, but the starting point is measuring and evaluating the amount of light present in the scene you want to shoot. This ability to evaluate a shooting

To evaluate a scene, use an incident-light meter to measure the light falling on different objects and areas

situation is essential to predicting what your image is going to look like. The fact that you evaluate a scene, though, does not mean that you won't change things. The process of evaluation by its very nature precedes manipulation.

Not only are there different volumes of light in most scenes, but these volumes of light are sometimes changing and always changeable. If you go into a room that is too dark, you turn on a light. When you do this, you change the physical amount of light in the room. Hence, there is more light. If there is a window in the room and it is sunny outside, the situation becomes more complicated. When we return to our original scene of someone in front of a window on a sunny day, this becomes evident. **SEE 13-8**

With the light meter, you can determine most of the light values within this scene. Let's speculate that you find the foot-candle values shown in the figure; the numbers used here behave nicely, all relating to specific *f*-stops. In real life the values you find would presumably settle in at many different levels: full stop, half stops, and such. For the sake of simplicity, the numbers given here will not complicate the issues.

For evaluation purposes, you can go through this scene and group the objects and areas in terms of the amount of light falling on them. **SEE 13-9** That is, you can group together all things lit to 640 fc, all things at 80 fc, et cetera. As you examine the scene, you find that there are nine different exposure values: 10 fc through 2,560 fc. (By exposure value we mean simply that this value of light, as we have measured it, exists within our proposed frame.) There are then nine different choices for exposing this image, each exposure value relating to an *f*-stop that is yet to be determined.

The variable in how all this relates to the *f*-stop is, of course, the EI. For this example, we will choose a color film stock that has an EI of 500, a stock that is presently manufactured by both Kodak and Fuji. Keep this film stock in mind; it will be our example throughout the text. Step 1, as always, is to set the EI on the light meter. **SEE 13-10**

Once you have decided on the stock and thus the EI, you've established a constant relationship between foot-candles and *f*-stops. By looking at the chart in figure 13-1, you see that the 640 fc of the shaded building converts to an *f*/16. If you want the shaded building to expose normally, you would shoot at *f*/16. Anything at 2,560 fc is going to translate to an *f*/32 at 500 EI. The 80 foot-candles

13-9

For evaluation purposes, objects and areas can be grouped in terms of the amount of light falling on them

2,560 fc	Sunny street
1,280 fc	Hot spot on windowsill
640 fc	Shaded building / Base of lamp / Backlight on person
320 fc	Book screen-left / Circle of light from lamp
160 fc	Left wall / Lampshade / Tissue box
80 fc	Person / Interior wall / Front edge of tissue box
40 fc	Under bookcase
20 fc	Shadow under table
10 fc	Ambient shadows

on the person in the room translate to an *f*/5.6. If you wanted the person to expose normally, you would shoot at an *f*/5.6.

This is straightforward. If you want something normally exposed, you shoot at the *f*-stop that corresponds to that foot-candle value. It is also important to note that when you shoot at a specific *f*-stop, only the things that are at that foot-candle value will expose normally. Everything else will come in at some level of over- or underexposure. These deceptively simple statements are the key to understanding how to produce almost any lighting effect.

13-10

When evaluating existing light, the first step is always to set the EI on the light meter

Shooting the 80 fc objects at an f/5.6 produces a normal exposure for that group

By deciding on the frame rate, shutter speed becomes a constant and can be plugged into the formula

When you decide to shoot at a specific f-stop, you have in effect chosen a specific group to be normally exposed. If you decide to shoot at an f/5.6, to normally expose the person, you have also chosen to normally expose the other elements in the 80 fc group. **SEE 13-11** Hence, choosing the objects at 80 fc and shooting at f/5.6 means that all the variables we have been suggesting come together to produce a normal exposure. You have already chosen the EI (500), so that is one variable out of the way. Another variable is the shutter speed. If you decide to run at 24 fps, the shutter speed also becomes a constant. **SEE 13-12**

There is a third variable that we will, at least for now, posit as a constant: the final exposure. All that has been discussed so far is normal exposure, but the possibility remains that you are pursuing something else. In fact, you will eventually come to see normal exposure as only part of the goal, as one part of the entire image; you will regard normal exposure as somewhat of a mythical beast, nice to scare and teach the children with, but only one element of a rich and multifaceted image.

The next two variables are the ones over which you have the most control: the f-stop and how much existing light there is in the proposed frame. The f-stop is clearly a key variable. At this point you are just evaluating an existing situation, so you will not be changing the amount of light on anything. (This is artificially imposed on the discussion and will change soon.)

Given the group of objects you have chosen—the ones at 80 fc—the next figure shows the elements you are combining to achieve a normal exposure. **SEE 13-13** We will call this a formula, though the + and = signs are somewhat misleading. It is not so much that you add these elements together to get this result, but that when these elements are present you get a specific result.

What would happen if you shifted the f-stop in this formula? If you shift the f-stop—say, to an f/8—things would change; something has to give somewhere else. Because you have established the first three elements as constants, the part that gives has to be the result. **SEE 13-14**

When you decide to expose at a particular f-stop, it is going to affect what happens to objects and areas that have different foot-candle amounts falling on them. What would happen to objects lit to 160 fc? Because 160 is twice 80, there is a one–f-stop difference. **SEE 13-15** Elements at 320 fc would overexpose by two stops. Elements at 40 fc would underexpose by one stop, and elements at 20 fc by two stops.

As suggested, the result can also be considered a variable. In that case you would just look at the formula in a slightly different order. If you wanted to underexpose for an effect, you would change the result variable first, and something else in the line would have to change. In this case the f-stop would have to change to get the desired result. Although this seems to be just a case of inverted logic, this is an important point: If you want something in the scene to be dark—underexposed—the result is indeed the starting point.

This suggests that the formula may be a helpful concept. Though as a metaphor it is somewhat problematic because you are not actually adding things, it does suggest a method of evaluating virtually everything in the frame. There are five variables here: EI, shutter speed, amount of light on subject, f-stop, and the final result: exposure. If you lock in four of the five, and remember that two are constants given certain preliminary determinations, the fifth has to be where the change is going to occur.

At this point the formula has just five variables. These are the basic variables for any image. The variable list will not necessarily be this short, however, as many things can complicate your considerations. As new topics are introduced, the list will get longer and more complex. We have demonstrated how to determine what is

13-13

The elements that when taken together produce a normal exposure

13-14

Because the first three elements are constants, changing the *f*-stop affects the final exposure

13-15

When the *f*-stop is set to normally expose the 80 fc group, the 160 fc group is one–*f*-stop overexposed

happening in terms of how specific elements in the image are exposing. The next step is understanding how this affects the way the film stock is going to render the image.

Latitude

The concept of latitude is absolutely crucial to an understanding of how light, and the image, is registered on the film. *Latitude* can most easily be defined as the "seeing range of the film." *It is the amount of under- or overexposure that the film stock can accept and still render objects with detail.* The best way to explain this is to compare it

13-16

The characteristic curve plots the density of grains on the negative against rising exposure

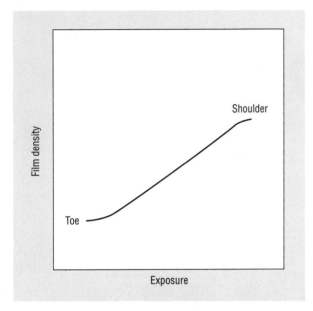

to the human eye. The eye can take in a wide range of lighting values and average them so you see all aspects with detail. If a person is standing in front of a bright light source, you have no trouble seeing detail in any area in which you look.[1] The film stock cannot do this. It can see only within a relatively narrow range of lighting values. That is, it can reproduce objects only to a certain level of under- or overexposure before it renders them completely black or clear, respectively.

Latitude varies from film stock to film stock. It can be quantified, and the manufacturer includes a graph in the product information, called a *characteristic curve*, that tells you how the film stock performs, by plotting the density of grains on the negative against rising exposure. **SEE 13-16** It shows the gradual consistent rise of exposure, called the *straight-line portion*, while also showing the precipitous drop-offs to under- and overexposure, called, respectively, the *toe* and the *shoulder*. Characteristic curves are quite difficult for beginners to interpret, and simple discussions with a knowledgeable source should tell you what you need to know. A working filmmaker or someone at a processing laboratory should be able to give you a good idea. The majority of film stocks have latitudes ranging from two stops to three and a half; that is, most stocks produce detail anywhere from two to three and a half stops on either side of normal exposure.

When learning exposure technique, many people find it useful to think of latitude as the "mistake factor." In other words, how badly can I miss on the f-stop and still get a usable shot? How badly can I be off and still get some detail in the subject? This is OK for starters, but eventually you will have to think of it in the more complex terms presented in this section.

To apply the concept of latitude to our example, you have a light meter reading of 80 fc (f/5.6) from the person in front of the window. There is substantially more light outside (2,560 fc). In just looking at this scene, your eyes have no trouble taking in these two extreme values and rendering a composite image. The film, however, can see only within a relatively narrow range of values; and, more to the point, it will expose normally for only one value at a time. What would be the likely result if you did shoot at an f/5.6? Obviously, the person in front of the window would be rendered normally, and the outside would be totally overexposed (blown out). The only other areas that would be normally exposed would be those also lit to an f/5.6. Everything else would be lit, and respond on the film, to some degree of over- (+) or underexposure (–). Your immediate response might be that you don't want that. If you think about it further, though, remember that you usually *do* want some form of gradation in terms of light in the image. If everything is normally, that is, evenly, exposed, the image will look flat and characterless. We expect areas to look shady (–) and bright (+). The point is that with a knowledge of latitude, you can begin to control which areas are over- and underexposed and to what degree. The film stock renders detail in the shaded and highlighted areas only to a certain point. The varying degrees of detail in over- and underexposed areas depends on how radically different the values are from the f-stop at which you are shooting.

Today's color negative film stocks have a latitude of roughly three to three and a half stops; that is, they render detail anywhere from three to three and a half stops on either side of normal exposure. If you shoot at an f/5.6 with your proposed stock, the film will see objects that are lit to the values in roughly this range. **SEE 13-17**

---

1. The eye also has an iris that facilitates taking in a wide range of values.

13-17

Color negative stocks have a latitude of roughly three to three and a half stops

An area that is lit to an *f*/11 (320 fc) will be two stops overexposed, and an area lit to an *f*/32 (2,560 fc) will be five stops overexposed. An area that is lit to an *f*/4 (40 fc) will be one stop underexposed, and if there were an area lit to an *f*/1.4 (5 fc), it would be four stops underexposed. Now, positing the latitude described, you can predict with a fair amount of accuracy what will happen in these four areas. An area at 320 fc will be two stops overexposed; but, because it is within the latitude of the film, it will be bright but rendered with at least some detail. The sunny street in the background (2,560 fc) will be five stops overexposed and, being outside the latitude of the film, will be totally overexposed. Areas at 40 fc will be one stop underexposed but rendered with substantial detail. Anything at 5 fc or less would be totally underexposed.

A good example of the interrelationship between latitude and exposure is a streetlight. (This is a hypothetical example, because you may never find a streetlight that gives you readings like these, even though we might sometimes wish that one would.) Let's say that your shot will be of a person walking from right to left under the light. With the activating button depressed, you just walk through the scene. The meter will respond as the light gets stronger and falls off again. To simplify things, go ahead and translate the foot-candle readings into *f*-stops. Again, there would be gradations, half stops, and so on between these readings, but we'll just show the full stops, assuming that the brightest spot is directly under the center of the light. **SEE 13-18**

If you shoot at an *f*/8, what is going to be the likely effect? The subject will be exposed normally only for that very brief point in the center of the light. With a

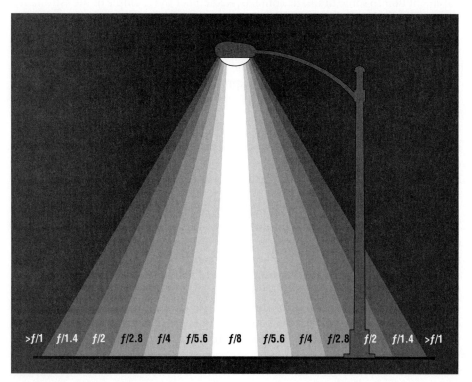

13-18

A hypothetical streetlight is a good example of the interrelationship between latitude and exposure

13-19

The subject exposes differently while moving

When the subject moves into an area where the light reading is:	The person is:
f/5.6	one stop underexposed
f/4	two stops underexposed—the subject is getting dark, but you still see detail
f/2.8	three stops underexposed—the subject is almost completely dark, nearly on the edge of the latitude
f/2	four stops underexposed—positing the latitude of three to three and a half stops, the subject has gone entirely to underexposure

knowledge of latitude, you can also predict where the subject is going to drop off to underexposure. The figure at left delineates the final exposure, given the various light readings of the different areas. **SEE 13-19**

Although you can see to the edge of the light with your eyes, you will find that the subject is lost much earlier on the film.

What would happen if you decided to expose this scene at an *f*/5.6 instead? Now you get a larger area of normal exposure, but it overexposes by one stop in the very center. It also extends the area of exposure one more stop at the edges. Where you lost the subject just above an *f*/2 before, you now keep him to just above an *f*/1.4. The subject, in a sense, traverses more area of exposure. Would that one stop of overexposure be acceptable in the center? That is always your decision, but if there is a strong top light, you can almost always expect its effect to be more amplified in the center. You can speculate that it would not only be acceptable, but you might like the effect more than the previous shot.

What would happen if you shot at an *f*/4? By following this method of evaluation, you can make what might be called an "exposure pyramid" with which you can predict what will happen at virtually any *f*-stop at which you choose to shoot. **SEE 13-20**

Are any of these possible exposures—that is, results—usable? Any of them might be usable, depending on what you want to achieve with the image; the emphasis is on *depending*, because that is the key. If realism is the goal, the *f*/8 shot might be acceptable. As suggested, with a realistic shot still your goal, the one stop of overexposure at an *f*/5.6 might be preferable. Would you accept the two stops over in the center that you would get with an *f*/4? That has to be your decision. Lower stops yield an effect that would be decidedly less realistic ("Beam me up, Scotty"), but might fit into some dramatic contexts. Remember the example of the astronaut's brightly lit quarters in Stanley Kubrick's *2001: A Space Odyssey.*

The question of exposure is dependent on what the filmmaker wants to achieve with a given image. If the image serves to provide dramatic context for the narrative (that is, if the image is at the service of the narrative), that may be the determining factor. If you want something more expressive or subjective, *that* becomes the determining factor. The effect you achieve should always be the effect that you want for the particular situation.

Armed with an understanding of latitude and an ability to evaluate a given situation, you have the ability to predict what will happen to any image at any exposure. You can meter any situation and set up an exposure pyramid. Then you have some decisions to make, each yielding an image that is a little different and has a different dramatic impact.

With a wide range of volumes of light in front of the camera, the *f*-stop must be used so that these volumes expose at the levels at which you want them. Think of this in terms of the filmmaker (you) using the *f*-stop as a response to a volume or, more accurate, volumes of light. The *f*-stop controls the light so that the correct amount of light for the desired exposure reaches the film plane. The choice of *f*-stop thus becomes one more creative tool in that its selection involves decisions as to the character and dramatic context of the image you are creating. If you do not treat exposure as a major consideration, you are saying—and I have heard it from people who should know better—that the image is unimportant to you.

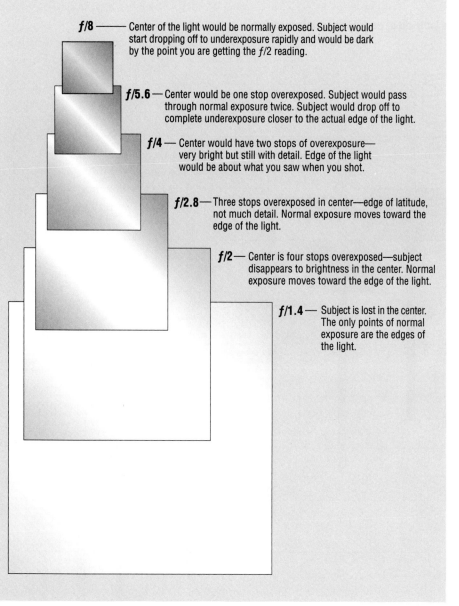

f/8 —— Center of the light would be normally exposed. Subject would start dropping off to underexposure rapidly and would be dark by the point you are getting the *f*/2 reading.

f/5.6 — Center would be one stop overexposed. Subject would pass through normal exposure twice. Subject would drop off to complete underexposure closer to the actual edge of the light.

f/4 — Center would have two stops of overexposure— very bright but still with detail. Edge of the light would be about what you saw when you shot.

f/2.8 — Three stops overexposed in center—edge of latitude, not much detail. Normal exposure moves toward the edge of the light.

f/2 — Center is four stops overexposed—subject disappears to brightness in the center. Normal exposure moves toward the edge of the light.

f/1.4 — Subject is lost in the center. The only points of normal exposure are the edges of the light.

13-20

With the "exposure pyramid," you can predict the outcome of virtually any *f*-stop at which you shoot

If we return to the original example of the person in front of the window (figure 13-8), some significant points become evident: As you evaluate shooting at different *f*-stops, you know what is going to happen to objects lit to the stop you are considering. Then, with a knowledge of latitude, you can predict with accuracy what is going to happen to objects lit to other stops. Are they within the latitude of the film?

If you can peg specific exposures to objects that are lit a certain way, you can make a graph of the relationships among a given *f*-stop, objects lit to that *f*-stop, and side effects of other things being over- or underexposed. Again, you are shooting with the EI 500 film stock. The following figure represents what will happen if exposure is decreased. **SEE 13-21** The lengths of the vertical lines represent the suggested three- to three-and-a-half–stop latitude. To see what and where things will fall into the latitude, extrapolate from the line to the left side of the chart.

The vertical lines represent the latitude at each individual exposure

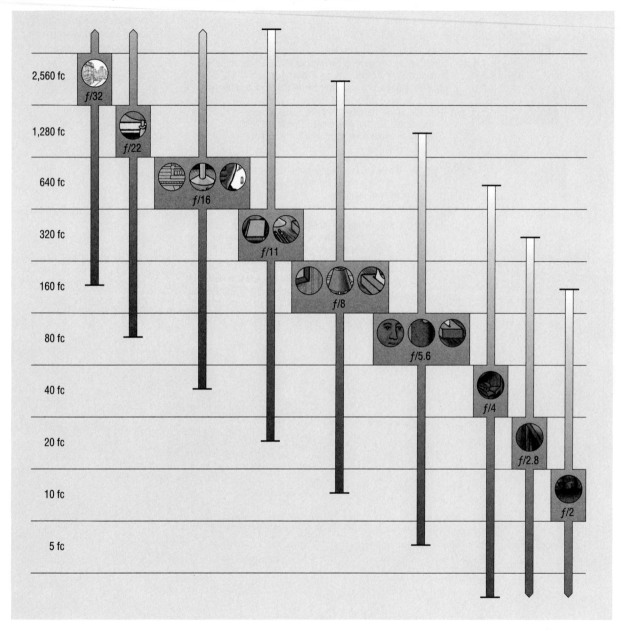

Again, if you decide that you want the subject normally exposed, you would choose an *f*/5.6 and would select the group shown in the following figure. **SEE 13-22** Areas at 640 fc—the shaded area on the building, the backlight on the person, and the base of the lamp—would be three stops overexposed. This would put you in the unenviable position of having a shaded area three stops overexposed on the edge of the latitude. Would this be an effect you like?

If you think about how you might perceive a scene like this normally, you might expect a person standing in front of a very bright background to look slightly dark, as if she were in the shade. How could you achieve this effect? If you want to see something as being dark, you underexpose it; so, rather than an *f*/5.6, what would happen if you shot at an *f*/8? The subject would be one stop underexposed and look more as though she were in the shade. Doing this, however, would change how all

13-22

When an *f*-stop is chosen, everything lit to other values will come in at different levels of exposure

13-23

As the *f*-stop is changed, the parameters of the latitude change

the areas lit to other values respond. In effect, you would shift the whole exposure range to the right on a standard *f*-stop scale. **SEE 13-23**

When you shot at an *f*/5.6, the objects lit to an *f*/2 were at the bottom end of the latitude. As you can see, they fall off the bottom when exposed at an *f*/8. All the objects lit to an *f*/16 were three stops overexposed when you shot at an *f*/5.6. They are only two stops overexposed when shot at an *f*/8. It begins to appear as though exposure is a structure imposed on a space, imposed on the scene you are shooting. When you expose at an *f*/5.6, you are imposing a structure on the scene that will bring a specific result on the film. If you change to an *f*/8, in a sense you pick up that whole structure and just move it to the right. If you were to shoot at an *f*/4, you would move the structure to the left.

You will often hear people talking about lenses in terms of how they "collect" light. When you expose at a specific *f*-stop, you are collecting what is in front of the camera in a certain way. If you expose at a different *f*-stop, you are collecting in a different way. And when you choose one *f*-stop over another, you are making a choice as to what you consider important in the image—what you value.

After postulating a possible lighting scenario, people often ask the question, "How would you expose this?" Or, worse, "How do you expose this?" I answer the question with a question: "What do you want?" You are not after some abstract, one-size-fits-all, perfect image. You are going for what you want.

Try thinking about latitude as being like a table: You can think of the range of exposures in the scene (that is, the range of light readings you have made with the meter) like objects spread out across a table. Call the center of the table "normal exposure," because normal exposure can be thought of as being halfway between total underexposure and total overexposure. One edge of the table represents underexposure, and the other overexposure. As you near either edge of the table, you get closer to total over- or underexposure until you drop off the edge. One should recognize this table analogy as a representation of the characteristic curve, the toe and shoulder being the edges of the table.

If your film stock has a latitude with a total of seven stops (three and a half stops on either side of normal exposure), the table is seven stops wide. If the film stock has a total latitude of roughly five stops (most black-and-white reversals would fall into this category), the table is five stops wide.

If you shoot the person in front of the window at an *f*/8, the objects that read 160 fc are in the center of the table, normally exposed; *f*/8 is also right in the center of the exposure values for our hypothetical scene. In this example the ambient shadows and sunny street fall off the edge of the table. **SEE 13-24** If you shoot at an *f*/22, different objects or areas are going to fall off the table. In this case a large part of the exposure range is dropping off the latitude table. **SEE 13-25**

With enough people and equipment, you could light any proposed image, including the person in front of the window, to the center of the table. In fact, that was precisely the goal in the story recounted earlier in this chapter about the Secret Service agents with their light meters. There are many reasons, most of which have already been discussed, why you would not want to do that. The image would be flat. This is why normal exposure is referred to as being a mythical beast. We talk about normal exposure, and it remains central to the discussion, but most of the images you see in films encompass a wide range of exposures. Yes, there will usually be areas that are normally exposed, but most images—and this is just common sense—have a wide range of values. As a beginner you may develop an abject fear of the edge of the table, but this is where you will want to learn to live. It is, simply put, where the texture and character of the image lives.

The scenario of the person in front of the window is an image that essentially has nine different exposure possibilities, *f*/2 to *f*/32, and nine distinctly different outcomes, again leaving out the fact that the readings have been simplified so that they fall exactly on the *f*-stops. Obviously, real life is not so cooperative.

If you can look among these results and find one of those many exposures that does precisely what you want, you are fine. The discussion, at least in terms of this image, can end here. But if your goal is to produce something that looks roughly like what you would see with your eyes, one can safely predict that none of the choices here would be acceptable. This pursuit of producing an approximation of human perception is generally referred to as *realism,* a concept that keeps the film world scrambling and thousands employed. Ahhh, realism. One might think that with all the interest in modernism and postmodernism, things would be different. But now, oddly enough, realism's hold on film is probably stronger than ever. However much artists and critics may rail at it, realism remains the stuff that fuels the engines of a substantial percentage of films, both in America and internationally.

This part of the discussion can be concluded by saying that if your goal is realism, the person in front of the window represents an image with incompatible extremes. There are simply too many differing values to get an acceptable compromise. The obvious answer to the problem is to use artificial light and/or to manipulate the existing light.

Reflectant Quality

The way objects and materials reflect light and how film responds to that light is referred to as **reflectant quality**, or *luminance*. Most people know that lighter objects reflect a high percentage of light, and dark objects reflect a small percentage. This, of course, is why we perceive them as light or dark. It stands to reason that objects that are highly reflectant—light objects—are going to photograph differently than will objects that are not so reflectant.

If you have ever worked with a monochrome monitor on a computer, you probably know that all objects can be measured and categorized according to the

13-24

The latitude "table"

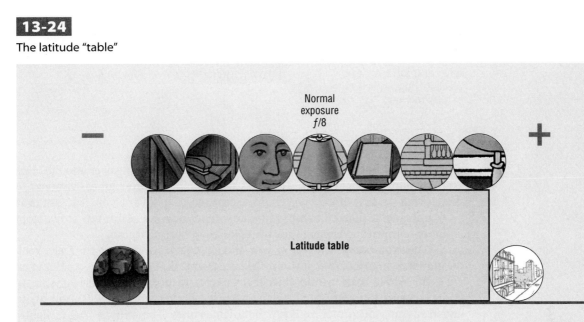

13-25

Shot at an *f*/22, many areas fall off the edge to underexposure

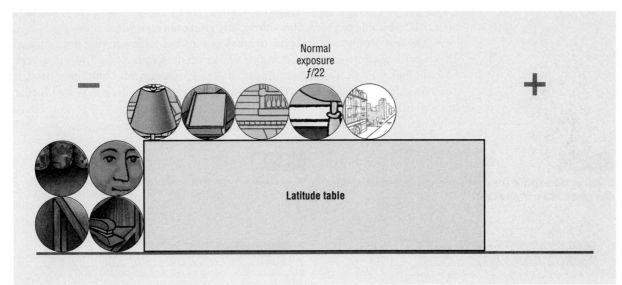

gray scale, which represents discrete points in how surfaces reflect light. The standardized gray scale represents all the possibilities, from the smallest amount of light (black) to the greatest amount of light (white). The gray scale starts from black and goes through a number of shades of gray before it gets to white. **SEE 13-26**

The relationship of the gray scale to exposure, and the general issue of how objects reflect light, are both of critical importance. If you light a gray scale to an *f*/5.6, what will be the result if you then set the lens to an *f*/5.6 and film it? It will be a normal exposure, and you will see the scale as you see it here. But what happens if you over- or underexpose the gray scale? If you underexpose it, you essentially take

13-26

The gray scale consists
of a sequence of discrete
reflecting tones, from
black through shades
of gray to white

the whole scale and move it to the right, the darkest grays shifting over into the black area. Medium and light grays, as well as white, shift to grayer tones. **SEE 13-27** A similar shift occurs with overexposure, except the scale shifts to the left. **SEE 13-28**

It should be noted that the gray scale will not respond in this way at five stops of under- or overexposure, latitude being the complicating factor.

When you change the *f*-stop, you shift all reflectant values on the scale. With the gray scale lit to an *f*/5.6, if you racked the *f*-stop all the way from an *f*/1.4 to an *f*/22, the whole scale would shift from overexposure to normal exposure to underexposure. Simply stated, this means that darker subjects will drop off to underexposure much more quickly than lighter ones. The same is true of lighter subjects on the overexposure end.

Thus reflectant quality obviously complicates any discussion of exposure. It should also be evident that latitude is not written in stone. Latitude is a general guide, and different subjects respond differently to over- and underexposure. This is also where a spot meter can help, although you really have to know how to evaluate the information it provides. To a certain extent, an understanding of reflectant quality is best gained through experience. You have to look at and shoot a lot of different materials to be able to predict how things are going to respond.

The way this issue affects exposure decisions has wide-ranging implications. This is particularly true when filming subjects with dark skin tones. You will quickly find out that most technical recommendations for exposure and light have been, to a certain extent, calculated with the Caucasian face in mind. This is explored further in chapter 15.

13-27

If you underexpose the gray scale, you essentially shift the entire scale to the right

13-28

If you overexpose the gray scale, you essentially shift the entire scale to the left

t-stops

Although we have encouraged the use of *f*-stops and foot-candles to measure and evaluate light, you will find that film crews actually communicate in ***t-stops***—a circumstance that requires some explanation. The *t* in *t*-stop stands for *transmission*. It might be useful to think of it as meaning the "true" stop. The *t*-stop takes into account the light that is lost by passing through a lens. Almost all lenses lose light due to lens complexity and *aberrations*— failure of a lens (or any refracting surface) to produce exact correspondence between an object and its image. In a perfect world, an *f*-stop, let's say an *f*/5.6, will let in a specific amount of light under given lighting conditions. But in our less-than-perfect world, if some light is lost in the lens, you are not getting a "true" *f*/5.6's worth of light to the film plane. If not compensated for, this results in a slight underexposure. The *t*-stop compensates for the lost light by using a slightly larger aperture.

The manufacturer calibrates *t*-stops for each individual lens. Virtually all professional lenses are calibrated in *t*-stops rather than *f*-stops. They are simply the point where a true *f*-stop's amount of light reaches the film plane. You use them just like you do *f*-stops. If you get a reading of *f*/5.6 and the lens is calibrated in *t*-stops, you set it to *t*/5.6.

By definition *t*-stops provide a wider opening, but none are as much as a full stop wider. This occasionally prompts the question of why one would bother to compensate when a single stop is well within the latitude of most film stocks. Just so you are forewarned, I've been on film sets where the DP was talking about light in terms of fifths of a stop. Needless to say, DPs are very exacting in determining how the film is exposed. This is partly an issue of maintaining consistent photographic quality, but it is mostly because different exposures produce different effects. Eventually, you will be the one making such choices.

14

Planning the Lighting

Thinking Out the Process

From this exposition of basic principles, we can move into some pragmatic examples of specific lighting setups. We can start by reiterating that when you are exposing an image, that is, choosing an *f*-stop, you are exposing for a dramatic effect that is important to you. Cinematographer Vilmos Zsigmond has made an interesting observation in this regard.[1] He states that misguided beginners often set up their lights and then stick out their light meter to get a reading. They then shoot at what the light meter tells them. This is a backward method. What most DPs do, particularly those involved in making narrative films, is start with the light meter reading that they want to achieve. They start with a value, in terms of an amount of light, and all subsequent decisions flow from that one piece of information.

On a less pragmatic level, you will hear many claims about the kinds of effects lighting can achieve. Lighting produces feeling. Lighting produces mood. Lighting creates visual text and subtext. You will hear many a cinematographer waxing philosophical, and sometimes a bit romantic, about all the things that lighting can do. This is as it should be. You have to be a bit of a romantic to want to express yourself with light, particularly when there are so many other attention-grabbing elements of film. But, on a gut level, *lighting is achieving the image that you want.*

This is both a technical and a creative process. It is a matter of knowing what you want and how to manipulate the materials to get it. The processes are inseparable. You cannot get one without the other. It is what has been referred to as *technique,* that application of the technical to produce the desired effect. Eventually you will probably be able to do much of your lighting to your eye. For now, however, you need to wrestle with the lights and the light meter to get them to do what you want.

Lighting: A Basic Strategy

Before getting into an extended discussion of lighting, it should be stated in all honesty, that thinking out the lighting of a scene is essentially an easy process.

---

1. Salvato, Larry, and Dennis Schaefer, *Masters of Light: Conversations with Contemporary Cinematographers* (Berkeley: University of California Press, 1984) p. 337.

Suffice it say to that we are simplifying immensely, but there is a certain amount of truth to this statement. The following strategy constitutes an easy way to think out your lighting:

1. Start by choosing an *f*-stop. There are many reasons to choose a particular *f*-stop (see the next section for an introduction to this critical aspect), but choose one that makes sense in terms of what you are trying to achieve. Once you have this fundamental piece of information, everything else falls into place.

2. Ask the question: *What areas or objects do I want to be normally exposed?* Then light those elements to the desired *f*-stop. Remember, you rarely want everything normally exposed. That would make for a flat and uninteresting image.

3. Then ask yourself: *What areas or objects do I want underexposed?* and *How much do I want them underexposed?* Light the areas you want underexposed, including the fill side of faces, to values less than your chosen *f*-stop. How much less is determined by how dark you want them to be, always remembering that eventually they will slip outside the latitude of the film.

4. The last question is, of course: *What areas do I want overexposed?* You light those areas to values greater than the chosen *f*-stop. As with the previous example, the amount of overexposure depends on how much you want, remembering again the latitude of the film.

With both underexposure and overexposure, you may want to exceed the latitude of the film for effect. The important consideration is to know where all the other light values are registering in relation to normal exposure, keeping in mind the limits of the film.

That is it in a nutshell. It sounds easy but of course it is not. The pragmatic part of executing a lighting setup is hard enough, but there are all kinds of side issues—such as quality, continuity, and coverage, to name just a few—that complicate the task. But consider this a good starting place.

f-STOP CHOICE

This is slightly premature, but the notion posed in step 1 above that the *f*-stop might be determined in advance needs some clarification. What factors might go into choosing a specific *f*-stop?

*   There is an existing light value to which it would be expedient to conform.

*   There are shots that require a predetermined amount of depth of field.

*   A preferred *f*-stop gives you the quality of light and lens resolution desired.

*   There are situations in which a specific value is easy to achieve and simply makes sense. This could be because of the type of instruments you are using, the size of the location, the way instruments that are going to be balanced against the key can be set, or a number of other reasons. There is simply some value that makes common sense given the situation.

Elaboration of these issues will continue as this discussion progresses, but be aware that frequently the choice of an *f*-stop is, as Zsigmond suggests, determined in preplanning rather than getting the lights up and simply sticking out a meter to get a reading.

Lighting Applications

Some of these basic principles can be demonstrated if you start with some simple tests that involve the key light and the fill light. Go ahead and load up a camera and shoot this. Before you shoot, though, there are a few general guidelines with which you should become familiar.

GUIDELINES

☑ **There are two basic movements used in trimming the instruments: panning and tilting.** These terms are used in the same way as with the camera. When you move a light from side to side, so the beam is sweeping horizontally, you are *panning* the light. When you move a light up and down, so the beam is sweeping vertically, it is called *tilting*. These movements are done frequently as you set up and make choices.

☑ **When using a focusable spot on a subject, always find and use the center of the light.** If you aim one of these lights at a wall, you will notice that it throws a round pattern. You should be able to discern its center—it's where it is the brightest. It is easiest to find the center of the pattern when the light is spotted in. Put it right on whatever you are lighting. Nine times out of ten, you'll get yourself in trouble if you start some other way. If you pan the light off the subject and/or area to get a lower reading, it will just look like they are not in the light, like the light is going past them.

☑ **Lighting is a very time-consuming process.** You will often be working with people who are new to film. Be sure to prepare both crew and talent for the kind of time that you are going to have to take. Lighting is a deductive process in which you keep creating and solving problems until you get what you want. You just have to be patient and go through the necessary steps. The most time I have ever seen go into lighting a single shot is about three hours, but in comparing stories with other film people that is pretty tame. A friend loves to tell about the time a crew he was on took eight hours to light a potato chip bag. The client did not like anything they set up. An efficient film crew can light a simple shot in ten to fifteen minutes, but the more complicated the shot and/or scene, the more time it takes. To get the result you want, the preparation and time have to be invested.

☑ **Take notes.** Without a guide for analyzing your test, you may have a difficult time reconstructing all the things you did. A sheet with columns for the foot-candle readings of all your lights is probably the best approach. Have a column for the key, fill, backlight, and so on. Also have a column for the *f*-stop. Most of these tests should be shot at the *f*-stop you get for the key. This is the usual, though by no means uniform, approach. I also recommend that you try shooting some of the setups you create at different *f*-stops. It can be instructive to see what happens when you expose for the fill light or the backlight. Experiment.

Learn these basic terms and practices because, if you get on a lighting crew, you will be expected to execute some straightforward tasks. Fellow crew members have little patience with anyone who slows them down.

TESTS

Start the test by setting up a key light to 160 fc, which translates to an *f*/8 with a 500 EI stock. We are choosing 160 fc for several reasons. First, it is a relatively easy value to achieve with the kind of lights you will probably be using. Also, there is plenty of room on either side of it for experimentation with over- and underexposure. Light meters, particularly inexpensive ones, do not always read small amounts of light with the kind of accuracy needed for an effective test. We will use values that you should be able to reproduce and measure with ease and accuracy.

If possible, use a focusable spot for the key. To achieve 160 fc, it is easiest to have an assistant move the light while you are at the subject with a light meter. Holding the meter at the subject, point it at the key and have the assistant move the light toward or away from the subject. Stop when the meter shows the desired value. Using the spot/flood capacity of the light is another easy method of getting the value you want.

Nose shadows receive significant attention. DPs generally try to have the light above and to the side of the subject so the shadow will go down into the lines to the side of the nose. **SEE 14-1** Other light positioning can make this shadow go to strange and irritating places, such as into the mouth, straight across the face, or even into the eye.

Next, set up the fill light and move it until you get an *f*/5.6 (80 fc). This is easiest to do with the key light switched off. Before shooting, check the total by taking another reading at the subject toward the camera. Sometimes the fill can add to the total, and you may have to back off the key light to reestablish the 160 fc. What will be the result if you shoot at an *f*/8? The fill light will underexpose by one stop—well within the latitude of the film—so the fill side of the face will be slightly darker but will be rendered with a fair amount of detail. Thus, the shadows are not very harsh, so you have an even, high-key image.

This relationship between the key and the fill is called the ***lighting ratio,*** or *contrast ratio* (see "Lighting Continuity" in chapter 15 for the specific formula). Remember that the intensity of the fill light in relationship to the key controls the dramatic quality of the image, and a ratio between the key side and the fill side of the subject can be calculated.

What happens if you walk the fill light out to an *f*/4 (40 fc)? Remember to recheck the total for 160 fc before shooting. The fill light is now underexposing by two stops. **SEE 14-2** Again, the shadow areas are well within the latitude of the film but darker than in the previous shot. It is not quite as flat as the previous image, but is still high-key. Continue backing off the fill light in this manner, always rechecking the total.

14-1

When the fill is underexposing by one stop, lighting will be high-key

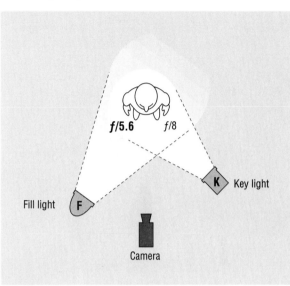

14-2

As the fill is drawn back, shadows on the fill side will become deeper

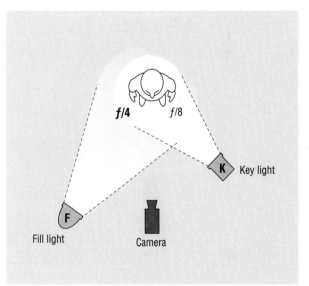

14-3

At 20 fc the fill is underexposing by three stops—still within the latitude of the film but very low-key

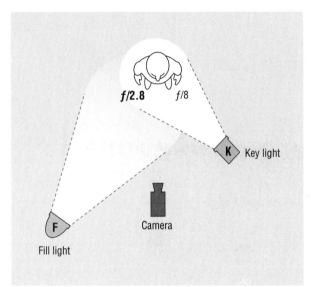

14-4

At 10 fc the fill will underexpose by four stops and will have little or no effect on the film

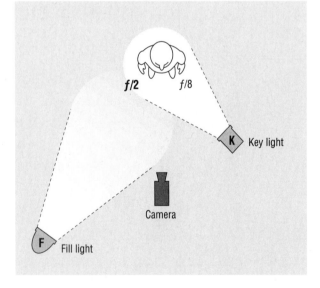

When backed off to an *f*/2.8 (20 fc), the fill light is underexposing by three stops and, though still within the latitude of the film, it is getting close to the edge of the table from our earlier analogy. At this point you have moved into lighting that would be considered low-key. **SEE 14-3** The shadow area is very dark, though still having some detail. It is an image with much more contrast. If you continue and back off the fill to an *f*/2 (10 fc), you are going to fall off the edge. **SEE 14-4** The fill is going to underexpose by four stops, and at this point we can predict—and all of this is about being able to predict results—that it will have virtually no effect on the resulting film. In fact, you might want to try switching the fill light on and off to see if there is any effect at all. Remember that latitude is not an absolute. There may be some effect, but you can be assured that if there is, it will be small.

Try to keep a visual record of how you see what you are shooting. When the fill is at an *f*/2, it is definitely producing an effect visible to the eye. The point is that the film will not see it. With this in mind, consider the following basic rules of lighting, which, at first glance, appear to be contradictory:

◆ **RULE:** *If it does not look good to your eye, it will not look good on film.*

This is common sense. If you are getting ready to film a shot and there is something about it that just doesn't look right, it is still not going to look right when you get the film back. Are there are too many shadows? Can the viewer see everything that is important? Are there shadows in the eyes that make the subject look like a raccoon? Is it just ugly light?

◆ **RULE:** *Just because it looks good to your eye does not mean it will look good on film.*

This is clearly a question of latitude. The light values have to fall within a relatively narrow range to show up on film. As you look at the last test with your eyes, the one filled to an *f*/2, you might say that it looks fine, but the film sees only a segment of what we see. The light meter and a knowledge of latitude are the keys.

Essentially, you treat all the rest of the lights as you have the key and fill. To start, try introducing a backlight. The light is usually set up above and behind the subject, pointing directly at the crown of the head. **SEE 14-5** How do you use the light meter to read it? The meter, in this case, should be pointed directly at the light, not toward the camera.

The light meter will be used in this fashion with more and more frequency. In many cases we are not so much interested in how much light is being seen from the camera position as we are in how many foot-candles are being produced by a particular lighting instrument. *Each instrument is set up to accomplish a specific purpose*—to light a desired area or subject, to create a certain effect—and its intensity is set to achieve a specific level of exposure. The goal may be as general as to give an overall fill to a large area or as specific as highlighting a glass on a nightstand.

The intensity you want for the backlight depends somewhat on the color of the subject's hair. These are very general guidelines, but if the subject has brown hair, many DPs like to keep the backlight the same number of foot-candles as the key light. If the subject has black hair, they go higher; if the subject is blond, they go lower.

To make the test interesting, trim the backlight to an ƒ/16 and walk the fill light back to an ƒ/4, so it is having an effect. **SEE 14-6** As you set up the backlight, try to make its beam hit only the back of the subject's head and not spill onto the face.[2]

If the backlight is at an ƒ/16 and you are still shooting at an ƒ/8, the backlight will overexpose by two stops, which will create a halo effect. Is this something you might want on occasion? Of course.

At this point there are three different values in the shot: ƒ/4, ƒ/8, and ƒ/16. What would happen if you shot at these ƒ-stops or others? If you shot at an ƒ/16, you'd be exposing for the backlight. The only thing that would expose normally would be the subject's hair. The face would be two stops underexposed. Could this be interesting? You may want to do something with the fill light, which is now out of the latitude of the film, but the overall answer is probably yes. What would happen if you shot at an ƒ/11? The possibilities are pretty much limitless, but you can continue to manipulate volumes of light and exposure to create different effects. Try shooting some different exposures and intensities on the three lights, as well as setting up other lights for other areas of the frame—the background, for example.

Remember that lighting is a very deductive process, particularly when you are just learning it. You can start with a question: What are the central points of interest in this image, and where do I want the viewer's attention focused? These are usually, though not always, the areas that you want keyed and normally exposed. Set up key lights for these points. Once you've done that, you will see that you have some problems. You don't like the shadow created by this key or whatever. Manipulate the lights until those problems are at least superficially solved. Do not overdo it; the other lights will cause problems, too. Once all the keys are set up and reading the foot-candle values you want, you then decide what you want to fill and how you want to fill it. Set up the appropriate lights. Again, this will create problems. Solve them. Then do the same thing with the backlights and other lights. You just keep trimming the lights and adjusting for their side effects until you get what you want. Remember

14-5

The backlight is measured by pointing the light meter at it

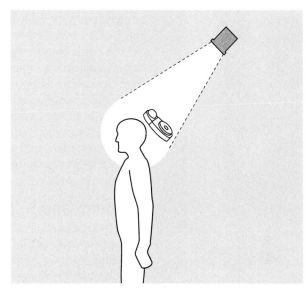

14-6

Trimmed to an ƒ/16, the backlight overexposes by two stops

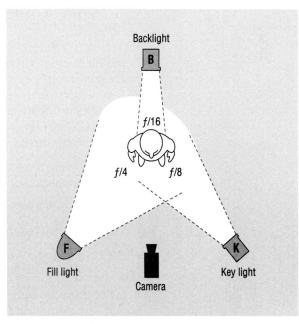

___

2. Technically speaking, trimming the backlight to an ƒ/16 would make it the key light. The key light can be thought of as the main source of light and it does not necessarily have to come from the front.

the methods for trimming instruments: repositioning, moving spot/flood, using modifying materials, and so on.

Clearly, character movement complicates these simple tests. Have the subject turn his or her head to the left and right, turn to see what the fill side looks like, and so on. Characters rarely look directly at the camera, so position the subject however you like. I generally prefer to have the key on the camera side of a subject's face, although this is more apt to leave the subject's shadow in the background of the shot. Many cinematographers take the easy way out and make the key side away from the camera, although this can make the nose shadow stand out.

Sometimes the hardest thing to do is to get started. You have all these lights and may not have a clear conception of what to do with them. These tests should give some basic direction. Be forewarned: Learning lighting is an experiential affair (isn't everything?). As a gaffer friend likes to put it, the best teacher is just spending a few years "putting it up, shooting it, and taking it down."

Problems and Solutions

The approach so far has been essentially evaluative. We have looked at several situations, such as the person by the window, the streetlight, and the table lamp, with one question in mind: What can I do with what exists here? Although evaluation is clearly part of the process, the approach has to be much more active in terms of changing things. The way to look at a shot or a scene is not to say, "What can I get?" but rather, "What do I have to do to get what I want?" The only reason a DP will walk through an unprepared location with a light meter is to find out what has to be changed to create the desired effect.

SHOOTING AN EXISTING SITUATION

We will start with several relatively simple situations and, for now, talk less in terms of specific instruments and more in the general terms of keys and sources. Let's say you're shooting in a room that has natural illumination from windows. You want to do a camera pan from person A to person B. **SEE 14-7**

With the light meter, you find that person A has 40 fc falling on him. Using the 500 EI stock, that is an $f/4$. Person B has 320 fc and an $f/11$. Consider the possibilities and make some determinations. If you shoot at:

$f/4$ Person A will be normally exposed, and person B will be +3, three stops overexposed.

$f/5.6$ Person A will be −1, and person B will be +2.

$f/8$ Person A will be −2, and person B will be +1.

$f/11$ Person B will be normally exposed, and person A will be −3, three stops underexposed, and rendered with only a small amount of detail.

If any of these choices represents the effect that you desire, you can go ahead and film. If your purpose is different, and it usually is, you have to bring in lights.

Let's say that you decide you want normal exposure on each person. The question always comes up: Could I simply rack f-stops? That is, rotate the f-stop ring from an $f/4$ to an $f/11$ as you are executing the pan, just as one would with a rack focus? That way you would get normal exposure on each person. If you did this, though, you would have an unwanted by-product. Think back to the discussion of reflectant quality and the gray scale. You are crossing over the wall as you execute the pan. If you change the f-stop, you shift where the wall is read on the gray scale. If the wall is white, as you close down you are shifting the white into the gray area,

14-7

Setup #1: using natural lighting from the windows

14-8

Setup #2: lighting person A to 320 fc

and the quality of the white wall will become darker. This effect can be very pronounced, depending on how radically different the values are.

Because of the three-stop difference between the two people, one must assume that there is also a shifting amount of light on the wall. Attempting to calibrate an *f*-stop rack to the changing values on the wall, however, would be an exercise in futility; it would be virtually impossible to execute.

So, again, given the desired result, you find uncompromisable extremes. If you want a normal exposure on both people, the best solution is to use an instrument to light person A to 320 fc.[3] There are other possibilities (and complications), but this is probably the most straightforward solution. So set up a light and modify it to 320 fc. **SEE 14-8** That will even out the two extremes, and you shoot at an *f*/11.

Another example of the problems involved with several different exposure values is shooting in a car. Several years ago I was involved in a film that had many

---

3. This recommendation is complicated by the color temperature of artificial lights. (See "Matching Color Sources" in chapter 15.)

daytime shots inside a car. Step 1 was to read the exposure values already present in the scene. First the DP metered outside and got a reading of 640 fc (*f*/16). Then he went inside the shaded backseat of the car and got a reading of 40 fc (*f*/4). This presented him with several choices. If he shot at an *f*/4, the subject in the car would be normally exposed and the outside would be—what?—overexposed, but by how many stops? an *f*/5.6 is +1, an *f*/8 is +2, an *f*/11 is +3, and an *f*/16 is +4. Positing the latitude of three to three and a half stops, the outside would be totally overexposed.

If we shot at an *f*/16, the outside would be normally exposed, but the subject would now be four stops underexposed and merely a silhouette. Each solution might be acceptable, given the dramatic approach of the scene, but in this case the director wanted detail in both areas. He essentially wanted a realistic look, even though the subject being filmed was a rather bizarre character. As much as people discuss breaking out of realistic modes of representation, it is amazing how often we find ourselves discussing pictorial realism.

Without manipulating the situation, what were our other choices? We could shoot at:

f/5.6 The figure would be –1, one stop underexposed, and the exterior would be +3, three stops overexposed, on the edge of the latitude.

f/8 The figure would be –2, and the outside +2. This is a possibility but, in my opinion, the worst of all possible worlds—neither one nor the other.

f/11 The figure would be –3, on the edge of the latitude, and the outside would be +1.

None of these seemed like a very acceptable solution, given the desire for a realistic image. The obvious solution was to bring artificial light into the car. In a film with a larger budget, there probably would have been a generator that the car could tow. But with the limited budget on this project, we simply wired some small lights onto the car's battery (you have to know what you are doing to do this!). The temptation might be to pump the interior light up to an *f*/16. This would be a real trick in pragmatic terms. Even if we could have done this, what would have been the result? A normal exposure inside and out—and it would look as though the sun were shining not only outside, but also next to the subject in the backseat of the car! I have seen this done, and the results are spectacular—spectacularly bad!

The idea here is to manipulate the lighting values so there is gradation that maintains the viewer's visual expectations—a gradation that, if you will, maintains our visual stereotypes. We perceive light and shadow in life; the absence of it on film makes the image unrealistic. Our solution was to light the person in the car to an *f*/8 (160 fc), which is pragmatically much simpler. We then shot at an *f*/11. The interior of the car and the subject were one stop underexposed, thus looking somewhat shadowed. The outside was one stop overexposed, giving it a bright, airy feel. **SEE 14-9**

For all intents and purposes, the foot-candle value that translates to an *f*/11 (320 fc) may not have even existed in this image. It probably did somewhere, but that is not what is relevant here. The point is to expose to achieve a specific effect. If there were no points at 320 fc (*f*/11) in the image, the final image simply would not have had any elements of normal exposure. Again, we were exposing less for the mythical beast—normal exposure—than for a specific effect. We exposed the image, knowing how all the areas were going to fall into the latitude. Again, the worst approach would have been to light the scene so that all the exposure values were equal and exposed normally.

14-9

Manipulating values to produce gradation maintains the viewer's visual expectations—a bright exterior and a more shadowed interior

	640 fc	Outside car
f/11	320 fc	Exposure setting
	160 fc	Interior of car

Averaging

The example of the car scene illustrates a concept that many people with a background in still photography may recognize as averaging. It is similar, but we are accomplishing something slightly different here. With *averaging,* when confronted with a range of ƒ-stop choices many still photographers choose a stop somewhere in the middle. That way they will have detail in all areas. If things are not precisely the way they want them on the negative, they can make printing adjustments at the darkroom stage.

Although averaging can be a reasonably good approach for still photographers, it has major drawbacks for most types of filmmaking. Films, of course, are made up of tens of thousands of individual frames, and it would be virtually impossible, without it becoming prohibitively expensive, to give them all individual attention. Each shot is analyzed before a final print is made, but it is analyzed for color and exposure correctness in the entire shot, not to find problems in small areas.

Even then, films are printed in reels, not in shots. In 35mm, reels are 10 minutes long; in 16mm, they are 45 minutes long. You cannot take a couple of printing tries to get an individual shot right and then move on to the next shot. If one shot is wrong, the entire reel has to be reprinted. You occasionally have to make a number of tries to get a whole reel right—and each try is very expensive. You do have control over individual shots. Without getting too far into the art and science of printing, the lights in the printer *can* be programmed to change with every shot, but you just can't print each shot individually and start again if you get it wrong. You make your best analysis of every shot, then print the whole reel.

This reinforces the importance of getting exposure and lighting right on location. This is true for virtually everything in the picture, particularly composition. Once you have the picture, it is pretty much fixed, at least for those who work with small budgets. There are ways to correct mistakes and manipulate preexisting footage, with optical printers and such, but they can be expensive and lead to plethora of matching problems. The more you get right on location, the fewer messy and expensive corrections you have to make in postproduction.

Again, people ask me, "In such and such situations, should I just average these different exposures?" My answer is an emphatic, *"No!* You should be choosing an exposure for some reason!" Averaging *can* be useful in some situations. Documentary shooting in particular has many circumstances in which you are unable to control the light. Finding an average can help you out of some complex situations, but in general the answer is no.

Working with Artificial Light

A good example of an exposure problem comes from a film that I directed several years ago. It called for two actors to come around a corner, stand in front of a door, and exchange dialogue. Then, still in the same shot, they approach the camera, stop, and exchange some more dialogue. The action took place in a dingy furnace room and was to initiate a segment of the film that was dark and mysterious.

I wanted the characters to enter a strong, narrow beam of light and have their first discussion. Still in the same shot, they exit the beam and approach the camera and have a second discussion in the darkened area of the furnace room. Setting up the beam of light was relatively simple. The problem became the darkened area outside the beam. The following figure illustrates what the proposed action looked like from overhead. **SEE 14-10**

We set up the beam and trimmed it to the foot-candle readings shown in the next figure. **SEE 14-11** Once we had the beam, we were able to check the other areas and see how all the other values settled out. The areas outside the beam—and we were just measuring ambient and bounce light, because the only light was the beam—were at 10 fc and less, mostly less.

14-10

Proposed character
movement for the furnace
room scene

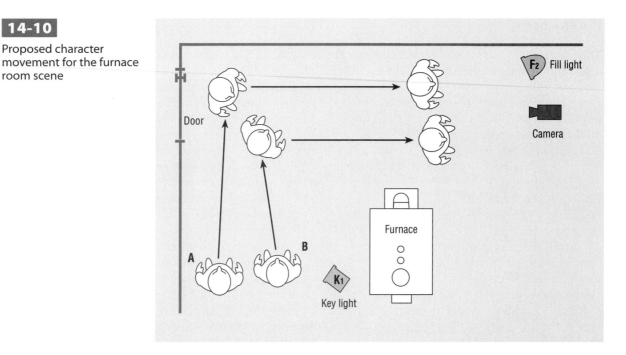

14-11

The foot-candle readings
after setting up the single
light source

I wanted the center of the beam to overexpose by one stop, because it would intensify the slash effect. We decided to shoot at the *f*-stop we got for 160 fc, an *f*/8 with our 500 EI stock. The areas at 10 fc translate to what *f*-stop? An *f*/2. The areas below 10 fc range below an *f*/2. Even though the maximum aperture on the lens we were using was an *f*/2.3, the light exists at these levels and can have an effect on the film. In this case, however, this is four or more stops less than an *f*/8, outside of the latitude of the film. I wanted the characters to have detail but still look as though they were in the darkened area, essentially a realistic image.

The solution was to set up a small light (softlight F2 in figure 14-10) that filled in the front area. I wanted a look that replicated the indirect quality of the ambient light, so we used a softlight. The question was: How strong did we want it to be? We wound up trimming it until we got 30 fc right by the furnace. That is two and a half stops less than the stop at which we were shooting. Always thinking in terms of what the film is going to register, that was within our proposed latitude. We could predict that the characters would be rendered very dark but still with some detail when they reached their final position. This was precisely the desired effect. It is not quite so clearcut as the example with the car, but again the areas of normal exposure in this image are exceedingly small—the edge of the beam. Think *effect.*

When I first started trying underexposure effects like this—and ones that were even more extreme—it took a lot of courage. I counted a few new gray hairs while I was waiting for the film to come back from the lab. In a sense what you are doing with this effect is plumbing the edges of the latitude. Occasionally, particularly as a beginner, you cross your fingers, hoping you have not fallen off the edge.

In the example in chapter 13 of the man in front of the window, it was suggested that the range of light values represents uncompromisable extremes for a realistic image. But here there is a range of six stops—10, 20, 40, 80, 160, 320—that are put together for a complex exposure. **SEE 14-12** Actually, there were more than six stops, because the fill for the dark segment of the shot was not a flat 10 fc across the whole space. It would have looked abnormal if the darkness were totally even. So, here we see a very wide range that works in the particular situation we created.

The Setup: Decision Making

The big question is: How do you work with individual lights? What follows is a lighting-plan walk-through. As stated, lighting is a very deductive process, and this discussion will elaborate on as much of the reasoning process as possible. You start with a basic premise about what you want the scene's lighting to accomplish and then go from there.

Knowing just what it is you want to accomplish is one of the hardest hurdles to clear. There is just no single answer and, regardless of what is said here, the answers have to come from you. Every scene is different. It is not as simple as saying that you have to do the right thing for a specific scene or that the material is going to determine the light. That leads to clichéd and stereotypical answers. Sometimes you have to play against type or create some kind of visual subtext. Sometimes you want to highlight specific subjects or areas. Maybe you want to hide something. Sometimes you just want to cheat conventional expectations.

The effect should nevertheless be appropriate to the context. I have a friend, an experienced director who closely supervises the lighting in his films, who was filming a scene in an all-night restaurant. The scene had a number of offbeat characters and ambiguous action. He had the scene lit in a very atmospheric, low-key way. A couple of months later, I noticed him hunched over the editing table with his head in his hands. He was looking at the scene and all he could say was, "How could I have done this? It's a @*#&%! all-night restaurant, not the Film Noir Cafe."

Our walk-through will start with the person and the table lamp. **SEE 14-13** The lamp is on, and the bookcase is about five feet behind the person. This is still a complex image. We will see many early mistakes with an image like this, particularly

14-12

This complex exposure incorporated a range of six stops

	320 fc	Two stops over
f/8	**160 fc**	Normal exposure
	10 fc	Four stops under

14-13

The starting point for the lighting walk-through

14-14

The range of readings represents someone's moving the meter along the surface of the table with the activating button pressed

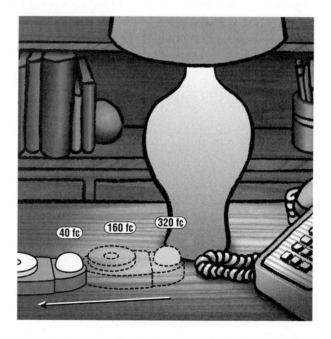

when using the automatic meters in Super 8 and video cameras. Let's say that we went through the scene and got the readings shown in the figure.

Notice the area just on the edge of the circle of light from the lamp, showing readings of 40, 160, and 320 fc. This represents someone's moving the meter along the surface of the table with the activating button depressed. **SEE 14-14** This response is very common when there is a strong light with a hard edge. You get a strong reading in the center, which drops off a little toward the edge; then you see a precipitous drop outside the circle. This is quite straightforward: We are just doing the necessary measurement of what is plain to see with our eyes. What is important to remark is that there is a four-stop difference between the first and last positions.

With this four-stop difference in mind, it is easy to see why so many beginners make mistakes when using the automatic meter on a camera. Again, the automatic meter does not know what to read in this image. Undaunted by the fact that he is getting no reading when the camera is pointed at the face, the novice will pan over to the light. The needle will respond with some kind of exposure, let's say an *f*/8. He will lock the *f*-stop, shoot the scene at an *f*/8, and be disturbed when it returns looking like the figure shown at right. **SEE 14-15**

14-15

The result of basing the readings of this scene on an automatic light meter pointed at the light

What happened is fairly obvious. The meter responded to, and the scene was exposed for, one of the brightest values. When the latitude of the film takes over, you are left with nothing. Looking at the scene with the naked eye, everything probably looked fine. Even through the camera, everything probably looked fine. But there was a rude awakening when the film came back. This kind of mistake is one of the most common exposure errors, and automatic light meters will do it to you with fair frequency. It is a prime example of the second rule of lighting: Just because it looks good to your eye . . .

Using more-accurate metering methods, you can determine that there are a number of possibilities for exposure in this example, none of them good. As with the first example, if pictorial realism is your goal, what you see here represents uncompromisable extremes. If you expose to get one thing right, something else in the frame is going to be at an unacceptable level. If you expose the person's face correctly, the lamp is going to be totally wrong, and so on.

Applying the method described earlier in this chapter, you should first determine the exposure at which you want to shoot. Looking over all the values, what would you choose? We will go with an *f*/8, which is what we get for 160 fc at 500 EI. Sometimes you want to choose values that are read from sources that pose problems. Part of the reason we are choosing an *f*/8 is because it is the reading off the lampshade. Lampshades are very difficult to manipulate to other values. You could put in a lower-wattage bulb, but this could create color problems and would change all the other readings in the scene. Another possible solution is to wrap the interior of the lampshade with spun and tape it in. This is relatively simple, but it must be done carefully, or seams and tape will show through the shade. Probably the most effective method is to bring your own lampshade, one that allows the amount of light that you want to pass through it. I have a number of lampshades around that I use for just such purposes.

With all that said, the reading off the lampshade is fairly reasonable, so there is really not much cause to manipulate it. I can look at that 160 fc (*f*/8) and feel comfortable with it. The lamp is one element that you might fear would jump out at the viewer if you shot at an *f*/8, but it is actually the one thing you are going to leave alone. When you shoot at an *f*/8, the ring of light on the table will overexpose by one stop, the base of the lamp will overexpose by two stops, and the very top of the lamp base will overexpose by three stops. This may seem to call for some attention on your part, but you will be surprised at how normal it will look on film. In a sense, we expect these areas to overexpose and we expect them to overexpose in this way. If you were to manipulate all these values to an *f*/8, the effect would look pretty silly. Lamp light is not flat.

For simplicity's sake, let's say you want a fairly even feel to the image—not flat, but not deep low-key. You already know what would happen if you shot at an *f*/8 without changing anything else. Where do you start with the actual lights?

As suggested, start with the key(s). Set up an instrument and light the person to 160 fc. Even here there is some room for maneuvering. If a person is sitting some

14-16

To duplicate the soft light coming through the lampshade, use tough-white diffusion in front of the key light

distance from a lamp, might you expect him to be a little dark? Rather than light the subject to 160 fc, you could light him to 120 fc, a half stop less. You would still shoot at an *f*/8, and the subject would underexpose by a half stop, looking slightly dark. This is not a bad option, but we will stay with 160 fc.

All the light on the subject is coming through the lampshade, so you can safely assume that it is fairly soft light. To duplicate that soft, warm light, we are going to put a piece of tough-white diffusion (#216) in front of the key light. You can still get 160 fc by spotting in the light or moving it forward. **SEE 14-16**

You have to be very careful that the light from the key does not hit the lampshade. You should be able to accomplish this with the barn doors, though you could also bring in a flag on a C-stand. If light from the key does hit the lampshade, there could be a shadow of the lamp on the table, an effect that would look very peculiar. Another reason to be careful of light hitting the shade is that it would actually boost the shade's foot-candle reading, which would then expose differently. You also want to control the spill off the bottom of the instrument onto the table. Light spilling onto the table could ruin the circle of light from the lamp. You should be able to accomplish this control, again, with the barn doors.

The Setup: Fine-tuning

Next you have to set up the fill light and the other lights. Once they are up, it is a matter of fine-tuning, what people call *tweaking*, the lights. You want an even feel to the image, so the fill should be relatively close to the key light in terms of intensity. Again, the lower it is in relationship to the key, the more contrast there will be in the image. I have found that having the fill light one stop less than the key creates an image that is too flat; it does not have enough texture and definition, even when I am going for a high-key image. Use a softlight and set it to 40 fc, two stops less than the key. **SEE 14-17** You still want a slightly darkened-room effect, and this should give the image some character. Occasionally, the shadow from the fill can cause a problem, even though it is very soft and diffused. You can generally put the light up high or move it until the shadow is hidden or out of camera range.

Next comes the backlight. **SEE 14-18** Because the person has dark hair, you probably want about 160 fc on the crown of the head. You have to be careful with spill coming off the backlight. You may want to use either aluminum foil or *black wrap*, a material specifically designed to wrap around the barn doors of lighting instruments.

People occasionally get the impression that spill from the backlight can or should be used to illuminate the background as well. Generally speaking, this is a bad idea. You will find that spill is hard to control, because you are attempting to use what is spilling off the bottom of the light. It is a good idea to keep the beam fairly

14-17

Adding the fill constitutes the first step in fine-tuning the lighting setup

The backlight beam should be fairly narrow and aimed at the crown of the head

narrow and have the backlight do just what it is supposed to do. If the background needs something, which it often does, supply it with other lights, called *set lights*.

This pretty much settles the lighting on the person. If you like it, you are done . . . with this part. Now it's time to take a look at the scene and see what else needs to be done. Because you have changed a number of things, use a light meter to check the ambient background light again. Let's say you get a range of low readings, 30 fc being the highest; 30 fc is going to underexpose by two and a half stops. This is getting toward the edge and may be darker than you want, particularly if the bookcase has a dark finish.

One solution would be to use a set light to throw an even 80 fc across the back wall. A softlight could be used if you want the light to be diffused and relatively even. What is the best position for this instrument? The fill for the person has been from frame-left, but is that the correct place for this fill? No, because the light from this softlight is designed to appear as though it is created by the lamp; it should come from the lamp's direction. Set it up fairly close to the key light. **SEE 14-19**

To boost the ambient background light, use an instrument positioned near the key, so the light appears to come from the lamp

To add character to the otherwise uniform background, move back the fill arrangement and add several highlights

The instrument is positioned close to the wall so that its throw will not affect the person. In doing this the right-front corner of the instrument is too close to the background. Setting up a net to cut down that side of the light is one potential solution. If you position it expertly, you should be able to get an even 80 fc across the entire background. Spun is also handy for cutting an instrument in the manner described; it is frequently used to cut a corner of a light or to knock out some unwanted spill.

Are you done? Again, step back and look. My guess is that your criticism will be that it looks too even, too flat. The lamp is the major source, and the light should fall off as you move frame-left. Now you could move the net and instrument so that the light will fall off from 80 fc on the right to 50 or 60 fc on the left. Even with this it may still look too uniform—it would lack character. The execution here was right, it was just the idea that didn't work.

Don't hesitate to abandon an idea when you determine that it is not going to work. Every filmmaker will have the experience of sitting in a screening room shaking his or her head, wishing that just a little more time had been spent to get it right. You cannot go in and do a little housekeeping without incurring major expenses.

So, what do you do? My recommendation would be that rather than junk the fill arrangement you had set up, just move it back. **SEE 14-20** It could still serve as a low-level fill, say, 40 fc. Then I would set up several small, direct lights that would have either very narrow beams or be trimmed so that they could throw some highlights on the background. The books behind the person might be a nice place for a little slash of light. The clock might be a good place as well. Might I even dare to bring a few small areas up to 320 fc? Having these discriminations in the background will help give the scene a sense of depth.

Putting these lights up on stands is one possibility. Another, and probably better, one would be to set up some kind of rigging and hang the lights. **SEE 14-21** More and more sophisticated poles and portable lighting grids are being developed so that everything does not have to be from the side and on cumbersome stands. I frequently run a 2 by 4 with holes drilled in each end between two C-stands: The tops of the stands go into the holes. The instruments would be in a position very similar to the backlight, only pointed in the opposite direction.

The specifics of what we did with the lights here are not so important. It is not the only approach. If you were to give this problem to twenty different lighting crews, you would get twenty different solutions. What is important is the approach, the process. What questions are being asked? What problems are being solved? You decide on a goal, you put up an instrument to achieve that goal, then you trim the instrument until you get what you want.

There are other options and other types of instruments. It is possible that you might want to use a kicker. The *kicker light* is always on the fill side and behind the subject. It comes in and brushes or rims the cheek when the fill is not covering the area as adequately as you would like. It also helps separate the subject from the background. There are *eye lights* that come in to highlight just an actor's eyes. You will hear many other lights mentioned—rim, side, underneath, special-effect, and so on. These lights tend to characterize direction or achieve specialized goals, rather than identify overall function (for example, an instrument creating the glow from a cigarette). *Underneath light* is usually key light. *Rim lights* and *side lights* are just types of key or backlights. Oddly enough, there are not that many identifiable overall functions of lights. This simplifies things somewhat, but for starters we'll stick with the four most important ones: key, fill, backlight, and set. You'll have your hands full with these.

It is not only a matter of problem solving for specific setups, it's a matter of being able to reflect on the context of what you are shooting and come up with the appropriate response for a given situation. Remember what my gaffer friend said about learning to light: "You just have to put it up and take it down for a few years." This means the ability not only to manipulate the technical aspects, but also to develop a vision of what you want things to look like. Your influences in this area are numerous: other films, painting, still photography, graphic design, or a variety of other media. Learning the technical and pragmatic aspects of working with lights is not an end in itself. You need to learn to do something with them.

That said, learning the technical side of lighting is an essential first step in learning the process of producing images. In the final analysis, that's all that is up there on the screen—light. You will not be served by ignorance about the tools available to you. A lack of knowledge necessarily limits your understanding of what is possible, much like a painter who has only two primary colors on a palette. Without a full understanding of and access to the range of technical possibilities, you can never reach the fullest expression of your ideas. If a painter has all the colors and still produces works of little interest, it is the artist who is lacking, not the materials.

Get out there and light. Too many people put it off. "The equipment is too heavy." "I'm not interested in the technical stuff." "I'm afraid I'll make mistakes." "I want to be a director." I've heard all the excuses. A fundamental, incontrovertible truth about filmmaking is that it is a process of producing images. To produce the images you want, you have to know what you are doing.

14-21

Set lights can be suspended from rigging

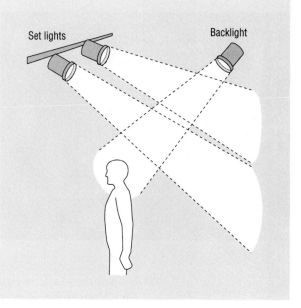

Set lights   Backlight

DIRECTION AND SHADOW

Refer again to figure 14-19. Why did we put the key where we did? The instrument is set up to the screen-right side of the subject, because the shot establishes the table

The dramatic underneath lighting of the close-up was justified by the master shot, showing the source

Eugene Corr's Desert Bloom

lamp as the source of light. If you were to put it to the left of the subject, the shot would not make any sense. If the light is not justified, the shot can evoke an unconscious feeling of something being wrong or out of place.

This issue of justification is a central concern. Reynaldo Villalobos's cinematography in Eugene Corr's *Desert Bloom* (1986) has an excellent example of light that creates a dramatic effect and is also justified. A scene involves a father (Jon Voigt) having a confrontation with his daughter (Annabeth Gish). In the master shot, we see light streaming through the window, creating a bright pool of light right in front of where the father is standing. **SEE 14-22A** When we see the close-up, the father has very ominous, Halloween-style lighting from underneath. **SEE 14-22B** This eerie light makes sense to the viewer, however, because we have seen its source.

You will hear substantial discussion on sets regarding shadows. Some crews devote an inordinate amount of time to trying to get rid of them. Sometimes a shadow can draw attention to itself and detract from the image, but the point is not that a character should have no shadow, but that the shadow should be in a logical place, and there should be only one. A hallmark of low-budget films is the multiple shadows wandering over every wall in the shot when characters move. Start watching how films treat shadows. I have seen beginning filmmakers run themselves ragged, trying to get rid of each and every one of them. Except for multiple shadows, it is often time and energy wasted. You will have to decide how to handle these constant companions, but beware of shots that are unintentionally otherworldly because the characters have no shadows.

Although trying to kill an unwanted shadow with another light is tempting, never solve a problem created by one light with another. The reasoning appears clear enough: If you don't like the shadow, just overpower it with another light, usually an instrument down low or up high. The effect, however, is an image that looks like somebody tried to overpower a shadow with something down low or up high. Solve the problem by either redirecting the original light (setting it higher is sometimes a good solution) or, often more to the point, changing the background. Faced with an ugly shadow on a wall behind a character, you can simply put something dark on the wall to cover it or soak it up. Find a poster or a plant—something that will break up the background and make it easier to work with the wall.

Natural Light

Beginning filmmakers often choose to shoot outdoors, wishing to avoid the issue of lighting altogether. They quickly find out that they have made a big mistake. The sun is not as loyal a friend to the filmmaker as might at first be imagined. If anything, shooting outdoors can be more complicated than shooting indoors. The foremost concern is understanding light well enough to know when what you are shooting is going to provide the results you want. Again, this is a process of evaluation. You will often hear of film crews "waiting for the light," and you will have to develop the skills to understand just what it is they are waiting for.

This is also an issue of being able to evaluate the *quality* of light. A good example of the quality difficulties you can experience is filming when the sun's rays are the most direct. From roughly 11 A.M. to 1 P.M., the light is very harsh, and you can get extremely dark shadows. Let's say that you are filming a medium shot of a person in bright sunlight. You want the image to read "nice sunny day," so you desire a pleasant, bright feel to the image. You take a light meter reading and find you have an $f/16$ in the direct sun. The immediate concern is the quality of all the shaded areas, particularly the fill side of the subject's face. How dark is it going to be? You meter in a shaded area, or just shade the incident bulb with your hand, and get a reading of $f/2.8$. You do the standard computation: an $f/11 = -1$, an $f/8 = -2$, an $f/5.6 = -3$, an $f/4 = -4$, an $f/2.8 = -5$. The nose shadow is going to be five stops underexposed and therefore totally black. Will this be a pleasant effect? No. The darkness of the nose shadow, and of all the shadows in general, will probably be too harsh for an appealing image.[4]

One solution is to bring in artificial light to fill in the shadow. Bouncing existing light off foam core or a reflector also works quite well. Obviously, you don't want to bring up the shaded areas to an $f/16$, because that would be flat and textureless. How far you bring them up depends on what you want the image to look like. Another solution is to shoot at a different time of day when the sun's rays are not so direct. We all know the dangers of sunbathing during those hours, and you can get burned, in a figurative sense, filming then, too. Only mad dogs and Englishmen go out in the midday sun. Filmmakers, even when unhindered by budgetary and scheduling concerns, generally try to stay away from it as well. Being totally unhindered, of course, is rarely the case.

Another equally important issue is *continuity*. Just as you have to think about objects and body position within the frame, you must be conscious of the consistency of light from one shot to the next. Still photographers and filmmakers less interested in conventional narrative scene breakdowns sometimes have the luxury of waiting a long time to get the right light. But when you have to execute a number of shots and you want them to appear to be occurring in real time, the activities of the sun and the sky can make you jump through a lot of hoops. Of course, we do not usually think of the sun and sky as having activities, but there are times when I have thought of them as unruly crew members whom I would fire in a minute if I could.

The sun has a nasty habit of rising in the east and setting in the west. If your subject is facing north or south, the fill and key sides will change from morning to afternoon. If the subject is facing east, the sun will go from being in front of the subject to being behind. Things change so rapidly that you can have substantial problems matching the light of individual shots.

---

4. Cinematographers will "light for black" to stay away from this peculiarly unpleasant phenomenon. That is, they will light a dark area to just outside the latitude of the film so that they get a richer black.

Even more difficult are the vagaries of weather and clouds. California is the home of a substantial percentage of the film business largely because of the quality of the light and the consistency of the weather. For those of us who work frequently in distant locations, a partly cloudy day can wreak havoc, making scenes that should have been shot in a few hours take twice as long. A rainy day can put you behind schedule, disrupt continuity from a previous day's work, and, in extreme cases, even change the environment in which you are working, such as by encouraging growth of underbrush. I once worked on a film in which we had to hand-dry a rain-soaked wooden wagon with hair dryers so it would match shots from the previous day. Another time a location was completely flooded out. Snow, wind, haze, fog, and smog can all work their special magic to make your life miserable.

There are all kinds of ways to cheat the elements, from bringing in instruments, to shooting from a high angle to exclude the sky, to moving people so they face different directions. Sometimes you have to wait it out. This happens to everyone, but larger-budget films are able to handle delays more easily than those precariously close to the financial edge. For lighting continuity, you have to know and understand the materials that are going to help you work despite the elements.

Finally, these issues of light quality and continuity can be interrelated. If there are very harsh shadows at noon, the shots will not match those made at a different time of day when the light was less direct. For anyone who has seen production stills from films that are largely shot outside—a John Ford western is a good example—it soon becomes apparent why there are often banks of lights and reflectors on the hills above the location. A high percentage of the time, the shadows that the sun creates and the fill necessary for a good photographic image do not go hand in hand. John Wayne needed some consistent fill light in some of those famous rides through Monument Valley.

Natural light can obviously be extraordinarily beautiful. There are two important points, though. First, you have to know enough about light to understand when it is going to photograph the way you want. Second, you have to be able to add to it when necessary to match individual shots to other shots. When working "in continuity," consistency of light is an issue whether you are working indoors or out. And it is particularly difficult to achieve lighting continuity when the quality of light can change unpredictably.

NIGHT SHOOTING

In the golden age of the Hollywood studios, much night shooting was done in a process called *day for night,* in which black-and-white film was shot with a combination of underexposure and red filtering to create a dark effect that represented night. Day for night is a lovely curiosity; some people love it and some people hate it, but it has rarely been seen in recent years. It does not really work in color, and newer, faster film stocks have made night filming quite practical.

The key to night filming is understanding that even at night there has to be a source of light. Darkness, as we generally experience it, and an absence of light are not the same thing. When there is an absolute lack of light, you cannot see your hand in front of your face. Night shooting must establish or incorporate some source of light. It might be a simulation of the moon or from a storefront or streetlight. Once you have determined the source, it becomes a matter of deciding how you want the elements to expose, just as in any other situation. Here, though, being willing to work on the edge of the table can produce remarkable effects.

Of course, the movement that fully explored night cinematography was film noir. The dark city streets and their claustrophobic interior counterparts fully incorporated all the shades from white to gray. Bob Rafelson's *The Postman Always Rings Twice* (Sven Nykvist, DP) has numerous examples of what can be achieved in

The strong side sources give both characters shape and definition while maintaining what night "should" look like

Bob Rafelson's *The Postman Always Rings Twice*

14-24

The character of the light emphasizes the subject's indecision

Jessica Lange in *The Postman Always Rings Twice*

color night cinematography. The sequence in which Cora (Jessica Lange) and Frank (Jack Nicholson) first try to kill her husband shows exceptional mastery of both interior and exterior shooting. Frank is outside talking to a policeman who happens by, as Cora paces nervously through the dimly lit restaurant. The exterior shots have two strong side sources, one established from a sign and the other from instruments by the gas pumps, which give both characters shape and definition while maintaining the logic of what night "should" look like. **SEE 14-23** The slight amount of detail that can be seen on the fill side of the characters' faces (particularly the policeman's) is evidence of the careful approach. This low fill would not be there had someone not wanted it there. The interior has Cora turning off the restaurant's lights as she builds up her nerve. Small sources inside have her passing from light to dark areas, emphasizing the indecision and heightening her dilemma, while light from outside casts stark patterns on the background. **SEE 14-24**

Night shooting, much like any shooting, entails determining the sources and, given the latitude of the film, how all the other values are going to fall in. Some boldness on your part is necessary, because many of the effects have to be around the edge of the latitude, with the idea that cinematographers often "light for black" complicating the job. It takes some experimentation with underexposure to achieve truly exceptional effects. Often, early experiments wind up having a too-bright foreground subject against a too-dark background. Do not let this deter you. Working with low values can be intimidating, but effective night shooting incorporates many different levels of exposure.

15

Executing the Lighting

A Checklist

To aid in lighting a scene, we can start assembling a checklist of questions you can ask yourself about every image. Everyone involved in lighting asks all or most of these questions for every shot, whether consciously or not. Eventually, you will internalize all these concerns, but in the meantime do not hesitate to simply go down the list before every shot. (You can be flexible in the sequence in which these issues are addressed.) What fundamental questions can be posed from the topics that have been covered in preceding chapters?

☑ *What do I want to achieve or accomplish with the image?*

☑ *What is the source of light? What direction does the viewer expect the light to be coming from?*

☑ *How am I going to expose the subject(s)? Am I going for normal exposure? Overexposure? Should the subject be darker, a little underexposed?*

☑ *What quality of light do I want? Do I want it to be soft? Hard? Should it be diffused?*

☑ *What goal(s) is each instrument accomplishing?*

These questions represent a starting point. What follows is a laundry list of all the other things you need to think about as well.

Lighting Continuity

As suggested previously, you'll find that it is not necessarily difficult to create beautiful and arresting images. Learn a few basics and you can do some great things. What is difficult is creating beautiful and arresting images that cut to other similar images. The task is formidable if your wish is to create the hallmark of conventional narrative film: a seamless sense of continuous time and space. This goal is referred to as *lighting continuity*.

If a shot that looks like it was done in the early morning is followed by a shot that appears to have been done at another time of day, the resulting images will not maintain the fiction of continuous time and space when edited together. Given the lengthy amounts of time required to execute shots, lighting for continuity is less the exception than the norm that has to be wrestled with every day.

Early in his career, one cinematographer shot a scene that had two characters sneaking up on a house as the sun was rising. The scene took about two hours to shoot, and the light was changing so rapidly that the first shots had an entirely different look from the last shots. The edited scene proved challenging to print due to the inconsistent quality of the light. The lab was able to fix it somewhat, but all DPs have to be able to come up with solutions in such situations.

The issue of lighting continuity has to be confronted not only when you are subject to the whims of the sun, but also when you work in interiors with artificial lighting. A good example is a simple shot/reverse shot sequence, the most common way to treat a dialogue scene between two characters. **SEE 15-1**

The foot-candle values below the two subjects (both 320 fc) represent readings off the key lights. The values above (160 and 40 fc) represent readings from the fill lights alone. Again, reading the instruments individually is the most effective way of finding out

15-1

A standard shot/reverse shot setup illustrates the importance of lighting continuity

what each one is accomplishing. With a hand or a card, you can block out the instruments that confuse the reading. Turning off the intrusive instruments can be equally effective.

As this scene is set up, you should immediately see a problem that is central to lighting continuity. The lighting on person A is even, with 320 fc key and 160 fc fill. The fill is one stop less than the key, thus underexposing by one stop. The fill side is rendered with a fair amount of detail and would be considered high-key. Person B has the same 320 fc key, but is filled by only 40 fc, three stops less. This is just on the edge of the latitude, and the fill side would be very dark and the image low-key. When the two images are cut together, they will have such different visual qualities that the people may appear to be in two totally different places. The difference may be something like trying to cut from a claustrophobic film noir to a romantic comedy. The two characters may not appear to inhabit the same universe.

It should be fairly obvious now that if you simply match the two fills, depending on which universe you want, you will be much closer to a continuous sense of space; the "ratio" between the key and the fill would be the same in each shot, and the look would be similar.

Comparing the key and fill is what has been referred to as lighting, or contrast, ratios. This ***lighting ratio*** is obtained by measuring the lights and plugging the foot-candle readings into the following formula. (Do not do this in *f*-stops, because the answer you get will not make any sense.)

$$\frac{key + fill}{fill\ alone}$$

Take a light reading at the subject with the key light and the fill light turned on. Then turn off the key and measure the fill alone. Divide the first figure by the second figure. We did this with person A and got the readings shown: 320:160 = 2:1, a two-to-one ratio. The ratio on person B (320:40) is eight to one. The lower the ratio, the more flat the image (high-key); the higher the ratio, the more contrast in the image (low-key). A four-to-one ratio is generally considered the rough dividing line between high-key and low-key.

What is at issue here is how much the fill light is underexposing. In a two-to-one ratio, it is underexposing by one stop. In an eight-to-one ratio, it is underexposing by three stops. It should be evident that this can be done with other instruments. How much is the backlight overexposing? How is the set light underexposing? Most of the time, however, you will hear ratios discussed in terms of key and fill.

Some variation in the ratios can be tolerated. An audience, unless it is composed entirely of filmmakers, is not going to catch minor errors or deviations. Audiences generally do not perceive this kind of thing on a conscious level. But if foot-candle values and exposure deviate very much, spatial continuity is going to suffer.

Lighting ratios are valuable for continuity, but they also can be helpful when you want to light a character consistently throughout a film. What would happen if you wanted the villain to be consistently filmed with low-key shadows? If you were indoors, you might consider the setup shown in the following figure. **SEE 15-2** Later in the shooting, you are outdoors and want to be consistent with previous shots. The sun gives 2,560 fc. How would you fill the subject to get the light to match? **SEE 15-3**

In the first example, the fill light is underexposing by three stops. What do you need off the fill to get it to underexpose by three stops? 1,280 fc is one stop under; 640 fc is two stops under; 320 fc is three stops under and is your answer. When you shoot at the appropriate *f*-stop, the fill light is underexposing by three stops in each shot. This leaves the quality of the light out of the quotient, but you have achieved at least some level of photographic consistency between the two images.

Lighting continuity, and the more general issue of photographic consistency, is not the goal in every film, but films that employ it are more numerous than one might imagine. Even films that deconstruct conventional narrative structures, such as Maya Deren's great experimental film *Meshes of the Afternoon* (1943) and Luis Bunuel and Salvador Dali's surrealist film *Un Chien Andalou* (1928), incorporate lighting continuity extensively.

☑ *Is lighting continuity important to what I am doing? Do I need to match to other shots the shot I am executing?*

15-2

A low-key lighting setup

15-3

A lighting setup for the same low-key effect outdoors

f-stops and Consistency

I frequently hear the question: "Should I always shoot at the same *f*-stop within a scene?" My answer, which I then go on to qualify, is yes. It is yes because I have seen too many mistakes from people who are not aware of the limitations. There is room for maneuvering, but you really have to know what you are doing.

A good example of this is a scene from a student film made several years ago. It was a relatively simple scene: A woman crosses a room and stands by another woman sleeping in a bed. **SEE 15-4** It was a night scene, and the filmmaker wanted to simulate a strong beam of light from a streetlight illuminating the bed. To accomplish that effect, he set up an instrument outside the window, throwing a big beam of hard light.

The filmmaker wanted the beam to overexpose by one stop, so, given his reading of 640 fc on the bed, he decided to shoot at an *f*/11. He then metered the rest of the room. The only other light was the ambient light created by the instrument he had set up for the streetlight effect. As you might expect, the readings were quite low, 20 fc and lower. Given the *f*-stop at which he wanted to shoot, he anticipated that everything lower than roughly 30 fc was going to drop off to underexposure. He wanted the room dark but not black, so he decided to put in a low-level fill. In a corner, he set up a bounce card and shot an instrument into it. **SEE 15-5**

From this the filmmaker got a nice, even fill of about 40 fc throughout the room, three stops underexposed. Dark, but not entirely lacking in detail. So far, so good. All the material of the woman in bed was shot from setup #1. Then he turned

Initial setup for streetlight effect

Adding low-level fill
by bouncing a beam
off a card

around to shoot from setup #2 the other woman approaching the bed. He already had a meter reading of 40 fc in the area through which she was moving. That translates to an *f*/4 at 500 EI, and he proceeded to shoot this part of the scene at that stop. Therein lay his big mistake.

Let's consider this scene. We have established that the woman is passing through a dark area. If we shoot her at an *f*/4, how will she expose? She will be exposed normally. But she is supposed to be dark. You might actually be able to get away with some slipperiness in the way she is exposed. Viewers might accept, if not demand, a slightly higher exposure in a close-up or a reverse angle than they did in a wider shot. The woman crossing the room is the main focus of the shot, so we expect to see her in more detail than in a shot where we see only her back. What happens to the character, however, is not the major problem. What is?

As is so often the case in situations like this, the problem is the background. In shot #1 we established that the walls are very dark, underexposing by three stops. If we expose at an *f*/4, what happens to the walls? They are suddenly at, or are very near to, normal exposure. The walls in this particular example were light blue. From the exposure the student did at setup #1, the walls were underexposed and thus a deeper blue. At the higher exposure of setup #2, the walls were a very light and airy blue, almost normally exposed. When he later attempted to cut the two pieces together, it just did not look like they were shot in the same room at the same time. The pieces did not look continuous, and the student had to reshoot that side of the scene.

The more experienced and confident you become, the more you should be able to shift *f*-stops without making mistakes. A normal exposure is a normal exposure, whether it is shot at an *f*/2.8 or an *f*/22. One filmmaker was shooting in an office building on a late winter afternoon and began losing the exterior light as evening approached. He could see on the meters that the light was dropping a half stop every fifteen minutes or so. Because the outside was in the background of all shots, he just had to trim each instrument (about six altogether) the same half stop every fifteen minutes. He started at an f/5.6, and by the time the shoot was over, the exposure was an f/2.3, the lowest stop on the lens.

If shifting the f-stop becomes unavoidable, you too can simply manipulate the light to the appropriate value. All experienced DPs know how to shift values around to match what has happened in other shots. Given a choice, however, a DP would probably opt to keep things at the same value just to prevent unnecessary complications.

A final point that refers back to the discussion at the beginning of chapter 14 about how we might choose a specific f-stop: Most DPs will go into a scene with an f-stop already in mind. This stop is not necessarily based on a value that they know is in the scene, the approach that was demonstrated in chapter 14. Rather, it is based on the fact that most DPs have an f-stop of choice, a preferred f-stop. The choice of f-stop has to do with their personal preference for the quality of light and the way the lens resolves at specific stops. Different DPs have different preferred stops, but they usually fall in a range from f/2.8 to f/5.6. There are situations, say, outside on a sunny day, where they may not be able to achieve their stop of choice, but when full control is theirs, they will almost always light to that particular stop.

There are two major reasons for this. Simply stated, the quality of light needed to achieve an f/2.8 is different from that needed to achieve an f/8. After years of experience, most DPs simply prefer certain qualities of light. Given scenes that do not need dramatic extremes, they will go with what they like. The second reason is more complicated: The image is sharper, with higher resolution, at lower f-stops. Even though there is greater depth of field at the higher f-stops, light refracts against the closed-down diaphragm, reducing sharpness. You may have more things in focus, but the overall image is a little softer. Sharpness and depth of field are different issues, and many DPs will sacrifice some depth of field for greater image clarity.

The idea of lighting for a specific f-stop seems to depart from the calculations presented earlier. Beginning with a given f-stop removes the f-stop as a variable. But eventually you will come to see that the true variables in the formula are the amount of light in front of the camera and the desired exposure.

The idea of a given f-stop casts a different light on our decision-making process, particularly when considering the basic strategy of lighting proposed in chapter 14. It was suggested that determining the f-stop is the starting point, and having an f-stop of choice makes this part of the decision-making process appear more arbitrary. If we go into a scene with a predetermined f-stop, the emphasis shifts to the manipulation of other variables in the formula—most specifically the amount of light present. The f-stop may not be quite as much of a constant as the shutter speed and the EI, but there are many professional cinematographers who treat it as a given.

Thinking of the f-stop as a constant changes our formula somewhat. **SEE 15-6**

15-6

The modified formula after changing the f-stop from a variable to a constant

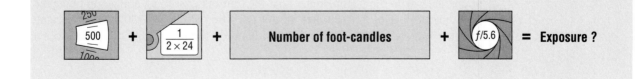

Most DPs will light for the f-stop of their choice. Many people on the West Coast love $f/5.6$. Other filmmakers will shoot only at an $f/2.8$. A DP's preferred f-stop can vary depending on the format—16mm, 35mm, and so forth.

Some DPs are extreme enough about wanting a specific f-stop that they will control situations that appear uncontrollable. If you are shooting exteriors and get a reading of $f/16$, is there any way you can shoot at a preferred $f/5.6$? Could you use neutral density as a front-filter on the camera to get there? The permutations become dizzying.

The question of lighting continuity does not have to be posed solely in terms of a preferred f-stop. It can be posed in a way that has already been suggested in the discussion of the lampshade and table lamp. Is there something in the image that is going to be difficult enough to manipulate that you are better off just shooting for that stop? For example, neon exposes well at an $f/4$ with 500 EI film. If there is going to be a neon sign in a shot, you can base the way you light everything else on that fact.

The specter of consistency will haunt you in almost everything you do. Exposure can be understood, though not mastered, relatively quickly. Matching shots is the tricky part. It is recommended here that as a beginner you try to shoot at the same f-stop in a given scene. It can possibly save you from some very difficult matching problems, and it is also good discipline to manipulate instruments to specific values.

☑ *Is there a particular f-stop at which I want to be shooting?*

Controlling Focus

The f-stop is a major variable in the production of the image, but it is also a major variable in depth of field. It is often necessary to light to achieve a specific depth of field. When you plan out a scene and do storyboards, you can begin to anticipate difficulties presented by specific shots. If there is a shot with two people on opposite sides of the room, you will have to consult the depth-of-field charts if you want them both in focus.

One film several years ago had a good example of this problem. One shot called for a man to be sitting on the edge of a bed while a woman in the background sat at a dressing table. Owing to the dimensions of the room and the action that had to occur, the closest they could be to each other was just under 20 feet. The man needed to be as close to the camera as possible. The DP was working with a lower-rated stock (EI 100) as well as small instruments and limited electricity. Thus he had to light the shot with a relatively low amount of foot-candles.

To maximize depth of field with focal length as a variable, the DP chose the widest-angle lens available: 12mm. This lens did not have the perspective characteristics he desired, but he needed the depth of field. He consulted a depth-of-field chart and found that his best option was to shoot at an $f/4$ and focus at 6 feet. This would bring into focus everything from 3 feet 5 inches to 27 feet. He planned to put the man a little less than 4 feet from the camera, just for some margin of error. The woman would be about 22 feet from the camera.

Thus, the DP needed to produce an $f/4$ on location. You essentially read the light meter backward to find out how many foot-candles you need. Start on the bottom of the meter with the f-stop, match to it the frames per second, and go up to see the resulting number of foot-candles. In this case the DP needed 250 fc. That became the base foot-candle value on which he planned the lighting of the entire scene.

When anticipating specific shots, you know you are going to need a certain *f*-stop to produce the necessary depth of field. Although all levels of production deal with lighting for depth of field, the complications described in this scenario, such as inadequate space, too short a focal length, limited electricity, and so on, are common on smaller projects. Filmmakers with more resources are less likely to paint themselves into corners. The solutions devised are typical of the kinds of compromises that often have to be made when you don't have complete control, compromises that affect the visual quality of the film.

☑ *Am I lighting to achieve an f-stop that will give a specific depth of field?*

Matching Color Sources

Matching the color temperature of light sources can be an almost overwhelming aspect of location shooting. As stated, it is an issue only when shooting color film, a not insignificant reason why students often choose to shoot in black-and-white.

The man in front of the window is an excellent example of a situation in which there are different light sources. **SEE 15-7** We have not yet actually put any artificial light on the person; we most certainly will, but for now we have only the lamp and its area of illumination. Assuming the use of tungsten-balanced film, what will the result be if we shoot this scene without an 85 filter? The area under the lamp will be normal, and the outdoors will be blue. If we shoot with the 85 filter, the area under the lamp will be amber and the outdoors will be normal.

The problem is: How do we match these two sources? There are two ways to do it. The first takes substantial experience to do correctly, is quite costly, and is the better approach. The second method is less expensive, requires fewer skills, and is less preferred. The second way, however, is probably the approach most students will take, at least at the outset.

The first method is to put rolled 85 gel on the window, the same material that you use in front of the camera lens. It comes in large rolls and can be laid smoothly

15-7

There are two common ways of matching color temperature when mixing daylight and tungsten sources

15-8

Reddish gel on the window brings the daylight color temperature down to match that of the tungsten instruments

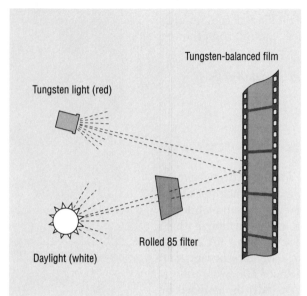

Tungsten-balanced film

Tungsten light (red)

Daylight (white)

Rolled 85 filter

against windows. The 85 adds an amber component to the light coming into the room from outside, as well as to the exterior light the camera sees. The tungsten film then reads this amber light as white light. **SEE 15-8** Do you use the 85 filter on the camera in this situation? No. What you are doing is bringing the color temperature of the daylight down to the color temperature of the tungsten instruments so that it will read correctly on tungsten-balanced film.

These filter rolls are quite expensive. You'll need experienced people to put up the 85 material, because if it's not applied properly you can be plagued by reflections, glares, and bubbles.

The second method is effective, but slightly more cumbersome. Rather than adding a color component to daylight, you can add one to the tungsten instruments. The material is called full-blue gel, and you will put a piece on each of the instruments. The *full-blue gel* also cuts the instrument down by one *f*-stop. In terms of color, the gel adds a blue component to the amber tungsten instruments, bringing them up to daylight color temperature. Do you use an 85 filter on the camera? In this case, yes. **SEE 15-9**

This is getting complicated, but here you take the amber of the tungsten light and add blue to match it to the white daylight. You then take this white light and, with the 85 filter, turn it amber again so the tungsten-balanced film will see it as white. Confusing? Perhaps, but it does make sense.

If it sounds as if the light is getting digested one too many times, you see at least one reason why the first method is so attractive. A general rule of lighting is: *Do not encumber an instrument unnecessarily.* Often enough, you will be doing other things to it, and putting on blue gel makes other adjustments more difficult. Along these lines, whenever you put something on an instrument that cuts the light in half (one stop), you are not using the instrument to its full capacity. You do not always want or need the full capacity of the instrument but, again, you don't want to impose limitations before you even start. There are always plenty of constraints built into the process without creating new ones unnecessarily. Anytime you want to do

15-9

Full-blue gel on the tungsten instruments brings their color temperature up to match that of daylight

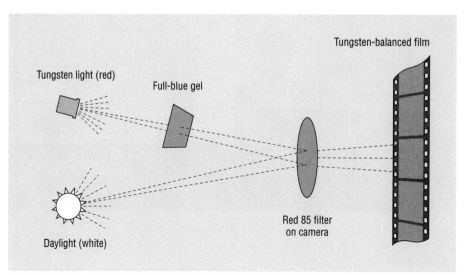

Tungsten-balanced film

Tungsten light (red)

Full-blue gel

Red 85 filter on camera

Daylight (white)

something with the instrument, such as pin spun on a corner, you have to deal with the blue gel as well. The blue gel just complicates your task.

You also have to use the 85 filter. As stated, it cuts out two-thirds of a stop, so you use the lower EI. You will be getting less light through the lens as well as less light from the instruments. The smaller output from the instruments makes matching light levels between the interior and exterior more difficult. All these factors only complicate your task and place an unnecessary limitation on your work. It will make achieving any significant depth of field difficult as well.

Having stated these negatives, we can reiterate that for the time being that the blue gel method is probably the way you will match the color temperatures. The expense and experience that it takes to use the first method may be beyond your means at this point. It also takes substantial preplanning to use the first method. The gaffer, electricians, and grips are well served by being early for the shoot. Setting aside the evening before or the early morning to put the materials in place will allow you to make better use of actual shooting time.

Given what has been said, you might consider it a toss-up between the two methods. The detail that tips the scale toward the "85 the window" method is that it also provides the ability to use *mixed gels*. This is where neutral density (ND) filter really comes in handy. Like 85, it also comes in large rolls and can be applied to windows. More significant, it can be mixed with 85 in a single gel.

Going back to the example of the man in front of the window, you not only have to solve the color temperature problem, you still have a major exposure problem. Assuming you want a realistic image, it would not be feasible to set up enough light to bring the foreground close, in terms of exposure, to the background. The solution is to bring down the background with ND.

A roll of 85ND3 gel would change the color temperature to tungsten color temperature (85) and cut out one stop of light (ND3). If it is an 85ND6, it cuts out two stops. Also remember that the 85 cuts out two-thirds of a stop, so the total light cut on an 85ND6 would be two and two-thirds stops. There are many other mixes; these are just a few examples.

To go back to the example of the formula, the ND and 85 filters become another variable. The figure below depicts the configuration you originally had on the shaded building (640 fc) of the man-and-the-window example. **SEE 15-10**

You will not always think of it like this, but when you put an 85ND6 on the window, you are reducing, at least from the camera's perspective, the foot-candle readings you found outside. Obviously, the actual readings on the shaded building and the street remain unchanged. You are simply putting a block between the filmed object and the camera, cutting down these areas by two and two-thirds stops. This can be treated as a subset within the equation: −1 = 320, −2 = 160, −3 = 80. The new reading would be a nominal 100 fc. **SEE 15-11** Although normal exposure may not be your goal here, changing the amount of light reaching the camera means that you have to change the *f*-stop for a normally exposed image. You consult the EI chart and find that 100 fc is a little over an *f*/5.6. You can do the same thing with the street, taking into account the 85ND6 filter on the window. **SEE 15-12**

It becomes evident that neutral density filters give you substantial control of the light outside and coming through windows. The material comes in enough

640 fc

15-10

The original formula for the shaded building in the example of the man and the window

15-11

The nominal change in foot-candle readings caused by the filter can be treated as a subset within the formula

15-12

The change caused by the 85ND6 filter on the window

gradations that you can even keep up, at least to some degree, with changing volumes of light as a day progresses. The ND approach allows you to bring down the values into a reasonably narrow range, eliminating the uncompromisable extremes identified earlier.

A *color temperature meter,* which resembles and is handled just like a light meter, is an aid to sorting out issues of matching color; with it you can measure the color temperature of any light source. Most color temperature meters also have a chart or an on-board computer that tells you what kind of filter is required to bring a given light source to the color temperature you want. Color temperature meters are complex and expensive tools, but are a necessity in professional production.

Another advancement that has made dealing with color temperature easier is the development of *HMI lighting,* a relatively new line of daylight color temperature instruments. Their use by professional crews has increased dramatically in recent years in spite of the fact that they are complicated and expensive to use. Most of them run on 240 volts and can be used only with crystal cameras. Although you probably won't have a chance to use them as a novice, you should be aware of their existence.

Again, this entire discussion applies solely to color film, as color temperature is not an issue with black-and-white. Pay attention to it, though, because even the most ardent black-and-white enthusiasts will eventually find some circumstance in which they want, or need, to shoot color.

☑ *Will I have to make adjustments to match color temperatures? If so, what materials and skills will I need?*

Electricity

Knowledge of electricity—how to use it and respect it—becomes a must when you start working with motion picture lights. Even the smallest instruments draw a substantial amount of electricity, so you need to know how to evaluate your power requirements.

When the subject of electricity comes up, it's amazing how many people admit to sheer terror at even the simplest of applications. It seems as though everyone has, or has heard, at least one horror story. We treat electricians as bearers of some mystical, dangerous secret, when it is actually something quite accessible. It is not necessary to become a highly trained professional electrician. You do need to exercise common sense, however. Specifically, you need to be able to determine your power needs and identify their source.

Access to electricity will always be an issue. At this point it means learning how to evaluate standard wall power—household outlets. Large-budget productions invariably bring large noiseless generators or go through a process called "tying in." *Tying in* requires the gaffer to use clamps that look like standard automotive jumper cables to tap into the main power of a building. This job should be handled only by qualified technicians, but it eliminates the time-consuming process of identifying the outlets and running extension cords all over the place.[1] Identifying outlets is the approach that, at least for now, you will have to take.

Every house or commercial building has multiple series of outlets referred to as *circuits,* which are tied to the main *breaker box,* often found in the basement or near where the electrical service enters the building. Most people have seen a breaker box, as found in most newer or rewired homes. Older homes often have fuse boxes instead, with the old screw-in style of round fuses. Breaker boxes and fuse boxes essentially amount to the same thing. The term *breaker* is used here. A typical breaker box is shown in the figure at right. **SEE 15-13**

Each breaker in the box represents a circuit. The numbers—15 or 20—on the breakers refer to the amount of *amperes,* or *amps,* that can be drawn from the circuit. Everyone knows that if you overload the outlets, you blow a circuit breaker. If you blow a breaker, you go to the breaker box, find the blown one, and put it back in service. In the type shown in the figure, the breaker simply snaps toward the *off* position and you have to flip it back on again. For the older, screw-in fuses, you must replace the fuse, which means that you should plan for that possibility and have spares on hand.

Obviously, you don't want to be constantly blowing fuses as you are filming, so you have to

---

1. In many localities tying in is highly regulated or, in some cases, illegal. Failure to check pertinent electrical codes may result in stiff fines or problems with insurance holders.

15-13

A typical electrical breaker box

apportion the instruments to the outlets so that excessive power is not being drawn from any one circuit. To do this you have to know how many amps each lighting fixture draws. There is a simple formula for this:

$$\frac{watts}{volts} = amps$$

In standard U.S. household circuits, *volts* are a constant: 120.[2] Virtually everything you plug in is based on 120 volts, except for some large appliances that have different plugs and receptacles and are 240 volts. *Watts* vary according to the specific lamp or appliance. Everyone has heard of 60-watt bulbs. If you had a motion picture instrument with a 1,000-watt bulb, and that is a pretty standard small lamp, you would use the formula to find out how many amps it required.

For a much simpler figure with which to work, 120 can be rounded down to 100 and used in a formula that is much easier to remember:

◆ **RULE:** *For every 100 watts, you need 1 amp of power.*

This is a simplification of the complex formula. For a 1,000-watt lamp, you need 10 amps (1,000 / 100 = 10). A 15-amp circuit cannot support two 1,000-watt lamps; you'd blow a fuse. Eventually, you will want to use the complex formula shown above, but the simpler rule both yields the information you need and gives you a margin for error.

So how do you go about determining which outlets are on which circuits? You have to go to the fuse box and do some simple testing. It is a fairly simple matter, but for some reason this is where people start to get cold feet. You turn off one breaker and see which outlets are no longer working. It is important that you turn off only one breaker switch at a time. If you are lucky, someone will have written on the faceplate which rooms each breaker controls; it might say "bathroom" or "east bedrooms," for example. If there is nothing written, you'll have to go through the whole house.

Once you have turned off one breaker, you can use a *circuit tester* to find out which plugs are not working. Circuit testers, also called *pigtails,* have two prongs with a small bulb on the end. You can buy one at any hardware store for about two dollars. You stick the prongs into an outlet; if the bulb does not light, the outlet is on the circuit you have turned off. Most multitesters, which are multifunctional battery testers, also have a position to test AC (alternating current). Other functions of the multitesters come in handy for other applications. If you have neither, you can use a small appliance, such as a radio, to identify which outlets are "hot."

By this method you can go through the entire structure and determine which outlets are on which circuits. As you do this, you should make a map, an overhead similar to that used for planning shots, that details the location of circuits and where the sources might be for the instruments you want to use. This is a time-consuming, albeit necessary, process.

Once you've determined where everything is, you can apportion the instruments to the outlets so that you never draw more power than a circuit can hold. If you find that a room has a 20-amp circuit, the most that you can plug into that room's outlets is a total of 2,000 watts; if two rooms are served by a 15-amp circuit, the most you can plug in is 1,500 watts, and so on. By the end, you may have a tangle of extension cords running from many different sources.

In the industry the size of instruments is spoken about in terms of *kilowatts (k).* This should not be confused with the *K* in degrees Kelvin. A 1k lamp is a 1,000-watt lamp; a 2k lamp is a 2,000-watt lamp, and so on. It is not uncommon, particularly when working in large spaces, for commercial productions to use 10k lamps and

---

2. Identifying 120 volts as a constant can be done only in terms of its use in a formula. Voltage as supplied from a local power company can vary from roughly 110 to 125 volts.

larger. If you plug 10,000 watts into the formula, you will find that you need 100 amps for a 10k lamp. It is clear that no standard household circuit, or even the whole house for that matter, can meet those power requirements. In fact, the use of any instrument larger than 2k necessitates an alternative power source.

Power limitations are an important issue because they force the novice to work with smaller instruments. Crews on bigger-budget films use large instruments—4k, 5k, 10k, and so on—fairly regularly, but it's virtually impossible for beginners to use them. This is probably fortuitous, for it takes a good bit of knowledge to deal safely with larger instruments, considering their heat, weight, and voltage requirements. This should never be used as an excuse or seen as a limitation, because you can do some wonderful things with small instruments.

That said, you can also do some things with big instruments that you just can't do with small ones. If you shoot a 1k through a silk, you won't have much light left to work with. If you want to add a deep color, you have the same problem. If you want a certain depth of field, you may not be able to create enough light to get the stop you want.

A substantial part of evaluating electrical requirements should occur in preproduction. As you become more secure with lighting, you will be able to anticipate the size, type, and number of instruments you will need. In fact, you should be prepared to the extent of knowing where almost every instrument will be placed. Drawing a map of your overall lighting design can be incorporated into the overhead that indicates the location of all the circuits. Planning may be hard at first, but keep it as a long-term goal.

☑ *Have I determined how much electricity I need and identified the source?*

Printing, Processing, and Exposure Manipulations

There are a number of ways to manipulate film images and these, of course, have a direct bearing on light and exposure. Techniques include under- and overexposure, color effects, and actually manipulating the film stock and the processing. Although most of your effort should be toward mastering basic exposure, you can still create some interesting effects and you may want to start experimenting with some of these. In any case it is important that you learn how to communicate to the processing lab what you have done.

Reference Charts

Gray scales or *chip charts* are used as references to communicate to the lab any changes. The gray scale is described in chapter 13. The chip chart is a series of colors on a chart—the photographic equivalent of color bars in video. Whichever you shoot, charts serve as a printing reference for the lab. You should shoot one of these reference charts at the head of every roll. When your film is processed, you will always request a workprint. To make the workprint, lab people analyze the chart and use it as a guide exposing the workprint. Manufacturers generally recommend the gray scale, and a number of labs and practitioners prefer the chip chart.

When your shooting is straightforward in terms of exposure, the chart is not so important. The lab will look at your shots and should be able to give you a reasonably good print. When you are trying for a difficult exposure or color effect, however, it is crucial that you have a chart and that it is shot correctly. Without a good reference, the lab may have no idea how to print your film.

Several years ago one student was shooting an exterior scene at night. It was mentioned earlier that people tend to associate the color blue with night. The student decided to try for a blue moonlight effect by putting the same full-blue gel that

15-14

Setup for creating a blue moonlight effect by putting full-blue gel on the instruments and omitting the 85 filter on the camera

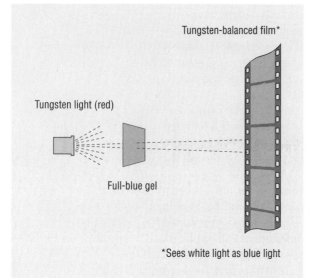

Tungsten-balanced film*

Tungsten light (red)

Full-blue gel

*Sees white light as blue light

corrects for daylight on the instruments, omitting the 85 filter on the cam. **SEE 15-14** If there is no filter, the film will read the light as blue.

He sent the film to the lab, justly pleased with creating an interesting, albeit relatively common, effect. The people at the lab took one look and said, "Too blue," so they filtered out the extra blue. He got his film back and hit the ceiling. The lab had murdered his beautiful blue effect. He made noises about never using that lab again until he was pulled aside and told what had happened. It was not "the lab's fault." It was his for not communicating to the lab what he was doing. All was not lost, of course, because the student's blue effect was still there in his camera original. When he went to a final print, the lab brought out the blue effect as it could have done from the beginning.

If the student had shot either a gray scale or a chip chart at the head of the roll, he would have been all right. In this case you just throw some light on the chart and shoot at the *f*-stop that the light meter tells you. You might ask if the student should have put the same blue light on his chart, because that was the effect he wanted. The answer is no. The lab dials the lights on the analyzing machine until the scale appears as it should. If there is blue light on the chart, whether it is a gray scale or a chip chart, the lab will dial out the blue to get to a normal representation. This will be exactly the opposite of what you want. If you shoot the chart normally, no changes will be dialed in, and your blue will make it to the workprint.

Many exposure manipulations bring up similar questions. One student wanted to do a number of underexposure effects. She knew that if the lab saw this without being informed, it would overexpose the workprint, or print it up, in the printing process and take away the effect. So the filmmaker exposed a chart normally at the beginning of the roll. The lab set its printing lights normally, and the underexposure effects made it to the workprint. Conversely, another student wanted the grainy effect of underexposed film printed up to look normal. She had underexposed her whole roll by one stop. If she had shot her chart normally, the workprint would have been one stop underexposed, which was not what she wanted. Instead, she underexposed her chart by that same one stop. The lab looked at the chart, dialed the lights up, and pumped more light through to the entire workprint. This was exactly what she wanted.

◆ **RULE:** *If you want the lab to preserve your effect, shoot the chart normally. The lab will set the printer lights to normal exposure, and your effect will be printed.*

◆ **RULE:** *If you want the lab to manipulate your print, shoot the chart with whatever modification you are attempting. The lab will make the necessary adjustments to correct the reference chart, and you will get the correction you desire.*

There is certainly a lot more to this, but these are some good general rules. If you shoot a chip chart, be sure to write on the packaging in big letters: "PRINT TO GRAY SCALE (CHIP CHART) AT HEAD."

In addition, be aware that manipulation of exposure will cause different effects in the final film. These effects vary between reversal and negative film stocks. With negative, underexposure causes greater visible grain and desaturation of color; colors will be more muted. Overexposed film will have less visible grain and greater color saturation. There is an old rule to this: When in doubt, overexpose with negative film. When going for commercial norms, which generally require tight grain and rich color, negative film stocks are more forgiving with overexposure. The rule is simply the opposite with reversal film: When in doubt, underexpose.

FORCE PROCESSING AND FLASHING

There are several other types of manipulations, the two most common being force processing and flashing.

Force processing, also called *pushing*, is the more common of the two. The easiest way to explain this is that if you find yourself in a situation where you don't have enough light, you can underexpose the film and then ask the lab personnel to "push" it. They would leave the film in the developer longer, overdeveloping it. Most labs have substantial experience with this and can be quite precise in how they match up what you have done with how they process the film. Care must be taken when you do this, however, because the quality of the image will change from the film that has been normally exposed and normally processed. The film will have a different look. Leaving the film longer in the *soup* (slang for the developing chemicals) generally increases contrast and creates more visible grain. As always, you have to think about how the pieces will match up with other things you are shooting.

Most DPs push film because they are trying to achieve a specific effect. It is great for producing a grainier, more abstract image. In cases like this, you build that one stop of underexposure into your filming by changing the film's EI. This relates to the concept of halving and doubling that was discussed earlier. Every doubling or halving of EI represents an *f*-stop, and you change the EI rather than make the mental computation each time. If you have a film stock normally rated for 500 EI and you want to push it two stops, what would the new EI be? One stop would be 1,000, and two stops would be 2,000. If you rate the film stock at 2,000, you will automatically be building two stops of underexposure into everything you film. You then tell the lab to push the film two stops, and the lab compensates for what you have done by leaving the film in the soup longer.

A couple of notes of caution: First, consult the lab before you attempt any experiments. The lab will have limits and recommendations on how much you should push specific film stocks. If you exceed these limits, you might not like what you get or the lab may flat out refuse to process it. Second, shoot tests before you commit a lot of time and footage to the concept. This is the only way to find out if the effect is what you want. Third, it costs more to push film. Labs have specific charges for pushing, generally additional cents per foot. Make sure it is in your budget. Fourth (and this should be obvious), if you want your film pushed, you have to do the effect consistently for the entire roll. A lab cannot push part of a roll or a single shot; it's the whole roll or nothing.

It is also possible to *pull* film, that is, build in overexposure. In this case you "underprocess" the film. Most labs will tell you that the resulting film will be flat and characterless and not worth the effort. I have seen people do a lot of odd things to their films, but the effect of pulling film is generally unpleasant, and I have rarely seen anyone who was pleased with the result.

Flashing, a procedure that the lab does to your unexposed film stock before you take it on location and shoot, is somewhat more complicated and not quite as common as force processing. At your request, the lab runs the unexposed film past a low-intensity light on one of its printers. This light builds an increment of exposure into the film. It is not quite this simple, but it adds a small number of foot-candles to your total. That increment of exposure brings up the shadow areas while not significantly affecting the highlights. If you add 5 fc to an area that has 10, that is a half stop. If you add that same 5 fc to 160 fc, the change is marginal. Again, DPs do this for effect. It gives the image a foggy feel, making the dark areas look milky and gray and the light areas washed out.

Vilmos Zsigmond, on Robert Altman's *McCabe and Mrs. Miller,* flashed everything that was shot. The resulting film has a washed-out, old look that is central to the elegiac tone of the film's action. He did similar work on the same director's *The Long Goodbye.* Another good example of flashing is Hal Ashby's *Bound for Glory* (Haskell Wexler, DP), the story of Woody Guthrie in the 1930s. The effect gives the film a worn-out, old feel that adds immeasurably to its texture. More accurate, these films were preflashed, because the exposure was done before shooting. You can also *postflash* film, that is, flash it after you have shot it, but the former is more popular.

Again, manipulating the EI of the film stock builds the desired exposure effect into your filming when force processing. This can be a dangerous piece of information, but the EI that you find on a film's packaging is only the manufacturer's recommendation. The number basically states that if you have a certain level of light, a specific f-stop will usually produce the best results. After years of shooting a specific film stock, many cinematographers will simply rate it slightly differently. By doing this they build in some level of underexposure or overexposure, at least relative to what the manufacturer says. They rate it differently, because they like the way the film stock exposes at that EI. Some cinematographers will rate the film stock differently and have the lab process it differently; for example, they will rate a 100 EI stock at 150 and have the lab process it for 150 EI. You may be scratching your head at this, and for good reason. To understand this you have to have substantial experience with labs and film stocks. The important thing to remember from this discussion is that all those things that we earlier established as constants start to have more indistinct boundaries.

That said, you should treat the EI as a constant until you feel confident that you fully understand it. As stated, pushing and flashing are done to achieve specific effects. These are only two ways of doing what DPs like to call "torturing" the negative. Characteristically, beginners often want to get right out there and apply their own thumb screws. Remember, as a novice it is incumbent on you to master basic exposure before anything else. One student, after reading some Martian film book, baked his film in the oven for several hours. He then proceeded to go out and misexpose the whole roll. Not only did this experience give him nothing to work with, it failed to communicate to him what a terrible idea the whole thing was to begin with. Before you try out all the settings on your microwave, figure out what exposure is all about. Then you can start playing with it.

✓ *Am I doing anything for an effect, in terms of exposure, color, or stock manipulation, that I should communicate to the lab?*

Slow Motion and Fast Motion

We have questioned the EI as a constant and now it is time to turn our attention to shutter speed. This is not as slippery a topic as the previous one. Shutter speed is tied to frames per second (fps) and it changes only when you change the frame rate. You do not change the frame rate arbitrarily—only when you want slow or fast motion. Recall from chapter 6 how frame rates slower than 24 fps produce fast motion and how those faster than 24 produce slow motion.

Consider the example of the man in front of the window. What would happen if you decided to shoot the scene at 48 fps? In this case you would change the shutter speed variable. If your desired result was still normal exposure on the person, how would the formula have to change? Something would have to give in

15-15

The modified formula after changing the shutter speed

the *f*-stop. Most light meters have a function that will tell you, but remembering that everything is expressed in halves and doubles, you should be able to figure it out arithmetically. **SEE 15-15**

In this example an *f*/5.6 produced normal exposure when running at 24 fps. If the film is running faster, there is less light reaching it. But how much less? Plug 48 into the shutter speed formula. The new shutter speed is ¹⁄₉₆ second, as opposed to the normal running speed of ¹⁄₄₈. So you are getting half as much light from the shutter speed. What shift in the *f*-stop will yield twice as much light? Wanting twice as much light, you change one stop. Which direction? If you want more light, you open the diaphragm (lower numerically). You open up one stop, which would be an *f*/4. **SEE 15-16** If you go the opposite direction to, say, 12 fps, you would have to close down one stop. **SEE 15-17** Again, the light meter will tell you. But if you can do fractions, you should be able to figure out the *f*-stop for any frame rate.

☑ *Am I shooting at standard sound running speed, 24 fps? If not, have I made the necessary adjustments?*

15-16

To yield twice as much light, you open the diaphragm one stop

15-17

To yield half as much light, you close the diaphragm one stop

Filming Various Skin Tones

Filming people of varied skin colors presents several issues that have to be addressed. Although this concerns people of many races, it is especially pertinent to filming African Americans and other people with dark skin, who will probably not have the facial detail you want if you use conventional exposure recommendations. Dealing with this issue will provoke a fair amount of discussion in the coming years. There have been brief references here and there but, to my knowledge, there has yet to be a definitive discussion. Experienced DPs have certainly learned to deal with this issue, but well-meaning novices, particularly when experimenting with latitude, can make mistakes that may have implications they do not want. The solution I recommend here is on the simplistic side and is not meant to be definitive. It will be helpful if it leads to a long-overdue discussion that could give beginners some direction in this area.

As stated in the section on reflectant quality in chapter 13, dark subjects respond to underexposure much more quickly than do light subjects. This is true of people as well. Without pointing fingers or laying blame, we can say that most photographic recommendations were designed considering surfaces that reflect an average amount of light, which includes the white face. This makes a modicum of sense because most things in nature and many things that humans create fall within this range. At the manufacturer's recommended EIs and f-stops, white objects are white, gray objects are gray, and black objects are black. The problem is that photographic black represents a lack of detail and, unless you are going for some effect, you always want detail in the face.

This will require some clarification, but to create normal exposure on a dark-skinned person, open up one stop more than standard recommendations; that is, overexpose by one stop. If the conventional translation of 160 fc is an $f/8$, expose at an $f/5.6$. This does not mean that you set up your instruments, get a reading, and shoot at a lower stop. It is not that you should choose a lower exposure, but that you manipulate light values to create higher levels of exposure.

Once again, using the example of the person and the table lamp, it is not that you shoot at an $f/5.6$ rather than the recommended $f/8$, for that would change how the lamp and everything else exposes. Rather, you still shoot at an $f/8$, but just manipulate the light to create more exposure on the person. **SEE 15-18** Rather than the 160 fc that you keyed the subject to earlier, you key to 320 fc. You will notice that the fill and backlight values have changed as well. In general, dark hair needs more backlight, so don't hesitate to go as much as two stops higher than the exposure. The fill is actually at the recommendation for normal exposure (160 fc).

This discussion is complicated by the obvious fact that dark-skinned people nevertheless have a tremendously wide range of skin tones. Again, experience will teach you, but try varying levels of overexposure. An African American with very dark skin will take the full stop that I have recommended. The image of a person with lighter skin might respond well at a half stop. There are some people with very light skin for whom the standard exposure recommendations will work just fine.

This becomes a bigger issue when you have a number of people with a variety of skin tones. A film on which I worked as the gaffer called for the staging of a discussion group. Persons A and D were African Americans with very dark skin, person B had somewhat lighter skin, and persons C and E were white. The room was quite large, so the scene presented many challenges, particularly for the wide shots. **SEE 15-19** There was a drop ceiling, so I started by pushing away some of the panels and rigging several broad lights shooting into foam core. This gave me a general fill of 80 fc in the area where the table was. I decided that this would be a nice level of fill if we were shooting for the f-stop that translates from 160 fc ($f/8$). We set up three instruments to serve as keys for the five participants. Persons A and B were keyed by instrument #3. I wanted person A to have 320 fc and person B to be a half

15-18

For better facial detail in a dark-skinned subject, set the key light one stop higher than standard recommendations

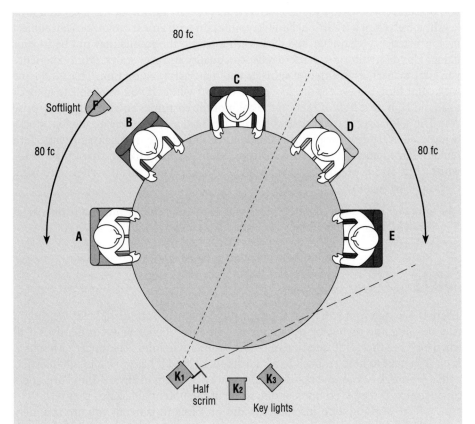

15-19

Lighting setup for a discussion group that featured panelists with a wide range of skin colors

stop less. This was accomplished by positioning the instrument in such a way that person B's distance from the instrument accounted for the difference. Person C had his own key (instrument #2) trimmed to 160 fc. Persons D and E were keyed with a single instrument (#3). In this case we put a half scrim on the right side of the instrument to cut the intensity on person E. Because the instruments that were rigged in the ceiling did not illuminate the back walls, we rigged set lights to bring the back wall up to 80 fc. We used several other instruments to accomplish specific purposes, but this was pretty much it.

In this setup persons A and D were overexposing by one stop, person B by a half stop, and persons C and E normally. When we moved in for close-ups and medium shots, we did a little more with backlights. We also used a traveling softlight on a rolling stand to give us the same consistent 80 fc on the background that we had previously accomplished with set lights. In setting up the entire shot as we did, we accomplished different levels of exposure without an overall change in the *f*-stop. Unless you are in a documentary situation, you do not accomplish this overexposure technique by simply getting a reading and opening one stop. As with everything it is a matter of manipulating the lights to get the levels of exposure that you want.

Though perhaps not definitive, this approach has yielded good results. It comes from using conventional exposure recommendations and having been disappointed with the results. Anyone with substantial experience filming African Americans will probably find this somewhat formulaic and simplistic; there are many other considerations, including the use of color gels. Be aware, though, of the issues identified here and the general guidelines provided.

Clearly, this has ramifications beyond the filming of people. When underexposed, dark objects lose definition much more quickly than do lighter objects. A black shirt is lost much faster to underexposure than a white shirt is. How people and objects reflect light also has a direct effect on any notion of high-key and low-key. If you attempt a traditional low-key situation with an African American subject or, for instance, a character in a dark leather jacket, the results may not be to your liking. This discussion goes back to reflectant quality and gray scales. From experience you start to learn how different subjects and materials read on film. This is an issue with color film, but even more so with black-and-white. If you were able to go back to an old Hollywood studio shoot, the color of the costumes and sets might surprise you. The colors were often chosen because they read a certain way on the film stocks being used. Very few people with this kind of knowledge of black-and-white film remain. For financial and creative reasons, many students like to shoot black-and-white, but some of the biggest mistakes in exposure occur when shooting black-and-white film.

☑ *Are there any subjects, objects, or areas in the shot that require adjustments in light levels or exposure?*

Safety

There is one question you must constantly ask yourself: *Is it safe?* Maybe we should take on the same menacing demeanor of Laurence Olivier with his dentist's drill when he asked that same question of Dustin Hoffman in John Schlesinger's *Marathon Man.* You have to hold yourself to a high standard, and it has to be a tough question with a thorough answer. Work-site accidents are a problem in any field, and beginners rarely notice, if they even think about, some of the potential hazards they face.[3]

When working with instruments and on films in general, you are routinely exposed to the following hazards.

▶ **Enough heat to cause fires** Shooting instruments into walls, boards, or other materials can build up heat that can cause problems ranging from serious burns to spontaneous combustion. Most materials made specifically for film work are designed to be nonflammable, but if used improperly a few can still catch fire. You also never know what is inside a wall. On one film, I was shooting an instrument into a wall until I was told that a previous owner had used shredded newspaper for insulation. We recommend using broad lights, because they distribute the heat across the length of the bulb. Focusable spots concentrate their light and heat in the center of the

---

3. Even very small shoots should be insured against accidents and other potential legal complications.

beam and, particularly when spotted in, can burn many materials. I have been on a number of sets where clothespins or foam core have started smoldering. *Keep a fire extinguisher handy!*

Always wear leather gloves when working with lights. They protect your hands from the heat. I have gotten burns that required first-aid treatment and a few that even left scars. *Always have a first-aid kit on the set.*

Be aware that heat will melt the glue on many adhesive tapes. Gaffer's tape is an indispensable aid on the set. You can use it to fix or put up anything. But if you put it on or near something that produces heat, it will lose its bond and not hold. Some companies make "tape-up" brackets with *spuds* (the mounting piece on most small light stands), and you can tape them to a wall and hang an instrument. If this is not done correctly, the tape can loosen and the instrument can fall. I was on a set where the gaffer taped up a backlight that fell and missed an actor by about a foot. This does not endear the crew to the talent—or to the insurance company. *Be careful.*

The sprinkler systems in many modern buildings can also present a problem. They can be triggered by heat, and if you place an instrument too close to one, you are really in for trouble. I was on a shoot where a system triggered, and the sprinkler heads put out a tremendous amount of water. Some gaffers tape Styrofoam cups around them. I don't know how effective this is; I just try to keep my instruments at least 3 or 4 feet away from any sprinklers. This constrains your lighting design, but the consequences of not taking these precautions can be worse.

▶ **Enough electricity to cause potential harm**   It would be impossible to go into all the potential hazards associated with electricity, and it is assumed that everyone has a healthy respect for what it can do. Suffice it to say that electricity should be dealt with only by trained technicians. Don't let anyone who thinks they know what they are doing do anything foolish.

Use common sense. Don't fiddle with a light or change a bulb unless the instrument is unplugged. If you are unsure if it is "hot," turn it on to find out. Always wear rubber-soled shoes. If somehow the worst happens and a crew member is getting a dose of electricity, never touch the person. Grab something that does not conduct electricity—a 2 by 4 will do quite nicely—and knock the person or the offending source away. Don't worry that doing so might hurt the person. That person is already getting hurt, and you just may be saving a life. If you are working with lights around water, take precautions that the two do not mix. Students thinking about shooting around swimming pools or in bathrooms should be either admonished to be extremely careful or discouraged entirely.

▶ **Heavy instruments on high, potentially unstable stands**   Many lighting instruments are heavy and, when you get them up high on a stand, they can be unstable. Put sandbags on the base of the stand for stability. You can find them at any lighting rental house or you can improvise. Never put a heavy instrument on a stand that is inadequate for its weight. Never build something with C-stands and extension arms that has the potential to fall over. Secure everything so it cannot fall accidentally or be tipped over by a careless crew member. You will hear the term *balanced weight* quite frequently on a set. Whenever there is uneven weight on a stand, be sure to use something to balance it.

When shooting outdoors be prepared for weather-related problems. On one shoot, we were filming a family sitting around a table eating lunch. As is so often the case, the beautiful natural light flooding through the windows was being provided by two 10ks outside. As we were shooting, some nasty-looking thunderheads appeared on the horizon. Always prepared for something like this, the gaffer and the key grip rigged up a tarpaulin to protect the lights from rain. As the thunderhead approached, the wind picked up. With ropes and tent stakes, they secured the instruments more firmly to the ground. As the storm drew nearer, it became obvious that it was not going to be an average downpour. The gaffer advised the director that they had better strike the exterior lights. Not wanting to lose a moment's shooting time, the director asked if it was absolutely necessary. When apprised of the potential danger, she ordered the lights struck immediately. The storm was short and violent, and we were back shooting within twenty minutes of its conclusion. We later heard that a tornado had touched down several miles away. *Do not take chances, and be prepared for the worst.*

▶ **People working up high on ladders, grids, and genie lifts**   Ladders are standard equipment on film sets, and you must learn how to be comfortable and work safely on them. Have someone steady the ladder and assist you with moving heavy equipment. I have seen people standing on all kinds of silly things to reach instruments. Be sure to stand on something stable that will hold your weight and have someone steady you. Location work can require numerous skills, from mountain climbing to the ability to do what almost amounts to high-altitude heavy construction. Learn how to work cooperatively in difficult situations.

Studio work also requires care. Most instruments are hung from grids; and though many studios have the traditional theater catwalk, most grids require ladders or genie lifts to reach them. A *genie lift* has extensions that allow it to elevate straight up. With this you can reach instruments from below. Genie lifts are handy, but they can tip over if not properly secured. They should be used only by people trained in their operation.

▶ **So many extension cords and stands on the floor that the potential for tripping or stumbling is a constant danger**   Lighting crews love to make what they call "grip jungles," where stands and modifying materials are so thick that you feel as though you need a machete to get through. I have seen setups that make it hard to get from one side of the room to the other. Everyone on the set must be sensitive to the fact that they have to be careful. That said, you should attempt to limit potential hazards. Gaffer's tape should be used to tape down extensions or any other cords. If you are not taping down cords, try to at least get them out of the way of high-traffic areas. Keep walkways open or cover the cords with mats. Do not have head-bangers sticking out into areas that people are going to be moving through. Again, use common sense.

Filmmaking requires a measured and careful approach that includes making sure that everything you have set up is properly secured. Watch how experienced crew members do things. Everything is done for a reason. Putting a heavy instrument on a stand is a two-person job and is done a specific way. This is the easiest and, more important, most predictable way—both people understand what they are supposed to do. I saw some Three Stooges imitators drop a 10k, and they were just lucky it didn't land on someone's head. Know your limits and learn how to work cooperatively. *Do not take shortcuts.*

☑ *Is it safe?*

Planning and Preparation

It should be evident from these discussions that a substantial part of the battle is won or lost in the planning and preparation. If you know what the challenges are and what is going to be asked of you, you can be equipped for, and do, virtually anything. If it happens to you only once, you will be lucky, but it is all too easy to back yourself into corners. You do a really beautiful shot that establishes a specific quality of, or direction to, the light. When it comes time to do the shots that have to match, you don't have the proper materials to create what is needed.

15-20

The reverse of setup #1 posed significant lighting problems

Early in my career, I worked on a scene that was being shot in a kitchen–dining room. The director wanted the scene to have a sunny feel, and, as always seems to be the case, the day turned out to be overcast. The improvised plan was to have a 2k outside the kitchen window, supplying the sunlight—the key for the scene. We set this up and proceeded to fill in all the areas that needed it. We shot all the material from setup #1, which was character A standing at an open refrigerator talking to character B. This all went fine. We had a 2k behind B, again to simulate strong morning light, and did some OTS shots from setup #1. **SEE 15-20**

The problems started when we turned around to shoot character B. Because we had established a strong morning light creating a nice backlight on B, the background from setup #2 had to be bright. It would have been impossible to light the entire exterior background, so the DP intended to draw the curtains in such a way that we saw only a single shrub just outside the window. We could then light the shrub with our tungsten lamps, thus simulating sunlight. We got everything up and then noticed an untenable problem: The bright light for the exterior was causing the backing of the curtains to reflect in the window. The reflection was large and unattractive, surely a distraction to anyone viewing the finished product. We scrambled while the talent waited. And waited.

Our solution was to tear down what we had done to the shrub, set up a large silk behind character B, and blow a lot of light into it. This also blew out the reflection. The character then had a very bright background that completely lacked detail. The director convinced himself that this solution would be adequate.

And that is all it was—adequate. The real problem was that by the time we had a solution, our time with the talent was limited and we had to rush through the shots. Almost invariably, you do your worst work when you are rushing. People are hired and money spent to make sure that directors have the appropriate, but by no means limitless, time to accomplish the task at hand.

In working with the footage later, the questionable quality of the image and the difficulties in editing the scene together reflected the conditions under which it was produced. Had the execution of the scene been completely thought out, we could have anticipated and dealt with the problem in a timely manner. Because the second setup was the more difficult of the two, it probably would have been better to shoot the material from setup #2 first. If we could not have found a workable solution to the background problem, we could have done different lighting for setup #1. I suppose the director and DP didn't even consider the possibility that what they had figured out for setup #2 would not work. Remember Murphy's Law: *Anything that can go wrong will go wrong.* Part of becoming adept at the craft of filmmaking is learning how to negate that law. If something can go wrong, you have to anticipate the problem and cannot let it stop you dead in your tracks.

On a more pragmatic level, you have to be able to anticipate all your equipment needs. Clearly, you have to know what instruments you will be using. This sounds more difficult than it is. One rule is to always bring more instruments than you think you are going to use. This anticipates malfunctions, and, more to the point, you will always have that one little instrument necessary for perfecting the image.

Not only do you need to anticipate the instruments, you need to know how you are going to rig them. If they will all be on stands, you need those as well. If you are going to hang them, you need the right kind of clamps. There is a great array of **grip equipment** to aid you in this task. From simple C-clamps with spuds to very sophisticated specialized clamps, there is something to help get that light just about anywhere you want it. Sometimes they have very exotic names, such as *mafer clamps* or *baby Matth pipe clamps*. On occasion it almost appears as though all the complex names are a foreign language designed expressly to exclude you. Just do everything you can to learn the lingo.

Not anticipating all your needs can slow you down or, in some cases, stop you altogether. Even the lack of something as simple as a *cheater*—the plastic adapter used to insert a three-prong plug into a two-prong outlet—can delay a shoot. Working quickly and efficiently is crucial, because your time with talent and locations is almost always limited. Again, experienced camera and lighting crews are able to anticipate and be prepared for just about any contingency. Many productions, particularly those with adequate budgets, will rent a *grip truck*. These are trucks that rental houses have outfitted with virtually everything you could need: instruments, grip equipment, heavy-duty extension cords, and **expendables** (such as spun, gel, cheaters, and so forth). Usually, you are charged both by the day and for what you take off the truck.

DPs often have longstanding working relationships with specific gaffers and key grips; they come as a team. If you are working with people who know what they are doing, they are thinking about more than the shot being done at that moment. They are thinking down the line to the shots that have to cut to what you are doing now. Is this light right for the emotional content of the image? Will the lighting continuity be correct? They should know all the right questions. They should know some answers too.

All these practical considerations are related to what is probably the most important aspect of lighting a scene: *having a plan*. Always visit a location before the day of the shoot. If natural light is going to be incorporated into the lighting scheme, try to visit the location at the general time of the shoot and chart how the light changes over the course of the day. As suggested, draw out an overhead of the positions of outlets and circuits. The overhead can serve a dual purpose to plot out an overall lighting plan as well. In conjunction with the director, sketch out where the action is going to occur and how the instruments will be set up. At this stage figure out electrical requirements, justification of light source, depth of field, and modifications for color temperature—in other words, just about everything.

The following question set is presented last, because having a plan includes consideration of all the previous items on the checklist. You will find, however, that frequently it is the appropriate starting point.

✓ *Do I have a plan? Am I prepared for all contingencies down the line, in terms of both equipment and thinking? Am I asking the right questions?*

Transferring to Video

There are significant changes in the film image when it is transferred to video. The notion that we are going to return to film complicates this, in that the final product should show no net loss. With the intent to finish on film, however, a question is posed. Even when finishing on film, video versions are almost always part of a film's exhibition strategy. Do we shoot for the video transfer or the finished film? The answer depends on what compromises you want to make between film look and video look. In addition, editing with an image that is a less-than-perfect representation of the original can cause problems in the quality of the final product.

VIDEO AND LATITUDE

One of the most significant raps against video is that it does not have as much latitude as film. Because videotape has a shallower latitude than film stock, detail in the darkest and brightest areas of the film will be lost in the transfer. In the early days of video, experienced film shooters often found that their darker shadow areas, in particular, were lost in the transfer. The visuals in Francis Ford Coppola's *The Godfather* (Gordon Willis, DP), which explored the deepest valleys of underexposure, are not quite as powerful when video represents its darkest elements poorly. It takes experience to determine how visual information will make it through the transfer.

Although latitude differences are clearly a matter of concern, when transferring film for video finish or shooting on video this criticism itself is largely specious. As the preceding chapters have demonstrated, you position the values of the instruments to the available latitude. This may pose difficulties because the discriminations between different light values have to be closer together, but videographers rapidly determined that they could light "film-style." When the final product is going to be video, some cinematographers have employed a two-and-a-half-stop window for exposure deviation from normal exposure. This assumes that everything outside that parameter is going to fall off at one edge or the other. The only arena where video's shallow latitude can truly be problematic is when you do not have control of the light. These situations include documentary and news filming, ironically two approaches in which film was largely doomed from the moment video became portable.

VIDEO AND THE CHARACTERISTIC CURVE

Another criticism has been that video responds poorly in the toe and the shoulder of its latitude. (The toe and shoulder are parts of the characteristic curve described in chapter 13.) This issue is the most difficult to dismiss. They are those areas in a frame just before the image drops off to complete over- or underexposure—the edges of the metaphoric table. In video the information in the toe and shoulder areas can become muddied. This is particularly true of the toe, that is, underexposure, resulting in a grayish, almost milky tone to the shadow areas. Although this is a significant complication, much as with latitude, crews have simply had to take it into account when lighting. Values are either placed within the straight line of exposure or outside of the latitude altogether. This clearly relates to the concern listed previously, where low-light situations are by definition going to be in the toe of exposure. You simply have to view it as one of the characteristics of video and come to appreciate it as part of the look of the medium. The only alternative is to add light or shoot film.

The quality of the transfer will have an impact on this as well. Inexpensive transfers will exacerbate the situation, yielding substantially more grain in the shadow area. A good transfer on state-of-the-art equipment with knowledgeable personnel should yield a dramatically improved image. It just costs an arm and a leg.

VIDEO IMAGE MANIPULATION

When the film is transferred, a video *colorist*—the video world's equivalent of the *timer*—has access to controls similar to, although much more extensive than, those found on a film printer. A significant consideration is that the telecine can be far more forgiving about exposure problems than film can be. The colorist can address much more drastic exposure problems than can be addressed in a film workprint or final print. This is fine if the final destination is video; problem shots will stay corrected to the end. But if you are going back to film, suddenly shots that looked great on the video monitor turn up looking terrible in the final film print. One low-budget film with a young cinematographer had extensive problems in this regard. The DP was missing on exposure in some of the night scenes, and the colorist was covering up the problem when transferring. He thought he was helping the DP. Without a workprint no one could anticipate how poorly the shots would print. When the director saw the first answer print, she was very disappointed in what the film look had given her. The colorist and the unit producer protected the DP in the video transfers, partially from a lack of knowledge about eventual problems and partially to keep the show on schedule, and the chickens came home to roost in the final print.

✓ *Is the film being transferred to video? What additional issues must be considered?*

ƒ-stop Choice and the Checklist Revisited

The notion that we will choose an ƒ-stop prior to shooting is critical. Again, the reasons:

- There is an existing light value to which it would be expedient to conform.

- There are shots that require a predetermined amount of depth of field.

- A preferred ƒ-stop gives you the lens resolution and quality of light desired.

- There is simply some value that makes common sense given the situation.

Lighting is about posing and answering questions. Addressing the checklist questions will eventually become almost automatic for you; they are all issues that have to be considered. Until the day when they become part of your subconscious, do not hesitate to just go down the list before you shoot. Be flexible in the sequence in which you address the questions. Different concerns will jump to the top of the list in specific situations. This list is not meant to be all-inclusive. You will certainly find many other things that demand your attention as well.

✓ *What do I want to achieve or accomplish with the image?*

✓ *What is the source of light? What direction does the viewer expect the light to be coming from?*

✓ *How am I going to expose the subject(s)? Am I going for normal exposure? Overexposure? Should the subject be darker, a little underexposed?*

✓ *What quality of light do I want? Do I want it to be soft? Hard? Should it be diffused?*

✓ *What goal(s) is each instrument accomplishing?*

✓ *Is lighting continuity important to what I am doing? Do I need to match to other shots the shot I am executing?*

✓ *Is there a particular ƒ-stop at which I want to be shooting?*

☑ *Am I lighting to achieve an f-stop that will give a specific depth of field?*

☑ *Will I have to make adjustments to match color temperatures? If so, what materials and skills will I need?*

☑ *Have I determined how much electricity I need and identified the source?*

☑ *Am I doing anything for an effect, in terms of exposure, color, or stock manipulation, that I should communicate to the lab?*

☑ *Am I shooting at standard sound running speed, 24 fps? If not, have I made the necessary adjustments?*

☑ *Are there any subjects, objects, or areas in the shot that require adjustments in light levels or exposure?*

☑ *Is it safe?*

☑ *Do I have a plan? Am I prepared for all contingencies down the line, in terms of both equipment and thinking? Am I asking the right questions?*

☑ *Is the film being transferred to video? What additional issues must be considered?*

Some of these questions, particularly the first one, will be real head-scratchers. If you do not have all the answers right now, don't be intimidated. Experience is the key. The more lighting you do, the more solutions will suggest themselves, not only in the pragmatic aspects, but in what happens in your head as well—the creative part. The process will be frustrating, time-consuming, and expensive, but you will never learn it unless you get out there and do it. It all leads to the most rewarding part: creating images of value and expressive power.

The checklist topics included here should eventually become internalized to the extent that you consider them automatically, or your approaches become so sophisticated that the basic language becomes almost obsolete. When I mentioned the three-point system as a starting point in a recent conversation with some colleagues, one DP remarked that she didn't think in terms of key and fill any longer. She went on to talk about lighting with a 5k and shaping and feathering the instrument with flags and silks and other modifying materials. Still, she had a source and needed to create detail in the shadows. On further questioning she admitted that she still worked with all the same issues, it was just that her language had changed. In addition, you are not going to have access to 5ks, much less any way to power them up. You have to face the fact that you will be working on a more limited scale than the "bigs." Use your creativity and ingenuity to find ways to be productive on that level.

Again, the key to lighting is not to look at a given location and say, "What can I get here?" but rather, "What do I have to do to get what I want?" Once you understand how light and exposure interrelate, you find that there are many things, small and large, you can do to improve the image in a substantive way. To produce on a high level with limited time and resources, you need to analyze a situation in advance, create a workable approach, and develop a plan to implement your ideas quickly and efficiently. Quick, however, does not mean instantaneous. Lighting takes time, and you need to allocate enough to do it right. Still, if you can envision the end product and work toward it logically and cooperatively, you can be productive without wasting time. Martin Scorsese's most significant early feature, *Mean Streets* (1973), was shot in about three weeks. Richard Linklater's *Slackers* (1991) was shot in a similar time frame. Given a creative and organized approach, producing shots of weight and value is both a worthy and an achievable goal. You can create tremendously beautiful images with a few well-applied resources. Moreover, the crucial concept to grasp is that virtually all images of character and interest are composed of complex levels of light and exposure.

A Typical Scene

By this point we have presumably created some narrative force to the contention that it takes an extensive investment of resources to create the images that so effortlessly reflect back at us from the motion picture screen. Once people get enough background to understand some of the complexities, I recount a story that a friend likes to tell. It is quite illuminating in terms of the process you have to go through. One of his clients, a hospital, was designing a commercial with a slow-motion close-up of a drop of water falling into a pool. My friend had been around long enough to understand immediately what producing an image like this would entail. The client felt that the shot was a metaphor for the beauty and fragility of the small things in life. My friend was unable to dissuade the client from this horrible cliché, nor could he faze the client by quoting an estimated cost.

The first issue is the camera. You do not need a sync camera, because sound is not an issue, but would a standard camera like a Bolex do? The top frame rate on general-use cameras that can vary speed is at most 72 fps. A drop hitting the water takes a split second. A camera running at 72 fps expands the action two and a half times. The action would still effectively take a split second. He knew he needed a specialized high-speed camera, the top rate on the cameras commonly available being 150 fps. This suited his purposes, expanding the motion more than six times. There are cameras that run at 10,000 fps, but these would break most any local commercial budget and were overkill anyway. He wanted a normal lens with close focusing powers, because a wide angle would push him farther from the action and a telephoto would reduce depth of field unacceptably. Although rental rates on high-speed cameras vary, the package with the lens he wanted was around $400. Although my friend had used such a camera before, he wanted a qualified AC to ensure against problems— another $400.

Preliminary decisions like this choice of camera set off a chain reaction of considerations. Moving one element makes all the other elements shift. When you run at a different frame rate, what changes? The shutter speed. Shooting at 150 fps, the effective shutter speed is $\frac{1}{300}$ second. When you lose light to the shutter, you have to regain it through the f-stop. He also wanted very tight grain structure, so he wanted to use a stock with a low EI, further minimizing the f-stop. Without some response he was looking at two factors that minimized depth of field: close focus and a potentially low f-stop. He risked having a shot that had a very narrow range of focus.

To address this, he decided to light the scene with a 5k plus a few other smaller lights. This was the smallest instrument that would create enough light to produce an f-stop that would give usable depth of field. This was fine except that the 5k demanded that the scene be shot in a studio, no other space providing enough power to fire up the instrument. He rented a studio and brought in a gaffer to assist him with the lighting and electrical needs. The gaffer brought in one electrician and one grip.

The last consideration was something that could reliably produce a drip on demand. The bottom line is that you have to make the action happen in front of the camera. If you do not have the right tools, you do not want to be waiting for something to create a drip while running at 150 frames per second. The camera is running almost 4 feet of film per second and can churn through a lot of film very quickly. He was able to find the appropriate piece of equipment at a medical supply store. A few PAs were also needed to help run this. Before long the costs on this "simple" image had escalated to where it became a major undertaking.

Though this image presents special problems, almost all images require the devotion of extensive resources. Every filmmaker has stories of lengthy shoots that began with someone claiming that they were "just going to do a few simple shots that will not take any time at all." Even the simplest of shots requires the time to get it right.

Part V
Editing

16

Principles, Procedures, and Equipment

Film Editing and Digital Nonlinear Editing

Digital *nonlinear editing (NLE)* systems have become the norm. Although the final goal frequently remains a film projected on a screen (and that is the assumption here), very few projects are edited on film in today's binary world of 0's and 1's. An NLE edit and subsequent return to the camera original to create a film print is the more common route, though it is fraught with pitfalls, many of which have already been discussed. Film is still being edited, however, with independents, students, and the occasional commercial feature being the largest user groups. This section presents an overview of both routes to a final film print: the traditional film edit as well as the NLE system edit and return to film. On the way, a substantial amount on the straight digital edit will be covered as well. Although this would occasion great debate in some circles, learning film editing remains the most comprehensive and intensive introduction to visual-media editing. On whichever side of the fence one falls on this issue, the approach of video-editing systems, whether analog or digital, is modeled on many of the features of the conventional film edit. As such, the discussions of NLE systems rely on a reading and understanding of the sections on film editing.

The Purposes of Editing

The inevitable clichés about editing are all true: This is where the real magic of filmmaking happens. This is where the film comes alive. The proverb that you can't make a silk purse out of a sow's ear applies to film, yet stories abound of films botched in their conception and shooting that were made substantially better in the editing. The flip side of this is the film that had great potential but was edited indifferently. *Editing* is the process of selecting the parts of the shots that are good and serve the needs of the film, and eventually discarding the rest. Editing with facility and authority in film requires extensive knowledge of the mechanics of cutting, an initially daunting though eventually easily mastered undertaking. In the digital domain, learning curves on software can be quite time-consuming, but once mastered editing is a reasonably streamlined affair.

Though this is a simplification, there are essentially three decision-making areas in cutting a film: cutting picture, cutting sound, and determining optical effects (dissolves, fades, and the like). For the picture, editing entails going through and determining the specific order of shots, then deciding on the precise transition point from one shot to the next. The order of shots may be predetermined in a narrative film, though that order may not be as rigid as first assumed. In documentary and experimental film, you may have to devise the order yourself. Cutting sound includes a number of approaches: from cutting sync tracks in conjunction with the picture; to determining the relationship between music and picture; to building complicated, layered sound effects after the picture is mostly cut. Optical effects are discussed in a following section; these choices relate to planning the available range of visual effects.

In his book *Cinema: Concept and Practice,* film director Edward Dmytryk has a chapter that should be required reading for all aspiring filmmakers, titled, "About a Forgotten Art."[1] In it Dmytryk puts forth the notion that anyone who wants to direct a film should spend time as an assistant in an editing room. No one learns better the kind of material that is necessary to edit a film than those who actually have to make the film work. If a director failed to get a significant close-up or botched a camera angle, it is the editor who both understands the problem and has to struggle to find a solution.

Thus it is imperative that you undertake editing your images from the outset. The production of images is a meaningless enterprise without the process of trying to fit them together. You can create beautiful images, but if there is no plan to their organization and employment, the outcome will generally be flat and uninvolving. To paraphrase a famous line from Orson Welles's *Citizen Kane:* It is not hard to produce beautiful images if all you want to do is produce beautiful images. A friend is fond of saying that editing is "the process of falling out of love with your footage and into love with your film."

The beauty of film is that it can take the chaotic and random nature of human perception and give it shape and form. The great Russian documentarist of the 1920s, Dziga Vertov, was fond of making grand emblematic statements on this subject:

> The starting point is: use of the film camera as a cinema eye, more perfect than the human eye for fathoming the chaos of those visual phenomena which evoke spatial dimension. . . .[2]

> Freed from the frame of time and space, I coordinate any and all points of the universe, wherever I may plot them. My road is towards a fresh perception of the world. Thus I decipher in a new way the world unknown to you.[3]

General Editing Principles

A number of key principles that influence both shooting and editing—the 180-degree rule, dramatic emphasis, and so on—have already been addressed, but a few additional topics merit discussion. As suggested, these concerns have such a strong impact on shooting that they must be considered from the very start.

TRANSITIONAL DEVICES

Shots that bridge one setting to another or that mark the passage of time are called *transitional devices.* This covers a wide range of approaches, but often transitional shots have the added burden of being establishing shots as well. The common approach is to show a setting, establishing both the place and, by extension, the time of day. If a scene that takes place in a dilapidated cabin in the mountains at night

---

1. Dmytryk, Edward, *Cinema: Concept and Practice* (Stoneham, Mass.: Butterworth Publishers, 1988), p. 144.

2. Vertov, Dziga, "Film Directors, a Revolution," *Screen* 12 (Winter 1971–72), p. 52.

3. Vertov, Dziga, "'Kinoks Revolution' Selections" in *Film Makers and Film Making,* Harry M. Geduld, ed. (Bloomington: Indiana University Press, 1970), p. 86.

needs to be established, the approach can be very general or very specific. The scene might start with a shot of mountains at dusk, rather than of an individual cabin. A cut from the mountains to the interior of an appropriately appointed cabin would be accepted.

This kind of employment of the long shot (LS) can be useful, but it can also become predictable. Several years ago I was hired for a day to camera assist on a feature film that had finished principal shooting several months earlier. We started the day by shooting the exterior of a warehouse. We then shot the exterior of a hospital. Next came a shabby bar. It soon became clear what we were doing. We were collecting transition shots for a film that was not connecting well. I saw a rough cut of the film several weeks later, and the establishing shots were not helping. The shot of the shabby bar preceded a scene in a shabby bar; the shot of the hospital was shown, then its interior. This sequence became painfully predictable. The film's problems were in the script, and no amount of transitions were going to make it more coherent. There was no apparent logic to the sequencing of the film's scenes, and no amount of establishment was going to change that.

Despite this, transition shots establishing location can be useful, although there are many ways to establish a shabby bar or a hospital without going outside—from planting some rationale in the script, to focusing on details, to employing wider interior shots. There are many ways to handle transitions, and you should find those that are effective but not predictable.

ECONOMY AND PACE

Economy and pace are very difficult to quantify. Each individual film, scene, and shot demands its own pace. Often this refers to employing each of the individual shots for the shortest time possible while still allowing them to achieve their purpose. This is generally controlled by the physical lengths of the shots, though there are many other elements that affect the sense of a film's internal rhythm. Usually, it is a question of the editor's consciously deciding how long each individual piece of film should be held. While cutting you can almost start an internal rhythm by snapping your fingers when shots are getting too long.

Pace also has cultural determinants. Mimicking the culture from which it emanates, the hallmark of American commercial film is that all the parts and the whole itself are exceptionally efficient in the way the material is presented. Any useless or redundant shots, scenes, or sequences are trimmed down or eliminated. American commercial features rarely hold shots longer than absolutely necessary, and scenes are played to their maximum efficiency. This attitude implies that if a point cannot be made in two seconds, it certainly does not need ten seconds devoted to it. Occasionally, subtle nuances of performance are sacrificed to moving the narrative forward.

This efficient approach has long been prevalent in American films, but it has been effectively challenged by numerous filmmakers, films from other cultural backgrounds often having a more leisurely pace. A slower pace forces the viewer to contemplate the meaning of the material more, particularly when coupled with an ambitious use of proxemic effects.

Michelangelo Antonioni has been one of the most adventurous directors in this regard, exploiting both a slower pace and the psychological intensity of the close-up. In *The Red Desert* (1964), he employs long, lingering, some might say too long and too lingering, close-ups of the main character (Monica Vitti), forcing the viewer to identify with her intense isolation and alienation. **SEE 16-1** Antonioni is quite remarkable in that he purposefully holds his shots well past what would be deemed their natural ending points by traditional American standards. In Antonioni films, scenes take two or three times longer than they would in conventional American films due to the inclusion of extensive visual detail and lengthy pauses between lines of dialogue. The approach has a much more contemplative and "environmental" effect, emphasizing the spaces within the conventional vehicle of meaning—the dialogue.

Keeping a film lean and efficient brings up the concept of *visual shorthand,* which refers to accomplishing an action visually in a minimum of images, again as economically as possible. It is an idea similar to the old "Name That Tune" television show. Rather than naming a tune by listening to a small number of notes, we can attempt to communicate an idea in the smallest number of shots. John Huston's *The Maltese Falcon* (1941) is often used as an example of the efficient "Hollywood classical style." Its terse pacing is crucial. The second scene of the film is an excellent example of this. It depicts the murder of Sam Spade's partner, Miles Archer, an action represented by a few sentences of description in the script. As always, this simple action can be thought of in terms of choices. It could be covered in an infinite number of ways—in one shot or thirty—all depending on the desired visual presentation and the amount of weight the scene should have in terms of the rest of the film.

The scene opens with a shot of a street sign (Bush Street), the setting having been mentioned in the previous scene. **SEE 16-2A** The next shot is a medium long shot of Archer walking into the frame. A gun, held by an unseen hand, comes up in the right corner and Archer is shot. **SEE 16-2B** The next shot is of a body crashing through a barrier and rolling down a hill. **SEE 16-2C** The entire scene is composed of three shots. The first shot serves to establish location and approximate time, the second is the action, and the third is the result of that action. The scene could have been drawn out to heighten suspense or emphasize other elements, but none of that was necessary. The action is a minor albeit significant plot point.

Visual shorthand is clearly a film-specific concept, although the idea of economy and pace exists in most media. Writers frequently speak about the necessity of presenting their ideas in as efficient a manner as possible, of getting straight to the point. Filmmakers such as Antonioni purposefully challenge that style. Although experimenting with any convention is always recommended, understanding and then mastering the conventional efficient approach to pacing is equally, if not more, important.

16-1

Lingering close-ups of the character force the viewer to identify with her isolation and alienation
Monica Vitti in *The Red Desert*

16-2

The terse pacing of this scene establishes, initiates, and completes the action in three quick shots
John Huston's *The Maltese Falcon*

Structuring the Editing

The vast majority of American films are cut so that their editing is as seamless as possible, what's known as *invisible editing*. In this approach any cut that is abrupt or calls attention to itself is considered a bad cut. All the rules that follow have their genesis in this conventional method. As always, these rules apply not only to editing but also to how you approach shooting a scene.

Though rules often are meant to be broken, the following represent years of acquired folk wisdom by many talented editors. As such, these concepts should be clearly understood. How they are applied is your business. An acquaintance once told me that her editing ability had almost been ruined by being forced to learn conventional editing techniques. Being polite, I held my tongue. If you consider yourself "ruined" by learning other people's approaches, you may be shutting off some important creative avenues. Listen to and learn from other people's experience. Rather than instantly treading new and exciting ground, most novice editors unfettered by conventional techniques wind up simply reinventing film editing.

THE BASIC RULE

Before going into specific concepts, the primary axiom of editing bears discussion:

◆ **RULE:** *There has to be a reason for a cut!*

This is the great overriding, unbreakable rule. When you cut from one image to another, there has to be a purpose for that choice. Often it is a narrative reason: A response has to be shown or an action must be emphasized. But do not get locked into the notion that a cut necessarily needs narrative justification—something that moves the story forward. Often the reasons are kinetic—to keep the shots from being too long or too static. Sometimes, as in many experimental films, a cut explores an element of film technique or an aspect of a character's subjective experience. Whatever the reason, when you are looking at a piece of film in the editing room, there has to be some positive reason why you feel one shot should end and another should come next.

CUTTING ON ACTION

A term that you will hear frequently is "cutting on action." This refers to match cuts and basically states that when choosing to cut from a long shot to a closer shot, or vice versa, the cut can best be masked by cutting on a character's movement. If a sequence requires a cut from a wide shot of a person taking a seat to a closer shot of her speaking when seated, the point to cut would be during the action of the person sitting. Cutting on movement usually occurs on emphatic rather than subtle character movements.

Once alerted to this technique, you will see it in almost everything you watch. In the scene from Alfred Hitchcock's *Notorious* mentioned in chapter 3, the cut that leads to the lengthy two-shot is an excellent example. **SEE 16-3** In a long shot, Alicia comes out on the balcony and is talking to Dev. The problem is how to get from this LS to the two-shot. The cut is masked by cutting on the action of Alicia's throwing her arms around Dev. If the shots were cut anywhere else, the cut would not appear as fluid as this particular choice makes it. Editors consistently cut on movement like this to create a fluid transition from one shot to the next.

16-3

The cut from the long shot to the two-shot is masked by cutting on the action
Alfred Hitchcock's *Notorious*

THE 30-DEGREE RULE

The 30-degree rule is tangentially related to the 180-degree rule but is not nearly as rigid and is less well known. It is more a matter of common sense than of the diagrammed schematic associated with the 180-degree rule. Simply stated, the *30-degree rule* says that if you want to cut to a closer shot of a subject or vice versa, the second shot should vary by at least 30 degrees from an axis drawn from the original camera position to the subject. The bottom line is that you should not move the camera toward the subject in a straight line; the possibility of a disagreeable jump is great if you do.

When you shoot a master shot, it is general practice to move in for closer shots. If you are doing a master shot of two characters, do not cut from setup #1 to setup #2, or it will look as though you are leap-frogging toward the subject. **SEE 16-4** The problem is compounded if you repeat the sequence. If you jump in and then jump back out again, it will look even more like the camera is leaping forward and backward. A more common sequence of cuts is to go from the master, to setup #1, to setup #3. **SEE 16-5**

The other key issue is continuity. If a character has his hands at his side in the long shot and at his waist in the close-up, the jump will stand out in a same-angle cut. Because so much else changes—the background, and the character's position within the frame—when the angle is shifted by 30 degrees or more, minor continuity flaws like this are much less noticeable. Small

16-4

Cutting from setup #1 to setup #2 would look as though the camera were leapfrogging toward the subject

16-5

In a cut from setup #1 to #3, background and character position change enough that minor continuity issues would go largely unnoticed

differences in body position during performance are unavoidable. The implication here is that if you can just get the continuity right, a same-angle cut will work. Most editors, however, would maintain that it is still a poor cut, even if the continuity matched.

Looking at the breakdown of the scene from *Something Wild*, you will notice that the overhead appears to have camera positions that specifically break the 30-degree rule. **SEE 16-6** The close-up of Ray (#3) is at the same angle as the over-the-shoulder shot of Ray (#2). The same is true of both Lulu (#4 and #5) and Charlie (#4 and #6). But as you analyze the scene, you will see that at no point does the film cut from an over-the-shoulder shot to a close-up of the same subject. If we see a shot over Ray's shoulder (#4), the next shot we see is from another direction.

EMPHASIS

Cutting on a subject or action exaggerates the significance of that subject. In essence the implicit message is that this subject is important enough to warrant more than a single perspective. If there is a shot of an object on a table, say, a knife, followed by a cut to a close-up of the knife, the implication is that the knife is an important element.

Sergei Eisenstein explored this idea in his landmark film *The Battleship Potemkin* (1925). The sequence has a dissatisfied sailor responding to rancid food on the ship. He looks at a plate inscribed with the motto "Our Daily Bread." Angered, he smashes the plate against a table. Clearly, this action could have been shot from one angle and been reasonably effective. But Eisenstein wanted the action to achieve much greater significance. He did a number of shots from the same camera angle of the plate being broken. He then started the motion in one shot and cut to the same action from another shot. Under normal circumstances the resulting cut would simply match. What he did differently was to start each new shot at a substantially earlier point in the movement than he had left it in the previous shot. This created overlaps of movement, exaggerating and intensifying the action.

16-6

Although several camera setups are at the same angle to a character (#2 and #3, for example), cuts are never made between them without an intervening shot from another direction

I once had a student who, given the assignment of creating several matched action cuts, decided to have some fun. She took the action of a car coming down a street and pulling into a driveway. She broke it down into about twenty separate setups, each covering a small part of the movement of the car. That this simple movement was given so much attention created the assumption that it was an immensely important part of the film. The anticipation was so great by the time the car finally came to a stop that when the occupants just got out and walked into the house, the letdown was comical.

VISUAL INTEREST

You have to go through the unedited footage to find the meat of the shots. What you have shot will inevitably have stretches that are not visually interesting. If you film a dance rehearsal, for example, there will be parts in which the dancer is turned from the camera or is framed poorly or when the action is just not engaging. Select the segments in which what was in front of the camera interrelates with the film frame in a visually exciting way. You should find moments when the physical makeup of the frame, the arrangement of shapes, the kinetic elements, the tension created by the parameters of the film frame—all make a shot speak.

In the best shots, not only is the subject exciting, but the way it is filmed increases visual interest. Find these points. As a beginner the infrequency of these moments can be discouraging, but they should increase as you gain experience. The goal of a cinematographer is to have exciting moments happening all the time. Great cinematographers have the ability to find the frame that gives the material an edge. As both an editor and a cinematographer, you must be able to recognize those moments when something is "happening" in the film frame.

VARIETY

Your shots must employ a variety of approaches: vary between close-ups and long shots, low angles and eye-level shots; images with different balances of compositional interest; moving and static camera, and so on. In other words, use the camera resources available to you.

If a film is composed entirely of long shots, it risks becoming visually dull and predictable. If the area of interest in all the compositions is in the same part of the frame, the same problems can occur. Obviously, there are exceptions. Several films that were done largely in long shot have been successful, such as Jim Jarmusch's *Stranger Than Paradise* and Chantal Akerman's *Jeanne Dielmann: 23 Quai du Commerce, 1080 Bruxelles* (1974). There are also films shot almost exclusively in close-up. But these are the exceptions; they do not represent the kind of explorations and experiments that provide useful learning experiences for beginners.

As with almost every facet of editing, camera perspective requires consideration during shooting. If you have not used a variety of perspectives, options in editing will be very limited.

CONTINUITY PROBLEMS

While cutting you will occasionally find continuity mistakes that were made in shooting, from minor problems to ones that will make you want to tear out your hair. If you have two shots with a bad continuity jump, for example, it may be possible to use a *cutaway*—a neutral shot between them that would mask the problem, such as a reaction from another character. This has the potential to work, but it can also have unfortunate side effects. The first is that it can destroy the pace of the scene.

Extra shots frequently slow down a scene and, though you may improve the individual cut, the overall shape of the scene suffers. The second problem concerns the logic of the visual presentation. It often just does not make dramatic sense to slip in a reaction shot or, more significant, some detail of the set. By cutting to it, that reaction or detail takes on an importance that it may not warrant. In both cases the operation is a success, but you lose the patient.

Sometimes you simply have to brazen your way through some of these minor continuity difficulties, and just make the cut. In the rush of frames, the dislocation for the viewer will be momentary, and new shots will quickly take center stage. As an editor you look at a cut with poor continuity over and over, in slow motion and frame by frame. It grates on all your sensibilities. You must realize, however, that the viewer is going to see it briefly only once, and, unless it sticks out like a sore thumb, it will generally go unnoticed.

Basic Terms

The following terminology applies to the basic principles and procedures of editing. Many of these effects can be created "in camera," but the norm is to plan them in editing and have them executed by the lab in the final print (see chapter 18). This gives greater control in positioning the effects and avoiding the inexactness that comes with being created by hand.

Fade-out and fade-in   A *fade-out* is simply where the picture fades to black. A *fade-in* is the opposite, where the image comes up from black. Fade-outs and -ins are generally used as transitional devices, either to get from one location to another or to signify the passage of time. Occasionally, filmmakers fade to shades and colors other than black. Ingmar Bergman fades to a brilliant red in *Cries and Whispers* (1972), amplifying the film's concerns with the symbolic aspects of blood. Films also occasionally employ a fade to clear or to white. These can be popular, though they tend to have a very stylized effect.

Dissolve   A *dissolve*, also called a *lap dissolve*, is a common technique in which one shot is faded out while the next shot is faded in on top of it. Similar to the fade-out, this is often used to signify a change of time or place. Although dissolves are immensely attractive to the novice, they are not used as frequently as you might imagine. There is an old put-down among editors: "If you can't solve it, dissolve it." As this suggests, the dissolve is frequently used to soften an otherwise terrible cut. Despite this it is also used to extraordinary effect, such as in Basil Wright's great British documentary *Song of Ceylon* (1934). The film dissolves between long tracking shots across temple ruins to create a poetic vision, emphasizing the timeless quality of setting and place.

Superimposition   Also called a *super,* a **superimposition** is composed of one shot overlaid on another. This effect is not common in features, but it has long been a staple of experimental films. Supers can be achieved in the camera while shooting or in the editorial and final printing processes. In the former case, the camera must have some backwinding capability. You make one pass on a section of film, wind the film back, then make a second pass on the same section. Each pass must be underexposed by roughly one stop, so the overlay does not result in overexposure. Tests should be shot to determine exact exposures, as different situations can present different problems.

The optical printer is used for rephotographing existing footage
Maritex JK-105 optical printer

Opticals This umbrella term indicates a graphic effect that is created in the lab. *Opticals* include split screens, keyholes, freeze frames, spins, wipes, and a host of other effects executed by the lab at the filmmaker's instruction and done prior to the final printing. They are difficult to get right and may take several tries to obtain the precise effect.

Most of these effects are produced on an optical printer. **SEE 16-7** Used to rephotograph existing footage, the *optical printer* is essentially a projector that has a camera shooting straight into it. Both the camera and the projector can be advanced one frame at a time. The camera can also be repositioned to focus on specific parts of the projected frame. The projected image can be manipulated in terms of both coloration and the speed the film is going through the gate. If you wanted to create a slow-motion effect, you could shoot two camera frames for every one projector frame. Any more than two frames creates a staggered effect between the individual frames, which can also have applications in creating time and image distortions. If you shoot seven or eight camera frames for every one projector frame, the result will be a staggered, almost balletlike distortion of the original movement. Ernie Gehr's *Eureka* (1976) uses this effect on a piece of film originally shot in 1908, in which the camera was mounted on the front of a trolley car. The effect created by the optical printer turns the content abstract, making it a play of shapes and form in stylized movement.

Optical printers are used most frequently to create optical effects, special effects, and titles in the editing stages of a film. A complicating factor is that film produced on a printer looks slightly different than the original film, because it is one generation away. If footage from the optical printer is mixed with first-generation footage, the difference will probably be apparent even to undiscerning viewers.

Effects that take extensive planning and calculations on an optical printer—such as *freeze frames,* in which multiple frames are made of an individual frame thus "freezing" the action—can now be executed in video in a few minutes. The NLE approach also completely eliminates generation problems. Although use of the optical printer has diminished, it is still instrumental in creating many visual effects and can be an exciting tool for beginning filmmakers, particularly those interested in formal experiments.

Procedures in Film Editing

The general process of completing a conventional film edit is covered in chapter 1. Central to the editing procedure are the people who do the work—the editorial staff—and the way in which the raw materials are organized for processing.

THE EDITORIAL STAFF

The head of the editorial staff is, of course, the editor. Though there are many different working relationships, the *editor* is generally responsible to the producer for creating a workable version of the film. Depending on how powerful they are, directors are often integral parts of the process as well, usurping the producer for editorial supervision. In the Hollywood studio days, directors often handed over their raw footage to the editor and that was the last they saw of it until it was finished. Today such directors as Woody Allen, Martin Scorsese, and Robert Altman have their hands in virtually every editorial decision.

The editorial staff can be large, with many members performing specialized or limited roles. The assistant and apprentice editors work most closely with the editor. The *assistant editor* is responsible for the overall organization of the editing room and all the materials of the film. The *apprentice editor* is responsible for many of the routine procedures that the editor does not do, such as syncing up, stringing out, configuring mixtracks, and so on. Beyond that, there may be a wide variety of specialists, including sound effects editors, music editors, Foley editors, and automated dialogue replacement (ADR) editors, among others. Each of these jobs is very specialized. British films often have a credit for a "footsteps editor," an individual whose sole responsibility is to edit in the sound of characters' footsteps.

Even if they have power in the editing stages, directors rarely spend much time in the editing room. Editing is too painstaking and laborious to be effectively supervised, or even watched, by an uninvolved second party. The editor is generally given the footage and then trusted to do the best job possible. The producer and/or director will occasionally be shown rough cuts of the film and will usually make detailed suggestions. The editor will generally give a rationale for any questionable sequences, and some compromise will be reached. Those with decision-making power thus negotiate the best possible cut of the film. Though film history is replete with examples of abuses of this process, this collaboration is generally the wisest path. A director must realize how a talented editor can enhance a project.

Having people critique the work is a crucial part of the process. Even if you are editing a film that you have written and directed, nothing is created in a vacuum. The person who thinks that anyone else's opinion dilutes his work is usually the person who is intent on producing one more trivial piece of self-indulgence. Watch out for the myth of the lone genius. There may have been a few in the history of art, but to assume that one is at that level is more than a touch pretentious. Even van Gogh had Cezanne.

ORGANIZATION

Organization in the editing room is essential. Students generally start working on short films without sound. Because the films are brief, organization is not too complicated because the footage is limited. Working without sound simplifies organizational concerns as well. This is a good discipline that gives valuable experience in telling a story visually. The spoken word can be a crutch, easily dominating the visual. When many beginners get their hands on sync equipment, they wind up just photographing the dialogue. They film head shots of actors conversing, derogatorily referred to as "talking heads." This is not by definition bad, but it can deny the power of visual storytelling.

All the material to be used in the film has to be extracted from the rolls of uncut footage, called *raw footage,* and be kept track of until it is incorporated in the edited workprint. All the outtakes and *trims*—frames trimmed from the shots you are using—must be stored so that they can be found if needed later.

There are many ways to organize when working with a small amount of material. One method is recommended here, or you can determine one that is workable. You should develop good habits from the beginning. However you proceed, be aware that there are accepted industry practices that you will learn if you ever assist in an editing room. But for now, it is important to just save everything and know where to find it.

APPROACHING THE EDIT

Project your unedited footage many times and make as many preliminary determinations as possible about the choice of shots. Go through the raw footage and take out the shots you want to use. Generally, you want to extract the entire shot from first frame to last frame (unless there are parts of the shot that are absolutely unusable). In most 16mm and 35mm applications, the beginning and end of each shot is easily identified by a series of *flash frames,* which have more exposure—look thinner—than the rest of the shot. This is because, while shooting, it takes a split second for the camera to get up to speed at the beginning of each new take as well as to come to a complete stop when shut down. In these brief periods, the entire mechanism is moving slowly, thus giving the first and last frames more exposure from the slower rotation of the shutter. Although at first appearing to be an irritant, these flash frames can be useful in identifying the beginnings and ends of takes in both the workprint and the original.

Professional editing rooms have *trim bins,* which provide a safe and clean place to hang the shots you intend to use. Outtakes should remain on the roll of raw footage. In the absence of a trim bin, you can make something on which to hang the shots: Set up a clean garbage bag in a large trash can and put a rod across the top from which to hang the film. Or you can simply tape the film up on a wall (be careful if you have a cat). Whatever system you decide on, the film should be hung with *film tape,* also called *white paper tape,* which is available from film-supply retailers. Do not use any other types of tape, because they will leave a gummy residue both on the film and wherever you hang it. This residue on the film will attract dirt and may cause problems in editing machines and projectors. Film tape also won't pull the paint off your wall.

Start a numbering system on the film tape. Cross-reference these numbers on a sheet of paper or, more convenient, on 3-by-5 cards, describing the type of shot (CU, MS, LS) and its contents. A simple list is all that is required. If you were making a film on a violin maker, the list of shots might look something like this:

1. CU, violin maker's hands
2. CU, glue being applied
3. LS, work area

And so on.

After all the shots are hung and numbered, the order can be determined by evaluating the list. If you are working on a nonstory film (such as an uncontrolled event, a self-portrait, or an impressionistic documentary), determining how the shots should be ordered will require significant thought. This is where 3-by-5 cards come in handy. You can arrange the film by ordering the cards and splicing the shots back together. I had a student once who just threw the cards in the air, and the order in which he picked them up was the order of the film. It was an awful film.

The next step is to cut all the pieces of film together in the order you have determined. The result of this process is called a ***first assembly***, or *string-out*. Once the shots are in order on a reel, you can start working on the individual transitions from one shot to the next. If two shots are not cutting together, do not hesitate to go back to the outtake rolls to look for help. Sometimes a shot that did not seem useful, or a snippet from a bad shot, can get you out of a major difficulty.

You start with the raw footage and keep rearranging it and whittling it down until you have a thoughtfully ordered and fluid piece of work. The first advanced cut of a film is called a ***rough cut***, from which you identify any superfluous material and work toward a ***fine cut***.

Film Equipment and Supplies

The *flatbed* tabletop editing machine is at the top of the film editing equipment pyramid. Even under the best circumstances, access to high-end gear is often limited. Students rarely get their hands on the good stuff until late in their educational careers, generally making do with more-rudimentary though perfectly adequate equipment. With film you can experiment with some very simple pieces of editing equipment. All you need is a film viewer and a splicer and access to a projector. Armed with these, you can work for quite a while.

PROJECTORS

Thomas Edison and his assistant, W. L. K. Dickson, are generally credited with creating the first motion picture camera; but it was the Lumière brothers, Auguste and Louis, who resolved the dilemma of an appropriate presentation device. In Paris on December 28, 1895, they projected a motion picture to a paying audience for what is recognized as the first time.

In design, the *projector* is very similar to the camera: The film is driven by sprocketed rollers; each frame is pulled in front of the gate by the pull-down claw, and the shutter hides the movement of the next frame as it is moved into position in front of the gate and then allows viewers to see the next frame. Just like the camera, the film must form top and bottom loops for the reciprocation between the constant motion of the sprocketed rollers and the intermittent movement of the claw. The biggest difference is obviously that a projector generates light, whereas the camera captures it.

The other major difference is that most projectors have a sound playback assembly through which the film generally needs to be threaded. Some projectors have a means of bypassing this sound head, but it is often a good idea to thread through the sound path to take advantage of its loop-restoring capabilities. Be sure to turn off the sound if you are analyzing workprint. The sound head will pick up the shape of the sprocket holes and make a machine gun–like popping sound.

Many of the newer projectors are *channel loading*, an automatic-threading feature. You slip the film into a slot, and the projector is closed on it. These projectors are generally not acceptable for viewing an edited workprint, because they tend to chew up films with splices. Try to get a manually threading projector, such as the Kodak Pageant, as it will be gentler on your film. **SEE 16-8**

All tips for cleaning a camera apply to a projector. Be sure to keep the projector free of dust and dirt. Even when you are handling a workprint, keep the film as clean as possible. The dirtier the film gets, the more difficult the evaluation of the overall quality of the project becomes. Projector cleanliness is particularly relevant when you finally get a projection print of your film, whether an answer print or a release print. Projection prints are very expensive, and one scratch can render the print unwatchable.

It is essential to view your raw footage many times before starting to cut. When you get the film back from the lab, the original film should be rolled emulsion-out. Workprints should be wound emulsion-in for correct projection. During the first screening of the footage, the condition of the workprint, and thus the original, should be thoroughly checked. The further the film advances in the editing process, the more it will show

16-8

Older, manually threading projectors are useful in editing stages
Kodak Pageant 16mm projector

wear. You may begin to wonder when the damage occurred if the film is not checked at the start. If scratches or dirt are seen in the first screening, their source must be identified. It is possible that they are in the workprint, so check it first. If you do not find the problem, have the lab check the original. Damaged or dirty film is generally discarded and reshot, so be conversant with any flaws and know whether they are in the workprint or the original.

As you view the uncut footage repeatedly before actually starting to cut, take extensive notes about which shots you want to use and how you want to cut the film. Evaluate the quality of your shots from a purely "plastic" standpoint, that is, quality of camera movement, efficiency of timing, overall composition, lighting, and so forth. Minor defects are often difficult to see on editing equipment. Lack of awareness about flaws in shots can lead to unpleasant surprises when you get a final print back.

16-9

The editing bench is a table that comprises rewinds, a viewer, a synchronizer, and other pertinent editing equipment

THE BENCH

The *editing bench* is essentially a less expensive version of the flatbed editing table. **SEE 16-9** While it appears, and to a certain degree is, cumbersome and archaic, its use has oddly enough remained the most significant part of the interface between digital editing and conventional film editing.

There will be a pair of *rewinds* for hand-winding the film. The rewinds are spaced roughly four feet apart. A film *viewer* is a standing viewing machine on which you can analyze the film at any rate you want, from frame by frame to normal movement. The greatest use of the viewer is in determining edit points—analyzing the shots and deciding on the beginning and end points of the segments of film that you intend to use. A *gang synchronizer*, consisting of interlocked rolling drums with sprocket teeth, is not required for simple picture cutting, but is necessary when working with sound. Sound and picture rolls can be locked to individual drums, called *gangs*, to be fed through the synchronizer in sync. With an amplifier/speaker, called a *squawk box*, and a sound head mounted on a gang, sound can be read and locked to the picture. With this equipment it is possible to outfit a workable and inexpensive editing room. Though flatbeds are preferable, you can do a substantial amount of effective work on an editing bench when resources are limited.

The *splicers*—used to cut and splice film—in general use are the Guillotine and the Rivas. **SEE 16-10** Inexpensive splicers that use precut splicing tabs are also available, but these are (or were, because of video) more for individuals and organizations that repair only a few home movies and institutional film prints. In terms of both the time they take to use and the durability of their splices, they are not adequate for extensive use.

Both the Guillotine and Rivas splicers have a setup block with a series of sprocket pins. When the film is set up on the pins, they ensure that it will be cut on the frame line and that it will line up correctly when the splicing tape is applied. Both models have blades that cut the film. Guillotine splicers use rolled tape, which is pulled across the film. A recessed, two-bladed knife trims off the excess splicing tape when you press down the handle; pins also come down and clear out the sprocket holes. The Rivas splicer also uses rolled tape, but the holes for the sprockets are precut. The tape is lined up and applied on the sprocket pins and then cut with a blade. The precut rolled tape is more expensive than the Guillotine's unperforated tape, but there is less waste.

On both types of splicer, the film is set up on pins, which ensure that it will be cut on the frame line and that it will line up correctly when the splicing tape is applied

Guillotine splicers have both a straight cutter for the film and an angled cutter for the sound. The angled cut cushions the splice as it crosses the sound head and makes it less apt to pop. Despite this, many editors do not use the angled cutter, having determined that they can cut the sound with the straight cutter without experiencing any difficulties. With the Rivas splicer, doing angled sound cuts requires using a second splicer equipped with the angled blade.

The frame line runs between the sprocket holes on both 16mm and 35mm, so the cut is right at a set of sprocket holes. Put splicing tape on only one side of the film so it is easy to take the splice apart if you do not like the cut. Editing is about trying different options until you find the desired cut. The tape splice method affords the best opportunity for experimentation.

Editing machines are designed to accept splices with one side taped, but be careful with projectors. If you are unfamiliar with a projector, run a test with some junk footage to see how the projector accepts splices. Sometimes, making the top loop very big will help a spliced workprint run through a projector. Be sure the sprocket holes near the splices are free of excess tape; if they're not, the film can jam or get chewed up—get "eaten" in film parlance—in a projector or editing machine. You will run across pieces of equipment that love to dine on messy splices.

Another type of splicer should be mentioned here. The *cement splicer*, also referred to as a *hot splicer*, works on a principle of welding the film together and, unlike a tape splicer, creating a permanent splice. Cement splicers are used largely for preparing rolls for printing, repairing projection prints, and, most important, in the negative-cutting process. Specifics about cement splicing are covered in chapter 18.

Supplies

The following supplies are necessary for basic editorial procedures. Many of these items are available only through labs, rental houses, or film-supply retailers. Always get more than you think you'll need.

Split reels All editing in 16mm and 35mm is done with the film on *cores*. Reels are too bulky for effective storage and are hard on the editing equipment. A *split reel* is used when film has to be projected or set up on a bench; it has the two flanges of a regular reel, with a threaded center so they can be detached. One flange has a pin to hold the core from spinning in the reel. The core should be set on the threaded center of this flange, and the second flange is screwed down on top of it.

Regular reels   Regular reels are used for take-up on the bench. These are simply the familiar reels used in projection that do not have detachable flanges.

Spacers   Donut-shaped plugs that are slid down the shafts of the rewinds, *spacers* replicate the distance between the gangs on the synchronizer so the reels do not turn flange to flange and the film does not come off the reels at an angle.

Clamps   Clamps are also slid down the shafts of the rewinds to lock the reels together so they spool in tandem.

Splicing tape   There are two types of splicing tape available: clear tape for the picture and white opaque tape for the sound. The clear tape tends to pull apart if used on the sound, causing damaged or lost frames. The only other difference is the perforated tape for Rivas splicers and the uncut tape for Guillotines. Do not use any substitutes—particularly, heaven forbid, Scotch tape; these leave a gummy residue, creating problems in projectors and editing equipment.

Grease pencils   Also called *china markers,* grease pencils are used to mark whatever information is necessary on the picture.

Permanent markers   Permanent markers are used for identifying leaders and making all marks on the sound. Do not use a grease pencil on the sound; the marks will rub off on adjacent layers and cause sound dropouts.

Frame rulers   *Frame rulers* are linear, rulerlike representations of film that are used to count frames in editing.

Film tape   Film tape should be used to close rolls, mark them, and hang up film in the trim bin. Again, use no other tape; anything else will leave a gummy residue.

Hole punch   A hole punch is used to mark the starting point of every roll, a reference by which to line up the film and mixtracks in the transports.

Extra cores   For editing you will need many cores to store outtakes and trims. Have a good supply handy. Although 2-inch cores are used almost exclusively in shooting, they are not used extensively in editing. The tight wind of the inner layers can damage the film's emulsion and be particularly hard on sound stock.

Small-trim container   It will be useful to have something to keep trims that are small, particularly those without edge numbers. Egg cartons are handy for storing frames, with identification written above each section.

Slug   Also referred to as *sound fill,* **slug** is leader or junk picture material that is simply used to fill in the empty spots on the sound rolls. The positioning of sound against picture is controlled by where it is cut on its individual mixtrack (dialogue, narration, music, sound effects, and so on). If there is nothing occurring in the intervening time between two sounds on a mixtrack, slug is used to span the distance between the two pieces. Unrecorded mag stock is *not* used to make up the gap between sounds, because even when blank it will give the sound a certain quality. Commercial films generally buy clear or colored leader for this, but picture from old projects can be used, or discarded prints can be purchased from film-supply stores. Any film with even a slightly complicated sound track will go through many feet of slug.

The Shape of Digital Nonlinear Editing

In purely pragmatic terms, the major goal of an NLE edit for film finish is to produce a usable list of *edge numbers* that will guide the negative cutter in conforming the original. In terms of sound, the goal is to produce a *mixtrack* that is full and rich and in sync. The routes to this end differ from the path described for film, although essentially the same things have to happen. General features of NLE systems are covered in chapter 17, but a brief description and the matchback to film deserve some attention here.

The primary image is acquired just as it would normally be with sync cameras and recorders. As described in chapter 8, the picture is transferred to presumably digital video and then captured. The location sound may be digitized from the analog source and captured or it can be captured straight from a digital source. If you do not have a good means to capture from digital audio, you may want to record it on the VCR function of a digital camera and then capture.

In the transfer *time code* numbers are generated that provide a permanent address for all video frames. As described in chapter 8, the time code numbers must be interrelated with the film's edge numbers. When a video frame is chosen in the edit as either a beginning point or an end point for a shot, that frame's time code number should be translatable to an edge number. When the digital edit is finished, the translated edge numbers are printed out in an *edit decision list (EDL),* which is used to guide the negative cutter's work. Many films, particularly features, have adopted a slightly modified approach, but the end product must be the same: information for the negative cutter. There are many other complexities of this deceptively simple operation.

With sound, the path to an optical master can take a number of directions, some of which are covered in chapter 18. Most NLE systems have the potential to mix projects internally. Even so, many editors output their sound to software specifically designed for audio, where tracks will be built and eventually mixed. It is also common to build the audio in this environment and then take it to a mixing facility, where the filmmakers can avail themselves of the services of professionals who can bring an extra dimension to the quality of the sound.

The essential job of most NLE systems is to emulate many of the functions commonly available in film editing. Although they do this well, they are also able to contribute useful additions, many of them coming from the video world. There are many different systems available, ranging from very powerful programs used in commercial production to systems that are limited to amateur doodling. They can be found on both PC and Macintosh platforms. Avid Technology currently has cornered a significant portion of the high-end market, with Final Cut Pro, Adobe Premiere, Media 100, D Vision, and a number of others also being major systems. Avid Film Composer™ is the chief Avid product for film matchback. Many of the lowest-end products do not warrant serious consideration. Every system has its own strategies for handling the chores of editing, storing the trims, screening the show, keeping the project organized, and so on.

Systems range from elaborate setups with dedicated hardware to those that run on a personal computer. High-end systems usually have two monitors, one for the source material and one for the edited program (although a second monitor can serve many other functions). A fast computer with a good capture card is required, as well as substantial internal or sideboard hard drive space. A video deck of your choosing (digital formats are the most common for high-end work) is needed for input to the system. Many systems offer their own *edit control unit (ECU)* with ergonomically designed functions, although a number of high-end systems use the standard keyboard, mouse, and menu structure. The simplest systems are run on home computers, with individual windows dedicated to playback, the edited program, and whatever else is necessary. All controls are also in the menus, at the click of the mouse, or on the keyboard.

Finishing

Now comes the hard part. It was suggested in chapter 8 that the conversion between video and film was problematic, with the changeover from 24-frame film to 30-frame video and the 0.1 percent slowdown being the chief complicating factors. Essentially, there are two ways to edit a program and then convert between the separate mediums. The first is to cut in NTSC (30-frame video), making frame adjustments along the way. The second is to reconvert to a 24-frame format when digitizing. The former has a number of inherent problems, and the latter, at least for now, is very expensive. The film world has struggled mightily with matchback. As with most great technical conflicts, a majority of film producers have settled on a compromise that employs the flexibility and speed of NLE systems while also relying on the integrity of the conventional film finish.

NTSC

As suggested, the biggest problem with cutting NTSC is that after three:two pull-down there are video fields and frames that do not correspond with film frames. Although there are some guerrilla filmmaking ways around this, it is recommended that you cut on a system that does the interrelated job of reconciling the difference between film/video frames and stops you from cutting on bad fields. To this goal the offending fields must be identified and avoided. The general strategy for accomplishing this is to designate all the individual fields by the letters of their corresponding video frame types (see figure 16.11 for the lettering diagram). In the display of the editing system, the letter designation will be displayed for every field. *Phantom fields*—fields that do not correspond directly to a film frame—are underlined. **SEE 16-11** If you attempt to cut on a phantom field, some systems invoke a dialog box that tells you to move the cut a field or two in one direction or the other. Other systems simply indicate bad frames with the underline and leave it up to the editor to cut correctly.

TEMPORAL ACCURACY VERSUS FRAME ACCURACY

The larger problem with all this is that though there are honest video frames that correspond directly with individual film frames, they still represent $\frac{1}{30}$ second whereas the film frame represents $\frac{1}{24}$ second. Even if we take the film frame represented by three fields, it is a difference of $\frac{1}{30}$ second for video versus $\frac{1}{24}$ second for film. We can edit honest frames but still come up with some time differences. The bottom line is that an absolutely frame-accurate matchback between a 30-frame system and 24-frame film print is not possible. You will simply have slight slippage between the two. Make no mistake, we are still talking about fractions of seconds here.

Although this is a problem, it is dangerous to overstate it, because you should not lose sight of the fact that if a shot is five and whatever fraction seconds in real time, it is going to be that length whether it is film or video. Most advanced software systems will protect you from any significant time discrepancies, recognizing the problem and either making, or prompting the editor to make, the necessary adjustments. Most systems will thus give you temporal accuracy, but there can be problems in frame accuracy. If a show is 20 minutes long on video, it will be 20 minutes on film. Frames, however, may slip one way or the other. Throw in the notion of the 0.1 percent slowdown, and this becomes even more complex. Any imperfection

16-11

Some NLE systems identify video fields that do not translate directly to film frames by underlining their corresponding letter

in the sequence of events will cause major sync problems with the sound. Filmmakers and lab personnel can recount horror stories about films coming back with the sound out of sync and with the wrong shots pulled. Many of these bugs are being worked out, but you have to be on top of every aspect to make this work.

Most editors are justifiably flip about all this. What problem really is a frame shift here and there? Who is going to notice? The feature world, however, which sees its films magnified 300,000 times, is loathe to allow sync to slip around and has largely stayed away from NTSC. The reason feature editors have abandoned NTSC is more far-reaching than this, but frame accuracy is nevertheless a fundamental issue.

24-FRAME DIGITAL VIDEO

Another solution is to work on a system that cuts 24-frame digital information. Avid's Film Composer is one of the best-known systems with which to do this. The key is that when you digitize, the 24-frame approach essentially undoes everything that occurred in the telecine process. It undoes three:two pull-down by removing the third field of every other frame. It also removes the 0.1 percent slowdown. With the film and captured video at 24 fps, a one-to-one frame relationship between film and video can occur. Theoretically, the output of edge numbers could be completely honest, eliminating the necessity of a workprint. This, however, is not the approach that has been adopted. What most features are doing is going ahead and generating a workprint, transferring the sound to mag stock, and doing a conventional sync-up of the sound (see chapter 17). Rather than interrelate time code and edge numbers, the film is given an independently introduced set of *code numbers*—a system that has been standard practice in Hollywood for years (see "Coding and Edge Numbering" in chapter 17 for a complete description). The edit is done in a 24 fps digital environment, and the editing crew uses time code and code numbers to conform not the original but the *workprint* to what is done in the NLE edit. The workprint is used for screening and eventual conforming of the original. As suggested earlier, correct transfer to video is absolutely essential for this to work.

Although this option still is used extensively, another possibility that has seen a great rise in use over recent years is either transferring straight to a 24-frame video format or shooting in a 24-frame digital video environment from the start—the latter approach leaving film out altogether. The Sony 24p system has been mentioned previously as has the fact that George Lucas is shooting the most recent *Star Wars* episode on a "Panavised" version of the camera. Along with the 24-frame version, a number of projects are being shot on the 25-frame PAL version of these cameras. Either way, entrance into the Avid, or any similarly capable system, and potential interrelationship with a film original become substantially more straightforward. Still, there are critical issues to be addressed.

Why create a workprint?   Why go to the added expense of creating a workprint and the added labor costs of cutting a workprint to an NLE decision list? Hollywood has experimented with this endlessly and has come to the conclusion that finishing in a digital environment and outputting a set of edge numbers, even when done in a 24-frame environment, is not workable. There are many reasons for this, but the following are three critical ones:

■ As suggested in chapter 15, camera crews found that they needed a workprint anyway to check their work. The camera crew needs to be able to evaluate the condition of the film, looking for scratches, dirt, lightstruck sections, focus problems, or any flaws that might not show up on a video representation. To save hard drive space, many features digitize at a low resolution, exacerbating the problems of evaluating the technical quality of the shots. The producers of one independent feature film that went the NLE route without a workprint were horrified when they got their answer print back, a few days before the premiere, and found some shots that were slightly, though unacceptably, soft. At that point there was no recourse. Substituting other shots would require replacing sound, remixing, and striking new prints, both an economic and temporal—given that their premiere was a few days away—impossibility.

Equally important, the camera crew and everyone else involved needs to know how the film has exposed. The shallower latitude of the video image can misrepresent the shadow areas recorded on the film. Understanding latitude differences is critical. In addition, video colorists can often create color and exposure effects in the transfer that are not possible when the final print is made (the reverse is true as well). On the previously mentioned film, the colorist thought he was helping the DP by compensating for some missed exposures. But when the compensations could not be or were not duplicated in the final film print, lighting continuity was compromised in a number of scenes.

■ Films headed for theatrical release are meant to be seen on a screen. During editing, watching a film on a monitor is acceptable to evaluate cuts, general pacing, and narrative cohesion, but when the discussion turns to how a film will do in the theater, a theatrical presentation is required. Film producers generally test their projects with both peers and general audiences before creating the final product. Both you and your viewers can look at it on the small box as many times as you want, but nothing substitutes for the experience of viewing the work in a theater. The presence of an audience, of whatever level of sophistication, is a must for general evaluation. You will feel every flaw magnified many more times when you sit in a room with either peers or strangers than when you see it on the monitors of an NLE system.

■ Negative cutters generally found printed lists to be a problematic guide to conforming the original. Although most of them have adapted to this new reality, the bottom line is that mistakes are simply more possible without the very real edited workprint sitting in front of you to check your work against. It is somewhat like being lost in the woods without a compass. The sun may give basic guidance, but you are never 100 percent sure of your bearings. If a negative cutter starts to question the accuracy of the list, there is absolutely nothing real to check the work against.

Although the need to generate a workprint had a big impact on the choice of NLE systems, the basic issue is still the synchronization of sound and picture. NTSC editing can give temporal accuracy but not frame accuracy. In addition, editors have found the steps that NTSC-based systems impose for checking frames to be an impediment to creative engagement with the material. It is difficult to focus on pacing and the like when there is a constant bombardment of technical requirements driving your cuts.

The feature world is thus integrating NLE edits with conventional film finishes. Though one never knows what is on the horizon, this method does not look like it will change significantly in the foreseeable future. The big change will come only when film prints are no longer the means of delivering a motion picture to a large audience. Digital delivery and projection is undoubtedly part of the future. The questions are when, and whether, they will completely replace film.

17

Cutting Picture and Sound

COVERING the mechanics of editing presents a number of pitfalls. Clearly, the practical aspects of editing must be introduced before going through the detailed finishing processes of a film, whether the final version is cut on film or on an NLE system. And yet the details of how a film is finished must inform all decision-making as the cutting is done. This chapter presents the traditional chronological sequence in which films are edited, as well as the parallel path that an NLE job would take. In both cases, however, you should familiarize yourself with the specifics of cutting the negative covered in chapter 18. There are many idiosyncrasies in the finishing process that simply must be understood.

The Film Edit

As stated earlier, flatbed editing tables are the norm when cutting film. Although the video revolution has forced many manufacturers of film equipment out of the market, there are still a number of flatbeds in common use, specifically Moviolas, Steenbecks, and KEMs. The six-plate, so named because it has two plates for each transport, one plate for feed, and one for take-up, is the table commonly available to students and independents. The more versatile eight-plates are preferred, because picture and sound are interchangeable on the fourth transport, giving the option of either picture searching or running a third mixtrack. Two-plates and four-plates are also available, both having been used extensively in television when news was shot on film; they receive limited use now. Several tables have interchangeable transports so the table can be switched between 16mm and 35mm.

The crucial concept to understand when cutting film and corresponding sound tracks is that all relationships between sound and picture are controlled by the frames. Once the tracks are threaded and locked together on the flatbed editing table, the picture frame has a corresponding sound frame on every mixtrack. Each frame on a sound head is theoretically in sync with the one that is in the picture gate. The relationship of each frame can be easily changed, but the goal is to create the relationships you desire.

Much of the mechanics of the cutting suggested here may appear complex at first, but these methods are relatively easy to master. The goal here is to describe some of the mechanical processes of cutting so you can refer to them during the actual process. Some descriptions may not become completely clear until you actually start trying some cuts. The terminology of the more popular flatbeds, such as *transports, locks,* and so on, are used, although effective editing can also be done on the bench, as well as on the older uprights.

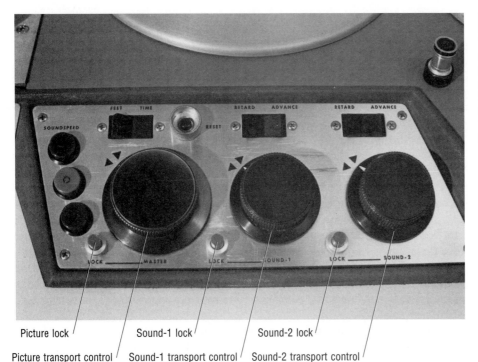

17-1

The transport controls and locks control the movement of the film and what tracks are interlocked to what other tracks

The control panel of the Moviola M77-AH

Picture lock

Picture transport control

Sound-1 lock

Sound-1 transport control

Sound-2 lock

Sound-2 transport control

THE CONTROL PANEL

The knobs and buttons on the control panel control the movement of the film and which tracks are interlocked to which other tracks. **SEE 17-1** Manufacturers employ a number of approaches to how a control panel works, but the general theory is consistent from one table to the next.

Transport controls   Each twist knob, called a *pot (potentiometer),* controls an individual transport, allowing you to run sound and picture independently. These hand controls can vary speed from creeping frame by frame to more than 100 fps; the maximum fast-forward speeds vary with manufacturers. The transports can be run forward or in reverse.

Sound-1 and sound-2 locks   The lock buttons do what their names suggest. By depressing the sound-1 lock, the first sound track is locked to the picture. The sound-2 lock does the same for the second sound transport. When the lock buttons are depressed, all rolls are fed at precisely the same rate across the sound heads and picture gate, thus providing sync. The sound tracks are said to be *slaved* to the picture pot. When a lock button is depressed, the corresponding pot no longer functions. This lock is electronic on some tables, mechanical on others.

Picture lock and soundspeed   Depressing the picture lock locks the picture pot to the soundspeed buttons at the left of the control panel. With this button the picture and any sound tracks locked to it are run at soundspeed (24 fps).

PRACTICAL CUTTING CONSIDERATIONS

Almost all cutting is done to the left of the transports. When you set up the starting hole punches and pass the film and mixtracks from left to right through the transports, you are in effect "committing the act of sync"; that is, any tracks that are locked together are in sync as they are fed through the transports. Clearly, permanency

When marking a frame, put the mark right in the middle of the frame

Cut on frame to right of mark

is fragile in this description of sync. You merely need to unlock the tracks or cut in different frames to vary the relationships between picture and sound. But the goal is to create and finalize the relationships between sound and picture that you want.

The process of cutting sound requires frequent marking of the magnetic stock, both designating cut points and identifying specific events in the sound. When marking a frame, put the mark right in the middle. **SEE 17-2** If you mark on the frame line, it might be unclear later which frame was being identified. In the context of this chapter, *cutting at the mark* means cutting at the first frame line to the right. You may eventually work out other methods, but for now consistency and clarity are key goals.

The terms *head* and *tail* are both used frequently in these discussions. **Head** is the beginning of a shot or roll; **tail** is the end of a shot or roll. As a film is set up on the bench or flatbed, the footage (the feed reel) is placed on a plate on the left side, with take-up occurring on the right. As the film travels, heads will be on the right and tails on the left.

Care should be taken to keep the workprint clean and trouble free while editing. The dirtier it gets, the harder it is to evaluate. In commercial situations clients or funders may view the film, so you will want to have a clean product with which to impress them.

The NLE System Edit

The general features of a typical NLE edit layout are outlined in chapter 1. Here is a quick review: Most programs have a **bin** for storing captured shots, a **viewer** for looking at and analyzing the shots, a **timeline** for putting together the edited program, and a **preview window** to monitor the edited project. Although NLE software almost universally calls the individual pieces of media **clips,** they will be referred to here as **shots** so as not to become too schizophrenic in the passage back and forth between film editing and NLE.

NLE systems are designed to be used by editors with different working styles. They employ multiple paths to execute the same function—designed for people who like to be keyboard-based, for those who prefer to work from menus, and for editors who work primarily with the mouse. Many NLE functions go by different names and forms in different software, but the general approach is almost always similar.

A number of typical functions found in NLE system windows need to be considered. The **playhead,** is generally a scrolling line that moves horizontally, indicating where you are in the clip or program. **SEE 17-3** There is a playhead in the viewer as well as in the timeline, the latter of which is usually tied to another one in the preview window. To move a shot into a specific place in the timeline, you generally position the playhead where you want the shot to go, then drop in the shot. The same work, as well as many other things, can also be done by typing the time code numbers into the appropriate places. The time code of the shots is displayed in a box in the viewer. Time code will also be created for the program, usually starting at 0:00:00:00 at the beginning of the timeline. Program time code generally shows up in a box in the preview window. The viewer and the preview

The playhead indicates the exact position within shots and the edited program itself
Final Cut Pro

window also have shuttle controls to *scrub* through the picture at whatever rate desired. Frequently, the arrow keys on the keyboard can be used for single-frame functions and to move between edits, a very useful function that is often found in other places as well. There will generally be a folder and/or menu choices for dissolves, fades, and a host of other effects. There should also be options for marking frames for future reference and other applications. The Toolbar in Macintosh Final Cut Pro (FCP), and its similar brethren in other NLE programs, also has many useful trimming and manipulating features.

Although analog *cuts-only video* systems, so named because you could do only cuts and no effects, are deservedly fast becoming a thing of the past, many of their general features have been assimilated into NLE systems. *Assemble editing* was the bane of the old analog method, but NLE has a much more humane approach for the harried editor. With analog the editor was forced to start at the beginning and build the show shot by shot. There was no way to go back to trim and refine earlier edits. In NLE the editor still generally assembles the project from the beginning but with complete freedom to go in and fine-cut the project. If the NLE editor uses the assemble edit function in the middle of a program, the added shot simply pushes all the material already in the timeline back, an outcome that was not possible in cuts-only analog editing. *Insert editing* is more for adjusting something that has already been edited in the timeline. The new shot overwrites the shot currently in the timeline, eliminating it rather than pushing everything back. All NLE programs have functions similar to assemble and insert, although they frequently use different names. FCP is the most confusing, with the insert function called Overwrite and the assemble function, just to confuse matters and stay away from copyright infringement, called Insert.

As suggested, all NLE software systems have different options to execute the same editorial procedures. FCP is no different, with a number of ways to bring things into the timeline. One way is to click on the chosen picture in the viewer and drag it to a menu embedded in the preview window (called the *canvas* in FCP) that gives options for whatever editing function you want. **SEE 17-4** There are also buttons to click at the bottom of the canvas that will execute the desired function. To further increase redundancy (a redundancy in and of itself), one can also drag the shot from the bin or viewer straight onto the timeline.

17-4

There are a number of
ways to perform assemble
and insert edits in all
NLE systems
Final Cut Pro

All viewers have methods for marking in- and out-points of the clips while they are being analyzed. There are either buttons on the window, keyboard com-0mands, functions in the menus, or all three. You scrub the shot and determine where you want to enter and exit the shot. You click "mark in" for entrance and "mark out" for exit. In initial stages doing general in- and out-points for both sound and picture is fine, but eventually you will want to be more discriminating in taking different amounts of audio and picture. Rationales for doing this are covered in the ensuing sections, but this allows you to overlap dialogue on other character's shots, finesse ambience differences between shots, and a host of other things. To do this in FCP, you use the menu function Mark Split. The submenu of Mark Split allows you to mark separately both video and audio ins and outs. Editors may handle this in different ways, but for complex projects this will be the norm.

Linking, a process that is not analogous to anything in cuts-only editing, is a frequently used option by many editors who are working with a film-related project. Sound and picture that were not already together in the capture process often needed to have a link created between them so they do not drift during editing. This is particularly true of picture and location sound that has to be matched. Linking is usually found in a menu and/or incorporated by a keyboard command.

Film: Preparing to Edit Sync Sound

Although many film departments justifiably have students start editing to sound effects and music tracks, the logical starting place for understanding the relationship between sound and image is working with *production sound*—the sync tracks. For those with experience in basic video editing, handling synchronous sound in film may appear cumbersome. The editorial staff must perform a number of procedures to prepare the film for viewing and cutting. A typical film takes days of prep work before you can start making any creative decisions.

Of the many things that should be done, two processes cannot be avoided: syncing up and creating the first assembly. *Syncing up* refers to matching the production sound, which has been recorded separately, with the image. Creating the *first assembly*, also called *stringing out*, involves choosing the desired takes and putting them in the order called for in the script. Two other processes are optional but highly recommended: ink number coding and A & B rolling the sound tracks. Both can save beginners many headaches. Though A & B rolling can be done at this time, the practical and theoretical aspects of this process are discussed later in this chapter in the section on actual dialogue cutting.

Professionally, syncing sound and picture is done on the editing bench. It can be done on a flatbed, but that is not recommended. It may look easier, but the process is very exacting and mistakes can be made because the relationship of frames is more fluid on the table. Syncing on the bench requires that picture and sound logs be completed scrupulously and the slate clearly filmed on location. Any discrepancies will cause confusion, particularly for novices. Whether on bench or flatbed, the logs themselves are indispensable for all cutting, and most questions should be easily answered by consulting them.

The methods of syncing, preparing rolls, setting up leaders, and cutting all the sound are very standardized in a professional editing room. This standardization maximizes efficiency when the editing crew is going through massive amounts of footage. It also sets up cues so that everyone involved in cutting, printing, and sound-mixing procedures will understand how the rolls are to be threaded in the various machines. Detailing all the procedures, codings, and markings is beyond the scope of this text, and several of them may not be that efficient for inexperienced editors working with a small amount of footage. Some general approaches are covered here, and what is presented should guide you through the initial stages and help you establish some good habits as well. That said, you should start becoming aware of what will be expected of you should you find yourself in a professional editing room.[1] The rationale behind the specific procedures and the general way in which editing is approached is *organization*. Without an organized approach, the creative aspects of cutting can and will be defeated.

SYNCING UP

The editorial staff starts with the production crew's work from the previous day. The film is picked up at the lab, and the mag stock transfers of the production sound, called *sync rolls*, are picked up from the transfer studio. Because the sound and the image are recorded separately, there are always different amounts of each. The assistant or apprentice editor must manually match them up. The hit of the slate is the reference point used to match the visual and audio rolls.

When you sync a roll of sound to a roll of picture, there are two basic procedures. The first sets up the rolls and puts the first shot in sync. Once the first shot is done, you employ the second procedure for every subsequent sync shot throughout the roll.

The first procedure is straightforward and logical: Thread the workprint into the picture transport and the sync-sound roll into one of the sound transports. With the transports not locked together, run the picture until the slate is hit. With some practice you will be able to control the transport to move the picture frame by frame and stop on the exact frame where the slate hits. This frame is easy to discern. The shot will start with the clapper/loader holding the slate bar up. You will be able to see the frame where the bar starts to come down and then the exact frame where

---

1. The responsibilities of and procedures used by the assistant and apprentice editors are detailed in Norman Hollyn's *The Film Editing Room Handbook* (Beverly Hills: Lone Eagle Publishing, 1990).

17-5

The hit of the slate is the reference point used to match the visual and audio

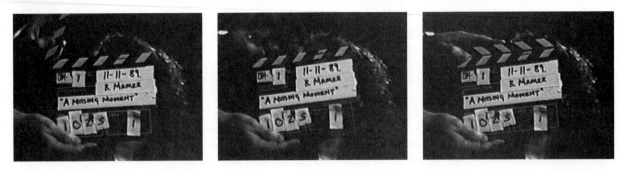

17-6

You can determine the first frame of sound—the attack—by moving the stock very slowly across the head

First frame of sound

it hits. The diagonal white lines of the bar and the board itself are designed so that you will be able to find the exact point where the two meet. **SEE 17-5**

With this frame resting in the picture gate, run the sound up to the hit of the slate. Play the sync track at roughly normal speed until you find the sound of the slate. It will be easy to find because it is accompanied by all the starting instructions and the verbal identification of scene and take by the 2nd AC or clapper/loader. Once you locate the slate, find the exact first frame of its sound.

Although the sound is not visible, it can be graphically represented. **SEE 17-6** You can determine this first frame, called the *attack,* by moving the stock very slowly across the head. The attack will be loud and raspy, as distinct from the silent frames before it. For future reference, use a permanent marker to indicate the exact frame where the slate starts. Lock the sound transport to the picture and you are set to go. At this point the first shot, and only the first shot, is in sync. Once the picture and the sound are set up, the second procedure is used to sync each subsequent take.

It is imperative that you find the exact first frame where the slate hits on both the sound and the picture. If this is handled carelessly, the shots will not be in sync. Once the slates are removed in the actual editing, the mistake will not be discernible and the shot will be wrong until the very end. If you are lucky enough to catch the problem at the mix, correcting it will be costly. If you do not catch it at the mix, it will be on screen in your final print. A mistake of a single frame may be difficult to see on a table, but when the film is magnified 300,000 times in a theater, it will be noticed by many. Mistakes of more than one frame will be visible to all.

One more thing must be done before rolling on to the next shot: With the transports still locked, roll back several feet toward the head and mark a picture frame and its corresponding frame on the sound roll. Roll these marks out and put a hole punch on each mark. This will be used as a reference point to load the rolls. Their positioning is somewhat arbitrary, because these punches will soon be replaced with the familiar countdown leader (see figure 17-12).

Once you have completed these setup procedures, roll on to the second shot. Nothing has to be done to the tail end of the first shot. The beginning of each new shot is always easy to identify because of the *flash frames,* the overexposed frames at the beginning of every shot. With the second shot, you will start the procedure that will remain consistent for all subsequent takes. It is broken down into simple steps

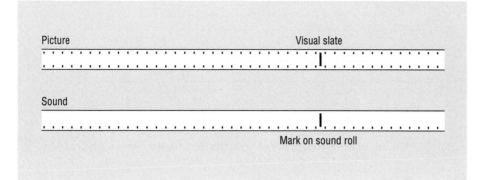

17-7

Step 1: Find the hit of the visual slate and mark on the audio straight across from it

(below) that are relatively straightforward. These steps will eventually be complicated by a number of issues that are important when working as an assistant or an apprentice in a professional setting, but those complications are easily surmountable once you understand the basic theory.

The following steps outline the second phase of syncing up and apply to all subsequent sync shots on the roll:

1. Find the hit of the visual slate and mark on the audio straight across from it.

2. Find the actual audio slate and mark it.

3. Roll the film out of the transports, cut from the first mark to the second mark, and splice the remaining pieces together.

Find the hit of the visual slate The hit of the visual slate is found in the manner previously described. Once you have the exact frame in the picture gate, mark the frame straight across from it on the audio track. **SEE 17-7** The positioning of this marked audio frame on the mag stock will be random, but it should occur in the start-up sequence ("Speed," "Camera," "Rolling," "Mark it").

Find and mark the audio slate With picture and sound still locked, roll to the actual audio slate. There is almost always more sound than image for each individual take, because the sound recorder is started before the camera in the sequence to initiate takes, so you will roll forward to find the audio slate. Find it in the manner described earlier and mark the exact frame. **SEE 17-8** You now have two marks on the audio: one on the frame that corresponds to the visual slate and the other on the actual audio slate.

17-8

Step 2: Find the actual audio slate and mark it

Step 3

Picture
Sound

A. Roll the film out of the transports, cut from the first mark to the second mark...

Picture
Sound

B. ...and splice the remaining pieces together

Roll out, cut, and splice the pieces Roll your marks out to the left of the transports. Cut from the right of the first mark to the right of the second mark. **SEE 17-9A** Then splice the remaining pieces together. **SEE 17-9B**

This simple process has to be repeated for every sync take throughout the entire roll. Before attacking the remaining slates, however, there are a number of ground rules to keep in mind. First, as with virtually all other sound and image cutting, all the splicing in the syncing-up process is done to the *left* of the synchronizer or transports. Any cutting to the right will disturb shots that are already synced, causing the rolls to go out of sync. Second, once you have locked the picture and the sound together in the setup procedure, keep them locked. If you unlock either picture or sound, you take them out of sync. Although picture and sound are relatively easy to get back in sync by going back to the last synced scene or the hole punches at the head, unlocking the tracks can lead to errors and consequently time-consuming repairs of sync. When you clearly understand what you are doing, this may not be important. Until then, *keep the tracks locked.* Third, "close" counts only in horseshoes and grenades. You have to find the *exact* first frame of the slate on both sound and image. If you make a mistake of a frame or two, it will follow you all the way through editing, mixing, and the final print.

With the exception of *MOS* shots, the picture should be kept intact and all cuts should be on the sound. Even the botched takes should be synced and left on the roll. All MOS shots and nonsync sound effects that the sound mixer recorded on location should be removed from the rolls and rolled onto separate cores. All pieces should be clearly labeled once they are removed from their original rolls. On the film tape used to close the rolls, write the scene and take numbers. To cross-reference with the pieces of film themselves, the assistant will also make lists with brief descriptions of both effects and MOS shots. Keeping this material organized is important to efficient editing and one of the primary responsibilities of the assistant editor.

Coding and Edge Numbering

Many postproduction facilities provide a service called *coding,* the process referred to in the section on film matchback at the end of chapter 16, wherein an entirely new series of code numbers are inked-in on both sound and picture. With *edge numbering,* the low-tech equivalent, one goes through the synced-up film and physically transfers all the edge numbers on the picture onto the corresponding frames of the sound. The former approach is vastly preferable, relatively affordable, and is the professional norm. Code numbers are usually composed of four letters followed by four numbers. **SEE 17-10** For the low-tech filmmaker with limited resources, edge numbering is easily done by hand with a permanent marker. Code numbers are preferable, largely because the edge number has to be held up to light and squinted at, whereas the other can be read easily.

Whichever approach you choose, the initial purpose is to provide a reference for sync. Once actual editing is started, you will obviously be cutting out the slates. Without the slate as a reference, the numbers allow you to reestablish sync when you make the unavoidable errors in removing sound or picture. The more experienced you become, the less this will be an issue. Mistakes should diminish, although it is still crucial to have a reference if any questions arise. The numbers can be used to correct everything from big errors to questions of individual frames. There is nothing more frustrating than looking at a shot and not knowing if it is in sync; and nothing is as time-consuming as going in and shifting frames to see if it is correct.

Moreover, code numbers are critical in organizing the workprint. The assistant editor uses code numbers to log, identify, and store virtually all the footage. They are the standard way of referencing everything in the editing room. In the process of trimming frames, storing them, and trying to find them later, things can get very confused—a situation that is unacceptable in a professional situation though an occasional reality for inexperienced editors. If it is unclear whether there are frames missing in a cut you are attempting to restore, checking to see if there are twenty frames between the code numbers (or the edge numbers if the film is not coded) will answer any questions. If there are not twenty frames, further searches are necessary. If the frames turn out to be lost, they can be slugged in with black leader, because the frames still exist in the original. The number of needed slug frames can be determined by simply counting. Due to their extensive use, code numbers are used as the critical film reference points in the way the feature world is presently approaching matchback from digital edits to film.

Edge numbering by hand is done on the synchronizer. Before starting, double-check the rolls to make sure that all slates are in sync. Mag stock has a base and emulsion just like film, and the film must be set up so you are writing on the base (you will have to retransfer and resync the sound if you write on the emulsion). Set up the film so it is running the opposite way on the

17-10

Coding numbers on both sound and picture reels

synchronizer, that is, from right to left instead of left to right. Set up the reels so they run off the top rather than from the bottom. This will put the sprocket holes in the appropriate position for the teeth on the synchronizer and the base facing up. Write each edge number on the precise corresponding frame of the mag stock. Do this for all rolls. This is the less-preferred method, with the numbers being more cumbersome to reference. Edge numbering is time-consuming but, to avoid costs, writing the numbers is a viable alternative. Either way, whatever time is expended initially will be saved many times over when you start the actual creative part of editing.

First Assembly

Creating the *first assembly,* or *stringing out,* involves arranging the film in rough order: taking out the desired shots, organizing them, then putting them back together in order. On a short film, the entire piece may be strung out at this stage, whereas a feature may be done one scene at a time. Don't worry about every subtlety; all you are creating is a rough sequence. You use the whole shot in this process, eventually trimming it down to the appropriate length.

The first step is to evaluate the synced film and pick your *selects*—the version or take—of each shot that you consider the best for your purpose. There are several deciding factors in evaluation, most notably performance, continuity with other shots, overall compositional integrity, and sound quality. In conventional narrative films, performance tends to be the overriding factor, though shots with poor formal qualities, such as sloppy camera movement, are generally eliminated out of hand. You do not remove these selects during this evaluative process, but rather circle the chosen takes in the logs. Pulling them out is a separate procedure.

The first assembly should be done on a bench rather than on the flatbed. On a synchronizer the relationship between frames is exceptionally clear and, as with every other stage, precision is a must. Any errors in removing the shots will cause major headaches in trying to reassemble the film both in order and in sync. The film should be strung out with all the slates and other information still intact. One end product of the syncing-up stage is that the sound and picture for each shot are exactly the same length in terms of frames. When you pull the selects, pull the picture from the beginning flash frame to the ending flash frame and the corresponding piece of sound.

To cut out the identified select, roll to the flash frame at the head of the shot. Mark the flash frame and the corresponding frame on the mag stock. Roll the film out to the right of the synchronizer and cut at the marks (the first assembly is one of the few stages in which you cut on the right). Roll to the tail of the shot, hanging the head of it in the trim bin. Mark the first flash frame of the next shot and the corresponding frame on the sound. Roll the marks out to the right and cut. You now have two pieces, one sound and one picture, representing the entire take, each piece being precisely the same length, frame for frame. With film tape, label the scene by its number. Keeping the material organized when it is hanging in the trim bin is essential.

In this manner pull each desired shot out of the sync rolls. It is imperative that what you pull out has an equal number of sound and picture frames. Any error will mean that the film will be out of sync that number of frames from the mistake on. Do not hesitate to check the shots by measuring them against each other. Stretch the two pieces out side by side and match up the sprocket holes for the length of the shot. **SEE 17-11** Sometimes the mag stock might be slightly smaller, requiring constant adjustment to make sure you are going frame by frame. If the two pieces are not the same length, you have made a mistake that must be corrected. Although this method may at first seem odd and cumbersome, measuring sound and image against each other is the central approach to controlling and maintaining sync in editing. When you have finished pulling the

17-11

Measuring sound and image pieces side by side is the standard approach to controlling and maintaining sync

Comparing sound and image pieces by matching
the number of sprocket holes

17-12

Standardized countdown leader is set up at the beginning of the edited workprint

selects, they should all be numbered and hanging in the trim bin. It is now a matter of putting them back together in order, creating two new rolls—one picture, one sound—made up entirely of the selects.

Before putting the film back together, standardized leaders should be set up with reference points, called *head start marks,* for cueing up the separate rolls. This is done with **SMPTE Universal leader** (*SMPTE* stands for Society of Motion Picture and Television Engineers), which is also referred to as *Academy leader* or **countdown leader**. The leader is made up of the sequence of descending numbers familiar to most readers. **SEE 17-12** The sequence starts with 8 and descends to 2. Each number lasts for 24 frames (1 second), with the exception of the 2, which is a single frame. This frame with the 2, the **Academy 2,** is used to sync up all the other elements in the printing process. The frame right before the actual countdown sequence—the frame before the first 8—should also be noted. Labeled "picture start," it is the point from which all shots are identified for the technicians engaged in the process of creating a final print. The footage counter is zeroed on the synchronizer, and picture start is set up on the zero frame of the gang. If a shot needs special attention, it is identified in footage and frames from this point (see chapter 18 for further discussion). Countdown leader can usually be bought at a lab or a film-supply store.

Set up a countdown leader in one of the gangs of the synchronizer. There will be an arrow symbol with "splice here" printed underneath it 47 frames after the 2.

Cut in the first frame of picture where indicated

SEE 17-13 Cut your first shot in here, leaving its corresponding piece of sound in the trim bin.

For the sound, set up 10 to 15 feet of white leader in the gang across from the countdown leader. On this white leader, mark the frame corresponding to the first picture frame and cut in the piece of mag stock for the first shot. Now the first shot, picture and sound, is attached to these leaders in sync. To cue up the separate rolls, the frame corresponding to the Academy 2 frame must be indicated on the white leader of the sound roll. Mark the frame corresponding to the Academy 2 and replace it with a *sync beep* or *sync pop*—a single frame of mag stock cut out of a longer piece with a constant tone recorded on it. **SEE 17-14** When it runs across the sound head at 24 fps, it provides the familiar beep at the head of all film reels.

It is now a matter of taking the shots hung in the trim bin and cutting them onto these rolls in order. If the scenes have been properly numbered and organized on the set, this should be a simple process of following the scene numbers, but have a copy of the script handy to make sure that the sequence is correct.

17-14

The sync beep is a single frame of mag stock that provides the beep tone at the head of film reels

If you have been accurate in pulling the scenes out frame for frame, you should be able to put all the shots back together without the synchronizer. It is recommended, however, that you use the synchronizer to double-check your work. All first assembly cuts should be straight across from each other when you roll them into the synchronizer. If they do not correspond, you have made a mistake. When you have reassembled the takes, you should have one roll with the film in order as well as a number of outtake rolls.

Handling MOS shots is also an issue. If MOS shots are designed as inserts into longer shots, I tend to leave them on their cores to be cut in later. If they are key pieces that drive the narrative forward, I go ahead and string them out with slug against them.

Once you have chosen a take, do not assume that you are locked into that decision. With the take in the context of the other shots, you may notice a problem, say, continuity or timing that makes the shot unsuitable. Do not hesitate to go back to the outtakes to see if there is anything that better fits the specific situation. Another take may have shortcomings but better continuity characteristics. If the shot you have to discard has better line readings, it is often possible to insert the better dialogue into the preferred shot.

Avoid the temptation to mix any of these processes or make creative decisions at this stage. Keep your parameters focused. It is important to see the raw material in each stage before effectively making decisions about the next one. You also get into a groove with each process, becoming very efficient. Trying to make decisions prematurely will draw straightforward activities out to painful lengths.

NLE: Preparing to Edit Sync Sound

There are a number of ways to approach syncing up with an NLE system. It can be done manually in virtually the same manner as a film sync is done or, if time code was used in shooting on location, the sound can be electronically locked in the telecine process.

SYNCING UP

In the time code applications, a camera and recorder with time code capabilities are used on location. Sync-up can be done on the telecine either when a time code interface is done or simply in the old-fashioned way. There are two options here: jam sync and record run. In the *jam sync* method, a small black box that provides a time code start point is plugged into the camera in the morning and then similarly plugged into the recorder. Both the camera and recorder are given a time code start point and are then recording the same time code numbers on each medium. After transferring picture on the telecine, the sound time code is chased internally and the slates are lined up. All the telecine operator has to do is stand back and watch. Though many producers have not developed the confidence to do this, the buzz has been that you can throw away your slate. In the *record run* method, the sound recorder produces the time code, which is sent to the slate via radio transmitter. The slate, referred to as a *smart slate,* hears it and sends it to a rolling LED clock on its face. When the slate is hit, the time code numbers stop for a second or so at the instant of the hit, then pick up again the appropriate amount of time later. The telecine operator finds the stopped number on the slate, types it into the computer, and the computer finds the corresponding time code number on the sound and records the two together. In both cases sound and picture are transferred onto the same videotape, eventually captured, and locked together throughout the editing process. Sound and picture are represented as one clip in the bin but are still displayed separately on their respective timelines, though they are internally locked or linked together.

The playhead here is shown a few frames before the hit of the slate

For us average citizens who have to do manual syncing, the picture and the sound are captured separately. As with so many things in NLE, there are many ways to go about this, even in an individual software program. In FCP one way is to scrub on the picture until you find the exact frame where the slate hits in a manner similar to film. Once you find the exact frame, click on "mark in" and use the assemble edit function. Bring the playhead back to the head of the shot on the timeline, open the sound take, and search through the waveform for the slate. Although you can both hear and see its visual representation, the audio hit of the slate should show a major deviation from the center of the waveform. **SEE 17-15** Place the playhead on the first frame of the audio slate, click on "mark in," and again use the assemble edit function. The audio and picture will appear together in the timeline but must still be linked. Though the material that you need is present, it can be irritating that the synced shot starts at the hit of the slate. FCP and other software have a function that allows you to extend the material ahead of the slate if desired. It is recommended that the newly synced shot be dragged back into the bin and renamed, say from 10A-1 to 10A-1S (the *S* is for sync), so it can be stored and retrieved for later use.

Telecine or electronic syncing appears to be a much more efficient way of doing it, but independents and professionals alike have found that they can sync up inexpensively and in a short period of time, rather than paying for it at an expensive telecine session.

First Assembly

All notions of creating a first assembly are significantly different in video. In the old analog video-editing arrangement, the notion of putting all the shots on one tape and then trimming them down is antithetical to the way analog information is handled. Instead, cutting is designed to occur between a video deck with a tape of the source material and a record deck where you build the edited program from the beginning. When the next shot is desired, it is found on the source tape and, after the in- and out-points are determined, transferred to the edited master. Due to the similarity in setup between analog and digital editing, the same is generally the case in NLE. In a digital approach, shots could be trimmed; but although there may be some editing staffs that lay it all out in order, it is usually a matter of collecting all the clips for a scene in the bin and then drawing them out as needed.

Dialogue Cutting

The statement that "every cut is an adventure" could not be truer than in dialogue cutting. Getting each individual transition to work is challenging enough, but the shape of the entire scene must be considered as well. It is possible to get the cuts to work well on an individual basis and still find that the scene is slow or awkward. As suggested, although there is no single correct place to cut between any two shots, there are myriad wrong places. The goal in conventional dialogue cutting is to find the cut point where the natural rhythms of human speech are maintained, the movement matches appropriately, the pacing in relationship to other cuts is right, and, of course, the dramatic emphasis is considered.

Straightforward shot/reverse shot sequences are used here as examples. Dialogue cutting obviously becomes much more complex than the simple examples used here, but the principles presented are the starting point for even the most advanced cutting. In a sense these simple cuts act as a window into the more complex cutting that can be learned only by doing.

The first cut discussed is the *straight cut,* a cut that tends to be abrupt. Although this is a good starting point, the fundamental approach to all dialogue cutting is the *overlapping dialogue cut.* This simply means that the picture cuts come in the middle of lines of dialogue. In many cases we see a character responding before the speaker has finished speaking. While we look at a film, we are rarely aware that someone has made a conscious choice between different shots and transition points, and, particularly, that these choices affect our response and interpretation of what we are seeing.

STRAIGHT CUTS: FILM AND NLE

A *straight cut* is one in which a character finishes a line of dialogue, and you cut to the next shot with the second character delivering his or her line. It is simple to execute, although there are some complications with the sound. Eventually, you will find that most cuts are more complicated than the simple, arbitrary straight cut demonstrated here.

An example is the exchange of two lines of dialogue suggested in the section on storyboarding in chapter 5. In shot #1 John asks: "Do you want to go to the movies?" In the second shot, Andrea responds: "I don't know. What times are the shows?" The first assembly still has the entire shot, including all the verbal and visual directions: the director's "Cut" on the outgoing shot and the start-up calls, the mark of the slate, and the "Action" on the incoming shot.[2] **SEE 17-16**

In film all synchronization is based on the relationship of frames. The following is a fundamental principle of the mechanics of film editing:

◆ **RULE:** *Whenever you make a cut in one roll—sound or picture— there must be an equal and reciprocal cut in all other rolls.*

When cutting sync footage, if 20 frames are cut out of the picture, the sound roll is now that same 20 frames out of sync. To get back into sync, you have to cut out 20 frames of sound that correspond roughly with the picture frames. This undoubtedly brings up a host of questions, but keep the idea of cutting equal amounts of picture and sound in mind.

---

2. Although film travels in a natural left-to-right movement, it forces the dialogue and other audio information to be represented in reverse in the illustrations.

17-16

The first assembly still has the slate and all verbal directions

A. To establish a 1-second pause, you cut out all but 24 frames between the two lines of dialogue…

B. …and splice the pieces together

The first step in making a straight cut is to determine the length of the pause desired between the two lines of dialogue; that is, how much time you want to elapse between the end of the first line and the beginning of the second. Generally, the goal is to re-create the natural cadences and rhythms of human speech. Experienced editors cut to the inherent pace of the scene. For our purposes it is helpful to think of a pause as a specific number of frames. When you cut the mag stock, you are dealing with increments of $\frac{1}{24}$ second. If there are 24 frames between two lines of dialogue, the pause will be 1 second long. An 18-frame pause will be $\frac{3}{4}$ second, and so on.

If you want the pause to be 1 second long, you need to plan 24 frames between the end of the word *movies* and the beginning of the word *I*. Although this represents an arbitrary approach, it nevertheless illustrates the process. To start, find the *decay*—a term that describes how sound trails off and reverberates—of the word *movies,* count 12 frames toward the tail, and mark on both the audio and the picture. Then find the attack of the word *I,* count 12 frames toward the head, and again mark both audio and picture. **SEE 17-17A** Then cut from mark to mark on both rolls. **SEE 17-17B** As always, check the two pieces against each other to make sure that you are removing the same amount of sound and picture.

The two 12-frame extensions add up to the 1-second pause desired. Taking 12 from one side and 12 from the other is, of course, completely random in terms of the example. You just need the total to add up to 24. That we have paid little attention to the picture's content suggests how arbitrary an example this is.

Pauses are shorter than one at first expects. Screen time is much more intense and concentrated than real time. If one second feels long, five seconds can feel like an eternity. Normal conversations generally have pauses of a little less than one second. If the pauses are too short, the lines will seem stacked on top of each other and unnatural; and if the pauses are too long, the dialogue will sound stilted or mannered. Very quickly you will internalize this and not think about specific times of pauses. You will just cut it until it sounds right. The performers themselves often provide the pauses in situations where the camera covers lengthy exchanges of dialogue. For now it is helpful to think out the pauses in specific numbers of frames.

As stated, this type of cutting tends to feel very abrupt. It can be useful for interruptions and dialogue that needs a punch, but if all cuts are straight cuts, a scene can resemble a Ping-Pong match, with the perspective abruptly flipping back and forth. Oddly enough, straight cuts work better on television than they do in films. Given the financial limitations and brutal deadlines of the medium, their greater ease makes more sense. Editors who can make a cut quickly are valued in television. This does not mean that the shows could not be cut better and that overlaps would not be appropriate, but the straight cuts do not look as abrupt on TV as they do on the big screen.

In NLE you would play the first clip in the bin and determine the out-point. The notion of a pause is again pertinent here. Remember that the frame count is 30 frames per second if you are editing NTSC. You will get used to multiples of 30, rather than the 24 of film (and 24-frame digital). Drag the first shot to the timeline. Open the second clip in the bin, consider the pause, determine the in-point, and drag it in behind the first shot. Clearly, this leaves out notions of where the first shot starts and the second shot ends, but the theory is straightforward. The notion of the nondestructive edit further helps you "size" the shots on the timeline. **SEE 17-18**

17-18

The layout of a typical straight cut

OVERLAPPING CUTS: FILM AND NLE

The overlapping cut is the bread-and-butter of narrative dialogue cutting, both conventional and otherwise. An *overlapping dialogue cut* is one in which the transition from one shot to the next occurs during a line of dialogue. In simple shot/reverse shot sequences, a common example is to cut from the speaker to the respondent before the speaker has finished speaking.

In film editing there are two basic steps to making an overlap between two shots. Eventually, your cutting will become complex and sophisticated enough that these simple steps will appear overly schematic, but they should be helpful for starters.

1. Make the audio cut.

2. Make the picture cut, displaced from the sound cut.

Make the audio cut   The rhythms and cadences of human speech are again the determining factors in making this first cut. Decide what pause you want between the lines and cut, paying no attention to the picture. This will leave the next shot out of sync, the removed piece of sound representing the exact number of frames the following shot will be out of sync. **SEE 17-19** To restore sync, you remove an equal number of frames from the picture.

Make the picture cut, displaced from the sound cut   Using the removed piece of sound as a guide, make the reciprocal picture cut, only displace it from the sound cut you made in step 1. If you were to cut the picture at precisely the same place as the sound cut, the result would simply be a straight cut. A good approach for determining the displacement is to find where you want to exit from the first speaker. If you decide that you want to exit during the word "movies," you would mark on the picture across from the word. **SEE 17-20A** Cut at the mark and stretch the sound against the picture toward the tail, cutting out an equal number of picture frames. The resulting cut will exit speaker A during the word "movies," overlapping speaker B over the word. **SEE 17-20B** The opposite approach would be to evaluate the cut in terms of where you want to enter the second person's dialogue.

For both straight and overlapping cuts, always cut the shot long before cutting it short. That is, cut the pause slightly longer than you think will be appropriate. It is much easier to trim the shots than to replace removed frames. Inexperienced editors tend to fiddle too much with cuts, adding frames in and taking them out, leaving both picture and sound frames prone to damage. Single frames are hard to line up on the splicing block, frequently resulting in frames at slightly skewed angles. This can make a picture cut hard to evaluate, because it will jump at the gate. It also

17-19

Step 1: Make the audio cut

Step 2

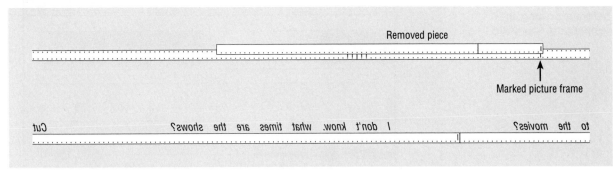

A. Make the picture cut, displaced from the sound cut...

B. ...resulting in an overlap

increases the possibility of the film's tearing on editing tables and in projectors. The sound is even more of a problem, because tight cutting on frames can increase glitches and dropout as the pieced-together area crosses the sound head. Keep in mind that the mag stock you are cutting is the mag stock that you will be taking to the final audio mix. Any imperfections will be difficult to keep out of the sound track.

One of the major reasons film editors never really accepted analog cuts-only video editing is that the systems made overlapping cutting very difficult, if not impossible. NLE systems make any kind of cut possible, and overlapping cuts are relatively straightforward. When picture and sound are linked, they can be shortened and lengthened individually while remaining together. Here different systems have diverse approaches for handling the overlap. Some require unlocking the sound to handle the elements separately, and others require handling the overlapped picture as a transition in the effects area. Essentially, what happens is that, rather than remove equal amounts of sound and picture from continuous pieces, one simply trims each individual clip to the amount desired and then fits the two pieces together like a jigsaw puzzle. **SEE 17-21** Although the parameters of the clips could be determined in the bin, it is easiest to bring the complete clips into the timeline and make decisions there, requiring nondestructive editing. The layout would be very similar to what was envisioned in film. If one or the other has not been shortened enough, it simply has to be trimmed appropriately to fit.

As suggested, the overlapping dialogue cut is the mainstay of conventional film editing, particularly cutting that attempts the invisible style associated with realism and the Hollywood commercial film. Fluidity is the key. The cuts are masked by being put in the middle of the dialogue, where they are least likely to be noticed. The technique also fits into the great tradition of dramatic emphasis, with focus on responses frequently being more important than showing the speaker.

17-21

Many NLE systems require that you "break sync" before executing an overlapping sound cut

Cutting Nonsync Sound and Picture

Cutting in effects, music, and narration makes up most of the rest of the editor's work. The sequence on a commercial feature is as follows: The editor edits the picture with dialogue until an acceptable cut of the film is produced. All editing on the picture is then declared finished, called *picture lock*, denoting that the picture will not be touched again and that all subsequent cuts will be in additional sound. Picture and sync-sound rolls are then turned over to the sound-effects and music editors. All their work is done on separate rolls, not cut into the sync rolls, to facilitate effective final sound mixing.

Effects, music, and narration in film are generally cut into *slug rolls*—rolls of junk picture or leader into which the nonsync sound is cut. Some source for long, uninterrupted stretches of good-quality slug will have to be located. In NLE sync sound is on the timeline against the dialogue. The number of tracks the software employs will play a big role in how complex the rest of the sound can be, though exporting the audio to proprietary sound software is common (see the last section of this chapter).

FILM: CUTTING SOUND EFFECTS

All the rolls used need to have reference points that correspond to the Academy 2. First set up a slug roll in the unused sound transport. Roll the Academy 2 on the countdown leader right in front of the gate. With the lock control, lock the slug roll to the picture and mark the frame straight across from the 2. Roll out the locked tracks and put a punch or cut a beep on the frame you just marked on the slug track. This frame is now lined up with the Academy 2 and is the reference for all future cueing of the rolls. What is referred to here as a slug roll would probably just be called a *mixtrack* in a commercial situation, and, again, clear leader would be used. These new rolls must nevertheless be distinguished from the sync rolls.

A film on which I was the sound mixer can serve as a good example of some of the hows and whys of effects cutting. It was a period piece, taking place in the 1840s, and featured several shots of a man chopping wood. Usable production sound was impossible, because the location was near a four-lane highway as well as being at the end of an airport runway (I think all locations are). For this reason all affected scenes were shot MOS, and the individual sound effects were collected later. This audio was transferred to mag stock, the result being a large roll of sound effects.

There are a number of approaches to cutting an effect like this, but one standard way is to find the desired effect in the sound-effects roll and cut it out. This entails running the effects on the flatbed at normal speed while listening for the appropriate sound. Once you have determined the effect you want, find the frame that has the attack and mark it with a permanent marker. This is similar to finding the attack of the slate. Generally, it is a good idea to cut a few frames before the actual sound. **SEE 17-22** These few frames of ambience before the effect allow the *rerecording mixer*—the studio employee who runs the mixing board at the final mixdown—time to soften the cut if necessary. Mark the last frame of the piece you want to take out as well. Be careful not to cut the decay too soon or it will sound incomplete, an outcome that will cause problems at the mix. A problem like this may not necessarily be unsolvable, but it will require expensive time to fix.

17-22

Cutting a few frames before the actual sound allows the rerecording mixer to soften the cut if necessary

17-23

A. To incorporate a sound effect, mark the frame on the picture roll and the corresponding frame on the slug roll…

B. …and splice in the effect

When the effect is cut out, you will have a piece of mag stock—9 frames in this example—with a single mark on it. Hang this in the trim bin, being careful to label it clearly by writing directly on the mag stock with a permanent marker or by using film tape.

The next step is to find the picture frame across from which you want the sound to be set up. This can be done by moving the film very slowly through the viewer or editing table. The individual frames will show a sequence of the movement. In the wood-chopping example, you would find the frame with the ax up in the air. The next frame might show the ax coming down. Then you can find the exact frame where the ax hits the wood. Mark this frame and the frame directly across from it on the slug roll. **SEE 17-23A** Once the slug roll has been marked, splice the effect into it so that the mark on the effect replaces the original mark on the slug roll. To accomplish this, cut on the slug roll the same number of frames before the mark, 2 frames in this example, as are on the effect to be cut in. **SEE 17-23B**

This approach can be streamlined on a six-plate, combining the process of searching for the appropriate effect with the cutting. Lock the picture together with a synced slug track in the first transport; the slug roll should be punched as described at the beginning of this section. Use the second sound transport for the unlocked sound-effects roll. Find the exact visual frame where you want the effect and leave it in the picture gate. Then listen to the unedited sound effects on the unlocked second transport. You can line up the desired effect with the visual, lock the second transport, and see and listen to it in sync. Once you find something you like, simply cut the sound effect from the unedited effects roll to the locked slug roll in the first transport.

The cutting of sound effects is generally a painstaking operation. Much of the extra sound heard in films is cut in individually. A representative example of the nature of effects cutting is the work of the footsteps editor, a credit frequently seen in British films. The footsteps editor literally goes through the entire film, cutting in the sound of footsteps as the characters move. While recording production sound, microphones are generally positioned to record the voice, so the sounds of footsteps are either too soft or completely nonexistent. The footsteps that are cut in are usually so subtle that they are not recognized on a conscious level. Their absence, however, can leave a scene with an otherworldly feel.

FILM: CUTTING TO MUSIC

Cutting to music has always been a popular starting place for students learning how to cut picture to sound. With the advent of music videos, it has become an even more significant part of the field. In the heyday of the Hollywood studios, music was generally timed to footage that was already edited. The composer, a full-time studio employee who produced multiple film scores a year, would score to the length of shots, complete scenes, or sequences (24 picture frames corresponding to 1 second of time in the composed music). The studio's orchestra would perform while viewing the edited film. The conductor could thus control the pace of the music to conform to the elapsed time of a given section of film.

Although this method has not been discarded completely, the norm today is to use a prerecorded piece of music and manipulate the picture to conform to its timing, pace, and rhythm. There are no house orchestras; that role is now performed by established orchestras hired for contract work. The old approach is still used occasionally but not with the same frequency; the facilities designed to time performance to projected picture are few and far between. As even the most casual viewer knows, music videos are prerecorded, and the song is played back as the performers lip-sync the lyrics. The prerecorded track is used as the guide to the timing of all the visuals.

The key to cutting image to music is to think of the sound as a specific length of magnetic film stock. A song that is, for instance, 5 minutes long will be represented as roughly 185 feet of film. Punch a frame in the beginning of the transferred mag stock, setting it to 0 feet and 0 frames on the frame counter. Specific events in the music, the singer hitting and holding a high note, for instance, can then be located and logged as occurring at specific footage and frames. You might find, for instance, that the first notes of the song start at 1 foot, 12 frames. The singer might start singing at 3 feet, 6 frames, and so on. Once you have these lengths, specific images can be cut against the sound.

The music can be further broken down into measures and even beats. Most music is in time signature, 3/4 and 4/4 time being two standards. Taking a song that is in 3/4 time as an example, you can make some determinations about the timing in frames. You might find that a specific measure is, for instance, 45 frames long or roughly 1.9 seconds. In 3/4 time each beat then occupies 15 frames. If the tempo increases or decreases, these measurements change as well.

With the sound analyzed, you can cut the image to the music to create very specific relationships. There are two lines of picture at the bottom of the following illustration to represent two possible approaches to cutting to the beat. **SEE 17-24**

17-24

With sound broken down to specific lengths of stock, you can cut an image to the music to create very specific relationships

If you wanted a shot to correspond to the precise length of a measure, it would be trimmed to 45 frames and cut to the beginning of the measure. If instead you wanted each new image to come at a beat in the music, each shot would be 15 frames long and started with the first beat. Persistent cutting on beats and measures would undoubtedly become schematic and predictable, but the approach can be applied in a less rigid manner.

FILM: CUTTING VOICE-OVERS

Voice-overs and narration are handled in a fashion similar to that for music, except that voice-overs generally offer more opportunity for manipulation. Once the recorded voice is transferred to mag stock, the text is represented as a specific length of film. Just as in the discussion of cutting to music, visuals can be positioned against specific events in the sound. Given certain limitations voice-overs can be cut and conformed to the visuals as desired, depending on the size and length of the text being spoken.

The first step is to get a good, clean recording of the speaker. Be sure to use a high-quality recorder and, more important, a high-quality microphone. Choose a speaker who has a strong, clear voice. Many people do not have "broadcast-quality" voices, and there may be intelligibility problems. Any weak link in the chain will cause difficulties down the road. Do everything in your power to obtain as clean a recording as possible. Use a sound-recording booth if one is available. If not, find an acoustically dead room and record at a time when there will be little or no interference.

Transfer this audio to mag stock—do not cut the original tapes. The following illustration gives a representation of the transferred mag stock. **SEE 17-25** Just as with music, the shots can then be cut to the desired length and positioned against the track. Pauses and line muffs can be changed or eliminated altogether through cutting the mag stock. If you identify certain events in the voice-over that you want to have specific images against, they can be located and the picture cut to match.

17-25

Narration is transferred to mag stock and can either be manipulated to match picture or have the picture matched to it

Mag stock

←——— Speech

17-26

To match specific images against certain audio events, you can slug black leader against the sound and cut in the appropriate images

One approach, which also works with music, is to slug black leader against the sound and cut in the images you know you want against the appropriate events. If you determined that you wanted shots 1, 2, and 3 to be against events A, B, and C, respectively, you could position them and address all the interim material later. **SEE 17-26** Again, pauses in the speech can either be shortened or lengthened by cutting the mag stock. If anything is lengthened, the interim space should be filled with slug. Unless there is music or some other covering sound, this will require some ambience to be cut on another track to fill the hole.

In the studio newsreel days, the picture was often cut first, then a narrator came in and read his spiel in a soundproof booth with the picture projected in front of him. Given the way the documentary form has evolved, the trend has been to record the narration first and then fit the picture to it. Although this has become the preferred method, it sometimes entails compromising visual efficiency to fit proscribed verbal timing.

NLE: CUTTING SOUND EFFECTS, MUSIC, AND VOICE-OVERS

Here the similarity in approach to film is apparent. Music and voice-overs are brought into the timeline and represented as a specific amount of time. Music can be scrubbed over and analyzed for specific events and measures and beats. Clips can then be fitted in where desired. Voice-overs can be trimmed and moved at will, either against picture or by themselves.

17-27

For a reaction shot, you replace the frames from the sync take with the same number of frames from the MOS shot

Effects are similarly easy. An effects clip can be opened in the bin and scrubbed on for in- and out-points. Once identified the clip is dragged onto the timeline and dropped into position. Although these types of cuts can be executed on an NLE system, it is very common to export the tracks to software specifically designed for sound editing (see "The NLE Mix" in chapter 18).

MOS Inserts: Film and NLE

Cutting shots that were executed without recorded sound takes on a variety of forms. In the most straightforward manifestation, MOS shots are used to break away from a character who is speaking. Called *reaction shots* or *inserts,* they are used either to show a reaction or to transition from one take to another. This is similar to the *cutaway,* but MOS inserts tend to have much more specific purposes. A cutaway is often poorly used as a repair or filler shot, but a well-placed MOS shot can be an important element, giving a flash of the eyes, a nod of the head, or some similar response as much weight as a line of dialogue.

The insertion of a reaction shot of one character into a long speech by another character is an example of this. In a case like this, the cuts are reasonably uncomplicated. If the goal is to cut to a character responding to someone's speech, you have to replace the frames removed from the sync take with the same number of frames from the MOS shot. In NLE you would simply drag in the desired clip and drop it where you wanted, with the new clip chosen to eliminate the original section.

One approach is to look at the sync shot and determine and mark where you want to exit and reenter the speaker's picture. In film you cut out the piece and identify an equal number of frames from the MOS shot that you want to use. Insert them in place of the removed section, using the removed piece as a guide for the length of the MOS piece. **SEE 17-27** If you cut out 72 frames of sync picture, you need to replace them with a 72-frame MOS piece. The speaker will pick up the speech in sync, because the eliminated sync frames have been replaced with an equal number of MOS frames. In NLE you would generally select a piece of a clip that was close to the same length, drag it in, then trim it to the correct length.

The only question is whether the length of the MOS insert is determined by what you want to take out of the sync shot or by what you want to insert. This depends on your goal in a given situation. You may want to be away from the speaker for a specific period, for pacing reasons or whatever. In this case you would conform the length of the insert to this requirement. On the other hand, you may have a good MOS reaction shot that is a specific length, in which case that determines how much you take out of the sync shot.

Although this example suggests an unmolested sound track, the cut to an MOS insert affords the editor the opportunity to manipulate the audio. If an actor gives a

17-28

When undesired material is edited out, the jumps in footage are covered with inserted reaction shots

perfect performance for the first part of a take but muffs the second part, you can cut between it and a take with a better second half. The jump resulting from the cut between the two takes can be covered in the manner just described. The same is true if the performance has a pause that is either too long or too short. In the former case, the offending frames would be trimmed out and covered by a cut to another character or object. In the latter case, slug frames would be used and attendant ambience cut on later mixtracks.

This approach for covering jumps in the footage can clearly also be used to cover jumps in interview footage like those described in the section on shot/reverse shot in chapter 3. **SEE 17-28** The ability to cover up problems can be a lifesaver, but use this technique judiciously, as it is often obvious that reaction shots are being placed to cover mistakes or soften awkward visual transitions. Eventually the approach to MOS will become more complex, with planned cutaways from a speaker being only a small part of the handling of MOS material.

A & B Rolling Sync Sound

A & B rolling the sync mixtracks refers to *checkerboarding,* or alternating, the original sync mixtrack on separate sound rolls to facilitate the final mixing process. You create two rolls for the sync tracks instead of the single strand that has been discussed up to this point. All the odd-numbered sound takes would be on the first sound roll,

17-29

The A & B–rolled sound alternates from one mixtrack to the other

and all the even-numbered takes on the second roll, though it does not always work out quite so cleanly. Although there are subtle differences, A & B rolling is generally done in both the film and NLE approaches. In the string-out, A & B–rolled sound tracks would resemble the illustration above. **SEE 17-29** Like edge numbering, A & B rolling the sync sound before the actual editing is optional but is highly recommended for the beginner. It is, however, not so much a matter of *if* as of *when*. The process of separating your sound has to be done before you go to the mix anyway; it is just a question of whether you do it in the beginning stages of editing or in the last few days before the mix. If at the beginning, A & B rolling would be done after the first assembly is completed but before the creative part of editing— the actual cutting—starts.

Four important rationales for A & B rolling the sound are given here. The first two must be considered in sound cutting at all levels of production. The third and fourth rationales are more considerations for inexperienced editors working on smaller projects. Commercial films generally have sophisticated resources to address these last two issues. Although the following requirements are presented in the context of a conventional film mix, the rationales can be extrapolated to laying out the sound on an NLE timeline as well:

- To facilitate volume control, equalization, and signal processing in the mix

- To allow interruptions and blending of dialogue

- To create ambience overlaps

- To avoid damaged splices and the problems associated with them

Volume control, equalization, and signal processing Each track in the mix is assigned to an individual channel on the mixing board. This channel will have a fader to control volume, as well as limited equalization capability. Each channel can also be assigned to sideboard signal-processing equipment, allowing for further equalization, reverb effects, echo effects, and other audio manipulations.

Thus each and every sound in your film will have the volume set for it in the mix and, if necessary, can be equalized or otherwise processed. If the sound for a shot is cut to the sound for the next shot, the rerecording mixer could not shift volume levels in the split second that the cut crossed the sound head, much less create any complex equalization. The slug between the takes allows the rerecording mixer time to anticipate and shift the necessary controls.

Interruptions and blending   It is impossible in the single-strand method to have an actor "step on" another actor's line of dialogue or to create any kind of *blending*, or layering, of dialogue. A & B rolling allows dialogue to be dropped on top of other dialogue. Robert Altman is famous for using this style of layered dialogue cutting. The frontier barroom scene that opens his *McCabe and Mrs. Miller* (Louis Lombardo, editor) has snippets of conversations underlying all foreground action. Although the cutting in this film includes other approaches to sound layering, sync tracks are frequently held and extended into surrounding shots.

Ambience overlaps   When executing any dialogue cut, you want to maintain the ambience that follows or precedes the voice, overlapping it between shots if possible. Also called *handles*, these **ambience overlaps** allow the rerecording mixer to soften any potential harshness of the cut. If there is substantial difference in the quality of ambience in any two shots, the sound may jump between the two levels if they are cut directly together. Despite efforts to avoid it, there will occasionally be gaps in the ambience where there is not enough audio to cover the pause. This is when the room tone that the sound mixer recorded on location comes in handy, with an ambience mixtrack created to cover any holes.

Damaged splices   Obviously, this applies to film only. As stated, editing film consists of trying different cuts until you find the one that works perfectly. You may like a cut one day and come back the next and wonder where on earth your mind was when you made that decision. If you decide that a cut is slow, you trim it down. If you decide a cut is too short, you add frames back in. Getting a cut right may take many attempts. This cutting and recutting can cause problems in the single-strand method. The cut becomes choppy, with several one- or two-frame cuts pieced together. With the picture this is not a significant concern, because you will be going back to the original.[3] But because this is the actual mag stock that will be used in the mix, too many quick cuts in a row can significantly affect audio quality. With the sound on alternating rolls, all trims and additions of frames made after the initial audio edit are cut in the slug, avoiding further splices in the mag stock. With limited time and resources in the editing room, it is better to keep the sound "mixable" all the way through the project.

The appropriate separation of sound is an issue for all the mixtracks and is essential for an efficient mix where the full potential of the sound can be fully explored (see "Film: Mixtrack Configurations" in chapter 18 for further discussion). Your sync sound is particularly critical, but if any or all of your mixtracks are a mess when you go to the mix, be prepared to have either an unpleasant mix or your project unceremoniously handed right back to you. A mix that is inappropriately configured is a clear sign to a mixer that the job is going to be one long headache.

With the NLE approach, there probably would not be much reason to separate the tracks as you go. Any separation of tracks could usually wait until just before the mix. If you found you needed "handles," the sound could be put on another track, and, if the system had nondestructive editing, it could be lengthened to provide some overlap.

---

3. This can actually pose a problem in compromising one's ability to evaluate the cuts as well as affecting how projectable the film is. When going to the mix or when working with clients of backers, you want as clean and trouble-free a version as possible.

A Typical Scene

As described, a significant part of the process of editing is building multiple sound tracks. Francis Ford Coppola's *Apocalypse Now* (1979) was said to have had more than seventy mixtracks. Jean-Luc Godard once made a feature film with only three mixtracks. When queried on why so few, he replied that it was because he had only three hands. Although individual films have their own requirements, the tracks for a typical project might look something like this:

Mixtrack 1:	*Dialogue*
Mixtrack 2:	*Dialogue*
Mixtrack 3:	*Extra dialogue and narration (if necessary)*
Mixtrack 4:	*Music*
Mixtrack 5:	*Additional music (if necessary)*
Mixtracks 6–10:	*Sound effects*
Mixtrack 11:	*Ambience*
Mixtrack 12:	*Additional ambience (if necessary)*

A scene from an independent feature that I worked on several years ago can serve as a good example of the way tracks are built. The scene involved a taxicab driver and his passenger caught in a traffic jam. In a single take, the passenger gets out and runs past the cars stalled in front of them to insert her business card under the windshield wiper of an arguing couple. Still in the same shot, she runs back to the taxi and starts yelling at the driver and honking the horn. As the sound mixer, I was on the floor of the cab, miking and recording the dialogue between the cab driver and the woman. It was senseless to jump out and record sound for the middle of the shot, given the phalanx of camera crew members, dolly and lighting grips, and sundry other personnel who were chasing after the action. As the actor and I waited in the cab, I continued to roll sound because turning off the recorder would have disrupted sync. When the woman returned, I had her hit the steering wheel next to the taxi's horn, faking the car honk. The horn may have covered key dialogue and would have been too loud for the volume levels I had set for the dialogue.

As I watched rehearsals, I started compiling a list of sound effects needed for the scene. After the shoot, I took the actor aside and had her run in place to get the clacking of her heels on the sidewalk. I also had to record the sound of the taxi's horn being honked to fill in where I had her fake it. For stylistic reasons the traffic jam was made up of classic cars. I went to each of the cars and recorded the distinctive sound of its horn. I asked the director if he wanted the sound of the engines idling, but he did not see that as part of the overall sound design. There were several other effects on the list that I knew could wait until postproduction.

The editor's first concern was the long, dead middle stretch of sync sound when the actress and camera were elsewhere, the remaining actor and I having filled the time with idle chatter. With the aid of the second transport, he simply measured out the piece of sync sound that he wanted to remove and replaced it with slug. As we were not intercutting sync sound, mixtrack 2 went unused. So the sync track (mixtrack 1) looked like the illustration on the facing page. **SEE 17-30**

As there were narration and voice effects in other parts of the film, the editor used the third mixtrack for the arguing couple in the lead car. We never really see the actors' mouths, so we took them into the studio after shooting and just had them improvise an argument for a while. They are not heard until the woman is close to their car, so their voices occupy the center part of the scene. To achieve the appropriate sound perspective, the rerecording mixer was instructed to start this track with the fader down, bringing it up as the woman approached the car and bringing it back down as she ran back to the taxi. **SEE 17-31**

17-30

Mixtrack 1: The unwanted sync sound is replaced with slug

Tail					Head
In car ←	— Running ←	— Card on windshield ←	— Running ←	— In car	

Picture

Sync   Slug   Sync

Mixtrack 1

17-31

Mixtrack 3: The couple's argument fades in as the woman approaches the car and fades out as she leaves

In car ← — Running ← — Card on windshield ← — Running ← — In car

Picture

Couple arguing

Mixtrack 3

17-32

Mixtrack 4: The woman's footsteps to and from the couple's car

In car ← — Running ← — Card on windshield ← — Running ← — In car

Picture

Footsteps   Footsteps

Mixtrack 4

Next came the footsteps. The editor found a section that sounded appropriate and cut them in from the car door slamming at the beginning to the end of her run. There was also a brief pause in the middle as she put her card on the windshield. **SEE 17-32**

Because the main focus in location recording had been on the dialogue, the sound of the car door as the woman entered and exited the taxi needed some attention. The camera was outside the car, and the recording inside made the sound perspective wrong. Something like this is usually, though not always, easiest to address in postproduction. I recorded the opening and slamming of the door on a number of older cars. As everything between the two sets of dialogue was being removed anyway, the sound of the car door being slammed was also completely replaced.

In both cases it was the combination of several sounds, the creak of the opening from one recorded door being mixed with the swing and slam from other takes. This took two tracks. **SEE 17-33** Another two tracks were built out of the car horns recorded on location. **SEE 17-34**

Last, the editor needed some light city ambience to fill out the overall sound design. This proved to be quite tricky to record, but the appropriate track was eventually found. It was cut uninterrupted into an ambience track. **SEE 17-35**

Just as we created an overview of an exposure in the lighting section, we can create an "exposure" of the way sound can be built. Although this leaves out several unused mixtracks, second sync, music, and so on, all the mixtracks can be viewed together. **SEE 17-36**

17-33

Mixtracks 5 and 6: The car door slamming, mixed from several takes

17-34

Mixtracks 7 and 8: Car horns recorded on location

17-35

Mixtrack 9: An ambience track to fill out the overall sound design

Mixtracks 1 through 9: The overall sound design

This chapter may at times have appeared to be recommending dense sound, but it is simply illustrating how to create a multilayered track. There will be situations in which you find one sound that is absolutely perfect for a scene or sequence. The point is to do what is good for the given situation. Determine what kinds of effects will give the scene the flavor, the ambience, and the lushness you desire.

Audio Finishing

Although many of the audio components of NLE programs are quite robust, it is common to export the audio tracks for a project to sound software specifically designed for building complex audio layering. Digidesign, Inc., with its Pro Tools™ software, and Sonic Solutions™ both make proprietary software that can be used for standard studio recording, say a musician performing a song, as well as interfaced with many NLE programs. **SEE 17-37** The typical approach is to cut picture in a program like FCP with dialogue tracks and minimal music and effects. Similar to picture lock in the conventional edit, once the picture is exactly the way you want it,

17-37

Pro Tools is a sound
design program in
common use

work can commence in a digital audio environment. The audio tracks, and in some cases the picture, must be exported from the NLE software and into the audio software. There are a number of ways to transfer the audio, but external hard drives or DAT are the most common options.

As always, synchronization is a critical factor. The whole conversation about the interplay between film and video comes back into play here. Being able to open the information exported from the NLE software in the audio software is also a significant issue. The general standard presently in use is the *Open Media Framework Interchange (OMFI,* or just *OMF)* file format. Developed by Avid Technologies but incorporated by most NLE program manufacturers, OMF provides the framework necessary to interchange any media information (picture and/or sound) between software applications. Be sure that your NLE software supports OMF architecture before making initial plans.

The OMF format has been a very stable and useful cross-software design, but it has had some limitations. The biggest is the maximum file size of only 2 gigabytes. Software designers are now at work on another format called the *Advanced Authoring Format (AAF)* which should provide greater flexibility. With either format, moving audio into a proprietary audio environment will remain a common way of doing a high-end completion of audio tracks. The actual final mix may be done in another environment altogether, with the building of tracks done very efficiently in the audio program.

18

Finishing the Film

WHETHER **edited conventionally** or on a computer, finishing on film involves the three previously mentioned significant processes: audio mixing, negative cutting (conforming), and final printing. The processes are generally performed in that sequence, although there is modest debate among film professionals as to whether to mix first or conform first. The audio mix is usually done at a commercial mixing house specifically designed for the purpose. Negative cutting is generally done by a professional, although students strapped for cash and willing to take risks can do it themselves.

These first two processes generate the *elements*—sound rolls and picture rolls—needed to create the final print. The final product of the mix is the *master mix,* the completed version of the film's sound. *Negative cutting* entails the return to the original film, generating a new version using the edited workprint as a guide. Final printing is done by a motion picture processing laboratory. The first print—the *answer print*—is essentially the lab's best shot at creating a print that you like. Although the goal is to get it right the first time, it occasionally takes the lab several attempts to produce an answer print that satisfies you. Once you have one you like, all subsequent *release prints* are made using the satisfactory answer print as a guide.

It is essential that these three processes be executed to the highest standard possible. An indifferent mix can ruin the most visually interesting film. Sloppy negative cutting can leave the film damaged and dirty and even out of sync. Unless you are attempting some specialized effect, you want the film to be as clean and polished as possible. Remember, there is no better advertisement for your talents and abilities than your work. Informality may be a desired aesthetic effect in certain circumstances, but generally viewers are left unimpressed by work that appears crudely executed.

The separate film and NLE paths will be continued, but when the goal is a final print these previously parallel tracks start to converge quite quickly. If the goal is a video finish—and the decision of which medium to finish on should be carefully considered—the endgame would be concluded on an NLE system or in an on-line environment at a commercial facility. For film purists, if such still exist, the traditional path of finishing a film "on film" has been dramatically affected by video and, particularly, digital sound technologies. The rounded aspiring filmmaker will need to understand as much as possible about both film and digital processes.

Titling

Films can have any kind of *titles*, from kids' drawings to scribbles on a chalkboard, although many filmmakers like the old-fashioned conventional white or colored text on a black background. In professional situations this last type of title is generally shot on an *animation* or *copy stand*, an arrangement with the camera mounted on a column designed to shoot fixed artwork. Without such a stand, shooting high-quality titles can be more difficult than one might at first anticipate, and nothing announces an amateur project quite as loudly as sloppy, crooked, or out-of-focus titles. A good film may never recover from a slipshod start. Obviously, professional titles do not automatically mean a high-quality film, an observation that is endlessly proven, but at a beginning level they say something about the filmmaker's attention to detail. Though an audience may forgive an error, those considering hiring you or funding and exhibiting your work will take a dim view of what can only be chalked off as carelessness. Take the time to make sure that everything is perfect.

For conventional titles, the first step is to build them on a card or paper stock. The title cards are then photographed on a large, high-contrast **sheet negative**, a standard film negative often referred to as a *Kodalith*. For independents and students, a standard way of building title cards used to be with the press-on lettering available at office-supply stores. This painstaking and time-consuming approach has largely been replaced with generating the titles on a computer. Titles must be output on a printer that produces completely opaque lettering, or there will be problems with the sheet negatives. These negative sheets are set up with strong backlighting and filmed, sandwiching gels if color effects are desired. It is possible to just shoot the cards themselves, but it is difficult to find an exposure that does not represent the blacks and whites as grays.

Anticipate all the titles you will need before creating and shooting them. Negative cutters, mixing houses, and the lab that produces the final print are frequently credited in films. Just as do crew members, postproduction personnel use a carefully crafted film as a résumé item, and it takes preplanning to determine who will do this work.

When shooting be sure that all titles are composed within the TV-safe frame. Video is the standard medium for submission of work for consideration, whether for grants, festivals, or job applications, so a transfer is a given.

Film: Preparing Leaders

For the conventional film edit, the Academy 2 on the countdown leader has been the sync mark during editing, but it now becomes necessary to incorporate a more complex set of leaders for the final mixing and printing phases. These leaders must be set up correctly, because they provide critical synchronization information to the mixing studio and lab. Check with either facility for pertinent details.

The leaders can be, and in many situations are, set up right from the start or at any point during the process. I tend to set them up at the end so they don't get dirty or damaged. Be sure that they are set up in the standardized way and that all the cuts and punches are accurate. Double-check everything you have done. Any mistakes will cause sound synchronization problems at the mix or during printing.

Final Sound Mixing

The audio mix has changed significantly in recent years. You might find places that still do a conventional film mix, particularly in school situations, but almost all commercial mixing studios now digitize all elements (picture and sound tracks).

Obviously, if you have edited on an NLE system, everything is already digital. Most editing software has internal mixing capabilities, although many filmmakers still like to go to a commercial mix for the extra dimension that can be achieved. Mixing is necessary only when you are combining two or more sounds. When all the sound is on one track of a timeline or on one piece of mag stock, the mix can be bypassed.

When you go into the mix, the position of all sound has been determined by your cutting. What is being finalized is the volume and character of the sound—the final product. The mix is always done with the film's editor present, although the mixing board is run by the studio's *rerecording mixer*. A good rerecording mixer can contribute much to a film. Although the original recording is presumably, though not always, of good quality, the mixer can clean up, or "sweeten," the sound, bringing it to its full potential. No matter how good you think your location recordings are, the magnificent sound reproduction of a mixing studio will unmask some heretofore unheard imperfections. Editing tables, particularly those in school situations, do not necessarily reproduce sound perfectly, so be prepared for a few surprises. Hopefully, there are no problems that the mixer cannot eliminate.

The mix is usually the first time you get to see your sound and picture together on a big screen. The experience usually produces that giddy feeling one gets when watching all the elements finally converge to create a finished product. This is where all the work and preparation start to come to fruition. The process is not without its tensions, however. This is the sound that your film is going to live with for the rest of its natural life. The pressure to get it right can be intense, particularly if the preparation has been incomplete or sound problems that have gone unnoticed in the editing turn out to be significant.

Mixes at smaller houses range from $150 to $250 per hour, whereas the most advanced mixing facilities run in the $700-per-hour range. A mix on an uncomplicated 5-minute film would probably take about an hour. Complex features can take a month or more.

FILM: MIXTRACK CONFIGURATIONS

When you take your film to a mixing house, the tracks must be laid out in a logical way, one that makes sense to the mixing-house personnel. As you are editing, you can be informal about which mixtrack each sound is on. You generally want the sounds where they are most convenient, particularly so you can view the film with the sound as complete as possible. Before going to the mix, however, the different types of sound should be segregated onto separate tracks. This allows the mixer to find specific sounds quickly and group together those that are to be treated similarly. This makes the mix simpler and faster. The mix is a substantial budgetary concern, so it should be as streamlined as possible.

Many mixing houses, especially those accustomed to commercial features, are very particular about how the mixtracks are set up. If your film is not set up appropriately, they may send you back to the editing room while still charging you for the time it took them to load and unload your mixtracks. Mixing houses in smaller markets might be a little more forgiving, but mixtracks not set up in a straightforward manner will require costly time to figure out.

In setting up the mixtracks for the mix, two requirements need to be emphasized. The first is this:

◆ **RULE:** *There should be no sound-to-sound cuts anywhere in the mixtracks.*

That is, the mixtracks should be cut in such a way that all pieces of sound are cut to slug rather than to other pieces of sound. If one sound effect follows right on top of another, it should be put on a different roll. The main reason for this is to allow the rerecording mixer scope to do sound manipulations; the rationales presented in chapter 17, the section on A & B rolling sync sound all apply here. Minimum slug length between any two pieces of sound should be four or five seconds. If the sound is dirty and needs substantial manipulation, you should plan on longer gaps. This will require spreading the sound effects through more mixtracks. One of the joys of the digital mix is that, if you make a mistake here, the mixer can cut the sound and paste it at another place on the timeline, thus allowing more-efficient treatment. Becoming too dependent on reconfiguring at the mix, however, can add time to an already costly procedure.

◆ **RULE:** *There should be no place in the film where there is only slug or an empty track on all the mixtracks.*

There must be some recorded sound on at least one of the mixtracks, even if it is just silence. What the listener perceives as silence is not the same thing as an absence of sound. If there is only slug on the head, the track will sound flat and empty. Mixing houses will generally be able to provide something, such as white noise or open-mic room ambience, to cover the gap if you make a mistake. Still, you should consider the quality you want for any quiet moments and provide the appropriate track.

THE "CONVENTIONAL" FILM AUDIO MIX

Commercial mixing houses for motion pictures provide a specialized service that until recently could not be duplicated in other contexts. In the old days of conventional film mixing (ten or so years ago), the key requirement was the interlock of mag stock playback machines, the projected film, and the sound's destination—the mag stock machine that recorded the master mix. The mixing studio itself was, and still is, a screening room with a mixing console at the rear with the aforementioned equipment in a separate booth. **SEE 18-1** The film was projected into the screening space, and the sound playback was routed through the mixing console, with each individual mag stock playback machine being fed into its own channel on the mixing console. The finished sound was on one uninterrupted, uncut piece of mag stock.

Though some of the particulars vary, the same theory applies to mixes done digitally. The film is displayed by video projection, with each track still connected to an individual fader. Interlock is electronic. When you drop off your material to be digitized, it is essential that the edited workprint and mixtracks be in good shape. Any broken sprocket holes or ripped picture should be replaced with black leader, and damaged mag stock should be retransferred and replaced. If anything breaks or is lost in the transfer, time-consuming repair will be required before the mix can start. The master mix will generally be in a computer file, which can be output to a variety of media—including, if desired, good old-fashioned mag stock.

Mixing equipment is set up so you can run back and forth on short stretches, scenes, and sequences of the film, working on the sound until you are satisfied. With *punch-in recording* the mixer can lay down one section of sound on one pass and then record over it if it needs to be redone. The mixer will make one pass on a section just to listen to what sound is there and see where it is located on the tracks. Then the picture and all the interlocked tracks are backed up; and if the mixer feels ready, he or she may try recording it. If the recording is not right, everything is backed up again and the mixer will take another shot at it, recording over the first attempt. Again, the mixer is determining volume levels, at your direction, and doing everything possible to maximize the quality of the sound. It usually takes a number of passes to get it right.

18-1

The mixing studio is a screening room with a mixing console at the rear

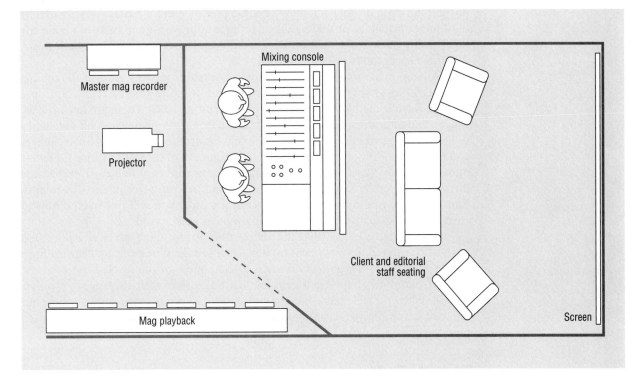

Many mixers require *cue sheets,* or *mixing logs,* that detail where all the sound is. Cue sheets list the mixtracks numerically across the top and the footage and frames or time down the side. This used to be obligatory, although mixers are increasingly discarding the practice. Be sure to ask when arranging a mixing date.

The mix is such a daunting expense that there is a great temptation to find ways to bypass it. In the "guerrilla days" of independent filmmaking, many producers outside the mainstream would search out any conceivable way to avoid the costly, conventional finishing processes. After years of puttering around the edges, most independents realized that this was a mistake. There are perfectly good reasons why things are done in certain ways, and established finishing technologies are designed to produce the highest-quality results possible. Although informality and roughness may be valuable aesthetic alternatives, the trade-off for trying to get by cheaply is often unintelligible sound.

I once assisted a young animator who had completed editing his first feature, a painstakingly executed puppet animation that had taken him more than a year to shoot. He was about to go to a mix, and I questioned him on how prepared he was. It turned out that he did not have the tracks appropriately separated and was going to mix at a rudimentary setup at a local college. I implored him to take some time to reconfigure the tracks and mix them professionally. He needed to meet a deadline and claimed complete poverty. I begged him to do anything to find the time and the money, but to no avail. At the premiere of his film, the sound was virtually unintelligible. There are many false savings between the beginning and the end of a film. It struck me as tragic that someone could take a film that far and not finish it properly.

Go into the mix with an open mind. The first mix of my work as a location sound mixer left me scratching my head. I went with a certain amount of cockiness, knowing I had done a thorough and competent job on a difficult location. It is not possible, however, to get back into the editing room without flaws. I was amazed by the dimension that the mixer was able to bring to improve the audibility of my already high-quality tracks. He was also able to identify and correct many flaws: cable noise, unwanted background noise, and so on.

A good mixer looks like an octopus, with hands moving all over the mixing board, twisting knobs, patching equipment, and tweaking volume levels. Your first mix will seem something like being in the cockpit of a 747: There are lots of dials, gauges, and indicators, and all you really know is that the plane takes off and lands. In the age of digital mixes, the mixer's job has become less physical. All the changes and effects can be programmed to drive the mixing-board controls, making the faders move on their own as if by an unseen hand. I recommend a commercial mix, because the better you understand the process, the more you can actively participate in it. And the better you understand the process, the more you will understand how to create mixtracks that give your film a rich and dynamic sound.

The master mix itself has the shortest life span among parts of a film. It is quickly transferred to the optical master. The photographic printing element for a film's sound track, the *optical master* is a blank piece of film except for a narrow strip of diamond-shaped patterns opposite the side with the sprocket holes. Occasionally, you will find a mixing house that can produce the optical track, but they are becoming increasingly rare. Usually, the motion picture processing lab produces the optical master.

THE NLE MIX

There are a number of ways to approach an NLE mix. Most software has internal mixing capabilities, with the potential of mixing a variety of numbers of tracks. All sound levels and fades are set on the timeline during editing. Although strategies differ, some use the rubber band method described earlier and some have a representation of a mixing board on which faders can be slid by clicking on them with the mouse. The mix can simply be executed to the hard drive and/or output to DAT. The optical master is then made, with a number of practitioners taking the intermediate step of transferring the finished mix to mag stock to check its length.

The most common approach is to premix a small number of tracks internally on the NLE system and then export this mixed sound to software created specifically for sound design. A number of excellent products are available, such as Sonic Solutions.™ The NLE timeline is typically used to create four relatively straight-forward tracks (e.g., two dialogue, one music, and one general effects). This is mixed and output to DAT. Then the complex process of layering the sound effects, ambience, and all other necessary information is done in another program.

Though a mix can be finished on typical software designed for editing sound, many postproduction teams still want a master mix from a professional mixing house. The completed tracks are usually output to DAT, input into the mixing facility's setup, then mixed in the manner described in the previous section.

In almost all cases, it is best to go to the people who have extensive experience with specific phases of production. A good rerecording mixer understands the possibilities and shortcomings of the final product, the particular character of the optical track being the most significant among many issues here, and can assist in producing the highest-quality product possible. Each person knows a specific area.

The editorial staff will have extensive knowledge about building and layering sound, but from the standpoint of understanding the mixing board, the sideboard gear, and the general process, they may not be qualified to get the best possible results in the mix.

Preparation for the Negative Cutter

The next step is *negative cutting:* to cut, or conform, the original film to what you have done in the editing process. The latent edge numbers are the reference points for replicating all cuts. The numbers will be read right off the workprint, or the time code used in the NLE approach will be translated back to edge numbers by the editing software. Cutting the negative is not undertaken until the picture is "locked," that is, until you are absolutely sure that the picture is exactly the way you want it. The old adage "measure your cloth many times because you can cut it only once" is applicable: Once you cut the original, there is no turning back.

Although students often conform their first film or two themselves, the job is usually handed over to an experienced professional, because careful handling of the film is so critical. The *negative cutter,* also called the *conformist* or *neg cutter,* is generally independent of the editorial department. This individual is brought on board after the editing staff has completed all its work, although filmmakers who anticipate complicated printing jobs may require consultation with the neg cutter early in the editing process. The neg cutter's activities facilitate the lab's work in creating the final print, so a professional neg cutter is completely conversant with the material the lab needs to finish a film. Complicated cutting, supers, mattes, fast cutting, mixing black-and-white and color, and so on generally require that the original be laid out in a specific way. A good negative cutter can give you guidance throughout the process.

One critical thing to keep in mind as you are preparing a project for the neg cutter is that everything you want in the final film must be present in the edited workprint and have a corresponding piece of original film. Things like freeze frames and all other optical effects have to be created on film by the time you get to this stage. There are also many fun video effects that can be created in NLE systems, but if they do not have a matching piece of original film, they will not be in your final film. Conversely, if you do not want something in the final print, it had better not be in the edit. Flash frames or lightstruck footage must be weeded out unless they are wanted for effect.

Your project must be appropriately prepared for the neg cutter. In film you mark the workprint, and the neg cutter reads all the information right off the film. In NLE you produce an *edit decision list (EDL)* that provides the neg cutter with everything he or she needs.

FILM: MARKING THE WORKPRINT

The edited workprint is marked with a grease pencil. Every actual cut from one shot to the next has to be clearly identified so the negative cutter clearly understands everything you are intending to do. All *unintentional splices,* that is, splices where you tried a cut but decided to put it back together again, must be identified as well. If there are standard effects such as fades, dissolves, or supers, they must be communicated to both the lab personnel and the neg cutter. When you are done, there should be a grease pencil mark on every splice in the edited workprint. All marks are done on the base side of the film, that is, rolled out on workprint.

Part V — Editing

All marks are done on the base side of the workprint, actual cuts being indicated with the letter *C*

18-3

Unintentional splices must be marked with an equal sign

18-4

Fade-outs and fade-ins are drawn on the workprint as well as indicated in writing

All actual cuts in the film are marked with the letter *C*. **SEE 18-2** All unintentional splices should be marked with an equal sign (=). **SEE 18-3**

Labs execute *fade-outs* and *fade-ins*—where the picture fades out to or up from black, respectively—at a number of standard lengths, called *fade rates*. The standard options are fades of 16, 24, 32, 48, 64, and 96 frames. Fades of 16 and 24 frames are the most common; anything longer feels very slow in the hyperanimated screen time. Slow fades (64 and 96) have their uses, but they tend to call attention to themselves and are frequently used in a stylized or mannered fashion. Fade-outs and fade-ins are literally drawn on the workprint. In both cases write a description of the effect next to the mark with a grease pencil, "16-frame fade-out" in the first example. **SEE 18-4**

Whenever you have a fade-out followed by a fade-in, be sure to cut in some black leader between the two shots. The screen will never achieve complete black if you do not. The length of the black depends on what you are attempting, but anything more than about a second will feel lengthy. Again, periods that seem brief in real life can seem like an eternity in screen time. Rather than going to or coming from black, you can go to colors or "fade to clear" for a more stylized effect. Check with the lab and negative cutter about executing such specialized effects.

Labs have the same standard *dissolve rates* as are available for fades. Also like fades, dissolves of 16 and 24 frames are the most popular. The effect of a dissolve

18-5

To indicate a dissolve, the workprint must be cut so the splice represents the midpoint between the two shots

can be only suggested in a workprint, because you cannot sandwich film stock. The workprint must be cut so that the splice represents the centerpoint of the dissolve between the two shots; that is, the point when we are seeing an equal amount of each shot. The lab and the negative cutter will not understand other configurations.

If you are doing a 24-frame dissolve, you count 12 frames from the cut toward the head for the beginning of the dissolve. For the end of the dissolve, you then count 12 frames (for a total of 24) from the cut toward the tail. The figure above shows how these are marked on the workprint. **SEE 18-5** Again, write a description of the effect with a grease pencil just before the mark.

The technical requirements of dissolves are explained later in this chapter, but suffice it to say at this point that they must be completely planned before they are called for in the workprint. You cannot go through your film and capriciously decide that you want specific cuts to be dissolves. Both shots of the dissolve will be extended in the negative cutting, so there has to be more usable footage than is represented in the edited workprint.

These are the basic marks. There are a few others, such as supers (a squiggle line), which should be discussed with the negative cutter. There are also detailed marks for replacing footage damaged or lost while editing the workprint—footage that is still intact in the original film and can be incorporated in the final print. Again, there should be a mark on every splice when you send the edited workprint to the negative cutter. Unclear marks create the potential for a mistake in the conforming process. If the mistake is a result of sloppy marking, it is no one's fault but your own.

NLE: Creating an EDL

In the method of matchback that Hollywood has adopted, there is a workprint that is marked and sent to the negative cutter. The process, in this case, proceeds just as it does in the conventional film edit. If no workprint is made, the NLE system software must be capable of generating a hard copy of an EDL. The EDL will have a list of beginning and ending time code numbers in two vertical columns down one side of the page, with two columns of their edge number translations down the other side. The negative cutter will perform the cuts from the numbers listed. Many conformists like to have a video of the work as well, with readable time code displayed in a *window burn*—a small window in a lower corner of the picture— or otherwise generated. In the absence of a workprint, they can check these numbers if any questions arise. Some negative cutters have even interlocked their synchronizers with a video playback deck to monitor their work. Window burns are often introduced in the original transfer from film to video as either a key or a supporting way of displaying matchback information.

Negative Cutting

It is with negative cutting that the two parallel tracks—film and NLE—that we have been following finally converge. The final product of this process is the same whether you cut on film or on an NLE system. Once the neg cutter cuts the original film, the final steps of making a print unfold in the same way.

Essentially, negative cutting is making an entirely new film out of your original, using the edited workprint or EDL as a guide. Cement splicers are used exclusively to create splices that will be clean and durable in the printers. The original film is not cut into a single strand but into two rolls—the A & B rolls—although there are instances where more than two rolls are needed.

Negative cutting is the least creative and least romantic of these finishing processes. The negative cutter never looks at the film and is completely uninvolved with sound. On the surface it is a dull and mechanical chore demanding little or no thoughtful involvement. And yet the process is extremely exacting, and any mistakes in handling or cutting the film can have serious repercussions. The negative cutter is dealing with a precious commodity: your original. Handling of the original in this stage must be scrupulous. If it is damaged or destroyed, you have nothing.

THE CLEAN ROOM

A professional negative cutter will have a *clean room*—a room designed to be kept as clean and dust-free as possible. Any dirt or dust that gets on the film will show up as spots on subsequent prints. If the dirt works its way into the film's emulsion, it can cause scratches and even worse damage. Fingerprints on the film must also be avoided. The negative cutter wears lint-free cotton gloves to minimize contact with the film. The rooms often have double doors to limit the dust coming in from the outside world and have air-transfer systems to clean and purify the air. The room is cleaned before every job, more often if it is a lengthy project.

The room generally has two pairs of rewinds. One set is used for the A & B rolls and the other is used to search for shots in the original. There is also a spool for the black leader needed to slug in the shots. A synchronizer and, of course, the cement splicer are also required items. Other equipment includes a trim bin, a pair of scissors, film tape, and a good supply of split reels, regular reels, spacers, and clamps.

How carefully and cleanly films are handled is the determining factor in a negative cutter's overall reputation. If the work consistently has dirt, fingerprints, or torn sprocket holes, no one is going to beat a path to that practitioner's door.

CEMENT SPLICING

The *cement splicer*, also called a *hot splicer*, works on the principle of overlapping and cementing the first frame of a shot on a small part of the last frame of the preceding shot. **SEE 18-6** Cement splices are permanent and strong and will hold up in the contact printers. The splicer has two film cutters, one for the head of the incoming shot and one for the tail of the outgoing shot. The head cutter does not cut on the frame line, but about an eighth of an inch into the bottom of the preceding unwanted frame. **SEE 18-7**

The neg cutter then scrapes the emulsion off this overlap with a small tool on the splicer. This scraped area allows the two pieces of film to bond together, which would not be possible if the emulsion were left on. A small amount of film cement is applied to the scraped overlap to create the bond. **SEE 18-8** If two shots were cut together, this overlap would be visible as the film is projected, a small blip appearing

18-6

A cement splicer is used to create a strong, permanent splice that will hold up in the contact printer
Maier-Hancock cement splicer

18-7

The head cutter cuts about an eighth of an inch into the bottom of the preceding frame, rather than on the frame line

First frame of shot

Overlap area (approximately ⅛")

18-8

The previous shot is laid on top of the overlap

Emulsion is scraped off so film cement can bond properly

Black leader for preceding shot (as used in A & B process)

Splicing block

Sprocket pins

on the bottom of the frame at every cut. The A & B process masks this by overlapping the cut on black leader. The cement splicing destroys the frames that are used for the overlap, an important consideration while cutting your film. (See "Notes and Cautions" later in this chapter for a discussion of these issues.)

The cement splicer has a small heating element in its base that keeps the splicer warm. This heat reduces the time it takes a splice to bond from about one minute to roughly fifteen seconds. The two pieces of film are not glued together, they are welded together. The splices should, if anything, be stronger than the film itself.

A & B ROLLING PICTURE

When working from an edited workprint, the neg cutter goes through the film and records the beginning and ending edge numbers of each individual shot, counting from the edge numbers to the actual frame where the cut is. In the NLE approach, the neg cutter simply consults the EDL for beginning and ending numbers. If the first shot runs from, for example, edge number 3247 minus 9 frames to 3291 plus 17 frames, the neg cutter will go to the original and pull out that piece.

Much as in sync sound, the original film is cut into two separate rolls, called *A & B rolls*. The process of *A & B rolling*, also referred to descriptively as *checker-boarding*, places black leader between alternating shots. This is done on the synchronizer. In the film approach, the edited workprint is set up in a gang to act as a guide. The SMPTE Universal leader (countdown leader) is put on the B roll, and the first shot is on the A roll. **SEE 18-9** Although it does not always work out this precisely, the A & B configuration puts all the odd-numbered shots on the A roll and all the even-numbered shots on the B roll, as discussed in chapter 17. This leaves the original film with no image-to-image cuts. All shots are cut to black leader at both the head and the tail. The black leader between shots is the same length, frame for frame, as the shot on the opposing roll. As one might suspect, the reasons for doing this are similar to those for preparing for the mix.

To understand the rationale for A & B rolling, it is necessary to jump forward to what the lab does with these rolls prior to printing. With a virgin piece of raw stock, a contact print from the A & B rolls is made in separate passes on a lab's printer. The A roll is generally printed first, printing all the odd-numbered shots. The raw stock is then rewound to the appropriate marks on the standardized leaders, and the B roll is printed. This second pass drops in all the shots missing from the printing of the A roll. The optical master is printed at a separate gate that exposes just the edge of the film. It is run at the same time as one of the A & B rolls.

The following are what A & B rolling allows the lab to do. Be aware that the negative cutter has no control over these elements, although he or she can usually answer many questions about the printing process. These are aspects of finishing that are facilitated by the neg cutter's efforts:

- Color and exposure corrections[1]

- Optical effects: fades, dissolves, superimpositions, and the like

- The creation of "invisible splices"

---

1. With black-and-white film, exposure is the only variable considered at this point.

18-9

In the A & B–rolling process, alternating shots are placed on separate rolls, with shots on the opposing roll replaced with black leader

Color and exposure correction Prior to printing your film, the A & B rolls take another trip to the Hazeltine (see chapter 8 for the initial discussion of this). The A & B rolls are loaded separately into the Hazeltine, and the timer goes through the entire film and analyzes each individual shot for color and exposure, a process called *timing*.

The *printer lights* for each individual shot—the actual volumes of red, green, and blue—are thus determined on the Hazeltine. The printer affords extensive opportunity to manipulate the character of the film's shots. The transmission of each primary color of light is broken down into a series of *printer points,* settings that correspond to the variable size of the valve that is in the path of each light and thus represent increments in the intensity of the individual colors. There are 50 points represented on a dial that controls the valve, with 25 theoretically representing perfect exposure. If a shot was overexposed on location, the lights can be dialed to compensate. If a shot is too red, the appropriate light could be dialed to contribute less red, and so on. The timer looks at each shot and uses his or her best judgment for both the appropriate color and exposure level. Although modern printers can "fire on a frame," the black leader between alternating shots gives the printer lights time to adjust for each individual shot.

These dials clearly allow substantial control over the image. Although there are limits, many difficulties can be corrected if there is enough information in the original. Material that cannot be corrected is that which is so overexposed or underexposed that there is no detail. Changes will generally affect the contrast range of the image as well as the amount of grain.

Another critical consideration is that the timer cannot manipulate specific elements in the frame, such as a blown-out window, without affecting the rest of the scene. Think back to the example of the man in front of the window: If the window area is overexposed, you cannot bring it down without bringing down the exposure of all the interior elements. Nor can you change the color in just one area of the frame without affecting other areas. If you had not corrected for the exterior color temperature with filters or gels, you could not subtract the resulting blue cast without affecting the interior. To do so would, for instance, make the lamp much redder.

Exposure on location is a tricky beast. As with the sound, your images frequently need to be tweaked for exposures that are slightly off. Labs do the bulk of their work with commercial clients and thus go for photographic normal. They will try to make facial tones accurate and generally push for realistic representation. If you have color or exposure effects built into your shooting, you must alert the lab to that fact. Individual timers have their own preferences, and experienced DPs will find timers they like and will work closely with them throughout all the printing-related aspects of a film.

Beginners tend to see this final printing phase as an opportunity to correct mistakes, as it most certainly is. Experienced DPs, however, are highly conversant with printer lights, and the role these lights play influences their plans before the first instrument is set up on a set. In fact, much of the discussion of lighting in part IV can be tied to the theory behind printer lights, but mastering basic exposure technique precedes these considerations.

Optical effects The A & B method allows the lab to execute the *optical effects*—dissolves, fades, supers, and so on—that were planned in the editorial process. Dissolves, as well as superimpositions and matte shots, clearly require two shots to be printed together. This would be impossible if a single roll of conformed original were used. The A & B method allows images to be on both rolls concurrently and thus printed together.

As the color and exposure are analyzed and recorded on the Hazeltine, the effects indicated on the marked workprint are similarly logged. In the path of the light in a printer, there is a master shutter—the *fader unit* (see figure 8-8)—which is

18-10

The dissolve occupies the same number of frames in the final film as its corresponding straight cut does in the workprint; the overlap portions simply are extended on the A & B rolls

opened and closed to create the overall effects. All fades and dissolves are created by this fader. A 24-frame fade programmed into the printer instructs the fader to close in 1 second at the appropriate point. A dissolve has a fade-out start at the programmed point on one roll. When the second roll is printed, a fade-in is started at the same point. The result of the fade-out on top of the fade-in is the dissolve.

On the workprint a dissolve is marked in the manner described in the previous section. As explained earlier, the cut in the workprint always represents the midpoint of the dissolve, that is, the point where there is an equal amount of each image. The negative cutter extends the shot past the centerpoint represented in the workprint. If it is a 24-frame dissolve, the negative cutter will extend each shot an extra 12 frames on the appropriate roll. **SEE 18-10**

To understand the requirements of dissolves, there are two issues that must be clear. The first is that the frames at the splice in the workprint are in the same position in the A & B rolls. Some people make the mistake of thinking that because the shots are being extended that the film somehow becomes longer, thus requiring some adjustments in the mixtracks. As figure 18-10 suggests, the dissolve occupies the same area, that is, number of frames, in the final film as its corresponding straight cut does in the workprint. The overlap portions of the shots simply are extended on the A & B rolls.

The second consideration is that there must be more usable frames than are represented in the edited workprint. In a 1-second dissolve, the negative cutter will be employing the 12 frames after the cut on the outgoing shot. They must be frames that you want to be visible. The same is true on the head of the incoming shot. You cannot cut on the last frame of a shot and then call for a dissolve in the edited workprint. If you did, the extended part of the dissolve would overlap into the next shot.

Superimpositions and matte shots are also printed together in the A & B method. A super is created by putting images in the same place on the A roll and on the B roll. The lab adjusts exposure to compensate for two pieces of film being printed together. Similarly, mattes are generally made of two or more components printed together. One part of the frame might be blocked off on one shot while the opposite side is blocked off on another piece of film. The two are printed together in the A & B method to produce a composite shot. Mattes and supers may have other requirements that should be clarified with both the lab and the negative cutter.

Numerous situations come up in which more than two images need to be combined, thus requiring the addition of more rolls—C rolls, D rolls, et cetera. Special effects and matte shots are the clearest examples of this. Ivan Reitman's *Ghostbusters* (1984) has an excellent example of this in the scenes of the giant marshmallow man coming down the street to confront the ghostbusters.[2] The shot consists of three elements: an animated miniature of the marshmallow man walking down a city street, a painted backdrop of the cityscape at night, and the ghostbusters on a roof with their backs to the camera. Many special-effects shots and animations are even more complicated. A shot from George Lucas's *Star Wars* (1977) is reported to have had more than seventy separate elements. In both of these examples, the elements would be combined before final printing, but the theory is the same.

Invisible splices   This refers to a method of masking the glitches inherent in the process of cement-splicing the film together. As stated, the cement splicer works by overlapping a small piece of the incoming shot on the outgoing shot. Left uncovered, this tab is visible when the film is projected. In the A & B method, this scraped tab is always covered by black leader laid on top of it and cemented. The picture is scraped and then covered by the outgoing frame of black leader.

CUTTING THE ORIGINAL

Negative cutters have their jobs broken down into efficient systems. Although there may be some minor differences in approach, the following is generally the sequence of events. The first step is to go through the edited workprint and log the beginning and ending edge numbers of all the shots. The next step is to go through the uncut original and find what sequences of edge numbers are on the individual rolls. The neg cutter will then have some idea of where all the pieces will be found. Given the huge amount of footage, longer films are often conformed one scene at a time.

The next step is to set up the appropriate leaders. The beginning of the A roll consists of white leader. The B roll has the Universal leader preceded by white leader. Once the leaders are completed, it is a matter of starting with the first shot and building both the A & B rolls from the original. The neg cutter gets the edge numbers from the first shot and determines on which roll of original it can be found. The neg cutter then winds through the appropriate roll until the shot is found. While winding through the original, the neg cutter rolls the film gently but not to the point of its being loose on the reel; any snapping or undue stress that will cause the layers of film to grind against one another is to be avoided. The shot is carefully cut out of the original with a pair of scissors, pulling the piece indicated in the edited workprint. The neg cutter actually pulls out an extra one and a half frames on either end of the shot, which are needed for handling and the area to be scraped on the cement splicer.

This first shot is then cut onto the A roll at the place indicated in the workprint or EDL. The B roll has black leader across from this first shot. Black leader is cut to the end of the first shot, with the second shot being cut onto the B roll, and so on. By this method a new version of the film is built out of the original.

Commercial feature films rarely cut the original. It is always kept intact, and all cutting is done with duplicates of the original, often the beginning of a complicated family tree of interpositives and internegatives. The film that you see at the theater may be many *generations* removed from the original piece of raw stock that was exposed in the camera on location. Strapped for cash, many students decide to conform their own originals. This is an acceptable route, although there are considerable risks. The more you get into film, the more the idea of touching the original becomes an issue of substantial concern. Any handling involves risk. When

2. A detailed description of this scene can be found in the June 1984 issue of *American Cinematographer*.

you start conforming, be as prepared as conceivably possible. If any element of the process gets confused or messy, the whole effort can start on a downward spiral, which at this stage jeopardizes all the time, effort, money, and, most significant, emotion you have invested in the project. This is why most people turn the process over to a professional.

NOTES AND CAUTIONS

Whether you intend to go to a negative cutter or do the conforming yourself, there are some basic considerations that should inform the process.

☑ All communication about specific shots, with both the negative cutter and the lab, is done in terms of footage and frames. The "picture start" frame in the Universal leader is stated as 0 feet, 0 frames, and everything is counted from there. If you have a shot that needs special attention, you would tell the lab or negative cutter that a shot at such and such a spot, say, from 125 feet, 12 frames to 128 feet, 32 frames, needs something done to it. Usually, this refers to alerting the lab to a shot that needs exposure or color correction, but there are also concerns that need to be relayed to the negative cutter.

☑ You should never be scraping black leader. Cement-splicing the tail of each shot presents a problem. The head of each shot feeds into the left of the splicer, so you are always cutting and scraping picture. When you cut the tail of a shot, however, the last frame would theoretically be dropped onto the scraped head of the black leader of the next shot. This scraped part would create a glitch that would be visible. To avoid scraping black leader, you have to orient the film so that you are still scraping picture when you cut the tail of all shots. This usually means bringing the tail of the shot from the right so that it feeds into the left of the cement splicer. **SEE 18-11**

This much handling of the fragile original justifiably makes some people nervous. Rather than twisting the film around, you may want to turn the splicer so it faces away from you and move to the opposite side of the table to make all your tail cuts. You will get a lot of exercise this way.

☑ The lost frames, referred to as *splicing frames,* constitute one of the most difficult mechanical editing concepts to understand. It concerns how the requirements of the negative cutter affect the way you cut your film—specifically, how you need to account for the frames that are ruined in cement splicing.

All frames of the unedited workprint have precise corresponding frames in the original. Thus, if you have to cut and scrape frames when cement-splicing the original, the ruined frames correspond to real frames in the workprint. These corresponding frames must be identified, catalogued, and set aside. If they are used elsewhere in the edited workprint, the negative cutter is faced with a problem. Looking at a piece of workprint and its corresponding original should clarify this. **SEE 18-12** If you were to pull section A from your raw footage and use it in your edited workprint, the negative cutter would go to the original film and pull that piece, plus an extra one and a half frames on either side of A, piece B in the original. Frames 2 and 3 are needed for the scraped emulsion overlap required by the cement splicer. The negative cutter also pulls frames 1 and 4, because they provide safe handling of the film. *Frames 1, 2, 3, and 4 in the original are thus destroyed in the negative-cutting process.*

18-11

To avoid scraping black leader when splicing the tail of a shot, orient the film so that you are always scraping picture

Splicing block

18-12

Always keep in mind that two frames on each side of a shot must be sacrificed when making the A & B rolls

Therein lies the problem. These ruined frames have corresponding frames that are intact in the workprint and could potentially, but wrongly, be used elsewhere in the edited workprint. If these workprint frames are used later in the film, the neg cutter will not find them when attempting to pull the shot. The shot in the original must be the same length as the one in the edited workprint or there will be sync problems with the sound. The negative cutter has to do some fancy footwork to fix your mistake, usually pulling the necessary number of frames from the tail of the shot or lengthening the next shot. Although these solutions can work, they can alter sync for individual shots and cause cuts to be less fluid.

A mistake like this represents poor planning on the editor's part. You must take into account that these frames are going to be destroyed and simply discard two frames, rounded up from one and a half, at the beginning and end of every shot that will be used in your film. Do not throw them away; mark them so you will know they are off limits if you consider using them later.

As with dissolves, this invariably leads to confusion about whether this makes the film longer. "If I have to add a frame and a half, doesn't that affect my sound?" The answer is no. The piece that is represented in the workprint coincides with the piece that will be in the conformed original frame for frame. The lost frames pertain solely to what is in your outtakes. The frames the negative cutter will need for cement splicing must remain intact in the unused portion of the workprint.

This rarely becomes a problem but does require attention to avoid mistakes. Shots have flash frames at the head and tail, and sync shots have all the starting and finishing information that make mistakes almost impossible. It becomes a problem only when you want to use different sections of the same shot at different places in the edited workprint.

☑ In the negative process, creating fades and stretches of black requires special handling. Using black leader on both the A & B rolls does not produce black on the resulting film print. Because everything is reversed, black leader produces clear or nearly clear film. Color negative, whether still or motion picture, has an orange cast to it, which is simply the shade that creates black in the resulting prints. So if you are working in color, you need to use *orange mask* in the A & B rolls to create black in an answer print. Fades require unusual treatment, with the two shots to be faded uncharacteristically cut together and the orange mask on the opposing roll. **SEE 18-13** The fader is closed on the picture during the pass on that roll. For the orange mask on the opposing roll, the fader is opened to produce black. A & B rolling negative requires knowing how the negative gets printed. Be sure to check everything with the lab if you are conforming your own film.

18-13

Fades require the two shots to be cut together, with orange mask on the opposing roll

18-14

Film pieces that do not have edge numbers must be identified and logged on paper for the negative cutter

☑ Special care must be taken when doing *fast cutting*—cutting of shots less than one second long. Any piece shorter than 20 frames has the potential to lack an edge number, which would leave the negative cutter without a clue as to where the piece came from. As you are cutting, pieces that do not have an edge number must be identified and logged for the conformist. The best way to do this is to lay the film that you intend to take the piece out of on a sheet of white paper. Put a pencil mark in each sprocket hole of the intended piece from one edge number to the next. Transfer the edge numbers to the page as well. **SEE 18-14** When you are done, you will have a line of more than twenty dots with the edge numbers indicated. Draw a line on the frames that are being used in the shot. This page is given to the negative cutter, with a note saying that this is the shot at this location in the film. Again, the location of the shot is indicated from "picture start."

☑ Nothing in the editorial process requires more practice than cement splices. Considering that you are working with the original, it behooves you to become completely comfortable with them before tackling the job. Scraping the emulsion on the overlap without damaging the frame is tricky. Try scraping many test frames, practicing not ripping sprocket holes or weakening the film. Practice applying the film cement so it does not spread onto the adjacent frames. These splices should be tested by gently twisting them to see if the edges separate. Holding the film in both hands and snapping it is the final test. The splice should be stronger than the rest of the film. Be absolutely comfortable with splicing before attacking your original.

As stated earlier there is modest debate among film professionals about whether to mix first or conform first. Most filmmakers mix first. If there are any structural problems with the film, they will show up as you watch it in all its glory in the mixing studio. Though it may be costly, you can always terminate the mix and return to the editing room. This would not be possible if the film were already conformed.

   The counterargument is that if there are any errors or miscalculations in the negative cutting, the mixtracks may need adjustments to compensate. If you have already mixed, all sound remaining in sync depends on the film's being conformed

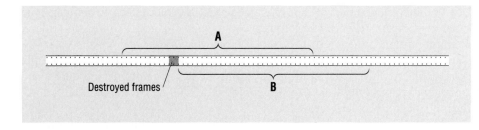

18-15

Destroyed frames

A

B

Misreading the edge numbers on a shot while conforming—pulling piece B rather than piece A, for example—results in irrevocably lost frames and a disruption of sync

frame for frame to the edited workprint. Given the complications of the process, lost frames, and so on, mistakes are occasionally made. If all guidelines have been followed and the negative cutter is an experienced professional, however, this should not be an issue.

Again, negative cutting appears to be mechanical and dull, but it is a critical process that must be done meticulously. Mistakes in conforming can be disastrous. Any errors or carelessness will result in ruined shots, difficulties in synced sound, or dirty, scratched prints. I worked on a film in which the negative cutter misread the numbers on one shot, a rare but costly occurrence. **SEE 18-15** Rather than pulling piece A, he pulled piece B and spliced it into the roll.

When the wrong piece is pulled, what resulting problem is immediately noticeable? Sync. When the otherwise perfect answer print was projected, we were stunned to see one shot in which the dialogue and the picture were completely mismatched. As the piece used was in front of the piece we wanted, correcting the head of the shot was no problem. The incorrect tail cut, however, occurred in the middle of the desired shot, thus causing substantial problems. The one and a half frames already pulled and destroyed were frames intended for the film. There was no getting them back. We were left with the unenviable choice of finding another shot with sound timed similarly to the already mixed sound or accepting a slight (two-frame) jump in the footage and a disruption of sync for the length of the shot. No suitable replacement shot worked, and the latter solution was reluctantly agreed upon. Though many viewers do not even notice it, I still flinch when I see the jump.

As stated at the beginning of this section, the film and NLE paths we have been following merge at this point. Proceeding under the assumption that a film print is the final goal, these chapters have sketched out two different routes by which to arrive at the same place. Regardless of your editing approach, the products of the mixing and negative-cutting processes are the elements required to make a final print.

The Final Print

With all the elements created, it is time to produce an *answer print*—the first attempt at making a final print of your film. The lab you choose needs a minimum of four elements to make a print: the A roll, the B roll, the optical master, and the marked edited workprint. If it is a complicated job, printing may require C rolls, D rolls, or more.

In many ways this last process is the most exhilarating. It is when you finally get to see a project that you have put so much into come to fruition. Be prepared for some disappointments as well. Too often beginning filmmakers expect the lab to magically create perfect exposures and correct all the deficiencies in shooting. Making an answer print involves many variables, and there may be trade-offs between what the filmmaker desires and what the lab can actually do. The lab workers make their best attempt to produce the print you want, but the lab cannot work miracles.

There is a certain irony in that the more ambitious you have been in lighting, filtering, and exposure, the harder the job is for the lab and the timer. A flat image is easy to time. When there are exposure gradations and color effects in an image, the timer may legitimately become confused about what you are attempting to achieve. Communication is the key. Let the timer know what you have done and what you want. Frankly, the biggest variable in printing is how well you have executed the shots. If the negative is exposed properly and the lighting volume and quality are consistent in continuity scenes, the timer's job should be easy. If the shots are a mess, the potential for problems grows.

There is an old joke among filmmakers about fixing films. When presented with problems in preproduction, the saying goes that "we'll fix it in shooting." Problems in shooting will be "fixed in the editing room." Problems in the editing room? "We'll fix it in the mix." And problems at the mix are "fixed in the answer print." This takes on a certain aspect of gallows humor, but the buck stops with the final print. There is no place to fix the film after this. There is a certain painful finality to going to a print.

You need to be aware of some of the pressures involved in finishing. Like the birth of a child, it is a joyous occasion. And, similar to a child's birth, there can be both a sense of separation and nervous fretting over what this wrinkly, squalling thing will look like to other people.

REVERSAL VERSUS NEGATIVE

Before discussing printing theory, the different approaches necessary for negative and reversal must be addressed. *Reversal film,* which has all colors and shades rendered normally on the original, is very straightforward. If a film is underexposed, you pump up the light to get a better exposure. If there is too much red in the original, the lab simply reduces the amount of red in the final print. If there is a light area in the original, it will be light in the print.

In *negative film,* however, everything is the opposite: The lights and darks are reversed from how they are normally perceived. An underexposed negative is very thin, that is, almost clear, so it would need less light from the printer. An overexposed negative is very dense, or thick, needing more light from the printer. In addition, when the lab increases a color, the result is *less* of that color in the final print. If there was too much blue in a print, for example, the lab would, paradoxically, need to increase the amount of blue. This last part is the most difficult to understand, and the novice may not have much immediate need to apply this knowledge. As with everything, though, the long-term goal is to understand every element of the process. And the process of printing—creating the final version of your film—is clearly one that demands significant attention.

THE PRINTING PROGRAM

As stated, the timer analyzes each shot for color and exposure. The resulting decisions are fed into a computer-generated decision list, called a *printing program,* which runs the printer lights as the A & B rolls are printed. The timer also checks the marked edited workprint for all cuts and effects and encodes all such *printing cues*—instructions to the fader unit—into the printing program. This decision list comes in a number of forms, but is usually an old-fashioned punched computer strip. Whatever the form, the decision list controls all the values at which the red, green, and blue printer lights will be set for each individual shot. It also instructs the fader unit to open and close for dissolves, fades, and any other optical effects.

The following figure shows the beginning of a typical printing program. It represents a simple short film employing just A & B rolls. It had no dissolves or fades and was shot on negative. **SEE 18-16**

The numbers under the *RD, GN,* and *BL* headings represent the red, green, and blue printer light settings for each individual shot. This film had 73 shots, with

```
                    PRINTING PROGRAM


          JOB NUMBER:       DATE:        SCENES:  73

          EFFECTS  CUES    MIN CUE      LAST CUE    MAX FPM

   A ROLL           36      4   00      357  00     2000

   B ROLL           37      5   00      357  00     2500
```

SCENE	FEET	FRAMES	A ROLL	RD	GN	BL	B ROLL	RD	GN	BL
	0000	25	ZC	00	00	00				
0001	0008	03					LC	10	13	06
0002	0013	08	LC	22	18	13				
0003	0014	20					LC	16	16	09
0004	0060	25	LC	22	18	13				
0005	0073	05					LC	16	16	09
0006	0074	15	LC	24	16	11				
0007	0077	05					LC	24	16	11
0008	0080	25	LC	28	27	34				

18-16

The beginning of a typical printing program for a short film employing A & B rolls

the cue total being slightly higher (75) because of head and tail leaders. A feature with, for example, 1,200 shots would have 1,200 settings. That some numbers are duplicated suggests that material from certain setups was used more than once, a shot/reverse shot in this case.

One of the first shots was evaluated at 22-18-13. Although the precise meaning of these numbers would not be consistent from lab to lab, this suggests that the shot was slightly underexposed and was a little too red. Because it is negative, less light is needed to get through the less dense negative. The higher number on the red is what suggests that the red component in the image had to be decreased. When the red is reduced, it affects overall exposure. This explains why the green and blue numbers are lower. The fact that the green light is set higher than the blue suggests that the red being eliminated had a little bit of yellow in it, the mix of red and green producing yellow. Remember, more is less in negative. The shot evaluated at 24-16-11 is similar to the one just described. The shot at 28-27-34 would suggest slight overexposure but with too much blue. Indeed, it was tungsten-balanced film shot in daylight without an 85 filter.

When the A roll is printed, the computer decision list created by the timer controls these settings on the light valves in the printer. The transition from shot #6 to #8 is a good representation of what occurs. The printer lights are set for 24-16-11 for shot #6. In the time that the black leader corresponding to shot #7, 140 frames, or almost six seconds, is masking the gate, the printer lights are instructed to change to 28-27-34.

This particular program had no fades or dissolves, so there are no effects cues. If there had been, the computerized printing program would have had instructions to the fader unit to create effects. Both the fader unit and the light valves require some response time to reopen or adjust to the programmed values. Short shots may not allow the fader unit or light valves sufficient time to adjust to new settings. Individual labs may require different response times, but it is generally less than one second. If your shots are very short, you may have to put some of them on a C roll.

THE FIRST ANSWER PRINT

The first answer print should be evaluated in terms of your standards. Although labs generally do a highly professional job, the print is rarely perfect—perfection is virtually impossible to achieve with so many variables. Sometimes you have to look at a print and decide whether it is worth the effort and cost to correct a few minor mistakes. If it is good enough, the lab makes all subsequent *release prints*—those designed specifically for distribution—from the printing program that has been created. If there are problems, you may have to negotiate with the lab about the cost of another answer print. If you can demonstrate that the mistakes were the lab's fault, the lab should absorb the cost of or cut a deal for the next print. If the mistakes are a matter of poor preparation or communication on your part, you will have to foot the bill for the next answer print.

The key complicating factor is that the lab tries to make the best print according to its established standards. Effective communication with the timer takes experience and a clear understanding of all the variables. Many times what the timer sees and what you are hoping to see may be two completely different things; it may be that what you are hoping to see is not possible. More often than not, disparities result because you have not communicated your desires effectively. In the final analysis, it may be that printing as well as shooting is an inexact art. There are situations in which even the most capable cinematographers are stymied by elements that are beyond their control.

In chapter 15 there was a story about a scene involving two people sneaking up on a house as the sun rises. The character of the shots was different enough that the filmmakers placed their hopes on the answer print. Their first step was to alert the lab to a potential problem. Not being familiar with a scene's context, the timer would have no way of knowing that it had problems. Once alerted, the timer can use only personal judgment to get the scene close. Although there are undoubtedly timers who can look at a negative and perfectly predict the look of the film, most mere mortals do not know precisely what a sequence is going to look like until it is printed. Once you see how close you have gotten, you can take another shot at it. In the sunrise story, it took three tries to get the printer lights set appropriately for the scene.

Again, be aware that most labs do the bulk of their work with commercial clients and thus are generally geared toward a reasonably straightforward photographic normal image: Flesh tones are normal, colors are true, exposure is within a certain range, and so on. If you want to create unorthodox images, this is simply a reality that you have to learn to accept. If you have any specific aims in either correcting or not correcting a shot, they must be clearly communicated to the lab both verbally and in writing. As stated, all communication is done in footage and frames, which are counted from the "picture start" frame in the Universal leader as 0 feet, 0 frames in the synchronizer. If a shot is too red in the workprint, you need to tell the lab that a shot at such and such a spot—say, 125 feet, 12 frames to 128 feet, 32 frames—needs some red eliminated. Or you may have another specialized effect that should not be corrected.

The finality of all these processes should be reemphasized. Corrections to a print are very expensive and in some cases completely impossible. In a film about chemical contaminants, for example, a director absentmindedly, and foolishly, used a 20-frame shot that included an identifiable product name. He had secured a well-known narrator and made multiple prints, anticipating wide interest in the film. When company representatives saw the film, they threatened legal action if the shot was not immediately removed. There was some unsubstantiated evidence that the company had produced the contaminant, but the director could never have afforded the protracted lawsuit that the company threatened to bring.

His options were all bad. On a final print, the picture and optical sound track are printed side by side. There is no way to replace one without affecting the other. He could go to every print and cut out the 20 frames, but the problem is that he would eliminate 20 frames of sound. Because of the displacement, it would not even be the corresponding sound. He could go back to his A & B rolls and cut out the offending shot, but then he would have to remix the sound and replace all the existing prints, both expensive propositions. He could replace the shot in the A & B rolls, but would again have to reprint everything. Someone recommended that he could take a permanent marker and blot out the offending shot, a wisecrack proposal until we noticed his expression, suggesting he was actually considering it.

He finally decided to cut the 20 frames out of one print, a radical action given the cost of an individual print. Mercifully, the sound that was cut turned out to be unimportant, and he cut the 20 frames out of the rest of the prints. While bemoaning his fate over a few beers, another documentary filmmaker pointed out the obvious: The shot should never have been there in the first place. If you are going to take on a corporation, go ahead and do so straightforwardly. Do not let 20 frames endanger an otherwise secure $80,000 project.

For most students and independents, a final print is just that: final. Commercial feature films can experiment with different versions, because most producers never cut the original. High-quality intermediate prints of the film are generally the source for prints. For those of you who have to cut the original, everything must be exactly the way you want it before you embark on any of these processes.

Despite all the possible headaches that have been described, the creation of the answer print is the most exciting part of the filmmaking process. You finally have something you can hold in your hands. This is what all the effort has gone toward. With all the hurdles that had to be jumped and the mountains that needed to be climbed to reach that moment, there is nothing as satisfying as seeing a project, no matter how complex or simple, come to fruition. And the more you understand the requirements of each individual step, the more those hurdles and mountains will become surmountable.

Once you have an acceptable answer print and begin making release prints, your film starts to take on an entirely different life: that of distribution and exhibition. In certain ways it can be a life that is even more demanding and draining than the actual production itself was, particularly for independent filmmakers. Although venues for nonmainstream films are becoming more plentiful, it is still a challenge to get a project out there and seen even if it is incredibly good. Festivals offer opportunities to get attention. There are also the "markets," convention-like events where "indies" can screen work for potential distributors. The direct-to-video market may hold possibilities as well, although the film you are making may not conform to the product commonly found on the shelf at your local video store. The Web is still a question mark.

While independents scramble to be recognized, we hear about only the successes. The story behind Robert Rodriguez's *El Mariachi* is generally well known: Studio executives saw it, snapped it up immediately, and offered the maker opportunities for future work. We rarely hear about the films that languish in some netherworld because they are not good enough or are perceived as unable to command a wide enough audience to attract a distributor. Despite all the pitfalls, the growing number of successful films—both independent and commercial— is greatly encouraging. Somebody has to make them, and it might as well be you. But all this is a different story, one that goes far beyond the one being told here. For students and novice independents, the key is to work and get experience. You have to make them before anyone is going to come to see them.

Glossary

⅓–⅔ rule States that one-third of the depth of field is in front of the focus point and two-thirds is behind.

16mm The midsized format used in many independent film projects and most intermediate and advanced film production classes.

24p A newer HD digital video format by Sony that records 24 frames of progressive video per second, achieving results that many consider close to motion picture film. Also known as *24-frame progressive.*

30-degree rule The principle that says you should not move the camera toward a subject in a straight line; that is, if a subject is shot from one angle, the next shot should vary by at least 30 degrees.

35mm The format in which the bulk of professional work is shot.

180-degree rule The principle used to create an understandable sense of the space in which the action is occurring. Also called *axis of action* and *the line.*

A & B rolling Alternating the original sync mixtrack on separate rolls to facilitate the final print. Also called *checkerboarding.*

A & B rolls The separation of the camera original onto two different rolls to facilitate printing effects.

A, B, C, and D frames A way of identifying the field arrangement of film frames that have been transferred to video.

Academy 2 The *2* at the end of the countdown leader.

Academy leader See *countdown leader.*

acoustics The total effect of sound and how it travels in a given space and particularly how it reflects off surfaces before arriving at the microphone or ear.

action The interrelationship of pull-down claw, shutter, and the other elements of the basic mechanism of the film camera.

adapter Connector that converts one type of audio or video plug to another.

Advanced Authoring Format (AAF) A framework in the planning stages that allows a large amount of digital information to be imported or exported to different software programs.

aerial shot Shot executed from a helicopter or an airplane.

ambience The character of the underlying sound in any given space.

ambience overlaps The overlapping of ambience between sync takes that allows the rerecording mixer to soften any potential harshness of the cut. Also called *handles.*

ambient light The general level of light in a space; the amount of light reflected off walls and other surfaces from the source(s) back into the space.

American Society of Cinematographers (ASC) Publishers of the *American Cinematographer Manual.*

amperes Rating of the load-bearing potential of individual circuits. Also called *amps.*

amplitude A measure of the strength (loudness) of a sound signal, determined by the distance from the baseline of the sound wave to the peak.

amps See *amperes.*

analog video The encoding of an electrical signal on a conventional magnetic tape.

animation A single-framing technique that puts inanimate objects in motion.

answer print The first attempt at creating a final print of a film.

anticipatory camera Rehearsed, highly choreographed camera movement that leads rather than responds to subject movement.

antihalation backing The antireflectant coating on a film stock.

aperture The place where each individual frame is exposed. Also called *gate.*

apprentice editor The person responsible for many of the routine procedures that the editor does not do, such as syncing up, stringing out, configuring mixtracks, and so on.

arm A crane-style device that has a suspended camera controlled electronically by a remote.

art department The crew members involved in the design elements of the image.

art director An expert in materials and building, responsible for executing the production designer's plans.

aspect ratio The film frame's width-to-height relationship.

assistant director (AD) The crew member primarily responsible for organization and efficiency on the set.

assistant editor The person responsible for the overall organization in the editing room.

attack The first frame of an individual recorded sound.

audio mixing The mixdown of the mixtracks created in editing. Also called *final audio mixdown.*

automated dialogue replacement (ADR) A method of creating and replacing dialogue in postproduction. Also known as *looping.*

automatic gain control (AGC) The function on a sound recorder that reads the audio signal and automatically adjusts the recording to an appropriate level. Also called *automatic level control (ALC).*

automatic level control (ALC) See *automatic gain control (AGC).*

automatic threading mechanism Feature on some cameras designed to feed the film unassisted.

axis of action See *180-degree rule.*

baby legs Short tripod legs used for low-angle shots.

background noise Distant traffic, refrigerators, fans, and similar interfering sounds.

backlight Generally positioned above and behind the subject, it provides texture and definition to the hair and separation from the background.

backwinding A function that allows the basic mechanism of the camera to be driven backward with a hand crank.

ball joint leveling Design used for leveling the tripod head.

banana plugs Used frequently on European-produced equipment; has the leads separated out into individual plugs.

barn doors Adjustable black metal doors mounted on the front of a lighting instrument, used to focus the beam.

barney A padded hood used to further dampen unwanted camera noise.

base In the construction of the film stock, it is the acetate vehicle for the emulsion.

batch capture After logging a number of clips, the NLE software's ability to capture them in one continuous procedure.

best boy The gaffer's first assistant.

Betacam SP An analog broadcast standard format that is heavily employed in television news and industrial applications.

bin The window in an NLE program where unedited shots and audio clips are stored.

bird's-eye view A shot from directly above that tends to have a godlike, omniscient perspective. Also called *overhead shot.*

black wrap A material designed to cut light by wrapping around instruments.

blocking for the camera Refers to staging action for the camera.

board See *storyboard.*

boom operator The crew member who holds the mic on a boom.

boundary layer microphone (BLM) Small, flat mic designed to sit on a piece of furniture or be taped to a surface.

bracketing Shooting a subject at what the light meter tells you, as well as at least one stop over and one stop under.

breaker box Generally, the main fuse box in a building.

breathing Effect created by the moving front element of the lens, a slight zooming effect that is a byproduct of a rack focus.

broadcast quality A nominally objective set of standards that represents the industry requirements for a video image that is of sufficient quality to be broadcast.

cable puller Sound crew member who helps with setup, keeps the mic cords out of the way during the shot, and often takes care of the sound logs.

call sheets Inform the talent and crew of the time they must be on the set, how much time is devoted to makeup and hair, and the like.

callbacks Used to take a closer look at talent after general auditions.

camcorder A combined camera and video recorder in one unit.

camera mounts Umbrella term that includes tripods, dollies, cranes, Steadicams, and many other specialized camera mounts. Also called *camera support systems.*

camera noise Problematic sound created by the camera during sync takes.

camera obscura A phenomenon in which light passing through a pinhole creates an upside-down representation.

camera operator On most commercial films, the person who does the actual shooting.

camera package Umbrella term for the camera, lenses, magazines, batteries, battery chargers, tripod, and any other camera needs specific to a shoot.

camera report The daily record of shooting kept by the 1st or 2nd AC. Also called *log.*

camera support systems See *camera mounts.*

camera tape An opaque tape with an adhesive that does not leave a gummy residue. One of its many purposes is to protect the film against light leaks.

Canon plug See *XLR plug.*

capacitor mics See *condenser mics.*

capture Acquisition of image and/or audio into a digital environment.

cardioid mics Microphones that pick up sound in a heart-shaped pattern; pickup is to the front of the mic to the general exclusion of sound sources behind.

cement splicer Cements shots together, used mainly in preparing rolls for printing. Also called *hot splicer.*

CGI (computer-generated images) Film frames and shots that are either manipulated or wholly created in a computer environment.

changing bag See *photographic darkroom bag.*

characteristic curve A representation of a film stock's latitude that plots the density of grains on the negative against rising exposure.

charge-coupled device (CCD) A flat board behind the lens in a video camera that is covered with thousands of light-sensitive pixels. The chip collects the light and turns it into an electrical signal. Also called *chip.*

cheating Shifting elements in the composition to balance the frame, thus improving an otherwise problematic shot.

checkerboarding See *A & B rolling.*

chip A flat board behind the lens in a video camera that is covered with thousands of light-sensitive pixels. The chip collects the light and turns it into an electrical signal. Also called *charge-coupled device.*

chip chart Used by the lab to set printer lights; a series of distinct colors on a chart that are shot at the head of every roll.

cinematographer See *director of photography (DP).*

circuit A series of outlets that are tied to a breaker or fuse in the main power box.

clapper/loader The crew member responsible for slating shots and loading magazines. Also called *second assistant cameraperson (2nd AC).*

clean room A space that is designed to be clean and dust-free for cutting original film.

clips The generic term in an NLE program for shots and audio takes.

close-up (CU) Essentially a head shot, usually from the top button of a shirt up. Variations are the *extreme close-up (ECU)* and the *medium close-up (MCU).*

coaxial A magazine design that has the feed roll in a chamber on one side and the take-up in a second chamber on the other side.

coding A set of numbers printed on both the picture and sync-sound rolls, used as a reference for sync.

color balance The way film stocks are designed to respond to different colors of light.

colorist The studio employee who operates the telecine transfer. The colorist has a wide range of color and exposure controls at his or her disposal.

color temperature The distinct color of a given light source, measured in degrees Kelvin.

color temperature meter Measures the color temperature of light sources.

component video A newer standard that breaks down the video signal into the conventional RGB elements plus a luminance component.

composite video The conventional standard that breaks down the video signal into RGB elements.

composition The arrangement of shapes and forms within an artistic frame.

compression The discarding of duplicating digital information to facilitate the efficient storage and easy retrieval of video footage. Some digital formats (such as Mini DV) compress very heavily, and many high-end formats employ no compression.

condenser mics Microphones whose signal is produced by battery power. Also called *capacitor mics.*

conformist See *negative cutter.*

contact print A print made in a lab by sandwiching the processed original film with a piece of raw stock.

continuity shooting The creation of shots that when cut together appear to be continuous, creating a real-time relationship between the shots.

contrast The play between light and dark in the photographic image.

contrast ratio See *lighting ratio.*

control track A type of track employed on some videotapes, devoted to a series of pulses that control the playback speed of the tape and that can be used to identify frames.

core A circular piece of plastic on which film is wound.

core adapters Used in the magazine to compensate for the larger centers of cores.

core loads Raw stock loaded on cores.

countdown leader The leader with descending numbers at the beginning of films. Also called *Academy leader* and *SMPTE Universal leader.*

coverage Shooting action from more than one angle to provide options in the editing room.

crane A camera support on a rolling vehicle with a single elevating arm.

crosshairs Two intersecting lines in the center of a camera's viewing screen.

crystal camera A speed-controlled camera that is required in order to record sync sound and effects.

crystal motor See *synchronous (sync) motor.*

C-stand Short for *Century stand,* a commonly used stand for setting nets, flags, silks, and the like.

cue sheet The log of mixtracks that assists the mixing process. Also called *mixing log.*

cutaway A shot to which the editor can cut away to show an action or solve an editing problem.

cuts-only video Basic video-editing system that performs only straight cuts from one shot to another.

dailies The footage from the previous day's work. Also called *rushes.*

daylight (D) Photographic white; that is, 5,500° K.

daylight spool Camera load that allows film to be loaded in subdued light.

DC servo-controlled motor See *synchronous (sync) motor.*

decay Describes how sound trails off and reverberates.

decibel (dB) An increment in the measurement of the amplitude of sound.

deck control The function of NLE software that controls playback operations of a video camera or deck.

deep focus A theoretical approach that keeps all elements in the frame in sharp focus. See also *shallow focus.*

depth of field The distance down the field of the camera's view that remains in sharp focus.

depth-of-field tables Charts of the near and far parameters of focus for the common focal lengths.

detent A click stop at a position on a moveable ring.

diffused light Light that has passed through a medium or that has reflected off a textured surface; it is indirect light.

digital audiotape (DAT) Digital sound-recording technology.

Digi Beta See *Digital Betacam.*

Digital Betacam A Sony format that is one of the high-end standards for NTSC digital video. Also known as *Digi Beta.*

digital video (DV) The storage of a digital signal (0's and 1's) on a conventional magnetic medium.

digitizing The process of encoding analog video information into a digital form.

diopter An adjustable glass element in the eyepiece that allows operators to adjust the viewing system to the peculiarities of their eyes.

director Usually the key decision-making force in all stages of a film.

director of photography (DP) Responsible for all things photographic for the film, primarily composition and lighting. Also called *cinematographer.*

dissolve Technique in which one shot is faded out while the next shot is faded in on top of it. Also called *lap dissolve.*

dissolve rates Rates of dissolves available at labs; 16, 24, 32, 48, 64, and 96 frames are the standard options.

dolly Wheeled vehicle with a camera mounting device on it.

double perf Film stock with sprocket holes on both sides. Also called *two row.*

double-system sound Audio-recording method whereby sound and picture are recorded separately.

downloading Unloading the film.

dramatic emphasis Use of the camera to show the action in the order and with the amplification desired.

dummy load A ruined roll of raw stock used for practice loading.

Dutch angle See *oblique shot.*

DVCAM Considered an industrial standard, a later upgrade from Mini DV that has proven both popular and durable.

DVCPRO Considered an industrial standard, the initial professional upgrade from Mini DV.

DVD (digital videodisc) Primarily familiar as a playback medium, mastering to DVD is fast becoming an important option in film production.

dynamic mics Microphones whose signal is produced by air movement within a magnetic field.

edge numbering The process of transferring edge numbers onto synced mag stock.

edge numbers Latent numbers encoded in all film stocks by the manufacturer. Also called *key numbers.*

edit control unit (ECU) Control hardware on which video-editing decisions are previewed, made, and programmed.

edit decision list (EDL) From an edited video program, a list that represents the beginning and ending points of all shots as well as all visual effects.

edited workprint (EWP) The workprint version of the film that is created during editing.

editing The process of selecting the shots and sounds that are good and serve the needs of the film, putting them in the order desired, and cutting them to the appropriate lengths in relation to each other.

editing bench A table with rewinds, viewer, synchronizer, and any other pertinent editing equipment.

editor Head of the editorial staff, responsible for creating a workable version of the film.

edit sync A hole punched at the head of rolls, used to sync them.

electricians Lighting-crew members responsible to the gaffer.

elements The sound rolls and picture rolls used to create the final print.

emulsion A gelatin bath that contains the silver halide crystals used in exposure.

equalizer Signal processor commonly used to manipulate the quality of sound, cutting or boosting it at specific frequencies.

establishing shot See *master shot.*

expendables Supplies used while shooting, such as spun, gel, gaffer's tape, and so on.

exposure index (EI) A numerical rating of a film stock's sensitivity to light. Also referred to as *ASA* (American Standards Association), *ISO* (International Standards Organization), and *film speed.*

external video device General term describing the video playback machine that is controlled by an NLE software system.

extreme close-up (ECU) A very tight close-up, essentially nose and eyes.

extreme long shot (ELS) Shot in which the subject is far away from the camera.

eye-level shot Shot taken with the camera near the eye level of the subject.

eye light Light used to highlight a subject's eyes.

eyeroom Compositional space given in the direction a character is looking. Also called *looking room.*

fade-in Where the picture fades up from black.

fade-out Where the picture fades out to black.

fade rates Lengths of fades that labs will do; 16, 24, 32, 48, 64, and 96 frames are standard fade rates.

faders The sliding amplitude controls on a studio mixing console. Also called *potentiometers (pots)* and *gain controls.*

fader unit A valve in the printer that is opened and closed to create the overall effects (fades, dissolves, and so on).

falloff The speed (degree) with which light intensity decreases as it gets farther from an instrument.

feature A film roughly seventy minutes or more that is intended for commercial release.

feed spool Holds the unexposed film in the film chamber.

field mixer Used for mixing microphones on location. Also called *mic mixer.*

fill light Fills in the harsh shadows created by the key.

film A work that can be projected photographically in a theater.

film chamber The space in the camera where the unexposed and exposed film is stored.

film noir Most identified with the 1940s, a style of film that used stark and atmospheric imagery to suggest a claustrophobic world filled with the darker and more ambiguous aspects of character motivation.

film plane The place where the film is exposed.

film speed See *exposure index (EI).*

film tape Used on the barrel of the camera lens for marking focus points and for hanging shots in the editing room. Also called *white paper tape.*

filter holders See *filter slots.*

filters *(audio)* Options on an audio recorder that affect a wide range of frequencies above or below a certain point. *(visual)* Glass or gel material that alters the color, quantity, or character of light.

filter slots Small slots either in the film chamber or on the exterior of the camera, where a filter in a holder can be inserted. Also called *filter holders.*

final audio mixdown See *audio mixing.*

fine cut In editing, the fine-tuning of the rough cut.

FireWire A connection that can transfer a high volume of information.

first assembly Putting the desired takes in the order laid out in the script. Also called *string-out.*

first assistant cameraperson (1st AC) The crew member responsible for everything to do with the cleanliness and operation of the camera.

fish eye A lens that sees almost a full 180 degrees in front of the camera.

flag A framed square or rectangular piece of black material used to block specific paths of light.

flange The lip on the back of the lens that is inserted into the camera.

flash frames The overexposed frames at the beginning and end of every shot.

flashing Running unprocessed film past a small light to create an effect.

flatbed Tabletop editing machine in common use.

flex file A data file created during the telecine process that interrelates film edge numbers with time code for matchback.

floodlight Lighting instrument that produces a diffused, indirect light beam; the three types are scoops, broads, and softlights.

fluid camera technique An approach to efficient shooting that smoothes out or eliminates bumpy camerawork.

fluid-effect head Similar to friction head, but moving parts are further cushioned with an enclosed viscous fluid that assists smooth pan and tilt movements.

fluid heads Common professional tripod head used to produce smooth movements.

flying spot scanner An approach to film-to-video transfer that employs a strong piece of light that is shot through the film; it rapidly scans each frame, separating out the RGB and luminance components to create the video image.

focal length The length of a lens, calibrated in millimeters or, less common, inches.

focusable spot Lighting instrument that produces a direct, specular light beam; can be lensed or open-faced.

focus ring Ring on the lens where focus is set for every shot.

Foley Method of creating sound effects in a specially equipped studio.

footage counter Indicator that keeps track of how much film has been shot. Also called *gas gauge.*

foot-candle (fc) Unit of measure of light based on volume of light 1 foot from a candle.

force processing Overdeveloping film, generally used to compensate for underexposure. Also called *pushing.*

format The size of the film stock and the image size. Three standard formats are in common use: 35mm, 16mm, and Super 8. In video, formats include Mini DV, DVCPRO, DVCAM, Digi Beta, and VHS.

frame Each individual photographic image on a piece of motion picture film.

frame counter Gauge on the camera that counts individual frames, helpful in such applications as animation.

frame line The hairline dividing one frame from another.

frame rate See *frames per second (fps).*

frame rulers Linear, rulerlike representations of film used to count frames in editing.

frames per second (fps) The number of individual frames photographed per second; the professional frame rate is 24 fps. Slower speeds create fast motion, and higher speeds yield slow motion. Also called *frame rate.*

freeze frame A printing technique that repeats individual frames to freeze the action.

French flag A small flag on an articulated arm that mounts on the camera, used to cut lens flares.

frequency range The spectrum of audible and inaudible sound, represented in hertz.

frequency response How evenly and completely a specific recorder or playback format reproduces the audible range.

Fresnel The most popular type of lensed lighting instrument, whose lens employs steplike concentric rings of glass. Named for its inventor.

friction head A type of tripod head that employs swelling rings to create resistance in pan and tilt movements.

front-filter A glass filter mounted in front of the lens.

front-surfaced mirror A mirror that is coated on a surface (of a shutter, for example) for optimal optical performance.

f-stop A diaphragm in the lens that is used to regulate the amount of light reaching the film plane.

full-blue gel Modifying material that cuts a lighting instrument's output by one f-stop and adds a blue component to amber tungsten instruments, bringing them up to the daylight color temperature.

full-body shot Shot that includes a person from head to toe. Also called *full shot.*

fullcoat See *mag stock.*

full shot See *full-body shot.*

gaffer Key crew member who heads the lighting crew and is responsible for the technical implementation of the DP's lighting plan.

gaffer's tape A 2-inch-wide tape used for a multitude of purposes on a set.

gain controls The sliding amplitude controls on a studio mixing console. Also called *faders* and *potentiometers (pots)*.

gang synchronizer Consists of interlocked rolling drums (gangs) with sprocket teeth; sound and picture are locked into gangs and fed through the synchronizer in sync.

gas gauge See *footage counter*.

gate See *aperture*.

gear heads Separate gears that control movement of the tripod head and are in turn controlled by hand cranks.

gel A colored cellophane-like material used on a light to change its color or quality.

generation The number of dubs away from the original recording. In the family tree of an image or a piece of sound, a first-generation copy is struck directly from the original. A second generation is a copy of a first-generation print (two steps away from the original), and so on. The greater the number of nondigital generations, the greater the quality loss.

grader See *timer*.

grain The silver halide crystals that are the building blocks of the photographic image; similar to pixels on a computer screen.

gray scale Represents a series of distinct shades of gray, from black to white.

grip The jack-of-all-trades on the set.

grip equipment Specialized clamps and tools used for mounting instruments.

half-moon shutter A half-disc–shaped shutter that rotates in front of the gate.

handheld camera An approach that can give a sense of urgency or chaos to action, often making the viewer feel like a participant.

handles See *ambience overlaps*.

Hazeltine Equipment used to analyze each individual shot prior to printing.

HDTV (high-definition television) A newer, high-resolution broadcast standard that employs a widescreen aspect ratio closer to standard 35mm theatrical presentation. Also known as *Hi-Def*.

head Mechanism with pan and tilt controls on which the camera is mounted. Also refers to the beginning of a shot or roll.

headroom *(audio)* Room above 0 VU where the recorder still reproduces an undistorted signal. *(visual)* Compositional space above a subject's head.

helical scan recording A rotating record head that multiplies the speed of tape travel, employed in video and digital audio-recording technologies.

hertz (Hz) Measurement of the pitch of a sound.

Hi-Def See *HDTV (high-definition television)*.

high-angle shot Shooting from above that tends to diminish a subject.

high-frequency attenuators (HFAs) Audio filters that cut frequencies above a preset level.

high hat A tripod head mount that stands about 6 inches tall, used for mounting a camera on a tabletop or other surface.

high-key Even, fairly flat lighting; one could call it nonjudgmental lighting.

high-pass filters Audio filters that allow high frequencies to pass through while filtering out low frequencies.

hiss Inherent system noise in analog recorders.

HMI lighting A relatively new line of daylight–color temperature instruments.

hot splicer See *cement splicer*.

hyperfocal distance The closest focus point that includes infinity in the depth of field.

inches per second (ips) The standard measurement of the rate of travel of audiotape—the running speed.

inching knob Used to manually move the camera's action backward or forward.

incident light The light that is falling on a subject. See also *incident-light meter*.

incident-light meter Measures in foot-candles how much light is falling on a subject; you point the meter into the light source or toward the camera.

inserts See *reaction shots*.

instrument Industry term for the equipment used to produce light—a lighting instrument.

interlaced video Video that interlaces alternating fields of information to create each individual frame. NTSC and PAL are interlaced.

intermittent movement The alternately moving and stationary state of the film as it is being exposed.

invisible editing Conventional approach to cutting in which the editing is designed to go largely unnoticed by the viewer.

jam sync A style of slating scenes in which the camera and sound recorder are fed a common time code at the beginning of every shooting day.

jump cut A cut in which there is a jump in time between the shots.

keepers Keep the film tight against the sprocketed rollers in the camera.

Kelvin (K) Measurement of color temperature.

key grip The head of the grip crew.

key light Usually the major source of illumination, generally a beam of light that casts harsh shadows.

key numbers See *edge numbers*.

kicker light A light that comes in and brushes or rims the cheek.

kilowatt (k) One thousand watts.

kinescope A motion picture camera designed to photograph video off a television monitor.

Kodalith See *sheet negative*.

lab The motion picture processing laboratory.

lamp Industry term for the bulb used in a lighting instrument.

lap dissolve See *dissolve*.

Latham's loops A bend in the film where the continuous motion of the sprocketed rollers and the intermittent movement of the pull-down claw are reconciled.

latitude The range of lighting values within which a film stock will produce a usable exposure.

lav See *lavalier mics*.

lavalier mics Small clip-on mics that are frequently used for interviews, although they have a wide variety of applications in film. Also called *lavs*.

lens The vehicle that transfers light to the film.

lens flare Effect caused by light shining into the lens, producing either washed-out areas or multifaceted patterns on the image.

lens mount The method with which the lens is attached to the camera.

lens perspective The way a lens represents space.

lens speed The maximum aperture—the widest the lens diaphragm will go.

lens support system Rods that extend from the body of the camera to support the weight of the lens, avoiding undue stress on the camera's lens mount.

lens turret A moveable plate in front of the film gate with which you can rotate different lenses in front of the film, allowing you to switch lenses between shots.

lighting The application and manipulation of artificial light for illuminating a scene—a key building block of the photographic image.

lighting continuity Creating photographic consistency between shots.

lighting ratio Representation of the relationship between the key and the fill. Also called *contrast ratio.*

light leaks Any unwanted light striking the film, caused by irregularities in the camera's tight-fitting junctions.

light struck Footage that is exposed to light in the loading process. All efforts are made to minimize the amount of film subject to this effect.

lighttrap Chamber where the film passes out of the magazine, designed to ensure that light will not seep in.

limiter Audio recorder feature that adjusts peak signals that are liable to be distorted.

line The principle used to create an understandable sense of the space in which the action is occurring. Also called *180-degree rule* and *axis of action.*

lined script A version of the script created by the script supervisor while filming; uses vertical lines to detail the action being covered from each setup.

line in Input jack for transferring an audio signal from another machine.

line jump Breaking the 180-degree rule.

line out Output jack for transferring an audio signal to another machine.

line signal Specific type of audio signal that is used to transfer sound from machine to machine.

location scouting The process of finding locations suitable for individual scenes.

lockdown Where a camera is securely fixed with weights or hardware so there will be absolutely no movement between one take and the next.

log See *camera report.*

long shot (LS) A shot that includes the full human body or more.

look The visual character of an individual film stock, mostly has to do with issues of grain, color separation, and how stocks respond to under- and overexposure.

looking room See *eyeroom.*

looping See *automated dialogue replacement (ADR).*

loop setters Small guards above and below the gate on automatic-threading cameras that create loops of the appropriate size and shape.

low-angle shot A shot in which the camera is below the subject, tending to make characters or environments look threatening, powerful, or intimidating.

low-frequency attenuators (LFAs) Audio filters that cut low-frequency signals.

low-key Contrast lighting that is atmospheric and might be considered judgmental.

low-pass filters Audio filters that allow low frequencies to pass through while cutting high frequencies.

luminance See *reflectant quality.*

mag See *magazine.*

mag stock Audio stock that is the same size and dimension as the film itself; the medium for audio cutting in conventional film editing. Also called *fullcoat.*

magazine A separate film chamber that is mounted on the camera. Also called *mag.*

married print A print in which the two entities—picture and sound—are finally joined together.

master mix The product of the mixdown of the mixtracks; the final sound for a film.

master scene technique Common approach to shooting scenes, in which the sequence of LS-MS-CU is used to move from general to very specific information.

master shot A shot that establishes the setting: where the characters are, any important objects that may be present, and so on. Also called *establishing shot.*

matchback The process of converting the frame information from a digital edit to the edge numbers needed to conform a version of original film.

match cut A cut in which the action matches from one camera angle to the next.

matte box An accordion-like bellows attachment that is mounted on the front of the lens on which to mount filters or to shade the lens from direct light.

maximum aperture The widest *f*-stop opening on an individual lens.

mechanical head A type of tripod head that employs swelling rings to create resistance in pan and tilt movements.

medium close-up (MCU) A shot of a person that is a little wider than a standard close-up.

medium shot (MS) A shot of a person from roughly the waist up.

memory Phenomenon in which a battery memorizes the small amount of charge it needs to be topped off if it has not been totally discharged often enough.

mic mixer See *field mixer.*

mic signal A specific audio signal that is created by a microphone.

Mini DV The most common consumer digital video format.

mini plug A smaller version of the quarter-inch plug, generally used as a microphone input on consumer cassette recorders and video cameras.

minimum aperture The smallest *f*-stop opening on an individual lens.

mirrored butterfly shutter Shutter shaped like a butterfly that, as it rotates, alternately sends light to the film plane and to the viewing system.

mixing log See *cue sheet.*

mixtracks The sound rolls created in the editing process.

modulometer See *peak program meter (ppm).*

mono Short for *monaural.* Single-signal channel presentation wherein the sound is presented as a single signal as opposed to separated as in a stereo or multi-channeled configuration.

MOS Shots executed without sound being recorded.

Nagra A popular audio recorder for sync-sound filming.

negative cutter Person who matches the original to the edited workprint. Also called *conformist.*

negative cutting The process of conforming the camera original to the edited workprint.

negative film Stock that has all the lights and darks reversed from how they are normally perceived.

nicad Rechargeable nickel-cadmium battery used for many cameras with electric motors.

nondestructive editing An approach found on some NLE systems, in which the shots and sounds can still be lengthened and shortened after being brought onto the timeline.

nonlinear editing (NLE) Hardware and software systems that permit editing digitized video on a computer.

nonsync sound Sound that is recorded at times other than when the camera is recording; includes location sounds, studio recordings, and prerecorded music tracks.

normal exposure The exposure that produces a clear and true-to-life picture.

normal lens A lens that essentially gives a normal representation of space.

NTSC (National Television System Committee) Organization that sets the standards for video signals in the United States. The 29.97-frames-per-second American standard is referred to as *NTSC.*

oblique shot Shot where the camera is tilted laterally; often used to suggest imbalance. Also called *Dutch angle.*

off-line editing Editing system in which time-consuming editorial decisions are made within a less sophisticated, less expensive, low-resolution environment.

ohm A unit of measurement of the resistance to a signal passing through a line.

omnidirectional mics Microphones that pick up sound in a spherical pattern, that is, equally in all directions.

one row See *single perf.*

on-line editing A high-end, high-resolution editing environment wherein projects can be finished at the highest quality possible.

Open Media Framework Interchange (OMFI or OMF) An open framework that allows the export and import of any media information among different NLE, audio, and graphics software programs.

optical effects Effects done during final printing, such as dissolves, fades, wipes, and supers.

optical master The photographic printing element for a film's sound track; it is a blank piece of film except for a narrow strip of diamond-shaped patterns opposite the side with the sprocket holes.

optical printer Used to rephotograph existing footage; essentially a camera shooting into an apparatus that projects the film.

optical track The photographic sound track that is printed on the edge of the final film.

opticals Graphic effects that are created at the lab prior to final printing, including split screens, keyholes, freeze frames, spins, wipes, and a host of other effects.

orange mask Leader that is the shade that creates black in the resulting color prints from color negative.

original The film that actually ran through the camera when shooting.

outtakes Unused shots, usually stored together on rolls for easy review.

overexposure Film that received too much light, resulting in overly bright images.

overhead Drawn view of a scene from above; helpful for planning blocking and camera positions.

overhead shot See *bird's-eye view.*

overlapping dialogue cut A cut in which the transition from one shot to the next occurs during a line of dialogue.

over-the-shoulder (OTS) A shot done over a character's shoulder.

pan A shot in which the camera is simply pivoted horizontally on the tripod. In lighting, it is turning the instrument on a stand in a similar fashion.

parallax A problem on rangefinder cameras, where the viewfinder is not seeing precisely the same frame that the film is seeing.

parallax adjustment A control to correct parallax problems.

peak program meter (ppm) An improvement on the VU meter that reads the peak of every signal from the microphone or line. Also called *modulometer.*

perforations See *sprocket holes.*

phantom mics Mics powered by the recorder's battery rather than an internal battery.

phasing A complex phenomenon in which specific frequencies are canceled out and thus not recorded.

phone plug See *quarter-inch plug.*

photographic consistency The challenge of creating shots that will match in terms of color and quality of light when cut together.

photographic darkroom bag A double-zippered bag used to load and download raw stock in total darkness. Also called *changing bag.*

pickup pattern Refers to how a mic picks up sound that is coming from different directions. Also called *polar pattern.*

picture gate The opening that light passes through to project the film on an editing machine or a projector.

picture lock The point when the editor determines that picture editing is completed, usually followed by extensive sound-effects and music editing.

pitch Distance between sprocket holes on the film stock.

pixel Short for *picture element.* The imaging sensing devices on the video camera's chip that translate the light it receives into an electrical signal.

plant mics Mics placed on a set to pick up sound in areas that are difficult to boom.

plastic memory Tendency of the film stock to stiffen in the shape in which it was left.

playhead A scrolling line in an NLE system that moves horizontally, indicating where you are in the clip or program.

point-of-view shot Shot that represents the vision or the viewpoint of a specific character.

polar pattern See *pickup pattern.*

postdubbing Recording replacement sync-sound dialogue in postproduction with the intent of editing into sound tracks.

postproduction The editing stages of a film, including scoring, titling, and all finishing processes.

potentiometers (pots) The sliding amplitude controls on a studio mixing console. Also called *faders* and *gain controls.*

preamp A small amplifier in a mic or line chain that boosts a weak signal to recordable or amplifiable levels.

preproduction The process of putting the film in position to shoot.

presence The innate audio ambience of a given space. Also called *room tone.*

pressure plate Holds the film flat against the gate area in the camera.

preview window The window in an NLE program where the edited program is played.

prime lens Any fixed-focal-length, that is, nonzoom, lens.

principal shooting Denotes the concentrated shooting schedule of a film's scenes.

printer A contact printer where film is duplicated.

printer lights The individual controls of the three primary colors of light—red, green, and blue—in a printer.

printer points Increments in the intensity of a printer light.

printing The general term for the process of duplicating processed original onto frame-for-frame copies.

printing cues The instructions to the printer lights and fader unit needed for every shot.

printing down Using the intensity of the printer lights to deal with overexposure.

printing program A computer-generated decision list that will run the printer lights and fader unit.

printing up Using the intensity of the printer lights to deal with underexposure.

producer The person who is the central organization and capitalization force in a motion picture's production.

production Includes all the actual shooting.

production assistant (PA) Generally responsible to the assistant director, PAs are go-fers who are available to handle any last-minute details on a set or in the production office.

production board A large board that cross-references the scenes with the resources needed to execute them. This is now largely computerized.

production designer (PD) The person responsible for the design of all of a film's settings.

production manager (PM) The person responsible for the day-to-day scheduling and running of a film's production.

production office Central command center for a film shoot.

production sound The sound recorded while filming. It is generally, though not exclusively, dialogue. Also called *sync sound*.

production values An umbrella term that refers to the amount of resources devoted to the image.

progressive video The sequential presentation of video information. Computer monitors and a number of high-end digital formats employ the progressive standard.

projection print A duplicate copy of the final product of a film project, produced for distribution and exhibition.

projector The equipment used to show a film on a screen.

proxemics From the word *proximity*, it refers to the distance between subject and camera.

pull-down The process of slowing down sound so it can stay synchronized with film transferred to video that runs at 29.97 frames per second.

pull-down claw The mechanism that advances each individual film frame for exposure.

pull-up The process of speeding up sound edited in NTSC to match the faster speed of film.

pushing See *force processing*.

quarter-inch plug An audio plug used extensively as a mic or line connection. Also called *phone plug*.

quick-release plate A detachable plate that is used to easily secure the camera to the tripod head.

rack focus Physically shifting the focus ring as a shot is being executed.

radio mic See *wireless mic*.

rangefinder viewing A viewing system in which the operator looks through a facsimile lens that is mounted on the side or top of the camera.

raw footage The rolls of uncut footage.

raw stock The unexposed film purchased from the manufacturer.

RCA plug Probably the most common audio line connection; found on a wide range of equipment from consumer stereos to VCRs.

reaction shots Wordless shots of characters reacting to action. Also called *inserts*.

recanning Putting a short end back in its packaging when rolls are downloaded at the end of a day or for any other reason.

record run A style of slating scenes in which the sound recorder produces the time code, which is sent to the slate via a radio transmitter.

reflectant quality The way objects and materials reflect light and how film responds to that light. Also called *luminance*.

reflective light Light that is bounced off the illuminated subject. See also *reflective-light meter*.

reflective-light meter Measures how much light is reflecting off a subject; you hold the meter close to the camera, pointed toward the illuminated object.

reflex viewing The industry-standard viewing system in which the operator is actually looking through the camera's lens while filming. Also called *through-the-lens (TTL) viewing*.

registration The stability, or lack thereof, of the film image as it is being exposed in the gate.

registration pin A small pin that holds the image steady as it is being exposed in the gate.

release print Designed for exhibition, all subsequent prints that use an acceptable answer print as the guide.

rendering A time-consuming process specific to certain NLE systems, in which an edited sequence must be saved to the hard drive before it can be played.

rerecording mixer An employee of the mixing facility who orchestrates the mix at the filmmaker's instruction.

resistance The force in a tripod head against the operator's movement.

resolution By width and height, the amount of pixels devoted to each digitized video frame. The general broadcast standard for a finished video is 640 × 480.

reversal film Has all colors and shades rendered normally on the original.

rewinds Mechanism on an editing bench for hand-winding the film.

RGB Abbreviation for the three primary colors of light: red, green, and blue.

riding gain The process of watching the display on an audio recorder, manipulating amplitude control to ensure that the sound is being optimally recorded at all times.

room tone See *presence*.

rough cut The first complete cut of a film.

rule of thirds Draws lines that divide the frame into thirds horizontally and vertically; used as guides for creating a balanced composition.

run-through Rehearsing a scene at normal speed, generally used to watch for technical problems.

rushes See *dailies*.

sandbags Used to secure tripods, light stands, and other equipment against tipping over.

scale The size of objects in relation to one another in the frame.

scene The basic unit of a script, with action occurring in a single setting and in real time.

scene correction Another name for a supervised transfer in which the colorist determines exposure and color for each individual scene during the transfer process.

scratch track A conventional sync track that serves as a guide in editing.

script supervisor The crew member responsible for keeping track of continuity as well as other general script considerations.

scrub To move slowly or frame-by-frame through picture or sound in NLE software.

second assistant cameraperson (2nd AC) The crew member responsible for slating shots and loading magazines. Also called *clapper/loader*.

selects The shots that have been selected for use in the first assembly.

series 9 filters The most common size of filters and ring adapters for 16mm zoom lenses.

set director The crew member responsible for planning the small items on the set.

set lights Instruments used to create effects in parts of the set.

setup The basic component of a film's production; refers to each individual camera position, placement, or angle.

shallow focus An approach in which several different planes of sharp and soft focus are incorporated within a single image. See also *deep focus*.

sheet negative Used to photograph title cards. Also called *Kodalith*.

shock mount A suspension system that absorbs any moderate shocks to the microphone or boom.

shooting for the edit Denotes the importance of considering while shooting a scene how it is going to be edited.

shooting script A detailed, annotated version of the script, usually put together by the director.

short ends The remaining unexposed portion of a roll at either the end of a day's shooting or when a fresh roll needs to be loaded.

short lens See *wide-angle lens*.

shot Commonly defined as the footage created from the moment the camera is turned on until it is turned off; a sequence of frames.

shot list A less formal alternative to the storyboard; a list of brief written descriptions of the intended shots.

shot/reverse shot Involves shooting all of one person's dialogue and then moving the camera to the reverse shot to shoot all of another person's dialogue.

shoulder The precipitous drop-off at the overexposure end of a film stock's latitude.

shutter Constantly rotating in front of the gate, it blocks the light while the film is being pulled down and then allows the light to reach the film when the frame is stationary for exposure.

shutter speed The amount of time each frame is exposed. In motion pictures it is usually a constant that is dependent on frames per second.

sightlines The direction that a character or characters are looking in a shot.

signal path The route that an audio or video signal takes.

silver halide crystals Crystals suspended in the film's emulsion that change their properties when struck by light and subjected to chemical developers.

single perf Film stock with sprocket holes on only one side. Also called *one row.*

single-system sound Audio-recording method whereby sound is recorded along the edge of the film.

slate The clapboard used to start sync scenes.

slug Leader or junk picture that is used to fill in the empty spots on the sound rolls. Also called *sound fill.*

slug rolls Rolls of junk picture or leader into which nonsync sound is cut.

smart slate A slate with a radio receiver that displays rolling time code on its face.

SMPTE Universal leader Standard countdown leader with descending numbers at the beginning of films; from the Society of Motion Picture and Television Engineers (SMPTE). Also called *Academy leader* and *countdown leader.*

sound Produced by the compression and separation of air molecules, generally represented as a wave.

sound effects (SFX) Incidental sound cut to action, not music or the spoken word.

sound fill See *slug.*

sound log Similar to a camera report, the log of the daily activity of the sound crew.

sound mixer The person who operates the tape recorder and is head of the sound crew.

sound perspective Refers to the way we expect to experience sound at specific proxemic positions.

sound track Can refer to any edited track of audio, but generally used to refer to a finished version of a program's sound.

specular light Light that is direct; it is generally produced by focusable spotlights.

spider See *spreader.*

spill Excess light from an instrument.

splicer The block on which one piece of film or sound is cut to another.

splicing frames The two frames that are sacrificed at each end of a shot when cement-splicing the original film.

split reel Reel with a threaded center so the two flanges can be detached.

spot printing A common practice on feature films, in which desired takes are circled on the camera report for later identification and printing.

spreader An apparatus with three extendable arms that is put on the floor to hold the tripod legs in position. Also called *spider* and *tri-downs.*

spring-wound motor A camera motor driven by a spring similar to that found in a mechanical clock.

sprocket holes Holes along the edges of a strip of film that facilitate movement past the gate. Also called *perforations.*

sprocketed rollers Feed the film into and out of the area where each image is exposed.

spuds The mounting piece on most small light stands.

squawk box An amplifier/speaker used on an editing bench.

standard legs Tripod that extends from roughly four to seven feet, used for shots that are done at a standard height.

Steadicam™ A device that mounts on the camera operator's chest, giving fluid movement to what are essentially handheld shots.

stereo Channel configuration wherein recorded sound is separated into two components and is presented on different speakers in amplification.

storyboard Has each shot drawn on one side of the page with the script material it covers—dialogue, action, and so on—on the other side. Also called *board.*

straight cut A visual cut at the end of one line of dialogue to the beginning of the next.

stress Aesthetic result of an unbalanced image. Also called *tension.*

string-out See *first assembly.*

studio mixing console A large audio mixing board generally used for mixing multiple sound components down to one master version of a program's sound.

sunshade Mounted on the front of a lens, it shades the lens from direct light.

super See *superimposition.*

Super 8 The smallest format in common use and the amateur standard for years.

Super 16 An adaptation of the 16mm format that uses the area of the film that would be taken up by the second row of sprocket holes for additional image area.

superimposition One shot overlaid on another; can be achieved either in the camera while shooting or in the editorial and final printing processes. Also called *super.*

supervised transfer A telecine transfer in which the video colorist determines settings for each individual scene.

sync The synchronization between sound and image.

sync beep A single frame of mag stock that creates a beep that is cut across from the Academy 2. Also called *sync pop.*

sync pop See *sync beep.*

sync rolls The mag stock transfers of the production sound.

sync sound Sound that is recorded as the camera is rolling on location or on the soundstage. Also know as *production sound.*

synchronous (sync) motor A speed-controlled motor that produces a virtually perfect 24 fps. Also called a *crystal* or a *DC servo-controlled motor.*

syncing up Using the slate to match the production sound with the image.

tail slate A slate done at the end of a shot as opposed to at the head.

tail The end of a shot or roll.

takes The number of attempts at a shot needed to produce at least several usable versions.

take-up spool Takes up the film after it has been exposed.

talent Umbrella term for all the performers in a film.

tape-direct switch Gives the choice of monitoring the playback or record heads.

target The series of markings on the viewing screen.

technical camera Everything concerning the camera except calling different shots.

telecine A high-end film-to-video transfer machine generally found at a film lab or video postproduction studio.

telephoto lens A long lens that magnifies the subject in a manner similar to binoculars.

tension See *stress.*

three:two pull-down The common strategy for converting between film and video frame rates in which the telecine prints three video fields of every other film frame.

three-point setup The textbook approach to figure lighting, comprising a key light, a fill light, and a backlight.

through-the-lens (TTL) viewing See *reflex viewing.*

tilt A shot with the camera moved vertically on a tripod head. In lighting, it is turning the instrument on a stand in a similar fashion.

time code A rolling clock encoded on the videotape that provides an address for each individual frame.

timeline Frequently used name for the master editing control window in an NLE system.

timer A lab employee who goes through the entire film and analyzes each individual shot for color and exposure. Also called *grader.*

timing The process of evaluating each shot before printing.

titles The credit lines for a film or video.

toe The precipitous drop-off to underexposure at the edge of a film's latitude.

track Specially built track used for fluid movement.

tracking shot A shot that follows alongside, in front of, or behind a moving subject.

transitional devices Shots that bridge one setting to another or that mark the passage of time.

transports The mechanism that moves the film or mag stock past the picture gate and audio playback head.

tri-downs See *spreader.*

trim bin Bin for hanging film during editing.

trimming Changing the shape, quality, or intensity of the light an instrument produces.

trims In editing, frames trimmed from the shots you are using.

tripod Three-legged camera support; what is referred to as a tripod is actually two separate pieces—the legs and the head.

tripod threading holes One or more holes in the bottom of the camera body that are used to attach the camera to the head.

t-stop Takes into account the light that is lost by passing through a lens.

tungsten (T) Lamps rated for motion picture photography that are 3,200° K. They produce the same color a black-bodied surface does when it is heated to 3,200°.

TV-safe frame A frame on the viewing screen that defines the boundaries of the image once transferred to video.

tweaking Fine-tuning what each instrument is accomplishing in a lighting setup.

two row See *double perf.*

two-shot So named because it shows two people from roughly the waist up.

underexposure Film that received too little light, resulting in dark areas of the frame.

unintentional splice Splice where an attempted cut was put back together again.

unsupervised transfer A telecine transfer in which general RGB settings are determined and then maintained through the entire process.

variable shutter A control on the camera that allows the operator to change the shape of the shutter.

video assist A tiny video pickup device that is mounted in the viewing system of the film camera, giving a video representation of the shot.

video field The two pieces of information that, when interlaced, create the video frame.

video workprint Generally a low-resolution, unsupervised telecine transfer used to make basic editorial decisions.

viewer In an NLE program, the window where clips are played back and analyzed for insertion into the timeline. Also refers to a traditional, standing viewing machine on which you can analyze the film frame by frame or at any other speed you desire.

visual shorthand Accomplishing an action visually in as economical a way as possible.

visual subtext Information that is not present in the content and structure of the narrative but implicit in the visual presentation.

VU (volume unit) meter Meter that gives a visual representation of the level of the audio signal being fed to the record head.

walk-through An initial rehearsal in which the technical personnel and the actors walk slowly through a shot to identify potential problems.

white balance The adjustments of the color circuits in a video camera to render light of various color temperatures as white.

white paper tape See *film tape.*

wide-angle lens A lens that gives a wide view of a scene. Also called *short lens.*

widescreen Created in the 1950s, widescreen is any presentation that has the aspect ratio of 1.66:1 or greater. In the United States, most widescreen is 1.85:1.

wild camera A camera that cannot do sync-sound filming.

wild motor A camera motor that produces a general speed rather than a precise one.

wind noise Unwanted sound created by wind hitting the microphone.

window burn A small window that can be created in the video frame where time code and any other pertinent information is visually represented.

wind shield See *wind zeppelin.*

wind zeppelin Has a baffle design that cuts much of the interference from wind. Also called *wind shield.*

wireless mic A mic, generally a lavalier, that is plugged into a radio transmitter; the signal is then sent to a receiver on a recorder. Also called *radio mic.*

workprints Duplicate prints made for editing that are frame-for-frame replications of the original and are made by a motion picture processing laboratory.

XLR plug The standard mic connection on most professional audio and video equipment. Also called *Canon plug.*

zero frame In the edge-numbering system, the frame on which the counting of each sequence of 20 frames starts.

zero VU (0 VU) Often presented as the point that the audio signal should not exceed because it will distort, although there is some room above it for viable recording.

zoom lens A lens with a variable focal length.

Index